ALSO BY WARREN ZIMMERMANN

*Origins of a Catastrophe: Yugoslavia and
Its Destroyers*

First Great Triumph

FIRST GREAT TRIUMPH

*How Five Americans
Made Their Country
a World Power*

Warren Zimmermann

FARRAR, STRAUS AND GIROUX
New York

Farrar, Straus and Giroux
19 Union Square West, New York 10003

Copyright © 2002 by Warren Zimmermann
Distributed in Canada by Douglas & McIntyre Ltd.
Printed in the United States of America
First edition, 2002

Some material in this book appeared in a different form in *The Wilson Quarterly*.

Library of Congress Cataloging-in-Publication Data
Zimmermann, Warren.
    First great triumph : how five Americans made their country a world power / Warren
Zimmermann.— 1st ed.
        p.   cm.
    Includes bibliographical references (p.) and index.
    ISBN 0-374-17939-5 (hc : alk. paper)
    1. United States—History—1865–1921—Biography.   2. Spanish-American War, 1898.
3. United States—Territorial expansion.   4. United States—Politics and government—
1901–1909.   5. Roosevelt, Theodore, 1858–1919.   6. Hay, John, 1838–1905.   7. Mahan,
A. T. (Alfred Thayer), 1840–1914.   8. Root, Elihu, 1845–1937.   9. Lodge, Henry Cabot,
1850–1924.   I. Title.

E663 .Z46 2002
973'.09'9—dc21
[B]

                                                                          2002025015

Designed by Debbie Glasserman

www.fsgbooks.com

10   9   8   7   6   5   4   3   2

This book is dedicated to my grandchildren

Louis Warren Metcalfe   Corinne Chubb Worthington
Percy David Metcalfe   Arthur Alsop Worthington
            Natasha Zimmermann

It is a great historical expedition, and I thrill to feel that I am part of it. If we fail, of course we share the fate of all who do fail, but if we are allowed to succeed (for we certainly shall succeed, if allowed) we have scored the first great triumph in what will be a world movement.

—Lieutenant Colonel Theodore Roosevelt to his sister Corinne
from the troopship *Yucatan* bound for Cuba, June 15, 1898

Contents

List of Illustrations

First Great Triumph

Introduction: Rising Empire

For Theodore Roosevelt, February 22, 1909, was one of the most satisfying days of his presidency. He was only ten days away from turning over the presidential mandate to his chosen successor, William Howard Taft, and only two months away from departing on safari to Africa. What was occupying him on February 22 was the return of the Great White Fleet, the sixteen first-class battleships that he had sent around the world as a show of American power. He had seen them off on December 9, 1907, at Hampton Roads, Virginia, at the mouth of Chesapeake Bay. Fourteen and a half months later he was back at Hampton Roads aboard the presidential yacht *Mayflower* to watch them come home from the longest cruise ever taken by any navy, nearly forty-five thousand miles.

The naval towns of Hampton and Norfolk were jubilant in expectation, their buildings arrayed with bunting and banners. Out in the bay, hundreds of steamers, yachts, and other pleasure boats of all sizes and varieties braved squalls to await the great ships. Emerging out of the mist and rain, they looked ghostly and strange in their brilliant white, set off by the black smoke from their three tall funnels. In fact, they were the navy's last white ships; while they were at sea, the Navy Department had begun the conversion to the less visible, more war-effective battleship gray. The white ships sailed in one by one in a column seven miles long, each flying three large ensigns. Simultaneously they fired a twenty-one-gun salute to the president, then each repeated the salute individually as it passed the *Mayflower*.

In top hat and frock coat, Roosevelt visited each division flagship in

the harbor and addressed the crews. Aboard the *Connecticut*, the
fleet's flagship, he told the assembled sailors:

> Over a year has passed since you steamed out of this harbor, and
> over the world's rim, and this morning the hearts of all who saw you
> thrilled with pride as the hulls of the mighty warships lifted above
> the horizon. You have been in the Northern and the Southern
> Hemispheres; four times you have crossed the line; you have
> steamed through all the great oceans; you have touched the coast of
> every continent. . . .
>
> As a war machine the fleet comes back in better shape than it
> went out. In addition, you, the officers and men of this formidable
> fighting force, have shown yourselves the best of all possible ambas-
> sadors and heralds of peace. . . . We are proud of all the ships and
> all the men in this whole fleet, and we welcome you home to the
> country whose good repute among nations has been raised by what
> you have done.

In attendance on a navy yacht were members of the House and
Senate Naval Affairs committees. Their presence was a quiet triumph
for Roosevelt, since in 1907 the chairman of the Senate committee,
Eugene Hale of Maine, had tried to block the cruise by withholding
funds. East Coast congressmen feared that a Pacific mission for the
fleet would undercut its primary objective of protecting America's
Atlantic coast. President William McKinley, Roosevelt's predecessor,
would undoubtedly have conciliated this point of view. But Roosevelt
ignored it, telling the senators he had enough money to get the fleet
into the Pacific; it would just have to stay there if they failed to appropriate funds to bring it home.

This episode, which Roosevelt relished telling in his memoirs, illustrated the growing power of the presidency over Congress, which
had dominated American politics since the Civil War. Roosevelt did
not customarily disregard Congress—he relied heavily on his closest
friend, Senator Henry Cabot Lodge of Massachusetts—but his two
terms had marked the resurgence of a strong executive.

One important absentee at Hampton Roads was greatly missed by
the president, Admiral of the Navy George Dewey, its only four-star,
who had been planning to attend but was ill with sciatica. Roosevelt,
as assistant secretary of the navy in the McKinley administration, had

lifted Dewey from an obscure post to the command of the Asiatic Squadron. Dewey had thus been positioned to destroy the Spanish fleet in Manila Bay at the start of the Spanish-American War in 1898.

Another absentee was Admiral Robley "Fighting Bob" Evans, who had commanded the Great White Fleet at the outset but had to retire for health reasons before it crossed the Pacific. Evans also had a distinguished war record. In 1898 in the victorious Battle of Santiago Bay, off Cuba, he had skippered the *Iowa*, to which the Spanish commander, Vice Admiral Pascual Cervera, had been brought as a prisoner. Evans had given Cervera full honors, and his sailors had cheered the vanquished Spaniard, moving him to bow his head for a full minute in gratitude and surrender.

The itinerary of the fleet recapitulated the distance the United States had come in the decade since the Spanish-American War. From Chesapeake Bay the battleships had steamed south to the Caribbean, which had become an American lake with the ejection of Spain from Cuba and Puerto Rico. They had then moved down the east coast of South America, through the Strait of Magellan, and up the west coast, stopping along the way in Brazil, Argentina, Chile, Peru, and Mexico.

The call at Valparaíso, Chile, would have stirred memories for Admiral Evans. In 1891, as captain of the gunboat *Yorktown*, he had dealt with a near war between Chile and the United States over the killing of two American sailors in a Valparaíso bar. One reason that the Harrison administration decided to settle the incident by diplomacy was its fear that the Chilean Navy might be superior to the American one. But by the time of Evans's visit with the Great White Fleet, that shocking disparity had been erased. The naval buildup now guaranteed American hegemony in the Western Hemisphere. Elihu Root, first as the secretary of war in charge of administering Cuba and Puerto Rico, then as a secretary of state who took Latin America seriously, had given political solidity to that dominance. Because of Roosevelt's aggressive diplomacy in wresting Panama from Colombia, a canal was under construction that would make the Caribbean central in saving future fleets from the long voyage around the Horn.

Even without the canal, which was not to open until 1914, the United States already had a two-ocean navy, the second strongest in the world behind Great Britain's. The difference with 1898 was dramatic. The naval victory in Cuba had been won with only four first-class battleships; these all were now supplanted by twenty brand-new vessels of the most modern fighting class. The military strategist Alfred T. Mahan had convinced American policy makers that naval power was the supreme expression of military supremacy and the proof of a nation's greatness.

The fleet's cruise also demonstrated, as Roosevelt put it, that "the Pacific was as much our home waters as the Atlantic." The ships had visited Hawaii, New Zealand, Australia, China, the Philippines, and Japan. Both Hawaii and the Philippines had become American colonies in 1898, the former by peaceful annexation, the latter by military victory. China was a growing focus of interest and the subject of the Open Door policy of John Hay, secretary of state under McKinley and Roosevelt. Japan, the emerging great power in Asia, was a principal reason for Roosevelt's dispatch of the fleet: He wanted to impress the Japanese with American strength while persuading them of his peaceful intentions. To his satisfaction, the reception in Yokohama had been friendly, warm, and highly respectful.

The fleet had left the Pacific for the Indian Ocean and the Red Sea, passed through the Suez Canal, steamed across the Mediterranean (units of it stopping to assist victims of a major earthquake in Sicily), and come home across the Atlantic. The cruise not only impressed the world with America's newfound military strength but excited the imagination of Americans as well. A million people had turned out in San Francisco to welcome the ships before their voyage across the Pacific. This enthusiasm laid the basis for a cherished objective of Roosevelt's: steady congressional funding of new battleships. Most important of all, the circumnavigation of the Great White Fleet gave substance to Roosevelt's assertion: "We have definitely taken our place among the great world powers."

Roosevelt noted in his autobiography that the day the fleet returned to Hampton Roads was George Washington's birthday. The first president, though remembered for his warning against U.S. entanglement in European affairs, was, like Roosevelt, an advocate of empire. In 1783 he referred to the United States as a "new empire" and a "rising empire," and three years later he said: "However unimportant America may be considered at present . . . there will assuredly come a day, when this country will have some weight in the scale of

Empires." That day came in 1898, when the United States burst upon the world scene with a spectacular series of conquests.

On April 25, 1898, two months after the sinking of the USS *Maine* in Havana Bay, the United States went to war with Spain over Cuba. On May 1, some eight thousand miles away in the Philippines, Dewey destroyed the Spanish fleet off Manila. On June 21 the U.S. Navy, a thousand miles to the east, seized the tiny Spanish-held island of Guam, with its fine harbor. The zigzag pattern of conquest continued from the Caribbean to the Pacific and back. On July 1, Lieutenant Colonel Theodore Roosevelt, attired in a brass-buttoned uniform he had just bought from Brooks Brothers, led his Rough Riders in an exuberant charge—on foot—up San Juan Hill, in eastern Cuba. Routing an overmatched Spanish force, the American soldiers took the heights overlooking Santiago Bay, where, two days later, the U.S. Navy won the battle for Cuba by capturing Admiral Cervera's entire squadron. On July 7, President McKinley, exulting in the expansionist fervor, annexed Hawaii, which had been under the de facto control of American sugar planters since 1893. On August 13, Manila fell to Dewey. The next day, the U.S. Army took control of the Spanish island colony of Puerto Rico after an efficient nine-day campaign launched almost as an afterthought to the action in Cuba.

On December 10, by the Treaty of Paris, Spain ceded to the United States the Philippines, Guam, and Puerto Rico, none of which had been an important prewar objective for the United States. Spain also renounced sovereignty over Cuba, which *had* been the principal U.S. target, thus opening the island to American military rule. And so by force of arms the United States in only a few months gained territorial possessions on both the Atlantic and Pacific sides of its continental mass.

Nor did imperial expansion end with 1898. In an 1899 division of Samoa with Germany, the United States acquired the strategic deep-water harbor of Pago Pago. The navy took Wake Island, an unowned and uninhabited atoll, in the same year. A jagged line of American bases, or coaling stations, as they were called in the age of steam, ran from California to Hawaii to Midway (which had been acquired in 1867) to Samoa to Wake to Guam to the Philippines. This chain of possessions made possible the extension of American political and economic influence to China, an opportunity that Hay's Open Door policy was designed to seize. The burst of imperial activity culminated in the plan to link America's Atlantic and Pacific holdings via a canal across the narrow waist of Central America. President Roosevelt set this project in motion in 1903 by subverting the sovereignty of Colombia and assisting a revolutionary Panamanian government that was willing to sign the requisite treaty.

America would never again acquire so much territory as it did during those explosive five years between 1898 and 1903. Roosevelt's presidency from 1901 to 1909 consolidated the country as a member of the circle of great powers. A turning point had been reached in the way the United States related to the world. Now Americans and their leaders could act with self-confidence, a sense of their own power, and an abiding belief that they could shape international life according to their values.

At critical periods of its history the United States has always managed to find leaders whose ability and character were equal to the great challenges they faced. The revolutionary period had Washington, Adams, Hamilton, and Jefferson. The Civil War produced Lincoln and Grant. In the years after World War II the neophyte President Harry Truman and a group of brilliant advisers were able to create a Western coalition, backed by American power, that could blunt the Soviet threat.

The birth of the American empire a hundred years ago was similarly endowed. Five major figures stand out not only because they were influential in establishing America's global power but also because their characters and beliefs helped determine how that power would be used. Of course these five men did not operate outside the context of their historical circumstances. The United States had been trying for decades to expand overseas, and the weakness of Spain, leading to insurrections in Cuba and the Philippines, offered an unprecedented opportunity. Nevertheless, the nature of that expansion, and its consequences right up to today, owe a great deal to the kind of men they were.

John Hay, Captain Alfred T. Mahan, Elihu Root, Henry Cabot Lodge, and Theodore Roosevelt can fairly be called the fathers of modern American imperialism and the men who set the United States on the road to becoming a great power. Mahan, Lodge, and Roosevelt devised the strategy that took the United States into the war with Spain. Mahan was the "man of thought," as he called himself, working out a rationale for expansion that made him the preeminent military strategist in all American history. Lodge was the political manipulator, deftly exploiting his prominence in the U.S. Senate to win support for the war. Roosevelt was the activist, using his position as assistant secretary of the navy to inspire and persuade higher-ups, including President McKinley himself.

Hay and Root made their mark after the victory over Spain. Both had doubts about the imperial venture, and both worked to moderate its consequences. Hay, as secretary of state under McKinley and Roosevelt, devised a coherent U.S. policy toward Asia and, even more important, cemented a close relationship with Great Britain that survives to this day. Root, as secretary of war under the same two presidents, created—in Cuba, Puerto Rico, and the Philippines—America's first colonial administration, transferring to it some of the best features of the American legal system.

These five were remarkable men by any measure. Two of them, Roosevelt and Root, won the Nobel Peace Prize. All were intellectuals and thought of themselves as such. All except Root were notable authors. Roosevelt wrote thirty-eight books, and Lodge twenty-seven, mostly on themes of American history. While much of this writing was perishable, Roosevelt's four-volume *The Winning of the West* deserves to be considered an American classic. Hay was a poet, a best-selling novelist, and coauthor of a popular biography of Abraham Lincoln. Mahan produced an analysis of the influence of sea power in history that profoundly affected American policy and became required reading in the British, German, and Japanese navies. Root, who had been one of the most talented corporate lawyers of his time, became after his government service a forceful advocate of the rule of law in international relations.

It may be argued that others have as great a claim as these five to be included in the parentage of American imperialism. The four principal outside claimants are treated extensively in this book: the naval hero George Dewey; the military governor of Cuba Leonard Wood; the colonial governor of the Philippines William Howard Taft; and President McKinley himself. The pugnacious Dewey was a brilliant sailor and a man of sometimes striking insight into the Filipino mentality, but he lacked Mahan's intellectual breadth as well as his fellow officer's ability to dominate opinion. Wood and Taft were conscientious public servants—Taft an exceptional one—but they were implementing a colonial strategy devised almost single-handedly by Root. McKinley remains a tantalizing enigma. The views of historians differ on whether he consciously masterminded America's war with Spain or was dragged unwillingly into it. The evidence seems to support the latter interpretation, thus reducing McKinley's importance as a force behind imperialism. Finally, one figure who is not usually considered an imperialist, Woodrow Wilson, was in fact a committed one. But his frequent interventions in Latin America followed a strategy mapped by Mahan, Roosevelt, and even his future nemesis Lodge.

Of the five fathers of imperialism, four were of the same generation, all but the precocious Roosevelt, who was twenty years younger than Hay, the oldest of the others. All were easterners except Hay, a midwesterner who was educated in the East. Roosevelt and Lodge were born wealthy and followed similar career paths: Harvard, writing, and politics. The other three came from the professional middle class: Hay the son of an Illinois country doctor; Mahan and Root the sons of teachers at West Point and Hamilton College respectively.

All except Mahan were active in the Republican party. They frequented the same clubs: the Century Association in New York, the Metropolitan Club in Washington. In the cozy atmosphere of small-town Washington they were mutual admirers and good friends who enjoyed one another's company at work and at leisure. Despite their diverse backgrounds, they used their abilities, their intellects, and their political ties with three of the most powerful states (Ohio, New York, and Massachusetts) to ascend to the small leadership class that ran the United States.

These five exceptional men were individually susceptible to human failings: arrogance, insensitivity, faulty analysis, impulsiveness or irresolution, shortsightedness. They were not omniscient and did not always see clearly the options available or the most productive paths to desired results. They reflected the collective prejudices of their class, particularly on matters of race. They were neither icons in a historical pageant nor villains in a morality play. Their actions and decisions, the consequences of which still affect Americans, were neither perfect nor inevitable but were often clouded by the fallibility that affects us all.

Hay, who owed his career to the luck of being hired in 1860 as an aide to President-elect Abraham Lincoln, was pursued all his life by self-doubt, depression, and difficulty in standing up to pressure. Yet he was a humane and entertaining companion, one of Washington's best storytellers. With Roosevelt, crude insensitivity often accompanied phenomenal energy; his inane exaltations of war must have jarred people like McKinley and Hay, who remembered the horrors of the Civil War. Mahan oscillated between remoteness and irascibility. Though an unmatched analyst of naval strategy, he was only a mediocre seaman. Lodge had a prickly personality and a large dose of Back Bay arrogance, but he worked selflessly and effectively to make his friend Roosevelt president. Root established an impressive system of colonial rule, yet he presided over a dirty war against an authentic Filipino rebellion.

The five combined to set the course of American foreign policy for the century to come. That course was not free of obstacles. Opponents of the war with Spain and the acquisition of the island colonies thundered their criticism in the Senate and across the country. The anti-imperialists came from a broad spectrum of American life: politicians like Grover Cleveland, industrialists like Andrew Carnegie, trade unionists like Samuel Gompers, immigrant commentators like Carl Schurz, and writers like Mark Twain. Their arguments against an American empire ranged from constitutional ones (betraying American traditions) to economic (taking on unnecessary burdens) and racist (bringing in inferior peoples). Criticism of the conduct of American forces in putting down a stubborn insurrection in the Philippines presaged a later debate over the behavior of American soldiers in Vietnam. The anti-imperialists failed to stop the imperial juggernaut, but they did help entrench human rights as a permanent concern of U.S. foreign policy.

Theodore Roosevelt never doubted that he was acting morally or that morality was a major feature of his policy. He was seldom blind to purely pragmatic considerations, as his skillful diplomacy with a rising Japan illustrates. Nor was he above using moral arguments for instrumental aims. His concern for the Cuban revolutionaries vanished after they had served their purpose of inciting the United States to war. But Roosevelt and Lodge were students and publicists of American history, and they really did believe that their country had a mission to spread the bounties of its civilization beyond its borders. Even John Hay, no ideologue, thought that the United States should pick up Britain's faltering flag and show that empires can operate for the good of their subjects. For all five men, the manifest destiny that had led the United States to defeat Mexico and conquer the American West should now unfold on a global scale.

Ironically, just as the United States was extending its influence into the world, it was in the process of attracting unprecedented foreign influences within its borders. The period of the new imperialism was also a time of the largest immigration America had ever received. Not surprisingly, the sweeping processes of imperialism and immigration influenced each other. Imperialists drew much of their intellectual sustenance from the racial doctrines that were then widely taught, including at America's finest universities. Their belief in Anglo-Saxon supremacy made them natural enemies of mass immigration from eastern and southern Europe and from Asia. For Henry Cabot Lodge, the fight against immigration was a sacred cause second only to his championing of imperialism.

Any balance sheet on the actions of Roosevelt and his four partners must abound in contradictions. By the end of the nineteenth century the United States had the wealth, the aspirations, and the accumulated frustrations to break out onto the world stage. Spain's mismanagement of Cuba, together with its striking military weakness, presented an issue made to order for the ravenous New York yellow press and the activists who were close to the vacillating President McKinley. Still, despite the growing jingoist sentiment, it was remarkable that Roosevelt, Lodge, and Mahan—a subcabinet official in the Navy Department, a senator yet to achieve a committee chairmanship, and a military intellectual—could persuade senior officials and finally the president himself that war was desirable.

There were strong strategic and humanitarian reasons for seizing Cuba, and the relatively rapid granting of independence to the island in 1902 showed a commendable sensitivity to Cuban concerns. On the other hand, from 1898 on, Americans tended to treat Cubans with arrogance, thrusting aside the revolutionaries who had made possible the U.S. victory over Spain and reserving the right to intervene at will in the future. The manic charges of Yankee imperialism made later by Fidel Castro, whose father had fought the American

Army in 1898 as a Spanish soldier, gained some of their effect from the consequences of the Spanish-American War.

The case for taking and holding the Philippines was dubious. Unlike Cuba, the Philippines had not been an object of American interest until late in the nineteenth century. The islands began to figure in the navy's contingency planning for a possible war with Spain, but Cuba was still the primary objective. Dewey's lightning victory posed the question of what to do with them. Even Mahan advocated retaining only part of the captured territory, but McKinley decided to keep the whole archipelago. The Philippines, and Hawaii, became the first pure colonies in American history.

The decade between 1898 and the end of Roosevelt's presidency began the long process of preparing the United States for global leadership as a great—ultimately *the* great—power. That leadership increased steadily throughout the twentieth century. America's hesitation over entry into the First World War was less a retreat from global involvement than the product of a debate, which continues today, over how closely America's security is tied to Europe. In World War II and the Cold War that followed it, American engagement was decisive in defeating the two terrible scourges of the century, Hitler's Germany and Stalin's Russia.

This is a book about imperialism, a word not very popular among Americans as a description of their past. It was not very popular in 1898 either. Even Roosevelt and Lodge, two full-blooded imperialists, found euphemisms. For Roosevelt the preferred description was "Americanism"; for Lodge it was the "large policy." For both, "expansionism" was a barely acceptable definition of U.S. policy.

Of the five, only Mahan had no fear of defining and using the word "imperialism." He gave its traditional territorial meaning—the acquisition and holding of colonies and dependencies—a political dimension as well. Imperialism, he wrote, is "the extension of national authority over alien communities." This broader definition implies that a country does not have to own the territory of an alien community in order to exercise imperial authority over it. This book uses Mahan's interpretation, but with the proviso that imperialism as practiced by the United States contained unique features.

Since the book assigns considerable importance to five individuals operating against a historical background of constraints and opportunities, Part One is largely biographical. It describes in some detail the lives and careers of Hay, Mahan, Root, Lodge, and Roosevelt and the elements of character that shaped their approach to imperialism before the war of 1898. Part Two focuses on the decade beginning with that war and running through Theodore Roosevelt's presidency: the birth of American imperialism, the work of the five men who created and shaped it, the great debate between imperialists and anti-imperialists, the essence and worth of the United States as a colonial nation, and its path to the status of world power. A final chapter traces the momentous effect of the 1898 period on America's journey to becoming the strongest power in the world during the twentieth century.

Readers of this book will not be treated to a saga of triumphant America led by a small company of heroic figures. Nor will they be assaulted by a revisionist diatribe against the use of American power to keep weaker peoples down. The reality of America's rise to great power status was much more complex than a stereotyped account from the right or the left can convey. There was both darkness and light in the characters and actions of the principal American protagonists. Those peculiarly American combinations of ideology and pragmatism, of power and principle, and of racism and tolerance were as much a feature of the United States of 1898 as they are of the United States today.

Theodore Roosevelt and his friends thus foreshadowed the often awesome ambiguities of America's global involvement throughout the twentieth century. One of Roosevelt's Harvard professors, William James, who detested the imperialism practiced by his former pupil, wrote of 1898: "We gave the fighting instinct and the passion of mastery their outing . . . because we thought that . . . we could resume our permanent ideals and character when the fighting fit was done." But the fighting fit did change America's ideals and character. Today, for better or worse, we still live with the consequences, and under the shadow, of the imperial actions taken a century ago.

Part One

THE
MUSIC MAKERS

We are the music-makers,
  And we are the dreamers of dreams,
Wandering by lone sea-breakers,
  And sitting by desolate streams;
World-losers and world-forsakers,
  On whom the pale moon gleams:
Yet we are the movers and shakers
  Of the world for ever, it seems.

With wonderful deathless ditties
We build up the world's great cities,
  And out of a fabulous story
  We fashion an empire's glory;
One man with a dream, at pleasure,
  Shall go forth and conquer a crown;
And three with a new song's measure
  Can trample an empire down.

We, in the ages lying
  In the buried past of the earth,
Built Nineveh with our sighing,
  And Babel itself with our mirth;
And o'erthrew them with prophesying
  To the old of the new world's worth;
For each age is a dream that is dying,
  Or one that is coming to birth.

—ARTHUR WILLIAM EDGAR O'SHAUGHNESSY
(1844–1881)

1. The Expansionist Impulse

1.

Americans like to pretend that they have no imperial past. Yet they have shown expansionist tendencies since colonial days. As early as 1613 Samuel Argall, a Jamestown ship captain in the employ of the Virginia Company, raided the settlement of Port Royal in French Canada. Overland expansion, often at the expense of Mexicans and Indians, was a marked feature of American history right through the period of the Civil War, by which time the United States had reached its continental proportions.

The War for American Independence, which created most of the founding myths of the Republic, was itself a war for expansion. The American revolutionaries were fighting to acquire all of Britain's possessions in North America, including the territories in Canada that the British had recently seized from France. General George Washington's raiding parties captured Montreal but failed at Quebec.

Thomas Jefferson nursed even grander plans for empire. Twenty years before he commissioned the Lewis and Clark Expedition, he had pondered an exploration of the Pacific Northwest. He interviewed sailors and explorers who knew the area and amassed the most comprehensive library on it in North America. In 1793 he organized a privately funded but government-sponsored expedition to seek a water route across the continent. The expedition was aborted when Jefferson discovered that its leader, a French scientist, was spying for France. But his aim was already to link the Atlantic and Pacific coasts via the Missouri and Columbia rivers.

Jefferson's greatest coup, the purchase from France in 1803 of vast but undefined western lands misleadingly known as Louisiana, brought this dream much closer to reality. The American president, Francophile though he was, won Louisiana by threatening to annihilate the French fleet and to fight any French troops who landed at New Orleans. Napoleon I had his own reasons for selling Louisiana. He was at a military disadvantage and feared the Americans would occupy the territory before he could get his army there. He boasted that by strengthening American power, he had given Britain "a rival who, sooner or later, will humble her pride." It was a clever calculation, since the two countries were at war nine years later.

With the addition of the land west of the Mississippi River stretching all the way to the Rockies, the Louisiana Purchase turned the hitherto square-shaped United States into a huge rectangle. In Jefferson's extravagant view the American entitlement went still farther, to the Pacific coast. Even before the mammoth land deal with Napoleon was concluded, he had secured congressional funding for Meriwether Lewis's expedition to find a water route to the Pacific Ocean.

After Jefferson's triumph with the Louisiana Territory, American presidents seized other new opportunities to expand. In the War of 1812 with Great Britain, the Madison administration made no headway in its attack on Canada but consolidated its hold on the Mississippi Valley. John Quincy Adams, President James Monroe's acerbic, depressive, and brilliant secretary of state, scored successes on both ends of the continent. His treaty of 1818 with Britain established the northwest boundary at forty-nine degrees latitude, where it is today. Also, in 1819 Adams bought from Spain the Floridas, comprising a strip along the Gulf Coast reaching to New Orleans as well as to what is now the state of Florida itself, for the modest price of five million dollars.

Adams's main historical legacy was the Monroe Doctrine, proclaimed in 1823 as Spanish colonies in Latin America were culminating their drive for independence from Spain. Adams was determined to blunt the not necessarily firm Spanish intention to use military force, with French support, to reestablish colonial control. The doctrine consisted of four noes: no new European colonization, no extension of European political systems to the Western Hemisphere, no intervention to put down revolutions, and (the U.S. quid pro quo) no American interference in Europe's internal concerns.

The Monroe Doctrine was a unilateral U.S. policy, not a treaty. It bound no country but the United States, nor was it uniformly enforced or observed. It was "violated" by Britain in the occupation of the Falkland Islands in 1833, by Spain in the reassertion of colonial rule over Santo Domingo in 1861, and by France in Napoleon III's brazen attempt to turn Mexico into a French puppet state during the American Civil War. There were other examples as well. Nevertheless, the consequences of the Monroe Doctrine were far-reaching, for Latin America became effectively a U.S. sphere of influence, off limits to its European rivals.

John Quincy Adams was a reluctant imperialist. He had opposed the Louisiana Purchase, and twice he renounced the U.S. claim to the territory that was later to become Texas, once as secretary of state and again as an antislavery congressman. But the desire in the South for more cotton land and an additional slave state prevailed. The agent of pro-Texas sentiment was a humorless, puritanical small-town Tennessee lawyer and former U.S. congressman. James K. Polk, a believer in Jeffersonian republicanism and a protégé of Andrew Jackson's, had no qualms about expansion. In his inaugural address as president in 1845, he said: "It is confidently believed that our system may be safely extended to the utmost bounds of our territorial limits, and that as it shall be extended the bonds of our Union, so far from being weakened, will become stronger."

Polk, unmatched among American presidents in his xenophobic belligerence, warned Great Britain not to challenge America's title to the Pacific Northwest and threatened Mexico with war if it interfered with the U.S. acquisition of Texas. He abandoned his attempt to expand the northwest boundary of the United States to north of Vancouver Island, settling for the earlier delineation at the forty-ninth parallel. But he fought a successful war against Mexico for Texas. By the Treaty of Guadalupe Hidalgo in 1848, Mexico recognized the Rio Grande as the international border and ceded to the United States what are now California, Nevada, and Utah, plus parts of the future New Mexico, Arizona, Colorado, and Wyoming. Mexico had lost half its land, and Polk had added 1.2 million square miles to U.S. territory, an increase of more than 60 percent. This achievement was completed after his presidency with the addition of the southern portions of Arizona and New Mexico, bought from Mexico in 1853. Alongside his hero Jefferson, Polk can claim to be the greatest presidential expansionist in American history.

Starting from the thirteen original states, the expansion from one contiguous area to another owed much to the diplomacy of Jefferson and John Quincy Adams and to the war policy of Polk. But expansion came from below as well. In the incorporation of the states between the Appalachian Mountains and the Mississippi River during the late eighteenth century, backwoodsmen like Daniel Boone were catalysts whose actions were far more important than the government's. In Texas the determination of its inhabitants to belong to the United States helped drive the U.S. government into war with Mexico.

From the very beginning of the Republic, American politicians debated whether new states should be permitted to enter the Union with the same rights as the original thirteen. The Northwest Ordinance of 1787, which Jefferson helped draft, provided for admission, with equal rights, of states between the Appalachians and the Mississippi. It proved to be one of the most important pieces of legislation passed under the Articles of Confederation. But it did not apply to not-yet-acquired territories west of the Mississippi.

Jefferson himself dithered about the western lands. His approach in 1780 was inclusive: "Our confederacy must be viewed as the nest from which all America, North or South, is to be peopled." As president he expressed the hope that the American continent would be settled by people "speaking the same language, governed in similar forms, and by similar laws." Yet he told Meriwether Lewis, as he sent him west, that the land beyond the Mississippi should become a giant Indian reservation and that whites, now free of the Indian threat, should limit their settlements to territory east of the river. Also, on Lewis's return, Jefferson seemed much more interested in exploiting the trans-Mississippi West for the fur trade than for settlement.

Jefferson's farsighted secretary of the treasury, Albert Gallatin, knew that Americans would rush to the West. He made sure that Lewis had instructions to test the new land's agricultural possibilities. Though Jefferson took a more tolerant view of Indians than he did of blacks, his policy was to divest them of title to their lands—by purchase if possible, by war if necessary—and to drive them westward. Even that restrictive policy clashed with the growing demands for white settlement of the West. Napoleon had predicted what Gallatin also foresaw: Americans were not going to leave the West to the Indians. Attracted by cheap land, settlers would spread out across the continent and ultimately establish claims for new states on the same basis as the original thirteen.

The Northwest Ordinance became the working model for regulation of this westward expansion in the nineteenth century. There would be no colonies, no second-class territories, except on a temporary basis. As it turned out, states were admitted on an equal footing until 1896, when Utah was compelled as a condition of admission to outlaw the polygamy practiced by the Mormons who had settled there. The inhabitants of newly acquired territories, with the significant exception of Indians and slaves, were expected and encouraged to seek equal rights as citizens. They were seen as prospective Americans, not as colonial subjects of a continental American empire. There was no challenge to this principle until 1898, when the United States acquired territory that was not to be settled by Americans and a colonial population that was not to be granted the rights Americans enjoyed.

Some Americans tried to go even further and take all of Mexico and Canada. These historical might-have-beens would have more than doubled the area of the United States. Polk's cabinet actually considered the annexation of Mexico following the American victory, but the idea died with the signing of the peace treaty in 1848. The drawbacks to expansion proved too strong. One was opposition in the American South to conferring citizenship on nonwhites. Another was a reluctance to acquire territory against the wishes of its people. A captured Mexico would have been the first territory taken without a diplomatic agreement or a clear expression of its people's desire to join the United States.

Canada was a larger and even more important target. From the birth of their Republic Americans had assumed that the large territory to their north would become a part of it. Jefferson in 1775 expressed the belief that "the delegates of Canada will join us in Congress and complete the American union." The Articles of Confederation invited an application by Canadians to be "admitted into and entitled to all the advantages of the union." A strategic objective, to deny the British the St. Lawrence River, dictated the American occupation of Montreal and Benedict Arnold's unsuccessful raid on Quebec in 1775. Similarly, in the War of 1812 Henry Clay, speaker of the House of Representatives, saw an attack on Canada as a way to break the British alliance with the Indians and to challenge the British Navy. Jefferson from retirement said that the conquest of Canada was merely a matter of "marching." To Canadians the War of 1812 was not about abstract principles like neutral rights on the high seas. They saw it as an American invasion, and they pushed the attackers back across the border.

Early in the Civil War, Canada escaped another American invasion when the United States and Britain narrowly avoided going to war over the British ship *Trent*, which had given two Confederate envoys free passage to London. After the British North American Act of 1867 created the Dominion of Canada, increasing both its unity and its autonomy, tensions with the United States abated. Still, cross-border raids continued, often stimulated by Irish-Americans, and American politicians, including Theodore Roosevelt, fulminated for annexation.

Why did the American appetite for Canada, often so rapacious during the century after the Revolution, go unsatiated? There are three main reasons. First, Canadians had no consistent desire to join the United States. Tens of thousands of Americans loyal to the British crown fled to Canada during the Revolution. They became a major political force in their rejection of American republicanism and produced in their descendants many of Canada's future leaders. The rhythm in the bilateral relationship discouraged merger of the two countries. Whenever the threat of annexation seemed strongest, as in 1775, 1812, and 1861, Canadians tended to band together.

Second, despite their annexationist jingoism in the early days of the Republic, Americans never reached a clear national position on Canada. In the War of 1812, Henry Clay's Kentucky urged attacks on Canada, but the New England states discouraged them. Over the issue of slavery, a triple dynamic led to standstill: Southerners opposed union with nonslaveholding Canada, northern abolitionists favored it, and most Canadians were appalled at the thought of joining a slaveholding United States. Rational American statesmen pursued moderate objectives. John Jay in 1795 and Daniel Webster in 1842 concluded boundary settlements with Britain; President Martin Van Buren enforced U.S. neutrality laws against American annexationists.

The third reason for Canada's independence from the United States was British power. For the British, retention of their primary territory in the Western Hemisphere was a high priority for which they were willing to fight. American presidents prudently refrained from challenging them directly. American imperialists had to rely on potential, rather than active, threats to ensure Britain's good behavior. For the United States Canada became a hostage instead of a target. It remained—along with Cuba, Puerto Rico, and a few Caribbean islands—one of the last European possessions left in the Western Hemisphere.

2.

The United States that emerged from the Civil War concealed a paradox. With the Confederate states reunited in the Union, it was a continental country from sea to shining sea. But it was not yet a continental nation, in a governmental sense. Only ten of the thirty-six states lay west of the Mississippi, and five of those touched the river. An overwhelming majority of the population lived in the states east of the river; the center of American population, by 1850 figures, was in West Virginia. The western lands—except for Kansas, Texas, Nevada, California, and Oregon—were territories, not yet states, when the Civil War ended.

By and large Americans after the Civil War thought of themselves as inhabitants of a middle-size country, bounded by the Atlantic Ocean and the Mississippi River. For them the "West" meant states like Illinois, Kentucky, and Tennessee; beyond the Mississippi was the "Far West" or the "Wild West," where buffalo, Indians, and very few whites roamed. Theodore Roosevelt's history *The Winning of the West,* published between 1889 and 1896, was about the border states *east* of the Mississippi, not west of it. Roosevelt did not have to explain to his readers what he was talking about. In the minds of most Americans the geographic West was not a full part of the United States, and their nation was much smaller than Americans would think of it in the twentieth century.

Between 1865 and 1898 the mental picture of an unfinished country began to change dramatically. Nebraska, Colorado, North Dakota, South Dakota, Montana, Washington, Idaho, Wyoming, Utah, and

Oklahoma all were admitted to the Union. Except for New Mexico and Arizona, which were to join in 1912, continental America was now whole. This change found its herald in Frederick Jackson Turner, a professor at the University of Wisconsin. In a famous address before the American Historical Association in Chicago in 1893, when he was only thirty-two, Turner defined the essence of America as a pushing back of the western frontier: "The existence of an area of free land, its continuous recession, and the advancement of American settlement westward, explain American development." But that epic period had vanished, Turner warned his listeners; according to the 1890 U.S. census, the frontier no longer existed. "And now," he concluded, "four centuries from the discovery of America, at the end of a hundred years of life under the Constitution, the frontier has gone, and with its going has closed the first period of American history."

In an article three years later Turner drew a foreign policy consequence from the ending of territorial expansion: "That these energies of expansion will no longer operate would be a rash prediction; and the demands for a vigorous foreign policy, for an interoceanic canal, for a revival of our power upon the seas, and for the extension of American influence to outlying islands and adjoining countries, are indications that the movement will continue." The energy for expansion, in other words, would vault from the gorged American landmass to the open seas, where new places beckoned.

Like many majestic conceptions, the Turner thesis did not fit all the facts, at least in foreign policy. The frenetic activities of William H. Seward, the most expansionist secretary of state of the late nineteenth century, occurred too early to have been affected by the completed settlement of the West. The breakthrough of 1898, which came after Turner's obituary for the frontier, marked less a new policy than the achievement of what American statesmen had been trying unsuccessfully to do for three decades. Where Turner's ideas had their greatest effect on foreign policy was in the minds of two of his friends, Theodore Roosevelt and Woodrow Wilson, the leading expansionist presidents of the coming generation.

America's political expansion to the Pacific coast was accompanied by an explosion in industry and technology that made the United States an economic great power before it was a political or military one. During the Civil War economic strength passed from planters to industrialists, financiers, and businessmen. American inventors and entrepreneurs were instrumental in bringing about most of the world's technical innovations of the late nineteenth century: turbines, internal-combustion engines, railway air brakes, telephones, phonographs, alternating current, incandescent electric lightbulbs, automobiles, cinematography, aeronautics, and radio telegraphy. Thomas Edison alone invented the lightbulb, the phonograph, and (later) the talking movie.

By the mid-1880s the United States was leading the world in the production of timber and steel, in meatpacking, and in the mining of coal, iron, gold, and silver. By 1890 it had become the leading global energy consumer. By the turn of the century it was producing more coal and steel than Britain and Germany combined. In the last decades of the century the United States advanced rapidly in other indices of economic importance. Population nearly doubled between 1870 and 1900. America achieved world leadership in mass media, putting out 186 million copies of newspapers and magazines. American businessmen began to look abroad for markets. Exports tripled between 1860 and 1897, surpassing imports in most years. By 1893 the United States had become the second-largest world trader, behind Great Britain. It was also in that year that a financial and industrial crisis came close to destabilizing the U.S. economy, but it proved resilient enough to withstand the fall in the market and the factory shutdowns.

Few barriers prevented entrepreneurs with initiative, energy, and luck from growing rich in those days. Of the more than four thousand American millionaires in the 1890s, none were more celebrated than the three industrial titans whose lives personified the growth of American economic power, Andrew Carnegie, John D. Rockefeller, and J. Pierpont Morgan. All were born between 1835 and 1838. All made fortunes before they were forty; Rockefeller, the most precocious, was the world's largest oil refiner before he was thirty. Carnegie's focus was steel, Rockefeller's oil, and Morgan's finance, but all three were amazingly versatile. They all were deeply involved in the railroad boom that was causing profound changes in the United States, not only industrially but culturally and politically as well. The railroads, even more than the Internet a century later, transformed and shrank space. They brought faraway places conveniently close, creating an enormous interior market for businessmen and farmers. Toward the end of the century railroads accounted for 60 percent of the issues on the New York Stock Exchange. According to Carnegie's biographer Joseph Frazier Wall, "all American business was related to and dependent upon railroading."

Carnegie's early career was dominated by railroads. He built bridges and sleeping cars and superintended, at the age of twenty-four, the western (Pittsburgh) division of the Pennsylvania Railroad. Rockefeller demanded rebates from the railroads in return for giving them transportation rights to his oil. He eliminated competitors in the oil business by threatening to deny them access to rail transport if they did not let him take them over. Morgan's first major financial success was in marketing New York Central stock. He moved on to taking over and reorganizing bankrupt railroads (the process was called morganization), ultimately controlling one-sixth of U.S. trackage.

With railroads, steel, oil, and finance, Carnegie, Rockefeller, and Morgan dominated most of the major elements of American economic power. Thanks mainly to Carnegie's management genius, American steel production tripled in the last thirty years of the century. When Carnegie sold his company in 1901, he helped create a conglomerate, the United States Steel Corporation, that controlled two-thirds of all American steel output. In the 1890s Rockefeller's Standard Oil Company marketed 84 percent of all the petroleum products sold in the United States, by then the world's largest crude oil producer. Morgan was so powerful that he sometimes functioned as a central bank. He helped pull the country out of the recession caused by the panic of 1893, saving the gold standard in 1896 and issuing $65 million in gold bonds for the benefit of the beleaguered Cleveland administration.

In the days before the regulation of trusts, American capitalism tended to monopoly rather than competition. Rockefeller was the most relentless in driving competitors out of business, but the other barons did it as well. Trusts dominated in oil, steel, copper, rubber, tobacco, and leather. As Rockefeller said, "The day of combination is here to stay. Individualism has gone, never to return." The Sherman Antitrust Act, directed against the Standard Oil Company and signed by President Benjamin Harrison in 1890, was so ineffectual that it was ridiculed as the Swiss Cheese Act. It did have the unintended consequence of weakening American labor unions, which were in any case pallid reflections of their European counterparts. Between the 1890s and the 1930s unionism was virtually absent in the largest industries, except for coal mining. Big business in America was free to do pretty much what it wanted.

The entrepreneurs and industrialists were lucky to have sympathetic, if often lackluster, American presidents in their corner. With only one exception, Grover Cleveland, every American president from 1861 to 1913 was a Republican. Throughout that period the Republican platform supported business interests: high tariffs, sound money, powerless unions, and weak controls on trusts. Rockefeller, Morgan, and Carnegie all were major contributors to the party.

Businessmen did not automatically favor territorial expansion—Carnegie, for example, was an ardent anti-imperialist—but they had a natural desire to control overseas environments for the sake of trade. In general, economic advances coincide with, if they do not always create, the emergence of world powers. That was the lesson of the Industrial Revolution in Britain and France and of the unification of Germany into an economic colossus. American imperialists believed that the economic transformation of their country would make it a great power. Business interests usually, though not always, shared this belief.

In the thirty-three years between the Civil War and the Spanish-American War, Americans began to discover the world. They had always had a love of the sea, exemplified by their fast clipper ships and chronicled in Herman Melville's whaling stories. Now the novels of Henry James and Anthony Trollope made them feel more at home in the drawing rooms of London and the Continent. William Dean Howells served a tour in 1861 as U.S. consul in Venice; his travel books on Italy made his name. Bret Harte, bard of the American West, moved to Europe in 1878 as a U.S. consul in Germany and Scotland and never came home again. Lafcadio Hearn settled in Japan in 1890, took a Japanese wife and name, and produced some of his best writing on that exotic culture.

Americans were beginning to shed their provincialism. Foreign tourism was becoming a big business. Ulysses S. Grant took a well-publicized two-year world tour after his second presidential term.

Cornelius Vanderbilt, one of the gaudier of the newly rich, built a 270-foot steam yacht for his first trip to Europe. More fastidious millionaires, like Theodore Roosevelt's father, used commercial liners to take their families to Europe as part of their education, while low-cost steamship fares made the Continent accessible to poorer students and middle-class tourists. In 1879 the two hundred thousand Americans who visited Switzerland were one-fifth of all foreign visitors that year to the Helvetian republic. Mark Twain satirized the gaucheries of American tourists on the grand tour in *The Innocents Abroad*, published in 1869. Henry James, more snobbishly, reproved their tendency to "stare and gawk and smell, and crowd every street and shop."

As the United States grew more receptive to foreign connections, two secretaries of state took initiatives to make it a global power. They were William H. Seward, who served under Abraham Lincoln and Andrew Johnson, and James G. Blaine, who was secretary under James Garfield, Chester A. Arthur, and Benjamin Harrison. Had the times been more propitious, these larger-than-life figures, both of them prominent Republican politicians and presidential hopefuls, would have made history as major expansionists. Their failure was not for lack of trying.

Seward was an irrepressible expansionist. He wanted to push the United States north into Canada, south into Mexico, and west toward Asia. His ambitions were grandiose, even delusionary. "Give me fifty, forty, thirty more years of life," he told a Boston audience in 1867, "and I will engage to give you the possession of the American continent and the control of the world." Rhetoric apart, Seward was a highly skilled diplomat. He frustrated Emperor Napoleon III's effort to take over Mexico in 1863 while the Union was distracted by the Civil War. Relying on diplomacy, since the ongoing war denied him the use of force, Seward bought time until Appomattox, then turned tough and, threatening to use force, achieved a French withdrawal.

Seward recognized that this attempt by France to catapult its power over the Atlantic Ocean, not unlike Nikita Khrushchev's deployment of missiles in Cuba a century later, was a major threat to American security and a challenge to the Monroe Doctrine. It almost certainly strengthened his instinctive belief that the United States had to control its continental neighbors. He must have known that his country lacked the power and the will to annex Canada and Mexico, but he made no secret of his hope that both would become states in the American federation.

Meanwhile, in joining the European powers in a scramble for territory, he focused on practical possibilities. In the Caribbean he sought a coaling station for the U.S. Navy in the Dominican Republic, signed a treaty with Denmark for the purchase of the Virgin Islands, and won the agreement of Colombia for the right to build a canal across the Isthmus of Panama. He also made tentative probes at the Caribbean islands of Cuba, Haiti, Culebra, French Guiana, Puerto Rico, and St. Bartholomew. None of these ventures prospered, usually because the Senate refused to approve them. Seward also had designs on Asia and on the Pacific Ocean, which he referred to as "the chief theatre of events in the world's great hereafter." He tried unsuccessfully to acquire British Columbia and to sign with Hawaii a reciprocity treaty that was finally concluded by his successor, Hamilton Fish. He did succeed, thanks to the U.S. Navy, in acquiring uninhabited Midway Island, strategically situated halfway from California to the Philippines.

Seward's imperialism was nothing if not eclectic. He was as interested in cold places as in tropical islands, and he courted Denmark for both Iceland and Greenland. His greatest imperial success, the purchase of Alaska from Russia, was ridiculed by a press that called the new territory a "national icehouse," a "polar bear garden," and "Seward's icebox." But Alaska was a steal, rivaled only in American history by the Louisiana Purchase. It cost under two cents an acre: $7.2 million, or slightly less than Seward had offered Denmark for the Virgin Islands. Yet he had great difficulty winning congressional approval and had to resort to a lobbying blitz that presaged the methods of modern politics. Seward's "education campaign" used briefing papers, letters of support from influential Americans, and the imaginative reprinting of absurd arguments from 1803 against the Louisiana Purchase. The secretary of state may even have resorted to bribery; the Russian minister in Washington certainly did. When Seward left office in 1869, the most committed imperialist ever to serve as secretary of state had only two trophies to show for his gargantuan efforts: the flyspeck Midway and the Alaskan colossus.

James G. Blaine was a perennial seeker of the Republican presidential nomination and succeeded only in 1884, when he lost to

Grover Cleveland. He served twice as secretary of state, briefly with Garfield and Arthur (1881) and nearly a full term with Harrison (1889–92). Blaine was as activist a secretary of state as he was a politician. His egotism, bombast, and assertiveness—he was known as the plumed knight, not always reverentially—belied what was actually a subtle approach to the diplomacy of expansion. He made a deal with Germany and Great Britain to establish joint control over Samoa, with its stategically attractive deepwater harbor of Pago Pago. Presciently anticipating 1898, he identified Hawaii, Cuba, and Puerto Rico as the only three islands "of value enough to be taken," but he made no effort to take them. Like his predecessors, he hankered after Canada in vain. In practice Blaine preferred trade to outright possession. In what was surely the most famous speech ever delivered in Waterville, Maine, his home state, Blaine said: "We are not seeking annexation of territory. . . . At the same time I think we should be unwisely content if we did not seek to engage in . . . annexation of trade."

Blaine cast his commercial gaze on Latin America, an area that he saw as vital to U.S. interests. He believed that better political relations would lead to better terms of trade, and in 1889 he presided over the First Pan-American Conference. Blaine encouraged American investments in Latin America and moved to protect them when they fell afoul of the instabilities of Latin politics. His concentration on the hemisphere coincided with the establishment of the United Fruit Company's broad and baleful influence in Costa Rica, Honduras, and Guatemala. Blaine's secretaryship was longer on potential than achievement, but his farsighted approach to cooperation with Latin America and his interest in the peaceful settlement of disputes anticipated two of his most clearheaded successors, John Hay and Elihu Root.

Paradoxically, Seward and Blaine pressed their expansionist policies in the absence of any serious foreign threats to the United States. By the late nineteenth century Britain, the traditional enemy, was perceived as less dangerous, and Germany had not yet attained the status of adversary, except in isolated places like Samoa. In arguing for bases in the Caribbean, Seward cited a past enemy (Confederate blockade-runners) rather than a present one. Moreover, although he was not above using anti-Russian arguments in his efforts to win the support of Congress for the purchase of Alaska, he never pretended that security against Russia was a major reason for acquiring it. In cases where foreign threats did exist, they were not always inducements to imperialism. France's bid to take over Mexico during the Civil War produced a strong American response, but no new claims on Mexican territory, and despite habitually belligerent words against Britain's hold on Canada, American efforts to annex their northern neighbor rarely got beyond rhetorical bravado.

Still, the record of American statecraft after the Civil War shows a persistent effort to increase influence and expand territory beyond the continental boundaries of the United States. Symptomatic of this effort was the attempt made by virtually every postwar secretary of state to broaden the scope of the 1850 treaty with Great Britain in order to build and control a canal across the Isthmus of Panama. On this and other issues there was too much consistency in the approach to ascribe the expansionist impulse solely to the personal agendas of several energetic secretaries of state.

3.

Whatever the effect of such physical phenomena as the expansion of the American frontier to the Pacific Ocean and the enrichment of the U.S. economy, much of the impetus for overseas expansion in the last third of the nineteenth century was mental. Old political ideas like the Monroe Doctrine were given a more expansionist cast, and newer ones like manifest destiny offered spiritual sustenance for aggressive behavior. Proliferating theories of racial superiority, often backed by science or pseudoscience, became accepted wisdom. It was a rare American, whether of higher or lower education, who did not believe that his country had a special mission, sanctified by geography and race, to lead and dominate less civilized peoples.

The Monroe Doctrine had been devised to help defend the United States against European encroachments in the Western Hemisphere, but it grew beyond John Quincy Adams's famous disclaimer that "America does not go abroad in search of monsters to destroy." Through the nineteenth century the doctrine became expansionist as well as exclusionist, a divine text for any president or secretary of state who sought to plant the flag in new lands. Polk invoked it to support his policy of depriving Mexico of Texas, California, and New Mexico and to ward off "any future European colony or dominion" on the North American continent. He had in mind British interest in the Pacific Northwest, but the language was general. He also cited the doctrine to ensure that the British did not take the Yucatán Peninsula, irrespective of the consent of the inhabitants.

After the Civil War the Monroe Doctrine was applied even more widely. Out of interest in the Dominican Republic, Secretary of State Fish prevailed upon President Grant to issue a no-transfer proclamation: "Hereafter no territory on this continent shall be regarded as subject of transfer to a European power." The ill-fated French effort to build a canal across Panama brought a ringing declaration in 1880 from President Hayes that "the policy of this country is a canal under American control." The next year Secretary Blaine badgered Britain for modifications of the Clayton-Bulwer Treaty of 1850, which barred either country from exerting exclusive control over a canal. Blaine argued that the treaty contravened the Monroe Doctrine and "our rightful and long established claim to priority on the American continent."

Even the Pacific Ocean and parts of Asia came under broad interpretations of the Monroe Doctrine. In a dispute over Samoa in 1886, the German Foreign Office complained that Secretary of State Thomas F. Bayard was interpreting the Monroe Doctrine "as though the Pacific Ocean were to be treated as an American Lake." A Russian official voiced a similar complaint with regard to Alaska; he said that the Monroe Doctrine "enters more and more into the veins of the people and . . . the latest generation imbibes it with its mother's milk and inhales it with the air."

When President Cleveland's last secretary of state, Richard Olney, opposed Japanese pressure on Hawaii in 1896, the Hawaiian minister in Washington exulted that the United States had in effect extended the Monroe Doctrine to Hawaii. Olney, who made more imperious claims for the Monroe Doctrine than any other secretary of state in the entire century, grandly informed the British that the United States was "practically sovereign" on the continent. The doctrine had been transformed from a ban against foreign interference to a vindication of unilateral American intervention. It had become a tool of American imperialism.

The phrase "manifest destiny," which first came into use in the 1840s, was a quasi-theological justification of America's continental expansion and of the Monroe Doctrine. In fact, John Quincy Adams himself had come close to coining the phrase when in his text of the doctrine he used the words "destiny" and "manifestation" in the same sentence. But the actual originator was a journalist named John O'Sullivan, who wrote in 1839:

> The far-reaching, the boundless future will be the era of American greatness. In its magnificent domain of space and time, the nation of many nations is destined to manifest to mankind the excellence of divine principles; to establish on earth the noblest temple ever dedicated to the worship of the Most High—the Sacred and the True.
>
> For this blessed mission to the nations of the world, which are shut out from the life-giving light of truth, has America been chosen; and her high example shall smite unto death the tyranny of kings, hierarchs, and oligarchs, and carry the glad tidings of peace and good will where myriads now endure an existence scarcely more enviable than that of beasts of the field.

O'Sullivan's phrase "destined to manifest" became "manifest destiny," a convenient catchword for American expansionists. The triumphal looseness of language made the phrase doubly attractive; it could be applied to the whole world or any desired part of it. It was an apt way to describe the ambitious American nationalism that had grown from the rich soil of economic success. In most cases it was used to justify overland expansion, with the emphasis on acquiring land rather than subject peoples. The West was won under the rubric of manifest destiny. The western territories were "destined" to be states of the Union, not colonies in a far-flung empire.

In that sense manifest destiny was consistent with imperialism, though not identical to it. Sometimes manifest destiny was given a frankly imperial spin. John Fiske, a popular lecturer, scoured the country with a set-piece presentation entitled "Manifest Destiny." He declaimed: "The work which the English race began when it colonized North America is destined to go on until every land on the earth's surface that is not already the seat of an old civilization shall become English in its language, in its religion, in its political habits and traditions, and to a predominant extent in the blood of its people."

The homegrown principle of manifest destiny was reinforced by the importation from Britain of Charles Darwin's theories of natural selection. "Social Darwinism," the application or misapplication of Darwin's biological theories to human society, had two major functions in the United States. The first was to justify the superiority of American capitalism. The Yale economist William Graham Sumner contended that millionaires were the product of natural selection and should be unimpeded in their accumulation of wealth. On a more popular level, the Baptist minister Russell Conwell gained nationwide distribution for his sermon "Acres of Diamonds," which preached: "It is your duty to get rich. It is wrong to be poor."

In the boardrooms of industrial America, social Darwinism appealed to businessmen who assumed that "survival of the fittest" was a description of them. Darwin's associate Herbert Spencer visited the United States in 1882 and lectured to 150 industrial and intellectual luminaries at a banquet in his honor at Delmonico's, New York's most famous restaurant. Darwinism gave scientific luster to the capitalists' defense of the status quo, validating their preference for laissez-faire over state interference and soothing their consciences about making money. The great railroad builder James J. Hill and John D. Rockefeller both invoked Spencer in justifying the trend toward monopoly in railroads and oil respectively.

If the Darwinian revolution reinforced the cult of capitalism on the economic side, the biological side validated the older American tradition of Anglo-Saxonism, which celebrated the superiority of the so-called Anglo-Saxon race. Anglo-Saxonists held that America's democratic institutions—e.g., the New England town meeting—came not from ancient Greece but from the early German tribes via England. They quickly incorporated Darwinism into their new approach to imperialism. The peripatetic Fiske argued that Anglo-Saxon expansion, based on Teutonic theories of democracy, justified any conquest.

An even more popular propagandist, the Reverend Josiah Strong, went farther. In 1885 Strong, the U.S. Evangelical Alliance's representative in Ohio, wrote a paean to Anglo-Saxonism, *Our Country*, which quickly became a best-seller. To the 185,000 Americans who bought the book, Strong cited Darwin in arguing that "the wonderful progress of the United States as well as the character of its people, are the results of natural selection." For Strong the Anglo-Saxon race represented civil liberty and "pure spiritual Christianity." North America was to be "the great home of the Anglo-Saxon, the principal seat of his power, the center of his life and influence." With its biological advantages, Strong predicted, the Anglo-Saxon race "will spread itself over the earth," to Mexico, to Central and South America, and "out upon the islands of the sea" to Africa and beyond. Shedding no tears for the "inferior races" doomed by the Anglo-Saxon advance, he asked rhetorically: "Is there room for reasonable doubt that this race, unless devitalized by alcohol and tobacco, is destined to dispossess many weaker races, assimilate others, and mold the remainder, until, in a very true and important sense, it has Anglo-Saxonized mankind?"

Strong's divine boosterism would be easy to dismiss if it had not been so popular or if echoes of it had not reverberated in some of the best American academic institutions. Universities of the late nineteenth century were steaming jungles of racial theories, some absurd, most misguided, but nearly all accepted as appropriate subjects for intellectual discourse. Darwin, often to his horror, set scholars scrambling to determine racial superiority by measuring facial angles, skull size, brain weight, even human hair. There was hardly a major university in the United States that did not include racially based courses in its core curriculum.

At Harvard Nathaniel Southgate Shaler, dean of the Lawrence Scientific School and one of the most respected professors on the faculty, taught white supremacy based on the racial heritage of England. The great Harvard historian Francis Parkman contended that Anglo-Saxon superiority was the key to the British victory over the French in North America. At Columbia the political scientist John W. Burgess wrote that the national state was the product of Teutonic political genius, a fact that "stamps the Teutonic nations as the political nations *par excellence,* and authorizes them, in the economy of the world, to assume the leadership in the establishment and administration of states."

At Johns Hopkins, Professor James K. Hosmer bragged: "The primacy of the world will lie with us. English institutions, English speech, English thought, are to become the main features of the political, social, and intellectual life of mankind." Hosmer's colleague Herbert Baxter Adams, who introduced the German seminar method at Hopkins, was a major advocate of the Teutonic origins of civilization, bringing this viewpoint to the American Historical Association, which he founded in 1884. David Starr Jordan, president of Stanford, held that "poverty, dirt, and crime" were the consequence of poor human material. Against this distinguished academic company there was little organized intellectual opposition. Racially tolerant scholars, like William James at Harvard, were the exception, not the rule.

Hierarchical racial theories helped shape the intellectual formation of virtually every American who reached adulthood during the second half of the century. Without even trying, well-educated American politicians carried into their careers large doses of Anglo-Saxonism administered to them in their universities. Theodore Roosevelt studied under Shaler at Harvard and Burgess at Columbia. Both Roosevelt and Lodge were close to Parkman at Harvard; Roosevelt dedicated his western history to him. Lodge imbibed the Anglo-Saxon tradition in Henry Adams's medieval history course. Adams, no ideologue himself, conceded the academic pressure when he admitted flinging himself "obediently into the arms of the Anglo-Saxons in history." Woodrow Wilson, as a graduate student at Johns Hopkins, was a protégé of Herbert Baxter Adams's.

With so much racial prejudice hanging in the American air, it is perhaps not surprising that the late nineteenth century was a time of considerable domestic violence, directed primarily against the two groups most easily branded as inferior: Indians and immigrants. The last major battle between the Sioux and the U.S. Army was fought near Wounded Knee Creek in South Dakota in 1890. In an exchange of fire that quickly became a massacre, a cavalry unit dispatched by General Nelson Miles killed 150 Indians, many of them women and children. Miles, a veteran Indian fighter, suffered no career setback for this disgraceful action. In 1895 he was promoted to commanding general of the army, a position he held through the Spanish-American War.

Rallies and strikes by disaffected workers, many of them immigrants and some of them anarchists, became a focal point for violence. At an anarchist-led workers' rally in Haymarket Square in Chicago in 1886, four workers and seven policemen were killed. Four foreign anarchists were convicted and hanged for inciting violence. Ten people were killed by militia fire in a strike by Slav, Hungarian, and American-born coke workers against Andrew Carnegie's autocratic partner Henry Clay Frick in 1891. The most famous strike of the 1890s broke out in the summer of 1892 against Carnegie's Homestead, Pennsylvania, steelworks. While Carnegie was on his annual vacation at his castle in Scotland, Frick brought in Pinkerton detectives as strikebreakers; about a dozen workers and Pinkertons were killed. Several weeks later Frick survived an assassination attempt by a Russian-born anarchist.

In 1894 a strike in Illinois by Pullman train workers, many of them immigrants, led to a widespread stoppage of rail traffic, extensive property destruction, the deaths of four workers, and a trial of the union's leader, Eugene Debs, that went to the Supreme Court. Sporadically throughout the decade, Italian laborers were lynched out of xenophobic hysteria: eleven in New Orleans in 1891, three more in Louisiana in 1892, six in Colorado in 1895. In the worst disaster of the 1890s, twenty-one striking Polish and Hungarian coal workers were shot to death by police near Hazleton, Pennsylvania.

America near the end of the nineteenth century was a restless and racist society. Those who believed the myth of Anglo-Saxonism could ascribe inferiority to masses of people at home and abroad: blacks, Indians, workers, immigrants, and most foreigners. Such a cultural atmosphere was extremely conducive to imperialist initiatives, because imperialism—like Anglo-Saxonism, social Darwinism, and manifest destiny—was also based on the principle of racial inequality.

4.

With a propitious intellectual and cultural climate, a burgeoning economy, a swelling self-confidence, and the preparatory activity of several vigorous secretaries of state, the United States seemed overdue for imperial adventure. But why was it so long in coming? Three elements were lacking and were not supplied until the 1890s: military power, a political consensus, and an imperial opportunity.

Before the air age the military power of a maritime country was assessed by the strength of its navy. The United States did not have a navy that could sustain an expansion overseas until late in the century. The U.S. Navy, one of the world's largest after the Civil War, had plummeted to twelfth by the 1870s, behind sleeping China, decrepit Turkey, and tiny Chile. It would not have been capable of taking and holding any territory contested by another power. But by 1898, as the result of a sustained shipbuilding program begun in the 1880s, the U.S. Navy was among the best in the world.

Behind the decision to build a world-class navy was a gradual but important political shift. The decades after the Civil War were a period of exceptionally weak presidents. Between Lincoln and McKinley, only Grover Cleveland had significant stature. The Congress was correspondingly stronger and jealous of its prerogatives, a point made by Woodrow Wilson in his precocious book *Congressional Government*, published in 1885. And in the early postwar period Congress was not disposed to support an imperial agenda; it beat back efforts by several presidents to buy offshore territories.

As the century drew to a close, Congress, enlarged by representatives of new states that themselves exemplified American expansion, became more amenable to assertive policies. In parallel, as the country and its economy grew, the executive branch and the federal bureaucracy became more necessary to the effective functioning of government and therefore more powerful. By the time William McKinley began his first term in 1897, Congress had become both a more cooperative and a less dominant branch of government. The large appropriations for the navy were a consequence of this redistribution of power.

In 1895, with possibilities becoming more favorable for a burst of imperialism, a revolution against Spanish rule in Cuba provided the opportunity. The strategic importance of Cuba, the U.S. interest in the island's sugar economy, and a well-publicized record of Spanish atrocities against the Cuban people combined to make war with Spain a realistic option. Hay, Mahan, Root, Lodge, and Roosevelt all had grown up in a period of weak presidents, an exploding economy, growing military power, rising expectations, and disappointing performance. Now the time for action had come, and they seized it. In helping make the United States a great power, they were more than simple agents of history. Conditioned by decades of frustration in foreign policy, they could now lead it into a new realm and become the movers and shakers of American expansion.

2. The Favor of Fortune

1.

The geography of John Hay's boyhood explains how far America had come as a country and how far it had to go. Hay's father, a physician, followed the frontier from Kentucky to Indiana to Illinois, pressing with each move to the bounds of settled America. John was born in 1838 in Salem, Indiana, and was taken at the age of three to Warsaw, Illinois, a small town on the banks of the Mississippi River and a point of transit to the primitive, undeveloped, and largely unknown West. When the Hays settled in Illinois, there were only three states west of the Mississippi, all of them touching it. As young John stood by the river, he could see the old America on the east bank and the new America on the west.

Hay took pride in being an early example of the American melting pot: "The first ancestors I ever heard of were a Scotchman who was half English and a German woman who was half French. My mother was from New England [Helen Leonard Hay was born in Middleboro, Massachusetts] and my father was from the South. In this bewilderment I can confess that I am nothing but an American." Dr. Charles Hay, John's father, even in a state where white racism predominated, was an opponent of slavery. John inherited his father's egalitarian spirit, asserting once, "We have no distinction of classes in this country. I believe and hope we never shall have."

Hay was an exceptionally bright child. He did well at Latin and Greek, picked up German, and displayed a knack for rhyming. His father, unambitious for himself, must have seen the intellectual spark in his son. He sent him away to school at Pittsfield, the seat of Pike County; to high school at Springfield, the state capital and a railroad town on the make; and, at sixteen, to university in the East. Hay had a legacy at Brown University in Providence, Rhode Island, a small Baptist institution where his maternal grandfather had been a member of the class of 1792.

At Brown Hay began to develop the wit for which he later was famous. At an undergraduate dinner in his first year he was asked to make a speech but was told it should not be dry. He responded, "Hay that is green can never be dry." He distinguished himself academically, making Phi Beta Kappa, and was elected class poet, as his grandfather had been. In his senior year he joined a literary salon run by Sarah Helen Whitman, a woman distinguished for having had a romantic relationship with Edgar Allan Poe. Hay, impressed, called her "the revered priestess." He also made a close friend of Nora Perry, a young woman whose poems were good enough to be accepted by the *Atlantic Monthly*. Shy and slow to make friends, Hay was not a leader; he was one of the last picked for his senior society. But he was a good writer and an even better talker; his classmates remarked on his brilliance as a storyteller. With a great sense of fun, he was good company, a pleasure to be around.

His class poem "Erato," delivered at commencement, was a 436-line half ode, half lampoon in rhymed couplets. It celebrated the poetic muse, Greeks, Trojans, Romans, the Crimean War, American Indians ("the glory of the dying brave"), and life at Brown ("How gleams the meerschaum, at the close of day"). Alternately formulaic, romantic, and satirical, the poem reveals a considerable, if somewhat pompous, talent. Its last eight lines, the serious part, define the kind of man Hay was becoming. They may be unique in the literature of commencement, since they exhorted the graduating seniors to aim low, not high:

> *Our words may not float down the surging ages,*
> *As Hindoo lamps adown the sacred stream;*
> *We may not stand sublime on history's pages,*
> *The bright ideals of the future's dream;*
> *Yet we may all strive for the goal assigned us,*
> *Glad if we win and happy if we fail;*
> *Work calmly on nor care to leave behind us,*
> *The lurid glaring of the meteor's trail.*

Back in Illinois after graduation, Hay became melancholy. The proximate cause was the conflict between his desire to be a poet and the duty he felt to become a lawyer. But the problem was much deeper. Already before the age of twenty-one Hay was a depressive, and he remained one all his life, probably with a manic side as well. He was given to sending Nora Perry his poems of love and death. "I have wandered this winter in the valley of the shadow of death," he wrote her. "All the universe, God, earth, and heaven have been to me but vague and gloomy phantasms."

With Hay's chronic depressions came a low sense of his own worth, unusual in a man who was to make a success in four unrelated careers. It may help explain the soft elements of his character: his languor, his sympathy toward others, his innate fairness and decency, his horror of confrontation, his conservatism, his lack of ambition, and his reluctance to challenge himself. Revealingly, he wrote to Nora, "I am not suited for a reformer. I do not like to meddle with moral ills. I love comfortable people."

John Hay had all the charm, wit, lack of enterprise, and laziness of the dilettante. It would have been a fair guess, based on his first two decades, that he would spend his life in Warsaw, or perhaps in Springfield, as a local lawyer with a flair for writing and for amusing people with funny stories. That he went so far beyond this, in spite of his undergraduate caution against following the "lurid glaring of the meteor's trail," was a constant source of wonder to him. "I never read of a man," he wrote late in life, "who has had so much and such varied success as I have had, with so little ability and so little power of sustained industry." At twenty-one and ever after, he was blessed with the one quality necessary to turn his potential into achievement, luck.

After agonizing over a career for nearly a year—poet? doctor? minister?—Hay reluctantly decided to accept his uncle Milton's offer to join his law firm in Springfield. Milton Hay ran a highly successful law practice and had been a financial guardian angel for John, having paid his way through school and university. This time he produced a miracle. When John Hay started work in Springfield, he soon met the occupant of the shabby office next to Milton Hay's more commodious one, a part-time lawyer and full-time politician named Abraham Lincoln. The two must have liked each other; they had in common a sense of irony and humor and a talent for storytelling. One imagines Hay sitting spellbound as Lincoln, already one of the best raconteurs in the United States, spun his yarns.

When Lincoln ran for president the next year, 1860, Hay was recruited to work in the campaign by an old school friend, John Nicolay, an immigrant from Bavaria and a journalist six years Hay's senior. Nicolay was secretary to Lincoln's campaign, and Hay helped him in canvassing and speechmaking. When Lincoln won the presidency in November, he made Nicolay his private secretary, and Nicolay suggested that Hay come along too as assistant secretary. Lincoln objected—"We can't take all Illinois with us down to Washington"—but relented: "Well, let Hay come." So at twenty-two John Hay, whose lack of ambition was matched only by his inexperience in politics, found himself half of the two-man personal staff of the president of the United States.

The minuscule size of the White House bureaucracy put the young man in close touch with the president from the very beginning. He and Nicolay slept in the Executive Mansion, as it was then officially called, in order to be available around the clock. Hay's duties included reading letters written to the president, drafting answers to them, directing Lincoln's attention to significant newspaper articles, dealing with visitors, protecting Lincoln from importunate office seekers, arranging the seating for receptions, supervising the clerks who kept White House records, and standing in for Nicolay when his friend was absent. More informally, Hay often accompanied the irascible Mrs. Lincoln when she went out, played with the Lincolns' two small boys, Willie and Tad, and in general allayed tension and boredom with his wit. Versatile, quick, and reliable, the young man won Lincoln's trust; soon the president was signing the letters Hay had drafted for him without reading them.

Less than six weeks after Lincoln's inauguration, Confederate gunners fired on Fort Sumter, and Lincoln became a war president. During the war he entrusted Hay with some sensitive assignments, including investigating the effectiveness of the Union ironclads in Charleston Harbor, testing Lincoln's political support in Florida, and monitoring a clandestine meeting in Canada to assess a Confederate peace overture that turned out to be a sham. To give Hay status for such missions, the president conferred on him the courtesy military rank of colonel. The title embarrassed Hay, though not enough to prevent him from using it all his life.

During the Civil War, Hay relished the excitement of the fighting and the stories from the front, as would be normal in a young man. He particularly enjoyed the company of General Joseph ("Fighting Joe") Hooker, whose defeat by Robert E. Lee at Chancellorsville failed to deter him from a lifelong ridiculing of Lee's ability. Hooker told Hay that Lee was not much respected in the army and had been surpassed by all his lieutenants in the Mexican War. Hay also recorded a comment by Hooker: "At dinner he spoke of our army. He says: It was the finest on the planet. He would like to see it fighting with foreigners." In three decades it would be.

As casualties mounted, Hay lost much of his callow approach to war. He was too close to Lincoln not to see the president's anguish at the massive loss of life. He read, and probably drafted, many of Lincoln's compassionate letters to parents who had lost sons in conflict. He almost certainly wrote Lincoln's celebrated letter to Mrs. Bixby, who had lost two sons in the war. Hay was himself under fire once, near Charleston. He saw one shell take a soldier's leg off and another strike a man in the face. His description of the sounds and sights of artillery conveyed his horror:

> The shells have singular voices; some had a regular musical note like *Chu-chu-weechu-weechu-b r r r*; and each of the fragments a wicked little whistle of its own. Many struck in the black, marshy mud behind us, burying themselves, and casting a malodorous shower into the air. . . . I often saw in the air a shell bursting,— fierce, jagged white lines darting out first, like javelins,—then the flowering of the awful bud into full bloom,—all in the dead silence of the upper air,—the crack and whistle of the fragments.

The war was only a part-time activity for this eligible single man. With his charm Hay was pursued by Washington hostesses. He was amorously linked to the daughter of a Massachusetts congressman, a Hooper from Boston. The small and debonair bachelor with his long, curled whiskers liked the attention. He injected a note of the flip in a letter to Nicolay, who was away on a health cure: "Nothing new. An immense crowd that boreth ever. Painters who make God's air foul to the nostrils. Rain, which makes a man moist and adhesive. Dust, which unwholesomely penetrates one's lungs. Washington, which makes one swear." Fortunately there was a powerful antidote to Hay's propensity to snobbishness: Abraham Lincoln. After some hesitation about taking his uncouth boss seriously, Hay became a hero-worshiper, a chronicler of Lincoln's humor, and a herald of his greatness.

Hay's descriptions of Lincoln—"the Tycoon," as he and Nicolay called the president—captured the comedy in Lincoln without making him ridiculous:

> Three Indians of the Pottawatomies called today upon their Great Father. The President amused them greatly by airing the two or three Indian words he knew. I was amused by his awkward efforts to make himself understood by speaking bad English; e.g. "Where live now? When go back Iowa?"

> At a dark period of the war, a gentleman of some local prominence came to Washington for some purpose, and so as to obtain the assistance of Lincoln, he brought a good deal of evidence to prove that he was the man who originated his nomination. He attacked the great chief in the vestibule of the Executive Mansion, and walked with him to the War Department, impressing this view upon him. . . . He walked back to the White-House with him, clinching his argument with new and cogent facts. At the door the President turned and, with that smile which was half sadness and half fun, he said: "So you think you made me President?" "Yes, Mr. President, under Providence, I think I did." "Well," said Lincoln, opening the door and going in, "it's a pretty mess you've got me into. But I forgive you."

> Today came into the Executive Mansion an assembly of cold water men and women to make a temperance speech to the Tycoon. They filed into the East Room looking blue and thin in the keen autumnal air. Three blue-skinned damsels did Love, Purity, and Fidelity in Red, White, and Blue gowns. A few invalid soldiers stumped along in the dismal procession. They made a long speech at the Tycoon in which they called intemperance the cause of our defeats. The President could not see it, as he said, "for the rebels drink more and worse than we do." At this they filed off drearily to a collation of cold water and green apples.

Hay felt a tenderness for Lincoln's humanity, even while he was making fun of him:

> A little after midnight . . . the President came into the office laughing, with a volume of Hood's Works in his hand, to show Nicolay and me the little caricature, "An Unfortunate Bee-ing"; seemingly utterly unconscious that he, with his short shirt hanging about his long legs, and setting out behind like the tail feathers of an enormous ostrich, was infinitely funnier than anything in the book he was laughing at. What a man it is! Occupied all day with matters of vast moment, deeply anxious about the fate of the greatest army of the world, with his own plans and future hanging on the events of the passing hour, he yet has such a wealth of simple *bonhommie* and good fellowship that he gets out of bed and perambulates the house in his shirt to find us, that we may share with him the fun of poor Hood's queer little conceits.

At times Lincoln treated Hay as his own son. In the summer the president would escape the Washington heat by spending the night at the Soldiers' Home on a hill in the northern part of the city. On one occasion Hay "went with him to the Soldiers' Home, and he read Shakespeare to me, the end of *Henry V* and the beginning of *Richard III*, till my heavy eyelids caught his considerate notice, and he sent me to bed."

In his closeness to Lincoln, Hay learned lessons that lasted him a lifetime. He shared the president's devotion to preserving the Union and his opposition to slavery. Those two principles drew Lincoln's protégé to a lifelong commitment to the Republican party; Hay never considered voting against a Republican candidate for president, no matter how unqualified he found him. His loyalty derived directly from Lincoln. "I consider Lincoln Republicanism incarnate," he wrote in 1866, "with all its faults and all its virtues. As in spite of some rudeness, Republicanism is the sole hope of a sick world, so Lincoln with all his foibles, is the greatest character since Christ." Hay's association with Lincoln also made him a lowercase republican. Lincoln's influence probably weakened Hay's inclination toward an elitist disdain for democracy. Hay's later diplomatic experience in four monarchies eliminated it altogether.

Hay admired Lincoln's charity toward political enemies. In one case he quoted the president as saying: "Perhaps I may have too little [personal resentment], but I never thought it paid. A man has not time to spend half his life in quarrels. If any man ceases to attack me, I never remember the past against him." The young aide was also touched by the effect of the war on the president:

> One of the most tender and compassionate of men, he was forced to give orders which cost thousands of lives; by nature a man of order and thrift, he saw the daily spectacle of unutterable waste and destruction which he could not prevent. The cry of the widow and the orphan was always in his ears; the awful responsibility resting upon him as the protector of an imperilled republic kept him true to his duty, but could not make him unmindful of the intimate details of that vast sum of human misery involved in civil war.

Lincoln taught the young aspiring writer the power of words to motivate and inspire. Hay's eyewitness account of the president at Gettysburg recognized the special nature of Lincoln's short address, though, interestingly, it failed to foresee an immortal future for his words:

> In the morning I got a beast and rode out with the President and suite to the Cemetery in procession. The procession formed itself in an orphanly sort of way, and moved out with very little help from anybody; and after a little delay Mr. Everett [the principal speaker] took his place on the stand,—and Mr. Stockton made a prayer which thought it was an oration,—and Mr. Everett spoke as he always does, perfectly; and the President, in a firm, free way, with more grace than is his wont, said his half-dozen lines of consecration,—and the music wailed, and we went home through crowded and cheering streets.

A month after the Battle of Gettysburg Hay sent Nicolay a memorable picture of a president at the top of his form:

> The Tycoon is in fine whack. I have rarely seen him more serene and busy. He is managing this war, the draft, foreign relations, and planning a reconstruction of the Union, all at once. I never knew with what a tyrannous authority he rules the Cabinet till now. The most important things he decides, and there is no cavil. I am grow-

ing more convinced that the good of the country absolutely demands that he should be kept where he is till this thing is over.
There is no man in the country so wise, so gentle and so firm.

The word "tyrannous" was no slip of the pen. Hay was enormously
impressed by Lincoln's toughness. He wrote Lincoln's law partner after the president's death: "It is absurd to call him a modest man. No
great man was ever modest. It was his intellectual arrogance and unconscious assumption of superiority that men like Chase and Sumner
never could forgive."

Compassion, dignity, reserve, charity, serenity, tenderness, wisdom,
gentleness: These qualities, which Hay respected and described
in Lincoln, became lodestones for Hay himself. But Lincoln's harder
virtues—power, tyranny, firmness, arrogance, superiority—were beyond the bounds of Hay's character. Though he reached the third-
highest executive position in the United States, he was never
comfortable with power or leadership. Firmness was difficult for him,
arrogance was incompatible with his habitually low self-esteem, and
"tyrannous" was never a word that could describe John Hay.

He fell short of Lincoln in one other important respect: He could
never achieve the touch that Lincoln had with common people. He
was horrified at Lincoln's willingness to welcome to the White House
office seekers, cranks, or just anybody. Though he respected ordinary
people, Hay was never comfortable in the company of fools, boors, or
adversaries. As secretary of state he was to pay for that failing in his
rancorous relations with Congress. He was not a demonstrative person; one of his closest friends commented, "No matter how intimate
you were or how merry the occasion, nobody ever slapped John Hay
on the back." Said Henry Adams, his friend of later life: "He no more
resembles the average American than a nightingale represents a
hawk."

Hay was with Lincoln when he died on April 15, 1865. He had
been with the president's son Robert at the White House on the
evening that John Wilkes Booth shot Lincoln at Ford's Theater. By the
time Hay and Robert Lincoln made the seven-block carriage ride to
Tenth Street, the president had been laid on a bed in a house across
the street. Hay stayed all night at the head of Lincoln's bed until the
president died shortly after dawn.

As Hay was at Lincoln's side at his death, in a symbolic sense Lincoln stayed by Hay's side for the rest of his life. Having worked five years for Lincoln the candidate and president, Hay was to devote another twenty years to writing and publishing, with Nicolay, a monumental ten-volume biography designed to secure the martyred president's place in history. Lincoln remained for him a mentor, teacher, and sometimes ribald companion. While he lacked Lincoln's greatness, Hay drew inspiration from Lincoln's great qualities, which drove him to achieve more in life than he had ever thought possible.

2.

The month before Lincoln's death, Hay accepted from Secretary of State Seward a diplomatic appointment as secretary of legation (the number two position) in the American mission in Paris. Hay had been trying to get out of the White House for reasons he considered too sensitive to explain. They probably had to do with the terrible-tempered Mrs. Lincoln, whom Hay and Nicolay privately called "the Hell-cat" and "the enemy." Hay had earned her dislike by curbing her personal use of public funds. Two weeks before Lincoln's assassination he wrote his brother Charles, "I am thoroughly sick of certain aspects of life here, which you will understand without my putting them on paper."

Hay had great respect for the dynamic Seward; he called him a "placid, philosophic optimist, . . . the truest and most single-hearted Republican alive." The older man must also have seen something special in Lincoln's young assistant, innocent as he was of diplomatic experience. Hay left for Paris in the summer of 1865, wafted by a letter of introduction to John Bigelow, the American minister, from Thurlow Weed, the Republican boss of New York State: "Hay is a bright, gifted young man, with agreeable manners and refined tastes. I don't believe he has been spoiled, though he has been much exposed."

With that faint praise, Hay launched a diplomatic career that he pursued intermittently for the rest of his life. But when he departed for France, he had no idea that he might become a lifelong diplomat. He had thought of running for Congress from Florida, of managing a vineyard he owned in Warsaw, of becoming a writer, or of going back to Uncle Milton's law firm. The chance to see the world for a year or two, thanks to Seward, relieved him of such larger choices.

In any case, there was no professional foreign service for Hay to join. Though a military giant because of the Civil War, the United States was a diplomatic pygmy. The major official U.S. presence abroad was in its nearly three hundred consulates, charged with assisting trade and protecting American citizens. Many of these were staffed by non-Americans, and others were filled by Americans who had other interests to pursue abroad, like the writers William Dean Howells, Bret Harte, and—at an earlier time—James Fenimore Cooper and Nathaniel Hawthorne. Diplomatic missions, established to represent American political interests and to report on local developments, numbered only thirty-six in 1870, with fewer than a hundred officers. So little importance did the government assign to its diplomacy that it did not create the rank of ambassador until 1893. Since until then the highest diplomatic rank was minister, American chiefs of mission were subordinated in protocol precedence to the ambassadors of all other countries, no matter how small.

American diplomacy was mostly a patronage operation. Great Britain had started a career service with entrance examinations for junior applicants in 1856. Though there were some efforts as early as the Grant administration to make U.S. diplomats more professional, the first competitive exams were not given until 1905 under Theodore Roosevelt. Ambrose Bierce, who observed American mores with a jaundiced eye, defined "consul" as "a person who having failed to secure an office from the people is given one by the Administration on condition that he leave the country." Presidential practice in Hay's youth was to appoint Civil War generals to diplomatic posts. In Paris and Madrid Hay served under former Union generals, neither of them competent and one of them under investigation for corruption.

Given such arrant neglect of the diplomatic function, the wonder is that the United States was able to manage an intelligent foreign policy. Yet for the most part it did. It benefited from the services of some first-rate diplomats, many of them named Adams. During the revolutionary period John Adams pleaded the American case as commissioner to France and Holland; later, as minister to Britain, he helped repair the relationship shattered by the War for Independence; and as president he kept the United States out of an impending war with France. His son John Quincy, even before becoming secretary of state and author of the Monroe Doctrine, represented the United States with prodigious talent in Holland, Britain, Portugal, Prussia, and Russia.

The third Adams in line, Charles Francis, was arguably the best envoy America ever sent to London. Serving during the American Civil War, Adams succeeded in keeping the British from intervening on the side of the Confederacy. Before his Vienna assignment, Hay stopped in London, lunched and dined with Adams, and traded political gossip with the older man. Hay's closeness to Lincoln had put him in touch with many senior Washington figures like Adams, and he was never bashful about exploiting such connections. Under Adams's wing he visited the houses of Parliament, saw Disraeli and Gladstone in action, and admired the Commons for the quality of its oratory and for its exclusion of the general public, a contrast with the more populist U.S. Congress.

Also in London was Adams's son Henry, serving as secretary to his father. Hay had met Henry Adams in Washington during the Civil War, when Adams was working for his father in the House of Representatives. The cerebral and acerbic Adams, just Hay's age, was on the threshold of a brilliant career as a Harvard professor, journalist, historian, and philosopher of art. In London he and Hay began one of the most famous American friendships of the nineteenth century. At the time, however, Henry Adams did not have much respect for what Hay was doing. "John Hay passed through London," he wrote in his autobiography, "in order to bury himself in second-rate legations for years."

In Paris, his first foreign service post, Hay served under another able diplomat, John Bigelow, who contributed to the two American achievements of preventing France from supporting the Confederacy during the Civil War and curbing Napoleon III's ambitions in Mexico. In the Mexican affair Hay could observe Bigelow's skillful diplomacy in helping Secretary Seward convince the emperor to back down. His role, however, is not apparent from his diary, which focused instead on his visits to galleries, museums, and the opera. He showed little

taste for helping Americans in trouble, one of the tasks of U.S. legations. When an American visitor asked for assistance in a dispute with
a hotel, Hay fobbed her off with the observation that the French
"make their living by plundering foreigners."

The young diplomat had as little regard for French royalty as he did
for French hotelkeepers. His experience with Napoleon III's court
sharpened his republican dislike of monarchy. He reveled in lampooning courtiers: a Bavarian official "who seemed moved by rusty strings,"
royal footmen "of portentous calf development." He left an astringent
picture of the emperor in the act of receiving the credentials of
Bigelow's successor, the corruption-tainted general John A. Dix:

> Gen'l Dix, followed by me and Hoffman [a junior officer in the
> U.S. legation], was then ushered into The Presence. The General
> looked anxiously around for the Emperor, advancing undecidedly,
> until a little man, who was standing in front of the Throne, stepped
> forward to meet him. Everybody bowed profoundly as the Duc de
> Cambacérès gave the name and title of the General. The little man
> bowed, and the General, beginning to recognize in him a dim like-
> ness to the Emperor's portrait, made his speech to him. . . .
>
> Short and stocky, [the emperor] moves with a queer, side-long
> gait, like a gouty crab; a man so wooden looking that you would ex-
> pect his voice to come rasping out like a watchman's rattle. A com-
> plexion like crude tallow—marked for Death whenever Death wants
> him—to be taken in half an hour, or left, neglected by the Skeleton
> King for years, perhaps, if properly coddled. The moustache, an im-
> perial which the world knows, but ragged and bristly, concealing the
> mouth entirely, is moving a little nervously as the lips twitch. Eyes
> sleepily watchful—furtive—stealthy, rather ignoble; like servants
> looking out of dirty windows and saying "nobody at home," and lying
> as they say it. And withal a wonderful phlegm. He stands there as
> still and impassive as if carved in oak for a ship's figurehead. He
> looks not unlike one of those rude inartistic statues. His legs are too
> short—his body too long. He never looks well but on a throne or on
> a horse, as kings ought.

Hay must have enjoyed writing that. It was close to his swan song
in Paris. In an inane example of how not to run a diplomatic mission,
General Dix insisted on bringing in his own staff and getting rid of his
by now experienced deputy. Back in Washington in early 1867, Hay

went straight to his patron Seward, who complained at the pressure he was under to get rid of Lincoln appointees but still offered to help his young friend return to Europe. Establishing what was to be a standard networking procedure, Hay made the rounds of the Washington political and social scene. He rekindled relations with such powerful political figures as Charles Sumner, chairman of the Senate Committee on Foreign Relations, and Salmon P. Chase, chief justice of the United States (who had been secretary of the treasury under Lincoln), called on other senators and representatives, and danced with well-connected young ladies at balls and cotillions. Seward did his best for Hay, but an expected appointment to Sweden went to a general, and the young diplomat went home to Illinois.

Back in Warsaw, he wrote a halfhearted job application to Uncle Milton: "I have forgotten most of the law I read with you and would have to learn it all over again. I am not even a good clerk as I know very little about money or business. It is nearly an even chance whether I would ever get to be worth my salt at the bar." After receiving such a low self-evaluation from his nephew, Milton Hay could be excused for telling him, as he did, that he had no openings. Hay's halfhearted job search as he pruned his vineyard exposed his real hope for another diplomatic assignment. Thanks to Seward, one finally came through: He was appointed chief of mission in Vienna.

It was a big assignment for a twenty-eight-year-old, since Austria, which had created a dual monarchy with Hungary that year, was still one of the great powers and ruled enormous territories in central Europe. Characteristically Hay threw himself into the cultural life: plays at the Burgtheater, art at the Belvedere, and music—opera, ballet, and operetta, with a preference for Johann Strauss and Offenbach. As always, he loved the parties and balls, followed the next morning by swims in the chilly Danube. He found Viennese women pretty and beguiling, "very easy and gay."

At a ball he was presented to Emperor Franz Josef, who commended the "wonderful resources" the United States had displayed in the Civil War. "He spoke of the difficult position [of President Johnson] and complimented him highly on his 'energy and courageous consistency.'" Hay must have bitten his lip here since he believed that Andrew Johnson, who had just escaped conviction in his impeachment trial, was doing his best to discredit the presidency.

Hay did find some time for work in Vienna. In February 1868 he sent Seward a thoughtful dispatch about the arms buildup by Prussia, Austria, and France, and the necessity of collective diplomacy to restrain it.

> The great calamity and danger of Europe today are these enormous armaments. . . . There is no menace to peace that could not be immediately dispelled by a firm protest of the peacefully disposed majority of nations. There would be, therefore, no danger to any people, but a vast and immediate gain to all from a general disarmament. . . .
>
> Why then is this awful waste of youth and treasure continued? I believe from no other motive than to sustain the waning prestige of Kings. Armies are to-day only useful in Europe to overcome the people in peace, or by groundless wars to divert their attention from domestic misrule. With the disappearance of great armies, the welfare of the people would become the only mainspring of national action, and that false and wicked equilibrium by which now the interests of one man weigh as heavily as those of millions of his fellow creatures, would be utterly destroyed.

The dispatch was the appeal of a man who had been through a war claiming the greatest human carnage since the Napoleonic era a half century before. European wars since then, like the Crimean and the Austro-Prussian wars, had been relatively short and light in casualties. Hay's warning against the thoughtless use of military power was of course unheeded. He was a junior diplomat, and America's political weight counted for little in the world.

Hay was no pacifist. His admiring account of the Italian revolutionary Garibaldi showed a belief in just wars: Garibaldi "loved liberty and peace so well that he is willing to fight for them. He hates war—as a doctor hates drugs, but he uses it, for the good of the world." Hay's sophisticated and compassionate view of war, based on sober reflection on his Civil War experience, stands in sharp contrast with the unalloyed and unexamined celebration of war by his future leader Theodore Roosevelt, who was six when the Civil War ended.

Hay's tour in Vienna toughened his intellectual fiber but was otherwise marked by self-indulgence and condescension. He left an unfortunate account of visits to the Judenplatz, the Jewish section of

Vienna, where he was both fascinated and repelled by the "stooping, dirty figures in long, patched, and oily black gabardines of every conceivable material, the richest the shabbiest usually, because oldest and most used, covering the slouching, creeping form, from the rounded shoulders to the splay, shuffling feet. A battered soft felt hat crowns the oblique, indolent, crafty face, and, what is most offensive of all, a pair of greasy curls dangle in front of the pendulous ears. This coquetry of hideousness is most nauseous."

In succumbing to the worst kind of American bigotry, Hay even blamed Viennese Jews for their poverty. "In America we always say, 'Rich as a Jew,' because even if a Jew is poor he is so brisk, so sharp and enterprising that he is sure to make money eventually. But these slouching rascals are as idle as they are ugly." One wonders if the opinions of the aspiring American intellectual would have been so jejune had he lived in Vienna a generation or two later and moved, as he would have, in the company of Freud, Schnitzler, Mahler, Hofmannsthal, Zweig, Kraus, and Schönberg, Jews who made the city a synonym for brilliance and sophistication.

In his year in Austria Hay found the leisure to visit neighboring countries, developing a taste for travel that his later trips with Henry Adams were to indulge. As he prepared to leave Vienna, he sent his former chief Bigelow a negative evaluation of the diplomatic profession. No two American diplomats, he wrote, "can catch each other's eyes without mutual guffaws, unless they have a power of facial muscle that would put the Roman augurs to shame." Nevertheless, after a few months lecturing on Europe to YMCA and other civic groups in the Middle West, he set out for Spain in mid-1869 as first secretary of legation at Madrid. Saddled with another incompetent ex-general as minister, the dissolute Gettysburg veteran Daniel E. Sickles, he decided to run things himself.

Spain was in the midst of a political crisis. Queen Isabella II had been deposed, and there was a struggle among those who wanted to restore absolutism, those who favored a constitutional monarchy, and those who wanted a republic. Hay was captivated by Emilio Castelar, the chief advocate of republicanism, and praised him beyond the bounds of judgment. In Washington Hay had learned republican values from Lincoln. In Paris he had written a poetic obituary for Napoleon III:

> *Afraid to fight and afraid to fly,*
>   *He cowers in an abject shiver;*
> *The people will come to their own at last,—*
>   *God is not mocked forever.*

From Vienna he had written Bigelow: "If ever, in my green and salad days, I sometimes vaguely doubted, I am safe now. I am a Republican till I die. When we get to Heaven, we can try a Monarchy, perhaps." Now in Madrid he was an unabashed republican in practice as well as theory.

Hay absorbed himself in covering parliamentary debates and cultivating politicians, especially Castelar. He studied Spanish history, the Spanish language, and the politics and culture of Madrid. Liberated from instructions by the lag of a month or more in the diplomatic pouch from Washington, he probably went too far in taking sides in the internal Spanish debate. But he knew, as he wrote later, that "most Americans will agree with those thoughtful liberals of the Peninsula, who hold that . . . reformation is impossible through the monarchy." However, republicanism was not to triumph in Spain, at least not during Hay's lifetime.

There was one issue on which the U.S. government did have a specific concern with Spanish policy: Cuba. Insurrection had broken out in 1868 against Spanish rule on the island, and the Spanish Army was using excessive force in trying to put it down. Hay read the Spanish government as favorable to American mediation leading to "the cession of Cuba to the Cubans" but believed it lacked the will for such an unpopular move. In frustration he wrote Nicolay in January 1870: "I am afraid Cuba is gone. This Government wants to sell out but dares not, and has no power to put a stop to the atrocities on the island. The only thing left to our Government is to do nothing and keep its mouth shut; or interfere to stop the horrors in Cuba on the ground of humanity, or the damage resulting to American interests."

Hay had come a long way. Now he was arguing a moral position as the basis for American policy; stopping the "horrors in Cuba" was in his view tied directly to American interests. Thirty years ahead of his time, he was contemplating U.S. intervention. He was convinced that in time Cuba would become part of the United States, and he welcomed the American gravitational pull. What is important is that Hay approached the Cuban issue through a belief in self-determination and human rights, not through manifest destiny, imperialism, or strategic doctrine.

He decided to end this diplomatic phase of his life in the spring of 1870 because of "pecuniary circumstances." He had lost four thousand dollars in the turpentine business, and his Illinois vineyard, however pleasant as a place for reflection, was not profitable. He was also fed up with the Grant administration, which he believed had filled the diplomatic service with "swine" and "nonentities." His mentor Seward was no longer there to advance his career, and American diplomacy offered no employment guarantees. He hated job seeking, complaining to Nicolay, "I am sure that by hanging around and eating dirt, I could get some office." The last thing this insecure young man wanted was to become a "whiteheaded old shyster of sixty loafing about the Capitol boring my Senator to get me an office to keep me from starving."

He had not wasted his five years as a foreign service officer. A diplomatic career that had begun inauspiciously with social and superficial diversions, and still reflected elements of snobbishness and racial prejudice, had taken on a new seriousness of purpose. He had used his experience with monarchist societies to examine his own views and had avoided clientism, the occupational disease of diplomats. His bout with monarchies had made him even more of a republican. He had developed a natural empathy with other cultures. In Spain he plumbed so deeply in his year that he collected enough material to write a first-rate book on the country. He was still a thirty-two-year-old of "agreeable manners and refined tastes," but there was now a greater depth to him. Even so, as his new friend Henry Adams put it rather cruelly: "No one would have picked out William McKinley or John Hay or Mark Hanna for great statesmen."

3.

Hay was constantly preoccupied with the specter of failure. He wrote his brother Charles from Europe: "I am confronted continually by the suggestion of middle age coming on me and finding me with no money, no home, no trade, nothing but the habits of a loafer. Up to a certain point it is a good and pleasant thing to knock around the world, but one must know when to hang up the fiddle and the bow and take up the serious shovel and the lucrative hoe." In pursuit of shovel and hoe, Hay's charm and networking skills came to his aid once again. He had not been off the boat from Europe for more than a few hours when he fell into a journalistic bonanza.

The possibly exaggerated story goes that after landing in New York, he looked up some of his friends and ended by dining at the Union League Club with Whitelaw Reid, deputy editor of the *New York Tribune*. After dinner Reid took Hay back to the *Tribune* offices, where Hay effortlessly turned some dispatches from Europe into an editorial. Horace Greeley, the legendary editor of the *Tribune*, said the next day: "I have read a million editorials, and this is the best of them all." John Hay had a job in journalism.

The *Tribune* was one of the most respected newspapers in America, with a nationwide circulation and, under Greeley's prodding, a commitment to "advance the interests of the People." Hay made fun of its nickname, the Great Moral Organ, but many took it seriously. Greeley had assembled a bunch of crack journalists, most of them, like Reid, around Hay's age. As Lincoln's aide during the Civil War Hay had accompanied Greeley to Niagara to interview the self-styled but bogus Confederate representatives. Greeley had been humiliated by the fraudulence of his interlocutors, but Hay at least had made a good impression on the famous editor. Greeley considered him the most brilliant of his young writers.

Hay spent four and a half years in New York, writing editorials on foreign affairs, national politics, and literary and cultural issues. He also did some new reporting. Reid sent him to Chicago to cover the aftermath of the Chicago fire of 1871. He managed a witty, if inappropriate, jauntiness in his visit to Mrs. O'Leary's house, where the fire started: "For out of that house, last Saturday night, came a woman with a lamp to the barn behind the house, to milk the cow with the crumpled temper, that killed the lamp, that spilled the kerosene, that fired the straw that burned Chicago." Hay interviewed "Our Lady of the Lamp" and her husband, who was too worried about damage suits to be communicative.

Though the *Tribune*'s editorials were unsigned and thus unattributable, Hay undoubtedly wrote many of those covering the international scene. He had to overcome a propensity to seek the middle on issues; as he confessed to Nicolay during his first year at the paper, "I do not like to blame and I mortally hate to praise." But on one subject, monarchy, his antipathy was still strong; the American Revolution had been successful and must now be extended to other countries. On domestic issues he was more conservative. When his employer Greeley ran for president on the Democratic ticket against the scandal-plagued Grant in 1872, Hay stayed home from the polls. Though he hated the corruption of Grant's administration, his loyalty to Lincoln's Republican party was still strong.

A colleague at the *Tribune*, Joseph Bucklin Bishop, who had been at Brown with Hay, left an admiring account of Hay's newspaper days. Hay "was always generous of praise for the work of others and depreciatory of his own." He had an unerring insight into character and an effervescent personality: "A more joyful companion could not be imagined, for there was in him no trace of that melancholy which became almost habitual with him in his later years."

Most striking to Bishop and to others was Hay's skill as a talker. In the main room, which the editorial writers shared, "some of the best talk it has ever been my privilege to listen to was to be heard almost daily. . . . [Hay] loved to talk and his keen joy in it was so genuine and so obvious that it infected his listeners. He was as good a listener as he was a talker. . . . He talked without the slightest sign of effort or premeditation, said his good things as if he owed their inspiration to the listener, and never exhibited a shadow of consciousness of his own brilliancy." For Elihu Root, his partner in the McKinley and Roosevelt administrations, the way he expressed a thought "in substance and perfection of form left in the mind the sense of having seen a perfectly cut precious stone."

Hay's years in New York were a flush time. He made friends among other intellectuals and was surprised and pleased that they took his own intellect seriously. The writers Walt Whitman, Bret Harte, and Mark Twain; the painter John La Farge; the sculptor Augustus Saint-Gaudens; the geologist Clarence King; and the financiers William Astor, William Vanderbilt, and Jay Gould all were within Hay's eclectic circle. He joined the Century Association, a club with a literary bent, and the more social Knickerbocker Club. Stimulated by his surroundings, he returned to his first love, poetry. Shortly after his return from Spain, he had written some dialect poems about his home county in Illinois. Thanks to his friend Reid, the first two were published in the *Tribune*'s weekly supplement. They caused a sensation, although since he had coyly signed them "J. H.," he did not at first achieve the fame that the poems did.

Hay's *Pike County Ballads* followed a dialect tradition that was already well established by 1871, when they came out in book form, now under Hay's name. James Russell Lowell had published stories in New England dialect in the 1840s. Hay's friend Bret Harte had been writing western dialect verse since the 1850s. Joel Chandler Harris's southern stories of Uncle Remus came out a decade after the Pike County poems.

The first of Hay's poems to be published was "Little Breeches." It tells the story of a four-year-old boy who is left on a wagon while his pa goes into the store for a jug of molasses. In his absence the horses bolt; the father, searching in a snowstorm, finds the horses in a snowdrift but not the child. Little Breeches is later found in a sheepfold, which he could not have reached on his own in the storm. "How did he get thar? Angels." The poem is as mawkish as this retelling, but its very sentimentality is what gave it public appeal. It ends:

> *And I think that saving a little child,*
> *And bringing him to his own,*
> *Is a derned sight better business*
> *Than loafing around the Throne.*

A much better poem is "Jim Bludso, or The Prairie Belle." It was based on a true happening on the Mississippi, and it brought to vivid life the world of the river. Jim is the engineer of an old steamboat, the *Prairie Belle*. He is something of a moral outcast, with one wife in Natchez and another in Pike. But his true worth is revealed when the boat catches fire in a race with a newer boat. To save the passengers, Jim turns it toward a willow bank and holds it there so they can get off: "I'll hold her nozzle agin the bank / Till the last galoot's ashore." They all make it, but Jim Bludso dies.

He were n't no saint,—but at jedgement
I'd run my chance with Jim,
'Longside of some pious gentlemen
That would n't shook hands with him.

He seen his duty, a dead-sure thing,—
And went for it thar and then;
And Christ ain't a going to be too hard
On a man that died for men.

The best of the *Pike County Ballads* is "Banty Tim," which gives a fascinating picture of race relations in Illinois and of Hay's own liberalism on the subject. The White Man's Committee of Spunky Point votes a resolution to expel a black man, Banty Tim, from town. One of the committee members, a former Union sergeant named Tilmon Joy, tells how Banty Tim saved his life in combat by crawling through Rebel fire and carrying Joy to safety, though Tim was hit many times. Joy concludes his speech with a delicious putdown:

"So my gentle gazelles, there's my answer,
And here stays Banty Tim:
He trumped Death's ace for me that day,
And I'm not goin' back on him!
You may rezaloot till the cows come home,
But if one of you tetches the boy,
He'll wrestle his hash tonight in hell,
Or my name's not Tilmon Joy!"

Ever insecure, Hay enjoyed his new notoriety while disparaging the quality of his "doggerel." He turned down a request to put some of his ballads in an anthology: "I am no poet. . . . I have never written a rhyme which deserved to be printed,—still less to be gathered up and kept as specimens of literature. I can do some things as well as most men of my weight, but poems are not of them. Let me up, and pass on to the next man in H.!" He was particularly embarrassed by "Little Breeches": "I shudder and hide in the cellar only when the boy with the small Knickerbockers is mentioned."

Some critics agreed with Hay's self-evaluation. "Poor poetry, foolish argument, wretched logic, and shameful theology," sniffed the *Hart-ford Post*. Religious reviewers were appalled at the glorification of sinners like Jim Bludso. One of them caught the spirit of Hay's verse in his satire of it:

> *You may murder or steal, keep a house of ill-fame*
> *And still go to Heaven*—if you only die game.

But Hay had some important intellectuals on his side. William Dean Howells, a major novelist and editor of the *Atlantic Monthly*, probably the foremost literary journal in the country, liked the poems well enough to publish them as a book. Howells complimented Hay for being a moralist in his writings. Even fussy Henry Adams, now an assistant professor of medieval history at Harvard, enjoyed the ballads, which he described as "better than anything Bret Harte ever wrote."

Hay was right to call them doggerel, but they were authentic in describing western virtues and attitudes, and they were told with humor and narrative skill. Jim Bludso is a real folk hero in the spirit of John Henry and Casey Jones. "Banty Tim," an American "Gunga Din," is a minor classic. The rhyme, meter, and brevity were incentives to memorize the poems, and thousands did. With his dialect verse, effete John Hay had found a means to stir the masses. Sadly, but characteristically, he never used it again. After, perhaps because of, the success of *Pike County Ballads* he never wrote another dialect poem.

In the same year, 1871, Howells published in the *Atlantic Monthly* several sketches that Hay had written about Spain, then brought them out in a book under the title *Castilian Days*. It is probably the best thing Hay ever wrote, an evocative description of a country rooted in a past both glorious and abhorrent and trying desperately to modernize. He drew enchanting pictures of Madrid, medieval Toledo, Spanish ladies ("built on the old-fashioned generous plan"), bullfights, proverbs, painters (he liked Velázquez and Murillo, but not El Greco), miracle plays, Cervantes, and duels. His description of bullfighting rates a place on the same shelf as the writings of Ernest Hemingway and Barnaby Conrad. It contains none of the normal American animal rights horror at the corrida, but portrays it as a fusion of cruelty and beauty. Hay's understanding and respect for tauromachy allowed him to sniff at its defects with the hauteur of an aficionado: "Now the bull is baited and slain by hired artists, and the horses they mount are the sorriest hacks that ever went to the knacker."

The political part of *Castilian Days* was a strong appeal for the transformation of Spain from a monarchy to a republic. Hay made an uncompromising defense of popular government: "There are those who think the Spaniards are not fit for freedom. I believe that no people are fit for anything else. . . . The people have the right to govern themselves, even if they do it ill." He had nothing good to say about Spain's priests and kings, calling Philip II a "fantastic bigot." He predicted inaccurately that they would soon be swept away. "The current cannot be turned backward. . . . Spain . . . is not condemned to everlasting punishment for the crimes of her kings and priesthood." These fighting words reverberated down the decades of American politics. In 1904, when Hay was Roosevelt's secretary of state, the cabinet heard a demand for his resignation by Irish-Americans still furious at his attacks on the Catholic Church more than three decades before.

4.

In early 1874, in the middle of his stint at the *New York Tribune*, Hay was a thirty-five-year-old with an enviable record of accomplishment. He had been a close adviser to a great American president, a diplomat of promise, a respected editorialist on a famous American newspaper, and an acclaimed popular poet. Politically he was a staunch Republican of the reformist Lincoln variety. The only Democrat he ever voted for was Samuel Tilden, elected governor of New York on a reform ticket in 1874. He preferred the company of intellectuals, but his elitism was based on merit, not birth. Moreover, at least in the abstract, he liked and trusted ordinary people, having ennobled some in the *Pike County Ballads*.

Hay in middle age was at five feet two inches a small and fastidious man. Curly hair and curving mustache made him suave with a touch of the bohemian. Mark Twain bubbled in superlatives about him: "a picture to look at, for beauty of feature, perfection of form, and grace of carriage and movement." A cautious, conservative approach to life was a permanent part of him. He saw himself as an improver more than a reformer. He hated controversy and shunned it. The paean to the ordinary that he had written into his class poem at Brown ("Glad if we win, and happy if we fail") returned in midlife in a poem published by Howells in 1871: "Try not to beat back the current, yet be not drowned in its waters."

For all his conservative style, Hay represented some of the best elements of the Illinois frontier. As the historian Frederick Jackson Turner wrote, the Mississippi Valley frontier promoted competitive individualism and a belief in equality. The pioneer heritage was "a passionate belief that a democracy was possible which should leave the individual a part to play in free society and not make him a cog in a machine operated from above; which trusted in the common man, in his tolerance, his ability to adjust differences with a good humor, and to work out an American type from the contributions of all nations." Abraham Lincoln was the great exemplar of this frontier tradition, of course. But the young John Hay, of Warsaw, Illinois, was part of it as well.

At thirty-five Hay took an important turn in the course of his life, one that took him far from his frontier origins. The second part of his life contained repetitions of the first—more diplomacy, more journalism, more writing, even a renewal of his association with Lincoln in the biography he coauthored with Nicolay—but the context was different. What made it different was Hay's marriage to Clara Stone and his move from Warsaw, Illinois, to Cleveland, Ohio.

Rural Illinois and the Mississippi River stood for the restless egalitarianism of the frontier. In contrast Ohio was an industrial giant in the making, a symbol of the post–Civil War boom that was turning America into an economic great power. Cleveland was a commercial hub, served by railroad and canal and occupying a central position between the iron mines of Minnesota and the coal and oil fields of Pennsylvania. It was a modern city, the first in the United States to illuminate its streets with electric arc lights. John D. Rockefeller, operating out of Cleveland, had already made his company the largest oil refiner in the world. Hay, floating along as usual, became a part of this new world of big business and even, by writing a disastrous novel, a propagandist for it. Late in Hay's life, Henry Adams defined his friend's new orientation: "John Hay was as strange to the Mississippi river as though he had not been bred on its shores."

Clara Stone was not a beauty, and Hay never pretended she was.

Like the Spanish ladies he described in *Castilian Days*, she was "built on the old-fashioned generous plan." He informed Nicolay that she was "large, handsome, and good." The two were married on February 4, 1874; at twenty-four, Clara was eleven years younger than her new husband. In many ways she was a perfect match for him. She was quiet where he was effervescent. Clover Adams, Henry's sharp-tongued wife, noted that Mrs. Hay never spoke but that was just as well, for Mr. Hay "chats for two."

Hay's geologist friend Clarence King observed that Clara's "rooted repose" and tranquillity made even nirvana "seem fidgety." King, a man of the world, adored Clara. He told Hay: "Only once in a million times does Providence pour out the *full cup* for man to drink. For you it has." Clara coped with life as it came; she had written in a school composition that without cold, there would be no ice skating. She was religious and intellectual. She helped her high-maintenance husband through disappointments, depressions, and increasingly bad health.

She was also able to keep up with his cerebral friends like Henry Adams, William Dean Howells, and Henry James. At Cleveland Academy, the institution of highest aspiration for the daughters of respectable parents, she had written an essay defending literary women and "blue-stockings." But Clara was a bit of a prude and did not enjoy the company of Hay's less kempt western cronies. Bret Harte, a lush and a moocher, must have been a trial for her. Mark Twain told of a Sunday when he and Hay "had been chatting, laughing, and carrying on . . . when the door opened and Mrs. Hay, gravely clad, gloved, bonnetted, and just from church, and fragrant with the odors of Presbyterian sanctity, stood in it. We rose to our feet at once, of course—rose through a swiftly falling temperature—a temperature which at the beginning was soft and summer-like, but which was turning our breath and all other damp things to frost crystals by the time we were erect—but we got no opportunity to say the pretty and polite thing and offer the homage due; the comely young matron forestalled us. She came forward, smileless, with disapproval written all over her face, said most coldly, 'Good morning, Mr. Clemens,' and passed on and out." Hay explained to his friend that Clara was "very strict about Sunday."

Clara's remarkable father, Amasa Stone, exerted a profound influence on Hay's life. Stone was a self-made millionaire who, like many settlers in Cleveland, had migrated there from New England. A Puritan in conduct and work habits, he began at seventeen as a builder in Massachusetts and soon had his own company for the construction of railroads and railroad bridges. At twenty-seven he was superintendent of the New York, New Haven, and Hartford Railroad. Having moved to Cleveland, he built railroads all over the state, as well as iron mills, woolen mills, and railroad car works. He also became one of the leading bankers of Ohio.

During the Civil War Stone was a brigadier general in the Union army and a trusted friend of Lincoln's; this must have been when Hay first met him. He was a philanthropist, founding a home for aged women, a children's aid society, and a college that came to be known as Western Reserve. Hay fell under the spell of this dynamic industrialist. Stone's persuasive powers, together with the lure of financial profit, wrenched his new son-in-law from a challenging journalism career in New York to a business sinecure in Cleveland.

In 1875 John and Clara Hay moved to Cleveland, where they spent nine of the next eleven years. The city remained Hay's financial and political base for the rest of his life. Amasa Stone lived on Euclid Avenue, called Millionaires' Row, in a mansion larger than the one John D. Rockefeller, a business rival, had moved into in 1868. Stone built a less capacious house for John and Clara on the same street.

Under the guidance of his father-in-law, Hay turned into a businessman. He had dabbled in investments before—in Florida real estate, in turpentine, in a diamond mine (on the misdirected advice of Clarence King), in his Warsaw vineyard, and in railroad stocks—but with no notable success. On his marriage his father-in-law made him a gift of ten thousand dollars in railroad bonds and an offer to have him help manage Stone's finances. With typical diffidence Hay described the job as "merely the care of investments which are so safe that they require no care." Yet he must have been good at it because the former journalist, scratching out an income from writing and lectures, suddenly became a very rich man, able to take long trips to Europe, to build a mansion in Washington and a summer home in New Hampshire, and to indulge himself in a life style that included lavish entertaining and collecting old master paintings.

If Ohio initiated Hay into a business culture in which he prospered, it also introduced him to a political culture that was to vault him to the top of American diplomacy. Ohio dominated late-nineteenth-century American politics as did no other state. Between 1869 and 1901 five of the seven presidents of the United States—Grant, Hayes, Garfield, Harrison, and McKinley—were Ohio natives. All five were Republicans and former Union officers in the Civil War. Hay knew them all and was particularly close to Garfield and McKinley. The Civil War icons William Sherman and Phil Sheridan were also Ohioans, as were two prominent politicians: John Sherman, secretary of the treasury, U.S. senator, and secretary of state, and Joseph B. Foraker, former Ohio governor and U.S. senator, who was to play a major role in American colonial policy toward Cuba and Puerto Rico.

With his ties to Lincoln, his unswerving party loyalty—"a little like the loyalty of a highly cultivated churchman to his Church," in Henry Adams's words—and his ability to charm, Hay soon became a popular member of the Ohio political machine. It brought him high office in 1879 when, after first refusing, he accepted from President Hayes a political appointment to be assistant secretary of state, the number two job in the department.

Hay's first service in the State Department lasted less than a year and a half, and it was not distinguished. The period did not call for dynamic diplomatic action; one historian has called it "the nadir of diplomacy." Washington between Abraham Lincoln and Theodore Roosevelt was more than usually corrupt. As an editorial writer Hay had railed against the Grant administration. In his novel *Democracy* Henry Adams described the city as a sinkhole of power seeking, bribery, and influence peddling. Now Hay was compelled to play a minor role in the shabby drama of Washington politics. As deputy to Secretary of State William M. Evarts, a New York lawyer whom he admired, he was in charge of dispensing patronage, an important lubricant to the wheels of power. A diplomatic post, said Adams in *Democracy*, was "the nearest approach to a patent of nobility and a government pension which the American citizen can attain."

Hay's diary is an often hilarious account of his tussles with office seekers. A Captain Brownell, representing a veterans' association, called: "He passed half an hour in conversation which was carried on exclusively by himself in which he spoke of himself with profound respect and admiration." Hay must have relished his conversation with the woman whose husband had beaten him out for the mission to Sweden in 1867: "General McCook brought in Mrs. Bartlett, the wife of General J. J. Bartlett, who went out to Samoa to make himself King, Emperor, or Pope of that country, and instead has got into jail. She wishes the Govt. to appoint him to something, and then send a gunboat for him and instal him in his office."

Hay's time at the State Department did nothing to improve his view of the shallowness of senators. An especially boorish one, Senator J. Donald Cameron of Pennsylvania, "sat with an unmoved countenance" and requested a high appointment for a friend from Pittsburgh or, if no appointment was possible, "that we would send him a note saying that there was not anything of the sort on hand; writing it on as large a sheet of paper as possible, and sealing it with as large a piece of sealing wax as the present financial condition of the Dept, would warrant." Hay sadly drew the conclusion that Secretary Seward had been right to say that "no man who is fit for a foreign mission ever asks for one." Yet Hay himself willingly played the patronage game. He even found a consulate for his importunate and boozy friend Bret Harte, though Harte was disappointed that it was not in a more salubrious city than Glasgow.

The most significant aspect of Hay's year and a half in Washington was the deepening of his friendship with Henry Adams. Henry and Clover Adams were Washington social figures of the most exalted kind. Their invitations were treasured by the political and intellectual elite. Henry Adams invented the power breakfast; it was served at noon and included a select guest or two. The Adamses entertained in the evening as well. On a typical workday afternoon Hay would leave his office in the State, War, and Navy Building (now the Eisenhower Executive Office Building, where the National Security Council and other presidential staff are officed) at four-thirty and walk two blocks to the Adamses' rented house across Lafayette Square from the White House. Tea was served at five and often turned into dinner.

Guests usually included the brilliantly mercurial geologist Clarence King and an exclusive sampling of the Washington power structure: the painters John La Farge and John Singer Sargent; the sculptor Augustus Saint-Gaudens; the scientist-entrepreneur Alexander Agassiz; the writers Henry James and Bret Harte; the German-American reformer Carl Schurz; and (later) politicians like Henry Cabot Lodge and Theodore Roosevelt. A thronelike chair was always brought forward for Clara Hay, who was deemed too heavy for the Adamses' oriental couches.

The main attractions on display at these gatherings were Adams's ruminations on American history, inspired by the research for his forthcoming history of the Jefferson and Madison administrations, and Hay's wit. An example was Hay's story (perhaps apocryphal but certainly typical) of taking an English visitor to Mount Vernon. The Englishman expressed doubt that George Washington could have thrown a dollar across the Potomac. "Why not?" said Hay. "He threw a sovereign across the Atlantic."

Hay and Adams could hardly have been more different. Adams was a Boston bluebood; Hay, the son of a western country doctor. Adams was a liberal and a Democrat; Hay, an increasingly conservative Republican. Adams had a deep and probing intellect; Hay's mind danced on the surface of issues. Adams was an elitist who took a crabbed approach to other people. Hay, though not without snobbish traits, was, in Adams's words, "always unselfish, generous, easy, patient, and loyal." Adams's view of history and the individual's role in it was pessimistic. Hay, on the other hand, was an optimist who believed in people. As Adams noted, he had "a singular facility for remembering faces, and would break off suddenly the thread of his talk, as he looked out of the windows on La Fayette Square, to notice an old Corps-commander or Admiral of the Civil War, tottering along to the Club for his cards or his cocktail." Adams feigned shock at Hay's friends: "[H]e has always managed to keep in what I think precious bad company. . . . [H]e knows intimately scores of men whom I would not touch with a pole, but who are more amusing than my own crowd."

Nevertheless, the two men formed a close friendship that was to last until Hay's death. Adams had an extravagant respect for Hay's political and diplomatic abilities. For his part, Hay considered himself an acolyte before the formidable intellect of his friend. In letters he took to addressing Adams with mock gravity as "My Beloved Mentor," "Brightest and Best," "My Own and Onliest," "Querido de Mi Alma," "My Cherished Livy," "My Angelical Doctor," and "My Dearest Boom De Ay." Adams responded in kind. The terms of endearment were so ardent that they even gave rise to a novel describing the relationship between the two as homosexual. That seems unlikely. After Hay's death his widow ruthlessly expurgated all dubious language from his letters before allowing their publication—she patrolled his legacy with heavy tread—but Clara Hay saw no problem in retaining Hay's affectionate language toward his friend.

Each man, perhaps, supplied something the other lacked. Adams, the heir of two presidents, never held political office. He may have wanted it, but he did not deign to seek it. He saw himself as "a stable-companion to statesmen, whether they liked it or not." His influence on Hay gave him a power that he was unable to wield in his own right. He was nourished by Hay's success and lived it vicariously. For Hay, Henry Adams was the acme of American aristocracy. The Rembrandts, Michelangelos, Turners, and Constables on the Adamses' walls; the introduction Clover gave Clara to the Paris couturier Charles Worth; Henry's learned disquisitions on the forces motivating humanity; and the Adamses' association with a political tradition older than Lincoln's all gave assurance to the unconfident westerner of nondescript background.

Self-confidence was the real key to this improbable friendship. Neither Adams nor Hay had it; both were given to long laments about their lack of worth. Adams's turgid autobiography, written oddly in the third person, is saturated with self-denigration. Hay was always concerned about being "a bore from Boresville." Even at the height of his fame from *Pike County Ballads*, he declined to take a diplomatic mission in Berlin because he felt he was "not up to it in many respects." Adams commented: "With all his gaiety of manner and lightness of wit, [Hay] took dark views of himself, none the lighter for their humor."

Neither man ever sought elected office. Adams spurned the legacy of his grandfather John Quincy, who had served with distinction in the House of Representatives after his presidency. Hay twice considered running for Congress, from Florida shortly after his time with Lincoln and from Ohio in 1880, but stopped short both times. Both men were given to publishing anonymously. Neither apparently dared face the literary judgment of possible critics. In their lack of self-assurance they seemed to take heart from each other and to push themselves farther than their innate despondency would have allowed. Their separate achievements were in part a product of the energizing effect of their relationship.

When James Garfield, another Ohioan, was elected president in 1880, he invited Hay to be his private secretary, saying he would upgrade the post to cabinet status. In a letter to his fellow Ohioan Whitelaw Reid, Garfield listed the qualities he liked in Hay: fidelity, comradeship, culture, statesmanship, and acquaintance with men required to make the White House powerful and brilliant. Hay nevertheless chose to regard the president-elect's offer of this potentially powerful office as a demeaning reprise of the position he had held under Lincoln two decades before. Hay's candid letter of refusal to Garfield revealed a deep-seated contempt for Washington and its ways:

> The contact with the greed and selfishness of office-seekers and bulldozing Congressmen, is unspeakably repulsive to me. It caused me last spring to refuse, definitely and forever, to run for Congress. It has poisoned all of the pleasure I should otherwise have derived from a conscientious and not unsuccessful discharge of my duties in the State Department. The constant contact with envy, meanness, ignorance, and the swinish selfishness which ignorance breeds, needs a stronger heart and a more obedient nervous system than I can boast.

After this blast it was a testament to Garfield's equanimity, and to Hay's relationship with an important Ohio patron, that the president continued to consult Hay on cabinet appointments.

Following a six-month stint editing the *New York Tribune* while Reid honeymooned in Europe, Hay returned to Cleveland to immerse himself in business affairs and to work on the Lincoln biography. By now his success as a businessman, combined with the influence of his father-in-law, was leading him toward political views that Lincoln might not have recognized. In Hay's view the Revolution and the Civil War had made America a great democracy; it was now necessary to protect the country against those who would subvert those achievements. This meant preserving the status quo. He identified private property as being most in need of protection. The political rights of the common man were important to political democracy, but his economic rights had to be weighed against the need for industrial stability and peace, as defined by the capitalist class.

Hay had been greatly agitated by the strikes and riots in Pittsburgh and Cleveland in 1877, while he was looking after Amasa Stone's interests during a European visit by his father-in-law. In panic, he had written Stone then:

> The government is utterly helpless and powerless in the face of an unarmed rebellion of foreign workingmen, mostly Irish. There is nowhere any firm nucleus of authority. . . . Any hour the mob chooses, it can destroy any city in the country. . . . There is a mob in every city ready to join with the strikers, and get their pay in robbery, and there is no means of enforcing the law in case of a sudden attack on private property. We are not Mexicans yet—but that is about the only advantage we have over Mexico . . . I feel that a profound misfortune and disgrace has fallen on the country, which no amount of energy or severity can now wholly remedy.

Now that he was back in Cleveland, his animus toward workers sharpened. He saw their challenge to property as an attack on American democracy rather than a demand for better economic conditions. He also focused on outside agitators instead of on the flaws in the system itself. The result of his ruminations was an ill-tempered novel, *The Breadwinners,* an early treatment of the class struggle that portrayed an urban strike in simplistic and tendentious terms. Howells turned it down for the *Atlantic* because of Hay's insistence on anonymity. It was published anonymously in the *Century* magazine in 1883 and then in book form.

Hay's choice of anonymity was curious, though there were precedents. Henry Adams's *Democracy* had been published anonymously, leading to speculation that it had been written by Clover Adams or even by Hay. But Hay's publicly stated reason was unconvincing: that he was engaged in a business in which his standing would be "seriously compromised" by disclosure. He seemed to be embarrassed at being identified with a tract that contradicted some of the political values he had stood for all his life.

The Breadwinners recalls the 1877 period of labor turmoil. It takes place in "Buffland," a transparent amalgamation of Buffalo, which Hay did not know, and Cleveland, which he did. The story turns on a strike against the city's largest rolling mill. Hay portrayed the managers of the mill sympathetically; the vice-president, who rose from cabin boy on a steamboat, seemed patterned on Amasa Stone. Captain Arthur Farnham, who breaks the strike through organizational talent and physical courage, is an army veteran and a heroic figure.

The strikers, members of a brotherhood called the Bread-Winners, are caricatures. They are led by an outside agitator named Andrew Jackson Offitt. "Andrew Jackson" allowed Hay to settle a historical score with an icon of the Democratic party, and "Offitt" exposed the Irish origin of the strike. Offitt is a labor radical, a thief, and a would-be murderer. Hay's description of him recalls his picture of Jews in Vienna:

> . . . a face whose expression was oleaginous, . . . surmounted by a low and shining forehead covered by reeking black hair, worn rather long, the ends being turned under by the brush. The mustache was long and drooping, dyed black and profusely oiled, the dye and the grease forming an unharmonious compound. The parted lips, which were coarse and thin, displayed an imperfect set of teeth, much discolored with tobacco. The eyes were light green, with the space which should have been white suffused by yellow and red. It was one of those gifted countenances which could change in a moment from dog-like fawning to a snaky venomousness.

Other union members fare little better under Hay's butcher's knife. He described them as "the laziest and most incapable workmen in the town—men whose weekly wages were habitually docked for drunkenness, late hours, and botchy work." One had been a streetcar driver "but had recently been dismissed for insolence to passengers and brutality to his horses." The strikers go on a rampage, threatening the residents of Algonquin (read Euclid) Avenue, try to steal money and jewelry from one of the rich families, and even talk of hanging rich people. Farnham beats them back with a pickup militia.

In all the drama Hay showed no interest in the strikers' grievances. Like Andrew Carnegie in the Homestead steel strike a decade later, he could sympathize with workers only if they did not organize or make concerted demands. He was horrified by the ideology of socialism. The leading agitators "were going from place to place, haranguing the workmen, preaching what they called socialism, but what was merely riot and plunder." At twenty-one Hay had contended that "the

temple of liberty is wide enough to admit every creed and every nation." Now, at forty-five, he had decided that the temple was too narrow to admit workers organizing for their rights.

If *The Breadwinners* was no more than a polemical defense of law
and order, it would not be so interesting as it still is. But John Hay,
even at his worst, had a sophisticated understanding of human nature
and a keen sense of fairness. He slipped into the book a subtle satire
of the Buffland upper classes, which revel in Indian names for their
boat clubs: The "Wissagewissametts" row against the "Chippagowax-
ems." He also had great fun with Victorian convention. His heroines
blush with regularity—"The hot blood came surging up, covering
neck and brow with crimson"—and he rarely missed an opportunity
to describe a young lady at her dressing table. One account of a girl
braiding her hair contains the following expressions all in one paragraph: "exquisite beauty," "luxuriant tresses," "pink and pearl of the
round arm," "the poise of the round head," "the full white column of
the neck," and "the soft curve of cheek and chin."

Even in this diatribe Hay managed to convey some sympathy for
working-class people, some sharp criticism for their betters, and some
familiar censuring of corruption and politics. He fell in love with one
of his lowborn creations, the sexy and ambitious Maud Matchin, described without Victorian reserve—her dress "fitted her almost as well
as her own skin"—and never criticized for her single-minded determination to win a position in a library. Hay lambasted the local power
structure for resorting to a corrupt deal to get Maud her job. He also
inserted some ridicule of the U.S. Congress, sharpened by his recent
tour in Washington. In discussing punishment for the labor agitators,
the vice-president of the rolling mill says, "We shan't be hard on
them. But one or two gifted orators will have to take the road. They
are fit for nothing but Congress, and they can't all go from this district."

The most surprising paragraph in *The Breadwinners* subverts the
very theme of the book by implying that the rich and the powerful deserve the disaster almost visited on them. It describes the scene after
the rioting has been put down:

> The rich and prosperous people, as their manner is, congratu-
> lated themselves on their escape, and gave no thought to the ques-

tions which had come so near to an issue of fire and blood. In this city of two hundred thousand people, two or three dozen politicians continued as before to govern it, to assess and to spend its taxes, to use it as their property and their chattel. The rich and intelligent kept on making money, building fine houses, and bringing up children to hate politics as they did, in fine to fatten themselves as sheep which should be mutton whenever the butcher was ready. There was hardly a millionaire on Algonquin Avenue who knew where the ward meetings of his party were held. There was not an Irish laborer in the city but knew his way to his ward club as well as to mass.

Try as he might, Hay could not completely identify himself with capitalist values. Still, *The Breadwinners* was seen by reviewers as a powerful attack on the working classes, a message that won it wide support among the reading public. It was the best-seller of 1883. But the critics, particularly those Hay cared about, hated it. The *Atlantic* and other liberal journals panned it for praising the capitalist aristocracy and for attacking collective bargaining. One critic wrote a parody called *The Money Makers*. The *Century* magazine, which had serialized it, dismissed it as "a piece of snobbishness."

Hay was stung by the criticism. He defended himself anonymously in the *Century*, arguing that he was attacking not a union but a "little society" run by a criminal who was swindling honest workers. He protested oddly that he himself worked for a living. Publicly he dropped his polemical defense of corporations. In fact, several years after *The Breadwinners* was published, he commented sourly: "This is a government of the people, by the people, and for the people no longer. It is a government of corporations, by corporations, and for corporations."

5.

Cleveland made Hay a rich man, but he grew restless and ill at ease there. For one thing, his father-in-law was succumbing to a slow-motion personal tragedy. In 1876 an Ohio bridge that Stone had built collapsed under a railroad train, casting eighty people to their death in the Ashtabula River gorge, the worst railroad disaster in American history. Stone was publicly pilloried for greed, dishonesty, and criminal

neglect. One of the sharpest critics was Hay's former publisher Howells, who came from Ashtabula. Howells later recanted after being
thoroughly informed of the facts by "a friend." But the disaster broke
Stone's health and spirit. He gradually lost interest in business affairs
and turned over to Hay the principal management of his personal finances. Finally, in May 1883, while the Hays were vacationing in Europe, Stone killed himself.

The loss of his revered father-in-law and his own worsening health
made the early 1880s a time of anxiety for Hay. He had never been robust, and depression followed him all his life, as it had Lincoln's. During his early days in Cleveland he suffered from headaches, partial
blindness, and heart problems. On a doctor's orders he had taken off
the summer of 1878 and traveled to Europe with his brother Leonard.
In 1882, plagued by depression and other maladies, he had decided to
take a whole year off and travel abroad. In Paris the famous neurolo-
gist Dr. Jean Charcot pronounced him to have "neurasthenia," a medical term of the time that described a neurosis characterized by
extreme lassitude and inability to cope with any but the most trivial
tasks. Depressives today will recognize the symptoms. Without the array of modern medical options, Dr. Charcot prescribed douche baths,
tonics, and bromides, which Hay considered mere palliatives. He
wrote Nicolay sadly, "I have given up all hopes of being twenty-one
again."

Hay's illnesses, the mental more than the physical ones, were a
lifelong millstone that made his creativity in so many fields all the
more remarkable. The Lincoln biography, on which he had worked off
and on for twenty years, was nearing completion, despite the collabo-
rative inconvenience of Hay's being in Cleveland and Nicolay in
Washington. Serial publication began in the *Century* in November
1886 and ran for four years. Hay seemed to get sick more in Cleveland than in Washington or New York, as Whitelaw Reid unkindly reminded him. Yet Cleveland continued to be good to him. Amasa
Stone had left him $3.5 million, and Jay Gould, an associate of
Stone's and one of the less fragrant of the superrich financiers, found
him a lucrative place on the board of Western Union.

Ever attentive to politics, Hay cemented his ties with Ohio politicians and the Republican party, to which with his burgeoning wealth

he became a major contributor. He had great affection for Garfield and grieved when the president was assassinated in 1881, the second presidential assassination for Hay but not the last. He campaigned for the scandal-plagued James G. Blaine, the losing Republican presidential candidate in 1884. After favoring the unsuccessful candidacy of Ohio Senator John Sherman for the Republican nomination for president in 1888, he supported the successful candidacy of the Indianian Benjamin Harrison, a former Ohioan. He also began to get to know William McKinley, a decorated Civil War veteran and popular Ohio congressman, whose name was attached to an important tariff act.

In 1886, bored with Cleveland, Hay decided to return to Washington. He wanted to get back to the center of things, but he had a personal reason as well. Clover Adams, Henry's sharp-tongued and unconventional wife, "off her feed" after the death of her father, as Henry uncharitably put it, had committed suicide in December 1885. The method she chose was particularly gruesome; a talented photographer, she swallowed a darkroom chemical, potassium cyanide. Her death threw Adams into a moroseness from which he never quite recovered. Hay wrote him a graceful condolence letter: "I can neither talk to you nor keep silent. The darkness in which you walk has its shadow for me also. You and your wife were more to me than any other two. I came to Washington because you were there. And now this goodly fellowship is broken up forever."

Adams and Hay had bought adjoining properties on Lafayette Square in 1883, and Adams had engaged a college classmate, Henry Hobson Richardson, a famous and portly (345 pounds) architect, to design the two houses. Now, with Clover dead, Richardson sped up his work so that the Hays could move from Cleveland to be close to Adams. Neither house survives, but behind the forbidding Romanesque façades both were extravagant and pretentious. Hay's dining room was larger than the one in the White House; his grand staircase could accommodate ten people abreast. When Adams was in Washington, they were in and out of each other's houses or taking long walks together. When Adams tried to escape his grief through obsessive foreign travel, Hay either accompanied him or pursued him to the ends of the earth with affectionate letters.

During the same period Hay became friendly with Henry Cabot

Lodge, a congressman from Massachusetts, and with Theodore Roosevelt, who arrived in Washington in 1889 to become the chairman of the U.S. Civil Service Commission. Hay was much older than both; in fact he had been a friend of Roosevelt's father. The Hays entertained Lodge and Roosevelt in their new Richardson house and visited the Lodges; often all three families met together at Henry Adams's. Lodge and Roosevelt were close friends, almost as close as Adams and Hay and, like the other two, were different in character. Hay found Roosevelt creative but ambitious and Lodge industrious but "tricky." Neither had the kind of humor Hay enjoyed. He once wrote Adams, "We had the Roosevelts and the Lodges to dinner once or twice, but I cannot make them gay."

From the time of his move from Cleveland in 1886 to his appointment as ambassador to London in 1897, Hay was unemployed. He took many trips to Europe, to Rome, Florence, Milan, Parma, Bologna, Dresden, Amsterdam, Aix-les-Bains (for his maladies, which seemed to grow worse), Paris, the Loire Valley, and always London. He visited Andrew Carnegie at his castle in Scotland; he and Clara attended Queen Victoria's Golden Jubilee; he even looked into the possibility of buying a country estate in England or Scotland. He built a summer house on Lake Sunapee in Newbury, New Hampshire. He traveled back to Cleveland frequently. He bought a Botticelli madonna and child for his Washington house.

And he had an affair. The lady in question was Nannie Lodge, the young wife of now Senator Henry Cabot Lodge. A wellborn Bostonian, daughter of a rear admiral, Nannie must have seemed to Hay everything Clara was not. She was pretty and witty, small and slim with dark hair and eyes extolled by Sargent as "unforgettable blue." So sharp was she of intellect that her vain husband depended on her to edit his speeches. John and Nannie fell in love and went to great lengths to arrange trysts that would not provoke gossip.

Clara, whose size was increasing and whose loyalty was staunch, remained in blissful ignorance, and the Hay marriage continued uneventfully and apparently happily. Hay finally seemed to think better of his extracurricular activity. At the end of a trip to Europe in 1891, far from both wife and lover, he wrote Clara a letter implying guilt and professing love. It radiated a sincerity that John Hay did not have it in him to fake:

> I feel stricken with remorse some times to think how much you have done for me and how little I have done for you. . . . For seventeen years your true heart, your rich and noble nature, your beauty has been mine, and have made me happier than it is possible for most men ever to be. . . . If Heaven grants me a return to health and to life, it shall be my study in the future to try to find some way of adding to your happiness. I am not half good enough for you—but I do love you with all my heart and nobody could love you more.

Now in his fifties, Hay was drifting into comfortable old age, though his illnesses were unpleasant and his depressions more frequent. He had nothing but leisure: no writing, no business, no government service. His and Nicolay's *Abraham Lincoln: A History*, really a chronicle of Lincoln's times rather than a biography of the man, was a critical success. Theodore Roosevelt said it made him proud to be a Republican. The authors offered no apology for portraying Lincoln as a full-scale hero, the father of modern American democracy. They were inevitably accused of northern bias, but they strove to be factual and accurate. They were certainly complete; the work ran to ten volumes and nearly five thousand pages, longer than Gibbon's *Decline and Fall of the Roman Empire*, with many maps and pictures.

The writing was not up to Hay's usual standard, though in places—for example, the chapter on Lincoln's assassination—it was moving. Nicolay, a good professional journalist, was not a native English speaker, and Hay himself took the shortcut of dictating long sections to a stenographer. The authors rigorously omitted references to Lincoln's private life. The death of the president's twelve-year-old son Willie, John Hay's playmate, went unrecorded, as did any explanation of how Lincoln wrote the Gettysburg Address. Still, this result of two decades' hard work was a majestic mark of gratitude to a president who had shaped the lives of his two young assistants. Even today it is an indispensable source for Civil War scholars.

Hay's return via history to the liberal Republicanism of his youth had little tempering effect on his conservatism, as is evident from his response to the litmus test of liberalism in the late nineteenth century, the effort to reform the federal civil service, still blemished by the spoils system. Moderate Republicans like Roosevelt and Lodge put civil service reform at the forefront of their concerns. Hay, who had railed against his task of patronage dispenser in the State Department, should have been in their ranks. But he was not; apparently his devotion to Ohio politics, which was a source of considerable corruption, outweighed his own experience. Hay remained faithful to the view he had expressed in 1881: "I have never met a reformer who had not the heart of a tyrant. Boundless conceit and moral selfishness seem the necessary baggage of the professional lover of liberty." Adams was unfazed by his friend's easy acceptance of political convenience: "Hay had treated the world as something to be taken in block without pulling it to pieces to get rid of its defects."

John Hay was better than he sometimes sounded. Throughout his life he was unfailingly generous to people in trouble. On his return from Paris in 1867 he had paid the train fare from New York to Washington for a lame and destitute black man whom he had encountered. He was constantly bailing out the impecunious Clarence King, once with a loan of one hundred thousand dollars that he did not expect to get back. When Hay discovered after King's death in 1901 that his friend had been secretly married to a black nursemaid for thirteen years, he established for her a trust fund that continued well beyond his own death. When Matthew Arnold visited Cleveland to give a lecture and stay with the Hays, Hay found out that only a few tickets had been sold; he quietly bought out the house and filled it with a nonpaying audience.

He was consistently loyal to Lincoln's legacy toward American blacks. He supported legislation to ensure black voting rights in the South; he invested close to a million dollars in housing for blacks in Washington; and in their work on Lincoln, he and Nicolay gave generous praise to black Union soldiers. His daughters, Helen and Alice, whom he adored, remembered his informality with his family, his uncomplaining patience with his illnesses, his righteous indignation with injustice, his impartiality and fairness, and his nervous dread while preparing a public speech.

For Hay friendship was the most important quality. He himself liked the company of powerful people, not unusual for political Washington or literary New York. Brooks Adams, Henry's younger brother, remarked that Hay had more notable friends than any other man of his generation. He found friends across the political spectrum, as long as they were talented or well-connected: the liberal Henry Adams, the imperial Rudyard Kipling, the anti-imperial Carl Schurz, the radical Mark Twain. Andrew Carnegie, another friend, said in his autobiography, "He inspired men with absolute confidence in his sincerity."

Hay was the most enthusiastic member of the Five of Hearts, the whimsical club whose entire membership was Henry and Clover Adams, John and Clara Hay, and Clarence King. He ordered special stationery for the Hearts and carved their emblem on a boulder high in the Colorado Rockies. The Hearts dissolved tragically with Clover's suicide and King's decline into dementia and death, but Hay and Adams remained inseparable. Hay said once, "I hate to lose my own friends. I do not remember that I ever lost one." He made the remark to Whitelaw Reid, ironically the only friend he almost did lose.

If Hay was hoping that his Ohio network would bring him high office, the time and money he spent on Ohio politics did not seem to get him very far. Hayes failed to provide him a top diplomatic mission. Garfield offered him a staff position that Hay considered menial. Harrison gave him nothing. The Republican candidates he backed seemed usually to lose. Blaine lost to Cleveland in 1884; Sherman lost the Republican nomination in 1888; Harrison, with Hay's friend Reid as vice-presidential candidate, lost to Cleveland in 1892. However, Hay had one political friendship in reserve, McKinley's. In the early 1890s, when McKinley moved from the House of Representatives to the Ohio governorship, Hay had contributed money to help him avoid a bankruptcy caused by a bad loan. McKinley and his political manager, the powerful businessman Mark Hanna, were in Hay's political debt.

When McKinley, whom Hay affectionately called the Majah, after his Civil War rank, won the Republican nomination for president in 1896, Hay mocked the office seekers who beat a path to the candidate's front porch in Canton, Ohio, from which he waged his unusual campaign. He wrote to Adams: "Cabot [Lodge] and Teddy [Roosevelt] have been to Canton to offer their heads to the ax and their tummies to the hara-kiri knife. He has asked me to come, but I had thought I would not struggle with the millions on his trampled lawn. Still, if you will go with me, and offer to pour out the bluest blood of your veins, I will go." Hay did go, without Adams, of course, and sent his friend a fascinating account of his interview with the next president:

I spent yesterday with the Majah. I had been dreading it for a month, thinking it would be like talking in a boiler-factory. But he met me at the station, gave me meat, and calmly leaving his shouting worshippers in the front yard, took me upstairs and talked for two hours as calmly and serenely as if we were summer boarders in Beverly [the Massachusetts town where Adams had a summer home] at a loss for means to kill time. I was more struck than ever with his mask. It is a genuine Italian ecclesiastical face of the fifteenth century. And there are idiots who think Mark Hanna will run him!

Hay and McKinley were a good fit. They both were friendly, generous to others, and pragmatic in their politics. Hay supported McKinley's run for the presidency in a major way, pouring thousands of dollars into Hanna's campaign coffers. In campaign speeches he lit into the populist Democratic candidate, William Jennings Bryan, the "baby Demosthenes" (Bryan was thirty-six); the "unclean spirits" that had captured the Democratic party; and the union leaders, "the moral dynamiters of society."

The rapport between Hay and McKinley went beyond Hay's financial contributions and partisan speeches. Both before and after his election to the presidency McKinley turned to Hay for policy advice. In 1895 Hay gave him an analysis of British thinking on foreign policy that McKinley remembered when he started to look for an ambassador to the Court of St. James's. The obnoxiously ambitious Reid wanted the job, but he rubbed McKinley the wrong way. Hay accepted the dirty task of trying to persuade his friend that running the *Tribune* was more important than being ambassador to Britain. It was Hay at his worst since, professionally idle for more than a decade, he wanted London for himself. He told McKinley with uncharacteristic unction: "There has been so much talk about my being sent to England that I presume you may have given some consideration to the matter. I do not think it is altogether selfishness and vanity which has brought me to think that perhaps you might do worse than select me."

The night before McKinley's inauguration, Hay gave a dinner for him at his Washington house; the next day McKinley wore for the ceremony a ring with strands of George Washington's hair that was a gift from Hay. The appointment to London was announced a few days later. John Hay's luck—first with Lincoln, now with McKinley—had once again propelled him to power. But the whole affair left Mark Twain feeling "sorry and ashamed" for Hay.

Hay was in fact a natural choice for London. He knew Britain well—too well, according to Roosevelt, who found him obsequious toward the British. It was not a fair criticism. Hay had little respect for the British monarchy, but he saw the country as a great democracy. As a private citizen he had actually delivered a tough message on behalf of the Cleveland administration to the British leaders in 1896, when the United States and Great Britain were in a serious dispute over the Venezuelan boundary.

With his appointment to London Hay entered the final and most important decade of his protean career; in less than two years he would be secretary of state. His preparation for the leadership of American diplomacy was unusual to say the least. He had served as a diplomat in four European capitals, though he had had only sporadic diplomatic exposure to Washington. He was far behind John Quincy Adams in breadth of diplomatic training, and unlike his idols Seward and Blaine, foreign affairs neophytes who became strong secretaries of state, he had no particular political stature. Compared with two modern secretaries, Dean Acheson and Henry Kissinger, Hay lacked conceptual and strategic grasp. He did not spend his time working out policy prescriptions, in contrast with Theodore Roosevelt, Henry Cabot Lodge, and Alfred T. Mahan.

Also in contrast with all these men, Hay was a bit of a dilettante. In fact, for a man of his experience, his ideas on foreign policy were curiously unformed. He had no strong political views except those he had inherited from Lincoln, and they applied mainly to domestic rather than foreign affairs and were growing more conservative as he aged. He did have a feel for human rights; in particular, he cared about the way governments treated their people.

In the growing debate over American expansion and in the policy deliberations leading to the attack on Spain in 1898, Hay was not a vocal participant. As a young man he had opposed American designs on Hawaii, but by now he strongly supported the Republican party's line that the islands should be annexed. His thinking on Cuba was liberal, in the sense that he opposed Spanish rule and favored some form of self-determination for the Cuban people. He admired imperialism on the British model but was too sophisticated to be a flag-waving American jingo. He would probably have considered himself a more moderate expansionist than Seward or Blaine. In sum, he thought little and wrote less about foreign policy. In this, as in so much else, he was a floater on life's seas. He preferred riding waves to making them.

On the other side, Hay was a man of the world who had excelled in four careers. While cautious and conservative, he had a clear set of values and good judgment informed by an understanding of history. His sense of humor was unmatched, and his charm was noticed by everybody. He knew America both as a westerner and as an easterner; he understood its greatness and its weaknesses; he valued its capacities and believed in its future. Most of all, he had a strong sense of public service, made all the more admirable by his deteriorating health and sustained by his extraordinary luck. As he wrote near the end of his life, "My early dreams consisted rather of a desire than of an expectation that I might do some service to the country in the way of politics and diplomacy. Through the favor of fortune and the kindness of friends my opportunities have been far greater than my dreams."

3. A Pen-and-Ink Sailor

1.

Life changed for Commander Alfred T. Mahan, USN, in the library of the English Club in Lima, Peru, in the late winter of 1885. Mahan, then in his mid-forties, was the son of a military officer, a graduate of the U.S. Naval Academy at Annapolis, and—after a career at sea—the commander of one of the worst ships in the navy. With unconscious irony the *Wachusett* was classified as a "third-rate screw," a sixteen-hundred-ton wooden ship of Civil War vintage, propelled by antique sails as well as infirm steam engines, underarmed, undermanned, underrepaired, and overused. Mahan had asked for a better ship, but it had gone to a fellow officer with a better reputation for seamanship, George Dewey. Mahan's mission was to sail the remote waters off the western coast of South America, putting in from time to time at Valparaíso, Chile; Callao, Peru (the port for Lima); and Guayaquil, Ecuador, and to provide protection for American citizens living or working in those countries.

It was no accident that Mahan found himself in a dead-end assignment. During his naval career he was never respectful of authority when he believed it was being used unfairly. His rigidly Protestant sense of right and wrong made him a natural whistle-blower. As an upperclassman at the Naval Academy he had challenged the tradition that senior classmen did not report one another for violations of regulations. As a young officer he had criticized the navy's emphasis in its curriculum on science and engineering at the expense of history and languages. He had also argued for greater recognition of the importance of line officers, who went to sea, over staff officers, who manned desks.

Mahan's boldest assault on naval decorum was to expose corruption at the Boston Navy Yard, to which he had been assigned in 1875. He discovered that the yard was a "football for local politicians" and that the workers there were defrauding the government. He dismissed a previous investigation as a farce and its chairman as a "scoundrel." He explicitly criticized the secretary of the navy, George M. Robeson, for tolerating corruption, wrote a judge and a senator demanding another congressional investigation, and, when it was held, testified before it. Embarrassed by the rectitude of this young officer, the navy detached him from the Boston yard and put him on "waiting orders" on half pay; he was without an assignment for a year. This punitive treatment failed to silence Mahan. He continued to rail privately against the navy. In 1885, from the Coventry of the South Pacific Squadron, he wrote a friend that the last three navy secretaries were "men eminent for nothing creditable."

Despite his skirmishes with the navy, Mahan found his South American command interesting and even exciting. As he took charge of the *Wachusett* in Callao in September 1883, war was raging between Chile and Peru over the nitrate-rich desert between the two countries. When the defeated Peruvians sued for peace, the U.S. government offered to assist the negotiations through its minister in Lima. The *Wachusett* and three other American ships were stationed in the harbor to ensure calm. Nearly a year later Mahan returned to Peru as the victorious Chilean Army ended its occupation. He watched as the Chilean-supported Peruvian puppet government was overthrown by violence.

The impression made on this later avatar of American imperialism was that the United States should not intervene. "The air is rife with expected strife and revolution and the American squadron which, *pace* the Monroe Doctrine, has the fewest interests and the fewest people to protect, is tied down to this place. . . . [L]uckily Mr. Blaine [the interventionist former secretary of state, now running for president] is not yet president so we will not probably interfere beyond taking refugees on board if necessary." Mahan was glad to avoid landing his sailors on the mainland to protect American lives and property. "If that magnetic statesman [Blaine] were in office," he observed sarcastically, "I fancy the American diplomats would be running around in the magazine with lighted candles."

Mahan used his experience in Latin America to develop a powerful—and, as it turned out, ephemeral—anti-imperialist doctrine. He wrote from the *Wachusett*: "The question of landing troops in a foreign country is very delicate. I trust it may be avoided. . . . The very suspicion of an imperial policy is hateful; the mixing of our politics with those of Latin republics especially. Though identified, unluckily, with a military profession I dread outlying colonies or interests, to maintain which large military establishments are necessary. . . . Having opposed secession I have no mind to see the country travel towards a like catastrophe via colonies or the Monroe doctrine."

Though not an imperialist, Mahan strongly believed in a big navy. The U.S. Navy had been reduced from a seven-hundred-ship fleet during the Civil War to one of the smallest navies among those of large countries of the world. It had even fewer armored vessels than largely landlocked Austria-Hungary. In 1882 Mahan complained that the navy had never before declined so far: "[W]e have not six ships that would be kept at sea in war by any maritime power." Prophetically he noted that "Spain[,] a near and troublesome neighbor[,] is our superior." To a friend with contacts in Congress Mahan poured out reformist thoughts: "The urgency is great; and although the horde of robbers that surround the Treasury and Congress will make it necessary to have caution in guarding the expenditures, yet they must be made and made very freely if the Navy is to be maintained." When he departed for the South Pacific command, he was seething: "The country cares nothing for the service nor will care, I think, till irremediable disaster in that quarter has overtaken it."

When Mahan took command of the *Wachusett* in Callao, he got firsthand glimpses of that lack of concern and felt personally humiliated by them. All three foreign ships in harbor—Chilean, German, and Italian—were superior to the *Wachusett*. On a Pacific cruise Mahan described his embarrassment when a French officer came on board the *Wachusett*, stopped next to an old gun, and remarked that the French Navy had had that model but had phased it out. "It was a summary of American naval policy during the twenty years following 1865," Mahan recalled. "We 'had' things which other nations 'had had.' " In his autobiography Mahan described the American custom of carrying "Quaker guns," simulated cannons made of blackened wood.

By 1885, he wrote, the entire U.S. Navy was a "Quaker navy"; "not the enemy, but our own people were deceived."

Thus on his obscure South American station in 1885 Mahan at mid-career found himself out of sorts with the navy, which accurately considered him a misfit and a complainer. His recompense for rectitude and zeal was a career that seemed to be going nowhere. He was far behind Hay, Root, Lodge, and Roosevelt, none of whom he had yet met. By 1885 Hay had been a successful White House aide, diplomat, journalist, and writer; Root had a lucrative corporate law practice; Lodge was a published author and a leading Republican politician in Massachusetts; and Roosevelt, eighteen years Mahan's junior, had already been minority leader of the New York legislature.

Mahan did have one option. In 1884, while on the *Wachusett*, he had been offered a post teaching naval history and tactics at the new Naval War College that was shortly to be established at Newport, Rhode Island. It was a fitting assignment in one sense. Mahan's father had taught at West Point, and Mahan himself was an intellectual and an omnivorous reader. On the other hand, association with a fledgling institution, whose creation had been opposed by naval traditionalists and whose funding depended on annual appropriations from an unreliable Congress, hardly seemed a promising career move for a naval officer whose service loyalty was already suspect.

Out of boredom and a characteristic desire to prepare thoroughly, Mahan used his downtime on the South Pacific station to read into his coming duties at Newport. He decided to steep himself in the study of history, a longtime interest. He had written for his ten-year-old daughter Helen an informal history of Europe, which reflected a close knowledge of the main events, honed down to a clear account that a child could understand. But he had not been immune to the U.S. Navy's antihistorical bias. He wrote later: "I shared the prepossession, common at that time, that the naval history of the past was wholly past; of no use at all to the present." During the *Wachusett's* frequent calls at Callao, Mahan would take a carriage to Lima, nine miles inland, and use the English Club's library. It was there that he came upon a translation of the great German historian Theodor Mommsen's three-volume *History of Rome*, written thirty years before. This was the book that changed his life.

Mahan was fascinated by the section in which Mommsen described the Carthaginian general Hannibal's invasion of Rome during the Second Punic War in the third century B.C. Mommsen, prescient for his time and even for our time, put great emphasis on naval power and on the superiority of the Roman Navy to the Carthaginian. According to Mommsen, it was this Roman superiority that forced Hannibal, elephants and all, to attack via a long overland route from Spain, across Gaul (France), and over the Apennines into Italy.

As he read, Mahan was suddenly struck by "how different things might have been could Hannibal have invaded Italy by sea, as the Romans often had Africa, instead of by the long land route; or could he after arrival have been in free communication with Carthage by water." The march, Mahan wrote later, cost Hannibal more than half his veteran troops—thirty-three thousand of sixty thousand—and enabled the Roman general Scipio to intercept his communications and confront him at the Trebbia River. The Roman legions, on the other hand, "passed by water, unmolested and unwearied, between Spain, which was Hannibal's base, and Italy." The Carthaginians ultimately lost the seventeen-year war, the victims, Mahan concluded, of their failure to control the sea.

The story of Hannibal, read in the English Club, struck Mahan with the force of revelation. The realization came on him that control of the sea was a historic factor never before systematically appreciated and expounded. He decided that his historical lectures at the War College should combine general history with naval history and explore their effect on each other. Before Mahan's time there had been narratives of naval warfare, but no overall approach focusing on the influence of sea power on world history. Mahan's study would be the first. "My self-assigned task [was] to show how the control of the sea, commercial and military, had been an object powerful to influence the policies of nations; and equally a mighty factor in the success or failure of those policies." His excitement, as he prepared, was almost indescribable: "Every faculty I possessed was alive and jumping."

With ideas churning, Mahan yearned to get home to a decent library where he could focus his preparations. The navy let him down, keeping him at sea for a year after he had requested a transfer to Newport. In October 1885 he finally received orders for the War College, together with permission to spend the next ten months in New

York City for research. He would miss the college's first academic year, which began in 1885, but would start his lectures in the fall of 1886.

Mahan's research was impressive. He read deeply in British and European history, relying heavily on English and French sources (he read French easily). He was particularly influenced by two military historians, both former soldiers. Sir William Napier's history of Wellington's campaign in Spain against Napoleon's army taught Mahan the possibilities of turning military studies into a science through the demonstration of cause and effect. The voluminous writings of Baron Henri Jomini, one of Napoleon's generals, had an even greater influence. From Jomini Mahan "imbibed a fixed disbelief in the thoughtlessly accepted maxim that the statesman and general occupy unrelated fields. For this misconception I substituted a tenet of my own, that war is simply a violent political movement." This insight, perhaps drawn from Clausewitz's famous definition of war as "the continuation of politics by other means," led Mahan to treat political and diplomatic factors as carefully as military ones, ensuring that his lectures would rise above the technical level. Jomini also inspired him to draw principles of universal validity from the details of land battles and adapt them to naval warfare.

The excitement with naval history that grew from Mahan's encounter with Mommsen and Jomini persuaded him to devote the rest of his naval career to study rather than to sea duty. He knew that this would destroy his chances of rising to the top in the navy; he would never make admiral or even commodore as a naval intellectual. This did not bother him; in late middle age he had found a vocation. One man above all made possible this "right about" in his career. He was Rear Admiral Stephen B. Luce, the founder of the Naval War College and an officer of vision and determination.

Luce had overcome bureaucratic opposition and a reluctant Navy Department to win approval for the establishment of the War College, the first in the world. His ideas were grandiose. As he described it, "No less a task is proposed than to apply modern scientific methods to the study and raise naval warfare from the empirical stage to the dignity of a science." As a young officer Mahan had sailed under Luce's command and had seen the brilliant seamanship for which Luce was renowned in the navy. When Luce began to staff the War

College, he thought of his bright former executive officer. Mahan accepted immediately. Actually he was not Luce's first choice for lecturer in naval history; the assignment had been turned down by an officer junior to Mahan. One wonders how history would have changed if that officer had accepted.

Luce played in Alfred Mahan's life the role Lincoln and McKinley played in John Hay's, that of a senior mentor who gives a talented subordinate the opportunity to spread his wings. Mahan recognized the gift and remained grateful and close to Luce for the rest of his life. After the *Wachusett* was decommissioned in October 1885, Mahan sought no more shipboard assignments; in fact he pulled all the strings he could to avoid them.

Many in the navy wanted to sink the War College at its launching or at least turn it into a technical school instead of an academy of history and strategy. Luce and Mahan had to lobby, cajole, and improvise to keep it afloat. In addition to the anti-intellectual hostility that affects every military service, there were personality problems. Secretary of the Navy William C. Whitney felt no attachment to the college, which had been established by his predecessor. Breaking a promise he had made to Mahan, he asked the Senate to merge it with an operational command also based in Newport, thus curbing its independent status. He shortened its curriculum. He even threatened to transfer Mahan abroad.

The superintendent of the Naval Academy at Annapolis, Francis M. Ramsay, was an even more implacable foe, since he saw his monopoly over naval education endangered. In opposing the Naval War College, Ramsay used the timeless bureaucratic argument that his own institution could do whatever postgraduate teaching needed doing. He even stooped to barring his Annapolis graduates from taking courses at Newport. Nor was Congress, undoubtedly stoked by Whitney and Ramsay, friendly to the college. It cut off the school's funding in the fall of 1886, driving the teaching staff to such expedients as selling scrap to make ends meet.

In this uncertain atmosphere Mahan arrived in Newport in the fall of 1886 with his wife, Ellen, his three children, and his dog, appropriately named Jomini. To his surprise he found himself acting president of the college because Luce had been promoted to command of the North Atlantic Squadron. Mahan began his lectures in a converted almshouse, a location appropriately symbolic of the college's financial plight. His permanent teaching staff consisted of one army lieutenant whose very presence infuriated the navy brass, who could not understand why land warfare should be taught at a naval institution. Mahan prepared his own maps and battle plans, scuttling around on the floor of his office, coloring cardboard ships and pasting them on drawing paper.

The lectures, a year in preparation, were of unprecedented breadth for a course of naval studies, an examination of the general conditions affecting the maritime development of nations and of the influence of naval power on Europe and America since 1660. The students, some twenty of them, were appreciative, and Luce, who had brought the Atlantic Squadron back to Newport for the term, was rapturous. He told the class he had found a naval Jomini "and his name is Mahan!"

In the fall of 1887, Mahan's second year at the college, he needed a guest lecturer on the War of 1812. He invited a young writer and politician whom he had never met but who five years before had published a book on the subject. Theodore Roosevelt's study, written mostly while he was an undergraduate at Harvard, caught Mahan's eye because it propounded a thesis that coincided with and perhaps even influenced Mahan's own thinking.

Mahan, like Roosevelt, was convinced that, contrary to the belief of the U.S. Navy and Americans in general, the United States had failed to learn the right lessons from the War of 1812. To Mahan the erroneous belief that the young America had brought Britain "to her knees, by the destruction of her commerce through the system . . . of single cruisers" had produced disastrous consequences. It had led to the U.S. decision to build "a navy of cruisers, and small cruisers at that; no battle-ships nor fleets . . . We wanted a navy for coast defense only, no aggressive action in our pious souls."

Just as Mahan and Roosevelt agreed with this analysis of American error, they also agreed on what had to be done: The United States needed a big navy with large ships and a global reach. At Newport that week they established not only a friendship but an alliance. Mahan would supply the brain and Roosevelt the brawn, and together they would set out to reform the U.S. Navy and, with it, American foreign policy in general.

2.

The preparation of his Naval War College lectures and their revision over the school years gave Mahan time to think through his entire philosophy of sea power. He confronted a major contradiction. He had always been an anti-imperialist. He feared that colonies would require a large armed force, which would in turn necessitate a strong central government. Having grown up "in the atmosphere of the single cruiser, of commerce-destroying, defensive warfare, and indifference to battle-ships," Mahan had arrived at Newport immune to the urges that had driven other countries to swallow up huge chunks of Africa and Asia.

Yet his mind, influenced by his reflections at sea, sharpened by his War College lectures, and reinforced by Roosevelt's militant activism, began to shed its anti-imperialist views, which he could no longer reconcile with his growing beliefs in a strong navy, in American interests in the hemisphere, and in a policy of global involvement. On sea duty off Latin America he had experienced the competition of other navies, and as an advocate of the Monroe Doctrine he believed in the need to exclude European powers from America's hemispheric preserve. A larger and stronger navy would be required to consolidate America's hegemony in the Caribbean.

Moreover, the necessary piercing of the Isthmus of Panama would create a new challenge. He made the analogy with the Suez Canal. The British needed a large navy to protect their passage to India through Suez; the United States would need a similar navy to protect its Atlantic and Pacific coasts, exposed by the opening of the isthmus. Such a navy, in his view, must do more than just defend U.S. ports with gunboats and dispatch single cruisers to raid an enemy's commercial shipping, thus far the U.S. Navy's principal missions. Naval strategy had to change from defensive to offensive. Battleships and heavy cruisers must replace light cruisers to make possible offensive operations far from American coasts, and fleets, with the ships trained at working together, must replace single ships. The new navy would need bases or colonies in which to rest, refit, and refuel. Without at first realizing it, Mahan was putting in place the military arguments for an American policy of imperialism. It remained for him to sweep them into a general philosophy of sea power. This was to be his great work at Newport.

While Mahan was embarked on his intellectual voyage, the U.S. Navy was engaged in a major rebuilding program. Beginning in 1882 in the Republican administration of Chester Arthur and continuing through the Democrat Grover Cleveland, Congress funded seventeen steel-hulled cruisers to replace the wooden ships on which Mahan had served. The new ships were hardly modern. Most still carried sail, and none had the armor or guns to contest the best European navies. The Naval Act of 1890 was a breakthrough to the new navy. It was inspired by Benjamin Harrison's secretary of the navy, Benjamin F. Tracy, a New York politician and former Civil War general. Tracy, the bureaucratic father of the modern American navy, introduced battleships, the largest and most heavily armed warships afloat, to give the navy what Mahan had been calling for, a mid-ocean capability.

Mahan had played no part in the naval reforms of the early 1880s and had even scorned their progenitors. But he may have influenced Tracy, who was friendly to the War College and knowledgeable about Mahan's views. As Tracy's solicitude put the college on a firmer footing, Mahan's personal situation also improved. In 1886 he had been promoted to captain, the highest rank he achieved on active duty. His lectures were going so well that with the encouragement of his wife and of Luce, he decided to turn them into a book. The timing was exquisite. Just as the navy was making itself a formidable fighting force, Mahan emerged to give it a rationale and a mission. *The Influence of Sea Power upon History 1660–1783* was Mahan's greatest achievement and probably the most influential work on naval strategy ever written.

He did not enter the writing business cold. In 1882 he had written a book for Scribner's in its series on the navy in the Civil War. His volume, *The Gulf and Inland Waters,* which covered the last phase, argued that the North's control of southern waters ensured its victory. This modest work helped move Mahan toward his ultimate revelation of the importance of sea power. In contrast, *The Influence of Sea Power upon History* was a work of breathtaking range: a history of diplomatic and military strategy, a survey of land as well as sea combat, and an assemblage of universal principles of naval warfare.

Majestic as his theme was, Mahan had great difficulty in finding a publisher. Scribner's was not interested; nor were others. He turned to J. P. Morgan, of all people, who declined to pay for the publication but did offer two hundred dollars toward the cost of printing. Thanks to the perseverance of Luce and Elly Mahan, and with the help of his War College colleague James Soley, Little, Brown finally agreed to publish the book in both the United States and Britain. It appeared in both countries in 1890.

Mahan wrote in his preface that he had tried to present a clear and accurate outline, without technical language, in hopes that "these matters, simply presented, will be found of interest to the unprofessional reader." The book is indeed clearly written, jargon-free, and easily accessible, even today. Mahan's prose, unlike John Hay's, does not dance. It plows forward confidently and steadily, occasionally weighted down by ponderous sentences, more often enlivened by generalizations that illuminate and excite. *The Influence of Sea Power* is a classic of style as well as substance. The key to its greatness is the degree to which Mahan marshaled data stretching over a century into a coherent, geopolitical analysis leading to major conclusions. He made no concessions to the trivial. The book is history in the grand manner.

Mahan's book described the age of sail, an era that was dying as he wrote. Pleading his credentials as interpreter of the imminent age of steam, he contended that in naval strategy "the teachings of the past have a value which is in no degree lessened." To fight effectively, modern naval strategists must understand why Hannibal lost to Rome and—two millennia later—why Napoleon lost to England. The reason was that the principles of naval warfare never changed: concentration on the enemy's weak point, refusal to weaken one's fleet by dividing it, and the primacy of attacking the enemy's fleet rather than his homeland. Such principles were "applicable to all ages" and "deducible from history."

Chapters 2 through 14 of a long book, five-sixths of the text, form a narrative account of the seven great maritime wars from the Anglo-Dutch wars of the 1660s to the American Revolution, with detailed descriptions of the great sea battles. Had these chapters constituted the whole book, the work would undoubtedly have been treated as a spirited but specialized account suitable only for historians and naval buffs. But Mahan wanted to reach a general readership. At the suggestion of his publisher, he added a hastily written sixty-five-page first chapter summarizing his views on sea power, often in a polemical manner. It was here that he tied his main themes to the present and applied them, invariably with disapproval, to American naval strategy. Chapter 1 made Mahan the most famous and subversive military commentator in the United States.

Mahan described the sea as a "great highway" or a "wide common, over which men may pass in all directions, but on which some well-worn paths show that controlling reasons have led them to choose certain lines of travel rather than others. These lines of travel are called trade routes." Trading ships "that thus sail to and fro must have secure ports to which to return, and must, as far as possible, be followed by the protection of their country throughout the voyage. This protection in time of war must be extended by armed shipping."

In these passages Mahan invented navies by the process of induction. He contended that "as a nation . . . launches forth from its own shores, the need is soon felt of points upon which the ships can rely for peaceful trading, for refuge and supplies"—that is, "stations" where "ships could lie in safety" and merchandise be stored. Such stations multiply and grow until they become colonies. But additional security is required. The dangers of the voyage itself require "stations along the road, . . . not primarily for trade but for defence and war." Mahan cited as examples Gibraltar, Malta, and Louisburg, at the entrance of the Gulf of St. Lawrence. By now Mahan's inductive brush had painted in colonies and bases.

He next outlined the six principal conditions affecting the sea power of nations. Three were physical, three human. The first was "geographical position." By this criterion Mahan found Britain, as an island nation, the most fortunate country. By contrast the United States was not so well placed since it had no ports near the great centers of global trade. For successful commerce destroying, Mahan observed, America would need to find bases in distant parts. This was the kernel of his later argument for the acquisition of the Philippines and other Pacific islands.

In examining geography, Mahan developed a strong argument for a canal across the Isthmus of Panama. If it were built, "the Caribbean will be changed from a terminus, and place of local traffic, or at best a broken and imperfect line of travel, as it now is, into one of the great highways of the world." But the canal would be a mixed blessing. Along that highway would travel the ships of the great European nations, coming closer than ever before to American shores and causing "international complications." Mahan believed the United States would have to take steps to establish its strategic primacy over the canal, as Britain had with the English Channel.

First, it would be necessary to shore up American defenses along the Gulf of Mexico coast, which was deficient in secure ports and repair facilities. Second, America needed bases ("stations") in the Caribbean to "enable her fleets to remain as near the scene as any opponent." Third, the canal would require a naval capability to defend it on the Pacific side. As he expanded his arguments about American power, Mahan was tearing to shreds his earlier opposition to imperialism. His inductive reasoning was leading him inexorably to the championing of an America in which imperialism marched from one logical stage to the next, imperialism begetting imperialism.

Mahan's second condition for sea power was "physical conformation." He described the seaboard of a country as one of its frontiers. Numerous and deep harbors, in peacetime a source of strength and wealth, in war would be a source of weakness if not properly defended. Mahan cited three examples drawn from American history. In 1778 the vulnerability of New York Harbor almost caused the British to lose it to the French, which would have forced Britain into an earlier peace. In 1814 an undefended Chesapeake Bay allowed the British to burn the new capital of Washington. Finally, during the Civil War the Confederacy's inability to defend the mouth of the Mississippi River brought disaster on the South.

Physical conditions led people to the sea or turned them from it, wrote Mahan. The French enjoyed too pleasant a land to be natural seafarers; the Dutch were driven to the sea by necessity; the English were drawn to it by geography and choice. Mahan saw Americans as going the way of the French. The United States had begun as a seafaring nation—"almost every one of the original colonies was on the sea or on one of its great tributaries"—but now the center of power was no longer on the seaboard, and the development of the interior had diverted interest, investment, and labor away from the sea frontiers. Mahan lamented, "Those who follow the limitations which lack of sea power placed upon the career of France may mourn that their own country is being led, by a like redundancy of home wealth, into the same neglect of that great instrument."

He conceded that the physical conformation of the United States had advantages. Its continental shape made the whole country, except for Alaska, fully accessible by land. Also, by the last decades of the century all important parts of the frontier could be reached rapidly by rail. The country was economically self-sufficient, not dependent on seaborne imports. Even its weakest frontier, the Pacific coast, was far removed from dangerous enemies. Yet should there be a new commercial route through the Isthmus of Panama, "the United States in her turn may have the rude awakening of those who have abandoned their share in the common birthright of all people, the sea."

Mahan's third condition affecting sea power was "extent of territory," the length of a nation's coastline and the quality of its harbors. Reviving the theme of his first book, he observed that sea power had been decisive in the American Civil War. The Confederacy's long seacoast and numerous harbors would have been a source of strength if its population had been larger and its navy more effective. A blockade against it could never have succeeded. Instead the combination of a long littoral and a small population was fatal. Mahan's purpose here was less to make a historical point than to launch a current warning. He was charging the naval hierarchy in the United States with a complacency bred of a misreading of history. In effect he was saying, "You think we have an adequate navy because we won the Civil War with it; in fact we were just lucky."

Mahan then turned to the three human conditions affecting sea power. The first two were a population habituated to the sea and "national character." Mainly because of their aptitude for commercial pursuits, the English and Dutch peoples came first in seaworthiness. In the capacity for planting healthy colonies, Mahan extolled Britain as unrivaled. In Americans he saw an unrealized and mainly potential talent for commerce and colonialism. Lacking a merchant shipping industry and a merchant marine, his countrymen had turned away from maritime vocations and therefore saw little need for the shield of a large navy.

Mahan's final human condition affecting sea power was "character of the government." National leaders could take advantage of sea power, as when Cromwell had built the English Navy. Or they could abuse it disastrously, as when the government of King George III had committed itself to a distant land war with the American colonies while France and Spain were waiting for an opportunity to attack Britain by sea. In Mahan's view, the system of government was also an important factor in the fate of navies. Here, as elsewhere, he vacillated in his preferences between autocratic and democratic systems. He noted that the most brilliant successes of sea power had come when the government reflected the will of the people. On the other hand, "such free governments have sometimes fallen short," while despotic powers have created successful navies "with greater directness than can be reached by the slower processes of a free people." Implicitly criticizing the United States, he observed that "popular governments are not generally favorable to military expenditures."

In peace, Mahan argued, governments, including his own, should encourage industries and vocations enhancing sea power and should build large merchant marines. In preparation for war, they should keep an adequate reserve of men and ships, maintain "suitable naval stations" in distant parts of the world, and protect them with military force, as the British protected Gibraltar and Malta. Mahan's model, indeed the collective hero of the entire book, was the British Navy. "England's naval bases have been in all parts of the world; and her fleets have at once protected them, kept open the communications between them, and relied upon them for shelter."

Mahan contrasted Britain's brilliant naval policy with the hapless approach of the U.S. government to naval matters. American weakness was most glaring in the absence of colonies that "attached to the mother-country afford . . . the surest means of supporting abroad the sea power of a country." In a striking image, he described the consequences of that deficiency: "Having therefore no foreign establishments, either colonial or military, the ships of war of the United States, in war, will be like land birds, unable to fly far from their own shores. To provide resting-places for them, where they can coal and repair, would be one of the first duties of a government proposing to itself the development of the power of the nation at sea."

The 452-page narrative section of Mahan's book featured cautionary examples of countries that had succeeded or failed. France, well suited for maritime power, had lost its primacy when Louis XIV chose to build a land, rather than a sea, empire. Britain, by contrast, had used sea power to achieve its epic expansion. The American colonies had won the Revolutionary War by exploiting the maritime resources of their allies, France and Spain, and by stretching thin the British Navy, which was preoccupied with the defense of Gibraltar and the Caribbean. Mahan quoted George Washington as telling his French allies that "a decisive naval superiority" was the key to success. But in the War of 1812—like the Civil War, a subject extraneous to the frame of his book—Americans had let down their guard, and "our coasts were insulted in every direction, the Chesapeake entered and controlled, its shores wasted, the Potomac ascended, and Washington burned."

Mahan preached that the United States could not wield the balance of military power in its own hemisphere or defend the Monroe Doctrine without an adequate sea force. He referred ominously to enemies and rivals but never named them. That was probably because he had no specific countries in mind. The traditional enemy of the United States was Britain, but Mahan was in love with the British Navy, and he saw Britain as a potential ally as well as a possible foe. Spain, prior to the revolution in Cuba in 1895, was not seen as a potential enemy. The United States did not yet own Pacific territories that would have brought Japan into the strategic picture. Kaiser William II's Germany was probably a future rival, but not yet a credible one. Mahan's warnings were against a putative threat, not a real one.

The Influence of Sea Power upon History received glowing reviews, some by critics who did not read beyond the polemical first chapter. One reviewer who did was Theodore Roosevelt, who devoured the entire book. He wrote Mahan excitedly: "During the last two days I have spent half my time, busy as I am, in reading your book; and that I found it interesting is shown by the fact that having taken it up, I have gone straight through and finished it. . . . It is a very good book—admirable; and I am greatly in error if it does not become a naval classic." Even more helpfully, Roosevelt wrote an enthusiastic review in the *Atlantic Monthly,* saying: "Captain Mahan has written distinctly the best and most important, and also by far the most interesting book on naval history which has been produced on either side of the water for many a long year."

Modern military historians have pointed out that *The Influence of*

Sea Power upon History was neither an original nor a wholly accurate work. Other writers, from Xenophon to British and American authors, had emphasized the primacy of sea power. Part of Mahan's thesis was undercut by the rise of nonmaritime powers like Germany and Russia. The victor of Waterloo might have been surprised at Mahan's assertion that sea power had defeated Napoleon. Anchored in the age of sail, Mahan was singularly insensitive to the technical innovations that accompanied steam and to new technologies like the submarine. Like most promoters of a single explanation for the complex sweep of history, he was a gross oversimplifier.

Nevertheless, his book was unprecedented for the audacity of its scope and for the brilliance of its application of history to modern naval strategy. Even more important, it was a masterpiece of popularization and propaganda. It was not a best-seller, but it found its targeted audience among educated nonexperts concerned with foreign policy. It made its author the reference point for all discussion of naval strategy. More than anybody else, Mahan now set the terms of the debate about the naval contribution to America's expansion.

3.

The Influence of Sea Power upon History represented the culmination of the life, experience, and intellectual formation of a remarkable man. Mahan has appeared in history as brilliant but austere, self-contained and remote, a bit fuddy-duddy, testy. He considered himself a superior person, though reticent and formal. Rivals saw him as peevish, irascible, and arrogant. The adjectives, none of them false, form a caricature of the man. The real Mahan was more complex and more interesting.

He was born in 1840, two years after John Hay, at West Point, New York, where his father, Dennis Mahan, was dean of the faculty at the U.S. Military Academy. Dennis had been reared in Norfolk, Virginia, the son of parents who had fled Ireland just after the failed revolution of 1798 against the British. Dennis attended West Point, where he was first in his class and an acting assistant professor before his graduation. His whole life as an army officer was devoted to teaching and writing. His book on civil engineering became a standard text and won him honorary degrees from Brown and Princeton. His courses at

West Point in mathematics and engineering were highly regarded, though he made life difficult for his students by his strict discipline and relentless cross-examination in class.

A workaholic who spent his vacations inspecting new examples of civil engineering, Dennis Mahan was in love with the art of war and used the great sieges and battles of history to enliven his lectures. He was also passionate about France, not surprising for the son of Irish immigrants accustomed to seeing France as the great enemy of Britain. He had been sent there for four years as a second lieutenant to study public works and military instruction. He came back a worshiper of Napoleon and the French Army, wrote a book about Napoleon's war tactics, and founded a Napoleon Club at West Point.

In one sense Dennis Mahan had as much influence on American military strategy as his more famous son. He taught most of the great American Civil War generals on both sides: Grant, Sherman, Jackson, Sheridan, Beauregard, Stuart, Hill. His book on field fortifications would have been particularly influential to that generation of military leaders. It emphasized the defensive character—pick and spade work—that the Civil War was to take. When Alfred Mahan as a young lieutenant met Sherman just after the fall of Savannah, the famous Union general was delighted to shake the hand of the son of "old Dennis."

Alfred Mahan, like John Hay, was proud of his polyglot ancestry: half Irish, a quarter English, and (through his mother) "a good deal more than 'a trace' of French." He said in his memoirs, "From my derivation, therefore, I am a pretty fair illustration of the mix-up of bloods which seems destined to bring forth the same new and yet undecipherable combination on the North American continent." Yet family life at the Mahans was not exciting. Alfred's mother was an extrovert who enjoyed the social life of the academy, but his father, though kind, was taciturn, sometimes going days without speaking. The family was devoutly Christian, with prayers every morning before breakfast. Alfred was sustained by religion throughout his life; toward the end of it he wrote a book about his faith. But from the age of twelve the boy no longer lived at home. For two years he attended an Episcopalian boarding school in Maryland, and for two more he went to Columbia College in New York, boarding with his revered uncle, a minister and prominent ecclesiastical historian.

Throughout his youth Alfred Mahan had a love affair with the sea. He devoured the mannered sea stories of the British naval officer Frederick Marryat and the American writer James Fenimore Cooper, who had served for five years in the U.S. Navy. Alfred's desire to attend the Naval Academy at Annapolis rather than stay at Columbia or transfer to West Point did not greatly dismay his father, who gave up trying to talk him out of it. Dennis even helped his fifteen-year-old son seek the assistance of Jefferson Davis, secretary of war and a West Point man, in securing an appointment to Annapolis. On September 30, 1856, three days after his sixteenth birthday, Alfred Mahan began a naval career that was to last four decades.

Mahan had a soft landing at the Naval Academy. With credit for his two years at Columbia, he entered as a third classman (sophomore). His father was a friend of the superintendent, and his mother was close to the wife of the commandant; two other professors had been at West Point too, so the sixteen-year-old had a support system that made up for his missing the first year. Though disciplined, academy routine included fencing and dancing lessons, prohibited hazing, unlike West Point, and was permissive enough to allow Mahan to read at least one novel a week.

Nor did it deter him unduly from his new major interest. As the sap rose, he seemed to have girls on his mind most of the time at Annapolis. Mary Esther Gill, Kate Brown, Julia Kent, Anna Franklin, Elizabeth Lewis, and Nannie Craven (the daughter of the commandant) all felt the hot breath of his affection. He kissed Elizabeth, and he told Nannie he wanted to be a brother to her. She teasingly accused him of being conceited, and he admitted it. He boasted to a friend he was considered the "smartest man in the class" and was "told frequently of my good looks and complimented sometimes by ladies in society." One day Mahan overstayed his leave three and a half hours, "the most serious infraction of the Regulations that I have ever been guilty of." The reason was "those infernal women."

Without working too hard, Mahan managed to distinguish himself academically. He was second in his graduating class of twenty, winnowed down from the forty-nine who had entered. He did not make friends easily, and his few close ones were mostly southerners who opted for the Confederacy when the Civil War began, two years after graduation. His friendship with Samuel Ashe of North Carolina was important to history, because Ashe saved the candid letters Mahan wrote him all his life.

He struck many of his classmates as a prig. His willingness to report on fellow students for breaking the rules earned him a period of silent treatment, plus the support of his usually silent father for his principled position. He once upbraided a fourth classman for eating the last piece of toast. On leave in New York City he sniffed in disapproval at the vulgarity of some of his fellow midshipmen on a ferry: "It takes at least twenty gentlemen to remove the bad impression made by one rowdy." But he enjoyed the affectations of youth, occasionally taking the seafaring man's drink of brandy and water and boasting of the number of cigars he smoked. In general he liked Annapolis and his classmates: "[Y]ou can form no idea what a nice class we have, my affection seemed to be wrapped up in them."

He was graduated at eighteen, a good-looking young man, tall (six feet one and a half inches), with a thin frame, blue eyes, and light brown hair. To go with a military bearing, he had an authoritarian bent, noting, for example, that "every great man that ever lived had the nature of a despot." He welcomed naval discipline, going so far as to credit the greatness of the British Navy to the idea of obedience "born, bred, and nourished" in Britons. But he hated discipline unfairly applied. He had a strong sense of justice and a conviction that he had been put on earth to dispense it.

Even in his Annapolis days he saw himself as a military intellectual. The future biographer of the naval heroes Nelson and Farragut told his classmates that the age of daring had passed and that he himself would win fame through intellectual achievement. He was not yet a maverick, but he was already a man of considerable independence of thought and action.

In light of later criticism of Mahan's competence as a sailor, it is worth noting that at Annapolis he was captain of the first crew, which won a commendation for seamanship and gunnery from a visiting board of commodores. He enjoyed the summer cruises, waxing literary over the first one: "In a stiff breeze, when the ship is heeling well over, there is a wild sort of delight that I have never experienced before." He suffered somewhat from seasickness—fortunately not as much as his friend Ashe, who had to leave the academy because of it—and was clumsy with knots, never managing anything more complex than a bowline. Though he confessed to a fear of gales, he was a genuine sailor and spent eleven of his first fifteen years in the navy at sea.

Mahan's first sea duty almost ended his career before it began. On graduation in 1859 he was assigned to the sloop of war *Levant*, but his orders were changed at the last minute, and the *Levant* sailed without him. It went down in the Pacific with all hands. Instead Mahan sailed to the South Atlantic, the Brazil Station, on the *Congress*, a frigate with a crew of about five hundred. Though the Atlantic had been first crossed under steam in 1837, the navy was slow to embrace the new technology, and the *Congress* was a pure sailing ship, like more than half the vessels in the inventory at the time. Mahan considered them "substantially worthless." Nevertheless, all the vessels on which he shipped after the *Congress* (including on his last voyage in 1893) carried sail as well as used steam.

Mahan, future strategist of the modern navy of steam and steel, had a real nostagia for the old sailing ships. After they had been phased out, he recalled watch duty on the *Congress*: "These eternities of the heavens and the deep abide as before; are common to the steamer and the sailing ship; but what weary strain of words can restore to imagination the beautiful living creature which leaped under our feet and spread her wings above us?" He also liked the tropics, their "pervading odor of rum and sugar" and of course their women; he described his "delight in a pretty face and dark Spanish eye."

As the *Congress* sailed north from Brazil, the American Civil War was beginning. Having returned home, the crew of the ship was compelled in Boston to pledge allegiance to the Union; four officers refused and were imprisoned. Mahan did not waver in his loyalty to the Union, even though most of his friends at Annapolis had been southerners, and a third of his class, including his friend Ashe, had opted for the Confederacy. He was not sure about the loyalties of his father. Dennis was distraught when his friend Robert E. Lee, a fellow Virginian, engineer, and colleague at West Point, resigned his commission to join the Confederate forces. Dennis remained loyal to the Union, but his brother Milo, the minister with whom Alfred Mahan had boarded in New York, left for Maryland because of his southern sympathies. The discord in the family, not untypical in 1861, paralleled the cleavage in Theodore Roosevelt's household: Roosevelt's mother was a southerner, and her brothers served the Confederacy.

If Mahan felt personally torn, he did not show it. He did not like the northern antislavery propaganda, but he liked slavery even less. He was repelled by his first look at the practice when some slaves fled to his ship off South Carolina early in the Civil War. He was also excited by the prospect of combat: "War, even in its incipiency, was new . . . and the enthusiasm aroused by a great cause and approaching conflict was not balanced by that solemnizing outlook which experience brings."

From the outset of the war Mahan was thinking creatively. He sent the assistant secretary of the navy a secret plan for capturing a Confederate pirate ship that had been attacking Union warships. It called for disguising an obsolete Union warship as a merchantman to decoy the raider into an attack, whereupon the hidden guns would be brought into action against it. Mahan offered himself to lead the enterprise. One can imagine what the Navy Department must have thought of the audacity of this twenty-year-old midshipman. It did not accept his proposal.

Mahan was assigned as first lieutenant on the *Pocahontas*, a steam corvette and in his enthusiastic view "one of the prettiest gunboats in the United States Navy." It patrolled the Potomac River against Confederate incursions, then ventured farther south to participate in the capture of Port Royal, South Carolina, and to blockade Charleston Harbor. Following the transfer of the captain, Mahan assumed temporary command as the *Pocahontas* roamed the inland waterways from South Carolina to Florida. He saw some combat but not much; the blockading he found "desperately tedious work." The Confederacy had practically no navy, a weakness to which he was to attribute its defeat in *The Influence of Sea Power upon History*. In his memoirs he made an ironic reference to Admiral Nelson's observation that "our men's minds are always kept up with the daily hopes of meeting the enemy." On Mahan's patrol there was no enemy to meet.

After a year combining excitement and drudgery on the *Pocahontas*, Mahan spent eight months on the faculty of the Naval Academy, which had been moved to Newport for security reasons. It was there that he met his future patron, Stephen B. Luce, then a lieutenant commander and head of the department of seamanship, to which he was assigned. Mahan also fell in love with an attractive older married woman, but his suit foundered on her unwillingness to seek a divorce. In the summer of 1863 Mahan sailed as executive officer under Luce on the Naval Academy's summer cruise to Europe, a curious indulgence for the navy in the midst of a war. The crew got the news of the victories of Gettysburg and Vicksburg while riding at anchor in the British port of Spithead.

Moving on to Cherbourg on the Normandy coast, the American sailors received word that Napoleon III's army had occupied Mexico City. Mahan mentioned the event in his memoirs without comment, but the contempt with which France treated the Monroe Doctrine seems to have stayed with him. One of the leitmotivs of his later writings was the warning that the Monroe Doctrine was only as good as the U.S. Navy whose mission was to uphold it.

After his short stint at the Naval Academy, Mahan was back on blockade duty, the boredom of which was relieved only once. His ship supported Sherman's march from Atlanta to the sea, and he was present at the fall of Charleston and the reraising of the Union flag over Fort Sumter. The city's two-year resistance to naval attacks had confirmed the conviction of Mahan's father in his book on fortifications that ships could not conquer forts. Charleston fell when Sherman, executing the principles in his West Point teacher's text, cut its communications to the interior. The action had a seminal effect on both Luce and Mahan. They realized that Sherman had been operating from a broad concept of military science, combining an understanding of land and sea warfare. The great general's example inspired the young naval officers to devote more intellectual attention to the science of war.

In the two decades between the Civil War and his epiphany in the English Club in Lima, Mahan saw a great deal of the world. He was executive officer on the *Iroquois*, a huge two-hundred-foot corvette that sailed to Japan and back. His two years in Asia proved an important intellectual experience. He read history and fiction omnivorously: Thackeray, Cervantes, Oliver Wendell Holmes, Motley's *Rise of the Dutch Republic*. He took extensive shore leaves, visiting the markets in Aden, witnessing a beheading in Japan, and playing billiards in Hong Kong and Shanghai. He shared his observations in chatty letters to his family. British soldiers made a lasting impression on him: "more the ideal of their profession in bearing etc. than anything we have at home." He sympathized with the Jews of Aden, "brutalized by ages of oppression and servility," a more charitable treatment than John Hay had given the Jews of Vienna.

Japan was the most beautiful country he had ever seen, but he wondered why the women blackened their teeth: "The unmarried girls have, many of them, as beautiful sets of teeth as you could wish to see." His puritanical but prurient soul marveled at the shameless-ness of the Japanese: "As for the exposure of the person no one thinks anything of it. Every third house you see women with their whole breast bare to the waist and men in swarms with a simple band that rather indicates than conceals their privates."

The *Iroquois* spent considerable time in Japan and China. She was given a seven-week overhaul in Hong Kong, where Mahan, indulging his nostalgia for sailing ships, was captivated by the junks plying Victoria Harbor. Mahan's ship, together with British, French, and Italian warships, took part in a show of naval power connected with opening Osaka and Kobe to Western trade. In effect he was participating in an early version of the Asia policy that was to develop more fully when John Hay was secretary of state. Mahan's two visits to Manila, a city with portentous importance for his and America's future, made less of an impression on him. As he remarked in his memoirs, "Long as American eyes had been fixed upon Cuba, in the old days of negro slavery, it had occurred to none, I fancy, to connect possession of that island with these distant Spanish dependencies."

Endless weeks and months on shipboard allowed Mahan plenty of time for reflection. He kept a diary to record his moods and to chastise himself for overindulgence. He suffered periods of tension and depression at sea when it was hard for him to get out of his bunk in the morning. He set himself goals—do not overeat, cut down on drinking—then graded himself on how well he had met them. He seemed consistently to fall short on the pledged abstemiousness. He fought his tendency to waste time by prescribing a reading program; luckily the *Iroquois* was large enough to have a good library. He compiled a set of "Rules for My Life." He spent considerable time in religious rumination. His faith was clearly a solace to him, then, as always, and he spent months trying to foist it on an erring shipmate.

Mahan's diary, unlike his letters, reveals a self-absorbed, introverted, often unhappy person, always failing to measure up to his own strict standards.

On the *Iroquois*, a ship with a crew of more than two hundred men, three-quarters of them non-Americans, Mahan had an opportunity to exhibit leadership qualities. He failed the test. He took an instant dislike to the skipper, Commander Earl English, whom he considered autocratic and petty. Mahan's hostility was more personal than professional—he conceded English's able seamanship—and he made no effort to keep it to himself. Even worse, he was often abusive to the crew. He detested their frequent swearing, drunkenness, thievery, malingering, and insubordination and was quick to punish. Though remorseful at his "violent fits of wrath," he seemed unable to curb them. "The more I reflect on my temper," he wrote his mother, "the more convinced I am that my natural disposition . . . is most abominable."

In Asia Mahan had two short stints of command: on the *Iroquois*, after the captain was transferred, and on a gunboat that was to be sold. An unexplained illness in Japan was serious enough to produce orders for his return home via six months of leave in Europe; he traveled as a passenger on an American merchant ship. His trip took him through the Suez Canal, which had been opened a few weeks before. Having been around Africa on his way out, he could measure the time the canal saved. In Europe he visited Rome and southern Italy, Paris and southern France, Spithead, and London. He had a surreal experience in Nice, happening on the woman he had loved in Newport six years before. Her husband had died, and she was unattached. Mahan proposed, and she turned him down.

It was one of the best things that ever happened to him. Within a year he met Ellen Evans, a serious young woman of nineteen. He pursued her to her affluent parents' summer home in the Adirondacks, where the dogged nature of his courtship was lampooned by her friends:

> *Elly had a big Mahan, whose teeth were white as snow.*
> *Everywhere that Elly went, Mahan was sure to go.*

They married on June 11, 1872. "Certainly not a great beauty," wrote Mahan to his mother, "she is very fair in my eyes." Elly Evans was a perfect wife for Mahan. She handled his moodiness with understand-ing, recognized and nurtured his talents, and gave him spiritual suste-nance. She also pitched in when needed, for example, typing the entire manuscript of *The Influence of Sea Power upon History.*

Dennis Mahan did not live to see his son inherit the mantle of mil-itary science that he himself had worn with distinction at West Point. He died in 1871, while Alfred was courting Elly Evans. The West Point academic board had recommended his retirement after forty years at the academy. The decision, though insensitive, could not have been unexpected; it nevertheless threw the elder Mahan into a depression. President Grant, his former pupil, reversed the board's ac-tion, but too late. Professor Mahan was in an emotional tailspin. On his way to seek medical help in New York City, he threw himself into the paddle wheel of a Hudson River steamer. From the age of thirty-one Alfred was now the "big Mahan," but it was not until he was in his mid-forties, at Newport, that he began to fill his father's shoes.

Following a cruise to England, which allowed him the leisure to visit English cathedrals, Mahan got his first regular command, the USS *Wasp*, and was sent back to the South Atlantic Station. Now a commander, he shipped at Montevideo with Elly also on board. His duties were similar to those of a diplomat. He was to report on politi-cal events and to advance and protect American interests in Ar-gentina, Uruguay, and Paraguay, including the two large cities of Buenos Aires and Montevideo. His two years on station were largely uneventful, though the *Wasp* did weather a revolution in Argentina. Mahan was then reassigned to the Boston Navy Yard. He returned home, in the leisurely tradition of the navy, via France, England, and Mount Desert Island, Maine.

When his run-in with the navy over the Boston Navy Yard resulted in the cancellation of his next assignment, he spent his enforced leisure with Elly and their baby daughter, Helen, in France, where Elly's parents were living. There he began the process of turning ad-versity into fortune by starting to write. His first two articles were on the architecture of French cathedrals and on the history of southern France, not the most predictable subjects for a naval commander on active duty. Aiming high, he submitted them to *Harper's* but was turned down. Nevertheless, Elly recognized his flair and kept him writing. On his next assignment as head of the ordnance department at the Naval Academy, he won third prize for an article on a more mainstream subject, "Naval Education for Officers and Men." It advocated a liberal arts curriculum and the cultivation of moral over mental qualities for the training of line officers: self-control, fearlessness, self-reliance, resourcefulness, calm.

After Annapolis, Mahan tried and failed to get an assignment at sea; perhaps he was still being punished for his aggressive rectitude in Boston. He was instead transferred to the New York Navy Yard, where he had to deal with the technical specifications of items of equipment, just the sort of thing he despised. He considered administrative details "interesting only to specialists"; now he was inundated with them. It must have galled him to write letters to the head of the Bureau of Navigation about the quality of the yard's miniature foreign flags, the cost of repairing drums, and the relative merits of different deck lanterns. He used his spare time to write *The Gulf and Inland Waters*. From New York Mahan was detached to take command of the *Wachusett* at Callao. In August 1883 he crossed the Isthmus of Panama by railway on his way to the obscure assignment that was to lead him to renown.

4.

When Mahan returned from Peru in 1885 to his billet at the Naval War College, he was forty-five years old and had been a naval officer for twenty-five years, more than half that time at sea. The rate of his promotions had kept up with that of such future leaders as William T. Sampson, who was to command the U.S. fleet against Spain; Winfield S. Schley, who was to defeat the Spanish at Santiago Bay; and George Dewey, the future hero of Manila Bay. But the momentum of his career was beginning to slow as the navy showed increasing irritation at his criticisms of it. The wretched *Wachusett* was a harbinger; he could not expect further responsible commands. Dewey, Sampson, and Schley all were to make admiral while on active duty; Mahan's career peaked at captain.

Yet his varied experiences proved an indispensable background to the important phase of his life he was entering. Virtually everything he would write about the American Navy and naval strategy was based on his personal observations. He could advocate naval reform because he had sailed on, and commanded, obsolete ships, had borne the ridicule of British, French, and even Chilean naval officers, and had battled inefficiency and corruption in American navy yards. While he had seen little combat (few naval officers had), his blockade duty in the Civil War had proved to him the effect of a dominant navy and had inspired his vivid description of the British blockade of Napoleon's ports.

Even before he had read Jomini on the relationship between war and politics or written a word about grand strategy, Mahan had exercised diplomatic functions along the coasts of Latin America, operating in the overlap between diplomacy and military strategy. In the Caribbean he had sailed the Windward Passage and been struck by the enormous strategic importance of Cuba. He had crossed the Isthmus of Panama by land and could see how much time a Panama Canal would save over the long passage around the tip of South America. He had even put an armed party ashore in Panama City, on the Pacific side of the isthmus, during one of Panama's frequent revolutions against Colombian rule.

He had sailed through the Suez Canal and seen its effect on the Mediterranean, giving him additional authority to argue that the Panama Canal would make the Caribbean thrive. He had been involved in the opening of Asia to an American naval presence and had seen opportunities there for trade as well as the keen interest of other powers. He had been twice to the Philippines and, though they made little impression at the time, was to remember the fine harbor at Manila Bay and the value of the archipelago as a stepping-stone to Asia.

Mahan's authority, based on his experience at sea and combined with the brilliance of his arguments for a big navy, made *The Influence of Sea Power upon History* a basic text for modernizers in the navy. An impressive number of U.S. naval officers, including Schley (who had been hostile to the War College) and Dewey, praised the book. But to the more orthodox officers, it simply confirmed that Mahan was a misfit and a troublemaker. Francis M. Ramsay, his old nemesis from Annapolis and now chief of the Bureau of Navigation, which supervised the War College, stated plainly: "It is not the business of a naval officer to write books."

Mahan was ecstatic at the book's reception, which boosted both his ambition and his confidence. But he was also aware of the limits of its influence, at least in the United States. "Except Roosevelt," he wrote Elly, "I don't think my work gained me an entree into a single American social circle." He was similarly realistic about his prospects in the navy. His career path was now set. He knew that he was a teacher and no longer a sailor, as he wrote Luce. He never wanted to go to sea again and henceforth used all the influence he could summon to stave off sea duty. He plunged into a sequel, which would carry sea power through the Napoleonic Wars, tossed off a less weighty biography of Farragut, and began to think about a biography of his hero, Nelson.

The sequel to his major work, *The Influence of Sea Power upon the French Revolution and Empire, 1793–1812*, published in late 1892, developed a point that Mahan had introduced in his first book: the primacy of the British Navy and its decisive importance in defeating Napoleon. The Napoleonic Wars provided a perfect set piece for Mahan's great theme, the contest between land power and sea power: "England had no army wherewith to meet Napoleon; Napoleon had no navy to cope with that of his enemy."

Mahan gave due regard to the attrition of land wars on Napoleon's military strength, but for him the cumulative effect of Britain's naval mastery turned the tide. "The world has never seen a more impressive demonstration of the influence of sea power upon its history. Those far distant, storm-beaten ships, upon which the Grand Army never looked, stood between it and the dominion of the world." This stirring tribute to the British Navy anticipated Churchill's later homage to the Royal Air Force during World War II.

His Anglophilia extended beyond history. The success of the British Navy and his admiration for the British Empire had helped turn him into an imperialist. His eyes were open to England's pretensions in the Caribbean, where he considered the British a rival to the United States, but he also saw England as a natural ally. He favored not a formal alliance but a "cordial recognition of the similarity of character and ideas [giving] birth to sympathy."

Mahan liked heroes, and in the 1892 book he produced both an individual hero and a collective one. The individual hero was William Pitt, British prime minister during the early years of the war against Napoleon. Mahan admired Pitt's painful decision to put aside a domestic reform program in order to contest Napoleon's imperial ambitions. Reading Pitt's speeches in the New York Public Library, he got so excited at the "unusual eloquence" that he was "strongly moved to rise on the spot and give three cheers." It was fortunate that Dennis Mahan, founder of the Napoleon Club at West Point, was not there at that moment.

Mahan paid close attention to writing as a craft and culled examples from his eclectic reading. "The besetting anxiety of my soul was to be exact and lucid," he explained in his memoirs. He drew inspiration from Samuel Johnson's injunction to "invent first, and then embellish." His writing, at its best, reflected this principle in his ability to get the thought right and then express it in the clearest way possible. He admired the discipline of Anthony Trollope, who wrote forty-seven novels, most of them while serving productively as a senior official in the British postal service.

In his meticulous way, Mahan fussed with details, abhorring split infinitives but accepting prepositions at the end of sentences. To his daughter Helen, aged eleven, he urged the use of short English words. She described it later:

> It is better to say I began than I commenced; better I went than I proceeded; better I wish than I desire; better I behave than I conduct myself. . . . When papa wrote his book a year ago he said: first, I will be careful to have everything right, no mistakes; next that everything shall be very clear, the sentences arranged that the reader shall easily understand; and then I will cut out all the big words I can and put short strong English words in their place. To do this papa had to write over and over again, and keep changing words he had written.

The phenomenon of a senior naval officer who was prepared to be critical of his own service and could write clearly was not lost on the magazine industry. In the wake of the success of *The Influence of Sea Power upon History*, Mahan began to write policy articles that were published not in obscure technical journals but in some of the leading magazines in America, more than 130 of them between 1890 and his death in 1914. His pieces in the *Atlantic Monthly* (which had also given John Hay a start), the *Forum*, the *North American Review*, and *Harper's New Monthly Magazine* made his views available to the small

February 22, 1909: The Great White Fleet returns to Hampton Roads in
Chesapeake Bay after its fourteen-and-a-half-month cruise around the world. The
battleships—so many that they disappear beyond the horizon—demonstrated the
new military power of a country which, less than two decades before, had hesitated
to challenge the Chilean Navy.

John Hay (left) and Henry Adams (below), shown here in their early forties in photographs by Adams's wife, Clover, built one of the great Washington friendships of the nineteenth century. The contemplative Adams lived vicariously through Hay's worldly successes as a diplomat and statesman. Hay admired Adams's deep understanding of American history and politics, as well as his friend's cynicism about them.

Hay's long career stretched from the Civil War, when he was an aide to Lincoln, to the McKinley and Roosevelt administrations, when he was secretary of state, as pictured here. Though afflicted by lifelong depression, he was a famously entertaining conversationalist whose sense of humor and irony reflected a refusal to take the world too seriously. He contributed a note of civility to U.S. foreign and colonial policy.

Alfred T. Mahan's austere personality is suggested by these portraits of him as a young officer and as a captain (at about the time he wrote *The Influence of Sea Power upon History*). An indifferent seaman, Mahan irritated traditionalists in the navy by publishing works on naval strategy. A rival scoffed, "It is not the business of a naval officer to write books." Though Mahan's works helped establish international respect for the U.S. Navy, he was not promoted to admiral until after his retirement.

Elihu Root was a lawyer's lawyer, with a sharp mind, a talent for finding clear solutions to complex problems, and a fierce loyalty to his client (from 1899, the United States government). He was the first American to be put in charge of an overseas empire. He, as much as Roosevelt, set the tone for America's involvement in the world of the twentieth century. Root was witty and irreverent, though intimidating; his friend Hay described his "frank and murderous smile."

Henry Cabot Lodge had two sides. The 1890 portrait by John Singer Sargent (above) captures the reflective intellectual who wrote twenty-seven books, reveled in the company of literary figures, and fathered a poet. The picture at right, taken almost a decade later at the time of the Spanish-American War, shows the dauntlessly intolerant politician who led the imperialist forces in the Senate, floor-managed the Treaty of Paris to a narrow success, and was later to humiliate Woodrow Wilson over the League of Nations.

William McKinley, one of the nicest men ever to hold the presidency, had seen the bodies piled up in the Civil War and did not want a war with Spain. He was pressed into it by a group of articulate warmongers around Roosevelt and Lodge, by a growing revulsion in the country at Spanish brutality toward Cubans, and by his own political instincts, to which he always deferred. In retrospect he called the war "the greatest grief of my life."

Always in a hurry, Assistant Secretary of the Navy Roosevelt—in his business attire of frock coat, bowler, and gloves—strides past the White House on his way home from the Navy Department. From his subcabinet position Roosevelt helped to prepare the navy for war and to encourage McKinley and his advisers toward greater militancy. His boss, Secretary Long, described him as "the best fellow in the world" but lacking "a cool head and discrimination."

Clara Hay (left), "a large, handsome, and very comfortable young woman," according to her husband, made Hay a rich man by marrying him. Her father was a vastly wealthy industrial entrepreneur from Cleveland.

Elly Mahan lived quietly in New York City and Quogue, Long Island; she rarely visited Washington. Mahan was devoted to her, writing touching letters from sea duty.

Clara Root also preferred New York to Washington. A shy woman, she accommodated her husband's workaholic ways easily, rarely venturing onto the social scene. Among friends she was vivacious and witty. Her marriage with Root was a strong one.

Nannie Lodge, whose effervescent beauty is not captured in this photograph (one of the few of her), charmed everyone with her vivid conversation, her brilliance, and what Corinne Roosevelt called her "sense of values." Given the personalities of their respective spouses, it may not be surprising that she and John Hay had an affair.

Edith Roosevelt was one of the best things that ever happened to Theodore. Her devotion to him, her political acumen, and her toughness of character were a perfect foil to his exuberance. She worked closely with Lodge to keep her husband grounded in political reality.

American foreign policy elite as well as to the educated lay reading public. Because they put current issues into a strategic framework, the magazine pieces had even more effect than his books on American policy.

In his journalism Mahan moved easily from high strategy to specific objectives. He described a world that had grown smaller and more dangerous. He saw threats to American interests in Samoa, the Bering Sea, the Isthmus of Panama, Curaçao, Haiti, and the Sandwich (Hawaiian) Islands. "To retain . . . the undisturbed enjoyment of the returns of commerce, it is necessary to argue upon somewhat equal terms of strength with an adversary," he wrote. But America was not ready for that argument. It had a defenseless seacoast and a weak navy. It needed to determine, first, its national interests, then the influence needed to assert them, and finally the size of the naval force necessary for that influence.

For Mahan, there were many reasons why America had to abandon isolationist thinking and look outward: its growing production, public sentiment, a geographic position between two old worlds and two oceans, the growth of European colonies in the Pacific, the rise of Japan, and the peopling of the American West with men favoring a strong foreign policy. He was not a warmonger; in fact he had a highly sophisticated view of how to prevent war through deterrence. Preparing for war, he wrote, will help prevent it. He urged on the United States a three-pronged naval policy: short-range warships to protect the chief American harbors, an offensive naval force to extend influence outward, and a national resolution that no foreign state should be allowed to acquire a base within three thousand miles of San Francisco. In his writings Mahan was introducing core concepts—deterrence, sufficiency, détente, globalism—that were to return as principles of American policy during the Cold War.

Mahan's geographic preoccupations in the early 1890s were the Caribbean and the Pacific. The isthmian canal continued to get his full attention for its disadvantages as well as its advantages. He foresaw that the Caribbean would become a strategic danger as the opening of the canal generated major European interest. "Like the Canadian Pacific Railroad, it will be a link between the two oceans; but unlike it, the use, unless most carefully guarded by treaties, will belong wholly to the belligerent which controls the sea by its naval power." Always ready with a prophecy of doom, he added: "The piercing of the Isthmus is nothing but a disaster to the United States in the present state of her military and naval preparation."

Hawaii, an independent kingdom under pressure from American sugar planters maneuvering to annex it to the United States, was another focus of Mahan's interest. Hawaii lay directly on any future route from the canal to China or Japan. If its islands fell into the hands of another power, not only would America's Pacific trade be menaced, but the whole Pacific coast from Puget Sound to Mexico would come under threat. In short, Hawaii influenced both the commercial and military control of the Pacific. Mahan favored annexing it.

There was an urgency in Mahan's advocacy during the 1890s. He wrote Horace E. Scudder, editor of the *Atlantic Monthly*: "If my belief that the United States is about to be forced out of her policy of isolation, is well founded, the age needs prophets to arouse the people." Settling in as America's naval prophet, Mahan was asked by Secretary of the Navy Tracy to deal with the U.S. crisis with Chile in 1891. Two American sailors had been killed in a barroom brawl in Valparaíso, and the United States went on a war footing. Mahan helped in preparing contingency naval operations and requisitioning military equipment. Deterrence worked; Chile backed down. But Mahan was left believing that the United States had behaved arrogantly. He also discovered that the American Navy might actually have been weaker than the Chilean, another proof in his case against American unpreparedness.

In 1892 Mahan became president of the War College, after modestly proposing other candidates without success. He was also beginning work on his life of Nelson. Unfortunately for him, Cleveland's victory in the presidential election that year led to the replacement of Secretary Benjamin F. Tracy by Hilary A. Herbert, a former congressman who had chaired the House Naval Appropriations Committee and had opposed the War College. Seeing his opportunity, Mahan's enemy Ramsay, now his immediate superior, ordered him to sea. Mahan offered a deal, agreeing to retire in three years, when he had achieved the requisite forty years of service, if he could remain at Newport. In his defense he cited others who had served fewer years at sea than he had, including Dewey and Ramsay himself.

Theodore Roosevelt, loyal as ever, weighed in with a letter to the new secretary, and enlisted the help of an even more influential politician, Henry Cabot Lodge, a key Senate imperialist. But however powerful Roosevelt and Lodge may have been, the navy's animus toward Mahan was even more powerful. He was ordered to the command of the USS *Chicago*, a first-generation steel cruiser and one of the last to carry auxiliary sail. She departed New York in May 1893 for Europe to return friendly visits made by European navies.

The twin destinations for Mahan's last voyage turned out to be heaven and hell. In the celestial sense it was an easy and even pleasant trip. The *Chicago* visited Ireland, England, France, Germany, Belgium, Spain, Italy, Turkey, Lebanon, Egypt, Malta, and Portugal on a leisurely two-year cruise. Mahan discovered that he was even more famous among political circles in Europe than in the United States. John Hay, with his instinct for attaching himself to people who counted, wrote him from a London sojourn that "all the people of intelligence are waiting to welcome you."

He was twice invited to dinner with Queen Victoria, who told him that she had heard of his book; was entertained by the first lord of the admiralty, Earl Spencer (great-great-uncle of the late Diana, Princess of Wales); and was closeted in tête-à-têtes with Lord Rosebery, the foreign minister and a large-navy man. Cambridge and Oxford both awarded him honorary degrees, and the *Times* of London compared him to Copernicus for having made sea power the sun around which all else revolved. In Germany Kaiser William II counted himself Mahan's first fan. He extolled *The Influence of Sea Power upon History* in a speech and wrote Mahan that he was "not reading but devouring" the book and had placed it on board all German ships.

Mahan's letters home bubbled with enjoyment at the adulation. He ticked off the invitations he had received in the south of France: reception, lunch, reception, dance, lunch, dinner, declined dinner, breakfast, declined dancing party, dinner, dance, symphony. He also indulged his favorite sport of girl watching. He did not think much of French women ("You never saw so many ugly women as there are in this country . . . not plain but downright ugly"). Spanish women scored little higher ("I am disillusioned with Spain. I have scarcely seen a pretty woman"). English women were his favorites. From Southampton he wrote: "While I do enjoy the animation of a crowded room or dinner my chiefest pleasure has been—a queer confession for a graybeard—in watching and talking with pretty young girls. . . . Like my father I love young things from young girls to puppies and kittens." The stability of Mahan's marriage may be measured by the fact that all these observations were made to his wife.

The infernal part of the *Chicago*'s voyage consisted in Mahan's being chained for most of it to a superior officer who hated him. Rear Admiral Henry Erben had been commandant of the New York Navy Yard and undoubtedly knew what Mahan thought of navy yards. Erben was promoted to commander in chief of the European Station and made his maiden cruise on the *Chicago*, which was designated the flagship for the station. Mahan skippered the *Chicago*, but Erben was the ranking officer in all other ways as well as Mahan's immediate superior.

Erben was an old salt of the old navy, bluff and hearty, but also anti-intellectual, blustering, profane, and irascible, just the sort of officer whom Mahan in his writings had consigned to obsolescence. The relationship between the two was sulfurous from the start and worsened considerably when the cruise turned into a literary victory lap for Mahan. Erben burned at the rapturous attention Mahan was receiving in nearly every port and actually tried to undermine it by giving him make-work projects on board so he would miss receptions. Erben also resorted to crude attempts to humiliate his subordinate officer. Once, while giving a dinner party on board, he sounded the fire alarm so that Mahan would have to take his station in his nightshirt in full view of the guests. He also placed canaries just outside Mahan's cabin in order to disturb his writing. Erben was determined to destroy this unconventional officer, this "pen-and-ink sailor," as he called him. He almost succeeded.

As Mahan's superviser Erben was called on to write a fitness report on him. Then, as now, these reports were the formal basis for promotions and assignments. Anyone who has worked in a bureaucracy will understand the horror with which Mahan must have read the following evaluation from Erben in January 1894:

> Captain Mahan always appears to advantage to the service in all that does not appertain to ship life or matters, but in this particular he is lacking in interest, as he has frankly admitted to me. His interests are entirely outside the service, for which, I am satisfied, he

cares but little, and is therefore not a good naval officer. He is not at all observant regarding officers tending to the ship's general welfare or appearance, nor does he inspire or suggest anything in this connection. In fact, the first few weeks of the cruise she was positively discreditable. In fact, Captain Mahan's interests lie wholly in the direction of literary work, and in no other way connected with the service.

In the lexicon of government personnel ratings, where criticism is usually implied rather than stated and delivered with a stiletto rather than a blunderbuss, this was about as devastating a report as a naval officer could possibly receive. As in most distortions, there was some basis for Erben's opinions, but there were mitigating circumstances in Mahan's favor. Always the victim of his own candor, Mahan had injudiciously admitted to Erben that the charm of ship life had vanished for him, but he had said the same thing formally to the navy in his effort to stay on at Newport. During the "discreditable" first weeks of the cruise, Mahan was laid up with a bruised knee and unable to supervise the shakedown part of the voyage.

As Erben implied, Mahan was not an attentive skipper, and Erben no doubt noticed that he spent his evenings with his writings (over the din of the canaries). Though aloof and humorless, Mahan seems to have been respected by the crew, an advance over his days on the *Iroquois*. His seamanship had also improved since he ran the *Wasp* aground and crashed the *Wachusett* into another ship. He got a fine rating from Erben's successor, who spent five months on the *Chicago* near the end of its cruise, and on return to New York the cruiser received a good inspection evaluation. By any objective standard Erben's report, driven by jealousy and vindictiveness, was grossly unfair.

Mahan understood immediately that he was in mortal combat. In his appeals to Washington he was driven to the embarrassment of documenting his own prowess and exposing evidence of Erben's deficiencies as an officer and superviser. He made the argument, a telling one, that to punish him would reflect badly on the navy, since its growing reputation was in large part due to him. He demanded a thorough investigation and turned again to Roosevelt and Lodge to ensure that he got it. The two rallied in support.

Roosevelt, acting as field general, sent Lodge to see Secretary Herbert and plead Mahan's case. Herbert told Lodge he had read and admired Mahan's books and shared Lodge's high opinion of him. But the case dragged on, with Erben making new and even more ridiculous charges, for example, crediting the good condition of the ship to junior officers. Mahan wrote Herbert plaintively: "As I am responsible for bad results, I cannot be denied credit for good."

In the end Mahan failed to win official vindication, but neither did he suffer unduly from Erben's campaign. The most important result of the affair was his new relationship with Lodge, who, he wrote Elly, "has always struck me as one of the chilly-tempered New Englanders." Now he considered Lodge, whom he had yet to meet in person, a man ready to fight for his views and career. From the time of Mahan's return to the United States in early 1895, he and Roosevelt and Lodge would form an effective triumvirate pressing for a larger navy, for the acquisition of Caribbean and Pacific bases, and for a war with Spain.

5.

Mahan returned to Newport, then retired from the navy in December 1896, no doubt with relief. Now he could devote himself to writing history, biography, and magazine articles and goading the country into taking its place among the great powers. He had already changed the landscape of America's strategic policy in unprecedented ways, developing naval science as an academic discipline, designing a philosophy of sea power, and helping provide the rationale for the building of a modern navy.

Roosevelt was right to say that "in philosophic spirit and grasp of his subject in its larger aspects he is not approached by any other naval writer whom we can at the moment recall." While Mahan did not initiate the American naval buildup that began in the late 1880s, his influence gave it the momentum necessary to make the nation a first-rate naval power. By 1898 the United States had the world's third most powerful navy. Mahan was in the peculiar position of stimulating, by his writings, the increase in the first and second navies, Britain's and Germany's, as well as his own.

Mahan had said in 1885 that he was an imperialist because he was not an isolationist. In his memoirs he amplified: "I am frankly an imperialist, in the sense that I believe that no nation, certainly no great nation, should henceforth maintain the policy of isolation which fitted our early history; above all, should not on that outlived plea refuse to intervene in events obviously thrust upon its conscience." His imperialism was not primarily directed at founding colonies or even outposts for trade. While he continued to give lip service to the commercial basis of sea power, his principal aim was strategic: to put dots on the map, bases that would enable the United States to control the Caribbean and enjoy unhindered access to Asia.

Mahan was not a political man, though he saw the use of politics in promoting policy objectives. His views were conservative, but not radically so. He voted Republican. He was for free trade, civil service reform, states' rights (not to include secession), and limits on the federal government. He opposed female suffrage. He tended to pick presidential candidates on the basis of their views regarding the navy. He was a humanist in much of what he said and did. A maverick himself, in the navy he encouraged individual expression and a curriculum strong in the humanities. His whole philosophy fixed on human beings. He wrote that good men were more important than good ships. He gloried in describing the great captains and the qualities of character that made them successful. For a consummate strategist, he saw the historic panorama of sea power in human terms.

He was also a good husband and a diligent father. His letters to his wife and daughters from shipboard were informative and affectionate, though rarely funny. He wrote Elly on their wedding anniversary: "May God always bless the day which gave you to me." He fretted about his younger daughter Ellen's safety in the surf on Long Island. To his elder daughter, Helen, he wrote long, didactic letters: on the importance of sympathy toward others, on how to read poetry (for meaning, not just melody and sweetness), on the value of religion. Perhaps he sheltered his daughters too much; neither married.

His natural austerity may have made him a better father at a distance than close up; in any case, he was less successful with his son, Lyle, than with Helen or Ellen. He had few friends—the best were Samuel Ashe, who pursued a minor political career as a North Carolina Democrat; George William Douglas, the canon of Trinity Church in New York; and his naval mentor, Luce—but he kept them for life. He had difficulty attributing malice to others, even to those who had clearly set out to hurt him. He even called the implacable

Ramsay a "gentleman" and described the contemptible Erben as not "willfully disagreeable" or "consciously malicious."

An important key to Mahan's character was his reliance on Christianity. His faith sustained him through boredom, depression, and controversy. His religion was of the quietist kind, far removed from the perfervid boosterism of his fellow imperialist, the Reverend Josiah Strong. Mahan's book on religion, *The Harvest Within*, written when he was an old man, was not at all confessional. In fact it rigorously excluded all personal detail; the reader could hardly have guessed from the text how the author had spent his life.

The book was a celebration of Christ's gift of love, the importance of the resurrection, and the efficacy of prayer. Mahan cited authorities from a wide literary repertoire: Boswell, Johnson, Mill, Guizot, Newman, Cowper, Browning, St. Paul. His approach was ecumenical; for example, he pointed out that Christ, "in the singular beauty of his character, drew his human nature from Judaism." Only once did Mahan drop the veil on his naval vocation in order to defend imperialism: "However men severally may regard imperialism as a political theory, the dominion of Christ is [essentially] imperial, one Sovereign over many communities."

If there is one figure of a later time with whom Mahan may be compared, it is George Kennan. Both were fathers of doctrines that inspired American policy—in Mahan's case sea power, in Kennan's containment. The two are remarkably close in character, background, and thought: austere without being starchy, somewhat remote, not given to humor. They had served in government organizations with which they were often at odds; in one sense they were bureaucratic misfits. Both were strong individualists, determined to press their ideas against the dogma of the day. They were original, creative thinkers and brilliant stylists, adept at exposing and explaining the core of issues. Each was better at the theoretical than the practical aspects of his government career. Mahan was not first-rate as a sailor, nor Kennan as a diplomat.

Their government experience gave them insight into the areas where military strategy, diplomacy, and foreign policy intersect. But their greatest contributions were as writers, not as officials. Their strengths, unmatched in their respective times, lay in influencing the historical, theoretical, and political lines of American policy. They were visionaries—or, as Mahan would say, "prophets."

4. A Lawyer's Duty

1.

Elihu Root had a perfect career, unblemished by failures, unmarked by serious defeats, crowned by regular successes. In his twenties he was already a highly regarded corporation lawyer, by his thirties his law practice had made him rich, and in his forties he was one of the most sought-after trial lawyers in the United States. He mixed hard work with long vacations, to Long Island, Martha's Vineyard, Colorado. Moving beyond some early associations with machine politicians in New York City, he earned a solid reputation as a political reformer.

He did not want political office for himself but excelled at identifying talented people who did, such as the twenty-three-year-old Theodore Roosevelt, whom Root supported when Roosevelt first ran for the New York Assembly. Without seeking either office, Root became secretary of war under McKinley and Roosevelt and secretary of state under Roosevelt. He represented New York State as a U.S. senator. He won the Nobel Peace Prize for his work on international law. He helped start two still-vibrant foreign affairs institutions, the Carnegie Endowment for International Peace and the Council on Foreign Relations. He died in 1937 at ninety-one, a revered elder statesman.

Root's inner life seemed as free of tension and ambiguity as his public career. His supreme self-confidence sailed him through choppy moral seas. He saw no inconsistency in his legal defense of the most corrupt politician in New York and his dedicated and effective work as a political reformer. He did not hesitate to castigate publicly the grasping and unjust behavior of big business even as he represented some of its most powerful exemplars. He extolled the government institutions he had established in the Philippines after the Spanish-American War, yet he presided over a cover-up of horrendous atrocities perpetrated by American soldiers against the Filipino people.

Root appeared untroubled by the inner demons that tormented his close friend John Hay. He was able to live with the contradictions of life and even to thrive on them. The smooth trajectory of his long career was marked by an economy of motion. His manifold activities—business, legal, political, social, even religious—all helped fuel the engine of his quiet ambition. Yet Root managed to avoid the odious image of the model boy in school who works just a bit harder, cultivates the teacher, and gets the best grades. Incredibly, his success made him few enemies. In fact one of his strengths as a lawyer and amateur politician was as a conciliator, a respected and trusted person accessible to all sides of a dispute.

Three qualities seem to have moderated the resentment that Root's seamless success might otherwise have engendered. The first was his trustworthiness. When he took on a commitment, he gave it the full measure of his effort. The thoroughness of his trial preparation was legendary. He was typically the hardest worker on ad hoc political committees dedicated to political reform or change. His fierce devotion to excellence made him a man who could be counted on to get things done. The second quality was an irrepressible sense of humor, which balanced his cold aloofness when he was in the intensity of work. Even his letters to his clients were full of jokes, lampooning the very values he was being paid to defend. He was a great teaser; he particularly liked to tease Roosevelt, even while Roosevelt was president.

Root's third quality was idealism, a seeming paradox in a man who had come to terms so easily with the ways of the world. Yet he had strong beliefs about the role of government; about the rights of individuals; about political campaigns; about business ethics; about immigration; about the rights of blacks in America; about the causes of war; about education; about the American seizure of Cuba, Puerto Rico, the Philippines, and Hawaii; about the Panama Canal; and especially about the importance of international law and arbitration. A popular after-dinner speaker, Root developed his beliefs in speeches rather than books. They situate him on the liberal side of the Republican party of his time, on Roosevelt's side. Root was a Republican but not an archconservative. With exceptions, his views were broad-minded, internationalist, and sympathetic to people, Americans and non-Americans, who lacked the privileges he manifestly enjoyed.

2.

Like Mahan, Root was born into a family of provincial New York State academics. His father, Oren, taught school in Syracuse, Utica, and Seneca Falls before becoming in 1849 a professor of mathematics at his alma mater, Hamilton College in Clinton. Elihu, four at the time, spent all his life in or close to the Hamilton environment. His maternal grandfather was the college's chief administrative officer. His father taught there for thirty-five years, to be succeeded by Elihu's older brother, Oren junior. His other older brother, Wally, also taught briefly at Hamilton before his early death of tuberculosis. Elihu himself attended Hamilton, returned often after graduation, spent many summer vacations in Clinton, and served as chairman of the college's board of trustees. Hamilton, today a small college in a state full of giant universities, was in the mid-nineteenth century the second-largest college in New York State, after Union College in Schenectady. It was bigger than any college in New York City, than John Hay's Brown, than Dennis Mahan's West Point, and than Alfred Mahan's Annapolis. It also had a fine academic reputation.

Elihu entered Hamilton in 1860 at the age of fifteen, the youngest of fifty-four freshmen. His college career seems to have been idyllic and unchallenging. He lived at home, in his parents' large and beautiful frame house with its wide porch and ample grounds. He was known as an intellectual, but he was also a joiner. No athlete, he was president of the college baseball team; no musician, he played the calliope in a college band. With a legacy from his two older brothers, he joined Sigma Phi and used it later to establish ties with fraternity brothers in business and legal circles in New York City.

He was social and sociable, participating in skating parties and beerfests, games of charades, and "socials" with girls. He was a churchgoer. He stayed out of trouble, refusing in one instance to join a student boycott of classes. He was an outstanding student, winning a prize for mathematics, earning praise for his public speaking, becoming the class valedictorian, and being graduated Phi Beta Kappa.

John Hay and Alfred Mahan both participated—"fought" would be too strong—in the Civil War. Root, seven years younger than Hay and five years younger than Mahan, did not. When President Lincoln called for volunteers at the end of Root's sophomore year at Hamilton, Elihu was a frail seventeen-year-old, and his attempt to enlist was rejected. Most of his class, all older boys, remained in college as well, nor did his two older brothers enlist. Since Root also played no role in the war with Spain in 1898, his first military experience was with the suppression of the Philippine insurrection between 1899 and 1902, for which as secretary of war he was directly responsible.

Root's valedictory address at Hamilton on the subject of education moved the reporter of a Utica paper to commend his broad-minded approach: "One of his conclusions was that educated men were only conservative when educated incompletely and narrowly. . . . Mr. Root's is an analytical, painstaking, far-reaching intellect, which will cut a deep furrow in life if we mistake not. . . . No wonder he left the stage loaded with boquets."

"Boquets" greeted Root at every phase of his life, but it is doubtful that he would have collected so many if he had selected as his career the ministry, teaching, or medicine, his contemplated alternatives to the law. He chose law because, he explained, two of his uncles were lawyers and several eminent New York State lawyers connected with Hamilton seemed like "Olympian gods" to him. These reasons seem incomplete. He appears also to have been persuaded by the lure of New York City (which he admitted) and his own ambition (which he did not). Elihu Root wanted to climb to the top of Olympus, and the law would get him closer to the summit than the other professions under consideration.

The two law schools in New York City, at New York University and Columbia (then in midtown), both were run by men with Hamilton connections, and Root was welcome at both. He chose NYU, headed by an 1847 graduate of Hamilton and a fellow Sigma Phi, because it offered the possibility of making money on the side. Root had to work his way through law school, and his NYU contact got him jobs teaching American history at girls' schools. One of the girls remembered him as "very tall" and "very shy." Her school was straitlaced; when the teacher finished his lecture, he was required to back out of the room so as not to expose his backside to the view of the young ladies. On one occasion, Root performed this departure ritual, only to find himself in a map closet instead of the corridor. He waited a long time in the closet, in a paroxysm of embarrassment, before he emerged and executed the proper exit. The self-containment of the girls exceeded his; not one made a sound.

That may be the last story about Root that describes him as shy. He quickly achieved the pretense, and ultimately the reality, of being at home in all situations. In New York he continued the extracurricular life he had enjoyed at Hamilton. Through his brother Wally, who was teaching at the Columbia School of Mines, Elihu settled comfortably into the companionship of the president of the university and several Columbia professors. He became a connoisseur of the best beer gardens in the city. With Wally he founded a mock literary, musical, and social society that offered scope for satire and mirth. Root got some of his humor from his family. His father and his brother Oren seem to have endured their nicknames—Cube Root and Square Root respectively—in a spirit of fun.

Exploiting another college connection, Elihu got to know Thomas Hastings (Hamilton '47 and a Sigma Phi), a Presbyterian minister who later became president of the Union Theological Seminary. Root's minister at home encouraged the contact, telling him that "a lawyer needs twice as much religion as a minister." Root taught in the Sunday school of Hastings's Presbyterian church. He also taught at a mission school and, after he had started a successful law practice, helped pay the tuition of some of the mission boys at Columbia. In addition, he was active in the YMCA, especially in its literary society.

One of Root's essays, written when he was twenty-one, gave a clear picture of where he wanted to go as a lawyer. He divided the world of business into three classes: first, those absorbed in the pursuit of wealth; second, those who concentrated on self-improvement, the emulation of eminent men, and the pursuit of "position and influence"; and third, those who put all their energies into helping others. Root identified with the second class—self-improvement, emulation, wealth, and position. In a YMCA paper a year later he was even clearer: "It is right that we should be ambitious. God means us to be ambitious." Even before he had become a corporation lawyer, Root espoused the Weberian concept that the Protestant religion encourages success in capitalist endeavor. According to his version of the Protestant ethic, ambition was sanctified, business was virtuous, and success was blessed.

After earning his Bachelor of Laws degree from NYU in 1867, Root took the advice of a family friend and joined an established law firm, Mann and Parsons. Again connections helped; John E. Parsons was another fraternity brother, a "Sig" from NYU. A letter of this period to Root's mother reflected a self-confident young man embracing the future. Root began with a prudent reference to his faithful churchgoing, then addressed the report that his mother had heard he was "blue." Wrong color altogether, he protested. There was some "irksomeness" while he had been teaching, but now he was "perfectly satisfied" with the legal profession, even though he was not making much money at it: "I enjoy myself thoroughly all the time while at work. . . . I go down to the office as I would to a turkey supper when in college. . . . As to the future I have no fears whatever. . . . With perfect health, a good education, good abilities, good habits of life and application, a well grounded and thoroughly acquired profession, lots of friends, a pleasant home for one that is not home, and an untarnished reputation, I feel like a well mounted firmly seated rider."

The young law graduate had joined a profession with a somewhat shady reputation in New York City. Unlike Root, many lawyers without law school educations took advantage of the lax licensing procedures to pursue shoddy and often corrupt practices. George Templeton Strong, an upper-class lawyer who fought successfully for higher standards, branded the legal profession as ranking "next below that of patent-medicine mongering." Prominent lawyers like Samuel J. Tilden and William M. Evarts—the first a future governor of New York, the second a future secretary of state—established in 1870 the Association of the Bar of the City of New York, an exclusive organization accepting fewer than a fifth of the lawyers in New York and reflecting the highest professional standards. The association became a model for reformist legal groups in other cities and led to the formation of the American Bar Association eight years later. Throughout his long legal career Root was active in both organizations.

After a year of practice Root formed his own partnership with several other young lawyers, and began to try cases. His mission school work brought him into touch with John J. Donaldson, a self-educated older man who had become a successful businessman and banker. When Donaldson late in life decided to learn Latin, Root volunteered to teach him. The Donaldsons became a surrogate family for Root, who entertained them at dinner with his humor and good cheer. Soon Donaldson began to direct legal business Root's way, and the partnership began to make money. By 1869, when he was twenty-four, he had far eclipsed his father's teaching salary and was earning a reputation as a first-rate trial lawyer.

That summer he took a celebratory trip west, getting as far as Omaha by train and steamboat, and in the fall he started a new firm. The next year Root made his first trip to Europe. It was not a happy occasion; he was accompanying his consumptive brother Wally, who was to die several months later. They happened to be in Dresden when the Franco-Prussian War began and were in the crowd of one hundred thousand when Kaiser William I, Prime Minister Otto von Bismarck, and Field Marshal Helmuth von Moltke appeared on the palace balcony. In the first recorded expression of his views on foreign affairs, Root found himself hoping that Prussia would lose the war.

In December 1871, when Root was twenty-six, William M. Tweed, boss of the Democratic machine in New York City and a grafter of epic proportions, was indicted for deceit and fraud on the basis of revelations exposed in the *New York Times*. Nobody could have been less like Boss Tweed in background, party affiliation, conduct, and moral standing than Elihu Root, yet Root, young as he was, became an assistant counsel for the defense of Tweed and his codefendants.

Why did he do it? There were personal reasons. One of the indicted men was a relative by marriage of a partner of Root's and had been represented by that partner in earlier litigation. There was also the philosophical argument that even the worst criminals deserve a defense. After all, Tweed's chief prosecutor, the reformer Samuel J. Tilden, had once represented Jay Gould and Jim Fisk, even grander swindlers than the New York City boss. Root always defended his decision to represent Tweed on this lawyerly ground. He told a Columbia Law School class years later: "No matter how vile the criminal, if he represents a constitutional right, you will do your country a service by defending him." Finally, there was the likeliest reason of all: The Tweed trial would bring the ambitious young Root into contact with some of the most prestigious lawyers in New York in an atmosphere of heavy and sustained publicity.

Lawyers might have understood why Root did what he did. But one nonlawyer did not: his mother. She wrote him uncertainly: "You know, my dear, that I have confidence in your integrity. Do you remember that you once said to me that 'every man had his price'? I only hope and pray that your price may be so high that even the Arch fiend himself cannot reach it." Root's price was not that high, and his mother's tone changed to cautionary. In a later letter she wrote: "You will not let your ambition make you forget what life is in its noblest most important aspect. Do not neglect that Book which is the only safe light to your feet and lamp to your path." Still later she wrote: "I will not for a moment, believe, that you are not strong and wise enough to profit by your intercourse with the distinguished men of your profession with whom you are brought in such close relation, and, at the same time, resist the unwholesome influence of their too liberal views in morality and religion."

The Tweed case went through two trials, with Root involved all the way. Tweed was finally convicted in November 1873 and received a prison sentence that effectively destroyed his political career and his health. He died five years later. Root's conduct at the trials, together with that of several other young lawyers for Tweed, was marked by steady resort to nettlesome technical and procedural arguments in support of their client. This annoyed Judge Noah Davis, whose anger was undoubtedly due also to the unsuccessful effort of the Tweed defense team to get him disqualified.

The young lawyers seem to have displayed an arrogance that got under the judge's skin. On the day of the sentencing Judge Davis scheduled a meeting with the defense lawyers, who feared a citation for contempt of court. Root's mother, by now a Greek chorus of mortification, wrote him: "Why do you try to do anything more for that wicked man? The verdict of the world is against him—the verdict of your own heart is against him. . . . I cannot believe, that you, who are always so cool, so self possessed, have been betrayed into doing anything that will subject you to the punishment of the Courts."

Judge Davis fined three of Tweed's lawyers for contempt, but Root got off with a withering reprimand: "I know how young lawyers arc apt to follow their seniors. . . . [Root and one other young lawyer] displayed great ability during the trial. I shall impose no penalty, except what they may find in these few words of advice: I ask you young gentlemen, to remember that good faith to a client never can justify or require bad faith to your own consciences, and that however good a thing it may be, to be known as successful and great lawyers, it is even a better thing, to be known as honest men." Root took the advice badly. In fact he got so angry at the judge that his mother intervened once again, to implore him not to "knock Judge Davis down."

Root never showed a shred of remorse for his participation and conduct in the Tweed defense. In fact the whole matter actually enhanced his reputation and boosted him higher on the ladder of success. His practice flourished, and his income increased. He was faithful in using some of it to support his impecunious family in Clinton. By the age of thirty Root was a quiet phenomenon in New York legal circles. In court his preparation was meticulous, his style witty, his presentation logical and to the point. His self-confidence was so supreme that it encouraged people to give him large responsibilities. His totally integrated philosophy unified his moral and material values in the joint pursuit of success. He seemed free of self-doubt and introspection—none of John Hay's brooding in his vineyard in Illinois. Not even the Tweed trial could deflect him from the path on which he had set out. In the plan of his future there would be no false starts, no detours, no moral crises, no waste motion at all.

3.

Root was never a corporation lawyer in the sense of being on the payroll of corporations. He always insisted on this distinction because he believed it preserved his moral independence. His practice was, however, increasingly involved with the banks and railroads that were in the vanguard of America's post–Civil War boom. His railroad work pitted him twice against the interests of Jay Gould, the nefarious railroad baron and political ally of Tweed's. Root's judicial pursuit of Gould showed that though he had defended Tweed, he had made no additional commitments to his ring.

Root in the 1870s did not seem very different from a young lawyer on the make today. He was awesomely industrious, highly competitive, and arrogant enough to rub some people the wrong way. An ex-

ample of his brusqueness was a reply he sent to a lawyer who had irritated him: "Sir: Your impertinent note of this date is received. If you
wish to see me, the information which enabled you to address the
note, will enable you also to find me at my office. Yours &c Elihu
Root."

He leavened his insolence with constant japery in his correspondence with clients. To a railroad vice-president, he wrote: "My dear
Sir:—I have received . . . your letter of the 17th of April desiring my
honest opinion. . . . Waiving any question of *honesty*, a subject which I
prefer to discuss before a tribunal more qualified to appreciate it than
one who combines the flagrant vices of a Bank President, a Railroad
Vice-President and a leather merchant, I reply in my opinion . . . [He
went on to set out a sober and clear legal opinion.]" On another occasion a railroad client called Root's attention to a difference of ten dollars in two expense statements Root had sent him. Root wrote back: "I
hereby vest that $10 in you in trust to found a hospital for the relief of
ruptured and crippled railway corporations."

As his law practice prospered, Root widened the scope of his activities and associations beyond the academic and religious ones.
Through the influence of a well-connected lawyer friend, he became
an avid playgoer, mountain climber, and friend of Charles A. Dana,
editor of the *New York Sun* and a major figure in American journalism.
Root was a regular guest at the Danas' weekly literary dinners, where
classics like *The Divine Comedy* and the Icelandic sagas were con-
sumed with dessert. He began to whet a growing political appetite by
joining the Union League Club through the help of yet another useful
Hamilton alumnus. The Union League had been founded during the
Civil War to assist Lincoln in the war effort; it survived as a bastion of
Lincolnesque Republicanism. All his life Root was a favored speaker
at Union League Clubs throughout the northern United States.

It was probably in New York City in the early 1870s that Root met
John Hay, who was in his nearly five-year period in New York writing
for Greeley's *Tribune*. Their biographers have not found evidence of a
meeting, but the two had enough mutual friends, like Dana of the
Sun and Greeley's deputy, Whitelaw Reid, to suggest that they knew
each other. In any case, Hay felt so positive about Root that he recommended him to McKinley in 1899 for secretary of war.

In January 1878 Root married Clara Wales, the daughter of a

prominent businessman, philanthropist, and Republican activist whom he had met at the Union League Club. The marriage helped consolidate his place in the New York Republican establishment, of which his father-in-law, Salem Wales, was a pillar. He wrote his mother that Clara was neither a genius nor a beauty, but he may have sold her short on both counts. A photograph from the period of her wedding shows a young lady with fine features and a slim figure. She seems to have had a sense of humor the equal of his. A good mimic and a witty storyteller, she also had a flair for the ridiculous. To protect him from unwanted telephone calls, she would answer the callers in the accent of an obtuse foreign maid and feign stupidity until they hung up in frustration.

Clara had little success in breaking Root of his high-intensity work habits. Before they were married, she complained that no man in the previous five years had paid her less attention than he had. As a married couple, they seldom went out in the evening because after his long working hours Root preferred a bottle of champagne with dinner at home. Sometimes he would be so absorbed in a case that he would not speak even to Clara for days at a time. Yet the two were very close and, in their growing antisocial habits, proved that they did not need the stimulus of others to enjoy each other's company.

Though he could be fiercely absorbed in his legal work, Root did come to believe in long summer vacations. He and Clara spent months at her father's summer houses in the Adirondacks and in Southampton, Long Island. He also learned to combine business with pleasure. His work on railroads and mines got him as far as Denver, and he used the opportunity to develop a lifelong interest in hunting game. He wrote to a friend: "Nothing in the east or in Europe could compare in charm with a good horse and high life in the open." He believed that this affinity for the West helped him get along with Theodore Roosevelt, a man of explosively different temperament. Root also joined an exclusive bass fishing club on Martha's Vineyard, the membership of which consisted of ten members of the Union League Club. In testament to the ease with which everything came to him, he caught the season's record of bass in his first year as a member.

As a lawyer Root was ambitious but not greedy. He did not charge exorbitant fees even when his corporate clients were well able to afford them. He often worked pro bono for individuals who had trouble paying, though the custom was not as normal in his time as it is now. To a general convicted of squandering funds given him for the erection of a statue, Root, who had lost the case, wrote: "If I sent you any bill at all, it would be for $500, but I dont wish you to trouble yourself about it and desire that you should first apply your means to the payment of the fine imposed upon you." He then offered to help the general win release from the court-imposed penalty. He declined to bill another client because he had delayed sending him his legal opinion. In yet another case, which he won, he offered not to charge if the client felt discomfited about paying.

4.

All his life Root insisted that he was not a political man. In truth he swatted back most efforts to get him to run for office, including for president against Woodrow Wilson in 1916. He protested that almost all the political positions he held were "lawyer's jobs"—e.g., U.S. attorney in New York State, officer of two New York constitutional conventions, and even secretary of war (since McKinley was looking for a lawyer, not a politician or a military expert). While he did not put secretary of state in the nonpolitical category, he did not seek that position either.

Yet Root was a thoroughly political man; he believed in the importance of politics, and he could not stay away from it. When Hamilton College invited him, at thirty-four, to be its commencement speaker in 1879, he left a political message with the graduating seniors: "The evil which makes all other evils possible, the most alarming symptom in a constitutional government, the most fatal malady by which a free people can be attacked, is the withdrawal of good citizens from the exercise of the governmental duties and the indifference to political affairs."

Root may himself have been guided by the principles he advanced at Hamilton, but he was also attracted by the power inherent in political office. In New York State two machines dominated the political landscape in the late 1870s. The Democratic Tammany machine, heir to Boss Tweed's organization, ran New York City, while a Republican machine controlled the state. It was headed by Roscoe Conkling, a U.S. senator, and his two lieutenants, Chester A. Arthur and Thomas C. Platt. As Root said, looking back on that period, "The governor did not count; the legislatures did not count; comptrollers and secretaries of state and what not, did not count. It was what Mr. Conkling said."

Chester Arthur was a well-educated (Union College), suave, upper-crust lawyer who belonged to the Century Association and the Union League Club, where he and Root became close. Arthur was a bit of a political chameleon. At twenty-four he had represented a black woman who had been kicked off a streetcar, but later in life avarice got the better of him. When he made enormous, and probably illicit, profits from his position as federal collector of customs for the port of New York, the scandal became so ripe that President Hayes appointed a blue-ribbon commission to investigate.

The commission put forward the name of Theodore Roosevelt's father, a prominent reformer, to succeed Arthur as customs collector, and President Hayes nominated the senior Roosevelt in November 1877. However, from his position as chairman of the Commerce Committee of the Senate, Conkling managed to block Roosevelt's appointment. The bitterness of the fight cannot have improved the elder Roosevelt's health; he died of stomach cancer, aged forty-seven, two months later. Hayes fired Arthur shortly after, leaving him tarred but unrepentant and unindicted.

At this time Root consolidated his friendship with Arthur. Root had been active in the Republican organization in his home district around East Fifty-fifth Street, an area rich in lawyers, bankers, and businessmen. In 1879 Arthur tried to get him to expand his horizons and run for judge of the court of common pleas. Root accepted the nomination but in a halfhearted way. He set the condition that he would not have to campaign; much to his relief, he lost the election.

A year later Arthur was on the national Republican ticket with James Garfield. Conkling had tried unsuccessfully to block Garfield and, as his price for supporting the ticket, had compelled the Garfield camp to accept his lieutenant Arthur as the vice-presidential nominee. Root, who had worked on the campaign, won a trip to Washington on a special railway car for the inauguration. Seven months later Garfield was dead of an assassin's bullet. Root happened to be in the vice president's New York home when the catastrophic news arrived in the small hours of the morning and was responsible for chasing down a judge to swear in the new president.

There were rumors that with his friend now in the White House, Root, still only thirty-six, might be offered the position of attorney general. They were unfounded, though flattering to Root's reputation as a hotshot lawyer. Root did exploit his closeness to Arthur to write for favors for clients, covering himself by writing the letters in a formal, nonpersonal style. He grew adept at fending off unwanted requests for political services. Tongue in cheek, he asked the New York City district attorney to tell the press that Root was "a liar and a horse thief, a scoundrel of the deepest die," so that office seekers would stop asking him to intercede with the DA.

His practice flourished. One series of cases, his defense of the New York City police commissioners against attempts by successive Democratic mayors to fire them, brought him notoriety. The issues were embroiled in city politics, and Root was both vilified and praised in the press. His friend Dana applauded him for trying to ensure a fair trial for his clients, while his critics accused him of trying to frustrate the efforts of liberal Democrats to reform the city. Root uncharacteristically lost his cool in responding to an attack in the *New York Times*: "We are not to be intimidated by the vulgar cry of an excited populace."

In the affair of the police commissioners, Root was supporting Arthur's political faction, the Stalwarts. In later years he mounted a chagrined defense of this stance: "Arthur's period is one in which the methods of political management and leadership characteristic of the Stalwart machine were in steadily growing disfavor, but one in which by a majority of the population such methods were regarded as natural, wise and correct."

Root remained loyal to Arthur in both action and memory. Unveiling a statue to the former president in Madison Square in 1899, he praised him for courtesy, sincerity, patriotism, integrity, and wisdom. He told the New York State Constitutional Convention in 1915, when Arthur had been dead for three decades: "I can never forget the deep sense of indignation I felt in the abuse that was heaped upon Chester A. Arthur, whom I honored and loved, when he was attacked because he held the position of political leader." In fact Arthur turned out to be more of a reformist president than expected, supporting the Pendleton Act, which was designed to base the federal civil service on merit rather than patronage, and launching a major reform of the U.S. Navy. Root seemed to have been drawn as much to Arthur's liberal side as to his thirst for power.

In the 1880s a contradiction began to open in Root's career. He was a friend of the leader of a corrupt political machine and sometimes even the machine's advocate. He was accumulating clients who represented large moneyed interests and had added to his portfolio several banks and the huge Havemeyer Sugar Trust. But at the same time he began to become an important voice for political reform in New York State.

His first significant reform action, in 1881, was to support young Theodore Roosevelt for state assembly from the Twenty-first District, where Root lived. Along with Joseph Choate, the most prominent trial lawyer in New York, Root signed a petition to nominate Roosevelt and even helped derail the candidacy of a rival for the nomination. Roosevelt was a reformer from the starting gate. It seems odd that Root would have backed him, in view of the nasty fight over the customshouse job between Roosevelt's father and Root's patron Arthur. Nevertheless, the two men liked each other instantly.

Root himself began to accumulate political jobs. In 1881 he served as a delegate to the Republican State Convention, and the year after he became a member of the newly elected Republican Central Committee as a reformer. In 1883 President Arthur made him, to his surprise, U.S. attorney for the Southern District of New York. This was then a part time position, allowing Root to spend half the day on his own practice. Most of his work was with customs cases, but he did get his first experience with international law. On behalf of the U.S. government he prosecuted ships assisting Haitian and Colombian revolutionaries for violating U.S. neutrality laws. He also handled a publicized case against a prominent banker for embezzling the bank's money, some of which was used as a loan to the son of former President Grant. Root's successful prosecution involved evidence meticulously gleaned from bank books that had been carefully drawn up for the purpose of avoiding detection. Even the *New York Times* was impressed.

Root attended the 1884 Republican National Convention in Chicago as a delegate and strategist for Arthur's renomination. The president was defeated by James G. Blaine, whose notoriety for personal corruption was even more flagrant than Arthur's. The young delegates Theodore Roosevelt and Henry Cabot Lodge opposed both candidates and even considered leaving the Republican party when Blaine was nominated. Root had no such reaction to the party, but he left the convention with a renewed determination to reform it.

Back in New York, he joined the effort to devolve power from the state and city political machines to the party rank and file. In 1886 he became the Republican party leader in New York City with Arthur's blessing and used the position to campaign against electoral fraud. In the same year he discouraged speculation about his own candidacy for mayor of New York—as party chief in the city he would have been a natural choice—and pushed for Roosevelt, who ran third in a race won by a Tammany-supported Democrat. In the 1887 campaign Root favored the nomination of two reform Democrats for the Republican ticket in New York City, horrifying Republican machine politicians with his bipartisan tendencies. The next year he helped get some of the Republican bosses expelled from the party. These reformist initiatives by an erstwhile Stalwart brought Root into increasing conflict with Thomas Platt, Arthur's former colleague, who had inherited Conkling's Republican machine. Platt retaliated in 1890 by ousting Root from the chairmanship of the Twenty-first District committee.

By the 1890s Root had moved well beyond his fling with the New York party bosses to the cleaner terrain of reform and good government. He worked in the trenches as well as on the hustings of reform, producing carefully prepared and well-argued proposals. He struck at election fraud by opposing the distribution of ballots to party faithful, the wholesale registration of tramps, the expedited naturalization of aliens for voting purposes, and the manipulation of primaries. He attacked vice with efforts to reduce the number of saloons and to curb gambling. He also hounded Tammany by urging the impeachment of a corrupt judge, sponsoring a bill to get the New York City police department out of the machine's control, and seeking greater separation of state and city political institutions. At the state constitutional convention of 1894 he won a major reform of New York's judicial structure and fought for the merit system in its civil service.

A strong believer in citizen activism in politics, he was a founder of several citizens' reform groups. He was constantly urging his wellborn friends to dirty their hands in politics. In one speech he remonstrated against rich people's claim to a natural entitlement: "The location of their residence or the fashionableness of their tailor gave them no right to dictate or rule others. If they wished to work for the good of the country they must do it as the humblest follower of Henry George did." (George was an advocate of tax breaks for the poor and an unsuccessful candidate for mayor of New York in 1886.) His view of good government was not populist. On the contrary, it foresaw leadership by the high-minded, public-spirited, and well educated, men like himself and his elitist friends in the Union League Club. He thought of reforms as a matter of changing laws rather than as a process of reaching out directly to poor people.

Interestingly, Root had no difficulty in biting the corporate hand that fed him. He represented the street railway company controlling most of New York's surface transit system, which consisted largely of elevated railroad trains drawn by steam locomotives. The company, headed by Thomas Fortune Ryan, a shady businessman with ties to Tammany, was a favorite target of muckrakers. Yet in 1897 Root strongly backed the initiative of his fellow reformer Seth Low, president of Columbia University, to put New York City's street railway companies under the city's control and make them conform to fair labor standards.

He also had no compunction about attacking the political power of corporations he represented. At the 1894 constitutional convention he introduced an amendment to set limits to, and require disclosure of, money used in campaigns. In words that sound strikingly contemporary, he argued:

Great moneyed interests are becoming more and more necessary to the support of political parties, and political parties are every year contracting greater debts to the men who can furnish the money to perform the necessary functions of party warfare. The object of this amendment is . . . to put an end, if possible, to that great crying evil of American politics . . . to prevent the great railroad companies, the great insurance companies, the great telephone companies, the great aggregations of wealth, from using their corporate funds, directly or indirectly, to send members of the legislature to these halls, in order to vote for their protection and the advancement of their interests as against those of the public.

Yet by the time he gave this speech he was representing National Cash Register, Western Union telegraph, United States Rubber, Standard Oil, the *New York Times*, many railroads, and the sugar, lead, whiskey, and watch trusts. The governments of the United States and the state and city of New York were clients. Individuals who turned to him included Theodore Roosevelt, Charles Dana, Frederick W. Vanderbilt, August Belmont, and William C. Whitney.

Root was not the least embarrassed by this contradiction; in fact he defended it. In his commencement address to the Yale Law School in 1904, after he had resigned as secretary of war, he told the fledgling lawyers: "To be a lawyer working for fees is not to be any the less a citizen whose unbought service is due to his community and his country with his best and constant effort." Then came a sentence that could have been taken from Judge Davis's reprimand of him in the Tweed trial thirty years earlier: "You will strive for your clients in many courts; but it will be your high privilege to strive also for the law itself, in the great forum of public judgment."

Although Root looked back on his Stalwart past without remorse or self-incrimination, he left no doubt what he thought of this period of "invisible government." He told the New York State Constitutional Convention of 1915:

> I do not remember how many years, Mr. Conkling was the supreme ruler in this state . . . and in a great outburst of public rage he was pulled down. Then Mr. Platt ruled the state. . . . The capitol was not here [in Albany]; it was at 49 Broadway; with Mr. Platt and his lieutenants. . . . The ruler of the state during the greater part of the forty years of my acquaintance with the state government has not been any man authorized by the constitution or by the law. . . . The party leader is elected by no one, accountable to no one, bound by no oath of office, removable by no one.

At this point in his speech Root came as close as he ever did to a confession: "I don't criticise the men of the invisible government. How can I? I have known them all, and among them have been some of my dearest friends. . . . But it is all wrong . . . that a government not authorized by the people should be continued superior to the government that is authorized by the people."

Root's intimate ties to giants of American capitalism did not leave him as free for crusading as he later tried to convince law school seniors. The 1890s found him busy advising his corporate clients how to get around the Sherman Antitrust Act of 1890. He counseled them to obey, not defy, the law, but he also found a dodge—forming new corporations and holding companies—that rendered the act toothless. His approach was so ingenious that one client, the newly incorporated American Sugar Refining Company, won a virtual monopoly of American sugar production in the years *after* passage of the Sherman Act.

Root never really tried to resolve the contradiction between his support of the status quo and his efforts to change it. It may have bothered him somewhat because he went to great lengths to defend both sides of his activities and to argue their mutual consistency. What is clear is that he was sincere and effective both as an advocate of reform and as a servant of capitalism. Other reformers, including Roosevelt, the most conspicuous of them, sought him out. He worked on reform issues in the same scrupulous way that he worked on corporate briefs. Moreover, he had real enemies among the leaders of the Republican and Democratic machines.

On the other hand, he would not have been one of the top lawyers in New York if he had not given his clients exactly what they wanted. To one client (there is no agreement on which) was attributed the remark "I have had many lawyers who have told me what I cannot do; Mr. Root is the only lawyer who tells me how to do what I want to do." The statement rings true; Root was ingenious at problem solving. But he did set ground rules. He claimed never to have advised a client to break the law. He believed that "a lawyer's chief business is to keep his clients out of litigation" and that "about half the practice of a decent lawyer consists in telling would-be clients that they are damned fools and should stop." By the standards of his time Root was undoubtedly on the side of clean government and political reform.

Root's support for Roosevelt was long term and consistent, from Roosevelt's first try for elected office in 1881 right through his presidency. When in 1895 Roosevelt became one of the four New York City police commissioners, he turned to Root for help in drawing up a brief against a fellow commissioner who was obstructing Roosevelt's reform efforts. Root's legal work persuaded the mayor to fire the commissioner. By then the pattern of the relationship had been set. To further his political career, Roosevelt was to turn to Root for his legal acumen, his political sense, and his superb judgment. Root gained in the exchange because Roosevelt's passion for reform helped keep the lawyer on his own reforming path.

Root and Roosevelt were friends, though not in the close sense that Roosevelt and Lodge, or John Hay and Henry Adams, were. Root was thirteen years older than Roosevelt and liked to emphasize the difference rather than minimize it. He teased Roosevelt as if he were an adolescent; Roosevelt, who enjoyed the teasing without returning it, called him "old man." In a letter congratulating Roosevelt, then president, on his forty-sixth birthday, Root wrote: "You have made a good start in life and your friends have great hopes for you when you grow up." Root was a witty man, but his wit, unlike Hay's, did not always narrow the distance between human beings. People, Roosevelt included, were not always sure where they stood with Root. His friend Hay remarked on his "frank and murderous smile." Roosevelt said many times that he considered Root the ablest man he knew, but he never really felt close to him.

5.

On the eve of the Spanish-American War, Root, at fifty-three, was one of the top lawyers in New York, a respected voice for political reform, and a rich man with a loyal wife and three children, aged twenty, seventeen, and fourteen. He was a classic workaholic, driving himself hard for nine or ten months a year, with little free time in the evenings or on weekends. In the summer he unwound at his father-in-law's house in Southampton—more fashionable than nearby Quogue, where Alfred Mahan went—or headed to the Rockies to hunt deer and antelope. Photographs show him with a well-trimmed mustache, no beard, and a direct and stern gaze. He wore his hair close cropped and in bangs, suggesting the aspect of a Roman emperor.

Root had so much self-confidence that he did not need the adulation or social acceptance that other political men, or even ambitious lawyers, required. Unlike Hay, he did not indulge in networking, did not dress with flair, and did not chase after fashionable dinner invitations. Hay's Clara was social; Root's Clara was not. His young law associates thought him cold until they realized that it was the intensity of his concentration that limited his conversation. His professionalism, not his manner, won their respect. His most famous junior partner, Henry L. Stimson, who followed Root's path to become secretary of war and secretary of state, worshiped him.

Root understood the workings of the world better than most. As an elder statesman he said: "Everybody knows that some rules for the conduct of life are matters of right and wrong, substantial, essential, and that other rules for the conduct of life are matters of convenience, of form, of method, desirable but not essential." While he did not particularly care for people's affection, he knew how to win their allegiance. After one massage session with Root, Boss Platt proposed him for the unwanted position of ambassador to London. "All he wanted, like a great many other people," said Root of Platt, "was to be treated with great admiration and respect." Without being a toady, Root knew how to do that.

Root's unique talents were to be tested in Cuba and the Philippines, where he established colonial governments on the debris of Spanish rule. His preparation for a task unprecedented in American political history was limited to his career as a corporate lawyer, his avocation as a political reformer, and his reputation for good judgment and effective problem solving. He was innocent of experience in national politics, government, and foreign policy. For so daunting a challenge, even a practical man would need a philosophy of government. In fact Root did have a reflective side. His public statements, most of which were made in retrospect after he had retired from government, shed light on the intellectual equipment he brought to his colonial mission.

Most striking was his analysis of the conflicting cultures of business and poverty in his Hamilton commencement speech in 1879, when he was only thirty-four. With trepidation, he saw in America a "war of poverty upon wealth":

> . . . a conflict of interests tending to the tyranny of a majority, a
> tendency on the one hand toward oppression, and on the other to-

ward revolution. Consider the influence of great corporations, how they are represented in Congress and state legislatures; how they sometimes mold and sometimes defy the law; how they stifle investigation; how they pervert public franchises; how grasping and unjust they are. Consider on the other hand, the condition of the poor; the paupers and laborers in the cities; the workmen in manufactories and mines. Of what advantage is this wealth to them? Why should they desire to perpetuate it? They do not desire to perpetuate it, but to destroy it.

Root was describing the very same social chaos that was the subject of John Hay's novel *The Breadwinners.* Unlike Hay, he showed a profound understanding of the iniquitous tendencies of big business and the legitimate grievances of the poor. In his novel Hay focused on the threat to order caused by strikes, riots, and mob violence. Root's deeper analysis found defects in the economic structure itself.

His sympathy for the downtrodden extended to his views of blacks in America. As a member and official of the Union League Club of New York he was a staunch loyalist to Lincoln's legacy. On the fortieth anniversary of the founding of the Union League in 1903, while he was secretary of war, he made a stirring appeal for the revival of the "failed" Thirteenth, Fourteenth, and Fifteenth Amendments giving black Americans citizenship, suffrage, and equal rights. "We can never throw off the responsibility that rests on our people for the well-being of these men who were held in bondage for so many years."

On the other hand, he reflected Republican party prejudice in rejecting the appeals of Susan B. Anthony and Elizabeth Cady Stanton, both New York residents, for women's right to vote. In a speech that sounds ludicrous today, delivered to the New York State Constitutional Convention of 1894, Root attacked an amendment on women's suffrage:

> In politics there is struggle, strife, contention, bitterness, heart-burning, excitement, agitation, everything which is adverse to the true character of woman. . . . Woman in strife becomes hard, harsh, unlovable, repulsive; as far removed from that gentle creature to whom we all owe allegiance and to whom we confess submission, as the heaven is removed from the earth. Government, Mr. President,

is protection. . . . the duty and the right of protection rests [sic] with the male . . . and I, for one, will never consent to part with the divine right of protecting my wife, my daughter, the women whom I love and the women whom I respect, exercising the birthright of man, and place that high duty in the weak and nerveless hands of those designed by God to be protected rather than to engage in the stern warfare of government.

Root's audience—all males, of course—interrupted him several times with applause.

Root believed in activist government. "I am a convinced and uncompromising nationalist of the school of Alexander Hamilton. I believe in the exercise of the executive, the legislative and the judicial powers of the national government to the full limit of the constitutional grants." He also believed in the preservation of the power of states and municipalities within the limits of their constitutional authority. He saw no contradiction between federal power and state power; what was important was that public bodies, state and federal, not deteriorate through the loss of their power. For that reason he opposed such proposals for popular democracy as direct election of U.S. senators (until 1913 senators were elected by state legislatures), compulsory referenda, recall of executive branch officials, popular review of judicial decisions, and recall of judges. He had no enthusiasm for the direct rule of the people, but in time he came to prefer popular democracy to the machine politics of his experience.

His long record of public service reflected his strong convictions about the responsibilities of citizens. Politics was the proper instrument for citizens who wanted to make a difference. In the New York of Root and Roosevelt, where politics was corrupt and machine-driven, most elite New Yorkers preferred to stay out of it. Roosevelt and Root plunged in, the former to challenge the system, the latter to change it from within. In a eulogy of Lincoln in 1920, Root dwelt on the great president's political acumen: "He understood the necessity of political organization for the accomplishment of political ends. . . . He was a politician, the best practical politician of his time." Root went on: "Politics is the practical exercise of the art of self-government, and somebody must attend to it if we are to have self-government. . . . The principal ground of reproach against any American citizen should be that he is not a politician. Everybody ought to be, as Lincoln was."

Root was a conservative with a conscience. He believed in order and tolerated change only if it came gradually and through traditional procedures. He trusted institutions, though he often subjected them to scorn. Like Hamilton, his idol and the namesake of his college, he thought that liberty must be balanced by law and that individuals must subject themselves to the control of an effective government. But government had responsibilities as well: It had to be honest, and it had to be authorized by the people. Although an apostle of American capitalism, he feared and opposed the political power of great corporations. He was comfortable working within a traditional political system, but his favorite words, his three Rs, reflected his distrust of the status quo: reform, restraint, and responsibility.

Root's views on foreign policy were less formed. Two short trips to Europe and a few law cases gave him little basis to develop a worldview. Once he assumed responsibilities for foreign affairs, his opinions fell comfortably into the imperial mode that Roosevelt and others had set. He recognized that the Monroe Doctrine, proclaimed unilaterally, was not part of international law, but he saw it as consistent with international law because it was founded on America's right to self-protection. He was a pragmatist, not a triumphalist. In a speech in 1904, while he was secretary of war, he disputed the arrogant claim of Cleveland's secretary of state, Richard Olney, that the United States was virtually sovereign on the continent. Root thought that America's right of self-protection had to be accompanied by responsible behavior: "Above all things let us be just."

Nor was he caught up in the fashionable view, held by Republican activists like Roosevelt, that war was purifying and ennobling. Unlike Hay and Mahan, he had missed the Civil War, but his reflections on war showed little taste for the alleged glories of combat. He saw war as negative but inevitable so long as selfishness, greed, and injustice existed. He believed in just war but also in the necessity of just peace. President McKinley somehow learned of Root's abilities and pacific views. In the spring of 1897, shortly after his inauguration, McKinley asked Root to meet him in Philadelphia to discuss the increasing tensions between the United States and Spain. According to Root's later account, McKinley said: "There is danger of war; there must not be war with Spain; there shall not be war with Spain. It must be and it shall be prevented at all hazards."

The president then asked Root to go to Madrid as U.S. minister (he even offered to elevate the position to ambassador) to try to work out a settlement with the Spanish government. Root considered the offer but turned it down. The reason he gave was that the negotiations would require informal, personal talks, and since he did not speak Spanish, he could not carry them out. Root's argument may have been sincere—he was after all a neophyte in diplomacy—but it was certainly erroneous. The history of successful negotiations is full of cases in which negotiators worked through interpreters.

In any case, Root left a favorable impression on McKinley because the president was to make him an even more important offer. To jump ahead in the story for a moment, some months after the smashing American military victories in Cuba and the Philippines in 1898, McKinley asked Root to become secretary of war, with the mission of providing civil government to America's first colonial territories. Despite Root's manifest lack of qualifications, McKinley had a clearly positive idea of the kind of man he was getting. He was getting a problem solver, an expert in the law, a reformer but not a radical, an elitist with a social conscience, a quick study, a person of loyalty and probity, a moderate who might make small waves but not big ones, and a man who understood politics but had no political ambitions himself.

For Root the mission seemed too important to turn down. He described the exchange, conducted over the newfangled telephone:

> I was called to the telephone and told by one speaking for President McKinley: "The President directs me to say to you that he wishes you to take the position of Secretary of War." I answered, "Thank the President for me, but say that it is quite absurd, I know nothing about war, I know nothing about the army." I was told to hold the wire, and in a moment there came back the reply, "President McKinley directs me to say that he is not looking for any one who knows anything about the army; he has got to have a lawyer to direct the government of these Spanish islands, and you are the lawyer he wants." Of course I had then, on the instant, to determine what kind of lawyer I wished to be, and there was but one answer to

make, and so I went to perform a lawyer's duty upon the call of the greatest of all our clients, the Government of our country.

McKinley knew his man. What he could not know was that Elihu Root would be the first of the modern "wise men," upper-class New York lawyers or bankers who give up lucrative careers to go to Washington and turn their talents to the service of their country. Root blazed a trail that has been followed by a remarkable group of public-spirited citizens, men like his own law partner and protégé Henry Stimson, John J. McCloy, Robert Lovett, Averell Harriman, Douglas Dillon, Cyrus Vance, Paul Nitze, and Robert Rubin.

All were men of accomplishment, energy, and character. None was perfect; nor was Root. There was in his moral universe an ambivalence that marked his entire career. In the perilous balance between serving a client and following one's own conscience, Root refused to recognize a dilemma. His "lawyer's duty" to his supreme client, the U.S. government, impelled him to ensure that it behaved with honor. But the same duty also carried an obligation, as he saw it, to defend his client when it went wrong.

As a colonial administrator he was to spur the U.S. government to effective, just, and sometimes enduring solutions in Cuba, Puerto Rico, and the Philippines. However, when American forces, under his charge, committed atrocities against the Philippine population, he considered it his duty to cover them up. Both his achievements and his errors sprang from his training as a corporate lawyer. They were the consequences of his tendency, on the smooth road to success, to ignore rather than confront any moral contradictions that might arise along the way.

5. Dauntless Intolerance

1.

In the first three months of 1895, Henry Cabot Lodge delivered a series of foreign policy speeches on the floor of the U.S. Senate. There was no great reason for his fellow senators to pay much attention to what he had to say. Lodge was only a freshman senator, having been elected from Massachusetts in 1892 after serving three terms in the House of Representatives. He was not yet a member of the Senate Foreign Relations Committee. In fact his voice on foreign policy was much less respected than that of the senior senator from his state, the venerable George Frisbie Hoar, who had advocated a nonexpansionist American approach to the world during his sixteen years in the Senate.

Moreover, Lodge was not an impressive speaker. Though tall and elegant, with a well-trimmed Vandyke beard, he had a high-pitched, grating voice once compared to the tearing of a bed sheet. His personality was chilly and austere, not of the type to make him popular within the Senate's convivial precincts. But he had energy, intelligence, determination, and foresight. His speeches accurately predicted the imminent revolution in American foreign policy.

In early 1895 Lodge was preoccupied with events on the Hawaiian Islands, a Polynesian monarchy whose mid-Pacific location and deep harbors had attracted the interest of the U.S. Navy. Americans had been involved with Hawaii for decades, successively as traders, as missionaries, as whalers, and as resident sugar planters. By the 1890s the divergent interests of Americans in Hawaii who favored annexation and native Hawaiians who opposed it were creating tension. In 1891 a nationalist monarch, Queen Liliuokalani, came to the

Hawaiian throne and began to reverse the growing influence of American sugar producers. In early 1893 a group of American annexationists staged a successful coup d'état with the support of the U.S. consul and overthrew the queen. But their plans were stymied when President Cleveland withdrew the outgoing Harrison administration's treaty to annex Hawaii. By 1895 the royalists were engaged in an uprising to restore Liliuokalani to the throne when Lodge rose in the Senate on January 19 to assail Cleveland's antiannexationist policy.

Lodge complained that the chief gainer from the queen's restoration would be Great Britain, which he accused of seeking to lay a telegraph cable on one of the islands and to establish commercial supremacy over all of them. Lodge claimed that the American people wanted the islands to be under American control, U.S. interests to be predominant, and administration of the government to be by "men of American blood." Most important, he argued that "the islands should become a part of the American Republic."

The Massachusetts senator was back at the charge three days later. In a second speech he widened his assertion of British greed with a catalog of their seizures of other islands in the Pacific. He also pointed to the presence of twenty thousand Japanese in Hawaii and of a Japanese warship off the coast. Again he urged an annexationist course: "I do not mean that we should enter on a widely extended system of colonization. That is not our line. But I do mean that we should take all the outlying territory necessary to our own defense, to the protection of the Isthmian Canal [not yet built], to the upbuilding of our trade and commerce, and to the maintenance of our military safety everywhere. I would take and hold the outworks, as we now hold the citadel, of American power." In a memorable conclusion Lodge said: "I cannot bear to see the American flag pulled down where it has once been run up, and I dislike to see the American foot go back where it has once been advanced."

On March 2, 1895, Lodge returned to the imperial theme, this time in a wide-ranging address on naval policy. Here, even more than in the previous two speeches, he revealed an enormous debt to the writings of Alfred Mahan. He used arguments from Mahan's first book on the influence of sea power as well as from some of the naval strategist's magazine pieces. He even referred to Hannibal's failure in the face of Rome's control of the sea, a central theme of Mahan's great work. Lodge did not yet know Mahan, who was still at sea on the *Chicago*. But he admired his writings and had interceded with the secretary of the navy on Mahan's behalf in the scuffle over Admiral Erben's poor fitness report.

Lodge set Hawaii in a larger strategic and commercial context. The Hawaiian Islands, "even if they were populated by a low race of savages, even if they were desert rocks, would still be important to this country from their position. . . . The main thing is that those islands lie there in the heart of the Pacific, the controlling point in the commerce of that great ocean. . . . Upon those islands rests a great part of the future commercial progress of the United States." The anticipated digging of a canal through the isthmus made Hawaii even more important, because all the main routes from San Francisco, Vancouver, and the canal itself would pass the islands.

Lodge sketched a comprehensive imperial strategy, using concepts and even language taken from Mahan. "The sea power has been one of the controlling forces in history. Without the sea power no nation has been really great. Sea power consists, in the first place, of a proper navy and a proper fleet; but in order to sustain a navy we must have suitable posts for naval stations, strong places where a navy can be protected and refurnished." Lodge then set up a standing map to illustrate to his fellow senators the large number of British bases around the world, marked with Maltese crosses. Great Britain, he cautioned, "has always opposed, thwarted, and sought to injure us; a Maltese cross must not be affixed to Hawaii." He also raised the specter of Japan as a rival.

The senator called for funding of three additional battleships ("the backbone of the modern navy") and nine torpedo boats, as President Cleveland's secretary of the navy had recommended. Lodge wanted a world-class navy that could be sent to foreign ports to safeguard American interests and citizens, could protect traders ("commerce follows the flag," he claimed), and could provide a first line of defense. He scoffed at arguments that this would be too expensive: "We have spent enough money in building ugly public buildings alone, to fit out the greatest navy in the world."

Lodge was carrying Mahan's strategic concepts into the politics of naval expenditures. He was addressing the practical issue of appropriations for the Navy Department, but his language rang with the authentic accents of a new American imperialism:

> It was the sea power in history which enabled Rome to crush Hannibal, perhaps the greatest military genius of all time; it was the sea power which enabled England to bring Napoleon's empire to ruins; it was the sea power more than anything else which crushed the rebellion in this country by blockading every port of the Southern States. It is the sea power which is essential to the greatness of every splendid people. We are a great people; we control this continent; we are dominant in this hemisphere; we have too great an inheritance to be trifled with or parted with. It is ours to guard and to extend.

Lodge's three speeches propelled him to the forefront of those Americans who were insisting that the United States assume its rightful place in the ranks of the great powers. As a Senate Republican, Lodge was better placed than his friend Theodore Roosevelt to make the case for expansion in opposition to a Democratic president whose policies both considered, in Lodge's words, "grotesque and miserable." At the time Roosevelt was a Republican holdover on the Civil Service Commission in Cleveland's Democratic administration, and he was soon to become a New York City police commissioner, a position that, like his previous one, lacked a foreign policy platform. So it fell to Lodge to become the point man for American imperialism.

He approached the task with gusto. In several magazine articles in 1895 he staked a claim for the United States as a great power:

> The great nations are rapidly absorbing for their future expansion and their present defence all the waste places of the earth. It is a movement which makes for civilization and the advancement of the race. As one of the great nations of the world, the United States must not fall out of the line of march.
>
> We have a record of conquest, colonization, and territorial expansion (Westward—as Washington taught!) unequalled by any people in the nineteenth century. . . . From the Rio Grande to the Arctic Ocean there should be but one flag and one country. . . . Every consideration of national growth and national welfare demands it.

When Britain disputed with Venezuela the mineral-rich border between British Guiana and Venezuela, Lodge sallied forth clothed in the mantle of Monroe, sword in hand. For nearly a decade the United States had shown sympathy for Venezuela's extravagant territorial claims, particularly since the antagonist was a traditional U.S. adversary. He wrote: "If Great Britain is to be permitted to occupy the ports of Nicaragua and, still worse, take the territory of Venezuela, there is nothing to prevent her taking the whole of Venezuela or any other South American state. If Great Britain can do this with impunity, France and Germany will do it also. . . . The supremacy of the Monroe Doctrine should be established and at once—peacefully if we can, forcibly if we must." Following up in a speech in the Senate in December, Lodge called Britain's claim against Venezuela "an absolute violation" of the Monroe Doctrine, an attempt to make the Caribbean Sea "little better than a British lake." The United States stood by the Monroe Doctrine, he said, "because it is essential to our safety and our defense. The Monroe Doctrine rests primarily on the great law of self-preservation."

Lodge's bellicosity and his growing knowledge of how to use the Senate to apply political pressure may well have stirred the Cleveland administration out of its torpor. At any rate he claimed credit for the president's uncharacteristically tough stand against the British. Secretary of State Olney's belligerent and arrogant note, delivered in London on July 20, 1895, and boasting that "the United States is practically sovereign on this continent," evoked a haughty British rejection. When Cleveland, in December, sent a message to Congress calling for the use of force against increasingly provocative British actions in the Caribbean, Lodge was jubilant, and Roosevelt, from New York police headquarters, talked about saddling up. In the end the British superiority in battleships (fifty to three), balanced by the fact that Canada remained vulnerable as an American hostage, produced a mutual decision to put the dispute to arbitration.

Final resolution was thus deferred for years. When it came in 1899, largely in favor of the British claim, the crisis had long been over. Though it had produced more bluster than action, the Venezuela affair in 1895 was a dry run for the war against Spain three years later. It provoked an outburst of nationalist fervor in the United States. Mahan, Lodge, and Roosevelt were among the loudest war hawks. Even the Anglophile John Hay, as noted in Chapter 2, was called on to convey a civilized warning to his British friends.

Revolution in Cuba gave Lodge even broader scope for his imperial inclinations. Under the feckless, corrupt, and sometimes brutal rule of Spain since the days of Columbus, Cuba had become a frequent target of American avidity during the nineteenth century. An insurrection against Spanish rule launched in 1895 offered another opportunity for expansionist impulses. With his strong view of America's global mission, Lodge was the natural leader of those senators who wanted to drive Spain out of the Western Hemisphere.

His interest in Cuba extended beyond the theoretical. He actually did some homework. On a visit to Spain in October 1895 he called on the Spanish prime minister, Antonio Cánovas del Castillo, and found him preoccupied with the Cuban insurrection and fearful of American intervention. He urged Cánovas to deal with the revolt quickly because the violence was harming American business interests. In a letter to Roosevelt, Lodge described Spain as a defeated country ready to be cast aside by history: "You never saw such desolate dreary plains and here and there a dying town. Even Madrid is bleak and cheerless. The people repel one. . . . They seem sullen and indifferent. The manners you meet and notice are cold and rude. They are beaten, broken and out of the race and are proud and know it."

In early 1896 Henry Adams, a zealous advocate of Cuban independence, put Lodge in touch with two representatives of the Cuban insurrection. They met clandestinely at the Washington house of Pennsylvania Senator J. Donald Cameron. The Cubans wanted American support for their independence struggle. Cameron complied by proposing a nonbinding resolution recognizing Cuba's independence. Lodge, now a member of the Senate Foreign Relations Committee and of its subcommittee on Cuba, strongly supported the resolution.

In meeting the Cubans secretly, Lodge and Cameron were trespassing on the executive powers of President Cleveland, who was strongly opposed to their position on Cuba. Lodge also encountered opposition elsewhere, from business interests in Massachusetts critical of the Cuban insurgents. General S. M. Weld, a Boston cotton broker, and Charles Francis Adams, Henry's older brother and a former railroad president, challenged the view that a war with Cuba would be good for business. Lodge was not to be deterred. To Weld he wrote haughtily: "The issues of war and peace . . . must be decided on higher and broader grounds than business considerations."

Lodge put himself on a collision course with Spain. To the plaudits of Roosevelt in New York, he peppered the Senate and the lecture circuit with bellicose speeches. "There is Cuba," he told the members of the Massachusetts Republican State Convention, "there it lies, that great island, athwart the Gulf, right in the pathway of our coastwise commerce, commanding the entrance to the . . . Canal." For Lodge the strategic arguments were unassailable: A free Cuba would be an American market, an American ally, and a bulwark against outsiders seeking control of the Gulf. Cuba was "a case of humanity" as well. "It does not, in my judgment, lie in American mouths to utter anything but sympathy for a colony struggling for independence. It is no answer to say to me that they cannot set up a government, if they win, as good as our government. They will set up a better one than Spain gives them."

Cleveland was not going to be drawn into an attempt to seize Cuba, any more than he had been susceptible to a bid for Hawaii. What counted was that Lodge had established himself as the rallying point for Republican attacks on an anti-imperialist president. When William McKinley, not a war hawk but a man open to persuasion, won the presidential election in November 1896, Henry Cabot Lodge became overnight the most powerful official advocate, by position and conviction, of an imperial policy for the United States.

2.

Lodge's view of America as a great nation with a record of conquest and an imperial mission came as much from his character as from his background. He was born in 1850 into a Boston family of wealth, privilege, and intellect. His mother's forebears, the Cabots, were among the earliest settlers in Massachusetts in the seventeenth century. His maternal great-grandfather, George Cabot, had been a prominent Massachusetts Federalist in the revolutionary period, a friend of Hamilton's, and a U.S. senator during Washington's presidency. The Lodges came later than the Cabots. Lodge's grandfather, a commercial agent, fetched up in Boston around 1790 after being caught in a slave rebellion in Santo Domingo. His father was a shipowner in the China trade.

As a boy Cabot—he was never called Henry—led the privileged and pampered life of the only son of an indulgent mother. He was exposed to the cream of Boston's intelligentsia, all friends of his father's: the Harvard historians William H. Prescott, Francis Parkman, George Bancroft, and John L. Motley; the naturalist Louis Agassiz; the famous surgeon Henry Jacob Bigelow; the poet Henry Wadsworth Longfellow; and the abolitionist U.S. senator Charles Sumner.

In the constant company of four of the greatest American historians, it was small wonder that the young Lodge made the study of history his passion. Nor, with a seafaring pedigree on both sides of his family, was it surprising that he devoured, as had Alfred Mahan, the sea stories of Frederick Marryat and became entranced by great navies. He was a voracious reader of the popular fiction of the day: Scott, Defoe, Hawthorne, Cooper, Dickens, Irving, *The Swiss Family Robinson*, the travel stories of Mungo Park, and the western novels of Mayne Reid. He learned the classical and medieval myths from Bulfinch's collections. His school training was so heavy in the classical languages that he was able without effort to sprinkle Latin tags throughout his future writing.

He was not too scholarly to love sports and the outdoors. In his memoirs he listed as favorite activities coasting, baseball, football, hockey, shooting, ice skating, swimming, boxing, fencing, rowing, sailing, riding, and indulging in the upper-class propensity to lie naked on the warm rocks under a hot sun. He also had an artistic bent, a good eye for architecture, and a passion for the theater. His father owned a large Boston theater, enabling the young Lodge to enjoy minstrel shows, circuses, comedies, melodramas, magicians, and monologists. He had a taste for music, especially Offenbach and later Wagner, and a love of sculpture, painting, and poetry.

Lodge took his aestheticism to Harvard, the inevitable academic destination for a Cabot and a Lodge. His theatrical bent got him into the Hasty Pudding Club, and his social standing won him a place in the exclusive Porcellian. He performed in Hasty Pudding productions, being photographed once as an uncomfortable and not particularly malevolent Lady Macbeth. He coauthored a rhymed burlesque of *Don Giovanni* (writing jingles to Mozart's music), acted as a supernumerary in Italian operas, and haunted Boston theaters. He heard readings by Fanny Kemble, who entranced him, and by Dickens, whom he found full of "cheap pathos" and "not quite a gentleman."

Under a new president, Charles W. Eliot, Harvard was casting aside its narrow classical curriculum and becoming the broad liberal arts university it has remained. Lodge relished the change and threw himself into English literature, taught by James Russell Lowell, and into a new course on medieval history started by Henry Adams. Adams must have been a brilliant teacher, though not to hear him tell it; the chapter about Harvard in his autobiography is titled "Failure." Adams's obsessive self-abnegation aside, Lodge found him inspirational. "Mr. Adams roused the spirit of inquiry and controversy in me. . . . He had the power not only of exciting interest, but he awakened opposition to his own views. . . . [F]or the first time I got a glimpse of what education might be."

While still a junior at Harvard, Lodge became engaged to Anna Davis, the eldest daughter of Rear Admiral Charles H. Davis, one of the top scientists in the navy and superintendent of the Naval Observatory. His daughter Nannie was tiny, blonde, pretty, and with a charm habitually noted by friends of the couple. She did not, however, rate more than a mention in Lodge's memoirs, published in 1913. For five full pages he burbled about her father: "To him and to the family into which I was then brought I owe in large measure the affection and the happiness which life has accorded to me. I have never known any man more charming or more lovable." Whether Lodge's curious failure to mention his own wife can be put down to a Bostonian sense of privacy or whether, as seems likelier, he simply took her for granted, one can begin to understand why in later years Nannie took up with John Hay, who was prepared to pay more attention to her.

Cabot and Nannie were married on June 25, 1871, the day after he graduated from Harvard. Both were just twenty-one. In July they embarked on a year's honeymoon to Europe. The length of time was not unusual; Henry and Clover Adams were also to take a year. The trip, Lodge's second to Europe, deepened his love of history, the arts, and literature; he was an inveterate sightseer and remained one all his life. Nine months and ten days after their marriage, Nannie gave birth to a baby girl in Paris. And soon Lodge made a brief but ardent friendship that helped set the course of his life. In Rome he ran into a Harvard classmate, Michael Simpson, who shared Lodge's aesthetic passions. They read Suetonius together, explored Hadrian's villa, took side trips to Naples and Paestum, "opened our hearts to each other."

Simpson clearly had an original mind and a good deal of moral courage. A New England Puritan like Lodge, he had, through intellectual struggle, abandoned the religious dogma of his childhood and become an agnostic. He wanted to devote his life to literature and public service, but he felt honor-bound to enter his father's business. In time he meant to pursue his literary inclinations and to engage in politics on behalf of the Republican party.

Simpson's sense of responsibility had a profound influence on his more callow friend. With no financial worries, Lodge had begun "to cherish some vague desires for a literary life." Just as he was "drifting vaguely," Simpson entered his life. "All this consideration given to serious things, all this thought about man's place in the universe, about the undiscovered future and the meaning and uses of life, coming from a man, a boy really, of my own age, were to me at once very strange and very impressive. . . . A life of unoccupied leisure no longer attracted me." Simpson's influence on Lodge was undoubtedly magnified by the young man's untimely death of typhoid just a few months after their intense relationship in Rome. More than forty years later Lodge wrote: "His death left a gap in my life which after all these years has still remained unfilled."

Simpson's death terminated the potential career of Cabot Lodge as aesthete. Lodge was to live vicariously a literary vocation through his son Bay, a poet who died at thirty-five, and through his own prolific, if mediocre, historical output. He even, at twenty-nine, edited a charming collection of fairy tales, based, with Harvard scrupulousness, on the oldest English texts, which was used in the Boston public schools. But Simpson's example, sealed by mortality, set Lodge on a path away from literature and the arts and toward politics and public service.

Something was lost in the passage. The semisybaritic, dilettante Lodge might have been more open, more tolerant, and more complex than the puritanical, political Lodge who was to define his career by American imperialism and unilateralism, opposition to immigration, and hatred of Woodrow Wilson. Sargent's portrait of Lodge at forty, two years before he won his seat in the Senate, captured the dreamy, artistic side of the man, a side that was to be sublimated to the single-mindedness of a powerful and ruthless politician.

After Simpson's death, Lodge wrote Henry Adams from Europe for advice on his future. His revered teacher urged him to look at things practically: "Keep clear of mere sentiment whenever you have to decide a practical question. Sentiment is very attractive and I like it as well as most people, but nothing in the way of action is worth much which is not practically sound." Adams followed with some no-nonsense counsel:

> The question is whether the historico-literary line is practically worth following; not whether it will amuse or improve you. Can you make it *pay*, either in money, reputation, or any other solid value.
>
> Now if you will think for a moment of the most respectable and respected products of our town of Boston, I think you will see at once that this profession does pay. No one has done better and won more in any business or pursuit than has been acquired by men like Prescott, Motley, Frank Parkman, Bancroft, and so on in historical writing; none of them men of extraordinary gifts, or who would have been likely to do very much in the world if they had chosen differently [an extraordinary put-down of four of America's greatest historians]. What they did can be done by others.
>
> Further there is a great opening here at this time. Boston is running dry of literary authorities. Any one who has the ability can enthrone himself here as a species of literary lion with ease, for there is no rival to contest the throne. With it, comes [*sic*] social dignity, European reputation and a foreign mission to close.

His mentor's crass advice persuaded Lodge to become a scholar. He plunged into the tedious study of the early law of the Germanic tribes, which Adams had taught as the foundation of the legal and political history of the English-speaking people. Paradoxically Lodge, who had studied classics intensively in school, gave no credit to ancient Athens for providing the seedbed for British and American democracy. He had not even visited Greece on his yearlong honeymoon, though he did admire the Greek temple at Paestum in southern Italy. In a way the ancient Greeks exacted revenge on their faith-less pupil: The German tribes bored him to the point of depression, and he abandoned them at the first opportunity.

Nevertheless, he made his "inexpressibly dreary" Germanic studies "pay," as Henry Adams said they should. They led to the study of Anglo-Saxon law, which he pursued under Adams in Harvard Law School and which became the subject of his Ph.D. dissertation. They also laid the basis of his careerlong opposition to non-Anglo-Saxon immigrants. By the age of twenty-six Lodge had a law degree and a doctorate from Harvard, plus a greater knowledge than he wanted or needed of medieval German law.

In his boredom with the first year of Germanic studies, Lodge jumped at an offer from Henry Adams in the summer of 1873 to become assistant editor of the *North American Review*, a respected intellectual quarterly that Adams had taken over as editor. Adams was a meticulous stylist, striking out superfluous words, especially adjectives, and writing clearly in short, simple sentences. Lodge never seemed to acquire this knack, even under Adams's benevolent tutelage. He had to rewrite his first book review eight times before Adams would print it. It took him three years to get a leading article into the magazine. His experience with the *North American Review* was nonetheless seminal. Together with his study of the law, it steered him toward the study of American history, which became his lifelong expertise.

His first book—twenty-six more were to follow—was a biography of his great-grandfather George Cabot. He followed it with articles on historical themes for the *Nation*, the *Atlantic Monthly*, and other high-quality periodicals. From 1875 to 1879 he taught American history at Harvard, covering the colonial and early postrevolution periods. Unlike Adams, he does not seem to have been a scintillating teacher; one of his classes shrank from fifty students to three.

Lodge's place on the Harvard faculty and the *North American Review* gave him intellectual stature, and he exulted in it. In his memoirs he listed with pride the professional clubs and organizations to which he was elected. At twenty-six he was offered membership in the Massachusetts Historical Society—"one of the youngest members ever chosen, I believe"—thus joining the company of the Harvard historians whom Henry Adams had encouraged him to emulate. He was also chosen by the Wednesday Evening Club, which met for talk and supper; it was graced by "many of our Boston worthies," including Adams's father, who had played such a key role as ambassador to London during the Civil War. He was admitted to the American Academy of Arts and Sciences and was made a trustee of the Boston Athenaeum, a distinguished library. He also joined some friends his own age in founding a dining society called the Porcupine Club (perhaps a wordplay on Porcellian) whose motto, in Latin, was "The people hiss at me, but I applaud myself."

Before he gave himself fully to politics, Lodge in his twenties and early thirties was a man at home in the natural superiority of his background, his taste, and his intellect. His memoirs began with a genealogical survey that, consciously or not, set the Cabots and Lodges in the Elysium of superior American families. As he looked back on his youth, he sensed a challenge to the old families from the newly wealthy: "To the modern and recent plutocrat the old American family means nothing. He knows naught of the history or traditions of his State and country and cares less. He has but one standard, money or money's worth."

Lodge made no effort to hide his confidence in the moral primacy of his own caste over the parvenus and "their lawlessness, their disregard of the rights of others, especially of others about whom they are not informed, and as they know only money, their information is limited. . . . They pay no regard to the laws of the land or the laws and customs of society if the laws are in their way. They seem to think that money warrants everything and can pay for everything, and that nothing must be allowed to stand in the way of what money wants."

Despising the newly rich, Lodge not surprisingly found society's natural leaders among the men with whom he had grown up in Boston—his fellow members of the Wednesday Evening and Porcupine clubs, for example. It was their standards he treasured: "a certain formality of address"; the respect of children for their parents; a belief that it was not good manners to discuss at dinner surgical operations, physical functions, diseases, and especially money; and a love of "the old and graceful art of letter-writing." Lodge admitted that civilizations decline when form becomes everything, but formlessness was in his view a poor substitute. What counted was "the careful establishment of standards by which, and by which alone, civilization, carrying arts and letters and thought in its train, has hitherto emerged after many conflicts from the bondage of barbarism."

Like many of his Boston friends, Lodge drew sustenance from his Puritan heritage, particularly its masochism and its independence. Like the Puritans, he believed that "work, after all, is the best of friends"; without it "one can never enjoy either leisure or a vacation." In a talk to the New England Society of New York in 1884, he said: "New England has a harsh climate, a barren soil, a rough and stormy coast, and yet we love it, even with a love passing that of dwellers in more favored regions." Harsh, barren, rough, stormy: Those adjectives all applied to Lodge himself in his later political years.

He said in the same speech that he admired the Pilgrims and Puritans for their search for religious freedom, but not for their denial of that freedom to others. He then made an eloquent appeal for the privileged to help the poor: "The destiny of the republic is in the welfare of its working men and women. We cannot push their troubles and cares into the background, and trust that all will come right in the end. . . . Legislation cannot change humanity nor alter the decrees of nature." But, he argued, it could encourage fairer working hours, emigration from overcrowded cities to the West, economical and energetic municipal governments, proper building laws, prevention of adulterated food, "wise regulation" of the railroads and other great corporations, extirpation of race and class in politics, and "above all every effort to secure to labor its fair and full share of the profits earned by the combination of labor and capital."

All in all, this was a relatively liberal agenda, comparable to the issues that Roosevelt and Root were pushing in New York at the same time. For Lodge at thirty-four it was based more on philosophy than experience; he rarely met the poor. In his memoirs he somewhat self-consciously described his role in the Boston fire of 1872, when, a year out of Harvard, he helped save the contents of threatened buildings, distributed food and clothing to the homeless, and followed up with periodic visits to the dwellings of poor people. He wrote that the knowledge of "how a part of the world lives which I had never possessed before" did him good.

Lodge's patrician sense of duty toward the poor did not extend to efforts on their part to take matters into their own hands. In his memoirs he was scathing about the presumptions of the working class and its champions. They wanted "to take money by means of legislation, through government action, from those who have it, either by earning it or by inheritance, and give it to those who have not earned it." This, he wrote, was "an effort to prevent those who work hardest and best from gaining any greater reward than those who work least and most ineffectively. Special privileges which are said to have existed for the benefit of the rich and successful seem to be on the way not to extinction, but to transference." The language here mirrors the narrow intolerance of John Hay in *The Breadwinners*.

Lodge had a strong belief in the greatness of American history, in the revolution that had shaken the country free of the hated England, and in the Civil War which had proved that Americans would be able to meet the future with confidence. On the issue of slavery he remained a liberal all his life. Like many Bostonians, he saw slavery as a "crime against humanity" as well as a "huge economic blunder and a social curse."

His heroic view of American history coincided with Roosevelt's, and sometime later, they collaborated on a book for juveniles, *Hero Tales from American History*. Published in 1895, it immortalized men who were lifelong heroes for the two authors. Many soldiers and explorers figure in the selections: George Washington, Daniel Boone, George Rogers Clark, Stonewall Jackson, Ulysses S. Grant, Robert Gould Shaw (who led a Massachusetts regiment of black soldiers in the Civil War), Philip Sheridan, David Farragut, Anthony Wayne, Andrew Jackson, and Stephen Decatur. Lodge added a special favorite, the historian Francis Parkman, but the overall emphasis was on derring-do rather than intellectual achievement.

The dedication to Roosevelt's wife Edith—there was no mention of Nannie Lodge—set the theme. *Hero Tales* was "the story of some Americans who showed that they knew how to live and how to die; who proved their truth by their endeavor; and who joined to the stern and manly qualities which are essential to the well-being of a masterful race the virtues of gentleness, of patriotism, and of lofty adherence to an ideal." The authors promised "feats of daring and personal prowess."

Not surprisingly, Lodge's approach to athletics was shaped in the same heroic mold; he saw sport as one of the martial virtues. As he told his twenty-fifth Harvard reunion: "The time given to athletic contests and the injuries incurred on the playing-field are part of the price which the English-speaking race has paid for being world-conquerors." Athletic victories, he preached, are the manifestation of a spirit "which subordinates the individual to the group, and which enables that group, whether it be a college or a nation, to achieve great results and attain high ideals."

As he edged toward a career in politics, Lodge was a mixture of unresolved tendencies. His Puritan heritage drove him to hard work, a determination to succeed, and a lugubrious sense that he must carry on the mission of his forefathers. His complacent association with upper-class Boston made him a prig and a snob but also ingrained in him a sense of duty to the less well endowed. He had an eye for the visual arts and might have developed a talent in that direction, but his dominant conventionality kept the aesthetic side of his character unformed and undeveloped. Though his friendships with Henry Adams and later with Theodore Roosevelt were deep, he was too austere and judgmental to make friends easily. He tended to bore his social equals and intimidate the rest.

His intellectual pretensions—three Harvard degrees and an irresistible compulsion to write—steered him toward American history. But he was not a very good historian. His heroes, like Hamilton, were two-dimensional, and so were his villains. He hated Jefferson, whom he called inconsistent, supple, feminine, illogical, crafty, selfish, and unpatriotic. In Lodge's description, Jefferson returned from Paris "with both body and brain dressed in the French fashion." Lodge's histories were epics dominated by strong government, by heroic exploits of expansion and battle, and by a sense of destiny. He was never to correct the weakness that Henry Adams spotted early on: "Your danger is a very simple one. . . . It is that of adopting a view of one side of a question. . . . Unless you can find some basis of faith in general principles, some theory of the progress of civilization which is outside and above all temporary questions of policy, you must infallibly think and act under the control of the man or men whose thought, in the times you deal with, coincides most clearly with your prejudices."

Adams caught the complexities of Lodge's character in a description written when Lodge was a prominent senator. It melds the early Lodge of Harvard, on whom Adams, his teacher and fellow Bostonian, had a profound influence, with the master politician of a later time:

> An excellent talker, a voracious reader, a ready wit, an accomplished orator, with a clear mind and a powerful memory, he could

never feel perfectly at ease whatever leg he stood on, but shifted, sometimes with painful strain of temper, from one sensitive muscle to another, uncertain whether to pose as an uncompromising Yankee; or a pure American; or a patriot in the still purer atmosphere of Irish, Germans or Jews; or a scholar and historian of Harvard College.

English to the last fibre of his thought,—saturated with English literature, English tradition, English taste,—revolted by every vice and by most virtues of Frenchmen and Germans, or any other continental standards, but at home and happy among the vices and extravagances of Shakespeare;—standing first on the social, then on the political foot; now worshipping, now banning; shocked by the wanton display of immorality, but practising the license of political usage; sometimes bitter, often genial, always intelligent; Lodge had the singular merit of interesting.

The usual statesmen flocked in swarms like crows, black and monotonous. Lodge's plumage was varied, and, like his flight, harked back to race. He betrayed the consciousness that he and his people had a past, if they dared but avow it, and might have a future, if they could but divine it.

3.

Lodge's choice of a political career was much more natural than Roosevelt's. In New York politics was largely in the hands of Democratic and Republican political machines; in Massachusetts it was a cleaner sport, practiced frequently by the upper classes. John Adams, his son John Quincy, and Daniel Webster all had contributed to the heritage of the state. So had George Cabot, a lesser light. A contemporary political figure probably made an even greater impression on Lodge: his father's friend Senator Charles Sumner, whose speeches against slavery so alienated Boston conservatives that he was ostracized from virtually all houses except the Adamses' and the Lodges'. Sumner's abolitionism had a heroic quality for the young Lodge, who may also have been impressed by the fiery senator's belief that Spain should be expelled from the Caribbean.

His own ancestry and his state's tradition drew Lodge into politics. So also did his own intellectual inclinations. His biographies of Washington, Hamilton, and Webster established paragons to be copied.

The book on Hamilton, published in 1882, reached rare heights of adoration. For his distrust of democracy, his favoritism toward the propertied classes, his belief in a strong central government at the expense of the states, and his drive to establish an American empire, Hamilton was Lodge's political model. Lodge credited Hamilton with the original conceptions for the Louisiana Purchase and the Monroe Doctrine. Thanks to his historical research, he was already, in his early thirties, a convinced imperialist.

These historical influences, plus the martyrdom of Michael Simpson, who had hoped to enter public service, made Lodge's move toward a political career easy. Adams, with his preference for living through the careers of others, helped. Lodge was Adams's first alter ego, several years before he acquired John Hay. Dismayed by the corruption of the Grant administration, Adams threw himself into his first and last sustained political initiative. He founded a new party of the center, opposed to machine politics and dedicated to civil service reform. In his mid-twenties Lodge became active in these efforts, making several trips to New York and Washington to sound out potential third-party adherents.

The membership list of Republican independents attracted to Adams's party was impressive. In addition to the founding members— Henry's father, Charles Francis Adams, and the German-American reformer Carl Schurz—it included Theodore Roosevelt's father, the laissez-faire Yale economist William Graham Sumner, Yale President Theodore Woolsey, the New York industrialist and philanthropist Peter Cooper, the Boston lawyer Moorfield Storey, and prominent journalists like E. L. Godkin, Charles Nordhoff, Samuel Bowles, and William Cullen Bryant.

But any effect the independents might have had was nullified by the Republican nomination in 1876 of Rutherford Hayes—not a reformer but not a spoilsman either—and the Democratic nomination of Samuel J. Tilden, who *was* a reformer. The independents broke up in disarray. The Adamses supported Tilden. Schurz joined many other independents in staying with Hayes, for which act of Republican loyalty he received a cabinet position. Lodge vacillated and finally voted for Tilden, the last time in his life he was to support a Democrat.

Lodge was still harboring moderate to liberal views as he began to find a home in the Republican party in the late 1870s. He favored reform of state and local elections, simpler ballots, longer terms of service for elected state officials, and more peace and order for the "laboring classes." With the help of a local Republican boss, he won the nomination for the state legislature from a district that included the working-class town of Lynn as well as his summer residence of Nahant.

Unlike Roosevelt, he did not immediately impress political observers. As a former independent and a Brahmin he was suspect as to both his party loyalty and his concern for common people. He was not a prepossessing campaigner, with his la-di-da airs and rasping voice. Senator Hoar called him "the worst stump speaker on this planet." A friend attending his campaign addresses remarked on the necessity of getting there early to be sure of a seat in the back row. But he had assets that assured his success. He was dogged in his efforts and undeterred by failure. Like Roosevelt and unlike Root, he was not squeamish about getting his hands dirty in the muck of politics.

Lodge was elected in 1879 for a one-year term to the lower house of the Massachusetts legislature, reelected a year later, and defeated in 1881 in the election for state senator. In 1882 he tried and failed to win the Republican nomination for the U.S. Congress. In 1884 he won it but lost the election. Undismayed by these Lincolnesque setbacks, he made himself useful to the party. In 1880 he had been chosen secretary of the Massachusetts delegation to the Republican National Convention, where he helped steer his state away from nominating Grant or Blaine, both of whom he despised for corruption, and toward Garfield, the eventual nominee. In 1883 he became chairman of the Republican State Central Committee, and engineered the defeat of a corrupt but popular Democratic governor, Benjamin F. Butler. He did it by meticulous planning, scrupulous attention to detail, and intensive vote canvassing, a harbinger of his legendary skills as a U.S. senator.

He led the Massachusetts delegation to the fateful Republican convention in 1884 in Chicago, where the front-runners were President Arthur and James G. Blaine. It was there that Lodge probably met for the first time Elihu Root, who was in Arthur's campaign brain trust. Lodge opposed both candidates but considered Blaine the more dangerous for his lack of morality, which had recently been portrayed fictionally in Henry Adams's *Democracy*, and for his disdain for reform.

Lodge found a kindred spirit in a young New York politician, Theodore Roosevelt, who had been a Harvard undergraduate while Lodge was teaching there but had missed, or been warned off, his American history course. The two had met casually through the years at the Porcellian Club and in Boston. Now Lodge suggested that they get together to promote a stop Blaine movement. The two convened at Roosevelt's house in New York, then visited Washington before heading for Chicago. Their lobbying activities at the convention were the butt of much ridicule because of their aristocratic accents, their dandified clothes, and their habit, as one reporter put it, of applauding "with the tips of their fingers, held immediately in front of their noses." This rare pair did manage to block Blaine's candidate for temporary convention chairman and insert their own choice, a black delegate from Mississippi. But they failed to stop Blaine, who was nominated on the fourth ballot.

This setback confronted Lodge and Roosevelt with a dilemma: Should they support the Republican ticket with the detested Blaine at its head? Both decided to hold their noses and stay with the party. Lodge summed up his anguish and his reasons: "It was the bitterest thing I ever had to do in my life. To bolt would have been the easiest thing in the world and the pleasantest, but in my eyes it was dishonorable. I . . . stood by the party. As a delegate I felt in honor bound to do so because if I had announced that I could not support Blaine I should never have been chosen a delegate. The pledge was tacit but distinct. Again, I was chairman of the State Committee, captain of the ship, trusted by the party & I could not in honor desert."

He also had a less high-minded motive for his loyalty to the party: He wanted to be a Republican candidate for the U.S. Congress. He was rewarded with the nomination three months later. Roosevelt's similar decision was less motivated by personal ambition and more fateful: Had he broken with the party in 1884, his eventual path to the presidency might well have been blocked. But both paid a heavy price for supporting Blaine, for they earned the enmity of the Republican reformers who had been their natural allies. From New York E. L. Godkin, editor of the *Nation*, launched scornful telegrams at Lodge. Friends in Boston, like the anticorruption lawyer Moorfield Storey and President Eliot of Harvard, turned on him. Eliot later called Lodge and Roosevelt "degenerated sons of Harvard" and blocked Lodge's election as president of the Massachusetts Historical Society.

Carl Schurz, conveniently forgetting that eight years earlier he had done exactly what Lodge did, begged him to abandon his fellowship with "the ordinary party politicians" and leave the party: "The more you try to satisfy them the less you will satisfy yourself." Lodge wrote Schurz a haughty reply: "Whatever the result of the elections, the parties will remain. By staying in the party I can be of use. By going out I destroy all the influence for power and good I may possess. . . . If I am to be banned because I vote according to what I believe . . . I will fight against such treatment with all my strength."

The split between Lodge and his erstwhile friends is important for two reasons. Many reform Republicans went on to support Cleveland against Blaine in the 1884 election, creating the Mugwumps, reformist renegades from the Republican party. Abandonment of the Republican party by the Massachusetts Mugwumps accounted for Lodge's narrow defeat in his run for Congress. A decade later the Mugwumps, still putting principle over party, became implacable foes of the American imperialism that Lodge was to champion. The very people who had broken with him over the Blaine nomination, Schurz, Storey, Eliot, and Godkin among them, later chastised him for advocating a foreign policy of expansion.

The second reason has to do with Lodge's political and spiritual development. In a reflective moment in 1890 he described it as sacrificing idealism for political reality. He had thought an independent party could be created but learned that "things political are only to be brought about by cooperation, or in other words, by organized parties where you act together because you agree in the main and submit to much that you do not like in order to advance larger principles of greater importance. Since I gave up trying to make a rope of sand, an independent party composed exclusively of good men, I have been in the school of party politics."

The 1884 experience caused him to distrust the more reformist elements in his party and to move toward its conservative center. The contradiction he had lived through in Chicago between party and principle convinced him to use his considerable organizational skills in the party's interest, sometimes at the expense of reformist policies. He lost the 1884 election, but he was never to lose another one. Using machine methods, he built a formidable party organization in Massachusetts. He abandoned the "rope of sand" for tighter and tougher bonds. Hardened by political defeats and, as he saw it, the betrayal of friends, he became narrower, more partisan, more combative, more closed, and more conspiratorial. The innocent idealism of his youth was dimming and dying.

4.

During the horrendous campaign of 1884, with Lodge running a losing battle for Congress, having to support the albatross Blaine, and undergoing attacks from friends and clubmates, his mother told a friend: "Only God and his mother know what that poor boy suffers." In fact there was one other person who knew—Theodore Roosevelt— because he was suffering the same thing. The ordeal of 1884 brought Lodge and Roosevelt very close; indeed it was the catalyst for one of the most extraordinary friendships in American history. Both men had a patrician heritage and were conscious of it, enjoying its perquisites and accepting its obligations. Though growing up in different cities, they had class, Harvard, and Porcellian in common. They both had lost revered fathers early in life, Lodge at twelve, Roosevelt at nineteen. They were aristocratic mavericks in the ungentlemanly game of politics. They also shared a commitment to honest government, the issue that brought them together to oppose Blaine.

There were more personal factors as well. When the two began their collaboration to stop Blaine, Roosevelt had lost his young wife just three months earlier; she was twenty-two, he twenty-five. He needed a cause and a friend. For Lodge, less needy, there was the thrill of embarking on a dangerous political course with a doughty companion. They were bound to annoy either the independent wing or the orthodox middle of the Republican party; in the end they annoyed both. At the Chicago convention regular Republicans accused them of having ice water in their veins and made a point of turning up their coat collars and shivering when Lodge went by. The independents, for their part, took their revenge on Lodge in the November congressional election. The exhilaration of venturing something dangerous, and failing at it, cemented a relationship that was in any case a natural one.

Still, it is remarkable how fast that relationship developed. Roosevelt, having put up Lodge in New York before the convention, visited him in Nahant after a postconvention trip to his Dakota ranch. He returned to Boston in October to campaign for Lodge. His new friend gave a twenty-sixth birthday dinner for him, convoking William Dean Howells, Thomas Bailey Aldrich, Oliver Wendell Holmes, and no Mugwumps. Roosevelt drew on the Chicago experience to tell the voters of Massachusetts that they had a candidate who was respected by "all our fellow-Republicans" and was "considered to be a representative American all over the country." The escalating warmth in their correspondence marked the growing bond between them. Roosevelt's letters began with the formal "My dear Lodge" until he wrote Lodge to console him after his election loss in 1884. Then it was "Dear Cabot," and soon it became "Dear old Cabot."

The friendship was not strictly equal. Lodge, eight years older, quickly became an adviser and even a mentor to the younger and more headstrong Roosevelt. Indeed he spent much of his life fending off charges that he exerted a malevolent influence over Roosevelt. The charges began early, just after their collaboration against Blaine, when Lodge was accused of using "my evil and unfortunate influence" to prevent Roosevelt from bolting the Republican ticket. Lodge denied the charge convincingly, but his example in staying with the party probably did influence Roosevelt, making Lodge the savior of his new friend's political career.

With his election to Congress in 1886, Lodge's political career finally took on a steady upward trajectory. He was reelected in 1888 and 1890, then elected (by the Massachusetts legislature) to the U.S. Senate in 1892, where he remained for more than thirty years. His ambition never rose beyond the Senate; he never considered himself presidential timber, nor did he covet a cabinet position. Yet he was passionately interested in the political career of Theodore Roosevelt. Like many others, he saw Roosevelt early on as a potential president, but unlike others, he was in a position to help him win the presidency.

Lodge could see that Roosevelt was trying to overcome his grief at the death of his young wife with bursts of activity even above his phenomenal energy level. His exertions at the Chicago convention proved it, as did his three trips west just after, when he shot everything in sight, knocked a bully senseless, tangled with a rival landowner, wrote a memorial volume to his dead wife and most of a book about the West, and still found time to come east to campaign for Lodge and the presidential ticket. In his binges of hyperactivity Roosevelt needed new fields of endeavor; indeed he needed to choose a profession or two. Lodge, three of whose biographies had appeared in the Federalist-inclined "American Statesmen" series, persuaded the editor that Roosevelt had the requisite political orientation and writing skills to produce some volumes.

The first was to be a biography of the Missouri senator Thomas Hart Benton, an advocate of western exploration and settlement and an idol of Roosevelt's. At work on the book at his ranch in the spring of 1886, Roosevelt wrote Lodge with an embarrassed but comic request:

> I have pretty nearly finished Benton, mainly evolving him from my inner consciousness; but when he leaves the Senate in 1850 I have nothing whatever to go by; and, being by nature a timid and, on occasions, by choice a truthful man, I would prefer to have some foundation of fact, no matter how slender, on which to build the airy and arabesque superstructure of my fancy—especially as I am writing a history. Now I hesitate to give him a wholly fictitious date of death and to invent all the work of his later years. Would it be too infernal a nuisance for you to hire some one on the *Advertiser* . . . (of course at my expense) to look up, in a biographical dictionary or elsewhere, his life after he left the Senate in 1850?

Lodge did help his careless friend, though he also suggested that Roosevelt check his facts in a library when he returned east. The two remained in close contact, encouraging and supporting each other. Roosevelt constituted a Lodge fan club, praising his friend's historical writings and encouraging him to run for the Senate. From the ranch he asked another favor of Lodge: to alert him if war with Mexico was imminent. He wanted to raise a company of horse riflemen "among these harum-scarum roughriders out here," a harbinger of his response to the war with Cuba twelve years later. Right after Roosevelt's defeat in the race for mayor of New York in 1886, Lodge, who had just been elected to Congress, rushed to New York to console his friend and see him off to London.

Lodge made sure that Roosevelt's career was heading in the right direction. He helped him get another writing assignment, this time a biography of Gouverneur Morris, the Federalist politician and diplomat in the early days of the Republic. Moreover, when the Republicans regained the White House in the election of 1888, Lodge urged the Harrison administration to appoint Roosevelt assistant secretary of state. The effort failed, probably because the new secretary of state was none other than James G. Blaine. Nannie Lodge made a fruitless effort to persuade Blaine. This was a case of life imitating art: Henry Adams's novel *Democracy* turns on the relationship between a Blaine-like senator and a beautiful society hostess. Still, thanks to Lodge, Roosevelt did get the relatively minor position of civil service commissioner.

Roosevelt dined with Lodge in his first week in Washington. With both now living in the capital city, their friendship deepened. The Roosevelts took Christmas dinner at the Lodges' five years in a row and saw them often at Henry Adams's breakfast gatherings, where John Hay was also a frequent guest. When their wives fled Washington's summer heat—Nannie to Nahant, Edith to Oyster Bay—the two were inseparable. In the summer of 1893 Roosevelt wrote his sister Corinne: "For the last fortnight, I have virtually been living with Cabot, for I take all my meals at his house, though I sleep at my own." At breakfast they spent an hour "in gloomy discussion over the folly of the Mug-wumps and the wickedness of the Democrats." They often dined alone as well. They found time to collaborate on *Hero Tales*. During this period Lodge dedicated his first book of speeches to Roosevelt, with the graceful inscription "To my friend Theodore Roosevelt, in token of personal affection, and of admiration for his work as a historian and for his services as a public man."

Corinne Roosevelt, whose uncritical devotion to her older brother made her memoir of him a mirror of his views, adored Lodge, whom she called a "brilliant scholar and statesman." Roosevelt himself was hardly less effusive. In a memorandum during his second term as president, he wrote:

From [the 1884 Republican convention] he was my closest friend, personally, politically, and in every other way, and occupied toward me a relation that no other man has ever occupied or ever will occupy. We have not always agreed, but our subjects of disagreement have been of but little weight compared to the matters upon which we did agree. For the past twenty-four years I have discust [*sic*] almost every move I have made in politics with him, provided he was at hand and it was possible for me to discuss it; and as regards many matters of policy and appointment, it would be quite impossible for me now to say whether it was he or I who first suggested the appointment I made or the course that I followed.

If Lodge exercised a Svengali-like influence over Roosevelt, as his detractors charged, it was less over issues than over the advancement of Roosevelt's political career. Lodge became increasingly convinced that his friend ought to be in the White House and planned to get him there with a determination of which even Roosevelt himself was incapable. Roosevelt's rise began in 1895, when he was offered the position of police commissioner, one of four in a reform administration in New York City. He was not sure he wanted to take it. But Lodge was, and with Roosevelt's acceptance and proxy in his pocket he went to New York to negotiate terms.

Roosevelt had not been at the police department six months when Lodge was urging another career move. From a vacation in Europe he advised Roosevelt to make a bid for the U.S. Senate. Roosevelt was a habitual pessimist about his future, and Lodge came on like a Dutch uncle: "I can judge of your standing and reputation better than you. . . . You will pardon all this advice but I am sure I am right as I was about your taking this place [at the police department]. My intense interest and belief in you do not mislead me, but the underestimate you always make of your own political position and weight may mislead you." Lodge did not hide his ultimate objective: "I do not say you are to be President tomorrow. I do not say it will be—I am sure that it may and can be."

He told his friend: "If you were like most men, I should not repeat these things to you but you so underrate your political strength that I fear you will neglect to use it and so miss the opportunity which will give you a big place in national politics." The imagination boggles at the picture of Theodore Roosevelt as a shrinking violet. But Lodge understood Roosevelt. His advice, at critical moments in Roosevelt's life, undoubtedly drove the younger man higher than he would have gone on his own more tentative self-evaluation. The return of a Republican to the White House in 1897, when McKinley succeeded Cleveland, began the fantastic series of events that were to make Roosevelt assistant secretary of the navy, army colonel and war hero, governor of New York, vice president, and president—all in less than five years.

When McKinley won the presidency in 1896, Lodge unlimbered all his weaponry to get Roosevelt a big job in Washington. Lodge and McKinley had had adjoining desks in the House of Representatives and had come to like each other. As a political strategist Lodge had some influence with the new president, even though he had backed House Speaker Thomas B. Reed against him for the Republican nomination. Lodge traveled to McKinley's home in Canton, Ohio, where the president-elect was reviewing appointments, to plead the case for Roosevelt as assistant secretary of the navy. At the end of the conversation he asked McKinley to appoint Roosevelt as the "one personal favor" he would ask. McKinley, dubious about Roosevelt's hotheadedness, delayed his decision.

Lodge also worked to reassure the newly appointed secretary of the navy, John D. Long, an aging ex-governor of Lodge's home state of Massachusetts. Long liked Roosevelt but wondered if the job might not be too small for a young man of his ambition. Lodge talked up Roosevelt to Mark Hanna, McKinley's closest political ally, and others in Hanna's coterie. He also successfully lobbied Roosevelt's New York political nemesis, the Republican machine boss Thomas C. Platt. When Roosevelt got to Washington, he persuaded the Metropolitan Club to remove the blackball against Platt's application for membership.

Given McKinley's hesitation and Platt's ill will, Lodge did a brilliant selling job for Roosevelt. In a letter to his protégé he disclaimed any generosity: "You will be kind enough to remember that in all I have done, I have been doing for myself and what I particularly want and that your interests are wholly secondary!" In a sense he was right. He saw in Roosevelt the battering ram he needed to achieve a powerful navy and a muscular policy of expansion. But his affection went far beyond those areas. He admired Roosevelt as a civil service and police reformer, as a historian and intellectual, as a man of courage and conviction, and as a person of such warmth that he could melt the frosty exterior with which Lodge shielded himself from normal emotions.

Thus there was a large measure of altruism in Lodge's activity on behalf of his friend. Roosevelt certainly thought so. He wrote that he would not try to express his gratitude, "for I don't suppose that between you and me it is necessary for me to say what I feel. . . . The main reason why I would care to go to Washington is to be near you." In later letters he said he felt ashamed when he thought of all Lodge was doing for him and even felt "a little like bawling." It took Lodge four months of hard lobbying to win the Navy Department position for Roosevelt. McKinley was already in office when Roosevelt cabled Lodge on April 6, 1897: "Sinbad has evidently landed the old man of the sea." The job was Roosevelt's first big break; it led to everything else. Without Lodge's efforts he would have had little chance for it.

In the Senate and outside it Henry Cabot Lodge had few friends and many enemies. One of his colleagues in the Senate compared him with the soil of Massachusetts: "highly cultivated but very thin." Most found him cold; many found him bigoted; some found him ruthless. In his relationship with Roosevelt, however, he displayed the best that was in him. To the younger and more brilliant man, he was unfailingly solicitous, sensitive, and selfless. The warmth he could not show his friends or even his wife he bestowed generously on Roosevelt. As Roosevelt clearly recognized, he owed his political successes to Lodge more than anyone else.

5.

Lodge spent thirty-seven years in Washington, D.C., starting as a thirty-six-year-old representative and ending as a venerable senator and slayer of the League of Nations. When he arrived in 1887, Henry Adams had been there for a decade and John Hay often made the trip from what Clover Adams had called "the fleshpots of Cleveland" to his grandiose new house on Lafayette Square. Roosevelt was to arrive in 1889.

Washington was still a muddy southern town, with none of the intellectual distinction of Boston or the showy richness of New York. Mark Twain found the city "a wide stretch of cheap little brick houses, with here and there a noble architectural pile lifting itself out of the midst." He loved the Capitol building, "a long snowy palace projecting above a grove of trees, and a tall, graceful white dome with a statue on it surmounting the palace and pleasantly contrasting with the background of blue sky." But the White House appalled him. "Beyond the Treasury is a fine large white barn, with wide unhandsome grounds about it. The President lives there. It is ugly enough outside, but that is nothing to what it is inside. Dreariness, flimsiness, bad taste reduced to mathematical completeness is [*sic*] what the inside offers to the eye."

The population of Washington when the Lodges arrived was about two hundred thousand, a third of it black. To affluent whites it was an invisible third. Few black Americans were lucky enough to achieve any of the twenty-three thousand federal jobs. They were banned from restaurants and ice-cream parlors, though not from saloons. Many worked in service trades, especially as caterers to guests in Washington's numerous boardinghouses. In an isolated case, one of Washington's most comfortable hotels, Wormley's at the corner of Fifteenth and H streets, was owned and managed by a black entrepreneur. The city's newspapers, like the *Post* and the *Star*, ignored black Washington to such an extent that their readers might well have thought the city completely white. Adams, Lodge, Hay, and Roosevelt—all staunch defenders of Lincoln's legacy toward black Americans—had little contact with real blacks in one of the country's most populous black cities. It would be interesting to know if John Hay's generous gift of train fare from New York to Washington to an indigent black was the closest contact he was to have.

By New York standards Washington was neither affluent nor fashionable. Mark Twain considered it inferior to St. Louis. There were no Morgans, Rockefellers, or Carnegies. Most houses lacked sewer connections; where there were sewers, mainly in the northwest quadrant, they emptied into and polluted Rock Creek, the border between Georgetown and the rest of Washington. The city's unelected administration did make efforts to beautify Washington for its large convention and tourist trade. The city fathers decreed the planting of sixty-five thousand trees, giving the capital a leafy character it still retains. A patented twig brush, pulled by horses, cleaned the streets daily. There were other touches of modernity. In 1876 the first commercial asphalt pavement in the United States was laid on Pennsylvania Avenue, already a parade route.

Architecturally the city was a major attraction, with imposing marble government buildings settling into Pierre L'Enfant's vistas. To add to the majesty, the Washington Monument was officially opened in 1885 to cascades of fireworks. Not all the buildings won favor; Adams unfairly referred to the gaudy, Second Empire State, War, and Navy Building next to the White House as an "architectural infant asylum." But he loved the natural setting of Washington, especially the woods ("Such a place for wild flowers I never saw") and the Potomac ("I know of no other capital in the world which stands on so wide and splendid a river").

Toward the end of the century the woodland dividing Georgetown from downtown was established and funded as Rock Creek Park, a favorite spot for walks, rides, and picnics. Roosevelt, who got most of his exercise hiking along Rock Creek, called it "as wild as a stream in the White Mountains." For the adventurous, excursions were common to the Great Falls of the Potomac, fifteen miles west of the city.

Creature comforts were inconsistent. In contrast with the dazzling variety of New York department stores, shoppers had to choose between Saks or Woodward and Lothrop's. As one shopper complained, Washington was not "a brag shopping place." Popular restaurants included Willard's Hotel, where Lincoln spent his first Washington night after his election as president; the Ebbitt House; Harvey's Fish House; and Hall's, which displayed a huge nude Venus over the bar. The prevalence of boardinghouses testified to the transient nature of Washington; while they were building their adjoining houses, Hay and Adams found Wormley's up to their fastidious standards.

The Corcoran School of Art was founded in 1888. But there was no public concert hall, and traveling opera companies limited their spectacles to a fortnight. Music lovers, unless they liked the outdoor band concerts of John Philip Sousa, were better off going to New York. African American music, especially choral music, was arguably of higher quality than any white music in the city. Washington was a literary wasteland; no great poet or novelist lived there. Adams, Hay, Lodge, and Roosevelt were actually among the most prominent local writers at the end of the century, vying for distinction with the likes of Frances Hodgson Burnett, author of *Little Lord Fauntleroy*.

Yet Washington had an indolent charm, even for foreign visitors. One Englishman remarked: "Compared with New York or Chicago, Washington, although it is full of commotion and energy, is a city of rest and peace. The inhabitants do not rush onward as though they were late for the train or the post, or as though the dinner hour being past they were anxious to appease an irritable wife." Another described the city's air "of comfort, of leisure, of space to spare, of stateliness you hardly expected in America. It looks a sort of place where nobody has to work for his living, or, at any rate, not hard." Charles Dickens had a less approving view; he called it "the city of magnificent intentions."

Washington society was almost by definition new, in contrast with the old families of Philadelphia, Boston, or New York. The first *Social Register*, published in 1900, listed twenty-one hundred families. Eight hundred and twenty of them were transients—army and navy officers, senior government officials, members of Congress, foreign diplomats, and people listed in one of the other five *Social Registers* who were temporarily in Washington. Families like the Adamses, the Lodges, and the Roosevelts raised Washington's social standing simply by moving there. "As there are so few cultivated people here," said Adams, "one's social value is out of all proportion to what it would be in London." Mark Twain, in his satire *The Gilded Age*, divided Washington's nobility into two categories:

> One of [the aristocracies] (nicknamed the Antiques) consisted of cultivated, high-bred old families who looked back with pride upon an ancestry that had been always great in the nation's councils and its wars from the birth of the republic downward. Into this select circle it was difficult to gain admission. . . . We will call [a second aristocracy] the Aristocracy of the Parvenus—as, indeed, the general public did. Official position, no matter how obtained, entitled a man to a place in it, and carried his family with him, no matter whence they sprang. Great wealth gave a man a still higher and nobler place in it than did official position.

Henry Adams's wife had been a quintessential Antique. Clover Adams had inherited a fine pedigree—her father was a wealthy, old Bostonian physician—and had married into an even finer one. Before her death in 1885, she set the city's social standard. Invitations to her almost daily small dinners of six or eight were greatly sought after, but few Washingtonians met her criteria. She disliked politicians, except for a few like Cabot Lodge and the bibulous Senator J. Donald

Cameron of Pennsylvania, whom she nevertheless derisively referred to as "the great Don." She ridiculed the ban decreed by President Hayes's wife on wine at the White House, where, as one politician complained, "the water flowed like champagne." Clover was not the first to call Mrs. Hayes Lemonade Lucy, but she did complain of getting sick "gorging on Potomac." She succumbed only grudgingly to John Hay's efforts to get her and Henry to call on Hayes's successor, the newly installed President Garfield from Ohio.

Clover's sharp eye and sharper pen inspired Henry James to call her "a Voltaire in petticoats." She produced a memorable picture of Washington society near the end of the century. An accomplished photographer, she provided some vivid verbal snapshots in her letters to her adored father, whom she addressed as "Dearest Pater." Clover Adams detested the ambition of political Washington: "The craving for the meanest kind of official existence is so intense as to form a division of lunacy by itself." She hated any politician tinged by corruption, like "that beast Conkling." James G. Blaine was never invited; Clover worried obsessively that her friend John Hay seemed to like "the rat." She detested flamboyance and warned Henry James not to bring that "vulgar cad" Oscar Wilde around. "I must keep out thieves and noodles or else take down my sign and go West."

Despite their refined natures, both Adamses preferred Washington to their native Boston. Henry wrote that it would be a very great city "if nothing happens to it." They enjoyed its earthiness. He described it as "the drollest place in Christian lands. Such a thin veil of varnish over so very rough a material." It was for him "a monkey-show . . . but like other monkey shows it is amusing." For her it was like a "prolonged circus." Her description of one of Henry James's visits to America from London said something about Washington and herself: "I think the real, live, vulgar, quick-paced world in America will fret him and that he prefers a quiet corner with a pen where he can create men and women who say neat things and have refined tastes and are not nasal or eccentric." On another occasion she wrote that she was having difficulty with the effete writing in *Portrait of a Lady,* that she preferred "the big bow-wow style." Washington, unlike the Adamses' Boston or James's London, was a "big bow-wow" city. As Clover put it, "A man's house is not his castle here but the public's bear garden."

The Antiques usually chose areas near the White House for their residences. The Adamses lived successively in two adjoining houses on Lafayette Square, with a view of the White House. Hay, who was not born an Antique, built right next to Adams. Lodge's house, at Massachusetts and Seventeenth, was a few blocks north. The male Antiques shuffled between club and home. The Cosmos Club had been founded in 1878 by scientists and literati, with Henry Adams as a founding member. Roosevelt, given associate member status because of his senior government position, used it frequently.

The Metropolitan, an older club, had opened in 1863; Hay and Nicolay were charter members. At Seventeenth and H streets, a stone's throw from the State, War, and Navy departments, the club attracted military officers, officials, and diplomats. By the 1890s it was boasting a who's who of budding American imperialists: civilian officials like Lodge, Roosevelt, Root, and Senator Cameron; naval activists like Commodores Dewey and Schley and Captain Robley Evans, all three of whom were to receive senior commands in the Spanish-American War; Mahan and his mentor Captain Stephen B. Luce; Colonel Leonard Wood, who was to command the Rough Riders in Cuba; and General Arthur MacArthur, destined to be military commander of the Philippines. Presidents and vice presidents of the United States were automatically honorary members, and chiefs of the major diplomatic missions were invited as well. So highly was club membership valued that in 1907, when Root was elected its president, he served out his term, even though he was secretary of state and later U.S. senator concurrently.

With little public entertainment in Washington, the Antiques enjoyed literary evenings and an occasional ball (Nannie Lodge loved balls), but mostly they entertained one another in their homes. Here the premium was on good conversation. According to Henry James, Washington was a "city of conversation." A period manual on the etiquette of social life in Washington decreed pompously: "No dinner, however superb in prandial show, can be agreeable if the *convives* are dullards. . . . No sordid computation of dollars can buy or measure the Promethean light of conversational effect."

The Adams table, which would certainly not have included the author of the words above, was considered the pinnacle of good conversation. Both Lodge and Clover Adams judged the best talkers to be John Hay and William M. Evarts, Hayes's secretary of state. After

Clover's suicide Henry stopped giving dinner parties, but his late-morning breakfasts became equally famous. When the Lodges arrived in Washington, Adams, a local fixture for a decade, a widower for a year, was eager to take them in and introduce them to the people who counted.

Over the years Adams had kept in touch with his erstwhile student, assistant editor, and protégé. At the outset of the relationship his correspondence with Lodge had reflected a schoolmasterly chiding, usually at Lodge's turgid writing style, accompanied by self-justification: "You will one day feel the advantage of my not having spoiled you by flattery." When Lodge was elected to the Massachusetts legislature, Adams had offered a little snobbish advice: "Social influence counts for whatever one chooses to make it. If you can make friends of the most influential members, including the Speaker, if you can occasionally bring one home to a family dinner, or to a talk in your library; if you can, in short, make yourself important or agreeable to the leaders, you will next year be in a position to claim a good committee and be a leader yourself." Adams also showed appreciation for Lodge's fidelity to their friendship: "I am much touched by your loyalty to your venerable Professor."

Hay, already a part of Adams's intellectually rarified Washington world, also befriended Lodge on his arrival, though he never found him amusing. In 1896 the two were close enough for Lodge to recommend Hay to McKinley as a possible secretary of state. However, following McKinley's reelection four years later, when Hay had actually been secretary of state for two years, Lodge conspicuously omitted to mention him to the president, proposing Root instead. Perhaps Lodge had found out about Hay's affair with his wife. In any case it had become clear that the temperaments of these two were not congruent. Hay found Lodge pompous, arrogant, and insensitive. Lodge saw Hay as lazy, weak, and something of a lightweight. The differences were reflected in their appearances: Lodge tall and rigid, Hay short and increasingly stout. Lodge once expressed to Henry Adams the "earnest wish" that "Hay would not look so exceedingly tired when approached on business." The bulldozer was encountering the embroidered pillow.

Despite his difficult personality, the Lodges were adornments to the social scene in Washington; they dined out, or entertained, four or five times a week. This popularity was due to Lodge's own background and ability (a combination of Antique and Parvenu traits), to Adams's patronage, and to Nannie Lodge's charm. Nannie combined classical good looks—stunning blue eyes, pure skin, and a small frame enhanced by perfect carriage—with wit, intelligence, a generous nature, and what Corinne Roosevelt called a "fascination possessed by no other." She seems to have been admired by all who knew her. Lord Bryce, the British diplomat, said of her: "She was one of those rare personalities in whom strength and elevation of character were united with sweetness, gentleness and a wonderful grace of manner." Henry Adams called her a dispenser of sunshine over Washington. Even Theodore Roosevelt, not the most perceptive of men when it came to women, remarked that Nannie "looked as queens ought to look, but as no queen I have ever seen does look."

When Nannie stepped out clandestinely with Hay, members of their set, including Adams himself, conspired to keep the liaison from Lodge, a clear sign of where their sympathies lay. After the Roosevelts arrived in Washington in 1889, Adams, the universal social catalyst, could exult, without reference to Hay's affair with Nannie Lodge or indeed to his own with Senator Cameron's wife, Lizzie: "Our little family of Hays, Lodges, Camerons, and Roosevelts has been absolutely devoted to each other."

6.

By the eve of the Spanish-American War Cabot Lodge had acquired the political traits that were to carry him through the rest of his career. He was not easy to type as either a liberal or a conservative. He was serious about upholding Lincoln's legacy of protecting the rights of black Americans. He consistently supported reform of the civil service, and he worked to make the consular service more professional and less political. Unlike many Republicans, he was not in the pocket of big business, perhaps because of his patrician disdain for new money. On the other hand, he opposed the traditional pattern of unrestricted immigration except for northern Europeans, a group in which he included the Irish, who formed such an important voting bloc in Massachusetts. He was a trade and fiscal conservative, favoring high tariffs and sound money backed by gold rather than silver.

Probably the key to Lodge's electoral success lay less in these general policies than in his scrupulous concern for the issues of his own state. He assiduously fought for Massachusetts products against foreign imports, for increased work for the Charlestown Navy Yard, and for the rights of the state's large fishing fleet. On the floor of the House and Senate, Lodge waxed rhapsodic about the Gloucester fishermen, urging the protection of their security against foreign intimidation on the high seas. Root called him "the senior senator from the fishing grounds."

Lodge's imperialism, which had become his greatest cause by the mid-1890s, owed little to his native Boston, where the home of Charles Sumner's antislavery crusades was to become the center of a passionate anti-imperial movement. In Boston opposition to slavery, America's homegrown colonial problem, had translated into opposition to colonialism overseas. But not for Lodge, for whom an antislavery position did not mean anti-imperialism. His own sense of superiority, reinforced by social Darwinism, made him a natural candidate for the imperialist philosophy, though he avoided using the word "imperialism," preferring "expansion."

More profoundly, his imperialism had twin roots in romanticism and technology. Lodge had a romantic belief in America's destiny, which he saw foreshadowed by the great figures of its past, like his biographical subjects Washington, Hamilton, and Webster, as well as the giants of *Hero Tales*. He believed in the importance of individuals in history: "The personal qualities and individual abilities of public men . . . make the history and determine the fate of nations." Nations have lives of their own. "We are a great nation and intend to take a nation's part in the family of nations," he said in a speech in 1896.

At the same time Lodge knew that a revolution in technology was gathering force beneath the surface of human activity. In a remarkable passage in his memoirs, published in 1913, he claimed that the "human environment has altered more in the last seventy years, since the first application of steam and electricity to transportation and communication, than it had in two thousand or, indeed, in six thousand years previously. . . . Moreover, since the first application of steam and electricity the revolution in the conditions of human existence has gone forward with constantly accelerating force and rapidity." He identified as elements of this technological revolution fast trains, sleeping and parlor cars, huge steamships, local transportation like street railways, telephones, wireless telegraphy, electric lighting, and motorcars. He noted that the men and women born between 1830 and 1870—Hay, Mahan, Root, Roosevelt, and Lodge himself all fell into that time frame—were personally affected by "these bewildering metamorphoses," which had radically changed the human environment and the conditions of life and had produced extraordinary financial and other material riches.

The attraction of a heroic past and the deterministic pull of the technological revolution combined to produce Lodge's view of America's imperial destiny. The United States had a mission and, through technology and wealth, possessed the means to fulfill it. But the country had to be prepared. The United States had been forced into the War of 1812 by lack of readiness: "We learned that weak defencelessness meant war, and strong, armed readiness meant peace, honor, and quiet." He and Roosevelt wrote in *Hero Tales*: "The only peace worth having is obtained by instant readiness to fight when wronged." Preparedness meant a large navy, a natural objective for a man whose own, and whose wife's, families had maritime backgrounds. Lodge ridiculed those who proposed "to meet the encroachments of a foreign power by a diplomat on a ferryboat."

A second need was a military strategy, which he developed in his speeches of 1895. He spoke of a "large policy," which meant control of the Caribbean and parts of the Pacific; seizure of strategic islands like Cuba, Hawaii, and the Philippines; and even the incorporation of Canada. Lodge's large policy was greatly influenced by the writings of Mahan and later by personal contact. He considered Mahan "the greatest authority living or dead on naval warfare."

He did not become as close a friend of Mahan's as Roosevelt did. But the two men did have a personal connection through Captain Stephen B. Luce, Mahan's friend and patron, whose son married Nannie Lodge's sister. From the years leading up to the Spanish-American War well into Roosevelt's presidency, Roosevelt, Lodge, and Mahan worked closely as an imperial triumvirate, colluding on military strategy and political tactics. Mahan kept in touch by letters from his homes in New York City or Long Island. Roosevelt and Lodge met frequently in Washington, often over Roosevelt's favorite double lamb chops at the Metropolitan Club.

In the Senate Lodge was a brilliant parliamentary manager. His forte was meticulous attention to organization and detail. He managed the successful effort in 1889 to make Thomas B. Reed speaker of the House over William McKinley. He understood and preached the arts of compromise. He had written of Hamilton: "He knew that the first rule of successful and beneficial statesmanship was not to sulk because one cannot have just what one wants, but to take the best thing obtainable, and sustain it to the uttermost." He told Harvard students in a speech: "Where there is no moral question involved do not, by insisting on the unattainable, lose everything." At least one of his critics found this attitude a vice, not a virtue. President Eliot of Harvard called Lodge "a compromiser on moral questions" and "an opportunist politician."

Whatever Lodge may have preached about flexibility, none of his colleagues found him easy to deal with. Hanna called him to his face the stubbornest man he had ever met. Another observer said that his ideas "formed a museum of wax figures which were not to be touched." Hay saw him as "a clever man and a man of a great deal of force in the Senate, but the infirmity of his mind and character is that he never sees but one subject at a time." Adams wrote that his methods "exceed the endurance of a coral reef." Lodge had known many defeats in his early political career; they had made him tougher and more intransigent than adversaries who had enjoyed better fortune.

Unlike Roosevelt, who was an inveterate flatterer, Lodge did not much worry about the impression he made on people. Strongminded, haughty, aggressive, partisan, persistent, acid, combative, uncompromising, conspiratorial: All these adjectives were applied to Lodge by his opponents. Hay remarked that he enjoyed "the furious kicking of his enemies." Sometimes he would even disrupt the urbanity of Adams's dinner table with his arguing and pontificating. A friend of his noticed that he had "a trick, even among his friends, of so putting things as to excite, when you do not agree with him, instinctive resentment. . . . He gives stimulants when wiser practice would prefer sedatives." Margaret Chanler, a prominent Washington hostess, said that "in discussion he was one of those who care more for downing his adversary than for discovering some common ground for possible agreement."

Lodge's overweening self-confidence often expressed itself in vanity, insolence, and superciliousness. Even Henry Adams found him tiresome, complaining once of enduring an hour of "dreary Senatorial drivel" with him. Recalling a memorable trip to medieval Normandy with the Lodges, Adams wrote: "In the thirteenth century . . . even a senator became natural, simple, interested, cultivated, artistic, liberal,—genial." The implication was that normally Lodge was none of those things. Adams, Roosevelt, and Hay loved to make jokes at each other's expense. But they did not tease their friend Lodge; only Nannie dared do that. She called him Pinky, a put-down for his stuffiness as much as a term of affection. Only Roosevelt seemed oblivious of the darker side of Lodge's character. To him Lodge was just "a delightful, big-boyish personage."

The best portrait of Lodge was never painted. Owen Wister, Roosevelt's novelist friend, tried to imagine how John Singleton Copley, the great American portraitist of the late eighteenth century, would have depicted Lodge: "It is unmitigated Boston that you see recorded; the eye of a robust, stiff-necked race of seventeenth and eighteenth century dissenters, with its plain living, high thinking, dauntless intolerance, bleak bad manners, suppression of feeling, tenacity in its stern beliefs, and its cantankerousness, stares down at you with cold disapprobation."

The supreme irony of Lodge's "dauntless intolerance" was that it pulled in opposite directions. The intolerant part of Lodge wanted to keep his world pretty much the way it was. He was opposed to constitutional changes, significant immigration, and the rise of labor. At the end of his career he fought a savage battle to keep the United States out of a league of nations that he feared would erode his country's sovereignty. At the same time he was a dauntless and consistent believer in expanding American power worldwide, through the creation of a strong military, through an aggressive diplomacy, and through the acquisition of overseas territories. Nobody, not even Theodore Roosevelt himself, did more to establish the United States as one of the world's great powers. Thus Lodge, who stood for so many traditional and reactionary principles, became a principal animator of a genuine revolution in American foreign policy.

6. So Brilliant and Aggressive a Man

1.

John Hay, Alfred Mahan, Elihu Root, and Henry Cabot Lodge all had strong, even remarkable fathers: Hay's a country doctor who pushed his practice to the territorial frontier of the new nation, Mahan's and Root's revered educators, Lodge's a patrician businessman who counted as friends some of the foremost intellectuals in the country. Theodore Roosevelt's father, in his character and in his contributions to his city, country, and family, was even more impressive than they.

The elder Theodore Roosevelt never had to compete for wealth or social standing. His family had settled in New York City in the seventeenth century, and his father, Cornelius, was one of the city's few millionaires. Cornelius expanded the family hardware business to plate glass imports and, more lucratively, to real estate, exploiting the mid-century construction boom in the city. After the financial panic of 1863 the firm moved to private banking and investment. As the youngest of five brothers Theodore senior would not have been expected to play a major role in Roosevelt and Son. In any case, business seems to have bored him, and he moved steadily toward what was to become his real life's work, philanthropy.

While in his thirties, Roosevelt helped found the Children's Aid Society to provide food, shelter, and moral sustenance to homeless boys, whose population in New York City was as much as twenty thousand by 1869. He regularly visited the Lower West Side, where gangs of boys gathered in the evening. To get them off the streets, he offered them religious instruction and access to a reading room, an industrial school, or a workshop.

Many of the waifs were newsboys, so Roosevelt on his own initiative founded a Newsboys' Lodging House with beds for a nickel. Every Sunday he taught a mission class in the morning and visited the Newsboys' Lodging House in the evening. The ultimate purpose of this welfare program was to return the boys to their parents or to re-settle them in the West. More than one hundred thousand were re-settled; years later, when the younger Roosevelt was president, the governor of Alaska told him that he had been one of those news-boys given a second chance. Roosevelt senior was also a cofounder of the New York Orthopedic Dispensary and Hospital, the Metropolitan Museum of Art, and the American Museum of Natural History. He had, as his friend John Hay put it, "maniacal benevolence."

The elder Roosevelt was a large, powerful man, with many of the attributes and experiences typical of his rarefied upbringing. He was educated privately. At nineteen he made the standard grand tour of Europe, where he was particularly sympathetic to the plight of Rus-sian prisoners he saw embarking for Siberia. He was fastidious about clothes, a trait his famous son inherited, and always dressed for din-ner. He belonged to the Union League and the Century clubs, as would young Theodore. His portrait shows a handsome but severe face; his son called it "leonine." He was a hands-on father with a strong sense of justice who refused to tolerate selfishness, cruelty, idleness, cowardice, or untruthfulness in his four children. "He was the only man," the younger Theodore wrote, "of whom I was ever re-ally afraid."

But he leavened his sternness with a love of fun and sport. He liked dancing, riding in Central Park, and driving a four-in-hand too fast. He was also devoted to his children—Anna, Theodore, Elliott, and Corinne—and they loved him back. In the family he was known as Greatheart, after the guide in *The Pilgrim's Progress* who slew four giants and a monster to enable the pilgrims to reach the Celestial Country. Among his many kindnesses was his habit of taking each child for a day in the country on her or his birthday.

Theodore senior was heroically attentive to his eldest child, his daughter Anna (nicknamed Bamie), whose back was hunched from a spinal disease that caused constant pain and required an uncomfort-able brace. He cared for her, entertained her, even took her on busi-ness trips to Washington. He was inspired by her plight to start the New York Orthopedic Hospital for the treatment of similar diseases.

On one occasion he demonstrated his brilliance as a fund-raiser by inviting to his house a large number of his affluent friends. When they arrived, they found arrayed on the dining table several indigent children who suffered, like Bamie, from spinal ailments. Next to them had been placed the steel braces that would be used in the new hospital. His small daughter Corinne, coached by her father, explained the value of the devices to the guests, who had thought they were attending a purely social reception. Thanks in part to Mrs. John Jacob Astor's highly vocal exclamations of sympathy and support, Roosevelt raised enough money on that one day to start the first hospital.

With his son Theodore, called Teedie, the elder Roosevelt was as solicitous as he was with Bamie. But his approach was different. The boy suffered from a debilitating asthma of the most serious and frightening kind. Without modern drugs to dilate his bronchial tubes Teedie was in danger of asphyxiation from the suffocating attacks, which usually struck in the middle of the night. They were often preceded by depression and always accompanied by panic. His parents treated the child with emetics and black coffee and made him smoke cigars in an effort to induce nicotine poisoning, which led to vomiting. They expended enormous loving energy on him. "One of my memories," he wrote, "is of my father walking up and down the room with me in his arms at night when I was a very small person, and of sitting up in bed gasping, with my father and mother trying to help me." The gruesome illness, and nearly as gruesome treatment, made Teedie weak and sickly, highly dependent on his mother and especially on his father.

Theodore senior somehow understood that the best treatment for Teedie's asthma was to make the boy self-reliant, responsible for his own future. He took him on hikes and climbs, pushing him to his limits. Teedie responded well. When he was eleven and suffering particularly acute asthma attacks, his father told him that he had a good mind but not a good body. To make the mind go as far as it should, "you must *make* your body." Theodore senior arranged for daily workouts at a gymnasium and set up a private gym in the Roosevelts' house. It took Teedie years to fill out and toughen his skinny body and pipestem legs, but he did it. His father's role was critical. The dreaded asthma had challenged Teedie at a young age; his father's compassion and determination helped him meet that challenge. In his autobiography Roosevelt called his father simply "the best man I ever knew."

Theodore and Corinne both noticed contradictions in their father's character. To Theodore he combined insistence on discipline "with great love and patience, and the most understanding sympathy and consideration." He was a beneficiary of wealth and privilege whose "heart filled with gentleness for those who needed help or protection, and with the possibility of much wrath against a bully or an oppressor." Corinne found it extraordinary that a man so full of tolerance and the milk of human kindness could be so single-minded and ruthless in the pursuit of his philanthropic objectives.

Teedie's mother, Martha Bulloch Roosevelt, known as Mittie, had less influence on him than his father, though she was every bit as solicitous about his asthma. A southern woman from Atlanta and noted for her beauty and hospitality, Mittie became one of the social leaders of New York. She was devoted to her children and affectionate to her husband, despite her lack of interest in his philanthropic endeavors. But she was also an odd woman and erratic in her behavior. She was habitually late for appointments, in fact could not be counted on to show up at all. She had an obsession about cleanliness, instructing her maid to run two successive baths, one for soaping and one for rinsing. When she said her prayers, a sheet was put on the floor so her knees would not touch the rug. From time to time she would go into a frenzy of housekeeping, driving herself to bed with exhaustion.

It was Mittie's Georgia family, rather than her character, that had the greatest effect on her husband and her son Theodore. The Civil War broke out when Theodore senior was twenty-nine and Teedie was two. As in the Vietnam War a century later, few members of the northern upper classes actually fought. It was accepted practice—especially in New York City, where businessmen were ambivalent about the war—for well-to-do men of fighting age to hire substitutes to join the Union army. Grover Cleveland, later to become president, did so without stigma; so did James G. Blaine.

None of the elder Theodore's four brothers went to war. But running from battle was not his style. There seems little doubt that being the man he was, he would have enlisted had he not had two brothers-in-law who were fighting for the Confederacy. James Bulloch, Mittie's half brother, became an admiral and built the Confederate warship *Alabama* in England; Mittie's younger brother Irvine served on it. The ship became a famous Confederate raider that sank fifty-eight merchant ships trading with the Union.

Before the firing on Fort Sumter, Theodore senior tried desperately to stave off a conflict that would divide his family. He joined other New York businessmen in antiwar petitions and demonstrations. After war broke out, he was wracked with conflicting responsibilities. He had to weigh his strong antislavery convictions against the damage his enlistment would do to his wife, all of whose sympathies were with the South. He decided to hire a substitute. Far from cowardice, it was an act of moral courage, made even more admirable by his activities during the war.

He devised a plan by which Union soldiers could send part of their pay home, instead of squandering it on drink, gambling, or the extortions of sutlers. His focus was on the soldiers' families, many of which were impoverished by the loss of income caused by the absence of their menfolk. He set out to win government support for the establishment of an allotment commission. Displaying a combination of compassion and brazenness that his son later emulated, he went right to the president of the United States. Lincoln's doorkeeper, young John Hay, was so impressed with Roosevelt's idea that he took him right to the president, who endorsed the plan on the spot.

The harder part was selling the scheme to the troops. He traveled on horseback, by train, and by boat from regiment to regiment. For two years he shuttled between Washington and the field, braving bad weather, train derailments, and illness to make a success of his initiative, now routine in the American armed forces. Magnificent as his achievement was, his conscience never let him rest. Bamie wrote much later that he "always afterward felt that he had done a very wrong thing in not having put every other feeling aside and joined the absolute fighting forces."

Another family member apparently felt the same way: Theodore's son. Teedie was a small child during the Civil War, but as an adult he never defended his father's decision not to fight. The passages in his autobiography that praise his father are blank on this episode. Corinne, who read her brother through the eyes of an adoring devotee, was convinced that all his life he felt the need to compensate for this single flaw in the life of a venerated father.

The younger Roosevelt lived most of his life in a period that knew no wars of significant duration between the American Civil War and World War I. It may have been understandable that ignorant of its horrors, he looked on war as romantic, ennobling, and purifying. Yet his constant exaltation of war was extreme even for a generation spared its experience. So also was his compulsion to participate. His eventual resolution to leave the Navy Department in 1898 to fight in Cuba, a decision considered mad by his family, friends, and superiors, was part of a lifelong obsession. When he was in his late twenties, he spoke of becoming personally involved in war against Mexico. Three decades later, during World War I, he was still at it, importuning President Wilson to give him, at nearly sixty, command of a division to fight in France. It is unlikely that Roosevelt would have been so pervid in pursuit of war, and his participation in it, had he not felt the need to absolve his father of cowardice. His near-hysterical warmongering over Cuba in the 1890s probably owed as much to filial guilt as to his views on American military strategy or political destiny.

2.

Much of Theodore's childhood was dominated by his asthma. In search of places he could breathe, his parents took him on frequent trips, including two summer visits to Europe. Except for a few months, his entire education before college was private. This was due more to his illness than to the mores of the upper class, but in any case, with no regular playmates, he was thrown on the considerable resources of a very close family. Bamie, though only three years older, was so matured by her spinal affliction that the younger children considered her a grown-up. Theodore, Elliott, and Corinne formed a tight trio, with Teedie clearly the ringleader.

Naturally inquisitive, Teedie had protean interests. Eclectically he read books that the young Cabot Lodge enjoyed too: Marryat's novels about the British Navy, Cooper's books about the sea and the frontier, Lewis Carroll, the Br'er Rabbit stories (recited and set down by Mittie long before Joel Chandler Harris made them famous), *The Swiss*

Family Robinson (which he disliked for getting its animals wrong), the second part of *Robinson Crusoe* (which he liked for the wolves), and girls' books like *Little Women*. In his autobiography Roosevelt noted several writings that had made an impression on him. One was a magazine titled *Our Young Folks*, which preached manliness, decency, and good conduct. The western stories of Mayne Reid gave him his first taste of the American West as well as a love of natural history. He also loved epics: Roland, Siegfried, and Longfellow's poem *The Saga of King Olaf*. It was the heroic he most treasured in all this reading: "From reading of the people I admired—ranging from the soldiers of Valley Forge, and Morgan's riflemen, to the heroes of my favorite stories—and from hearing of the feats performed by my Southern forefathers and kinsfolk, and from knowing my father, I felt a great admiration for men who were fearless and who could hold their own in the world, and I had a great desire to be like them."

He read widely in natural history, devouring Darwin, Audubon, and the American naturalist Spencer Fullerton Reid. He collected live animals and stuffed dead ones, taking lessons in taxidermy from a man who had explored the West with Audubon. He was given his first shotgun at thirteen and, when he failed to hit anything, a pair of spectacles. It turned out that his eyes were so weak that he could not see beyond ten yards. With a new gun and corrective lenses, he became the fearsome hunter he was to remain all his life. He began on the next family vacation by decimating the bird life of Upper Egypt. His approach to natural history—reading, shooting, skinning, stuffing—was typical of his approach to everything. It was enthusiastic, dogged, and heedless of what others might think. Most of all, it was marked by an obsessive effort, encouraged by his father, at self-improvement.

In his memoirs Roosevelt told a revealing story about character building. After an attack of asthma, he was sent by stagecoach to Moosehead Lake in the wilderness of northern Maine. On the coach he was taunted by two boys his own age. Looking at his weak physique, "they found that I was a foreordained and predestined victim, and industriously proceeded to make life miserable for me." He tried to fight but discovered that either adversary could handle him singly, toying with him without hurting him much, yet preventing him from striking back. Typically he learned from the experience. "I made up my mind that I must try to learn so that I would not again be put in such a helpless position; and having become quickly and bitterly conscious that I did not have the natural prowess to hold my own, I decided that I would try to supply its place by training." Again with his father's help, he learned to box, taking lessons from an ex-prizefighter in a sweaty New York gym.

The young man took his mental toughness to Harvard, a college for which he was equipped intellectually but not socially. Private tutoring had deprived him of learning how to get along with people outside the circle of his adoring family. He was, as an affectionate classmate recalled, "a bundle of eccentricities," with a weird appearance in dandified clothes and powder puff side whiskers, a high-pitched falsetto voice that clipped off words like a paper cutter, a nervous laugh (or "sharp, ungreased squeak," as his mother uncharitably described it), and a habit of oscillating between arrogance and extreme lack of confidence. His speech betrayed his lack of assurance. He spluttered; either the words would not come or he would rush them too fast.

Too supercilious to make many friends, he found refuge in intellectual achievement and the company of the very rich. He was vice-president of the Natural History Society, editor of the undergraduate magazine, and an officer in various social clubs. His grades were good enough to put him in the top 10 percent of his class and win him a Phi Beta Kappa key. Like Cabot Lodge eight years before, he was elected to the Hasty Pudding and Porcellian. Despite his bizarre attitudes, he was in his way a big man on campus.

At Harvard Roosevelt lived a life of conspicuous wealth, consorted only with "gentlemen," and wrote snobbish letters to Corinne putting down his social unequals. His annual income of eight thousand dollars was much more than any professor's stipend and nearly twice President Eliot's. His senior year he kept his own horse and buggy. Still, he did not fit the stereotype of the indolent aristocrat. He boxed and wrestled as a lightweight (five feet eight inches and 130 pounds), once winning admiration for allegedly forgiving a boxing opponent who had hit him after the bell.

He also rowed, skated, shot, and rode, though by his own admission his athletic prowess never caught up to his enthusiasm. Following his father's lead, he taught Sunday school class. He was respected for his tenacity and sense of fairness. Nevertheless, most of his classmates simply did not like him, according to the wife of one of them.

At this stage of life he showed no concern for the working class; the coal and rail strikes in Pennsylvania in 1877, which terrified John Hay into writing *The Breadwinners*, left no imprint on the Harvard undergraduate.

President Eliot's reforms in Harvard's curriculum allowed Roosevelt to choose from the large menu of elective courses. He plunged into natural sciences, at which he excelled, political economy, German, rhetoric, and English. He avoided Lodge's course in American history but enjoyed William James's class in vertebrate biology. Ironically, Lodge was to become his partner in imperialism, and James a political enemy. Looking back at Harvard from a vantage of three decades, Roosevelt wrote guardedly: "I thoroughly enjoyed Harvard, and I am sure it did me good."

His shaded assessment of Harvard's value may be connected with the death of his dream of being a scientist. He had arrived at Harvard intending to be a naturalist. He kept snakes and a live turtle in his rooms and got the highest grade in his class in zoology. But he found in the science faculty a contempt for the outdoors and a concentration on biology as "purely a science of the laboratory and the microscope." Since he "had no more desire or ability to be a microscopist and section-cutter than to be a mathematician," he abandoned science. His thoughts were in any case moving in other directions. He began at Harvard a naval history of the War of 1812, and he told a classmate that after graduation he wanted to help the cause of better government in New York City.

Roosevelt's time at Harvard saw two important changes in his personal life. During his sophomore year his father died at forty-six of stomach cancer, two months after the U.S. Senate had blocked his appointment as President Hayes's reform nominee for New York collector of customs. Theodore's grief was deep and long-lasting; the bond between the two had truly been strong. The young man reacted characteristically, first with guilt ("I realize more and more every day that I am as much inferior to Father morally and mentally as physically"), then with determination ("How I wish I could ever do something to keep up his name"). The loss energized him to study harder; his grades shot up.

The second event took place in the fall of his junior year. He met Alice Lee of Boston, a pretty blue-eyed blond girl with a sense of humor and a radiant disposition. Through the Cabot line she was related to Henry Cabot Lodge. She seemed a younger version of Theodore's mother and may have resembled Mittie Roosevelt in light-headedness as well. Theodore and Alice were married in October 1880, the autumn after his graduation from Harvard.

Roosevelt lost much of his asthma problem while at Harvard but was given a new concern his senior year. The college doctor told him that he had a weak heart and ought to live a quiet life without strenuous exertion. His reaction was defiant. To make his point, he went off with Elliott on his first trip to the West, where the two managed to kill more than four hundred birds. The next year, on his honeymoon with Alice in Europe, he climbed the Matterhorn—no easy feat, although there were fixed ropes at dangerous places after the loss of four lives during the first ascent sixteen years before. Roosevelt's muscular approach to life, the direct result of his father's injunction to build his body, was by now irreversible. It affected everything he did.

The newly graduated, newly wed young man spent his first year after Harvard toying with career options. He attended Columbia Law School but disliked the fashionable emphasis on corporation law, Root's specialty, and soon abandoned his studies. He and Alice cut a social swath in New York, making the scene at the theater and the balls that followed and joining social and literary clubs. Theodore went fox hunting and played polo on Long Island. But he also had a serious project under way. At Harvard he had written two chapters of his history of the Naval War of 1812, then lugged the manuscript to Europe on his honeymoon. Now he spent afternoons at the Astor Library and snatches of time at home to finish it. Alice was bemused. Once she observed, "We're dining out in twenty minutes, and Teddy's drawing little ships."

The Naval War of 1812 came out in 1882, and its twenty-three-year-old author found himself praised by both scholars and popular reviewers. Four years after publication the book was placed, by regulation, on board every American naval vessel; this was four years before Mahan's great work on sea power was published. At this early stage in the symbiotic relationship of the two men, it was Roosevelt who had the greater effect on Mahan, rather than the other way around.

Roosevelt's precocious history was all the more remarkable, given his lack of experience with boats. His childhood reading of Marryat and Cooper had been supplemented by his mother's sea stories, based on the experiences of her naval officer brother. Also, as a boy Roosevelt had sailed off Long Island, though he preferred rowing. But this was skimpy background for an authoritative history of America's greatest naval success. So, characteristically, he plunged into a campaign of research of such depth that he was able to refute the chief British authorities on the war. He taught himself the full sailors' lexicon and used it with the ease of an old salt, as shown in his jargonistic description of the beginning of the famous battle between the *Shannon* and the *Chesapeake*, the only British naval victory in the war:

> At midday of June 1, 1812, the *Chesapeake* weighed anchor, stood out of Boston Harbor, and at 1 P.M. rounded the Light-house. The *Shannon* stood off under easy sail, and at 3:40 hauled up and reefed top-sails. At 4 P.M. she again bore away with her foresail brailed up, and her main top-sail braced flat and shivering, that the *Chesapeake* might overtake her. An hour later, Boston Light-house bearing west distant about six leagues, she again hauled up, with her head to the southeast, and lay to under top-sails, top-gallant sails, jib, and spanker. Meanwhile, as the breeze freshened the *Chesapeake* took in her studding-sails, top-gallant sails, and royals, got her royal yards on deck, and came down very fast under top-sails and jib.

Already bumptious, Roosevelt shredded the account of the most eminent British historian of the war, William James, whom he later accused of systematic and malicious misstatement, of direct lying, and of explaining away the British defeat. His own view, which has been accepted for the most part ever since, was that courage and resolution were shared equally by both sides, that the Americans usually possessed a material advantage, and that they won primarily because of their superior fighting skills.

Roosevelt's history was filled with themes that returned in his writings and his life: efficiency, courage, self-reliance, hard work, discipline, determination, and preparedness. In his description of the Battle of New Orleans, added to the third edition in 1883, he gave hints of the heroic backwoodsmen who were to star in his future epic *The Winning of the West*. He described the Tennesseeans marching into the city as "gaunt of form and grim of face, with their powder-horns slung over their buckskin shirts; carrying their long rifles on their shoulders and their heavy hunting-knives stuck in their belts; with their coon-skin caps and fringed leggings."

The Naval War of 1812 was not the work of an American jingo. Roosevelt's scholarship was exact and fair, sometimes to the point of being stultifying. He himself wrote that the initial chapters were so dry that "they would have made a dictionary seem light reading by comparison." Moreover, he was not full of praise for the American naval tradition. Quite the reverse. He used the victories of 1812–14 as a stick with which to beat contemporary naval policy. "It is folly," he wrote in a passage that anticipated Mahan, "for the great English-speaking Republic to rely for defence upon a navy composed partly of antiquated hulks, and partly of new vessels rather more worthless than the old. It is worth while to study with some care that period of our history during which our navy stood at the highest pitch of its fame." The "highest pitch" of fame was certainly not the situation in 1882, when Roosevelt's book was published. In fact American naval preparedness was at its nadir, just before the first reforms.

Roosevelt distinguished himself from his dilettante acquaintances not only by his writing but by his plunge into Republican politics at the grass roots in 1881. In both vocations he was running a parallel course with Lodge, whom he knew only slightly. Unlike Lodge, already in the Massachusetts legislature, Roosevelt did not have full family support for his move into politics. His adoring sisters cheered him on, but his uncle and two cousins urged him not to soil his hands. Moreover, many of his acquaintances—"the men in the clubs of social pretension and the men of cultivated taste and easy life"—tried to talk him out of a "low" profession not controlled by gentlemen.

Roosevelt's reaction was typically contrary. He countered that he would not accept the political dominance of the "saloon-keepers" and "horse-car conducters" but would contest it personally. This first tangle with New York's patrician lawyers and businessmen shaped his combative relations with them (except for Root) for the rest of his life. His instincts, like Lodge's, told him that the way to succeed in politics was to experience it from the bottom up. He may also have been looking for a way to get back at the Conkling machine, which had defeated and perhaps destroyed his father. From the moment he stuck his toe in the sewer water of New York politics, he was a reformer.

The Twenty-first District in New York City, studded with the brownstones of bankers, businessmen, and lawyers, was safely Republican. Some, like the superlawyers Elihu Root and Joseph Choate, were politically active, though none deigned to run for office. The ward boss, Jake Hess, was a German Jew who acted as agent for the Albany Republican machine. His lieutenant and secret rival, Joe Murray, was an Irishman who could use his brains as well as his fists. In 1881 Murray successfully ran Roosevelt against Hess's candidate for Republican nominee for the state assembly. Amassing the support of well-heeled reformists like Root, who signed a letter for him, Roosevelt won easily.

At this point in his young life Roosevelt had no thought of making a career out of politics. If he had, he might not have shown such disregard for what people thought of him. His debut in the Albany legislature was described unforgettably by a fellow member:

> His hair was parted in the center, and he had sideburns. He wore a single eye-glass, with a gold chain over his ear. He had on a cutaway coat with one button at the top, and the ends of its tails almost reached the tops of his shoes. He carried a gold-headed cane in one hand, a silk hat in the other, and he walked in the bent-over fashion that was the style with the young men of the day. His trousers were as tight as a tailor could make them, and had a bell-shaped bottom to cover his shoes. "Who's the dude?" I asked another member.

Just as his dress was designed to call attention to himself, so was his parliamentary behavior. He was constantly importuning the speaker for the floor and ridiculing veteran members. He had, as even a worshipful biographer admitted, a swelled head.

Roosevelt's vanity and ostentation made him a laughingstock, but not for long. On legislative issues he did his homework and came up with explosive proposals that shattered the assembly's comfortable toleration of corruption and sleazy government. He had not been in the assembly three months when he was calling for the impeachment of a corrupt judge for collusion with the crooked financier Jay Gould. The judge was involved in a scam by Gould designed to take over one of New York City's elevated railroads. Roosevelt went after Gould as well, calling him a shark, swindler, archthief, kleptomaniac, and member of "the wealthy criminal class." He defeated an effort, backed by Gould's supporters, to rebate taxes owed by the financier.

Roosevelt was not always an authentic reformer—he opposed legislation setting minimum wages and working hours for laborers—but overall, in his three terms in the assembly, he inspired and achieved several victories for reform. He led the drive to make the civil service more professional. He pressed for a bill to outlaw the manufacture of cigars in tenements, where working conditions were deplorable. Taking aim at both the Democratic and the Republican machines in New York City, he sponsored legislation to strengthen the mayor at the expense of the corruption-prone aldermen, to set a debt limit, and to raise the fee for liquor licenses. His effectiveness in the assembly changed the members' view of Roosevelt from harmless fop to formidable eccentric.

In his second term, while he was still the youngest member of the assembly, his Republican colleagues elected him their candidate for speaker, an ambiguous gesture, since he was foreordained to lose to the Democratic majority. Still, it was no small thing to be the leader of his state's legislative party at the age of twenty-four. Ironically, the next year, when the Republicans held a majority, he lost the nomination to a machine man, an indication that the Republican bosses were content to promote the young maverick as a sure loser but not as a sure winner.

Because of long recesses, Roosevelt's three sessions in the New York Assembly totaled only a little more than a year. But they exposed some important existing character traits and developed new ones. The qualities he brought to Albany and displayed there included enormous capacity for work, genuine commitment to reform, driving ambition, fearlessness, tenacity, and indifference to being popular. His first experience in politics also brought out two latent qualities: an ability to get along with others and a sympathy for how the other half really lived.

For all his traveling to Europe and the West, Roosevelt had actually led a sheltered life. His schooling had given him no social breadth; education at home and four years at Harvard were hardly an exercise in diversity. On trips to the Maine woods while in college, he had made a lifelong friendship with a Maine guide, Bill Sewall, who became a sort of mentor to him. But it was not until he reached Albany that he had to work regularly with people of all stations—from farmers and mechanics to liquor dealers and pawnbrokers. He discovered that he enjoyed it and was good at it.

He particularly relished dealing with New York machine politicians, something he would have to do, with diminishing pleasure, through most of his political career. At Morton Hall, Republican headquarters of the Twenty-first District, he sat in on the political discussions. "Some of them sneered at my black coat and tall hat," he recalled. "But I made them understand that I should come dressed as I chose. . . . Then after the discussions I used to play poker and smoke with them." In his autobiography he devoted no fewer than seven pages to Joe Murray, the ward heeler who gave him his start in politics. Roosevelt endowed this Irish immigrant with all the virtues of a saint, "a man to be trusted in any position demanding courage, integrity, and good faith." He was only slightly less lavish about such fellow members of the assembly as Billy O'Neill, a storekeeper from the Adirondacks who was his closest friend in Albany, and Mike Costello, a Tammany Irishman whom he considered "as fearless as he was honest."

Roosevelt was undoubtedly showing off in describing these patrician-plebeian friendships, but his enthusiasm was real. The lesson he learned from Murray seemed equally authentic: "I do not think that a man is fit to do good work in our American democracy unless he is able to have a genuine fellow-feeling for, understanding of, and sympathy with his fellow-Americans, whatever their creed or their birthplace, the section in which they live, or the work which they do."

Much as he admired his father, Roosevelt had so far shown little interest in pursuing the charitable work that ennobled the elder Roosevelt's life. But he did inherit from his father a strong sense of social justice, which his time in Albany gave him the opportunity to exercise. The most famous example was his visit to the tenements where cigars were made. This was at the persuasion of Samuel Gompers, an official of the cigar makers' union and an unlikely man to consort with the effete young legislator. Gompers was a Jewish immigrant from London and himself the son of a cigar maker.

Roosevelt had opposed the bill to ban cigar making at home for a classical Republican reason: It injected the long arm of government into the sanctity of the home. But he agreed to an inspection tour with Gompers and made two others afterward. In his memoirs he described the scene:

> In the overwhelming majority of cases . . . there were one, two, or three room apartments, and the work of manufacturing the tobacco by men, women, and children went on day and night in the eating, living, and sleeping rooms—sometimes in one room. . . . The tobacco was stowed about everywhere, alongside the foul bedding, and in a corner where there were scraps of food. The men, women and children in this room worked by day and far on into the evening, and they slept and ate there. They were Bohemians, unable to speak English, except that one of the children knew enough to act as interpreter.

The visits turned Roosevelt into a champion of the cigar bill. Passed by the assembly, it was voided by the courts for the same classical Republican reason and, Roosevelt believed, because cigar manufacturers had greased the right palms. But the effect on him was permanent. He had discovered on-site inspection as the surest path to just decisions, surer than political beliefs, moral convictions, or theological dogmas. He was to employ the technique again and again, in visiting slum housing as New York City police commissioner; in throwing over a desk job under McKinley for the experience of fighting in Cuba; and, as president, in personally inspecting his beloved creation, the great canal across Panama. With his visit to the tenements, Roosevelt also redeemed the legacy of his father. The vision of the two Roosevelts was the same: to make the lives of the poor better. His father had chosen the way of charity; the son would choose the way of politics.

Roosevelt's third and final year in the New York Assembly was marked by an unimaginable tragedy. His mother and his wife died in the same house on the same day, February 14, 1884, St. Valentine's Day. Mittie died of typhoid fever at the age of forty-eight, and Alice of Bright's disease two days after childbirth at only twenty-two. Summoned from Albany, Roosevelt arrived at the family house in New York in time for the deaths of both women, who were so like each other in beauty, charm, and lightness of personality.

Now an orphan, a widower, and a father at the age of twenty-five, Roosevelt reacted oddly but typically. Later that year he wrote a touching remembrance of Alice: "She was beautiful in face and form, and lovelier still in spirit; as a flower she grew, and as a fair young flower she died. . . . And when my heart's dearest died, the light went from my life forever." Then he struck her out of his mind and drew a black line under his star-crossed marriage. With only rare exceptions, he never mentioned her again. He turned their newborn baby, Alice, over to the ever-faithful Bamie, who acted as mother and father to the child during her first years. Together with his siblings, he sold the house they had grown up in and Mittie and Alice had died in. He also sold the house he had lived in with Alice. However, he kept his property in Oyster Bay, Long Island, which he had bought for weekends with Alice, changing the name from Leeholm, after her family, to Sagamore Hill, in memory of indigenous Indian chieftains.

Manically Roosevelt threw himself into work. Three days after the double funeral he was back in the assembly, in a paroxysm of activity that lasted for the rest of the session. But he decided not to stand for a fourth term. It was during this period of grief that he consolidated his friendship with Lodge. Less than four months after the deaths the two men traveled to Chicago to engineer the selection of a reform candidate at the 1884 Republican National Convention. After their failure Roosevelt entrained alone for the Dakota Badlands to stake his claim as a ranchman and cowboy. In the fall he was back east to campaign for Lodge and the Republican ticket. He still had no focus, no commitment to politics, writing, or ranching. Nevertheless, with the double tragedy his life had reached an important turning point.

Looking back on Roosevelt's first twenty-five years, one is struck by the amount of adversity he was able to overcome. His childhood asthma inflicted on him enormous pain, mental stress, and depression. His eyesight was horrible, and he was so dependent on spectacles that he sewed multiple pairs into his clothes when he went soldiering in Cuba or hunting in Africa. He lost his revered father while still in college. Moreover, his reaction to the simultaneous deaths of Alice and Mittie should not be underestimated just because he suppressed most of it. He overcame all these trials by extraordinary mental and physical toughness. Hardly a promising Darwinian specimen—in fact a four-eyed weakling—he built up both his body and his confidence in himself.

It is no surprise, then, that it was effort, not talent, that counted. He would have agreed with an admiring biographer that he had "not a particle of genius." He himself wrote: "I never won anything without hard labor and the exercise of my best judgment and careful planning and working long in advance." Though constantly beset by self-doubt, endlessly poured out to Lodge, Roosevelt turned himself into a matchless engine of self-reliance, determination, and accomplishment.

Before he reached his twenty-sixth birthday, he had written a naval history that was recognized as the best survey of its subject, had become a Republican leader in the legislature of his state, and had challenged the national Republican leadership at its presidential nominating convention. The qualities of character he had achieved through misfortune combined with his precocious record of achievement to make people talk—already—of the highest office for him. While he was still in the state assembly, one of America's most distinguished educators and diplomats, Andrew D. White, first president of Cornell University and later ambassador to Germany, told his history students: "Young gentlemen, some of you will enter public life. I call your attention to Theodore Roosevelt, now in our Legislature. He is on the right road to success. . . . If any man of his age was ever pointed straight at the Presidency, that man is Theodore Roosevelt." Wherever he was headed, Roosevelt was moving fast, propelled by adversity as much as success. As he wrote later, "Black care rarely sits behind a rider whose pace is fast enough."

3.

To hear him tell it later, Theodore Roosevelt spent a considerable part of his life in the West, running his two ranches, roping and branding cattle, chopping cottonwood, shooting buffalo and grizzlies, punching out bullies, arresting desperadoes, and swapping yarns with the locals on long winter evenings. He devoted three substantial books, numerous magazine articles, and a long chapter in his autobiography to his western adventures. On the strength of his first writings about his exploits, Roosevelt became the first of the three major late-nineteenth-century popularizers of the American West. The other two were also easterners and friends of his, Owen Wister of Philadelphia and Harvard, whose best-seller *The Virginian* was published in 1902, and Frederic Remington of Canton, New York, and Yale, the great sketcher and sculptor of cowboys and Indians.

Actually, Roosevelt spent a total of less than two years in the West, mostly spread over the four years from 1883 to 1887. He never owned any land there but was a squatter on his two ranches in the Badlands, named the Elkhorn and the Maltese Cross. His financial stake was divided between a house in the Little Missouri Valley, which his Maine friend Bill Sewall built for him, and the purchase of cattle. In all, he spent about eighty thousand dollars in the Dakota Territory, a large sum for those days, and lost about seventy thousand of it. His cowboy skills were, by his own admission, meager. He was a poor roper, an average rider, and a bad shot. Nor was he much of a trailblazer. A deranged French nobleman was already ensconced in the cattle town of Medora, which he had named after his wife. Several of Roosevelt's Harvard friends and even his father-in-law had preceded him with investments in railroads, land, or cattle in the Dakota and Wyoming territories.

Despite the narrowness of his experiences on the frontier, Roosevelt was as profoundly affected by the West as he pretended. Wister and Remington went west for their health. So, in a way, did Roosevelt. Before Alice's death he had spent a few weeks on the Little Missouri, in what is now North Dakota, in September 1883. After she died in February 1884, his visits became frequent, a kind of therapy for him. He squeezed in three trips in the year of her death, fitting them around the Republican National Convention in June and the presidential election in November. "I owe more than I can ever express to the West," he wrote in his memoirs, without breaking his silence about his lost love to explain why.

The Dakota Territory was for him a gigantic arena for the discharge of the explosive energy he always amassed in times of crisis. He did everything to excess. He outlasted everybody on hunts. He killed a nine-foot grizzly. He exulted in icy downpours that chilled his cowboy partners into querulous bad temper. He worked the roundup with a broken rib and a chipped shoulder. He rode great distances, sometimes a hundred miles in a day, once going through five horses by riding forty hours straight. Giving way to his natural combativeness, he decked an armed barroom tough who teased him about his glasses.

He also nearly provoked a duel with his French neighbor, the lunatic Marquis de Mores, a crack shot who had already put two rivals underground. Had he not drawn back, Mores probably would have killed him. He and two pals chased three boat thieves a hundred miles down the Little Missouri, caught them, and brought them ashore after floating downriver another six days. Roosevelt, by himself now, then walked them under his guard for forty-five miles in two days to deliver them to prison. During the episode he managed to read all of *Anna Karenina*.

By valiant exertion, Roosevelt sublimated most of his grief over Alice's death. But not all. Sewall, whom he had lured to the Badlands from Maine, described his bouts of melancholy, in which he despaired of having anything left to live for. In his descriptions of western landscapes, he returned again and again to the themes of loneliness, separation, and solitude. Some of his best writing embodied his feelings, as in this evocative passage from one of his books on the West, every sentence sounding a note of doom:

> When the days have dwindled to their shortest, and the nights seem never-ending, then all the great northern plains are changed into an abode of iron desolation. Sometimes furious gales blow down from the north, driving before them the clouds of blinding snow-dust, wrapping the mantle of death round every unsheltered being that faces their unshackled anger. They roar in a thunderous bass as they sweep across the prairie or whirl through the naked canyons; they shiver the great brittle cottonwoods, and beneath their rough touch the icy limbs of the pines that cluster in the gorges sing like the chords of an aeolian harp. Again, in the coldest midwinter weather, not a breath of wind may stir; and then the still, merciless, terrible cold that broods over the earth like the shadow of silent death seems even more dreadful in its gloomy rigor than is the lawless madness of the storms.

Roosevelt's grief, compounded by the political setbacks at the Republican convention and in the presidential election, was human enough. What was almost superhuman was the strength of his refusal to be defeated by it. It was not the barren beauty of the Badlands that sustained him—Sewall said that anyone who preferred them to the East must be depraved—but their hardship and challenge, the naturalist's thrill in new birds and animals, the physical excitement of riding and hunting, and, perhaps most of all, the people.

As usual, Roosevelt made no sartorial efforts to blend in. His clothing and equipment were gaudy and top of the line; to the locals he was a "dude" to be made fun of. He wore a hundred-dollar buckskin suit, carried a custom-made Winchester rifle, and sported a steel hunting knife with a sterling silver sheath and handle from Tiffany's. His overall appearance—"all teeth and eyes," as a village doctor described him—and his reedy New York accent did not help make him invisible. He did learn to keep quiet and put up with the ridicule—up to a point. He finally made himself popular with the cowboys because he admired what they did, learned how to do it himself, and displayed toughness and courage.

His descriptions of cowpunchers and ranch hands had an idyllic quality. He enjoyed, ignored, or denied the low sides of their characters—"meanness, cowardice, and dishonesty are not tolerated"—and extolled their virtues. To him they were honest, hardworking, humorous, faithful, resourceful, heroic. Even more than his friends in New York politics, the westerners became prototypes of average Americans endowed with the simple virtues. This highly romantic view that Roosevelt the aristocrat held for these men of commoner clay became a permanent fixture in his philosophy of life. It was to emerge in his historical picture of Daniel Boone and the Kentucky frontiersmen in *The Winning of the West*, earlier prototypes of his beloved cowboys. It was also to surface in real life in his assembling of the Rough Riders, a fighting force that mixed cowboys and dudes and exemplified heroism and comradeship.

Roosevelt's stint in the Dakota Territory got him over his depression, gave him a muscular physique, brought him some income from his western writings, and restored his confidence in himself. In the words of a friend, it also "taught him the immense diversity of the people, and consequently of the interests, of the United States. It gave him a national point of view." He was lucky to leave the Badlands when the leaving was good. He sold much of his cattle business at a substantial loss just before the blizzard of 1886–87 took care of the rest and turned Medora into a ghost town.

He left behind some clairvoyant admirers. The local doctor, describing their first meeting, wrote: "I told my wife that I had met the most peculiar and at the same time the most wonderful man I had ever come to know. I could see that he was a man of brilliant ability and I could not understand why he was out there on the frontier." The publisher of *The Bad Lands Cow Boy*, who knew him better, told him flatly: "You will become President of the United States."

Back in New York City in 1886 and still unsure about a commitment to politics, Roosevelt let the Republican bosses talk him into running for mayor in a three-way race. His opponents were Abram Hewitt, a centrist Democratic businessman, and Henry George, a left-wing proponent of the single tax. He was the youngest candidate for mayor in the city's history. Supported by Elihu Root and other prominent reform Republicans, Roosevelt ran on an anticorruption platform distinguished by an effort to win the black and immigrant vote and spiced by his self-depiction as the "cowboy candidate." He confided to Lodge that he knew he had no chance of winning: "In all probability this campaign means my final and definite retirement [at twenty-eight!] as an available candidate." He did hope to finish second.

On election day, when it became clear that George was cutting into Roosevelt's vote, the Republican leaders began to urge their party faithful to vote for Hewitt in order to stop the socialist. Roosevelt finished a poor third. Disappointed and bitter about this act of political cynicism, he cabled Lodge, who had just won his first seat in Congress: "Am badly defeated, Worse even than I feared." His six-hundred-page autobiography contains not a word about the mayoralty race.

Some two years after Alice's death, Roosevelt had begun seeing Edith Carow, a close friend of his sisters'. He had courted her at Harvard before meeting Alice but had not seen her for seven years. Edith was good-looking (though not as pretty as Alice), wellborn but impecunious, intelligent, strong-willed, sensible, and, especially in her later years, intimidating. She loved Theodore deeply and probably always had. The two disguised their engagement for reasons of propriety and because he considered the relationship a political liability during his run for mayor. Their wedding was also semiclandestine. A month after his election defeat in November, they were married in London instead of New York; the best man was a young English diplomat whom Roosevelt had just met on the boat.

Theodore's marriage to Edith, though conceived in shadow, began for both of them a luminous, happy, and successful relationship. She was a calming, supportive, and loyal wife, whose strengths often compensated for his weaknesses, such as his recklessness about money. More perceptive and less flighty than Alice, she was also politically astute and a keen judge of people, a genuine asset to her husband in his multiple careers. When Cabot Lodge wanted to press a course of action on Roosevelt, he often had the good sense to check it out with her first. Theodore and Edith spent a modest honeymoon of only fifteen weeks in Europe. While the social pace wore Edith down, Roosevelt had "a roaring good time." Pursuing his version of relaxation in Rome, he wrote six articles there on ranch life for the *Century*. In Sorrento, he wrote to Corinne, "I generally take a moderate walk with Edith every morning, and then a brisk rush by myself."

On his return he resumed his pattern of zigzagging between politics and writing, following his bid for mayor with the biography of Gouverneur Morris. He had tossed off the biography of Thomas Hart Benton in four months; Morris took him only three. By the beginning of 1888 his restless energy was again craving new activity. In January he founded the first environmental organization in the United States, the Boone and Crockett Club, dedicated to the preservation of game and forests. But that was clearly not enough.

Roosevelt kept resisting a choice between history and politics. He was prepared to embrace whichever career might bring him greatness. He did not think it would be politics. He saw himself as too controversial, even hated. In 1884 he had written to a New York state editor: "I have very little expectation of being able to keep on in politics. . . . I will not stay in public life unless I can do so on my own terms; and my ideal, whether lived up to or not, is rather a high one." The New York mayoral experience can only have reinforced his pessimism. In 1888 he wrote a friend: "I shall probably never be in politics again. My literary work occupies a good deal of my time; and I have on the whole done fairly well at it; I should like to write some book that would really take rank in the very first class, but I suppose this is a mere dream." That year he started on just such a book, *The Winning of the West.* It expanded to four volumes and took him nine years to complete.

When Benjamin Harrison defeated President Cleveland in 1888 and the presidency returned to the Republicans, Roosevelt, true to form, looked for a political office that could be combined with his writing. Predictably, Secretary of State-designate Blaine was not keen to follow Lodge's advice that he take as his deputy a sworn enemy of his presidential ambitions. Interestingly, the explanation that Blaine gave Nannie Lodge went beyond the painful memory of the 1884 convention. It would be heard again as Roosevelt moved into national politics: "My real trouble in regard to Mr. Roosevelt is that I feel he lacks the repose and the patient endurance required in an Assistant Secretary. Mr. Roosevelt is amazingly quick in apprehension. Is there not danger that he might be too quick in execution? I do somehow fear that my sleep at Augusta or Bar Harbor would not be quite so easy and refreshing if so brilliant and aggressive a man had hold of the helm."

Even though Roosevelt was about to enter the only relatively fallow period in his entire political life, his absence of "repose and patient endurance" disturbed the sleep of other prominent politicians, including the president himself. Still, Harrison did offer Roosevelt, again through Lodge's mediation, the post of civil service commissioner. Roosevelt was already known as a committed advocate of a merit system for federal appointments, but the job had none of the power or glamour for which the brilliant and aggressive man of Blaine's description must have yearned. It is difficult to resist the conclusion that Roosevelt's germinating work of western history was on his mind, and he was glad to have a sinecure that would give him the leisure to write it.

His days were less hectic than normal. He left the office at four or five in the afternoon, often to play tennis at the British legation with his friend Cecil Spring Rice, the junior diplomat who had been best man at his London wedding. He spent long summers in Oyster Bay, out of the Washington heat. From time to time he dashed to the Elkhorn ranch for a week or two in pursuit of bear and elk. Nevertheless, being Theodore Roosevelt, at the Civil Service Commission, he mounted crusades against the spoils system, catapulting himself into controversies that more prudent men would have avoided.

One of his first acts was to force the dismissal of a personal friend of Harrison's, a corrupt postmaster in the president's hometown of Indianapolis. Having elbowed himself to the leadership of the commission, he incurred the wrath of Harrison's postmaster general and financial backer, John Wanamaker, the Philadelphia department store tycoon and a spoilsman of traditional stripe. When Wanamaker stalled on the commission's recommendation to dismiss twenty-five Baltimore postal employees for electoral fraud, Roosevelt called him a "hypocritical haberdasher" and engineered a congressional investigation. Wanamaker was disgraced, and the young reformer vindicated. Harrison did not seem amused at these assaults on the ramparts of patronage. Roosevelt wrote wistfully to Lodge, "I do wish the President would give me a little active, even if only verbal encouragement." In part because of Roosevelt's zeal, corruption became an issue in Harrison's losing race against Cleveland in 1892.

In his six years with the Civil Service Commission, Roosevelt could take legitimate pride in what he called his "applied idealism." He extended the merit system to many new offices and brought genuine enforcement to civil service regulations. "I have been a real force," he boasted to Lodge early in his tenure. He never abandoned that enthusiasm. In his memoirs, published nearly two decades later, he saw fit to devote thirty self-congratulatory pages to these achievements. As commissioner he earned favorable press copy from the *New York Times* and the once-hostile *Washington Post*. He was portrayed in a cartoon as David the giant-killer, slaying the spoils system.

Still, he was restless in what he must have considered a second-rate position. He complained to Corinne that his life was growing more sedentary and that he was beating his head against the wall. Two years into his job he was singing his usual threnody to Lodge: His career was over; he had "spent and exhausted" his influence with the party and country. After four years, he wrote Bamie: "I do not see any element of permanence or chance of permanent work for me in the kind of life where I really think I could do most." After completing six successful years on the commission, he still saw only a dead end. He wrote Lodge: "My victory here does not leave me with any opening. It leads nowhere."

He also made some unwise political decisions. In the contest for speaker of the House in 1889, he campaigned for Tom Reed against

William McKinley, even though he believed McKinley would become president and told him so. In 1894 he let Edith talk him out of running for mayor of New York; the Republican candidate won. Yet his ambition never flagged. On the way to the commission, he wrote years later, "I used to walk by the White House, and my heart would beat a little faster as the thought came to me that possibly—*possibly*—I would some day occupy it as President."

During their six years in Washington, the Roosevelts, young as they were—on arrival he was thirty, she twenty-eight—made their mark socially. Thanks to their family backgrounds and the indulgent patronage of the Lodges, the young couple moved easily into the social circle around Henry Adams. Their friends and contacts included senators, cabinet officers, foreign ambassadors, and others of ranks exceeding Roosevelt's. Roosevelt throve on power dinners. As he wrote Bamie, "I always eat and drink too much. Still, I have enjoyed them greatly, for here I meet just the people I care to. It is so pleasant to deal with big interests, and big men." He won an admirer in Adams, who was fascinated by his dynamism. He was "pure act," said Adams, who himself was no act.

It was at this time that Roosevelt got to know John Hay well. Roosevelt appreciated Hay's friendship with his father and his support for the senior Roosevelt's allotment plan for Union soldiers. As a small boy Theodore had first met Hay, who was twenty years older, when his father brought him to their country house in a rainstorm. Hay's umbrella blew out in the wind, and Teedie and Corinne enjoyed his comic struggle to fix it. Theodore's father introduced Hay to the children as a young man who would "make his name well known in the United States."

Now, in Washington, Roosevelt could enjoy Hay's humor and friendship. Despite their mutual admiration, however, there was always a shadow between the two men. Like Adams, Hay found Roosevelt too ambitious and pushy, while for Roosevelt Hay was something of a wimp. He was unwilling, Roosevelt once said, to "face the rather intimate association which is implied in a fight." Hay was charming, but Roosevelt's aggressiveness and pugnacity found their true echo not in him but in Lodge.

During his Washington period Roosevelt consolidated his alliance and friendship with Alfred Mahan, who had invited him as guest lecturer at the Naval War College in Newport in 1887. While Roosevelt was at the Civil Service Commission, Mahan was often either at Newport or at sea, but the two kept in touch. Roosevelt acted as self-appointed press agent for *The Influence of Sea Power upon History*, published in 1890, and intervened several times against the navy's efforts to derail Mahan's career. He was such a Mahan booster that John Hay told Bamie Roosevelt of his delight that Mahan had finally made his name, "as Theodore would now no longer feel obliged to make [his friends] all go to Annapolis to hear his lectures."

By 1895 Roosevelt's frustrations were keeping pace with his bellicosity. He had been six years in Washington on the Civil Service Commission, the last two under the Democratic president Grover Cleveland, who had unexpectedly kept him on. There was now a reform Republican administration in New York City under Mayor William L. Strong, whose new office Roosevelt had decided not to compete for. Strong offered him street cleaning commissioner, probably less of an insult than it appears, but Roosevelt allowed Lodge to talk him into a more visible job, one of the four police commissioners.

Roosevelt's sidestep back into New York politics left him no tribune for national pronouncements, but it did increase his national reputation. The state and the city were perennially ripe for the reformer's ax. As Roosevelt had written in his Benton biography, "New York has always had a low political standard, one or the other of its great party and factional organizations, and often both or all of them, being at all times most unlovely bodies of excessively unwholesome moral tone."

Roosevelt threw himself into the work of police commissioner with his usual energy. He put his civil service convictions into practice by rewarding merit and punishing corruption and graft. In enforcement of the blue laws, he took a political risk by closing down saloons on Sundays, then discomfited the organizers of a German-American meeting protesting the closures by unexpectedly accepting their invitation to attend it. In the company of the celebrated muckraking journalist Jacob Riis, he visited the poorer districts of the city. When the Jewish community complained about the forthcoming address of an anti-Semitic demagogue from Germany, Roosevelt assigned forty Jewish policemen to protect the visitor's right of free speech.

All this was done with a keen eye to populist publicity: the sleeping patrolman finding the commissioner staring down on him, the tenement dweller meeting a sympathetic city official for the first time, the criminal catching a glimpse of the commissioner himself on one of his famous night prowls, the crowds watching him ride his bicycle to work. He invited reporters along on some of these escapades. To the press he was Haroun-al-Roosevelt, emulating the caliph of Baghdad in protecting his flock and rooting out evil. The portrait of the fighting police commissioner fitted nicely alongside the picture of the courageous cowboy.

The political infighting in New York City, generated partly within the four-man board itself, caused Roosevelt great frustration. Still, in correspondence with Bamie, his most trusted confidante, he expressed satisfaction. He loved the "glimpse of the real life of the swarming millions." He also believed he was doing some good. "I am more than glad that I went into it; and it will be a year that I shall always consider as perhaps the best spent of my life, in point of actual, hard, useful, disagreeable and yet intensely interesting and exciting labor." But, as he put it, it was "not work that can be done on a rosewater basis," and by the 1896 presidential election he thought he had done all he could with the police. McKinley's election offered him the possibility of another career move.

4.

By this time Roosevelt had developed a strong and consistent opinion of what the United States stood for and what it could become. He outlined this view of his own country in two works of history. The first was his biography of Thomas Hart Benton, published in 1886. Benton had become Missouri's first senator when the territory was admitted to the Union in 1821 as the westernmost state; he served thirty years in the Senate. Roosevelt admired him for his fidelity to two goals: preservation of the Union (even though Benton was a slaveowner) and westward expansion.

Roosevelt's second and far more ambitious work, *The Winning of the West*, was published in four volumes between 1889 and 1897. The primary subject of the work was not the conquest of what was then called the Far West or the Wild West beyond the Mississippi River, but the settlement between 1769 and 1807 of lands west of the original thirteen states and east of the Mississippi, the current states of

Kentucky, Tennessee, Ohio, Indiana, and Illinois. Roosevelt's narrative account of their acquisition and settlement contains serious blemishes, among them an often insensitive approach to Native Americans. But it has great strengths as well, which make it his finest piece of writing, a still-underrated American classic. It is broad in scope, impressive in research, incisive in interpretation, and gripping in style. The vivid accounts of frontier adventures and intrigues, the skirmishes between settlers and Indians, the long-running duel with the British, and the competing strategies of the grand adversaries make absorbing reading. One would like to believe that if he had done nothing else in life, Roosevelt would still be remembered for *The Winning of the West*.

His epic theme was that the conquest of the lands between the Allegheny Mountains and the Mississippi made possible all the westward expansion beyond the great river. Indeed, without the wresting of those lands from the British, the Spanish, and the Indians, Jefferson's Louisiana Purchase would not have led, in Roosevelt's view, to the populating of the trans-Mississippi West. A belt of hostile territory would have lain between the United States and the vast domain it had purchased. Between the Alleghenies and the Mississippi, Roosevelt wrote, the American Revolution "was fundamentally a struggle between England . . . and the Americans, triumphantly determined to acquire the right to conquer the continent." If the Americans had failed, "we would certainly have been cooped up between the sea and the mountains; . . . the Alleghanies [sic] would have become our western frontier." But they succeeded, and their success, for Roosevelt, confirmed the success of the American Revolution.

How were the lands pacified and settled? Roosevelt gave due credit to the American military victory in the Revolution and to the negotiating skill of John Jay and John Adams in gaining British recognition of the Ohio River valley as American territory. But there was a more important factor. Fortunately the American negotiators of the Treaty of Paris "represented a people already holding the whole Ohio Valley, as well as the Illinois." It was those people who were the real heroes of Roosevelt's epic, the backwoodsmen, handy with ax, rifle, or knife, who seized or occupied the land and made it safe for settlement.

Roosevelt's icons among these frontier types were Daniel Boone, George Rogers Clark, John Sevier, and James Robertson. Roosevelt was too good a historian to ignore major defects in these figures: Sevier, Clark, and Boone, for example, all conspired with the Spanish enemy. But their accomplishments made them "emphatically American worthies . . . men of might in their day, born to sway the minds of others, helpful in shaping the destiny of the continent." Roosevelt also saw them as representing an even larger collective force: "the movement of a whole, free people, not of a single master-mind." The members of this collective force—the explorers and settlers—were simple, rough, commonsensical, warlike, daring, truculent, ruthless, and industrious. Though ranging over hundreds of thousands of square miles, they merged for Roosevelt into a single American type, "one in speech, thought, and character." He saw them as quintessential Americans: "Nowhere else on the continent has so sharply defined and distinctively American a type been produced as on the frontier."

Roosevelt portrayed the frontiersmen as unique. In fact, however, they were familiar characters in a romantic epic that he had been staging all his life. They were the embodiment of Bill Sewall, the Maine guide who had taught him woodcraft, and of Billy O'Neill, the small-town storekeeper from rural New York whom he had known in the New York Assembly. They resembled the gaunt Tennesseeans with their powder horns and rifles, who marched on New Orleans in *The Naval War of 1812*, and the Badlands cowboys with whom he had hunted, rode, and roped. They were like the characters in his and Lodge's *Hero Tales from American History*, which contained chapters on Daniel Boone and George Rogers Clark. Moreover, they were to appear again as the Rough Riders, whose very name conveyed the human attributes that Roosevelt found so appealing.

The backwoodsmen who won the West were, for Roosevelt, part of a historical continuum that stretched from the American Revolution to his own time. Like Frederick Jackson Turner, whose great thesis on the American frontier was published while Roosevelt was writing *The Winning of the West* and from whom he derived inspiration, he saw American history as the history of expansion: expansion from the Old World to the New, then expansion overland to the Mississippi, finally expansion to the western continental limits. Roosevelt actually planned to write a sequel to *The Winning of the West* to cover the seizure of Florida and Oregon, the incorporation of Texas, and the acquisition of New Mexico and California.

At times Roosevelt implied that expansion was just a question of showing up. He simply brushed the Indian inhabitants out of existence, assuming fatuously that all that was needed was to fill in empty spaces: "We . . . have seized the waste solitudes that lay near us, the limitless forests and never ending plains, and the valleys of the great, lonely rivers; and have thrust our own sons into them to take possession; and a score of years after each conquest we see the conquered land teeming with a people that is one with ourselves." In more realistic moments, he understood that the "waste solitudes" were occupied by British, Spanish, and Indians. These adversaries had to be pushed aside. War was irrevocably, if regrettably, necessary for expansion. The military victory of the Virginia governor Lord Dunmore over Chief Cornstalk and his Shawnee nation in 1774 opened the way for Boone to settle Kentucky, for Robertson to control Middle Tennessee, and for Clark to conquer Illinois. Roosevelt was not squeamish about the fate of the Indians in this process: "Unless we were willing that the whole continent west of the Alleghanies [sic] should remain an unpeopled waste, the hunting-ground of savages, war was inevitable; and even had we been willing, and had we refrained from encroaching on the Indians' lands, the war would have come nevertheless, for then the Indians themselves would have encroached on ours."

In speaking and letters, Roosevelt often used racial expressions. Latin Americans were Dagoes, Chinese Chinks, Spanish Dons, British Jacks, Japanese Japs, and American Indians savages. The late nineteenth century was a time of credence in racial theories that have no intellectual standing today. Like most graduates of major American universities, Roosevelt believed that some races were dominant and some inferior. As a Lincoln Republican he was a strong opponent of slavery and a nominal backer of rights for black Americans, but he considered them members of a stupid and backward race whose presence in the United States was a tragic but irreversible error. For him racial superiority dictated that the inferior races be displaced, rather than assimilated. It was thus "of incalculable importance that America, Australia, and Siberia should pass out of the hands of their red, black, and yellow aboriginal owners, and become the heritage of the dominant world races."

These racial beliefs translated directly to Roosevelt's treatment of the American continent and the American Indian: "The conquest and settlement by the whites of the Indian lands was necessary to the greatness of the race and to the well-being of civilized mankind. . . . Such conquests . . . are sure to come when a masterful people, still in its raw barbarian prime, finds itself face to face with a weaker and wholly alien race which holds a coveted prize in its feeble grasp." The necessary victory of the "dominant world races" swept away appeals to morality: "Whether the whites won the land by treaty, by armed conquest, or, as was actually the case, by a mixture of both, mattered comparatively little so long as the land was won. It was all-important that it should be won, for the benefit of civilization and in the interests of mankind."

Roosevelt's picture of Indians was a stereotype of inferiority. They were "filthy, cruel, lecherous, and faithless," and their life was "but a few degrees less meaningless, squalid, and ferocious than that of the wild beasts with whom they held joint ownership." In describing them, Roosevelt habitually used words like ferocious, treacherous, bloodthirsty, duplicitous, and skulking.

In defending warfare against the Indians, Roosevelt was not reflecting a particularly extreme view. Nor was his thinking out of line with the expansionist policies of most United States administrations throughout the nineteenth century. Not even in the twentieth century was there any widespread movement to return the West to the native tribes that once roamed it. However, Roosevelt crossed the line into racism when he elevated the Indian wars to a high plateau of virtue: "The most ultimately righteous of all wars is a war with savages, though it is apt to be also the most terrible and inhuman. The rude, fierce settler who drives the savage from the land lays all civilized mankind under a debt to him."

Yet Roosevelt was not completely comfortable with this racist baggage. In *The Winning of the West*, he returned repeatedly to the paradox of how a people could claim to be civilized if it behaved as barbarously as its barbarous foes. He tried to resolve the dilemma by asserting that justifiable conquest is inseparable from regrettable costs:

> Every such submersion or displacement of an inferior race, every such armed settlement or conquest by a superior race, means the infliction and suffering of hideous woe and misery. It is a sad and

dreadful thing that there should of necessity be such throes of agony; and yet they are the birth-pangs of a new and vigorous people. That they are in truth birth-pangs does not lessen the grim and hopeless woe of the race supplanted; of the race outworn or overthrown. The wrongs done and suffered cannot be blinked. Neither can they be allowed to hide the results to mankind of what has been achieved.

In accepting the need for appalling brutality in the warfare against the Indians, Roosevelt was also honest and concerned about the human consequences of his position. For a genuine racist, racial superiority would be justification enough for atrocities against the Indians, but Roosevelt was bothered by the assumption that a superior race could be excused for doing whatever it wanted to fulfill its destiny. At any rate, such an assumption was not his only defense of the seizure of land from Indians who had gotten there first. To supplement it, he resorted to three additional arguments.

The first was the legalistic claim that the Indians did not really own the land: "Every good hunting-ground was claimed by many nations. It was rare, indeed, that any tribe had an uncontested title to a large tract of land; where such title existed, it rested, not on actual occupancy and cultivation, but on the recent butchery of weaker rivals." To this argument Roosevelt added an economic one: that the whites used the land better than the Indians. "As for the whites themselves, . . . they cannot be severely blamed for trespassing upon what was called the Indian's land; for let sentimentalists say what they will, the man who puts the soil to use must of right dispossess the man who does not, or the world will come to a standstill." A third argument was a combination of the law of the strong and manifest destiny: "It was our manifest destiny to swallow up the land of all adjoining nations who were too weak to withstand us."

Roosevelt, uneasy with a purely racist defense of the conquest of Indian-occupied land, treated individual Indians in ways that did not always square with a view of their racial inferiority. He was often, though not always, evenhanded and generous. His description of cease-fires was balanced: "Any peace which did not surrender the land was sure in the end to be broken by the whites; and a peace which did surrender the land would be broken by the Indians." His writing was replete with unfeigned sympathy for the tribes victimized by American expansionists. He called the brutalities of the Georgians toward the Cherokees a "shameful wrong" and "indelible blots on our fair fame." He also deplored the removal of the Seminoles and the fact that their "great . . . leader" Osceola was captured by American treachery. He acknowledged that "the most cruel wrongs have been perpetrated by whites upon perfectly peaceable and unoffending tribes like those of California, or the Nez Perces."

As a connoisseur of war Roosevelt gave the Indian enemies high marks for their endurance, discipline, use of cover, and mastery of surprise. He called them "the most formidable savage foes ever encountered by colonists of European stock" and rated them, on their own ground, "far more formidable than the best European troops." The Wyandots, in particular, "were the bravest of all the Indian tribes, the most dangerous in battle, and the most merciful in victory, rarely torturing their prisoners." He also gave due credit to the great Indian chiefs. He wrote a moving account of the Shawnee chief Cornstalk's defeat at the Battle of the Great Kanawha in 1774 against Governor Dunmore's superior forces. Cornstalk, "as wary and able as he was brave," was the best general in the field, in Roosevelt's eyes. Cornplanter, an Iroquois chief, was a "valiant and able warrior" who sincerely desired peace with the settlers. Another Iroquois chief, Joseph Brant, was "a mighty warrior, and a man of education, who in his letters to the United States officials showed much polished diplomacy."

In addition, Roosevelt pulled few punches in condemning whites when they cheated or brutalized Indians. He devoted a whole chapter to the massacre in 1782 of ninety-six Moravian Indians by backwoodsmen whose conduct he found "utterly abhorrent, . . . a subject of just reproach and condemnation." He wrote: "More than a hundred years have passed since this deed of revolting brutality; but even now a just man's blood boils in his veins at the remembrance. It is impossible not to regret that fate failed to send some strong war party of savages across the path of these inhuman cowards, to inflict on them the punishment they so richly deserved. We know that a few of them were afterwards killed by the Indians; it is a matter of keen regret that any escaped."

Roosevelt reported as a matter of course that the whites, like the Indians, broke treaties and routinely took scalps. He described many incidents of American ruthlessness toward Indians, including one by his hero Sevier. He condemned the treachery of the U.S. government in failing to defend a friendly Indian tribe, the Chickasaws, against their enemies the Creeks. But his sympathies did not stretch to Indian tribes that were hostile, like the Sioux or Cheyennes. He defended the massacre of several hundred Cheyennes by the U.S. Army in 1864 at Sand Creek, Colorado, as "on the whole as righteous and beneficial a deed as ever took place on the frontier." He did concede "certain most objectionable details," without specifying that they included the indiscriminate slaughter of men, women, and children, whose chief, Black Kettle, was flying a white flag.

Roosevelt's praise of peaceable Indian tribes and brave chieftains and his implied guilt regarding American conduct toward Indians make him much less than a pure racist. The same inclusive tendencies affected his behavior. On his ranch he claimed to have established a rule that Indians should be treated as fairly as if they were whites: "We neither wrong them nor allow others to wrong them." On the Civil Service Commission he worked with the Indian Rights Association to reduce corruption in the Indian Service. He was to select several Indians for the Rough Riders in 1898 and to praise their bravery after the war. When it came to the basic issue of western expansion, however, Roosevelt blinded himself to the plight of those Indians who found themselves unwittingly in the path of the locomotive of history and who resisted their foreordained defeat.

5.

The fourth volume of *The Winning of the West* was published in 1897, the same year that Roosevelt became assistant secretary of the navy, his first position in foreign policy. The four books had come out to a rising chorus of popular and scholarly praise, which made them bestsellers and established their writer as an authority on expansion. During his intense and prolonged concentration on overland expansion, Roosevelt had developed a related theory of imperialism that he was now to apply, and sometimes to misapply, to his work with the navy.

Like Turner, he saw a direct connection between expansion to the end of the continent and expansion beyond it. He explained this connection in a new foreword to *The Winning of the West*, written a year after the Spanish-American War, while he was governor of New York. "We of this generation," he wrote, "were but carrying to completion the work of our fathers and of our fathers' fathers." He went on to describe the context of his historical concepts:

> The whole western movement of our people was simply the most vital part of that great movement of expansion which has been the central and all-important feature of our history—a feature far more important than any other since we became a nation, save only the preservation of the Union itself. It was expansion which made us a great power. . . .
>
> At bottom the question of expansion in 1898 was but a variant of the problem we had to solve at every stage of the great western movement. Whether the prize of the moment was Louisiana or Florida, Oregon or Alaska, mattered little. The same forces, the same types of men, stood for and against the cause of national growth, of national greatness, at the end of the century as at the beginning.

Roosevelt saw America's expansion to the Pacific coast and then abroad as part of a still-larger movement that had its roots deep in history. In the very first sentence of *The Winning of the West* he wrote: "During the past three centuries the spread of the English-speaking peoples over the world's waste spaces has been not only the most striking feature in the world's history, but also the event of all others most far-reaching in its effects and its importance." Americans were entrusted with a mission on behalf of the "English-speaking peoples" not only to continue this spread but to create a nation covering "a region larger than all Europe." Roosevelt believed that the emergence of an American great power was inevitable. The British might try to stop it, but they were doomed to fail. "The British fought against the stars in their courses, while the Americans battled on behalf of the destiny of the race."

Among colonial rivals, Roosevelt voiced his greatest antipathy toward Spain. He saw it as a weak and corrupt power given to a diplomacy of delay, treachery, and intrigue. It had secretly roused the Indians against the United States and had tried to drive wedges between the western settlers and the seaboard Americans. "Her colonial system," he said in *The Winning of the West*, "was evil in its suspicious exclusiveness towards strangers; and her religious system was marked by an intolerance still almost as fierce as in the days of Torquemada." Roosevelt showed no such hostility to Britain or France, other rivals on the American continent, though he did favor the annexation of Canada and wrote that (British) Columbia, Saskatchewan, and Manitoba should be American states. His feelings toward Spain could only have intensified his desire to make war on it in 1898.

Roosevelt understood that expansion would create the constitutional problem of how to deal with settlers to the new lands or, more vexing, with people already there when the lands were taken. As always, he preferred the first case—"The time to have taken the lands was before settlers came into them"—but he was prepared to deal also with the second. In doing so, he developed a theory of colonialism based on his view that the United States had invented a superior kind of colony. It was unique in history since it combined freedom and strong central government. In America, "no State was subject to another, new or old. All paid a common allegiance to a central power which was identical with none." Reminding his readers of the provisions in the Northwest Ordinance of 1787, he asserted that all people who entered the Union should have the same rights as those already in it. This equality would apply to settlers and also to conquered peoples (Roosevelt envisaged Canadians): "We want no unwilling citizens to enter our Union." In fact Roosevelt's constitutional solution was not based on equality; Native Americans were not included. It was soon to become clear that the people of Cuba, Puerto Rico, and the Philippines were not to be included either.

America's territorial expansion turned out to be a flawed model for the imminent expansion overseas. Cuba, Puerto Rico, and the Philippines were not areas of sparse habitation waiting to be peopled by Americans. They were densely populated islands with native cultures far more integrated than those of the American Indians. Moreover, their inhabitants fitted neither of Roosevelt's categories for the West. They were neither Indians to be pushed aside nor potential American citizens who would enjoy equal rights. Roosevelt never showed the same passion about Cubans, Puerto Ricans, and Filipinos that he had showered on the backwoodsmen and even, at times, the Indians. They simply played no major part in his historical epic.

Nor was there any thought of bringing to the islands the main element that had contributed to the winning of the West, American settlers, the most important characters in Roosevelt's saga. In the last paragraph of *The Winning of the West* he wrote: "Much had been accomplished by the deeds of the Indian-fighters, treaty-makers, and wilderness-wanderers; far more had been accomplished by the steady push of the settler folk themselves, as they thrust ever westward, and carved states out of the forest and the prairie." But settlement by Americans was entirely missing from his future justification of the seizure of the Spanish islands. They were not to be populated by Americans but to be exploited for political, military, or economic reasons. The role of settlers was to be played by the U.S. Army and the American colonial administration.

The experience of 1898 was to shatter the consistency of Roosevelt's view on colonialism. But it did not refute two of his central theses: that it was America's manifest destiny to become a great power and that war was the only way to do it. Roosevelt loved the backwoodsmen because of their fighting skills and because they were ready to fight even without the backing of the government in Washington. He was not loath to use them as a stick with which to beat his pusillanimous contemporaries, "men of the present day who are either so ignorant or of such lukewarm patriotism that they do not wish to see the United States keep prepared for war and show herself willing and able to adopt a vigorous foreign policy whenever there is need of furthering American interests or upholding the honor of the American flag."

This man who had never seen conflict believed that war was an end in itself. Those who had seen it, like McKinley and Hay, were much less enthusiastic about taking on Spain. But he was not to be diverted. The bitter experience of his father's failure to serve in the Civil War contrasted with, probably even created, his passion for heroes who were courageous, manly, and pugnacious. It also merged with his philosophy that war was necessary for expansion and that expansion would fulfill America's destiny to become a great power. The outcome was a fierce desire to have a war and to participate personally in it. In this, as in so many other elements of his approach to foreign affairs, his study of western history was seminal.

6.

During his years as civil service commissioner in Washington and police commissioner in New York, Roosevelt began to take strong and specific policy positions based on his evolving theories of imperialism. In 1891 he was even more of a war hawk than Mahan over the confrontation with Chile. At Henry Adams's table or in the Metropolitan Club dining room, he railed against what he considered the limp-wristed American response. In 1893 he wrote a friend: "I am a bit of a believer in the manifest destiny doctrine. I believe in more ships; I believe in ultimately driving every European power off of this continent, and I don't want to see our flag hauled down where it has been hauled up." Hay, who always found Roosevelt's belligerence comical, wrote to Adams that Roosevelt "goes about hissing through his clenched teeth that we are dishonest. For two nickels he would declare war himself, shut up the Civil Service Commission, and wage it sole."

Hay was right. Roosevelt was annoyed at the softness of the Cleveland administration. He wrote Bamie: "I hope there is no truth in the rumor that Gresham and Bayard [respectively Cleveland's secretary of state and ambassador to Britain] have considered the wisdom of abandoning Samoa. It is a great misfortune that we have not annexed Hawaii, gone on with our navy, and started an interoceanic canal at Nicaragua." During a dispute with Britain over sealing rights, he fumed to Lodge that "Great Britain's conduct about the seals is infamous. We should at once take her action as a proof that she has abrogated the treaty and should ourselves treat it as abrogated, and seize all Canadian sealers as pirates." His red blood boiled when the Venezuelan crisis erupted at the end of 1895. He urged the Cleveland administration not to back down and stressed to an audience at Harvard that the crisis came within "the strictest view" of the Monroe Doctrine. To Bamie's husband Will Cowles he confided: "If there is a muss I shall try to have a hand in it myself!"

Roosevelt's bellicosity made him scornful of all he considered weak, including members of his own social set as well as men like Carl Schurz who had loyally supported him on civil service reform. He vented his disgust to Lodge:

I see that President Eliot [of Harvard] attacked you and myself as "degenerated sons of Harvard." It is a fine alliance, that between the anglo-maniac mugwumps, the socialist working men, and corrupt politicians . . . to prevent the increase of our Navy and coast defenses. The moneyed and semi-cultivated classes, expecially of the Northeast, are doing their best to bring this country down to the Chinese level. If we ever come to nothing as a nation it will be because the treachery of Carl Schurz, President Eliot, the *Evening Post* and the futile sentimentalists of the international arbitration type, bears its legitimate fruit in producing a flabby, timid type of character, which eats away the great fighting features of our race.

When insurrection broke out in 1895 against Spanish rule in Cuba, Roosevelt was intellectually, psychologically, and emotionally driven to get the United States, and himself, into war. Having shown himself ready to join a fight against the Mexicans over America's southern boundary and against the British over Venezuela, he now wanted to take on an even better target, the weak and decadent Spanish.

He importuned the governor of New York to give him a commission in any state regiment that might be sent to fight Spain. He told Bamie that not only did he desire to drive the Spanish out of Cuba, but he also wanted a policy leading to "the ultimate removal of all European powers from the colonies they hold in the western hemisphere." He wrote: "I am a quietly rampant 'Cuba Libre' man. I doubt whether the Cubans would do very well in the line of self-government; but anything would be better than continuance of Spanish rule. I believe that Cleveland [a lame duck when this letter was written] ought now to recognize Cuba's independence and interfere; sending our fleet promptly to Havana. There would not in my opinion be very serious fighting; and what loss we encountered would be thrice over repaid by the ultimate results of our action."

McKinley's victory over Bryan in 1896 brought the Republicans back to power and gave Roosevelt the chance to turn his imperial theories into activism. He was no crony of McKinley's, but he stumped loyally and effectively for him during the campaign. Still, when Lodge, who was in better odor with the president-elect, went to Canton to plead for Roosevelt's appointment as assistant secretary of the navy, McKinley was dubious. He hoped that Roosevelt had "no preconceived plans which he would wish to drive through the moment he got in." A few days later McKinley told another Roosevelt emissary: "I want peace, and I am told that your friend Theodore—whom I know only slightly—is always getting into rows with everybody. I am afraid he is too pugnacious."

McKinley had Roosevelt's number, but Roosevelt understood McKinley pretty well too. He told Bamie before the election: "McKinley himself is an upright and honorable man, of very considerable ability and good record as a soldier & in Congress; he is not a strong man, however, and unless he is well backed I should feel rather uneasy about him in a serious crisis, whether it took the form of a soft-money craze, a gigantic labor riot, or danger of foreign conflict."

Concerted pressure by a bevy of Roosevelt's supporters, led by Lodge and including Hay, who was greatly amused by the supplicant's naked ambition, finally won him an appointment as assistant secretary of the navy. It was not a particularly auspicious assignment. As the second-ranking position in the Navy Department, it did not carry cabinet status. Nor did Roosevelt's way of achieving it bode well. McKinley was clearly wary of him, and his old rival New York Republican boss Thomas Platt approved the appointment only because Platt decided he would be less dangerous in Washington than in New York.

Still, Roosevelt could count some assets. Since Washington was a small city, he would have plenty of access to McKinley himself. Foreign affairs and defense were in the purview of only three departments, State, War (Army), and Navy. The secretary and assistant secretary in each department constituted the six primary officials in the national security structure. As Roosevelt took the measure of the three secretaries, he could feel even more confident. The secretary of state, John Sherman, a former senator, was senile. The secretary of war, Russell A. Alger, a Michigan politician, was in Roosevelt's view an incompetent. His own boss, John D. Long, was a likable politician with a real fondness for Roosevelt, a propensity to take long vacations, and a tendency to be easily manipulated. McKinley had no White House staff to deal with foreign affairs; his chief adviser, George Cortelyou, handled everything, including politics. In such circumstances a young man with strong ideas and colossal energy could make his mark.

Roosevelt, still only thirty-eight, brought back with him to Washington a reputation for dynamism that both attracted and intimidated. He had elevated the Civil Service Commission from a bureaucratic backwater to a highly visible center of reform, at the cost of some damage to his own party. He had dazzled politically inert intellectuals like Henry Adams with his energy and effectiveness. He had proved himself to be a competent intellectual, holding forth with the nation's scientific elite at the Cosmos Club. He had established a creditable reform record with the New York police in a dauntingly challenging assignment. Yet his battering ram style worried Republican leaders, who mistrusted his judgment and feared his impulsiveness. He was seen as a renegade, not a team player.

Whatever the bosses might think, Roosevelt was developing a nationwide base of support independent of them. His cowboy exploits assured him a never-ending stream of national publicity, which he kept replenishing with his prolific writings. His youth, virility, largeness of spirit, and apparent self-assurance merged with his image as easterner/westerner and intellectual/roughneck to make him a popular, almost a populist figure. He crackled with kinetic energy. As his friend the naturalist John Burroughs said of him, "Roosevelt was a many-sided man and every side was like an electric battery."

He was the political counterpart of Carnegie, Rockefeller, and Morgan, the brash, successful entrepreneur exuding wealth, optimism, and power, and representing a new America ready for greatness. Only his sisters and Lodge knew of his doubts about himself. To a growing number of Americans he was a dynamic young man destined for political stardom.

Part Two

IMPERIAL AMERICA

Imperialism, the extension of national authority over alien communities, is a dominant note in the world-politics of today.

—A. T. MAHAN, *RETROSPECT AND PROSPECT: STUDIES IN INTERNATIONAL RELATIONS, NAVAL AND POLITICAL* (1902)

7. Island Fortress, Cuban Blood

1.

On Tuesday, February 15, 1898, the American battleship *Maine*, just beginning the fourth week of a visit to Cuba, blew up in Havana Bay and sank with the loss of 268 Americans. President McKinley had ordered the *Maine* to Havana to protect the small American population there. Cuban rebels were waging an armed struggle for independence, and Spain was understandably annoyed at this challenge to its sovereignty over the island. Frustrated Spanish Army officers provoked violent demonstrations in the city against Spain's recent concessions to the rebels. Fitzhugh Lee, the excitable American consul general, asked for a show of force to prevent the violence from spilling over to the American community.

The Spanish authorities in Cuba were apprehensive about the presence in Cuban waters of a three-hundred-foot-long armored American warship sporting ten heavy guns. According to traditional naval protocol, however, they had no choice but to accept the American request for a "courtesy" visit; to save face, they sent a Spanish warship on a "return" visit to New York. Nobody knows to this day if, in the tense atmosphere between the United States and Spain, the *Maine* became the victim of an act of sabotage by the Spanish or the bituminous coal in its hold ignited by spontaneous combustion. Whether by sabotage or by accident, the destruction of the *Maine* dramatized and aggravated the serious differences between the two countries.

When the *Maine* exploded, John Hay, U.S. ambassador to Great Britain, was in Egypt with Henry Adams on an extended holiday up the Nile. Apparently the thought never occurred to Hay to curtail his vacation. Complaining of the shortage of meat on his Russian ship, he went on to Athens, shopped, and met the king of Greece. He stopped in Venice and Paris before making his leisurely way back to London in late March. Theodore Roosevelt remarked disparagingly to Henry Adams's brother Brooks on Hay's dereliction of duty.

Hay himself eventually showed some chagrin at being away from his post at such a critical time. From Venice he wrote his capable deputy chief of mission, Henry White, that he felt "a certain remorse at having been idling on the Nile while you were so full of anxieties and cares. But you have borne up under it splendidly and covered yourself with glory, and so there is nothing to regret on public grounds." Hay also offered a lament for the president: "McKinley has had a terrible stress and responsibility in the end of his first year. I think he has borne it with great wisdom and energy, and I hope he may come safely through."

Back in London, Hay threw himself into defending American support for the Cuban rebels to a sympathetic British government, while making sure that Britain's critics at home knew that America had one sure friend in Europe. He lectured Cabot Lodge, a perennial twister of the lion's tail: "I do not know whether you especially value the friendship and sympathy of this country. . . . I find it wherever I go— not only in the press, but in private conversation. For the first time in my life I find the 'drawing room' sentiment altogether with us. If we wanted it—which, of course, we do not—we could have the practical assistance of the British Navy. . . . The commonest phrase is here:—'I wish you would take Cuba at once. We wouldn't have stood it this long.'"

Hay did not neglect to tell Lodge how hard he had been working for his country and in what difficult circumstances. In the eternal grumble of all diplomats chafing at their foreign ministries, he wrote: "You may imagine what it is to me, absolutely without light or instruction, compelled to act from day to day on my own judgment, and at no moment sure of the wishes of the Department. What I should have done, if the feeling here had been unfriendly instead of cordially sympathetic, it is hard to say." Hay was discovering, and nurturing, the first seeds of a bilateral relationship that was to grow throughout the twentieth century between two countries accustomed to seeing themselves as enemies and rivals.

When the *Maine* blew up, Alfred Mahan was two years into retire ment in New York City. Now free to say what he wanted, he was turn-ing out magazine pieces and enjoying his growing stature as an icon of naval wisdom. He had completed an important biography of the great British Admiral Horatio Nelson, had accrued degrees from Oxford, Cambridge, Harvard, and Yale, and had been elected to the Ameri-can Philosophical Society. He had also become a trusted adviser to Theodore Roosevelt, now assistant secretary of the navy, who devel-oped the habit of sending his consistently bellicose ideas to Mahan for evaluation and praise. Roosevelt urged Mahan to write him "from time to time, because there are many, many points which you will see that I should miss." Mahan was glad to comply.

Mahan's writings in the year before the *Maine's* destruction made a forceful strategic case for the United States' taking control of Cuba. As usual, his approach was global. In *The Interest of America in Sea Power, Present and Future,* published in 1897, he fulminated against the American tendency to isolation: "No nation, as no man, can live to itself or die to itself." He saw the United States as an extension of Eu-ropean civilization and the Atlantic Ocean as a link, rather than a di-vider, between the two continents.

The great task before the European/American civilization was to "receive into its own bosom and raise to its own ideals those ancient and different civilizations by which it is surrounded and outnum-bered," by which he meant China, India, and Japan. A fortified canal through the Central American isthmus was essential, for it would bind the Pacific outposts to the main body of the "European family." It would also advance by thousands of miles the frontiers of European civilization in general and of the United States in particular, as well as link the eastern side of the American continent to the western. Ma-han viewed this mission in the most grandiose terms: The "world of civilized Christianity" must fulfill it or "perish."

But the canal project depended on control of the Caribbean, and Spain was in the way. "In the cluster of island fortresses of the Caribbean is one of the greatest of the nerve centres of the whole body of European civilization; and it is to be regretted that so serious a portion of them now is in hands which not only never have given, but to all appearances never can give, the development which is re-quired by the general interest." The key "island fortress" was Cuba, which Mahan, with some justification, considered continental in size.

Cuba is 760 miles long. Superimposed on a map of the United States, it would stretch from Washington, D.C., to the Mississippi River. In area it is larger than Ohio, Virginia, Tennessee, or Kentucky and one and a half times the size of Ireland. For Mahan its "positional value" was extremely great, and not only because its northern coast lies only 90 miles from Key West. A superior navy in Santiago Bay in Spanish-held Cuba "could very seriously incommode all access of the United States to the Caribbean mainland, and especially to the Isthmus."

In Mahan's graphic description, Florida, Cuba, Haiti, and Puerto Rico formed a long peninsular line broken by narrow sea passages; if the passages were under hostile control, the United States would be blocked from the Gulf of Mexico. Cuba's size, geographic situation, population, number of seaports, and resource potential made it for Mahan the most important single position in the Caribbean, with "no military rival among the islands of the world, except Ireland."

Believing so strongly in Cuba's strategic significance, Mahan should have been alert to signs of U.S.-Spanish confrontation, especially since in New York City he could not escape the hysteria of the warmongering tabloid press. In the week following the *Maine*'s explosion, William Randolph Hearst's *New York Journal* devoted more than fifty pages of coverage to the disaster. Despite the absence of evidence, Hearst left his readers in no doubt about responsibility for the *Maine*'s destruction. The *Journal*'s second-day story was headlined THE WARSHIP *MAINE* WAS SPLIT IN TWO BY AN ENEMY'S SECRET INFERNAL MACHINE. Hearst advertised a fifty-thousand-dollar reward "for the conviction of the criminals" who had sent the American sailors to their death.

Curiously, Mahan did not react immediately. He was intellectually prepared for a war that he considered necessary, but he did not seem to appreciate its imminence. When tension was rising in the weeks before the sinking of the *Maine*, he had been on a lecture tour in Boston and absorbed in correspondence with magazine publishers. He was finishing a chapter for a British history of the Royal Navy. He was also deep into American history, working on several articles about John Paul Jones. If there was a contemporary foreign policy issue claiming his immediate attention, it was Hawaii. He had been pouring into Roosevelt's receptive ear the importance of taking the Pacific archipelago.

Yet Mahan could not avoid a growing concern about the Cuban cockpit. He began by encircling the problem, rather than focusing on its essence. Ten days after the explosion he complained to a publisher that the United States was not as ready for war as it should have been: "How absurd that the U.S. should be anxious about Spain. We might and should have had a navy, in which our only anxiety would have been to do right." To an English friend who had sent him condolences at the loss of American sailors, he took a measured approach, disclaiming any evidence of Spanish treachery and expressing the hope that the tragedy would draw Britain and America closer. It was Roosevelt, from his key position in government, who got Mahan to think seriously about preparing for war. In the weeks after the *Maine* disaster, Roosevelt peppered Mahan with plans for attacking Spain and was gratified that Mahan's views in reply were as hawkish as his own.

Mahan did worry about leaving the country on a planned trip to Europe. Shortly after the *Maine* went down, he queried the Navy Department on whether he should cancel his plans to sail in late March. He was told to go ahead. Still nervous as his departure date loomed, he asked Roosevelt if he expected war. The question caught Roosevelt in a period of exasperation that the president, whom he considered to have "no more backbone than a chocolate eclair," was ignoring his belligerent advice. Out of frustration he told Mahan that hostilities were not inevitable and he could leave. On the eve of his departure Mahan still failed to grasp the importance of the *Maine* disaster: "The year 1898 . . . seems to me now doomed to unproduction; possibly the respite [in Europe] may restore my working powers, for though I dont feel tired out, I feel near it."

He duly sailed for Europe on March 26, with a promise from Roosevelt to recall him if war broke out. When it did, on April 25, a telegram found him in Rome, instructing him to report to Washington immediately. He took ship for home, in disguise and under a pseudonym. From that point on Mahan was to become a key military adviser to the U.S. government. He returned to Washington with the satisfaction of having helped prepare his country for its imperial mission. He had provided an overall strategy for imperialism, badgered the navy into a state of fighting trim, developed a tactical approach to the war for Cuba, and roughed out the rudiments of a role for the colonies-to-be.

2.

When the *Maine* went down, Hay and Mahan were bit players in the unfolding drama of 1898, and Elihu Root, in private life in New York City, was a nonplayer. But Lodge and Roosevelt were stars. Lodge, a member of the Senate Foreign Relations Committee's subcommittee on Cuba, had consorted with Cuban insurrectionists, extolled the strategic and economic value of Cuba for the United States, and publicly advocated Cuba's independence from Spain. Moreover, he was clear on who the enemy was. He despised the "unsmiling" Spanish as "a broken race" and hated their country, right down to its "brutal, savage, and disgusting" bullfights.

Thanks to Lodge's powers of persuasion with President McKinley, Roosevelt settled into his ample office overlooking the White House grounds on April 19, 1897, ten months before the *Maine* disaster. The new assistant secretary of the navy was already clearing the decks for war. To secure his base, he lost no time in appeasing his boss, Secretary Long. This rotund and amiable politician was one of only two college graduates in McKinley's cabinet. He had no qualifications for running the Navy Department other than his old friendship with McKinley in Congress. Cautious and peaceable by nature, Long was intimidated by his deputy's expertise and activism. He vacillated between anxiety about Roosevelt's animal energy and gratitude for his unrivaled competence. His lack of sureness made him a pushover for the young firebrand with his urgent and pugnacious agenda. Roosevelt found Long "just a dear, . . . a man of whom one really becomes fond."

Within a week of taking office, Roosevelt was already alerting the president to possible trouble with Cuba in a memo on his favorite subject of preparedness. Within two months he was at the Naval War College in Newport delivering a fire-breathing speech that might have cost him his job under a more disciplined president than McKinley. The speech displayed most of Roosevelt's cherished themes: the need for America to become a world power, the urgency of being prepared for war, the duty of Congress to fund more and bigger ships, the superiority of offense over defense in naval strategy, the uselessness of diplomacy without force, the delusion of "peace at any price," the immorality of "the soft and easy enjoyment of material comfort," the inevitable clash of races, and, most of all, the virtue of war. The speech was a hymn to war in the spirit of Frederick the Great or Napoleon. Roosevelt actually used the word "war" sixty-two times, a striking anomaly for an administration pledged to peace. War for him was the test of greatness:

> All the great masterful races have been fighting races, and the minute that a race loses the hard fighting virtues, then, no matter what else it may retain, no matter how skilled in commerce and finance, in science or art, it has lost its proud right to stand as the equal of the best. Cowardice in a race, as in an individual, is the unpardonable sin, and a willful failure to prepare for danger may in its effects be as bad as cowardice. The timid man who cannot fight, and the selfish, short-sighted, or foolish man who will not take the steps that will enable him to fight, stand on almost the same plane.

It might have seemed odd for this audience of military intellectuals, some of whom had fought in the Civil War, to hear from a four-eyed Harvard man with no combat experience that sometimes "education merely serves to soften the fibre," while only "the men who have dared greatly in war, or the work which is akin to war, are those who deserve best of the country." No doubt Roosevelt believed, and expected his listeners to believe, that he himself had done work "akin to war," punishing abusive cowpokes, tracking down rustlers, running a municipal police force, and devising a robust naval policy. In any case his reputation as a naval pundit was secure at the War College; *The Naval War of 1812* was required reading there. So he possessed the authority to deliver the punch line of his speech: "No triumph of peace is quite so great as the supreme triumphs of war. . . . As yet no nation can hold its place in the world, or can do any work really worth doing, unless it stands ready to guard its rights with an iron hand."

Roosevelt's intention was to use public platforms to push the government toward a war footing. He understood that speeches by officials are not just private opinions but expressions of government policy. His War College speech was probably not cleared in advance;

neither was it refuted afterward by his superiors. President McKinley in fact told a friend, "I suspect that Roosevelt is right," though he cannot have enjoyed having his hand forced by a thirty-eight-year-old upstart. The speech got great publicity not just because of Roosevelt's growing fame but because it was interpreted as a significant hardening of American policy.

In private Roosevelt went much further. After only two weeks as assistant secretary, he wrote Mahan exuberantly that if he had his way, he would construct a canal through Nicaragua "at once," build a dozen battleships, annex Hawaii, expel Spain from Cuba "tomorrow," and acquire the Danish Virgin Islands. It was quite an agenda for a man who had taken offense at McKinley's suspicion that he might have "preconceived plans."

Recognizing that his views were out of kilter with his president's, Roosevelt cautioned Mahan, "I speak to you with the greatest freedom, for I sympathize with your views, and I have precisely the same idea of patriotism, and of belief in and love for our country. But to no one else, excepting Lodge, do I talk like this." He told Mahan that Lodge had just lobbied the president on similar lines. In August he wrote Lodge that "it would be everything for us to take firm action on behalf of the wretched Cubans. It would be a splendid thing for the Navy, too." Moreover, on Mahan's tip, he raised from oblivion the hawkish war plans that Mahan had commissioned while at the War College and put them into play in governmental discussions.

Roosevelt conspired with Lodge to persuade McKinley to agree to a treaty of annexation of Hawaii. This time the cautious Long was on board probably because of the temptation to overturn the antiannexationist policy of the previous Democratic administration of Grover Cleveland. Roosevelt colluded with the Washington agent of the proannexation Hawaiian "government," filling him in on where the different players stood in the U.S. administration. He also lobbied McKinley directly. The president submitted the treaty to the Senate on June 16, 1897. Though it languished on the Hill for a year, it marked the first major step toward America's imperial future. Roosevelt continued to fuss. He wrote a friend later: "If we don't take Hawaii it will pass into the hands of some strong nation [his fear was Japan], and the chance of our taking it will be gone forever."

The assistant secretary took advantage of Long's generous summer 1897 vacation on his beloved farm in Massachusetts ("Now stay there just exactly as long as you want to") to improve naval readiness and, equally important, to ingratiate himself with the president. Lodge encouraged Roosevelt to act "entirely independently" during the secretary's seven-week absence, and he did. McKinley was charmed by him, taking him driving in the presidential carriage and entertaining him at dinner at the White House.

Roosevelt in turn thrust on the president a proposed war plan or, as he described it to Lodge, an outline of "what I thought ought to be done if things looked menacing about Spain, urging the necessity of taking an immediate and prompt initiative if we wished to avoid the chance of some serious trouble." He proposed harassing the coast of Spain with cruisers, dispatching the main fleet from Key West to attack Cuba, landing an expeditionary force on the island, and blockading, and possibly capturing, Manila. During their talks McKinley expressed the desire to avoid trouble with Spain and was noncommittal on Roosevelt's audacious initiative, although he agreed to continuing the naval buildup.

Roosevelt was as enthusiastic a networker as he was a strategist. He took advantage of the Metropolitan Club, just a block up Seventeenth Street from the Navy Department, to share lunch or dinner with an array of politicians, military officers, or cultural figures who might help advance his military aims. Apart from Lodge, his most important fellow diners were Leonard Wood and George Dewey. Wood, who was to become the commander of the Rough Riders and a colonial governor of Cuba, was a rangy army officer from Massachusetts, a former Indian fighter, and a physician. He was currently serving as McKinley's doctor. Roosevelt admired him for his derring-do, the strength of his character, and his imperialist views.

Dewey was different: a small, debonair naval officer whose humdrum career—he had recently been in charge of lighthouses—concealed a steely determination and a willingness to take risks. Over brandy and cigars he may have conned Roosevelt with war stories exaggerating his prowess. But Roosevelt, a keen judge of character, saw a spark of greatness in Dewey. In Long's absence, he used his political connections—principally Redfield Proctor, a senator from Dewey's home state of Vermont—to get Dewey appointed commander of the Asiatic Squadron over the secretary's favored candidate, a more senior officer. Thus was Dewey positioned to attack the Philippines.

With uncharacteristic understatement, Roosevelt confessed to Hay in London in November 1897, "I am a bit of a jingo." A fortnight later he explained the two reasons for his desire to fight Spain: "First, the advisability on the grounds both of humanity and self-interest of interfering on behalf of the Cubans, and of taking one more step toward the complete freeing of America from European domination; second, the benefit done to our people by giving them something to think of which isn't material gain, and especially the benefit done our military forces by trying both the Army and Navy in actual practise."

Humanity, hemispheric domination, self-improvement, practice for the armed forces: All these motives became immediately attainable with the explosion under the *Maine*. Roosevelt, like Lodge, saw the sinking of the battleship as a new and powerful argument for the conflict with Spain that he had been urging for years. He now approached the problem of Cuba with a new passion. A typical example of his fervor was a letter to Brooks Adams, a fellow jingo: "The blood of the Cubans, the blood of women and children who have perished by the hundred thousand in hideous misery, lies at our door; and the blood of the murdered men of the *Maine* calls not for indemnity but for the full measure of atonement which can only come by driving the Spaniard from the New World."

Roosevelt wasted no time in assigning blame for the sinking. In Hearst's *New York Journal* two days after the blast, the subhead of the lead story proclaimed: "Assistant Secretary Roosevelt Convinced the Explosion of the War Ship Was Not an Accident." When Roosevelt was not leaking to journalists for ulterior motives, he showed some uncertainty about the ship's demise. "The *Maine* was sunk by an act of dirty treachery on the part of the Spaniards *I* believe," he wrote a friend. But to Bamie he said: "No one can as yet tell what the cause of the disaster was." The facts were of no particular consequence to him now that he had a pretext for war. He reprimanded a professor at the Naval Academy for speculating in the press that a coal bunker fire, rather than a mine, had sunk the ship. Roosevelt was using the *Maine* as an excuse to go to war, as Bismarck had used the Ems dispatch and Lyndon Johnson was to use the Tonkin Gulf incident.

January 25, 1898—The *Maine* arrives in Havana Bay where, three weeks later, it will be sunk by an explosion in the hold. The American flag was attached to the wreckage on Memorial Day, 1902, by the newly independent Cuban government. The destruction of the *Maine* intensified the war fever against Spain, even though there was no evidence that the Spanish had set off the explosion. The consensus today is that it was caused accidentally by heat from a fire in a coal bunker next to a powder magazine.

Cuba

General William R. Shafter (right), commander of the Fifth Army Corps in Cuba, was a product of the second-rate U.S. peacetime army. Roosevelt criticized him for his bulk and his timidity, but he succeeded in achieving the surrender of Santiago without a battle.

Theodore Roosevelt (left), as a Rough Rider in his Brooks Brothers uniform, strikes a typically bellicose pose. His nine days of combat in Cuba set him on the path to the presidency, via the governorship of New York and the vice presidency of the United States.

Leonard Wood, a physician and army general, was military governor of Cuba from 1899 until 1902, when the island became independent. He achieved major administrative, economic, and educational reforms, but failed to recognize the strong desire of Cubans to manage their own affairs.

Spanish admiral Pascual Cervera was a tragic figure in the war. He knew that Spain would lose and that he would be the man who ended four centuries of empire. He met his fate with courage and, when he surrendered, was applauded spontaneously by the crew of the *Iowa*.

The Philippines

Commodore George Dewey (left) owed to Roosevelt the Pacific assignment that led to his destruction of the Spanish fleet in Manila Bay on May 1, 1898, and made him an admiral. Dewey was vain, arrogant, and feisty, but he also sympathized with the aspirations of Filipinos more than any other U.S. military officer.

Emilio Aguinaldo (right) first fought against Spain, then against the United States when it refused the Philippines independence. An enigmatic figure, he oscillated between ruthlessness and moderation. Roosevelt and Root called him a "Chinese half-breed," while Dewey held him in respect. His failure to win a mass following among Filipinos and his inept generalship contributed to his defeat in the war against the United States.

The U.S. Army's three-year war in the Philippines was brutal, as suggested by this picture of two American soldiers contemplating the corpses of Filipino soldiers. Atrocities were committed by both sides; Root and Roosevelt covered up many of the American ones.

William Howard Taft devoted eight years to the Philippines—as president of the Philippine Commission, the first civil governor, and U.S. secretary of war. His integrity and energy, en-cased in a 325-pound body, made him the most effective colonial administrator in U.S. history and helped him to win the presidency in 1908.

Jingoes

Even before he became a senator at the age of thirty-six, Albert J. Beveridge had earned a reputation for imperialist oratory. Nobody's speeches in defense of America's conquests in 1898 were more eloquent, more fervent, or more filled with a crusader's ardor. Like Roosevelt, Beveridge was a progressive as well as an imperialist, leading the fight for meat-packing standards, trust regulation, income tax, and laws against child labor.

William Randolph Hearst did not invent the yellow press, but he took it to new heights (or depths). In his *New York Journal* he pressed tirelessly for war against Spain, often exploiting or inventing human interest stories deifying Cubans and demonizing Spaniards. A genuine populist, Hearst hated the Republican aristocracy represented by Roosevelt, Lodge, and Root.

Goo-goos

Carl Schurz had the look and language of an Old Testament prophet. A political refugee from Prussia, he acquired a distinguished record in the United States as a Civil War general, a senator from Missouri, and a publisher of political journals. He believed that U.S. behavior in Cuba and the Philippines betrayed the very American values which had inspired his immigration to the United States.

Senator George Frisbie Hoar of Massachusetts was the strongest opponent of imperialism in the Senate. He urged the independence of Cuba, Puerto Rico, and the Philippines, and was one of only two Republican senators to vote against the Treaty of Paris. A descendant of several fighters in the American Revolution and of a signer of the Declaration of Independence, he quoted the Declaration and the Constitution against the jingoes.

Andrew Carnegie provided the steel for the buildup of the U.S. Navy during the 1890s, but that did not stop him from passionately opposing the annexation of the Philippines. He signed letters to John Hay, whom he had entertained at his castle in Scotland, "Your Bitterest Opponent."

Finley Peter Dunne, the Chicago newspaperman who created the Irish American sage Mr. Dooley, had a huge following for Mr. Dooley's satires on the wars against the Spanish and the Filipinos. Mr. Dooley treated Roosevelt and his allies as foppish, pretentious, autocratic, insensitive, and stupid.

Roosevelt.   Gage.   Knox.   Long.   Hay.   Wilson.   Root.   Hitchcock.   Smith.

In this picture of Theodore Roosevelt's cabinet, Hay (secretary of state) and Root (secretary of war) are immediately to the president's left. Navy Secretary Long stands just behind Hay's head. Roosevelt considered Root the ablest member of the cabinet. His opinion of Hay was much lower, though Hay's Open Door policy marked the beginning of a long-term U.S. interest in the Pacific and his Anglophilia helped launch a century-long friendship with Great Britain.

The State, War, and Navy Building (now the Eisenhower Executive Office Building) was the locus of most U.S. policy-making in the period of the Spanish-American War. When completed in 1888, it was the largest office building in the country, with 900 exterior columns and more than 550 rooms. Roosevelt, Hay, Root, and Mahan all had offices in the building, which also served for McKinley's and Roosevelt's cabinet meetings. On their way to the presidency, William H. Taft, Franklin Delano Roosevelt, Harry Truman, Lyndon Johnson, Richard Nixon, Gerald Ford, and George H. W. Bush all worked in the building. Visually, it has always been controversial. Mark Twain called it "the ugliest building in America," whereas its admirers consider it the finest example of Second Empire architecture west of Paris.

President Theodore Roosevelt, here with the props of author and statesman, exudes the confidence of a newly powerful nation. His domination of the Caribbean, his role in wresting Panama from Colombia so he could commence construction of a transisthmian canal, his successful mediation between Japan and Russia after their war, and his creation of a powerful navy added substance to Lodge's boast in 1898, "We have risen to be one of the world's great powers."

On Friday, February 25, 1898, he found an opportunity to spring into action. Underlings in a bureaucracy know that Fridays are often good days to exercise authority, as superiors begin departing for the weekend. It was on that Friday that Long left the office at noon to get a massage and visit a doctor for his aching corns, leaving his excitable deputy in charge. He was well aware of the risk he was taking. He left Roosevelt a clear instruction, written in his own hand: "Do not take any such step affecting the policy of the Administration without consulting the President or me. I am not away from town and my intention [is] to have you look after the routine of the office while I get a quiet day off. . . . I am anxious to have no unnecessary occasion for a sensation in the papers."

Roosevelt should probably have taken some time off too—Edith was seriously ill with suspected typhoid fever, and that very morning her husband had summoned a doctor from Johns Hopkins. But instead as acting secretary he took command of the cable machine, alerting the far-flung fleet that war might be imminent, assigning rendezvous points, organizing maximum supplies of coal, ordering supplemental ammunition, and urging Congress to extend the authorized recruitment of seamen. Most important, he sent a famous cable to Dewey, commander of the Asiatic Squadron thanks to Roosevelt's foresight: ORDER THE SQUADRON, EXCEPT THE MONOCACY [a Civil War relic], TO HONG KONG. KEEP FULL OF COAL. IN THE EVENT OF DECLARATION WAR SPAIN, YOUR DUTY WILL BE TO SEE THAT THE SPANISH SQUADRON DOES NOT LEAVE THE ASIATIC COAST, AND THEN OFFENSIVE OPERATIONS IN PHILIPPINE ISLANDS. KEEP OLYMPIA [Dewey's flagship] UNTIL FURTHER ORDERS. ROOSEVELT.

On return to his office Long did not welcome his deputy's act of insubordination. He vented to his diary: "I find that Roosevelt, in his precipitate way, has come very near causing more of an explosion than happened to the *Maine*. Having authority for that time of Acting Secretary, he immediately began to launch peremptory orders. He has gone at things like a bull in a china shop. It shows how the best fellow in the world—and with splendid capacities—is worse than no use if he lacks a cool head and discrimination."

Roosevelt's head was cooler than Long thought. The impulsive assistant secretary had taken the trouble to invite an influential member of the Senate Foreign Relations Committee, his friend Lodge, to his office on that fateful Friday afternoon. Lodge saw what Roosevelt was doing and no doubt approved it, thereby putting the stamp of the jingoes in the Senate on it. It is no wonder that neither McKinley nor Long countermanded Roosevelt's order to Dewey. In any case Roosevelt's strategic sense was flawless. If the United States was to fight Spain, the lightly defended Philippines was the ideal place to initiate hostilities. He brushed right past the fact that the United States had no grievance with Spain over the Philippines, while Cuba had been a cockpit of contention for years. Not only did Roosevelt's cable presage the course of the war, but in a broader sense it also started the United States on its journey to becoming a great power.

3.

In 1898 Spain was in a centuries-long decline from its great days of exploration and expansion in the sixteenth century. Its downward slide was accelerated by two major nineteenth-century rebellions in its Cuban outpost, where disparities in wealth piled social grievances onto political ones. The United States, on the other hand, was on the rise, propelled by the unprecedented economic boom after the Civil War and by the growing power of its navy. It is hard to avoid the conclusion that if it came to war, Spain could not win and the United States could not lose.

The calamity for Spain was that the United States was focusing its new power and ambitions directly on Cuba. For Americans the island was a traditional objective; for the Spanish it was a possession not to be surrendered, no matter what the odds. After the loss of nearly all their Latin American colonies in the early part of the century, Cuba remained their last major possession, a source of wealth, an outlet for colonization, and the last frayed symbol of their greatness. It was the "ever faithful isle"; it must remain Spanish. As a Spanish foreign minister had said in 1848, "Spaniards sooner than see the island transferred to any power . . . would prefer seeing it sunk in the ocean." Cuba was particularly important to the Spanish Army, and the army's loyalty was necessary to the stability of the monarchy in Spain.

Trouble began with a revolution in Spain in 1868. A military rebellion overthrew the Bourbon queen Isabella II and established a constitutional monarchy with a king recruited from Italy. At the same time, in Cuba, a Creole (Cuba-born) planter aristocracy mounted a revolution against Spanish rule. The Spanish prime minister, the moderate general Juan Prim, grew concerned that nearly one hundred thousand Spanish troops were being tied down in Cuba and launched an attempt to conciliate the rebels. But his efforts managed to alienate both conservatives, who wanted a tougher approach, and republicans, who complained that because of the war, neither conscription nor taxes were being reduced. Not for the last time, Spain's policy in Cuba became entangled in domestic politics.

The "war of 1868" in Cuba also brought the United States into contention with Spain in a way that foreshadowed the issues of 1898. The rebel leaders, whose sugar production was mainly directed toward the American rather than the Spanish market, sought annexation by the United States. Short of that, they wanted U.S. recognition of their rights as a belligerent. President Grant and several of his cabinet secretaries were tempted to accord them such recognition, but Secretary of State Hamilton Fish was wary. Fish opposed Spain's dominion in Cuba, but he was reluctant to antagonize the Spanish at a time when they were moving toward a more liberal political system at home. Nor was he encouraged that the rebels had not come out against slavery; some were slaveholders themselves.

To square this diplomatic circle, Fish persuaded Grant to follow two of his predecessors, Polk and Buchanan, and try to buy Cuba. In 1869 the president sent General Dan Sickles off to Madrid to negotiate with Prim. The young first secretary of embassy who greeted him on arrival, John Hay, was enamored of Spanish republicanism and had been lobbying for American support for Cuban independence. Now Sickles brought an approach Hay could support with enthusiasm. But there was no sale. Political conditions in Spain were moving again to the right. Prim was assassinated in December 1870, and his successors, goaded by the army, launched a crackdown on the rebels in Cuba. A shaky Spanish republican government, which took office in 1873, was so preoccupied with domestic violence at home that it could neither reverse the brutal tactics of the army in Cuba nor respond to the American interest in buying the island.

The U.S. government was thus stymied, but there was considerable unofficial American support for the Cuban rebels. Senator John Sherman, later McKinley's secretary of state, pleaded their case in

Congress. Horace Greeley of the *New York Tribune*, undoubtedly aided by Hay, just signed on as an editorial writer, advocated action to help them. Private filibustering ships were launched from New York and Florida for raids on Cuba; the U.S. Navy intercepted some, but many got through. One that did not was the *Virginius*, a Cuban rebel supply ship flying U.S. colors. The Spanish captured it off Cuba and executed all fifty-three people on board, including its American captain. This extreme act led Secretary Fish to seek to lower the temperature of U.S.-Spanish relations through negotiations. An ensuing bilateral agreement staved off war but could not dilute the bad blood between the two countries.

The decade-long war in Cuba petered out in 1878 with the failure of the rebellion. It had cost some 208,000 Spanish and 50,000 Cuban lives and left on both sides a residue of bitterness and distrust against the United States. Future Spanish governments would not forget American covetousness over Cuba or the transparent sympathy voiced by prominent Americans for the rebel cause. The rebels for their part felt betrayed: The United States had not granted them belligerent rights, had frustrated their filibustering efforts, and had failed to force Spain into concessions. For the Grant administration the main sticking point was the rebels' failure to condemn slavery. That would not be a stumbling block in the next Cuban rebellion in the 1890s; slavery was abolished in Cuba in 1886.

Except for slavery, virtually all the other bilateral issues from the 1868–78 war returned in the Cuban uprising of 1895–98: belligerent rights, U.S. interest in the purchase of Cuba, American sympathy for the rebels, and Spanish inability to deal with Cuba independently of the political situation at home. Moreover, on the Spanish and Cuban sides, the major actors were almost all the same. The leading Spanish conservative politician during the first rebellion, Antonio Cánovas del Castillo, was prime minister at the outset of the second. The Liberal party leader from the 1860s, Práxedes Sagasta, succeeded Cánovas as prime minister in 1897. On the rebel side the outstanding military leaders in the 1868–78 war, Máximo Gómez and Antonio Maceo, both led troops again in 1895 after long spells of exile.

War in Cuba began in 1895 in the rural and mountainous east, like the 1868 war and like Fidel Castro's rebellion six decades later. The intellectual leader of the rebels, José Martí, who was killed in the early weeks of the war, had framed a radical agenda that embraced not only independence from Spain but also social revolution within Cuba. For Martí the conflict was between black and white—some 80 percent of the rebels were black—and between country and city.

In Gómez and Maceo, who was black himself, the rebels had skillful and veteran leadership. In eastern Cuba they controlled the countryside, pinning the Spanish soldiers to roads and towns. Even in the west, where the capital city lay, there was considerable sympathy for the revolution among all except the Spanish-born minority, the *peninsulares*. The rebel plan was to move west to threaten Havana; by the end of 1895 they had advanced across more than half the country. Their war was a guerrilla war of movement, avoidance of confrontation, raids, and sometimes acts of terror.

The Spanish Army was in no doubt about the necessity of crushing this formidable challenge. During the war two hundred thousand troops were dispatched to Cuba, the largest military force ever to cross the Atlantic to that time. The Spanish commander, General Arsenio Martínez Campos, who had governed Cuba as captain general after the earlier rebellion, submitted gloomy reports to the prime minister. He feared that it might be necessary to force the peasants into the towns in order to cut off the rebels' source of support. Martínez Campos, an intelligent and reflective officer, confessed that he had not used his "full powers" to carry through such a ruthless policy. The man he identified as being willing to use them, General Valeriano Weyler, a veteran of the First Cuban War, replaced him in early 1896.

Whether the Spanish pursued a conciliatory or a tough military policy, the prospect of its success was inhibited by the tangled political situation in both Spain and Cuba. Cánovas, prime minister in a restored monarchy under a queen regent, hoped to prevent developments in Cuba from upsetting stability at home, as they had done in 1868. But the army, guarantor of stability in Spain, was the instigator of violence in Cuba. Lodge had urged Cánovas to deal with the rebellion quickly, but the Spanish leader found himself hardly able to deal with it at all.

Some sentiment existed in Spain for giving Cuba autonomous status under loose Spanish rule; there was even an Autonomist party in the Spanish parliament. But its Autonomist counterpart in Cuba, composed largely of rich Creoles, found itself frustrated by the

Unionist "Spanish party," consisting mainly of the Spanish-born *peninsulares*, which controlled local government on the island. The Unionists warned that autonomy would lead quickly to Cuba's separation from Spain and, especially, to the end of the preferential customs arrangement with the home country, from which they derived considerable economic benefits.

In fact Spain's mercantilist approach to its colonies, dating back to the sixteenth century, militated against autonomy. For the Unionists the colonies were, as always, supposed to trade first and foremost with Spain. But when Cuba's major products, sugar and tobacco, began to attract lucrative markets in the United States, the traditional system lost its viability for most of the non-Spanish Cuban population. The Creole plantation owners, who naturally favored free trade over protection, became increasingly disenchanted with a colonial rule that discriminated against their profits. The tendency of these Creoles and the peasants who worked for them was to move toward a clean break with the mother country. The tendency of the Spanish *peninsulares*, tied to the old ways, was to support military repression. It was a dynamic stalemate, of the sort visible after the 1970s in Northern Ireland, between a hard-line party insisting on a rigid association with the homeland and a disenchanted separatist population with ties to another country.

Cánovas was hamstrung. Concessions to Cuba would destroy his Spanish constituency there, but a crackdown would risk losing the island altogether. Though a conservative, he probably understood that a grant of autonomy would be the best way to end the war and avoid the loss of Cuba. But the army, supported by the *peninsulares*, objected. Since the army was necessary for the preservation of the Bourbon monarchy, and indeed of his own government, Cánovas acceded to a strategy designed to crush the rebels. General Weyler, promising "a salutary rigor," was given the license to carry it out. Weyler had learned about scorched-earth tactics from close study of William Tecumseh Sherman's campaigns in the American Civil War. Within weeks of his arrival in Cuba, he expanded on Martínez Campos's idea of forcing the peasants in from the countryside by ordering their confinement in secure military areas.

Weyler was not the only military strategist to resort to what he called reconcentration against guerrillas. A similar approach was used only a few years later by the British in the Boer War and much later in Malaya and by the Americans in the Philippines and later in Vietnam. But in Weyler's hands the policy was particularly disruptive and cruel; close to one hundred thousand Cubans died as a result of it. It provoked criticism in Spain as well as America. To placate the queen regent, Maria Christina, the opposition Liberals, and the United States, Cánovas distanced himself from Weyler. He also gave lip service to reforms but, to appease his conservative constituency, decided to postpone them until military victory had been won.

During 1896 Weyler rolled back some of the rebel advances in the west, and in December Spanish troops killed the charismatic black general Antonio Maceo. Cánovas moved in February 1897 to give Cuba greater autonomy, but his policy of balancing reform with repression ended with his assassination in August by an Italian anarchist, possibly with Cuban complicity. A Liberal government under Sagasta, who was partial to Cuban autonomy, took office; within weeks Weyler resigned. His successor immediately announced the cessation of all offensives and offered a full amnesty for all political prisoners. Confident of winning the war, the rebels rejected it.

The Sagasta government began work on constitutional changes that went farther than Cánovas's limited gestures toward autonomy for Cuba. But Sagasta's reform fell between the widening poles of political opinion in Cuba itself. For most Cubans it failed to satisfy the growing appetite for independence, while for the Unionists it was a sellout of Spanish interests and Spanish citizens. It was the violent Unionist demonstrations against Sagasta's policies and American complicity with the rebels that brought the *Maine* to Havana Bay to protect the American community.

Neither harsh nor lenient policies could save Spain's weakening hold over Cuba. In truth Spain was no longer capable of colonial rule. Its economy was shaky, its army and navy were retrograde and spiritless, and its political structure had been unstable since the revolution of 1868. The Bourbon monarchy was back in place, but it was presided over by a twelve-year-old boy (the future Alfonso XIII) and a foreign queen regent, the Austrian Maria Christina. Spain's choices were bleak. Its frail constitutional framework might not survive the independence of Cuba; neither could it withstand a ruthless and draining war against the rebels.

As it was, fifty thousand Spanish soldiers died in Cuba: two thousand in combat, the rest of disease. Four centuries after Columbus's discovery of the island, Spanish rule there was lurching to Armageddon; it was only a matter of time. The U.S. Navy was not necessary to end an empire already condemned by Spain's internal contradictions.

4.

Nevertheless the United States did become massively involved in Cuba, and that involvement only made things worse for Spain. By 1894 American imports from Cuba were three times U.S. imports from all other Latin American countries. As a source of imports to the United States, Cuba was, amazingly, exceeded only by Britain and Germany. Moreover, Cuba accounted for more than half the United States' export trade to Latin America. Cuba was even more dependent on this bilateral trade: Its exports to the United States were 87 percent of its total exports; its imports from the United States were 38 percent of the total. McKinley's Tariff Act of 1890, which had made sugar duty-free, helped produce those stunning statistics. But U.S.-Cuban trade continued at a high level even after sugar was taken off the free list in 1894.

The Sugar Trust, a consortium of eight leading American refiners started in 1888 by Henry Osborne Havemeyer and represented by Elihu Root, established U.S. domination over Cuban sugar production by using its monopoly position to force down producers' prices in Cuba. Havemeyer joined a Boston refiner, Edwin Atkins, to buy sugar plantations in Cuba. Other American businessmen followed, eroding further the Spanish economic hold on the island. These sugar barons had no love for Spanish rule because it was exercised by conservative politicians who favored protectionist policies to the advantage of Spain over the United States.

On the other hand, the rebellion that began in 1895 was a potentially dangerous threat to American profits. It could not be trusted to remain in the hands of the Creole planters; indeed peasants were beginning to burn plantations. In early 1896 Atkins urged Senator Lodge not to press for recognition of the insurgents as belligerents, on the ground that recognition would remove Spain's legal responsibility to defend U.S. property in Cuba. Atkins also expressed doubts that the insurgents could establish a stable government. Lodge agreed with him but was too committed to the rebels to abandon his support for their rights as belligerents and, indeed, their independence.

Atkins was also a good friend of President Cleveland's secretary of state, Richard Olney, whom he talked into pressing for a Cuban autonomy that stopped short of independence. In April 1896 Olney, under Atkins's influence, offered to mediate between Spain and the rebels. Prime Minister Cánovas, at that point anticipating a victory by Weyler, turned him down. The Cleveland administration then retreated to a policy of strict neutrality, hoping for the increasingly unlikely resolution of the war on the basis of Spanish sovereignty and Cuban autonomy. In the McKinley administration the business community, represented politically by McKinley's friend and political mentor Mark Hanna, now an Ohio senator, continued to flinch from the prospect of a destabilizing war but produced no alternatives to it. American business was finding itself increasingly incapable of propounding and selling a coherent strategy on Cuba.

Another U.S. concern, the humanitarian, was a major and still-underrated factor in shaping the American view of Spanish Cuba. Three of America's earlier wars had been fought for specific principles: political liberty in 1776, freedom of the seas in 1812, and preservation of the Union in 1861. The Spanish-American War was the first in which Americans were activated in large part by the way a foreign government treated its subjects. Catholic, retrograde, obscurantist Spain already had a poor reputation in the late nineteenth century American culture of dynamic Protestantism. Even Hay's *Castilian Days*, as objective a picture of Spain as the American reader was likely to get, was scathing in its denunciation of the oppressive influence of the Catholic Church on the Spanish people.

Spain's efforts to put down the rebellions in Cuba in 1868 and 1895 met heavy criticism in the United States. When General Weyler started forcing peasants into camps, he became the ideal villain; Butcher Weyler, he was called. The rebels, on the other hand, enjoyed a fantasized image among the American public: the men proud and heroic, the women pure and beautiful. The sensationalist press played on these stereotypes. Hearst's *New York Journal*, for example, made a heroine of Evangelina Cisneros, a winsome young Cuban woman with rebel connections who was imprisoned and probably abused in a

Spanish jail. A Hearst reporter smuggled her out of prison and into the United States, where she stayed at the Waldorf-Astoria, dined at Delmonico's, and was received at the White House by the president himself. Fed on such stories and on the cruder fare of Weyler's atrocities, Americans developed a real concern for the human rights of Cubans, and made their representatives in Congress pay attention. Human rights—or moral rights, as they were called in the 1890s— were also an issue that could easily be exploited by those, like Roosevelt and Lodge, for whom strategic objectives were paramount.

When McKinley took office in March 1897, he found among Americans a growing opposition to Spanish rule in Cuba, sympathy for the aims of the Cuban revolution, and even willingness to consider war with Spain. He had a Republican Congress that, unlike Republicans in the first half of the twentieth century, held expansionist views. Strategic and humanitarian interests were moving the country toward war. These interests contained a potential division over what kind of Cuba a war ought to produce. For the master strategist Mahan, Cuba was an island fortress to be controlled, even annexed by the United States. For those moved by human rights and the suffering of Cubans, the island should be independent, run by its own people.

The last thing the new president wanted was a war in Cuba. As an advocate of American business interests he did not dare shake the stability of the American economy, which was recovering nicely from the panic of 1893. A decorated veteran of the Civil War, McKinley once asserted: "I have been through one war; I have seen the dead piled up; and I do not want to see another." He was by nature gentle and pacific, one of the nicest men ever to sit in the Congress or the White House. Hay called him a man of "unfailing courtesy and good will" with "a rare power of making friends and keeping them."

McKinley had hoped that the Cuba problem could be settled on Cleveland's watch. When it was not, he told the outgoing president the night before his inauguration that if he could avert war with Spain during his term, he would be "the happiest man in the world." The next day in his inaugural address he assured the American people: "We want no wars of conquest; we must avoid the temptation of territorial aggression. War should never be entered upon until every agency of peace has failed; peace is preferable to war in almost every contingency." Shortly afterward, he told Root, whom he was trying unsuccessfully to send to Spain as his envoy, that war must be prevented "at all hazards." He attested to Carl Schurz, an outspoken anti-imperialist, that "you may be sure there will be no jingo nonsense under my Administration."

In the national security area McKinley's cabinet was strikingly weak. The force of Roosevelt's kinetic personality overwhelmed the secretary of the navy's conciliatory preferences. Long could wring his hands but do little else. The War Department, in charge of the army, was presided over by Russell Alger, a former governor of Michigan, whose leadership and substantive abilities were as scanty as Long's. Alger had the additional baggage of a suspect record as a Civil War commander, having been accused of being absent from his command during a military action. He was inclined to compensate by urging a demonstration of what the army could do. But he was not a consistent hawk; McKinley remarked on his "war days" and his "anti-war days."

The State Department, traditional repository of the view that diplomacy was preferable to war, was the weakest institution of the three. Secretary John Sherman, when an Ohio senator, had been a fierce Hispanophobe and backer of American intervention on behalf of Cuba's independence. But by 1898 he had turned into an opponent of war and expansion, even though he was the brother of the general whom Butcher Weyler so admired. Sherman was only sixty-five, but his growing senility made him a cipher and an embarrassment. Most of the foreign policy work passed into the hands of his two deputies.

The senior assistant secretary, Judge William R. Day, another Ohioan and a friend of McKinley's, was personally antiwar but too timid to stand up for his views. The other assistant secretary, Alvey A. Adee, a rare career diplomat, was an indispensable master of diplomatic issues and practice, but his eccentricity and his deafness made him ineffective as a peace advocate. So State, the natural center of opposition to war, was led, as a foreign diplomat wickedly observed, by a secretary who knew nothing, a first assistant who said nothing, and a second assistant who heard nothing.

Even among his own appointees, McKinley thus had no effective advocates of alternative approaches to Roosevelt's promiscuous war-mongering and to a groundswell in Congress for forceful action. Personally the president was not as strong as Cleveland had been in withstanding pressures for intervention. Moreover, he was himself appalled at the brutality of the Spanish actions to put down the rebellion. In his public statements he consistently invoked civilization and humanity in expressing sympathy for the Cuban people. He even initiated a relief drive for Cuba and contributed the huge sum of five thousand dollars from his own pocket. Most of all, he kept his finger to the winds of American politics. He was a follower, not a leader, of opinion. As it shifted toward war, he shifted with it, though to Roosevelt's exasperation, he agonized all the way.

Set against this background of rising American belligerence, McKinley's diplomatic objectives never got close to what the Spanish, mired in their own inflexibility, could be expected to accept. U.S. policy on Cuba had two objectives, one stable, one shifting. The humanitarian goal remained consistent: a genuine end to the reconcentration policy and a relief program for its victims. The political goal began with autonomy for Cuba, then tilted toward independence, and finally settled on political and military intervention and control by the United States.

The tensions inherent in these policy shifts were mirrored by the views of McKinley's representatives in Madrid and Havana. In the tradition of American diplomacy since the Civil War, both were former generals. The consul general in Havana, Fitzhugh Lee, was a bombastic Confederate Army veteran and Democratic Virginia politician; he was a Cleveland appointee who had been kept on. Lee openly sympathized with the Cuban rebels and wanted Washington to intervene in the war militarily with the aim of annexing Cuba. The minister in Madrid from July 1897 was Stewart Woodford, a former Union general and New York Republican politician. Woodford had a keen eye for Spanish politics and a deep commitment to a peaceful settlement of the Spanish-Cuban dispute via autonomy for Cuba. He was a friend of McKinley's, and at the outset of his mission, his views were close to McKinley's own. In his ten months in Madrid, Woodford varied little. It was the president who changed.

Woodford's initial démarche in the summer of 1897 urged the Spanish government to adopt a policy favoring Cuban autonomy but warned that the United States might recognize the Cuban rebels and even intervene if there were no progress. The Liberal government that took over after Cánovas's assassination helpfully promised major concessions that allowed McKinley, in his annual message to Congress on December 6, to ask that Spain be given a "reasonable chance" to end the war. If it failed, the president raised the possibility of intervention by force, though he ruled out annexation as "criminal aggression." While Woodford in Madrid believed that autonomy could work, Lee, in Havana and closer to the insurgency, saw no possibility of a negotiated settlement on that basis. He ridiculed the idea that the rebels would ever accept anything short of independence. Indeed the rebel general Gómez had threatened to shoot any of his soldiers who supported autonomy.

The Spanish, deeply suspicious of American motives since the Ten Years' War of 1868–78, had talked themselves into the conviction that the rebels' strength came mainly from American support rather than indigenous factors. As Woodford reported, "all Spain has been led to believe that all help to the insurrection comes from us and that the rebellion only lives because of our sympathy and assistance." It was true that the rebel leaders had planned most of their strategy from the sanctuary of New York City apartments and that filibustering expeditions from American ports had reached Cuba about a third of the time. So a leitmotiv of Spanish diplomacy was to urge America to stop supporting the insurgents. The queen regent asked Woodford plaintively whether the United States would denounce the rebels and break up the New York junta if Spain granted autonomy to Cuba. The Spanish would not, or could not, face the reality that the main issue in Cuba was their colonial policy, not American meddling. They fastened on autonomy because independence would destabilize Spain and theaten the monarchy. But if autonomy failed, in Woodford's shrewd analysis, "the Queen will have to choose between losing her throne or losing Cuba at the risk of war with us."

One idea fleetingly offered by McKinley as a way back from the brink of war was the sale of Cuba to the United States. For the president this approach, attempted unsuccessfully by three of his predecessors, would satisfy both doves and hawks. It would avoid war, solve the human rights problems, and bring Cuba under full American influence. But for Spain the prospect was not enticing, though as a last resort it might be less humiliating than a rebel victory or a lost war against the United States. For the Cuban rebels it was not attractive. Martí, who would certainly have opposed it, was dead, but even his successors were wary of replacing one colonial overlord with another.

Back in the summer of 1897 McKinley had used unofficial contacts to sound out the Spanish about a purchase. In March 1898 he tried again through Woodford, who was enthusiastic about the idea. An offer of three hundred million dollars—more than forty times what the United States had paid for Alaska—was floated. The queen regent had previously refused to contemplate the alienation of Cuba from her son's inheritance. Now the unraveling of Spanish rule in Cuba compelled her interest. After discussing the issue with her advisers, she scheduled a meeting with Woodford. But the meeting was canceled; evidently Maria Christina could not achieve a critical mass of support. With the purchase of Cuba a nonstarter, mutually acceptable options dwindled to nothing.

To make matters worse, in the first months of 1898 a series of disparate events in the United States brought bilateral relations to the snapping point. On February 9 Hearst's *New York Journal* printed the facsimile of a purloined letter from the Spanish minister in Washington, Enrique Dupuy de Lome, to a friend in Cuba, in which Dupuy de Lome insulted McKinley, calling him "weak," "a would-be politician," and a "bidder for the admiration of the crowd." At the exposure of his indiscretion the chagrined minister did his diplomatic duty by cabling his resignation forthwith to the Spanish Foreign Office. But the image of Spain was tarnished further.

Americans were still shaking their heads and their fingers when the *Maine* went to the bottom a week later. The general view was that the Spanish had blown up the ship with a mine. The reaction of the press and public, an orgy of anti-Spanish invective and calls for war, was so predictable that in itself it constituted the best evidence for why the explosion could not have been the work of the Spanish government. Why would Spain in its weakened state want to provoke such American hostility? McKinley responded to the rising clamor by pushing through the Congress, in only two days and with no opposing votes, a fifty-million-dollar appropriation for national defense. Woodford reported that the Spanish were stunned at the size and the speed of the appropriation. He forecast that the bill would severely reduce the chances of gaining autonomy for Cuba since it would encourage the rebels to fight on.

Into this superheated atmosphere burst an unexpected event that electrified the Senate and the country. On March 17 Redfield Proctor, the Republican senator from Vermont and a respected businessman, delivered a short speech to the Senate about his recent visit to Cuba. It was Proctor who on Roosevelt's suggestion had persuaded McKinley to put George Dewey in command of the Asiatic Squadron. But the senator had not been a hawk on Cuba. Now, focusing on the violation of human rights on the island, he described the pitiful condition of the four hundred thousand Cubans who had been displaced by Weyler's reconcentration policy and concluded that the entire native population of Cuba was "struggling for freedom and deliverance from the worst misgovernment of which I ever had knowledge."

Proctor's reputation for probity brought home to Americans the evils of the Spanish reconcentration camps. His speech had a special effect on the business community, which was still hesitant about fighting Spain. Former President Benjamin Harrison commented that no parliamentary speech in the past fifty years had "so powerfully affected the public sentiment." House Speaker Reed, a determined opponent of war, commented bitterly in reference to Proctor's marble business: "Proctor's position might have been expected. A war will make a large market for gravestones."

Four days after Senator Proctor's bombshell, the report of the naval court of inquiry on the *Maine* was completed. The investigation had been conducted by four naval officers headed by William T. Sampson, an ordnance and gunnery officer who within weeks was given command of the Cuban naval campaign. It was better than a whitewash, but not much. The court questioned survivors, visited Havana, and sent divers down to examine the wreckage, which was in shallow water. It did not, however, call the two naval technical experts who had publicly expressed the view that the explosions had come from inside the ship.

The court's conclusion, not surprisingly, was that the navy was not to blame. It decided that the first of two explosions was caused by a mine under the bottom of the ship. Equally predictably, a Spanish inquiry concluded that the ship had blown up from inside. (An investigation carried out in 1976 by U.S. Admiral Hyman Rickover, then in command of America's nuclear submarine program, largely agreed with the Spanish conclusion.) While the Sampson inquiry pronounced itself unable to assign blame, McKinley knew that its findings would resonate in the country with hardly less force than the explosions themselves. The president sat on the report for nearly a week, then delivered it to Congress. Fine print aside, its political effect was to incriminate Spain.

Reluctance among Americans to take their country into war had been based on antijingo feelings held by McKinley and others who remembered the carnage of the Civil War, on the view that the United States had no right to interfere in the affairs of another country, and on the reluctance of American business to disturb a profitable, if crumbling, status quo. The *Maine* disaster, the Sampson report, the lurid press accounts of Spanish atrocities, and Senator Proctor's eyewitness description undercut all these antiwar arguments.

The country was now speeding toward war. Lodge, playing with deft flattery on McKinley's party loyalties, warned him of the consequences of weakness. He wrote the president on March 21:

> The unanimity with which you are supported at this moment has never I think been equalled at any crisis in our history. . . . It is an awful trust which is thus placed in you Mr. President at this moment. . . . It is equally true that this unanimity of support, so freely and patriotically given, would disintegrate in a day if there were to be hesitation or weakness shown in dealing with the *Maine* incident or the Cuban question at large, and instead of silent union of all we should have warring factions and bitter debates.

Roosevelt was at the limits of frustration. He made a nuisance of himself in cabinet meetings, which, thanks to Long's generosity or laxness, he was allowed to attend. To his brother-in-law Will Cowles, he wrote on March 30: "I have advised the President in the presence of his Cabinet, as well as Judge Day and Senator Hanna, as strongly as I know how, to settle this matter instantly by armed intervention; and I told the President in the plainest language that no other course was compatible with out national honor, or with the claims of humanity on behalf of the wretched women and children of Cuba." Roosevelt accurately saw the divisions in the government: "The President is resolute to have peace at any price. . . . Congress as a whole wishes either war or action that would result in war." But he failed to see that McKinley was moving toward the more belligerent congressional position.

Elihu Root, the New York Republican with corporate ties and no enthusiasm for war, perfectly reflected the shift among American moderates toward a war policy. In a letter on April 2 to Cornelius Bliss, fellow New York reformer and now McKinley's secretary of the interior, Root showed himself ready to bow to reality in order to preserve the influence of the president and the Republican party: ". . . when it is once certain that diplomacy has failed and that the Government of the United States is about to engage in war with Spain, the duty of restraint is ended and the duty of leadership begins. Fruitless attempts to retard or hold back the enormous momentum of the people bent upon war would result in the destruction of the President's power and influence, in depriving the country of its natural leader, in the destruction of the President's party."

But he found the decision for war a difficult one and laid out an undoubtedly heartfelt argument against American military action: "I deplore war. I have earnestly hoped that it might not come. I deny the obligation of the American people to make the tremendous sacrifices which it must entail, not only of treasure but of life, for the purpose of aiding the Cubans or any other people. I agree with the President that it is not his duty to sacrifice his own people for the benefit of others."

As a lawyer he put together a case against Spain based on human rights: "I cannot doubt that if the American people wish to make war upon Spain because of her acts in Cuba, if they are willing to make the sacrifices required, they have a moral right to do so. The Cuban cause is just. The Cubans are exercising their inalienable rights in their rebellion. They have a hundred times the cause that we had in 1776 or that the English had in 1688. When we take up their just quarrel we are doing no wrong to Spain and violating no law divine or international."

Finally, as an American Root argued for resolve from the president and loyalty from the people: "I prefer that we should not do it; I would prevent it if I could; I think the President has been right in trying to prevent it; but if it is to be done, then every American ought to be for the war heart and soul, and first and foremost and without the slightest uncertainty or question should be the President of the United States." Bliss showed the letter to the president, who was impressed with it, no doubt because it was close to his own thinking.

The shift was also apparent in U.S. diplomacy. By the end of March American and Spanish positions had begun to diverge even more. The one thing on which the two sides could agree was that the reconcentration must end. But even here Washington found Madrid too slow in dismantling Weyler's camps. The Spanish, maddeningly, kept trying to exact political payment again and again for small steps to eradicate reconcentration.

On the other demands, put forward by Woodford on instruction, American officials found the Spanish even more obdurate or dilatory. The Americans wanted a cease-fire. The Spanish agreed but, in deference to the army's pride, said it would have to be at the request of the rebels, who, as everybody knew, would not initiate or even accept an end to the fighting. Washington also wanted to be the "final arbiter" in peace negotiations between Spain and the insurgents. The Spanish, sensing this clear threat to their sovereignty, demurred. For the Americans autonomy had ceased to be an acceptable constitutional settlement for Cuba. But beyond this they were ambiguous about what they did want. A message to Woodford on March 27 referred to "full self-government." When Woodford asked Assistant Secretary Day, now effectively in charge because of Secretary Sherman's dotage, what that meant, he was told it meant "Cuban independence."

Woodford himself was still hoping for a solution that would bring autonomy to Cuba but retain Spanish sovereignty. He did not inform the Spanish of the U.S. support for "full self-government," a phrase that was not in the operative part of his instructions and that he knew would widen the breach between the two countries. His omission was unprofessional but understandable. In any case the Spanish undoubtedly assumed by now that no solution contemplating Spain's continued presence in Cuba would be acceptable to the United States, and that was why they did not want it as a final arbiter.

Woodford was acting in the freewheeling and counterproductive tradition of political appointees in diplomatic posts, but to his credit, he was desperately struggling to prevent war. He had been assured by Assistant Secretary Day in writing that "the President's desire is for peace," and he believed he was the last American official left who could deliver it. He was no further out of bounds than Roosevelt, whose oath of service to the president did not deter him from coaching Lodge on how to defeat a McKinley-backed resolution that he considered too weak. Woodford was a good man relegated by failure to the scrap heap of history.

Diplomacy offered the embattled president no alternatives. In fact diplomacy in the final two weeks before the war was a classic exercise in futility. Woodford concluded that the Spanish knew they had lost Cuba, but he still hoped, against his own analysis, that war could be avoided. On April 3 he cabled Washington that the Spanish initiative to bring the pope in as a mediator offered an opportunity. The reply was a knuckle-rapping turndown from Day, with a snide question appended: "Would the peace you are so confident of securing mean the independence of Cuba?" On April 5 Spain made a concession: an immediate cease-fire on condition that the U.S. Navy move its fleet north from Key West. Woodford, for whom advocacy had by now overcome analysis, cabled his belief that "this means peace." But it was too late; the administration was counting votes for a war resolution in Congress.

The other European states, having failed to develop a common approach to Spain's terminal agony, were conspicuous nonplayers in the diplomacy of the crisis. On April 6 Britain, France, Germany, Italy, Austria-Hungary, and Russia finally made a last-minute appeal to McKinley to resume negotiations. The president, courteous as ever, did no more than listen to the resident ministers who descended on the Oval Office to present their joint démarche. He conceded nothing.

On April 9 Spain made its last bid: an unconditional armistice. Woodford predictably saw a ray of light, cabling: "I hope that nothing will now be done to humiliate Spain." When the Spanish minister delivered the news to the State Department, Assistant Secretary Day asked him if Spain was finally prepared to recognize Cuban sovereignty. The answer, as expected, was no. McKinley now had no alternative; his war message was read by clerks in the House of Representatives on April 11.

In his message the president brushed by the final Spanish offer and concentrated on the grounds for U.S. intervention. It was noteworthy that the American security interest—"the present condition of affairs in Cuba is a constant menace to our peace"—was placed fourth in priority. Third was the commercial interest. Second was the need to provide Cuban citizens protection and indemnity for their life and property.

The principal ground cited for intervention, the primary reason why the United States initiated the war, was human rights. McKinley's war message was replete with phrases evoking the suffering of the Cuban people: "cruel, barbarous, and uncivilized practices of warfare"; "dependent people striving to be free"; "people perishing by tens of thousands from hunger and destitution." American intervention was required "in the cause of humanity and to put an end to the barbarities, bloodshed, starvation, and horrible miseries now existing there, and which the parties to the conflict are either unable or unwilling to stop or mitigate."

In his unusual treatment of human rights McKinley was writing the first words of a new chapter in American foreign policy. "It is no answer to say this is all in another country, belonging to another nation, and is therefore none of our business," the president argued. "It is specially our duty, for it is right at our door." Even allowing for the time-honored custom of placing altruism ahead of narrower interests in the public description of policy, McKinley's words were extraordinary. For the first time in American history a U.S. president was contending that the United States had both a right and a duty to intervene when another country abused its citizens.

In these words of 1898 was born the doctrine that a country's sovereignty cannot protect it from outside intervention on human rights grounds. The priority given human rights by later presidents from Jimmy Carter through Bill Clinton owes its inspiration to a president who had seen suffering and who, regardless of other motives, felt a personal concern for Cubans under oppression.

Yet McKinley did not draw the logical conclusion from his emphasis on "dependent people striving to be free." His message contained nothing that would make them free. He made no call for independence. In fact he explicitly excluded independence: "To commit this country now to the recognition of any particular government in Cuba might subject us to embarrassing conditions of international obligation toward the organization so recognized. In case of intervention our conduct would be subject to the approval or disapproval of such government. We would be required to submit to its direction and to assume to it the mere relation of a friendly ally." In other words, if the United States invaded Cuba, it did not want the Cuban rebels to be in a position to tell it what to do.

Even worse, McKinley put the Cubans on the same level as the Spanish. Forcible intervention by the United States as a neutral to stop the war, he said, involved "hostile constraint upon both the parties to the contest." The president did leave to the Cuban insurgents the prospect of later, if conditional, recognition. He said that when "there is within the island a government capable of performing the duties and discharging the functions of a separate nation," then it "can be promptly and readily recognized."

Was McKinley setting up Cuba for annexation by the United States? There are arguments both ways. His unwillingness to concede independence in his war message was consistent with his earlier attempt to purchase Cuba; he could hardly have wanted to buy the island merely to turn it over to the insurgents. His war message was thus of a piece with the efforts made by three of his predecessors to gain American control over Cuba. Cuban independence had not flamed brightly for the earlier presidents who had coveted the island either.

On the other hand, there is no compelling reason to believe that McKinley was engaged in a disguised American takeover of Cuba. He had publicly ruled out annexation, and the State Department had made clear to Woodford in Madrid and to the Cuban minister in Washington that the United States favored independence. Perhaps, in ruling out immediate independence, the president was simply focusing on short-term contingencies. As he prepared for war, pressure on him grew to keep his options open. No doubt the army and navy were pleading for maximum flexibility; they, not the rebels, had to be in control of the military agenda. In any case McKinley was not a forward thinker. The odds are he had simply not thought through the consequences of the war he was being dragged into.

Moreover, even at this late stage the hawks around McKinley were not advocating annexation. While the war message was being drafted, Roosevelt told a friend he was opposed to a "land-grabbing war": "I should be doubtful about annexing Cuba, and should most emphatically oppose it unless the Cubans wished it." Lodge, a consistent advocate of independence, wrote disingenuously after the war that if congressional resolutions favoring independence had been followed, war would have been prevented altogether. At the moment the critical need for both Roosevelt and Lodge was to get the war started and the Spanish driven out of the Western Hemisphere. Like the president, they had not given much thought to the issues of sovereignty and Cuba's future.

Congress was thus presented with a presidential war message that was rife with ambiguities, full of language on behalf of the rights of the Cuban people but empty of support for those fighting in their name. Congress debated it for eight days, then on April 19 approved—by a comfortable majority in the Senate (42 to 35) and an overwhelming one in the House (310 to 6)—a joint resolution that was strikingly different from the president's message. It was not at all ambiguous. It plainly called for Cuban independence.

The Senate reached into American history for suitably dramatic language. Paraphrasing the Declaration of Independence, it proclaimed that "the people of the island of Cuba are, and of right ought to be, free and independent." There was even an effort to include language recognizing the insurgent government; it passed the Senate but was killed by McKinley's allies in the House. In response to effective lobbying by the Cuban junta's lawyer—and apparently the greasing of senatorial palms with some two million dollars—an amendment sponsored by the anti-imperialist senator Henry M. Teller from the beet sugar state of Colorado was added. It explicitly renounced annexation: ". . . the United States hereby disclaims any disposition or intention to exercise sovereignty, jurisdiction, or control over said island except for the pacification thereof, and asserts its determination when that is accomplished to leave the government and control of the island to its people."

The rest of the joint resolution conformed to McKinley's approach. It demanded that Spain relinquish at once its authority and government in Cuba and withdraw its armed forces. It "directed and empowered" the president to use the nation's "entire land and naval forces." Still, the contradiction between executive and legislative branch decisions could not have been more stark. The president was explicitly opposing independence; the Congress was explicitly supporting it. Had McKinley felt strongly about the matter, he would have refused to sign the resolution and sent it back for revision. But he did sign it without delay on April 20, making it in effect a declaration of war, to be formalized by Congress five days later. That evening of April 20 Secretary Long, to the jubilation of his deputy, ordered William Sampson, newly promoted to rear admiral and now in command of the fleet at Key West, "to move at once to blockade Cuba, which, of course, is the beginning of the war."

Thus the United States launched its first overseas war in conditions of puzzling ambiguity. The only objective on which the president and Congress could agree was that Spain had to be driven out of Cuba. There was no agreement on what Cuba's status would be after the expected American victory; indeed there was no strategy. The contradiction between the president's message and the joint resolution—the two founding documents of American imperialism—left unresolved the crucial issue of who would inherit Cuba from Spain. Would it be the United States or the Cuban people? That fatal ambiguity has scarred American relations with Cuba ever since.

5.

It is natural to look for consistency in McKinley's actions leading to the Spanish-American War. Some historians are convinced that he was determined to deny independence to Cuba. Others, including one of the first, Lodge, interpreted the war message as accepting independence. The probable truth is that McKinley, a weak strategist but a keen interpreter of political realities, was content to live with policy contradictions. He may have been, in Henry Adams's alliterative tribute, "a marvelous manager of men," but as Roosevelt had observed, he lacked backbone. The verdict of Professor Ernest R. May of Harvard seems on the mark: McKinley "led his country unwillingly toward a war that he did not want for a cause in which he did not believe."

Still, it was McKinley's war. How had he let himself be pushed into it? The most important reason was that Cuba was the right issue at the right time. America's political, economic, and military power had reached a point where the country could assert itself in ways unimaginable before. Cuba presented the perfect opportunity. It was close to American shores and newly vital for military strategists. It was a traditional object of American desires. It was a potential target of unfriendly countries prepared to ignore the no-transfer clause of the Monroe Doctrine. It was also a focus of horrendous human rights violations. The American public, press, and Congress were clamoring for a solution that freed the Cubans from Spain's bumbling tyranny.

McKinley tried every way to achieve this peacefully. But his options were limited. Autonomy was unacceptable to the Cubans, and independence equally unacceptable to the Spanish. The hoped-for deus ex machina, the purchase of Cuba, proved an impotent deity. Faced with Spanish and Cuban intransigence, McKinley's diplomats resorted to word games in the hope of bringing the sides together. They preached autonomy when they meant self-government, self-government when they meant independence. The Spanish saw through this approach; for them the Americans simply kept raising the bar. There was no American antiwar strategy except to improvise and hope for the best.

As the situation deteriorated on the ground, in the two foreign ministries, and in the eyes of the American public, the hawks in McKinley's party went airborne. For Roosevelt and Lodge war was an objective per se, any war against almost any opponent. (Germany would have done as well as Spain.) The caution of the business interests represented by Mark Hanna and of the doves led by Speaker Reed began to look spineless and even unpatriotic. The Senate, which had frustrated the imperial designs of previous presidents, was now so appalled by the atrocities against the Cuban people that it was spoiling for battle.

Elihu Root, with his genius for clear analysis, got McKinley's dilemma exactly right. He told Roosevelt that he sympathized with McKinley but believed that "if the administration does not turn its face toward the front and lead instead of being pushed, it seems to me it will be rolled over and crushed and the Republican party with it." McKinley was driven by inertia rather than design. In the end he went to war for the same reason as his Spanish opponent: to preserve the influence and leadership of the government in power.

Spain marched toward its final debacle with a certain tragic grandeur, exemplified by its senior naval officer, Rear Admiral Pascual Cervera y Topete. Cervera, a fifty-nine-year-old nobleman who had been a sailor since the age of nine, was a brilliant naval strategist with a keen sense of realism about Spain's feeble capabilities. He assessed the American fleet as at least three times stronger than the Spanish one. Short of Spain's finding a powerful ally, he believed that "the best thing would be to avoid war at any price." Yet he bore himself with a sense of fatalism. He wrote to his brother on January 30, 1898: "My purpose is not to accuse, but to explain why we may and must expect a disaster. But as it is necessary to go to the bitter end, and as it would be a crime to say that publicly today, I hold my tongue, and go forth resignedly to face the trials which God may be pleased to send me."

Cervera understood, though he did not share, the views of those politicians who believed that Spanish pride would be better served by losing Cuba in a war than by negotiating it away. Under their hawkish leadership Spain continued on a collision course. Eleven days after the sinking of the *Maine*, Cervera sent a moving message to the minister of marine:

> Do we not owe to our country not only our life, if necessary, but the exposition of our beliefs? I am very uneasy about this. I ask myself if it is right for me to keep silent, make myself an accomplice in adventures which will surely cause the total ruin of Spain. And for what purpose? To defend an island which was ours, but belongs to us no more, because even if we did not lose it by right in the war we have lost it in fact, and with it all our wealth and an enormous number of young men, victims of the climate and the bullets, in the defense of what is now no more than a romantic idea.

A few days later he was even more explicit: "It would be foolish to deny that what we may reasonably expect is defeat, which may be glorious, but all the same defeat."

Cervera's fatalism captures the inexorable nature of the road to war. The Spanish knew they would lose but could not stop. McKinley hated the thought of war but could not avoid it. America's launch into imperialism had several propellants: the conflict between a declining and a growing power over a territory important to both of them; the lack, exposed by diplomacy's failure, of credible alternatives to war; the welling up of public and congressional opinion; and, not least, the determined and effective activities of American advocates of war. In the end William McKinley was led to recognize that the only acceptable course was the one he had so firmly ruled out at the beginning of his presidency.

8. The Supreme Triumphs of War

1.

"It was my fortune to be in command on May 1, 1898, of an American squadron in the first important naval action against a foreign foe since the War of 1812." Thus began Commodore George Dewey's laconic description of the Battle of Manila Bay. Thanks to Theodore Roosevelt's manipulations, Dewey had been made commander of the Asiatic Squadron, which had been strategically placed at Hong Kong, a few days' sail from the Philippines. He was already putting his ships on a war footing when, on April 25, five days after the declaration of war, he received from Secretary Long orders that reflected the athletic prose of Roosevelt: "War has commenced between the United States and Spain. Proceed at once to Philippine Islands. Commence operations particularly against the Spanish fleet. You must capture vessels or destroy. Use utmost endeavor."

When the first conflict of the Spanish-American War broke out in the Philippines, few Americans knew where the islands were. President McKinley confessed to difficulty finding them on the map, and the chatty Chicago saloonkeeper Martin Dooley, Finley Peter Dunne's fictional commentator on politics, wondered whether they were islands or canned goods. On assuming command of the squadron, Dewey had discovered that the latest naval intelligence report on the Philippines was twenty-two years old. Where it counted, however, the U.S. Navy was up to date. As a result of the long-range planning program instituted by Captain Mahan, the Naval War College had begun in 1894 to consider tactical options in a potential war with Spain. Some of the contingency planning called for an attack on the Philippines.

Roosevelt, who kept in touch with the War College strategists, moved their ideas from the theoretical to the operational plane with his momentous February 25 order to Dewey to prepare for "offensive operations" in the Philippines. The American objective there was straightforward: to strike the Spanish enemy where it was weak in order to force an early end to the war. The Philippines were a means to an objective. The objective was Cuba.

Steaming six hundred miles east, Dewey was just off Manila Bay on April 30. He was blessed by a superior quality of ships and armament and by the incompetence of the Spanish defenders, who vastly underrated their American adversary. The captain general of the Philippines, Don Basilio Augustín, ordered a proclamation read to the Spanish forces claiming that the United States was a country "without cohesion or a history," that its people were composed of "all the social excrescences," and that Dewey's squadron was "manned by foreigners, possessing neither instruction nor discipline." Spanish military preparations were no more than the inadequate efforts of a sleepy imperial outpost with no expectation of ever facing a war.

As Dewey's squadron bore down on the islands, the Spanish admiral Patricio Montojo, finally aroused, decided to make a stand at Subic Bay, an excellent defensive position thirty-five miles north of Manila Bay. But on inspection he found that no shore guns had been mounted there, so he abandoned the idea. Montojo compounded this failure in preparations with a blunder in tactics. In order to spare Manila from American gunfire, he placed his ships at the southern end of the bay, where they could be protected neither by the city's heavy guns nor by the shore batteries, which were unable to lower their sights to hit ships at a range of under two thousand yards. Brave as they proved to be, the Spanish lacked a basic seriousness in their preparations. The very evening of Dewey's arrival off Manila Bay, Admiral Montojo left his ship to attend a reception in the city.

Dewey decided on a bold move: to sail right into the bay under cover of darkness. He demonstrated considerable courage in waving off a junior officer's warning that it would be prudent to sweep the entrance of mines. The ships—five cruisers, one gunboat, and a revenue cutter—stole in at four knots, attracting only desultory fire against the last vessels in line. They raised the lights of Manila at 3:00 A.M., and an hour later Dewey gave his crew coffee, failing to hold his own down. Three miles from Manila and now under fire, Dewey turned his ships toward the outgunned and outweighed Spanish squadron clustered south of the city. At 5:22 A.M. he gave his famous order to the captain of his flagship, *Olympia*: "You may fire when you are ready, Gridley." Seven U.S. fighting ships were now engaged against seven inferior Spanish vessels.

By the end of the morning it was all over. Dewey's squadron sank or burned all the Spanish ships. The Spanish suffered 161 killed and 210 wounded. The Americans lost 1 sailor to heat stroke; 9 were wounded. By risking his ships to save Manila from the American guns, Admiral Montojo lost his squadron and made the city hostage to American power. When Montojo was later court-martialed, Dewey was glad to write a letter commending his gallantry in action, though not his professional competence.

It was almost a week before the news of Dewey's victory reached the United States. As Secretary Long prepared to break the news to an eager Washington press corps, he discovered that his deputy, Roosevelt, had already done it. The irrepressible assistant secretary might be excused for taking proprietary pride in Dewey's achievement. As he bragged to a friend, "Didn't Admiral Dewey do wonderfully well? I got him the position out there in Asia last year, and I had to beg hard to do it; and the reason I gave was that we might have to send him to Manila. And we sent him—and he went!"

Dewey became an instant hero. Mahan commended the rapidity and audacity of his "dash" as reflecting "the highest credit upon his professional qualities." Roosevelt cabled him: "Every American is your debtor." From London Hay, ever quick with a compliment, praised the "mingled wisdom and daring" of his thrust into Manila Bay. The navy promoted him to rear admiral, and Congress appropriated ten thousand dollars for a Tiffany sword for him. When he completed his service in the Philippines and returned to the United States in September 1899, he was given a parade in New York City, and a huge, though disposable, triumphal arch was erected in his honor on Madison Square. In one sense none of this enthusiasm was misplaced. Dewey's victory at Manila made America overnight a Pacific power. It was also the first hard evidence that the United States, after decades of being a laughingstock, was now a military force to be reckoned with. It took a similar lightning naval victory in Cuba to consolidate that fact.

The outbreak of war had caught Alfred Mahan in Europe, but the American strategy of launching a blockade of Cuba was based on proposals he had provided in March. Two days before Dewey's victory, Mahan sent William R. Day, now secretary of state following Sherman's resignation, a concise and useful analysis via the U.S. Embassy in Paris. He predicted accurately that the Spanish fleet would not seek refuge in Havana Bay, where the Americans had a light blockade in effect. He also discouraged the diversion of U.S. ships to guard American coastal ports, which he knew Spain would not threaten. Here he had a strong ally in Roosevelt, who was compelled to deal with demands to the Navy Department from politicians and well-heeled private Americans for the defense of their favorite East Coast summer resorts. Mahan was convinced that the American ships should be concentrated where they could blockade and defeat the enemy, not along the U.S. coast but in the Caribbean. The navy's acceptance of this advice was a major factor in the American victory.

Mahan reported for duty on May 9, a few days after the news of Dewey's triumph had reached Washington. He was asked to serve as number two on the three-man Naval War Board, which had advisory and some command responsibilities over the disposition of naval forces. True to his maverick style, he began his service by proposing that the board be abolished and its functions assigned to a single naval officer. He was not thinking of himself for the position; he had in mind an officer on active duty. His objective was to get away from a corporate approach and fix responsibility on a single individual. As he wrote Secretary Long, ". . . individual responsibility . . . alone achieves results in war." Long was not impressed with Mahan's arguments; the Naval War Board continued as originally constituted, with Mahan its dominant figure.

Mahan's irascibility, which seemed to grow with his authority, made him difficult for Long to handle. He had a pronavy bias and a contempt for Secretary of War Alger, whom he dismissed as an ineffective strategist and manager. He showed no sympathy for the unprecedented logistical challenge facing Alger of mounting military campaigns on two oceans. He was a team player only as long as his team was the navy. On tactics he wavered over whether to launch operations against Puerto Rico or alternatively to give priority to Cuba. When Admiral Cervera took his fleet into Santiago Bay, the navy was finally able to bottle it up there. Mahan's experience with blockades now came into play. Despite an impatient and frustrated American public, the War Board under Mahan's guidance helped maintain the monthlong blockade that proved the key to victory.

While Dewey was stalking the Spanish fleet in the Pacific, Roosevelt was making plans to abandon his navy ties and enlist in the army. For years he had been telling anyone who would listen that if the United States went to war, he intended to fight. His reasons were mixed. In the first place, his vociferous warmongering was not always welcome in McKinley's cabinet, where his judgment was distrusted. He believed that his usefulness in Washington would end when war was declared, and he confessed to his brother-in-law Will Cowles: "Remember . . . how limited my power is; all the more so, as I am now suspected by the administration because of my entire dissent from their views about what our honor and dignity demand." Added to this career-oriented reason was a moral one: "One of the commonest taunts directed at men like myself is that we are armchair and parlor jingoes who wish to see others do what we only advocate doing." For a man with Roosevelt's activist philosophy of life, the front was the only place he could imagine being.

Roosevelt never clearly articulated the most important reason for signing up—his father's failure to fight in the Civil War—though he came close in his autobiography: "I had always felt that if there were a serious war I wished to be in a position to explain to my children why I did take part in it, and not why I did not take part in it." Roosevelt's father, as fine a man as his son, could not make such an explanation to his children. The younger Roosevelt could, and his daughter Alice, who heard his war stories countless times, was convinced that he had enlisted to pay off the debt contracted by his father. As he put it in his autobiography, when a man believes in a war, "he ought to be willing to make his words good by his deeds. . . . He should pay with his body."

All of Roosevelt's friends, Lodge in the lead, tried to talk him out of "paying with his body." Secretary Long, who also tried to dissuade him, confided to his diary:

> My Assistant Secretary, Roosevelt, has determined upon resign-
> ing, in order to go into the army and take part in the war. . . . He has
> lost his head to this unutterable folly of deserting the post where he
> is of most service and running off to ride a horse and, probably,
> brush mosquitoes from his neck on the Florida sands. His heart is
> right, and he means well, but it is one of those cases of aberration—
> desertion—vainglory; of which he is utterly unaware. He thinks he
> is following his highest ideal, whereas, in fact, as without exception
> every one of his friends advises him, he is acting like a fool.

Long then added a sentence that turned out to be prophetic: "And
yet, how absurd all this will sound if, by some turn of fortune, he
should accomplish some great thing."

The assistant secretary of the navy went to the secretary of war for
help in getting himself into the army. Despite his low view of Alger,
Roosevelt sensed an ally, "almost the only member of the Administration who felt all along that we would have to go to war." Alger made
him a handsome offer. Three voluntary cavalry regiments were being
formed. Would Roosevelt like to command one of them? Generous in
his turn, Roosevelt declined the command on the basis of his military
inexperience and suggested his friend Colonel Leonard Wood, a career army officer and, not incidentally, Alger's family doctor. Roosevelt
as a lieutenant colonel could serve as his number two. Arrangements
made, Roosevelt resigned from the Navy Department on May 6 and
left Washington for San Antonio, Texas, six days later to train with his
regiment.

The First Volunteer Cavalry Regiment had a peculiar composition.
Three-quarters of its soldiers were recruited in the Southwest, from
Arizona, New Mexico, Oklahoma, and the Indian Territory. Many of
the rest were seduced by Roosevelt from the upper-class precincts of
Harvard, Yale, Princeton, and the Knickerbocker Club. The new lieutenant colonel, fitting his sturdy frame into the uniform he had ordered from Brooks Brothers, reveled in the racial and social mixture
of his men. Harvard quarterbacks, Ivy League tennis stars, high
jumpers, polo players, steeplechasers, and the captain of the Columbia crew shared latrines and chow with cowboys, hunters, gamblers,
mining prospectors, sheriffs, New York City policemen, Indian fighters, and Indians. The only common factor in the motley backgrounds

of the soldiers was that they all had been brought up to ride and shoot and could therefore be sent to war with only three weeks' training.

Roosevelt felt at home with them all. Although the cowboys who made up the majority came from a part of the country unfamiliar to him, they were cut from the same bandanna as his Dakota friends and the westerners he had celebrated in his historical writings. His enthusiasm for the troops was reciprocated. He even earned a reprimand from the austere Wood for standing rounds of beer for subordinates as a reward for a good day's training. He wrote Lodge exuberantly: "You would be amused to see three Knickerbocker club men cooking and washing dishes for one of the New Mexico companies." He told his friend it was America in microcosm, "as typical an American regiment as ever marched or fought."

The publicity value of such a diverse band with its flamboyant leader (Wood was practically invisible) was not lost on the national press. Various names, like Teddy's Terrors or the Rocky Mountain Rustlers, were tried on the public. Finally, in deference to the regiment's cowboy component, a name was borrowed from Buffalo Bill's Wild West Show. It became known to contemporaries and to history as the Rough Riders.

After a scant two weeks of high-spirited training with his troops in Texas, Roosevelt shepherded the regiment, complete with horses and mules, onto a train headed for Tampa, Florida, the embarkation point for Cuba. With Wood he was given the unpleasant task of cutting their numbers; a third of the regiment would have to stay behind. So would the horses, a serious problem since, as Roosevelt later remarked, the cowboys were not used to walking.

Roosevelt felt no qualms about using his high-level contacts to seek favors. He even wrote President McKinley to ensure that the Rough Riders made it to Cuba in the first wave. Alger turned down his appeal through Lodge to reinstate the horses, but Roosevelt did credit the secretary of war with helping in his irregular requests for equipment. He also quickly earned a reputation as a whistle-blower. He suggested to Lodge that the president be told about the "frightful" mismanagement at the Tampa port, a criticism that was true but not entirely fair about the largest overseas embarkation that the American Army had ever staged. He also took a swipe at the three-hundred-pound General William R. Shafter, the commander of the American expeditionary force and his superior officer, pontificating to Lodge that "men should be appointed as Generals of Divisions and Brigades who are physically fit." Roosevelt's access to important people in Washington made him a man, junior though he was, not to be trifled with.

His influence was not up to getting his regiment a place on the troopship, however. He accomplished that feat through his own resourcefulness and determination. When the embarkation order came from the president, Roosevelt commandeered some coal cars to get his men to the dock before the other regiments. He then hurried them onto a transport ahead of two regiments that had priority. On June 14, after a delay occasioned by the false sighting of enemy warships, the forty-eight-vessel fleet carrying some sixteen thousand men left Florida for an undisclosed destination, either Cuba or Puerto Rico.

On the ship Leonard Wood mused to his wife: "Hard it is to realize that this is the commencement of a new policy and that this is the first great expedition our country has ever sent oversea and marks the commencement of a new era in our relations with the world." Theodore Roosevelt, who had providentially sewn spare pairs of eyeglasses into his hat and his uniform, had similar musings. As the band on the *Yucatan* played "The Star-Spangled Banner" and "The Girl I Left Behind Me," his thoughts were on posterity. "It is a great historical expedition," he wrote Corinne from shipboard, "and I thrill to feel that I am part of it. If we fail, of course we share the fate of all who do fail, but if we are allowed to succeed (for we certainly shall succeed, if allowed) we have scored the first great triumph in what will be a world movement."

2.

The core of the force that shipped out of Tampa was the regular army, which before the war numbered fewer than thirty thousand officers and enlisted men. The proportion of soldiers to the American population was the smallest it had been since the War for Independence. Most of the leaders of this second-rate service had been junior officers during the Civil War or Indian fighters after it. The commanding general, Nelson Miles, had captured the great Sioux chief Geronimo. Miles was a capable officer, but by 1898 he had grown so egotistical and demanding that he was a thorn in Secretary Alger's side. The mastodon Shafter was a typical officer of a peacetime army that had lost its edge; he was politically compliant, risk-averse, and incapable of earning the respect of his men. Below the level of general officer there were some good men, of whom Leonard Wood was the best example. But the army had such a poor reputation that one National Guard regiment, the Seventh New York, refused to serve under regular army officers.

President McKinley acted quickly during April to win congressional approval of large increases in the regular army and the National Guard. Within months the size of the regular army doubled, and more than 200,000 volunteers were on active service. Besides National Guard forces, the volunteers included the three new cavalry regiments, of which Roosevelt's was the most publicized. In all, some 264,000 men saw duty in the army during the war; three-quarters of them were volunteers, most of whom were relegated to the home front.

The navy was in much better shape. As the result of the reforms of the previous decade and a half, it had better equipment and greater esprit, though still only four first-class battleships. Thanks to Mahan's management of the Naval War College, its younger officers were experienced in strategic planning. Also, largely because of Roosevelt, it was in a high state of readiness. Roosevelt was not far off when he boasted: "If only the Army were one-tenth as ready as the Navy, we would fix that whole business in six weeks." Rear Admiral Sampson, the commander of the North Atlantic Squadron and the senior naval officer in the Caribbean, affected a professorial demeanor, but Mahan knew and admired him as a competent and bold strategist.

The inevitable bickering between the army and the navy began in Tampa, when General Shafter was given command of the convoy operation. From his perch on the Naval War Board Mahan huffed that in the world's greatest sea power, Great Britain, transport service was a prerogative of the navy. In his passionate opinion, awarding it to the U.S. Army was "radically vicious." There were disputes over tactics as well. Each service, as averse to casualties as today's U.S. military, expected the other to bear the brunt of fighting the Spanish in Cuba. Shafter wanted close-in shelling of ports by the navy; the navy, except for Sampson, who was prepared to take risks, favored extensive ground operations by the army.

McKinley's objective was to win the war with as few casualties as possible. That meant avoiding confrontation with Spain where it was strong. No serious consideration was given to an attack on the Spanish mainland, and separate proposals by Alger and Sampson for assaults on Havana, the best-defended city in Cuba, were rejected as too risky. Dewey's attack on Manila was a low-cost operation on the periphery of Spanish power. The decision to mount a naval blockade of Cuba was born of this cautious attitude. The blockade, begun on April 23, was designed to yield three principal results: to cut off food and supplies to the Spanish Army in Cuba, to disrupt Spain's seaborne commerce with the Caribbean, and to deny Havana Bay to the Spanish fleet. It would also buy time to train the new and cumbersome American Army, and it would allow postponement of the decision about where an American force should be landed on the Cuban coast.

When Spain's naval commander, the melancholy Cervera, left the Cape Verde Islands heading west, alarm bells sounded in Washington. The Americans overreacted; in fact the Spanish had blundered in sending Cervera across the Atlantic with only seven ships, and those in parlous condition. The Spanish also broke the rule to which the Americans, under Mahan's prodding, adhered: They divided their fleet. Without the rest of the fleet, kept home for the unnecessary task of guarding Spain's coastline, Cervera would be no match for the American Navy. He knew it himself and invoked defeatist images of Don Quixote and Trafalgar. Nevertheless, his disappearance in the ocean's vastness sowed panic in the United States, and Sampson was sent to find him. The American commander sought the Spanish admiral as far east as Puerto Rico. He shelled San Juan while he was at it but returned empty-handed.

In late May, thousands of miles from home and denied access to Havana by the American blockade, Cervera finally took his squadron into Santiago Bay, on the southeast coast of Cuba. Sampson with four ships raced for Santiago. On June 1 he began to seal the narrow mouth of the harbor, bringing reinforcements to strengthen the blockade. The navy's action to block Cervera's exit effectively ended the

American debate on where to land troops on the Cuban coast. A landing on either side of Santiago Bay could silence the shore batteries and open the way for an attack on the city. Cervera's ships and the Spanish troops defending Santiago would be trapped between the American Army and the American Navy. Whether Cervera stayed in the harbor or came out to face the navy's guns, his squadron would be in peril. Though Roosevelt and the others departing Tampa did not yet know it, they were headed for the coast of Cuba just east of Santiago with the mission of capturing the city and contributing to the destruction of the Spanish warships.

The naval blockade had been in effect for nearly a month when the American forces landed at Daiquirí, a town still noted more as the birthplace of a frosted rum cocktail than for its importance in the Spanish-American War. As the transports neared the beach, Roosevelt, who always seemed to travel in style, spied his former Navy Department aide commanding a converted yacht and hitchhiked to shore aboard it. The Americans made immediate contact with Cuban insurgents who controlled the countryside in eastern Cuba. This meeting—Shafter and Sampson on one side, General Calixto García on the other—dramatized the Spanish dilemma. Spain now had to fight two wars in Cuba, one against the rebels and one against the Americans.

The Americans' plan was to fight their way from the coast and up the hills overlooking Santiago Bay. The first skirmish at Las Guasimas was victorious but costly. In Roosevelt's vivid description of his initial exposure to combat, the Americans were frustrated by their inability to see the enemy soldiers, who were using Mauser rifles with invisible smokeless powder. The Rough Riders had just been issued Krag-Jorgensen repeating rifles, which were also smokeless, but had never fired them. Confessing to anxiety, Roosevelt nevertheless pushed his men forward with the Spanish bullets "singing through the trees over our heads, making a noise like the humming of telephone wires."

The Rough Riders lost eight dead, half the American total. The very first man killed by a Spanish bullet was Hamilton Fish, Columbia crew captain and grandson of the secretary of state who had favored the Spanish side in the Cuban war of 1868–78. The dead Rough Riders were buried in a common grave on a hillside, "Indian and cow-boy, miner, packer, and college athlete," in Roosevelt's elegiac tribute. The neophyte soldier was lavish in his praise for Wood, who had moved the Rough Riders at breakneck speed to engage the enemy, for the white and black regulars who had fought alongside them, and for two Cherokees in his regiment.

After Las Guasimas Wood was promoted to replace a general stricken with malaria, and Roosevelt found himself in command of the regiment. Shafter ordered two assaults, one on a fortified Spanish position at El Caney, northwest of Santiago, the other on the heights overlooking the city. While the fighting at El Caney was inconclusive, though costly, the attack on the two hills, Kettle and San Juan, proved decisive. The Rough Riders were one of the six regiments assaulting Kettle Hill. Roosevelt was resourceful and aggressive in leading his men into battle. The only Rough Rider to be mounted, he ensured that his regiment was one of the first to the top of the hill. It was during this charge that Roosevelt shot his first and only Spaniard, appropriately using a revolver that had been salvaged from the wreck of the *Maine.* The Rough Riders also played a useful supporting role in scaling the higher San Juan Hill, which was taken primarily through the use of rapid-firing Gatling guns covering the infantry attack. The capture of the heights opened to view the bay and the city of Santiago and exposed the Spanish defenders to imminent attack.

The Spanish had 150,000 regulars in Cuba, but the civil war had dispersed them around the island. In the three engagements on July 1—El Caney, Kettle Hill, and San Juan Hill—the Americans greatly outnumbered their foes. Shafter sent into combat more than 15,000 troops, nine times the Spanish numbers. Despite such a numerical advantage, the U.S. troops suffered alarming casualties for a single day's operations: 225 killed and 1,384 wounded, or a tenth of their force. By Roosevelt's figures the Rough Riders sustained the heaviest losses of any regiment that stormed the two hills, nearly 20 percent of all troops engaged. In his account of the Santiago campaign he attributed this high casualty level to the toughness of the Spanish soldiers, their Mauser rifles, and the difficulty of offensive warfare against a well-armed and dug-in enemy. Roosevelt was undoubtedly right about the obstacles, but it is also true that with the American advantages, a defeat was almost unimaginable. At home it would have been seen as a disaster.

Was Roosevelt a hero in the Santiago campaign? Certainly he was.

He demonstrated great powers of leadership, coaxing, cajoling, and threatening his troops, and even those of other regiments, into battle. At Las Guasimas he was aggressive in engaging the enemy, and in the storming of the San Juan heights the Rough Riders under his command made a signal contribution. Unlike W. S. Gilbert's Duke of Plaza-Toro, Roosevelt led his regiment from the front, not from behind. In the fog of war, he was decisive, sometimes anticipating orders rather than waiting for them. He was embarrassed to be riding a horse while his men were on foot, but this made him a bigger target for snipers. He was magnanimous in victory, commending the Spanish enemy and praising his fellow soldiers, including those from black regiments. His book *The Rough Riders*, published less than a year after that fateful July 1, is a generally reliable and fair-minded account. Roosevelt therefore deserved much of the praise he received from the public as the "hero of San Juan Hill."

Yet he was a shameless self-promoter. He kept close to the war correspondents at the front, especially Richard Harding Davis, a thoroughbred in William Randolph Hearst's expensive stable, whom Roosevelt invited to accompany the Rough Riders. Davis gave the regiment and its leader generous, even worshipful coverage; he was a cocreator with Roosevelt of the mystique of the cowboy-soldiers. Roosevelt also kept Senator Lodge abreast of his exploits, and his friend acted as a publicity agent in Washington for his derring-do. Lodge was happy to circulate to Washington offices and dinner parties accounts such as the following, no doubt written with an eye to verbatim distribution: "On the day of the big fight I had to ask my men to do a deed that European military writers consider utterly impossible of performance, that is, to attack over open ground unshaken infantry armed with the best modern repeating rifles behind a formidable system of entrenchments. The only way to get them to do it in the way it had to be done was to lead them myself."

The Rough Riders, for all its candor, was also a subtle attempt to cast its author in the most positive light. Roosevelt showed himself engagingly mortal in admitting to confusion in his first battle and in trying to run with his sword caught between his legs. He projected an image of fairness (justified, to be sure) with enlisted men, blacks, Indians, and even the white regiments that were not getting as much publicity as the Rough Riders. Most of all, the Roosevelt of the book was a heroic exemplar, a leader of men who spared no effort to do his manly duty and win victory. The impression conveyed was of triumph by a gallant commander storming the heights by himself rather than of a team victory in which the Rough Riders constituted less than a tenth of the U.S. forces. Mr. Dooley commented dryly that Roosevelt should have titled his book *Alone in Cubia*. Alger, by then feuding with Roosevelt, barely mentioned him in his highly defensive account of the war, published in 1901.

Two days after the capture of San Juan Hill, General Shafter nearly threw the victory away. Prostrated by the heat, depressed by the unexpected casualties, harassed by the Spanish who were still firing up the hillsides, and concerned about Spanish reinforcements moving in from the west, he felt unable either to attack Santiago, less than a mile from his lines, or to destroy the shore batteries threatening Sampson's ships. He saw his own army as underarmed, underfed, and undermanned. He tried unsuccessfully to persuade Sampson to force the entrance to the harbor. He even considered withdrawing five miles until he was talked out of this loss of nerve by his senior officers and by Alger.

Even Roosevelt succumbed to momentary panic. "We are within measureable distance of a terrible military disaster," he wailed to Lodge two days after San Juan Hill. Though Shafter's analysis was the same, Roosevelt had no use for the corpulent general who came so close to reversing the victory that had made Roosevelt a national hero. By Roosevelt's code, leaders should lead, but Shafter was "too unwieldy to get to the front" and never came within three miles of it. To Lodge's publicity mill Roosevelt complained: "Not since the campaign of Crassus against the Parthians has there been so criminally incompetent a General as Shafter."

To Secretary Alger July 3 was the "darkest day of the war." But while the Americans in Cuba bitched, bickered, and vacillated, the Spanish came to their rescue. Admiral Cervera, for whom defeat was a matter of predestination, reconciled himself to facing it on the open sea rather than sandwiched between the American Navy at the harbor entrance and the American Army in Santiago. In Cervera's opinion, and that of all his captains, it would be suicide to run the blockade. The four Spanish armored cruisers and two destroyers were no match for the four U.S. battleships and two armored cruisers. But in Havana the captain general of Cuba, Army General Ramón Blanco, had won from Madrid command responsibility over the naval squadron. Blanco believed that the moral effect would be worse if the fleet surrendered meekly in the harbor than if Cervera tried to fight his way through the blockade. Blanco wanted Cervera out as soon as possible, and the admiral succumbed to his destiny.

So, on the morning of July 3 in broad daylight, the Spanish squadron steamed toward the harbor entrance and the American guns with the traditional signal "Viva España" flying and the bugles blaring. In the lead was the flagship *Infanta María Teresa*, commanded by Captain Victor Concas, who had as keen a sense of tragic history as his commanding officer. Concas memorialized the moment: "The sound of my bugles was the last echo of those which history tells us were sounded at the capture of Granada. It was the signal that the history of four centuries of grandeur was at an end and that Spain was becoming a nation of the fourth class."

Sampson's "judgment, energy, and watchfulness" (Mahan's words) in blockading Cervera had brought brilliant success. His captains had been exercising their crews for a month against what was now happening, the Spanish squadron heading right toward the superior American firepower. By a quirk of fate the American commander was not present at his own victory. He was on his way to shore to confer with General Shafter. The sudden battle was in the hands of Commodore Winfield Scott Schley, a flashy and erratic officer who had lost his nerve weeks before while searching for Cervera and was later to appear before a board of inquiry because of it. Even though Schley now compounded his earlier error by nearly ramming another American ship as the Spanish squadron came out, he was not destined to lose this battle.

Like Manila Bay, it was half a day's work. All of Cervera's ships were run aground, burned, or sunk. Three hundred and twenty-three Spanish sailors were killed, while, as at Manila Bay, only one American died. The Spanish fought so bravely that they elicited sympathy from their enemy. As the seamen on the *Texas* began to cheer the sinking of the *Vizcaya*, which had visited New York only months before, the American skipper called out: "Don't cheer, boys, the poor devils are dying." When Cervera boarded the *Iowa* to surrender, he was cheered spontaneously by the American crew. As Lodge wrote later, the Spanish had courage, but not the kind of courage that leads to victory.

From shore Admiral Sampson reasserted his authority. Evoking Gettysburg and Vicksburg, also victories close to Independence Day, he cabled Washington: "The fleet under my command offers the nation as a Fourth of July present the whole of Cervera's fleet." With the victory of Santiago Bay the Spanish-American War was effectively over. Though neither Havana nor Manila had yet been taken, everyone knew that the destruction of the Spanish fleet made the two capitals defenseless.

It would be hard to imagine a more convincing proof of Mahan's dictum that control of the sea was the key to military victory. Although the American Army was instrumental in driving Cervera out of Santiago Bay and would be needed to take and hold Havana and Manila, the war was won by naval victories accomplished with stunning rapidity and concentration of force. The fighting had produced romantic heroes from both services: Dewey for the navy, Roosevelt for the army. All this was in marked contrast with the four-year agony of the previous American war, when McKinley remembered seeing the bodies stacked up. No wonder the Spanish-American War has been called the most popular war in American history.

3.

Three days after the naval victory at Santiago Bay, on July 6, 1898, the Senate, spurred by Lodge's skillful parliamentary maneuvering, approved by a vote of 42–21 a joint resolution to annex the Hawaiian Islands. The House on June 15 had passed a similar measure by an even more comfortable margin. On July 7 President McKinley signed the annexation bill, making Hawaii a colony of the United States. The Hawaiian takeover was not directly tied to the Spanish-American War—the Pacific islands had never been a Spanish possession—but its timing was closely connected to the war. The incorporation of Hawaii was also a direct outcome of the growing imperial spirit that dominated the McKinley years and inspired the thrust against the Spanish territories.

From 1778, when the European discoverer of Hawaii, the British sea captain James Cook, set foot on Kauai, the islands were in perpetual tension between Asian natives and white newcomers. The great explorer's death in 1779 was a metaphor for the contradictions in the relationship: He was worshiped as a god but was killed and partially eaten by members of the Polynesian population.

From the beginning Americans were at the center of the Hawaiian ambiguity. Merchants were attracted by sandalwood, used to make perfume, and whalers relaxed and refitted in the capacious harbors. Eleven years after Cook's disaster, Simon Metcalfe, the skipper of an American merchantman, fired on a group of natives in reprisal for the shooting of a sailor, killing or wounding more than one hundred. In the early nineteenth century American sailors settled in Hawaii and supplied their entrepreneurial and commercial talents to grateful native rulers. Two who thus ingratiated themselves, Isaac Davis and Oliver Holmes, won the title of governor and lived well under King Kamehameha of Hawaii's hereditary Polynesian monarchy. Holmes had 180 retainers whose duties included serving roast dog to his guests.

With the arrival of the first Protestant missionaries in 1820 American influence in Hawaii became paramount. It might seem incongruous to think of missionaries as swashbuckling, but many of the stern New Englanders who sailed to Hawaii were. They came to save souls, and they did so with marked success—by 1840 they had won some fifteen thousand converts—but they stayed to insert themselves with great skill into the economic and political power structure of the islands. Nineteenth-century Hawaiian history brims with the often eccentric exploits of Americans, many of them missionaries, and their offspring.

The U.S. government took an early official interest in Hawaii. Though naval visits in the 1820s were limited to compelling Hawaiian chiefs to pay their debts to American traders, energetic missionaries soon extracted a stronger American commitment to the islands. In 1842 William Richards, one of the first American missionaries and a clever political operator, visited Washington as a royal envoy to persuade the U.S. government to guarantee Hawaii's independence against threats from Britain and France. President Tyler, deciding that the threats were real, announced that the United States would look with dissatisfaction on any foreign attempt to take possession of the islands. Tyler's fears proved actual when a British naval officer took over Hawaii briefly in 1843. In the same year Britain and France signed a pledge not to annex the islands. The United States, with five-sixths of the commercial ships in Hawaii's harbors, did not sign.

During the same period Gerrit Judd, another missionary with grandiose political aspirations and a firm power base, was pressing for Hawaii's outright annexation by the United States. Having gained despotic control over the government's finances and patronage in the 1840s, Judd dreamed at first of abolishing the monarchy to which he owed allegiance and turning the country into an American-style republic with himself in charge. He changed to an annexationist position after a meeting with Senator (later Secretary of State) Seward on a visit to Washington. In 1853 Judd found an ally for annexation in the resident American commissioner, David Gregg, who, apparently acting without instructions from Washington, tried to negotiate a treaty of annexation with the Hawaiian monarchy. The attempt failed, but Gregg, backed up by several U.S. warships off Honolulu, had set an example of gunboat diplomacy on behalf of American expansion.

The American Civil War damaged the whaling industry, but the termination of sugar sales from the South to the North brought Hawaii a sugar bonanza and increased the U.S. economic stake in the islands. Sugar exports to the mainland shot up nearly twelvefold between 1860 and 1866. The sugar boom, plus the assurance of secure property rights, produced a frenzy of land purchases; by the later years of the century whites owned four times more acreage than native Hawaiians. Huge fortunes were made on Hawaiian sugar. A San Francisco refiner, Claus Spreckels, cornered most of the Hawaiian sugar crop in the late 1870s, started a large sugar plantation of his own, and for a time controlled much of the finances of Hawaii until King Kalakaua expelled him in 1886 for overreaching.

After the Civil War the U.S. Navy began to focus on the strategic value of Hawaii. The navy coveted Pearl Harbor, near Honolulu, which it considered the best-protected anchorage in the entire Pacific. Henry Whitney, a journalist and "missionary boy" (the local phrase for a descendant of missionaries), proposed in 1872 that the Hawaiian government lease it to the United States in return for a reciprocity treaty that would give Hawaiian sugar duty-free access to the American market. Though reciprocity was in Hawaii's clear economic interest, native demonstrations and a near mutiny against the cession of Hawaiian territory delayed the deal. It was revived in 1874 during the first-ever visit by a Hawaiian king to the United States, where King Kalakaua was received by President Grant and by a joint session of Congress. The Reciprocity Treaty, negotiated with Secretary of State Fish and passed by both houses in 1875 after frequent delays, allowed Hawaiian sugar to be admitted to the American market free of duty. But the king stood firm against leasing Pearl Harbor. As a sop to the United States, Hawaii agreed not to alienate any territory to foreign powers or to accord reciprocity to any other nation.

The burgeoning relationship between the United States and Hawaii made Congress increasingly insistent on influencing Hawaiian affairs. In 1887 it refused to renew the Reciprocity Treaty unless the navy was given exclusive use of Pearl Harbor. This time Kalakaua gave in, opening the way for Pearl Harbor to become the largest U.S. naval base in the Pacific. Worse was to come for the unlucky king. The Harrison administration, which took office in 1889, decided to lower the U.S. tariff on sugar from all foreign sources, an act that would destroy the privileged position Hawaii had gained through the Reciprocity Treaty. Secretary of State Blaine, an expansionist, offered to preserve Hawaii's advantage in sugar in exchange for making the United States the guarantor of the country's independence with the right to land troops there. When Kalakaua resisted this challenge to Hawaiian sovereignty, Congress passed the McKinley Tariff, which, by making all sugar duty-free, eroded Hawaii's economic stability.

Domestically things went no better for the beleaguered Hawaiian monarch. Other Americans followed Gerrit Judd to heights of political power. Walter M. Gibson, a shady adventurer as well as a Mormon missionary, became prime minister under Kalakaua in 1882. He immediately launched the monarch onto an ill-advised and unsuccessful imperial policy, declaring Hawaii the foremost Polynesian state and trying to snap up the islands of Midway and Samoa. Two missionary boys, Lorrin A. Thurston and Sanford Dole, formed the clandestine Hawaiian League in 1887 to challenge Gibson and his royal patron. The league had an all-white, mostly American membership and its own militia. In a showdown with Kalakaua it forced the king to dismiss Gibson and to form a new government composed of its members. Thurston, Dole, and company then rammed through a white supremacy constitution that excluded two-thirds of the native Hawaiian voters and caused the weakening and humiliation of Kalakaua.

The bizarre pattern of official and unofficial relations between the American Republic and the Polynesian monarchy throughout the nineteenth century boded ill for Hawaii's fate as an independent country. Local Americans proved adept at insinuating themselves into positions of power in the islands by taking advantage of a naïve, credulous, sometimes greedy, and often corrupt Hawaiian monarchy. They got used to throwing their weight around, as missionaries, entrepreneurs, political operators, sugar barons, royal advisers, naval captains, and even diplomats. They demonstrated a range of intimidation techniques, from gunboats to racial intrigues to private paramilitary forces. They also knew how to play on Washington's desires for a naval stronghold in the Pacific.

Officially, the United States posed as the defender of Hawaiian sovereignty; privately, local Americans undermined that sovereignty nonstop. The contrast with Cuba was striking. On the Spanish island Americans were outside the power structure. In Hawaii they had honeycombed it. In Cuba Spanish oppression supplied a serious human rights issue to help legitimize American strategic and economic interests. In Hawaii it was the Americans who threatened the human rights of the native peoples by amassing political power at their expense. But unlike General Weyler's depredations, this seemed not to concern the American people.

In talking about potential territorial acquisitions, nineteenth-century American statesmen were given to metaphors involving ripe fruit. For John Quincy Adams and others, Cuba was an apple. Hawaii, by contrast, was usually described as a pear. The U.S. minister to Hawaii from 1889, John L. Stevens, proclaimed in 1893: "The Hawaiian pear is now fully ripe." The distinction, though accidental, is meaningful. Like an apple, Cuba had a tough outside, proved hard to bite into, and could taste sour. By contrast the softness and sweetness of the Hawaiian pear made for easy, if messy, consumption. Minister Stevens would know, because he was to play a key role in ending Hawaii's independence.

Stevens's background encapsulated the tradition of American encounters with Hawaii. He was a Universalist minister, a Republican politician from Maine, and a diplomat with experience in northern Europe and South America who had a close relationship with the two major imperialist secretaries of state of the century, William Seward and James G. Blaine. In Hawaii Stevens was a faithful defender of the country's economic interests, alerting Washington to the distress caused by the McKinley Tariff and supporting the Hawaiian government's unsuccessful efforts for a free trade treaty with the United States. But he also became a foe of Polynesian sovereignty and an advocate of annexation.

Stevens first exercised his influence in 1890, when he and his British counterpart in Honolulu helped block King Kalakaua's effort to revise the white-oriented 1887 constitution in order to increase the power of the monarch and the native population. When the king died in 1891, his sister and successor, the formidable Liliuokalani, resolved to complete his mission to change the constitution. Stevens made clear to the new queen that he considered her authority limited. She disagreed. In one sense the Hawaiian revolution of 1893 was a test of wills between these two strong individuals.

It was easy to ridicule Liliuokalani as a comic opera figure, as many in the U.S. Congress were wont to do. Indeed she was an unusual monarch, even for Hawaii. Tall and striking in appearance, with a most unfeminine tongue, she was also a devout Christian and contributor to charities. Her hobby was writing songs in the Hawaiian language; one of them, "Aloha Oe," is still popular. She had an an iron will but put herself under the influence of a German medium, a dependence that may seem less eccentric with the recent knowledge that President Ronald Reagan's appointment schedule was sometimes set by his wife's astrologer. Liliuokalani's reign contained elements of farce but also of tragedy. At issue was her determined but doomed attempt to preserve her country's sovereignty and to protect the rights of native Hawaiians against growing pressure by a small minority of powerful whites for annexation to the United States.

Liliuokalani's intransigence on the constitutional issue, plus the economic depression visited on Hawaii by the McKinley Tariff, set most of the whites against her. Lorrin Thurston, a relentless opponent of Hawaiian rights and coauthor of the white power constitution of 1887, founded a clandestine Annexation Club to plot her overthrow. On a visit to Washington Thurston heard encouraging words from senior members of the Harrison administration, including Secretary Blaine. Throughout 1892 Queen Liliuokalani wrangled with the white-dominated legislature. Out of frustration in January 1893, she made plans to put a new constitution into effect without parliamentary support. The outcome was revolution.

Hearing of the queen's intentions, Thurston and the other conspirators swung into action to overthrow her. They checked with Minister Stevens and with Captain G. S. Wiltse of the USS *Boston*, a cruiser anchored in Honolulu Harbor. Both were sympathetic and offered to land troops from the *Boston*, if necessary to protect American lives and property. Stevens, by Thurston's account, said that if the provisional government could demonstrate that it was in control, he would recognize it. In fact this mid-level diplomat in a lame-duck administration—Harrison had just lost the presidential election to the Democrat Grover Cleveland—had no authority to convey recognition. But Thurston took Stevens's support as a green light to move.

A newly formed Committee of Safety, an aboveground version of Thurston's Annexation Club, in a letter to Stevens accused the queen of committing revolutionary acts, menacing lives and property, and (worst of all) proclaiming a constitution that reduced white influence. The committee sought the protection of U.S. forces. On Thurston's request, Stevens delayed acting on the letter but did refuse Liliuokalani's appeal for support against the insurrection. On January 16 troops from the *Boston* landed in Honolulu. Two of the queen's ministers urged Stevens to order them back to their ship; Stevens declined.

The next day Thurston wrote a proclamation announcing the end of the monarchy and the intention of the provisional government to seek "union" with the United States. After some minor skirmishing between Thurston's irregulars and the queen's troops, the committee seized the government building. Stevens, by letter, recognized the provisional government. Liliuokalani, bereft of resources, gave up. Her surrender, as she put it, was not to the Hawaiian insurrectionists but to the "superior force of the United States of America, whose minister plenipotentiary, His Excellency John L. Stevens, has caused United States troops to be landed at Honolulu and declared that he would support the said provisional government." The queen got it right: Stevens had been a coconspirator in her overthrow.

Following his coup d'état, Thurston scurried to Washington to persuade the dying Harrison administration to ram through the Senate an annexation treaty conveying territorial status on Hawaii. The president did send a treaty forward on February 14, but it failed to pass before Cleveland's inauguration in March. Meanwhile Liliuokalani had dispatched her own envoys to Washington. They made headway with Cleveland's advisers, who convinced the president-elect, no imperialist, that the queen had been illegally deposed. On taking office, the new president withdrew the annexation treaty and sent an antiannexationist former congressman, James H. Blount, on a fact-finding mission to Hawaii.

Blount's subsequent report accused Stevens of helping overthrow the monarchy and expressed the belief that if annexation had been put to a secret ballot among Hawaiians, it would have lost by at least a two-to-one margin. Stevens's successor as minister, Albert S. Willis, was instructed to try to regain the throne for Liliuokalani on the condition that she give amnesty to the insurrectionists. Disastrously she refused the condition; in fact she told Willis that the revolutionaries should be "beheaded." Though beheading was not a form of execution in Hawaii, she had certainly found a graphic way of making her point.

Liliuokalani's bloodcurdling obstinacy lost her the goodwill of the Cleveland administration, which recognized the July 4, 1894, inauguration of the upstart republic and its president, the durable missionary boy Sanford Dole. A new constitution, free of all royal restraints, was slanted steeply against the interests of native Hawaiians. It required an oath of allegiance to the republic from all citizens, stringent property qualifications for voters and officeholders, and fluency in English. There were also provisions excluding Japanese and Chinese, significant minorities in Hawaii, from political participation. An abortive attempt to overthrow the republic in 1895 brought Liliuokalani a short spell in prison. With the end of her monarchy there was no political force left to champion the interests of native Hawaiians or to prevent the Hawaiian pear from finally dropping from the tree.

It is doubtful that Roosevelt, Mahan, or Lodge knew or cared much about the erratic history of American influence in nineteenth-century Hawaii. What they did care about was Hawaii's strategic importance to the U.S. Navy, and that was why they strongly favored annexation. During the Cleveland administration all three advocated American control of the islands. While there was no hope of annexation under Cleveland, McKinley had surprisingly few scruples. Before his inauguration he met the Hawaiian foreign minister, an American citizen, in Canton, he appointed an annexationist as minister to Honolulu, and in the fourth month of his administration he sent the Senate an annexation treaty. It was delayed for more than a year because of Liliuokalani's lobbying, the opposition of the protectionist Sugar Trust, and McKinley's failure to give the treaty a high priority. As it had in Cuba, the Sugar Trust acted as a brake on the U.S. incorporation of Hawaii.

As storm clouds gathered in U.S.-Spanish relations in early 1898, Hawaii took on a new importance. McKinley, under blandishments from Roosevelt and Lodge, told his chief of staff in March: "We need Hawaii just as much and a good deal more than we did California. It is manifest destiny." The same month the Senate Foreign Relations Committee reported the annexation bill favorably to the floor. The committee made a strategic defense of the acquisition, with Japan implied as a rival: "The issue in Hawaii is not between monarchy and the Republic. . . . The issue is whether, in that inevitable struggle, Asia or America shall have the vantage ground of the control of the naval 'Key of the Pacific,' the commercial 'Cross-roads of the Pacific.' " The closest the committee came to a moral argument was to cite a spurious genetic connection, "a duty that has its origin in the noblest sentiments that inspire the love of a father for his children . . . or our Great Republic to a younger sister that has established law, liberty, and justice in a beautiful land that a corrupt monarchy was defiling."

Dewey's victory at Manila Bay strengthened these arguments and supplied new ones. Now Hawaii was a critical station on the way to the Philippines and would be even more vital when the isthmian canal was built. The Hawaiian government was quick to see this. Overcoming a fear of Spanish reprisals, it offered the United States a ship and a National Guard battalion and provided coaling and shore facilities to the transports carrying troops for the capture of Manila.

Annexation, now inevitable, became official on July 7, 1898. The American flag was raised in Hawaii on August 12. Liliuokalani, her royalist allies, and native and mixed-race Hawaiians boycotted the ceremony. Citing the American Declaration of Independence, they complained that the annexation did not rest on the consent of the governed. So Hawaii became a territory of the United States.

Most of the arguments in Congress against Hawaii's annexation had been racial. Representative Champ Clark of Missouri speculated on what would happen if the territory became a state: "How can we endure our shame when a Chinese Senator from Hawaii, with his pigtail hanging down his back, with his pagan joss in his hand, shall rise from his curule chair and in pigeon English proceed to chop logic with George Frisbie Hoar or Henry Cabot Lodge? *O tempora! O mores!*" As it happened, Hawaii's first senator, elected in 1959, *was* of Chinese extraction: Hiram Fong, a self-made millionaire and a graduate of Henry Cabot Lodge's law school, Harvard.

The strongest arguments in the United States in favor of Hawaii's acquisition were strategic. Economic opinions were divided, with continental Americans largely opposed and Hawaiian whites strongly favorable. A human rights rationale was virtually nonexistent. In the end a determined drive for power by a local American minority—seeking profits from sugar, relying on Mammon as well as on God, and now aligned with America's foremost strategic thinkers—had overwhelmed a feckless native monarchy claiming the right to govern, well or ill, in the name of the majority of Hawaiians. Notwithstanding the benefits that were to accrue to Hawaii from its incorporation in the United States, its annexation took account only of the interests of the annexers, not the interests of the annexed. In that sense it was imperialism in its purest form.

4.

"Hurrah for Hawaii!" exclaimed Roosevelt in a letter to Lodge from his bivouac on the San Juan heights overlooking Santiago. But the Rough Rider had little inclination to give Hawaii more than a passing mention. For one thing, he was thinking about Cuba and his own place in history. "Did I tell you," he wrote Lodge, "that I killed a Spaniard with my own hand when I led the storm of the first redoubt? Probably I did." For another thing, he was worried that Shafter would fail to insist on unconditional surrender but would instead allow the Spaniards "to walk out unmolested." Most of all, he was angry at the "stupidity and inefficiency" of the military authorities, especially their failure to provide enough transports to unload supplies and their inability to cope with the rising incidence of malaria, which had killed or prostrated three hundred of his men.

Shafter seemed to be living down to Roosevelt's low opinion of

him. He was feuding with the navy over how to take Santiago, disput-
ing orders from Washington to attack the city rather than besiege it,
and, as Roosevelt feared, negotiating a surrender agreement permit-
ting the Spanish to evacuate their troops. The dissension in the field
was mirrored in Washington. In the presence of the president, Secretary of War Alger disparaged the navy for its failure to take the lead in
attacking Santiago. At this insult to his service, Mahan lost his temper
and accused Alger of ignorance about the use or purpose of the navy.

The Spanish obligingly saved the Americans from falling into an
abyss of recrimination. On July 14 they agreed to surrender on the
American terms, which, an idea of Mahan's, required repatriation of
their troops all the way back to Spain. They wanted to keep their
weapons but gave in when the Americans insisted on taking them.
Against the views of Roosevelt and others, Shafter had been right:
Spanish capitulation proved possible without an attack that might
have cost many American casualties. The surrender of Santiago on
July 17 confirmed the American military victory in Cuba. With the
destruction of the Spanish fleet, the fate of Havana could be left
to the peace negotiations, which were beginning in Washington
through the mediation of the French ambassador.

The Cuban insurgents under General Calixto García had been a
key factor in America's military victory. Before any American soldier
set foot on the island, they had weakened the Spanish Army, thrown it
on the defensive, and inflicted huge casualties. They had denied the
Spanish troops food and equipment, thus making their dependence
on foreign supplies vulnerable to an American naval blockade. As allies of the Americans, however, they had a mixed record. During
Shafter's military operation from Daiquirí to Santiago they helped prevent the Spanish from reinforcing their troops, but two weeks before
the Spanish surrender they failed to prevent a relief force from replenishing the garrison at Santiago.

The rebels were scorned and ridiculed by the U.S. soldiers, who
failed to take into account that they were fighting in their own country for their own independence. The Americans had a different
agenda—to establish military hegemony—and they could not understand why the Cubans were suspicious of that aim. The fact that most
of the insurgents were black provoked racist reactions among some
Americans. Lieutenant John Parker, who led the Gatling gun detach-

ment up San Juan Hill, called the Cuban soldier "a treacherous, lying, cowardly, thieving, worthless, half-breed mongrel." Brigadier General Samuel B. M. Young—"as fine a type of the American fighting soldier as a man can hope to see," according to his subordinate Roosevelt—dismissed the insurgents as "a lot of degenerates, absolutely devoid of honor or gratitude . . . no more capable of self-government than the savages of Africa." Roosevelt himself, while eschewing racial slurs, scoffed at the rebels' unmilitary deportment and found them useless as fighters and even as scouts. General Shafter despised them as "no more fit for self-government than gun powder is for hell" and cut them out of his military planning and his negotiations with the Spanish on capitulation.

All this bad blood welled up in the surrender ceremony in Santiago. Shafter did not invite General García to take part, nor were Cuban troops allowed into the city with their arms. The War Department had made clear that Spain was to surrender to the United States and that Cuba would be under American military occupation. There would be no role for the rebel army and no recognition of a rebel Cuban government. In anger and despair, García addressed Shafter: "We are not savages ignoring the rules of civilized warfare. We are a poor, ragged army as ragged and poor as was the army of your forefathers in their noble war for independence, but like the heroes of Saratoga and Yorktown, we respect our cause too deeply to disgrace it with barbarism and cowardice." Then the old Cuban soldier, who had been fighting the Spanish for thirty years, resigned his command and withdrew his forces.

As the military operation in Cuba drew to a close, one further task remained in the Caribbean. Puerto Rico, five hundred miles east of Cuba and more than a thousand from the United States, was still in Spanish hands. Mahan had argued consistently that Cuba could not be defended if Spain retained control of Puerto Rico, which also commanded one of the entrances to the Caribbean and an approach to the future canal. The history of this tiny island, smaller than Connecticut and one-thirteenth the size of Cuba, was related to Cuba's. Like the larger island, Puerto Rico had been Spanish since its discovery by Columbus, had remained a colony during the wave of Latin American independence in the 1820s, and had been buffeted throughout the nineteenth century by the alternation of liberal and authoritarian regimes in Spain.

But in Puerto Rico there had been no armed insurrection against Spain, though there was a revolutionary movement that, as in Cuba, began in 1868 and used New York City as a base. Unlike the Cubans, the Puerto Ricans sought their rights from Spain through the political process. By November 1897 they had achieved significant constitutional concessions, mainly because of the pressures of revolution in Cuba, the U.S. demands on Spain with regard to Cuba, and the influence of a new Autonomist party on the island. On April 25, 1898—ironically, the very day the United States formally declared war on Spain—the first parliament met under what one Puerto Rican scholar has called the most advanced charter of self-government of any Caribbean colony until after the Second World War.

In contrast with Cuba, Puerto Rico had no interest for the U.S. government other than strategic. Taking a cue from former Secretary of State Blaine's identification of Puerto Rico in 1890 as a target for acquisition, Mahan, Roosevelt, and Lodge all wanted to control the island. While Roosevelt was in Texas training the Rough Riders, Lodge wrote him: "Porto Rico is not forgotten and we mean to have it." Roosevelt replied that Puerto Rico had to be annexed. An assault on Puerto Rico also fitted McKinley's strategy of picking off lightly defended Spanish possessions so as to minimize American casualties.

Sampson bombarded San Juan from the sea on May 12 but broke off the action because his main mission had been to find Cervera. It was not until late in the war that planners turned again to Puerto Rico, which was lightly defended by eight thousand Spanish soldiers. After the usual internecine squabbling between the army and navy leaderships, General Miles, the army chief of staff, set forth from Charleston with thirty-five hundred men on July 8, five days after the Battle of Santiago Bay. He landed on July 25, captured the city of Ponce (Lodge's son Bay, a naval cadet, took the surrender), established martial law, and began a major offensive August 5. He had nearly subdued the whole island by August 14, when Spain and the United States suspended hostilities. American casualties were minor: seven killed and thirty-six wounded.

The reception of the conquerors by Puerto Ricans was mixed. Although the writer Stephen Crane described the Americans as being "bombarded with cigars and bananas," Prime Minister Luis Muñoz Rivera, who had negotiated the advantageous autonomy agreement with Spain, was not hospitable. "We are Spaniards," he said as the invasion force gathered, "and wrapped in the Spanish flag we will die." Such bravado did not survive the overwhelming American military superiority. But it did indicate that Puerto Ricans were not about to treat the Americans as liberators.

The surrender of Santiago and the easier operation in Puerto Rico did not solve all the Americans' problems. As Leonard Wood put it to his wife, "Having soundly thrashed the enemy, we are now in a struggle with nature and to a certain extent disease." He was referring to the debilitating effect of malaria, misdiagnosed at first as yellow fever, which was claiming far more American lives than had been lost in combat. The solution of the surgeon general in Washington was to move the troops to higher altitudes, in the mistaken belief that the disease was a sea-level phenomenon. The men in Cuba were vehemently opposed. Shafter sensed disaster approaching. He told the War Department: "In my opinion there is but one course to take, and that is to immediately transport the Fifth Corps . . . to the United States. If it is not done, I believe the death rate will be appalling."

As Washington's order to shift camp was read at Shafter's staff meeting, Roosevelt saw the resignation on the faces of the regular officers. He realized that as a volunteer with close ties to people in power, he could take an initiative unavailable to soldiers with careers on the line. What became known as the round-robin incident demonstrated Roosevelt's peculiar role as a soldier/politician. He could be a destructive whistle-blower; his criticisms to Lodge of Shafter and Alger undoubtedly made the rounds of high-level Washington and blackened the reputations of the two men. But he could also use his position and influence to help Shafter and his fellow soldiers, as he now did.

In consultation with the other officers and probably with Shafter himself, Roosevelt wrote Shafter a letter that was designed to put pressure on McKinley and Alger to bring the troops home. Roosevelt cited fifteen hundred cases of malaria and warned that more than half the army, if kept in Cuba, would die "like rotten sheep." A second letter to Shafter, which Roosevelt did not draft, made the same points in less dramatic language; this round-robin letter was signed by the eight commanders in Cuba, including Roosevelt.

Both letters were sent to Alger. Even if they had been transmitted by secure means, they would surely have caused a stir since they came close to accusing the president and the secretary of condoning murder. In fact they were handled in a much more inflammatory manner. They were handed over to the Associated Press correspondent in Santiago in Roosevelt's presence and—who can doubt?—by his hand. The leak was a high-risk action, inviting the Spanish to pounce on their debilitated conquerors had they been so inclined. It also exposed weakness and dissension in the American command, and that was what infuriated Alger, who blamed everything on Shafter and Roosevelt. But the ploy achieved its purpose: It generated immediate orders to accelerate the evacuation of the Fifth Army Corps to Montauk Point on Long Island in New York. The first embarkations began August 7.

Roosevelt's willingness to take on the Washington brass had helped avert a major calamity for the disease-ridden American Army. But in personal terms it probably cost him a coveted prize. He had launched a determined campaign to get himself awarded the Medal of Honor. The effort began in the field and continued even after he had won the governorship of New York largely on his exploits in Cuba. Why he felt he needed this extra boost to his ego is unclear; perhaps the ghost of his father still hovered. Making a pest and a boor of himself, he got his commanders, his fellow officers, and even his orderly to write letters attesting to his bravery. As late as 1913 he had the oafishness to publish them all in his autobiography. He persuaded the faithful Lodge to make the case for him in Washington. He himself wrote the general in charge of decorations.

There was probably a reluctance within the regular army to award the Medal of Honor to a volunteer officer. Moreover, Roosevelt's major military exploits were confined to a single day, and his whole combat experience was limited to two weeks. Wood, by contrast, had won the Medal of Honor through an entire year's dangerous duty of chasing down the Apache chief Geronimo. Roosevelt's major problem was undoubtedly Alger, who resented his relentless self-promotion and his growing criticism of the secretary's administrative mismanagement. In a letter to Alger from Cuba shortly before the round-robin incident, Roosevelt had bragged that the Rough Riders were "as good as any regulars, and three times as good as any State [National Guard] troops."

Alger, for whom Roosevelt's regiment was just one of thirty fighting in Cuba, replied sharply: "I suggest that, unless you want to spoil the effects and glory of your victory, you make no invidious comparisons. The Rough Riders are no better than any other volunteers. They had an advantage in their arms [thanks to Wood's determined scrounging, they had modern Krag-Jorgensen rifles and smokeless powder], for which they ought to be grateful." Alger told Lodge that Roosevelt would not get the medal, and he was right. His effort to block the commander of the Rough Riders remained successful for more than a century. President Bill Clinton finally awarded Roosevelt the Medal of Honor posthumously in January 2001.

Before leaving Cuba with his men, Roosevelt indulged in a characteristic adventure. He decided to swim out to the collier *Merrimac*, which had been sunk at the entrance to Santiago Harbor in an unsuccessful effort to trap Cervera's fleet. Jack Greenway, one of the more intrepid of the Rough Riders, swam with him and left this account:

> We weren't out more than a dozen strokes before [Consul General Fitzhugh] Lee, who had clambered up on the parapet of Fort Morro, began to yell.
>
> "Can you make out what he's trying to say," the old man [Roosevelt] asked, punctuating his words with long, overhand strokes.
>
> "Sharks," says I, wishing I were back on shore.
>
> "Sharks," says the colonel, blowing out a mouthful of water, "they" stroke "won't" stroke "bite." Stroke. "I've been" stroke "studying them" stroke "all my life" stroke "and I never" stroke "heard of one" stroke "bothering a swimmer." Stroke. "It's all" stroke "poppy cock."
>
> Just then a big fellow, probably not more than ten or twelve feet long, but looking as big as a battleship to me, showed up alongside us. Then came another, till we had quite a group. The colonel didn't pay the least attention. . . .
>
> Meantime the old general was doing a war dance up on the parapet, shouting and standing first on one foot and then on the other, and working his arms like he was doing something on a bet.

Finally we reached the wreck and I felt better. The colonel, of course, got busy looking things over. I had to pretend I was interested, but I was thinking of the sharks and getting back to shore. I didn't hurry the colonel in his inspection either.

After a while he had seen enough, and we went over the side again. Soon the sharks were all about us again, sort of pacing us in, as they had paced us out, while the old general did the second part of his war dance. He felt a whole lot better when we landed, and so did I.

There in cameo was the Roosevelt of the Cuban campaign: impetuous, inquisitive, heroic, omniscient, charismatic. It was the story of San Juan Hill, replayed as comedy.

Roosevelt landed at Montauk Point with the Rough Riders to find he was an American legend. His every word was telegraphed to newspapers across America. He radiated the confidence of victory; he had even become the symbol of America's triumph. "I am feeling disgracefully well!" he boomed on arrival, then, after a graceful expression of sympathy for the weakened condition of his soldiers: "Oh, but we have had a bully fight!" President McKinley, with Alger in tow, visited Camp Wikoff and made a point of descending from his carriage to shake Roosevelt's hand.

The camp, a coronation for Roosevelt, was a humiliation for Alger. Preparations for receiving the troops were inadequate, in part because the pressure from Roosevelt and Shafter had hastened their arrival. Alger became the scapegoat for what had gone wrong, a position Roosevelt was delighted to keep him in. From the camp Roosevelt complained to Lodge of lack of transport, bad food and water, and overcrowding, and expressed the hope that the president would remove Alger before the November election: "He simply can't do better; he can not learn by experience." Americans killed in the Cuba campaign totaled only 1,014, a stunningly successful result, despite the carnage on July 1. But three-quarters of the deaths were from disease, not combat. Alger would have to pay the price for that statistic.

As for Roosevelt and the Rough Riders, his military career and theirs passed into history and myth on September 13, when the regiment was mustered out. In a moving ceremony the soldiers gave him a Remington sculpture of a broncobuster, then filed by one by one to shake his hand. His tribute to "this peculiarly American regiment" and the emotion and loyalty the men displayed toward their commander left no doubt that in their eyes, Roosevelt was an exceptional leader.

5.

A major challenge to the American armed forces throughout the Spanish-American War was to fight on two fronts eight thousand miles apart. Even before the battle for Cuba reached its climax, a large operation was also being mounted to capture the city of Manila. Admiral Dewey's victory in Manila Bay had been easy and cheap. Now the question was how to follow it up. The primary war aim was control of Cuba. Did the United States also seek control of the Philippines? The military planners wanted to keep the pressure on the Philippines in the belief that it would hasten the Spanish surrender. But did this mean only seizing Manila or subduing the entire archipelago of seven thousand islands?

Major General Wesley Merritt, the second-ranking general behind Miles and commander of the military expedition to the Philippines, asked the president point-blank. McKinley avoided a direct answer. The two American purposes, he said, were "completing the reduction of Spanish power" and "giving order and security to the islands while in the possession of the United States." He seemed to be saying that the United States should take the whole of the Philippines but hold it only temporarily. But was he?

The ambiguity over objectives caused confusion over the force structure needed. Manila was more than seven thousand miles from San Francisco, and Merritt, playing it safe, wanted a large force because of the length of the supply lines and because he assumed, prematurely, that the local population would be hostile. The decisive U.S. naval victory had weakened the threat from the twenty thousand Spanish soldiers in the archipelago. Dewey, believing that the mission was limited to taking and holding Manila, thought that five thousand U.S. troops would suffice. General Miles, reflecting the disorder over strategy in Washington, oscillated from an occupation of the entire archipelago to an operation limited to Manila. Merritt was finally given more than twenty thousand men, more than Shafter got for Cuba. But McKinley, the reluctant imperialist, would not resolve the issue of what to do in the Philippines. He later mused that if Dewey had just sailed away after smashing the Spanish fleet, what a lot of trouble he would have saved.

En route across the Pacific one of the American ships was diverted to capture Guam, the largest of the Mariana Islands. Guam was important for its location, about two-thirds of the way from Hawaii to the Philippines and within easy sailing distance of Shanghai, Canton, Hong Kong, and Yokohama. The history of Spain's control of Guam had begun and now ended with a theft. Ferdinand Magellan, its European discoverer, named the island chain the Ladrones (thieves) because one of the inhabitants stole a boat from him. Now, nearly four centuries later, the Americans purloined Guam itself.

The circumstances were comic. When on June 20 the USS *Charleston* lobbed a few shells at two abandoned forts on the island, two local officials rowed out to the American cruiser. They thought the attack was a salute and had come to apologize for their inability to return it. Captain Henry Glass explained that Spain and the United States were at war, that he was in fact attacking the island, and that they were under arrest. After some protocolary folderol, the governor and his garrison of fifty-six dumbstruck Spanish marines surrendered. Guam thus became America's second overseas colony, after Midway.

Dewey's reinforcements found the newly minted rear admiral in what he himself called "a period of anxiety" as he blockaded Manila Bay. Warships from Britain, France, Japan, and Germany, all interested in the newly vulnerable strategic archipelago, had swarmed toward the harbor after the battle. Most of the ships observed the protocol of a blockade, reporting to Dewey and anchoring where they would not impede his blockading operations against the Spanish. But the Germans, who had brought in five ships comparable in power to the American squadron, got shirty about recognizing American authority. They often failed to report, anchored where they chose, and displayed ostentatious chumminess with Spanish officials in Manila, even exchanging visits with the Spanish captain general. When a German warship interfered with the Filipino rebels' operations against the Spanish, Dewey decided to get tough with the German commander, Vice Admiral Otto von Diederichs.

By the accounts of both German and American eyewitnesses, the American admiral lost his temper with Diederichs's flag lieutenant and threatened war if the Germans did not stop violating the blockade. The confrontation never got beyond rhetoric, and Dewey chose to play it down. Perhaps embarrassed that his temper had nearly propelled him into an unauthorized conflict with a powerful adversary, he did not even report it to Washington. President McKinley eventually heard of it but chose to pass it off lightly the first time he met Dewey face to face. From a more spartan president the feisty little admiral would have merited a reprimand, but McKinley knew better than to take on a war hero.

The skirmishing in Manila Bay demonstrated Germany's predatory interest in the Philippines; Diederichs told Dewey he was there "by order of the Kaiser." It also showed the British in a favorable light. The skipper of the one British ship in the harbor strongly backed Dewey in his successful effort to face down the German commander. The German challenge in the Philippines, though weakened by British cooperation with the American squadron, added complexity to Dewey's problems and made him increasingly anxious for reinforcements. It was becoming difficult just to "sail away"; Manila at least had to be taken.

As in Cuba, an indigenous independence movement was in the field against Spain. In the Philippines it had been fighting off and on since 1896. In both cases the U.S. armed forces had the incredible good fortune of coming in behind a domestic insurrection that was harassing and weakening the Spanish enemy. In both cases military necessity forced on the American government the need to develop strategies toward the rebels. Those strategies not only affected the military outcome but also determined the character of American imperialism during the war and for the century after it.

Even before the American expeditionary force set foot on Philippine soil, there was a substantial history of connections between American officials and the insurgent leader, Emilio Aguinaldo. As a local rebel commander in his native Cavite, Aguinaldo, a young middle-class Filipino of mixed Tagalog and Chinese ancestry, had shown himself a resourceful and ruthless fighter. He challenged and defeated his leader, Andrés Bonifacio, engineered Bonifacio's trial and execution in May 1897, and several weeks later proclaimed a republic headed by himself.

The Spanish were looking, as in Cuba, for a compromise with the insurrection; in contrast with Cuba, they achieved one in the Philippines. In late 1897 they agreed to pay Aguinaldo eight hundred thousand pesos and to temper some of their colonial excesses, in return for his commitment to leave the Philippines and give up the rebellion. Neither side kept strictly to the bargain. The Spanish made no reforms and failed to pay the insurgents the full amount promised. Aguinaldo, faithful only to the higher calling of revolution, arrived in Hong Kong and immediately began to buy weapons for the next round.

It was in Hong Kong, then, as now, a listening post and center of intrigue, that Aguinaldo began his relationship with the United States. Earlier in 1897, even before his arrival, his agent had approached the American consul general there, Rounseville Wildman, about an alliance whereby the Americans would provide arms to enable the rebels to establish a republic, and the rebels would cede two provinces and the lucrative collection of customs to the United States. Wildman showed interest until the State Department refused the deal and rapped his knuckles. In March 1898, as war was growing imminent between Spain and the United States, Aguinaldo made contact with Dewey's squadron in Hong Kong. He claimed later that one of Dewey's officers had encouraged him to lead the revolt in the Philippines and had promised American support. The claim, though unsupported, is credible; Dewey, stoked by Roosevelt, was preparing for war, and a Philippine insurrection would be helpful.

As war drew closer, Aguinaldo unaccountably left Hong Kong, bound for Europe for the alleged reason of escaping legal problems. By a trick of fate, his ship stopped in Singapore just as the conflict broke out, and he was taken to another American official who seemed ready to support insurrection. This was Consul General E. Spencer Pratt, who promised, or perhaps merely hinted at, American backing for Philippine independence under an American protectorate. Pratt telegraphed Dewey that Aguinaldo was ready to return to Hong Kong to establish cooperation with the U.S. Navy; Dewey wired back that Aguinaldo should come "as soon as possible." By the time Aguinaldo got back to Hong Kong, Dewey had departed for Manila Bay. He had, however, taken one of Aguinaldo's men with him, and he had authorized Aguinaldo's passage on the U.S. Navy cutter *McCulloch*, which arrived at American-controlled Cavite in Manila Bay on May 19.

Aguinaldo and American officials later provided contrasting accounts of this tangled set of contacts and discussions. Evidence is lacking whether the Americans made firm commitments of military support for Philippine independence, as Aguinaldo alleged, or Aguinaldo was magnifying mere expressions of sympathy, as the Americans claimed. The two American consuls, Wildman in Hong Kong and Pratt in Singapore, were diplomatic entrepreneurs after the fashion of Stevens in Hawaii. They had their own agendas and did not feel overly tethered by guidance from the State Department, which in fact tried to restrain them both. In any case they would not have been either the first or the last American diplomats who failed to tell Washington everything they were doing. In a climate of hostility toward Spain, they, and Dewey as well, undoubtedly thought they were serving the national interest by encouraging Aguinaldo's anti-Spanish activity.

For his part, Aguinaldo, who was not yet thirty and looked like a teenager, dreamed big dreams and was prone to hear what he wanted to hear. He might not have understood whatever nuances and caveats may have fallen from American lips. But he was also a man toughened by revolutionary intrigues and the judicial murder of a rival, a man who knew how to manipulate and how to recognize manipulation by others. When he arrived back in the Philippines, he may have believed that he had already won American support for independence. But even if he did not, he could hope to maneuver the Americans toward that goal by making himself indispensable as a military ally.

Even more important than the commitments the free-lancing American consuls may or may not have made was the fact that Dewey sailed Aguinaldo back to a revolutionary situation in the Philippines. The American consul in Manila, Oscar F. Williams, was reporting that Aguinaldo's absence had not quelled the insurrection against Spanish rule. Dewey's act to repatriate him was incendiary, similar, though on a much smaller scale, to the German decision two decades later to send Vladimir Lenin back to Russia on a sealed train.

Later, when the United States was at war against Aguinaldo, Dewey tried to downplay his relations with the rebels. He testified to Congress that "these little men" had been bothering him in Hong Kong when he was getting his squadron ready for battle and that it was just an "act of courtesy" to give them passage to the Philippines. In a more reflective mood in his memoirs, he offered a more credible reason: "Obviously, as our purpose was to weaken the Spaniards in every legitimate way, thus hastening the conclusion of hostilities in a war which was made to free Cuba from Spanish oppression, operations by the insurgents against Spanish oppression in the Philippines under certain restrictions would be welcome."

Determined to maximize assets for the capture of Manila, Dewey saw the clear advantages of a domestic rebellion. He thus found it convenient to believe the erroneous assertions of the Hong Kong and Manila consuls, Wildman and Williams, that Aguinaldo wanted the Philippines to be an American colony rather than an independent country. The policy makers in Washington had no such illusions; they moved quickly to attach a leash to Dewey. Aguinaldo had been back in Cavite only a week when Secretary of the Navy Long cabled the admiral his instructions for dealing with the rebel leader. He ordered Dewey to report in detail on every contact he had with the insurgents. As for the political relationship, "it is desirable, as far as possible, . . . not to have political alliances with the insurgents or any faction in the islands that would incur liability to maintain their cause in the future."

Long did not divulge any plan to annex the Philippines; such a decision was months away. He did indicate a deep suspicion of the rebels, also shown in Cuba, and a willingness to use them only on the condition that they be denied any military or political power. Dewey, who did not share this suspicion, exchanged intelligence information with Aguinaldo and turned over to him captured Spanish arms. The rebels also received a large shipment of rifles and ammunition from China, courtesy of the entrepreneurial consul Wildman, who later absconded with a large share of Aguinaldo's payment.

Dewey's cooperation with the insurgents paid off. Advancing on Manila, they surrounded the city on the three land sides, closing the ring with the American naval squadron in the bay. Less conveniently, Aguinaldo accompanied his military advance with political pronouncements. While offering due gratitude to the United States, they left no doubt of his intention to establish an independent government throughout the islands. On June 12 he declared independence; on June 23 he formed a government with himself at its head.

Washington resolved to block this process of incremental independence. Secretary of State Day reprimanded Consul Pratt in Singapore for apparently pledging to recognize Aguinaldo's political claims. Navy Secretary Long reiterated to Dewey his obligation to report "any conferences, relations, or cooperations, military or otherwise, which you have had with Aguinaldo." Dewey blithely reported that he had excellent relations with the insurgent leader, whom he treated as a friend and who had "kept me advised of his progress, which has been wonderful." The admiral denied any commitments to the rebels but made no secret of his admiration for them: "In my opinion, these people are far superior in their intelligence and more capable of self-government than the natives of Cuba, and I am familiar with both races."

The U.S. Army commanders who were beginning to arrive in the Philippines were more in tune than Dewey with Washington's hard line toward the rebels. American troops, the first of four detachments, landed on June 30 at Cavite, along the bay south of Manila. Cavite, a former Spanish naval base, was a beachhead of American territory, having been taken by Dewey on May 1. Subsequent landings were even closer to Manila; in his memoirs Dewey credited rebel advances with allowing the Americans to get "within easy striking distance" of their objective.

The first American commander ashore was Brigadier General Thomas M. Anderson, a Civil War veteran, a lawyer, an advocate of military reform, and a skillful diplomat. He took the insurgents seriously, reporting, "They are not ignorant, savage tribes, but have a civilization of their own." He also respected Aguinaldo for housing and feeding the American forces. Yet he understood that Aguinaldo's transparent drive for independence would bring him into conflict with the American Army. Like all the other Americans, he told Aguinaldo that the United States desired no colonies, but his orders left no leeway for any concessions to rebel claims of independence. Disagreements grew. Aguinaldo took a rigid position on his status; he insisted on being treated as a president. When he was not, he began to withdraw his cooperation with the arriving Americans.

Anderson's commander, General Merritt, who came on July 24, ended for good the honeymoon phase of U.S. cooperation with Aguinaldo. Merritt broke off contact with the Philippine leader, a foolish action since he needed the insurgent forces, which were positioned between the American beachhead and Manila. It was the insurgents, not the Americans, that surrounded the city. Merritt was not above tricking Aguinaldo. He sent an emissary to offer the rebels several artillery pieces if they would exchange places with the Americans in a rebel-held sector south of Manila. Aguinaldo accepted on the condition that the American general sign the request, thus furthering the rebel leader's goal of achieving U.S. recognition. Trusting Merritt, he withdrew his troops, but the American delivered neither the artillery nor the document. Merritt's duplicity and disdain gave substance to Aguinaldo's fears, already aroused by the numbers of U.S. soldiers pouring in. He saw that as the Americans increased their troops and their military capabilities, they would have less need of his local army. The swelling American force was becoming as much a threat to Aguinaldo as it was to the Spanish defenders of Manila.

For their part the commanders of the Spanish garrison in Manila decided that they would rather surrender to the Americans than to the insurgents. Troop levels on the Spanish and American sides were equal, at about thirteen thousand, but the Spanish had to contend with the additional liabilities of Dewey's guns in the bay, insurgent forces surrounding Manila, and incipient starvation among the city's seventy thousand besieged residents. The new Spanish military governor general, Don Fermin Jaudenes y Álvarez, faced a problem: If he surrendered Manila without a fight, he would be court-martialed for cowardice. His predecessor, Augustín, had just been sacked the week before for defeatism. Moreover, as Jaudenes explained indelicately, he would prefer to surrender to white people than to "niggers." So he worked out a deal with Dewey through the good offices of the Belgian consul. Both sides would pretend to fight, and after a demonstrational exchange of fire the Spanish would surrender.

The rebels were neither consulted on nor informed of the deal. As it unfolded on August 13, both Spanish and U.S. forces showed excessive enthusiasm, and the Americans actually lost more casualties in the sham battle for the city than they had in the real battle for the bay. Apart from that, the plan worked, and the American flag was raised over Manila. The odd man out was Aguinaldo. The night before the battle, General Anderson had told him that the American forces had been ordered to prevent Filipino soldiers from entering Manila. On August 13 American troops, after finishing with the Spanish, began to carry out that order. There was great tension and some violence as the two sides jockeyed for position, but Aguinaldo decided to give in and conserve his troops for another day.

After the devastating naval victory of Manila Bay, it was only a matter of time before Manila fell. Fortunately Dewey, like Shafter at Santiago, had the patience to wait until the city could be taken with minimal American losses. The Battle of Manila, like the battles of Santiago and Havana, was important because it was never fought. The three nonevents spared thousands of American lives. Ironically, on August 12, the day before Manila surrendered, Secretary of State Day and Jules Cambon, the French ambassador in Washington who was representing Spain, had signed a protocol ending hostilities. The news did not reach Manila until several days later. Dewey's efforts to avoid casualties had been doubly repaid.

The Spanish-American War was over. Spain had been eliminated as a Caribbean and Pacific power and thereby weakened as a European power. Though the monarchy did not fall, the loss of the Cuban market and the humiliation of defeat diminished its wealth, its self-confidence, and its control over separatist tendencies at home. Henceforth 1898 was referred to in Spain as *el Desastre*. In the Philippines the war ended in conditions of extreme uncertainty. The Spanish were no longer a major factor there, but the Philippine rebels who had done so much to assure the American victory were seething with discontent. The city they had fought two years to capture had been turned over to a foreign power; they were not even allowed to attend the surrender ceremony. The Battle of Manila completed the process by which they were transformed from allies to adversaries of the Americans. Soon they would be enemies.

How had the United States managed to set itself athwart an indigenous movement that seemed to share so many of the same goals? First, the American ingratitude stemmed from an obsession with the strategic importance of the Philippines and a tendency to see the rebels as pawns rather than people. There was an element of racism in this attitude. General Merritt treated Aguinaldo as a subordinate, and his men were likely to refer to Filipino soldiers as "niggers." Second, the activity of the three highly unprofessional consuls in Hong Kong, Singapore, and Manila confounded rational planning with their bad analyses and bad advice. They reported inaccurately to Dewey and to Washington that Aguinaldo was seeking annexation rather than independence, and they exaggerated to the insurgent leader the degree of unity between his views and the Americans', misleading him into thinking that the United States supported independence. Third, nobody on the American side understood, or much cared about, local conditions or the circumstances giving rise to Aguinaldo's rebellion. Fourth, there was confusion from the president on down about America's true interests in the Philippines.

The American victory was tainted by a rancor on the rebel side that exploded into war within months. Dewey, who probably understood and sympathized with Aguinaldo more than did any other American official, had serious forebodings. Several months after the fall of Manila, he urged his government to promise the people of the Philippines "a large and gradually increasing degree of autonomy under American rule." In a letter to his son he said of the insurgents: "We don't want a war with them if we can help it and perhaps it would be better to give up the islands rather than have one." But as Dewey undoubtedly knew, it was too late to give up the islands and, in the wishful thinking of his commander in chief, sail away. He was left to lament in his memoirs that after Aguinaldo's rebellion against the United States had broken out, "now . . . we must establish our authority by force against the very wishes of the people whom we sought to benefit."

6.

The satisfactions of military victory did not obscure, at least not to President McKinley, the urgency of the tasks that lay ahead. Most pressing was the need to fill the gap in the State Department. With the senile Sherman shuffled off at the outset of the war, his deputy, the cautious Day, had been filling in as secretary. McKinley wanted someone better qualified. A month after the Spanish capitulation he turned to another member of the Ohio political establishment, John Hay. Characteristically, the thought of becoming secretary of state threw Hay into a depression. He told Henry White the job would kill him in six months. Without Hay's knowledge, White tried to save his mentor from the burdens of office. He asked outgoing Secretary Day to get the appointment killed, but McKinley was adamant. Henry Adams, who was staying with Hay in England, counseled his friend that "no serious statesman can accept a favor [i.e., the London embassy] and refuse a service." Suppressing his fears for his health, Hay accepted the appointment and agreed to report for duty in late September, in time for the negotiation with Spain over a peace treaty. He was to serve as secretary for nearly seven years.

For McKinley the appointment of Hay was an astute political move. Hay had made a brilliant success of winning the British to the American side in the war. Three weeks after its outbreak, British colonial secretary Joseph Chamberlain, to whom Hay was close, proposed "permanent amity" with the United States and an Anglo-Saxon alliance. As a novelist, poet, and journalist Hay was awesomely articulate in speech and writing. He was the last American in political life to have been close to Lincoln, a huge asset in Republican and national politics. He also genuinely admired McKinley. His drawbacks—an unwillingness to confront (the president had the same weakness) and a disdain for Congress—seemed minor.

In his youth a romantic advocate of Cuban independence, Hay had sympathized with the Cuban revolutionaries. But unlike his friends Roosevelt, Lodge, and Mahan, he took a skeptical view of the war, much as the president himself did. Just weeks before the United States declared war, he had cautioned his wife: "You and I had better have no opinion about the Spanish War except the President's." His famous celebratory letter to Roosevelt was nuanced. "It has been a splendid little war," Hay wrote, "begun with the highest motives, carried on with magnificent intelligence and spirit, favored by that Fortune which loves the brave." But he added an often overlooked cautionary note: "It is now to be concluded, I hope, with that fine good nature, which is, after all, the distinguishing trait of the American character." Hay had his eye not only on the coming settlement with Spain but also on the potential problem with the subject peoples who now found themselves under American rule.

Hay was not the sole prominent American whose fortune was changed dramatically by the victory against Spain. Nobody surfed the wave of success more skillfully than Theodore Roosevelt. Secretary Long's reluctant prophecy at the beginning of the war had proved right: Roosevelt had indeed accomplished "some great thing." His main achievement had been to help get the United States into the war in the first place, but it was his exploits on San Juan Hill that brought him national renown. He was suddenly the most famous political figure in America. Hay, always ready with an ingratiating word, told him: "You have written your name on several pages of your country's history, and they are all honorable to you and comfortable to your friends."

After the war Lodge told Roosevelt that now he could pretty well name his political position: "Ordinary rules do not apply to you." Lodge favored the House, as a stepping-stone to the Senate, over the New York governorship. Roosevelt replied that he would prefer national over state politics but had noticed that "the good people in New York at present seem to be crazy over me." His first idea for presenting himself to those good people was a parade of Rough Riders up Fifth Avenue, but his nemesis Alger scotched that initiative. Nonetheless, the New York Republican leadership, though not keen on his reformist credentials, saw a sure winner in the hero of San Juan Hill. For once Roosevelt ignored Lodge's advice and declared his candidacy for governor.

At the nominating convention his opponents distributed evidence that he had once declared Washington, D.C., to be his residence. The charge was true; he had been trying to avoid New York taxes. Panicked, he appealed to Root for help, and his friend showed why he was one of the best political lawyers in the country. In a demagogic speech to the convention, he argued sentiment rather than fact. He proved to the delegates' satisfaction that Roosevelt's heart had always been in New York, even if his wallet had occasionally strayed. In a frantic whistle-stop campaign around the state, Roosevelt carted along six Rough Riders in uniform, while the bands played the war's hit tune, "There'll Be a Hot Time in the Old Town Tonight." On November 7, two weeks after his fortieth birthday, he won a close victory. In six months he had gone from a second-level position in the Navy Department to governor of the most populous state in the Union.

During a single year America's role in the world had changed forever. A country whose power and influence had been largely limited to the continent of North America had suddenly acquired a global reach that it would never relinquish. Throughout the nineteenth century the United States had expanded steadily, but its growth had been overland, to the contiguous territories in the Hispanic South and the sparsely populated West and to noncontiguous Alaska. Now the expansion was overseas. In fifteen weeks the United States had gained island possessions on both the Atlantic and Pacific sides of its continental mass. It had put under its protection and control more than ten million people: whites, blacks, Hispanics, Indians, Polynesians, Chinese, Japanese, and the polyethnic peoples of the Philippine archipelago. This burst of offshore conquests made America a genuine overseas empire.

The military and political strength of the United States had finally reached the same level as its economy, which was outproducing almost all the industrial countries of Europe by 1898. The lightning triumphs in Manila and Santiago bays made the navy almost overnight one of the five best in the world. Even the army outgrew its derisory reputation as an Indian-chasing cavalry to earn acclaim for battles won in two hemispheres with fewer than four hundred killed in action. In Latin America the United States had for the first time given the Monroe Doctrine an authority backed by force; the hegemonic American position in the Caribbean was now protected by military might. America's first acquisitions in the Pacific also inspired a permanent preoccupation with that ocean and with the Asian mainland that was to span three bloody twentieth-century wars. The country had entered the war against Spain with the limited aim of winning control of Cuba, but it emerged as a world power. To White in London Lodge summed up the specific achievements: "One of the most important is the friendly relations which have been established with England. Another is the expulsion of Spain from this hemisphere. Another is our entrance into the Pacific by the annexation of Hawaii and our securing a foothold at last in the East. . . . Lastly we have risen to be one of the world's great powers."

The decision to go to war had been popular with the American people, who had enlisted in droves to fight in it. The ensuing victory, quick in coming and sparse in casualties, gave rise to a triumphalism that the tragic Civil War a generation earlier could never have produced. The saloonkeeper of Archey Road echoed the theme satirically: " 'We're a gr-reat people,' said Mr. Hennessey earnestly. 'We ar-re,' said Mr. Dooley. 'We ar-re that. An' the best iv it is, we know we ar-re.' " Lodge, to whom Mr. Dooley's comment certainly applied, rhapsodized: "What a wonderful war it has been. What a navy we have got and what good fighters our soldiers are. Nothing but victory and at such small cost." Even the skeptical Hay fell prey to the euphoria. From London he wrote the president: "We have never in all our history had the standing in the world we have now."

9. Jingoes and Goo-goos

1.

The necessity of presenting peace terms set President McKinley on a cycle of agonized indecision. The defeat of the Spanish had been so conclusive that the issue was not what they would concede but what the Americans would demand, so the debate was exclusively American. At stake was whether Cuba, Puerto Rico, and the Philippines should be independent states or American properties—in other words, how much of an imperial power the United States should become. McKinley never thought of himself as an imperialist, but the very scope of the American victory was pulling him inexorably into the imperialist camp.

The course of the war, even before it ended, put the Americans in an enviable negotiating position. The Spanish Navy had been effectively destroyed. The Spanish garrisons in Cuba, Puerto Rico, and the Philippines could not be either reinforced or supplied. Even the Spanish coast now lay open to attack by the U.S. Navy. Mahan's principle of naval primacy was again graphically demonstrated: Spain lay prostrate before American power. The Spanish prime minister, the Liberal Sagasta, had always been critical of the way Spain managed its empire and was thus unlikely to pursue a hard line in the coming negotiations. In approaching the Spanish in June and again in July, as the war neared its end, McKinley took little risk in putting forward a tough American going-in position. Cuba, according to the U.S. government, would become independent after an indeterminate period as an American protectorate. Instead of exacting a cash indemnity from Spain, the United States would take in territory what it considered it was owed—specifically, Puerto Rico and Guam. Only with respect to the Philippines was it ambiguous. For the present it would hold the city and bay of Manila pending conclusion of a peace treaty that would determine the final status of the whole archipelago.

Spain was prepared to accept Cuba's independence, though ironically it would have preferred Cuba's outright annexation by the United States since it feared that the Cuban revolutionaries would exact reprisals against Spanish inhabitants and sympathizers. But it balked at the cession of Puerto Rico and Guam, recalling that the United States had not annexed all the territory it had taken in the Mexican War. It believed that it should maintain sovereignty over the Philippines and that Aguinaldo's insurgents should be barred from the peace negotiations.

As in the period leading to the outbreak of war, Spain had no real cards to play except delay, but by August 1898 the Americans would have none of it. His temper flaring, Mahan urged on Secretary Long an ultimatum to the Spanish, with the threat behind it of resumption of hostilities. McKinley, himself annoyed at the foot-dragging, approved a tough line. The Spanish, out of options, caved. The protocol ending the war was signed in Washington on August 12 by McKinley and French ambassador Cambon, representing Spain. Spain conceded the independence of Cuba and the cession of Puerto Rico and Guam. The Philippines remained the major point of contention.

In American designs, tiny Puerto Rico never had much of a chance. McKinley had been uncharacteristically firm; as early as June 3 he had told Hay in London of his intention to annex the island. Its strategic value overshadowed other considerations. It was vital to the plans to build and protect an isthmian canal; moreover, no American strategist wedded to the Monroe Doctrine would want to leave a Spanish military base in the vicinity of Cuba. Cuba itself was a more complex problem. The Teller Amendment prescribed eventual independence, but a loophole in the wording allowed postponement of that day until "pacification" of the island; meanwhile, a U.S. military government would have full powers. The greatest conundrum was the Philippines. McKinley, who had not been able to find the islands on a map, now had to decide whether they should become an American colony.

The principal jingoes in his administration were not of one mind. Roosevelt never wavered in his conviction that the archipelago should be annexed. But Dewey, the hero of Manila Bay, favored considerable autonomy for the Philippine people, a position that did not help the annexationist side. Mahan wanted to keep the island of Luzon, with Manila and Subic Bay, for strategic reasons, but he was prepared to leave the rest to Spain. Lodge fluctuated between a firm policy of annexing all the islands and a temptation to trade them. He actually proposed ceding all but Luzon to Great Britain in exchange for the Bahamas, Jamaica, and the Virgin Islands (which, in his scheme, the British would buy from Denmark and then give to the United States). In this cacophony it was no wonder that McKinley decided to buy time by postponing a decision until the peace conference was under way.

In setting up the peace negotiations, the United States met Spanish concerns on only two points, neither of which was really an American concession. It agreed to have the negotiations in Paris instead of Washington, the American preference. As the capital city of the victorious power Washington was clearly an inappropriate, even an insulting site; it was cost-free to give it up. The Americans also agreed to exclude the Philippine insurgents from the talks. They could hardly have been less willing than the Spanish to have Aguinaldo, with his insistence on independence, at the table.

The five-man American negotiating team was chaired by former Secretary of State Day, who had just turned the State Department over to John Hay. Day was uncomfortable with the territorial acquisitions, but he had been a pragmatist at State and would not be forceful in opposing them. A second peace commissioner, Democratic senator George Gray, had voted against the annexation of Hawaii and was dead set against any more U.S. colonies. The other three members of the commission—two Republican senators plus Whitelaw Reid, Hay's friend and the publisher of the *New York Tribune*, which had moved off the fence to become an imperialist daily—were expansionists. The three senators on the commission were members of the Foreign Relations Committee, which would be responsible for dealing with the treaty that emerged; McKinley was cannily beginning to co-opt the Senate.

The Spanish negotiators, mostly Liberals, were not intimidating. The Conservative party, which would have insisted on a firm negotiating stance, refused to serve on the commission, thus protecting its position that the defeat was entirely the responsibility of the Liberals. Early in the negotiations the Spanish ambassador to France, Fernando de León y Castillo, sought out Whitelaw Reid to say: "Do not forget we are poor; do not forget we are vanquished; do not forget that after all it was Spain that discovered America; do not forget that this is the first great war you have had with a nation on the continent of Europe, or with any foreign nation; that you have had an astonishing victory, and that you cannot complete it without showing magnanimity." The Spanish were compelled by adversity to lead from weakness.

In the late summer and early fall of 1898 a debate raged in McKinley's head about whether the United States should annex the Philippines. The president had been an uncertain imperialist at best. With Puerto Rico and Guam he had crossed the line he himself had drawn in 1897 against "territorial aggression." But the Philippines were more important, a true litmus test. He admitted to not knowing what to do with them when they "dropped into our laps." He seemed to have in mind a "hitching post" for the navy, not a major acquisition of territory. Lodge had found him "a little timid" about the islands, but his appointment of an imperialist majority on the peace commission indicated a slight tilt toward annexation. By the time of the commissioners' departure for Paris in mid-September he had accepted Mahan's argument that the island of Luzon was a strategic necessity.

McKinley's guidance to his negotiators reflected the turmoil in his mind. The instructions were clear and specific on Cuba and Puerto Rico and even on an interim solution for the Philippines: Luzon was to be ceded "in full right and sovereignty" to the United States. Regarding the archipelago as a whole, however, McKinley gave the negotiators nothing they could use. They were left to read between the lines of a set of cryptic philosophical musings indicating indecision rather than purpose. The tone, in its grandiosity, seemed generous and self-denying:

> It is my earnest wish that the United States in making peace should follow the same high rule of conduct which guided it in facing war. It should be as scrupulous and magnanimous in the concluding settlement as it was just and humane in its original action. The luster and the moral strength attaching to a cause which can be confidently rested upon the considerate judgment of the world

should not under any illusion of the hour be dimmed by ulterior designs which might tempt us into excessive demands or into an adventurous departure on untried paths. It is believed that the true glory and the enduring interests of the country will most surely be served if an unselfish duty conscientiously accepted and a signal triumph honorably achieved shall be crowned by such an example of moderation, restraint, and reason in victory as best comports with the traditions and character of our enlightened Republic.

Even as the president preached magnanimously, he inclined toward an annexationist position:

> . . . without any original thought of complete or even partial acquisition, the presence and success of our arms at Manila imposes [*sic*] upon us obligations which we cannot disregard. The march of events rules and overrules human action. Avowing unreservedly the purpose which has animated all our effort, and still solicitous to adhere to it, we cannot be unmindful that, without any desire or design on our part, the war has brought us new duties and responsibilities which we must meet and discharge as becomes a great nation on whose growth and career from the beginning the ruler of nations has plainly written the high command and pledge of civilization.

"Moderation, restraint, and reason"? Or "obligations which we cannot disregard"? Within five weeks the answer came. On October 26 McKinley's rudderless ruminations were succeeded by a crisp cable to Paris from Hay instructing the commissioners to insist on the entire Philippine archipelago. When this demand was presented to the Spanish negotiators, they were thunderstruck at what they understandably saw as a total absence of the moderation that they had been led to expect. What had made McKinley change his mind?

A key factor was the expert advice he sought and received. McKinley was a hands-on president, a manager who insisted on learning the details of problems. The advisers whom he considered best informed all argued that the islands could not be divided. An article by a respected Western expert on the Philippines, an Englishman named John Foreman, impressed McKinley in its argument for annexation on the grounds that an independent native government would only provoke civil war. The president also consulted a U.S. naval officer, Commander R. B. Bradford, who had decades earlier made an on-site study of opportunities for naval bases and coaling stations, the current primary U.S. interests in the islands. Bradford's conclusion was that Manila was not viable without the rest of Luzon, and Luzon was not viable without the other islands; it was all or nothing. A more recent visitor to the islands, General Francis V. Greene, who had commanded the second U.S. expeditionary force just a few months earlier, also foresaw anarchy and civil war without firm American control. Greene described Aguinaldo as a South American type of dictator and emphasized to the president the rebel leader's limited appeal in the archipelago as a whole.

The most thorough and up-to-date examination of the Philippine situation never reached McKinley's desk. It was compiled by two young naval officers whom Dewey had sent on a two-month survey of Luzon. Their conclusion was that most Filipinos opposed annexation and wanted independence under American protection. Dewey praised the report but sat on it for weeks before forwarding it to Washington, where the naval high command buried it. As far as McKinley knew, the experts agreed that no form of self-government, even under an American protectorate, was viable. Annexation was the only answer.

McKinley was also sensitive to the arguments made by most senior military officers that the Philippines would be snapped up by another power if the United States failed to annex them. The Monroe Doctrine ensured that an independent Cuba could not easily become a lodestone for rapacious great powers. But there was no Monroe Doctrine for the Pacific; an independent Philippines could be prey to the acquisitiveness of others. Indeed, Admiral von Diederichs's tussle with Dewey in Manila Bay had been followed by further German expressions of interest in the islands. Germany actually reached a secret understanding with Spain in September envisaging cession of three islands in the Caroline chain. (It was concluded in February 1899 with Germany's acquiring all of Spain's remaining Pacific colonies except Guam.) Japan was also thought to covet the Philippines. The British, looking to the security of their colony in Malaya, were urging the U.S. government to annex the Philippines as a means of denying them to Germany or Japan. As the leader of a new entrant to the great power club the president could not ignore these considerations of high strategy.

An even more important pressure pushing McKinley toward annexation was the weight of public opinion. Americans were by no means unanimous in their support of annexation; as Mr. Dooley had remarked, there was confusion on whether the Philippines were islands or canned goods. Some Protestant groups saw an opportunity for evangelizing the Filipinos, perhaps forgetting that most of them were Christians already, albeit Roman Catholics. American business interests, not including the anti-imperialists Andrew Carnegie and Mark Hanna, were animated by the idea of having the Philippines as a stepping-stone to the China trade. More convincingly to the president, polls of newspaper editorial opinion showed a growing sentiment for annexation. In an annexationist frame of mind, McKinley left the White House in mid-October for a ten-day campaign trip that allowed him to test opinion for himself.

Eighteen ninety-eight was a congressional, not a presidential, election year, but McKinley hoped to protect the Republican majorities in the House and Senate. His October 11–21 trip took him to six midwestern states with large Republican constituencies and a generally positive view of American expansion and of McKinley himself. He had won Indiana, Illinois, Iowa, and his home state of Ohio in 1896 and had lost only narrowly in Missouri and Nebraska (where he nearly beat his rival, William Jennings Bryan, in his own backyard). McKinley used his campaign speeches to test audience reaction to a forward-leaning approach to annexation. He had a stenographer measure the applause to each rhetorical thrust:

> —Tamai, Iowa: "We do not want to shirk a single responsibility that has been put upon us by the results of the war." (Strong applause)
> —Omaha, Nebraska: "Shall we deny to ourselves what the rest of the world so freely and so justly accords to us?" (Audience: "No!")
> —Charlton, Iowa: "Territory sometimes comes to us when we go to war in a holy cause, and whenever it does the banner of liberty will float over it and bring, I trust, blessings and benefits to all the people." (Great applause)
> —Springfield, Illinois: "Having gone to war for humanity's sake, we must accept no settlement that will not take into account the interests of humanity." (Prolonged applause)
> —Columbus, Ohio: "Whatever obligation shall justly come from

this strife for humanity, we must take up and perform and as free, strong, brave people, accept the trust which civilization puts upon us." (Applause and cheers)

If McKinley had uttered the same words in New England or the South, he might not have heard the same positive reactions. As it was, the views of heartland America could not have surprised him; he heard what he expected to hear. The popular validation of a course he was leaning toward anyway was nevertheless crucial to this consummately political president. McKinley had sought the support of the American people for the declaration of war against Spain; he sought it again on the momentous issue of annexing the Philippines. A year later, to a group of Methodist clergymen, he described his decision in more celestial terms:

> I walked the floor of the White House night after night until midnight; and I am not ashamed to tell you, gentlemen, that I went down on my knees and prayed Almighty God for light and guidance more than one night. And one night late it came to me this way—I don't know how it was, but it came: (1) That we could not give them back to Spain—that would be cowardly and dishonorable; (2) that we could not turn them over to France or Germany—our commercial rivals in the Orient—that would be bad business and discreditable; (3) that we could not leave them to themselves—they were unfit for self-government—and they would soon have anarchy and misrule over there worse than Spain's was; and (4) that there was nothing left for us to do but to take them all, and to educate the Filipinos, and uplift and Christianize them, and by God's grace do the very best we could by them, as our fellow-men for whom Christ also died.

There is no cause for doubting this account; McKinley was a devout and honest man. What he left out, however, was the scrupulous care with which he had researched each of the four reasons he cited to the Methodist ministers. Those reasons may have come to him as divine revelation, but he had subjected them to rational analysis beforehand. Nor did he share with his clerical audience the fifth and most important reason: The American people, like God, had told him to annex the Philippines.

The Spanish response to the new American position presented by Chairman Day in Paris on October 31 was angry and intransigent. The foreign minister told his chief negotiator: "I consider . . . that the intention of the Americans is to annex everything of value in the colonial empire of Spain with the least sacrifice possible, and we should exert ourselves to prevent this." Sticking to their claim of sovereignty over the Philippines, the Spanish hoped that the American congressional elections, a week away, might turn public feeling against McKinley. In the event the Republican majority in the House was reduced but not erased, and the Republicans won enough state legislators to ensure that the indirectly elected Senate would also remain comfortably in their hands. McKinley now felt reinforced in taking a position that even most of his commissioners thought was going too far, that annexation was justified by right of conquest.

The Spanish, negotiating in the fear both of an American military attack and of domestic unrest, began to buckle on the two most contentious issues. They came off their extravagant claim that the United States should assume the huge (four-hundred-million-dollar) Cuban debt, and they finally accepted the U.S. annexation of the entire Philippine archipelago, settling for a compensation of twenty million dollars for the loss. The Treaty of Paris, a short document of seventeen articles, was signed by the five commissioners on each side on December 10. Spain ceded the Philippines, Puerto Rico, and Guam to the United States. It relinquished "all claim of sovereignty" to Cuba, which would be "occupied" by the United States for a time not specified in the treaty. In addition to the twenty million dollars paid for the Philippines, Spanish merchant vessels were to receive equal treatment with American vessels in Philippine ports for ten years. Except for a few minor concessions, the United States extracted from Spain everything it wanted. Far from offering the magnanimous gesture for which the Spanish ambassador had pleaded, the Americans showed no mercy and sent the Spanish negotiators home humiliated.

There was little mention in the peace treaty of the people who actually inhabited the territories that were changing hands except that they would be given free exercise of religion and that their "civil rights and political status" would be determined by the U.S. Congress. No representatives of the Philippine, Cuban, or Puerto Rican people had been admitted to the negotiations. Aguinaldo's representative, after being received by McKinley at the White House, failed to get a single meeting with a commissioner in Paris and was also rebuffed by Secretary Hay on his return. McKinley was serious about the welfare of the native populations—he had privately expressed the belief in July that it would be "cowardly and dishonorable" to give them back to Spain—yet by his instructions the war fought partly in their name was brought to an official end without any effort to consult them or take their views into account.

2.

It had been less than eight months from the declaration of war to the treaty of peace, not much time to build a national debate on the momentous issue of whether, and under what conditions, the United States should hold overseas possessions. That debate began in earnest when McKinley sent the Treaty of Paris to the Senate for advice and consent to ratification. Polling of the editorial positions of newspapers throughout the country, then an accepted form of opinion sampling, revealed strong support for the treaty in all parts of the country except the solidly Democratic South. The West, itself the product of expansion, was especially enthusiastic. The administration enjoyed an additional advantage in that it expected the new Senate, to convene in March 1899, to be more expansionist than the current one. If the treaty failed among the lame ducks, it would probably have a better chance with a more Republican Senate in the spring.

The administration entered the debate confident that it could win well over the two-thirds (sixty votes of the ninety total seats) needed for ratification. Although the Republicans held only forty-six seats, a bare majority, Lodge, one of the floor managers, expected the opposition to be confined to those few senators who had opposed the war. He was wrong. Democrats, under the coercive leadership of the lameduck Arthur P. Gorman of Maryland, began to unite against ratification.

One of their approaches was constitutional. George G. Vest of Missouri argued that the Constitution provided for the acquisition of territory only for the purpose of creating states, not colonies. William E. Mason of Illinois introduced a resolution contending that the United States could not govern a foreign people without their consent. A second Democratic approach was prescriptive. Augustus O. Bacon of Georgia submitted a resolution, parallel to the Teller Amendment on Cuba, promising eventual independence for the Philippines. A third approach was blatantly racist. Senator John W. Daniel of Virginia, speaking for many of his southern colleagues, called the Filipinos "a mess of Asian pottage." In the House of Representatives John F. Fitzgerald of Massachusetts, John F. Kennedy's grandfather, inquired: "Are we to have a Mongolian state in this Union?"

The Republicans countered the Democratic arguments point by point. Orville H. Platt of Connecticut, a learned imperialist, developed a convoluted constitutional theory that later proved critical to the governing of the Philippines and Puerto Rico. In rebutting Senator Vest, Platt contended that the Constitution entitled the United States to acquire territory and to govern it, but that constitutional rights did not extend automatically to the inhabitants of new territories. As the Treaty of Paris made clear, Platt maintained, their civil rights and political status would be determined by Congress rather than the Constitution. Republican orators also attacked Senator Mason's appeal to self-determination, arguing without shame that self-government had not been offered to Alaskan Eskimos, Indians, or Negroes. Republicans also invoked the foreign threat as a reason for annexation.

The fight for votes was marked by cloakroom intrigues and considerable arm-twisting. Gorman on the Democratic side played dirty, and the Republicans, with more patronage to dispense, matched him with threats and inducements. Lodge's Republican colleague, the senior senator from Massachusetts, George F. Hoar, defected from the party's annexationist line. Mark Hanna blew up at Hoar's refusal to take the German threat seriously, complaining that Hoar was "crazy": "[He] thinks Germany is just fooling."

McKinley's wisdom in appointing a Democratic anti-imperialist senator to the negotiating team paid off when Gray switched to support the treaty. He received a judgeship for his good sense. Lodge wrote to Roosevelt: "We were down in the engine room and do not get flowers, but we did make the ship move." In the end the Republicans, suffering the defection only of Hoar and of one other senator, enticed a few Democratic votes. The final tally was 61–29, a slim margin of two votes. Seven no votes were cast by lame ducks, indicating that the treaty might have had an easier time if held over to the new Congress. Lodge told Roosevelt: "It was the closest, hardest fight I have ever known, and probably we shall not see another in our time when there was so much at stake." Lodge's sincerity was manifest, though his prediction was wrong. In two decades he was to be embroiled in an even tougher fight, his battle with Woodrow Wilson over the Treaty of Versailles.

The Republican victory was assisted, perhaps even produced, by two factors far from the halls of Congress. The first was the bizarre set of positions taken by the leader of the Democratic party, William Jennings Bryan, who had lost the presidency to McKinley in 1896 and was to lose to him again in 1900. Bryan had never been keen on the war with Spain, but when it was declared, he, like Roosevelt, won approval to raise a regiment. Either he was too late or political factors intruded. In any case, while the Rough Riders were winning glory, Bryan's Third Nebraska was mired in the dust of Florida.

Bryan carried his ambivalence into the debate on the treaty. He exhorted his supporters in the Senate to vote in favor so the Democrats could make Republican imperialism an issue in the 1900 presidential election, when they would urge Philippine independence. His expedient tactics did nothing but give his Republican opponents a victory he might have been able to prevent. Andrew Carnegie, who had been lobbying vigorously against the treaty, complained in disgust: "One word from Mr. Bryan would have saved the country from disaster."

The other factor that ensured passage of the treaty was Emilio Aguinaldo. The Filipino rebel had gone from one frustration to another. He had been blocked from the attack on Manila and cut out of the Spanish surrender. He had been barred from the peace treaty negotiations and had seen his views ignored by the negotiators. His army had received no assurances from American officers about future independence, nor had independence been promised in the Senate debate. Aguinaldo felt driven to the only option left him, a military uprising. In the fall of 1898 the rebels began to consolidate their hold on the countryside of Luzon and to challenge the debilitated Spanish power in the other islands. By mid-October Dewey believed they were in control of most of the islands and began to worry that the United States might have to fight them.

In late December McKinley implemented the annexation provisions of the Treaty of Paris with instructions to the military commander in Manila that left no further doubt about American intentions: "With the signature of the treaty of peace . . . the actual occupation and administration of the entire group of the Philippine Islands becomes immediately necessary, and the military government heretofore maintained by the United States in the city, harbor and bay of Manila is to be extended with all possible despatch to the whole of the ceded territory." Additional clauses called for winning "the confidence, respect, and affection" of the inhabitants and asserted that "we come, not as invaders or conquerors, but as friends." The Americans in the Philippines bowdlerized the tough parts of their instructions and emphasized the positive ones when they informed Aguinaldo. But he saw through the coats of sugar and, concentrating on the assertion that the U.S. Army intended to occupy all the Philippines, responded with a harsh warning: "My government is ready to open hostilities if the American troops attempt to take forcible possession of such portion of the territory as comes under its jurisdiction. I denounce these acts before the world, in order that the conscience of mankind may pronounce its infallible verdict as to who are the true oppressors of nations and the tormentors of human kind. Upon their heads be all the blood which may be shed."

On February 4, two days before the scheduled Senate vote on the Treaty of Paris, a rebel patrol exchanged fire with an American sentry in Manila. The incident quickly escalated into a rebel assault on the city. The insurgents were driven off, but they left 238 American casualties, including 44 killed. Suddenly it was full-scale war, and it was to last for more than three years. When McKinley received the news of the fighting from a newspaper dispatch, he said to his staff: "It is always the unexpected that happens, at least in my case. How foolish these people are. This means the ratification of the treaty; the people will insist on its ratification." He was right; national security emergencies usually lead to a closing of the ranks behind the president. In those last two days three senators switched their votes to yes. The McKinley administration had won an important victory. But the policy now confirmed was earning it the enmity of a majority of Filipinos and was plunging America into a long and atrocious war against a citizen army defending its homeland.

The Spanish parliament, the Cortes, had as much difficulty in registering a defeat as the American Senate had in ratifying a victory. The Treaty of Paris, which contained few face-saving provisions, was seen as a national humiliation in Spain. But the Cortes faced the same problem as the Spanish negotiators: Spain had lost a war and, if it resisted, would lose another one. It approved the treaty by two votes, not enough to satisfy constitutional requirements, and the queen regent had to use her authority to override the parliament. Thus Maria Christina, who had once tried to find a consensus for the sale of Cuba, became the agent for Spain's uncompensated loss of the island. Sagasta's Liberal government, never fully committed to the retention of Cuba, fell from office after the treaty was approved.

El Desastre did not have the effect many had predicted on the Spanish political system. Parliamentary monarchy survived for several more decades. There was no near-term military takeover or lurch to the right; Liberal governments later returned to power. There may even have been some relief that Spanish rule in Cuba, which had poisoned political debate in Madrid for three decades, was no longer an issue. The real effect of the Spanish defeat seems to have been psychological and moral. Now it was no longer possible to pretend that Spain was a power whose voice counted for much in the world or even in Europe. The forced turn inward opened the way for a Spanish cultural renaissance of writers, artists, and musicians known in Spain as the Generation of '98. Miguel de Unamuno, José Ortega y Gasset, Federico García Lorca, Pablo Picasso, Joan Miró, Salvador Dali, Manuel de Falla, Isaac Albéniz, Enrique Granados, Pablo Casals, and Andrés Segovia all developed and practiced their artistry in the baleful shadow of the Spanish military disaster.

On February 16, a week and a half after the Senate vote, McKinley spoke about the Philippines before a huge Republican audience in Boston. He stood beneath portraits of Washington, Lincoln, and himself, united by the theme, emblazoned in large letters, "Liberators." The outbreak of war twelve days earlier between occupiers and occupied could hardly have assuaged the doubts that habitually plagued McKinley about his colonial policies. But his attitude in Boston was triumphal rather than apologetic. He asserted that the United States would aid Filipinos toward self-government. Until they were ready, however, they must understand that "their welfare is our welfare, but that neither their aspirations nor ours can be realized until our authority is acknowledged and unquestioned."

The new fighting on Luzon showed that it was premature to seek the consent of the governed; it was not a good time "for the liberator to submit important questions concerning liberty and government to the liberated while they are engaged in shooting down their rescuers." The president tried to soften this pre-Orwellian paradox—liberating the Filipinos by fighting them—by escaping into a benign future: "I cannot bound my vision by the blood-stained trenches around Manila,—where every red drop, whether from the veins of an American soldier or a misguided Filipino, is anguish to my heart,—but by the broad range of future years, when . . . [Filipinos] shall for ages hence bless the American republic because it emancipated and redeemed their fatherland, and set them in the pathway of the world's best civilization."

McKinley was grappling with the core contradiction inherent in the U.S. seizure of the Philippines and Cuba: Americans may have seen themselves as liberators, but they were regarded by large elements of the local populations as oppressors. Having pushed the contradiction into the future, where he could predict it would be resolved, the president tried to argue that it did not exist in the present either: "No imperial designs lurk in the American mind. They are alien to American sentiment, thought, and purpose. Our priceless principles undergo no change under a tropical sun. They go with the flag." McKinley's sincerity gave him some credibility in disclaiming imperial intentions even as he was acting on them. But a growing body of opinion in the United States was prepared to challenge him, his party, and his military on both their actions and their aspirations. The debate thus launched was the first major discussion of colonial issues since the Mexican War and the first national examination ever of America's role in the world.

3.

The inside-out debate began among official policy makers in the executive branch and Congress, then spread to writers and other opinion makers outside the government only after many of the key imperial decisions had been taken. The names the opposing sides called each other were often pejorative. For the anti-imperialists Theodore Roosevelt was "a dangerous and ominous jingo," as Henry James called him from the safe distance of his expatriate life in London. The term "jingo" came from a London music hall ballad of 1878, when Disraeli's British government was deciding whether to defend Turkey against Russia: "We don't want to fight / But by jingo if we do, / We've got the ships, we've got the men / We've got the money too."

Roosevelt did not particularly mind being called a jingo; he sometimes used the term to describe himself. But he rejected "imperialism" as a description of his approach. He tolerated "expansion." The word he preferred was "Americanism." Opponents of empire embraced the term "anti-imperialist." Roosevelt had other names for them. The most polite was "goo-goos," his contemptuous reference to self-proclaimed advocates of "good government." Behind their backs he called them "unhung traitors."

The two administrations of Grover Cleveland (1885–89 and 1893–97) had provided a dry run for the great debates of 1898 and after between jingoes and goo-goos. Cleveland was temperamentally opposed to expansion. In his first inaugural address in 1885, he stated baldly: "I do not favor a policy of acquisition of new and distant territory or the incorporation of remote interests with our own." He reversed his predecessor Benjamin Harrison's decision to annex Hawaii by withdrawing the treaty from the Senate. When the Cuban rebellion began against Spain, he avoided a commitment to U.S. intervention. Now in retirement Cleveland railed against the "Hawaiian monstrosity," the Treaty of Paris, and the lengthy occupation of the Philippines. He argued that "the mission of our nation is to build up and make a greater country out of what we have, instead of annexing islands." He was the first great anti-imperialist of the 1890s.

During McKinley's administration the chief jingoes—Roosevelt and Lodge, with Mahan as their intellectual backup—were successful at framing the debate on their terms. Roosevelt went further than most imperialists in exalting war as an end in itself. Lodge found inspiration for imperialism in the American past, even citing the despised Jefferson as "the greatest expansionist in our history." He saw the expulsion of Spain as "merely the last and final step of the inexorable movement in which the United States has been engaged for nearly a century." Mahan filled his writing with Darwinian references to strife among nations, "the struggle of life," "the race of life," and the importance of extending "Anglo-Saxon control." He, like the other jingoes, believed fervently that American expansion would benefit the whole world: "What the nation has gained in expansion is a regenerating idea, an uplifting of the heart, a seed of future beneficent activity, a going out of self into the world to communicate the gift it has so bountifully received."

The other men around McKinley and the president himself had no strong views and no clear strategy. Hanna, McKinley's closest political ally, had shared the hesitancy of the business community about a war over Cuba, though he supported the peace treaty. Secretary of State Sherman, in his dwindling moments of lucidity, opposed the war and resigned in senile protest when it was declared. His deputy and successor, Judge Day, was not keen on territorial acquisitions; neither was Roosevelt's chief in the Navy Department, Secretary Long. Secretary of War Alger was inconsistent in his views.

Despite his reference to a "splendid little war," Hay was not a natural jingo. As late as August 22, 1898, even after his appointment as secretary of state, he congratulated Andrew Carnegie on an article in which the industrialist had called for American withdrawal from the Philippines, though Hay questioned the practicability of such action. By the time he settled into the State Department in September, he had become comfortable with the imperial course he had been selected to pilot. He showed no hesitation in instructing the American negotiators in Paris to demand the entire Philippine archipelago from Spain.

The internal debate within the McKinley administration never amounted to much since only one side was debating. Unlike Hoar in the Senate, neither the president nor his more dovish advisers even tried to marshal anti-imperial arguments. They were practical politicians, and their decisions were taken out of pragmatism rather than principle. It was not until the war was over and the island territories were acquired that the real debate began over whether the United States should be an imperial power.

The first institutional expression of opposition to the Spanish-American War and its imperial outcome came as it neared its end. A group of private citizens opposed to the war met on June 15, 1898, in

Faneuil Hall in Boston, the scene of incendiary gatherings in revolutionary times. The group met again on November 11 and constituted itself as the Anti-Imperialist League. At that time it issued an "Address to the American People" that subjected McKinley's policies to comprehensive criticism, elements of which surfaced later in the Senate debate over the Treaty of Paris.

The anti-imperialists strongly opposed the projected annexation of the Philippines, contending that the U.S. Constitution had no provisions for vassals and that good government depended on the consent of the governed. They expressed concern about the perversion of American values; in their view the war had been fought for humanity and freedom, not conquest. They contended that the law of might and the pursuit of commercial gain were destroying the principles on which America had been founded. They feared that the nation's domestic needs would be sacrificed to colonial ambitions. In short, they were convinced that republican and imperial values were incompatible.

The Anti-Imperialist League contained a few national figures, like Carnegie and Mark Twain. For the most part, however, the members were graduates of Harvard and Yale and limited to the Northeast, especially the Boston area. About half were lawyers, and many of the others university professors. Harvard supplied much of their intellectual firepower. Members included Charles W. Eliot, the president of the university; Charles Francis Adams, Jr., longtime member of the Harvard Board of Overseers; and two of its most famous professors, William James and Charles Eliot Norton. Eighty percent of the league's members could trace their American roots back five or more generations. Like their enemy and fellow Bostonian Cabot Lodge, they reflected a strong abolitionist tradition. They were elitist, seeing themselves as natural leaders, but their elitism rarely descended to the level of social issues. While not uniformly probusiness (Carnegie was the major exception), they were not typically proimmigrant or prolabor either. In foreign policy they tended to be noninterventionist, and a few (including Carnegie) leaned toward pacifism.

Most members of the Anti-Imperialist League were Republicans with a strong streak of independence; they valued principle higher than party and reform higher than politics as usual. Their politics in fact dated back to the 1884 split in the Republican party, when the Mugwump faction turned away from the Republican candidate Blaine because of his corruption, thus helping the Democrat Cleveland win. The German-American politician Schurz, the Harvard professors James and Norton, the journalist Godkin, and the two Boston businessmen Edward Atkinson and Charles Francis Adams, Jr., all had been Mugwumps in 1884.

Now, in 1898, all were anti-imperialists. Roosevelt and Lodge, who had stayed with the party in 1884 and were leading it on the imperialist path in 1898, despised them as traitors, first for selling out their party, then for betraying their country. After he won the race for governor of New York, Roosevelt vented to an English friend: "I was opposed by the professional Independents, like Carl Schurz, Godkin, . . . and the idiot variety of 'Goo-Goos,' partly because they objected to my being for the war with Spain, and partly because they feared lest somebody they did not like might vote for me."

4.

It is noteworthy that three of the leading anti-imperialists, Carnegie, Godkin, and Schurz, were immigrants who had not been born to the values they fervently espoused. Their careers had strikingly different definitions: Carnegie the opulent industrialist; Godkin the misanthropic writer; Schurz the earnest political reformer. But for all three America, with its values and institutions, had a sacred quality because they had come to it by a process of achievement rather than inheritance. The dramatic uprooting and replanting that characterize every immigration gave them a commitment to American ideals that many native-born did not feel. If the United States was in their mind and memory a grail, then it was important to preserve that grail essentially as they found it. Reform was legitimate because it could make the grail shine brighter. But imperialism, the perilous thrust beyond continental limits and the unfamiliar encounters with strange peoples, was a threat to the pristine nature of the America of their experience and their dreams. So they opposed it.

Carnegie, the exemplar of a rags-to-riches American career, was the son of a radically inclined Scottish handloom weaver who had emigrated with his family to the Pittsburgh area in 1848. At thirteen Andrew began work as a bobbin boy in a cotton factory; his skills at

bookkeeping and telegraphy soon brought him to the attention of a
Pennsylvania Railroad executive, Thomas A. Scott, who nurtured his
career from then on. While still a young man, Carnegie involved himself in many of the industries that were making the United States an
economic giant: railroading; construction of telegraph lines, sleeping
cars, locomotives, and iron bridges; and, most profitably, steel.

His business philosophy had two precepts: Reduce prices by cutting costs and "put all good eggs in one basket and then watch that
basket." He observed both principles in cornering steel by under-
selling his rivals and seizing control of every stage of the business
from iron ore through the coking process to the finished product. By
1898 this small, precise Scotsman with a genius for organization had
become one of the richest men in America.

He held pronounced political views. From his early days he had a
streak of pacifism, though he enthusiastically supported Lincoln's war
to bring the South back into the Union. He opposed the demands of
Roosevelt, Lodge, and Mahan for a strong navy but eventually succumbed to the profit motive and in 1886 won the contract for armor-
plating four new battleships, two of which, the *Oregon* and the *Iowa*,
were to destroy the Spanish flagship off Santiago Bay in 1898. He
salved his conscience for a while by refusing to make naval guns, but
this self-restriction also fell away in 1894.

Like many self-made industrialists, Carnegie was a social Darwinist and a disciple of Darwin's associate Herbert Spencer, whose
phrase "survival of the fittest" proved so useful to the pursuit of monopoly. But he rejected the more lurid extremes of Spencer's natural
selection school. He did not see life as a bloody jungle, nor, though he
believed Anglo-Saxons to be a superior race, did he seek to impose
their values on the whole world. He was not even a doctrinaire advocate of laissez-faire, the favored economic doctrine of social Darwinists; in fact he had no principled objection to government intervention
in the economy. Beginning in his early thirties, he sought through
philanthropy to reduce the inequalities of biological competition. Despite his wealth, he had a pronounced democratic and egalitarian
streak.

In foreign policy Carnegie was strongly critical of British and
French imperialism. He favored home rule for Ireland and hankered
for Canada's union with the United States. Regarding his adopted

country, he was an unabashed advocate of the Monroe Doctrine. He wrote Secretary of State Blaine in 1882: "America is going to control anything and everything on this continent. That's settled." He supported war against Spain in 1898 because he favored Cuban independence, wanted to drive Spain out of the hemisphere, and hoped the war would bring together the United States and Great Britain, whose citizenship he had not given up.

In none of these respects was Carnegie much of a thorn in McKinley's foot. He did become objectionable, however, over annexation of the Philippines. His humanitarian instincts, which had put him on the side of the revolution in Cuba and thus on that of McKinley, drove him in the opposite direction in the Pacific, where American soldiers seemed to be crushing a local population. In an article in the *North American Review* in August 1898, he established his claim to be an anti-imperialist: "Are we to exchange Triumphant Democracy for Triumphant Despotism? Is it possible that the Republic is to be placed in the position of the suppressor of the Philippine struggle for independence? Surely, that is impossible."

This was the article that John Hay admired. But the new secretary of state soon changed his mind, complaining to Whitelaw Reid, in Paris negotiating with the Spanish: "Andrew Carnegie really seems to be off his head. He writes me frantic letters signing them 'Your Bitterest Opponent.'" Toward the end of the negotiations Reid received his own diatribe from Carnegie: "It is a matter of congratulation that you seem to have about finished your work of civilizing the Fillipinos [*sic*]. It is thought that about 8000 of them have been completely civilized and sent to Heaven. I hope you like it." His bitterness over the Philippines gave him a special, if temporary, enmity for Roosevelt, whom he called "a dangerous man."

Carnegie seeded the British and American press with articles and letters condemning "race imperialism" and lobbied both McKinley and Bryan in person on behalf of American withdrawal from the Philippines. In August 1898 he proposed in the *Times* of London that the archipelago be traded to Britain in exchange for the British West Indies and Bermuda. During the negotiations with Spain he made a spectacular, and probably illegal, intrusion into the conduct of American foreign policy by offering McKinley twenty million dollars—the amount the United States was to pay Spain for the Philippines—in order to forestall annexation, make them independent, and "restore our Republic to its first principles."

His primary concern was for his adopted country, not for the Filipinos. He feared that annexation would threaten American security: "As long as we remain free from distant possessions we are impregnable against serious attack." He also worried that expansion would change the character of America itself by embracing untrustworthy aliens, "foreign races bound in time to be false to the Republic in order to be true to themselves." He foresaw a negative effect on American farmers and workers, a decline in industrial growth, and a rise in social instability at home. Perhaps most important, he feared that the glorification of violence would weaken America's moral fiber and reduce international respect for its just voice. The nation would be forsaking the democratic principles that had made it unique.

Carnegie's worries about the country that had welcomed him and allowed him to prosper was a leitmotiv in the attitudes of other anti-imperialist immigrants as well. Godkin, who had emigrated from Ireland at the age of twenty-five, quickly established a career as a journalistic curmudgeon. From the editorial desks of the influential *Nation* and *New York Evening Post*, he railed against the corruption in industrial society, the spoils system, and the growing belligerence of American foreign policy. Like Carnegie, he saw the United States as an exceptional, exemplary, and pristine country in danger of contamination by foreigners. But unlike Carnegie, he was an out-and-out racist in social Darwinist clothing, contemptuous of the poor and the foreign. He disliked immigration, proposing that all foreigners be excluded unless they could read or write English, and he favored restricting the suffrage for immigrants once they were in. He was a xenophobe who described Mexico as "a disgusting country peopled by ruffians, into which a Christian and a gentleman is a fool for venturing."

Godkin differed from Carnegie in his lack of interest in the plight of the Cuban rebels; he took the Spanish side against them and opposed the U.S. war with Spain. His arguments were constitutional and racial. He contended that there was no American system for governing dependencies and that governing people against their will was "un-American." He objected to admission of "alien, inferior, and mongrel races," believing it would deepen corruption in America's large cities. He feared that imperial expansion would create the need for swollen military and colonial bureaucracies.

With all his prejudices Godkin possessed an unshakable integrity that gave him a large audience among intellectuals. He cared deeply about domestic issues, setting them higher in priority than foreign ones and stressing that "social and political problems of the gravest order remain to be solved before we can consider ourselves fit at all for the role of armed evangelists." Roosevelt wrote Godkin off as a "malignant and dishonest liar." Though cruder than Carnegie, Godkin, like the millionaire industrialist, saw himself as a guardian of America's first principles and ideals. His pessimisim about America was rooted in a desire to preserve it as it was when he saw it for the first time from New York Harbor.

The spiritual leader of the anti-imperialists was Carl Schurz, also an immigrant who represented many of the strengths, and some of the weaknesses, of the movement he personified. A native of Prussia, he emigrated to the United States at twenty-three, having been a student radical in the European revolutionary movements of 1848. Schurz established a political base in the Midwest as the chief spokesman for the many German immigrants who had settled there. He was an early opponent of slavery, a friend of Lincoln's, a Union major general who commanded a mostly German division at Second Manassas and fought bravely at Gettysburg, a U.S. senator from Missouri, and secretary of the interior under Hayes.

A tall, imposing man with a full beard and absolute moral convictions, Schurz excelled as an orator and journalist. He ran several German-language papers, including one in St. Louis that employed a young Hungarian Jew named Joseph Pulitzer. He was a pioneer of civil service reform, coauthoring the Pendleton Act of 1883. The twenty-two-year-old Hay saw Schurz frequently in Lincoln's White House and considered him something of a role model: "Schurz is a wonderful man. An orator, a soldier, a philosopher, an exiled patriot, a skilled musician [at the piano]! He has every quality of romance and of romantic picturesqueness." The young Hay noticed something else about Schurz: "He will make a wonderful land pirate; bold, quick, brilliant, and reckless. He will be hard to control and difficult to direct." Schurz was indeed indefatigable, humorless, inflexible, importunate, and self-righteous—a scold and a gadfly. Because he could get out the German vote, no Republican president could ignore him. He gave advice, often unsolicited, to every Republican in the White House from Lincoln to Roosevelt. Yet he was always ready to abandon the party when his principles demanded.

He bolted in 1884 over Blaine's candidacy, refused to support Roosevelt's bid for mayor of New York in 1886, and, as an anti-imperialist, opposed Roosevelt again when he ran for governor in 1898. But he had supported Roosevelt for civil service commissioner and worked with him on civil service reform. Such incidental cooperation was not enough for Roosevelt, who reviled Schurz as a "prattling foreigner" and "a champion of dishonor in national relations and of dishonesty in civic matters." Schurz's revision of Stephen Decatur's epigram would have seemed unpatriotic to a flag-waver like Roosevelt, but it struck a clear note: "My country, right or wrong. If right, to be kept right; and if wrong, to be set right."

With the exception of his desire to annex Canada, Schurz was a consistent anti-imperialist. As early as 1870 he opposed President Grant's attempt to annex Santo Domingo, setting a theme that became a lifelong conviction. He argued that because the natives were unprepared for self-government, annexation would contradict the principles and traditions of the United States and threaten its constitutional and social integrity. Harrison's bid for Hawaii gave Schurz the opportunity to denounce manifest destiny, the doctrine of choice for imperialists. If the American people, he thundered, "yield to the allurements of the tropics and embark upon a career of indiscriminate aggrandizement, then Manifest Destiny points with certainty to a total abandonment of their conservative traditions of policy, to a rapid deterioration in the character of the people and their political institutions, and to a future of turbulence, demoralization, and final decay." He was not opposed to American primacy in international trade, but he found it "a barbarous notion that in order to have a profitable trade with a country we must own it."

Throughout the 1890s Schurz, from his position as chief editorial writer of *Harper's Weekly*, was a major journalistic opponent of imperialism. Moreover, as a showdown with Spain approached, he barraged McKinley with antiwar messages. Once war was declared, he could tolerate American participation only on human rights grounds:

"Our real compensation for our sacrifices and risks . . . will consist in our moral consciousness of having delivered Cuba of Spanish misrule." On May 9, 1898, he wrote the president: "If we turn this war, which was heralded to the world as a war of humanity, in any sense into a war of conquest, we shall forever forfeit the confidence of mankind." Carnegie, a fellow member of the Anti-Imperialist League, so admired Schurz's polemical journalism that he financed the reproduction and distribution of his writings.

Schurz took the position that under the Constitution, territories acquired by the United States would have to become states. Assuming that the United States would annex additional Caribbean islands and territory on both sides of an isthmian canal, he saw an inevitable disruption of the American system: "That would bring us another lot of about 13,000,000 of Spanish-Americans mixed with Indian blood, and perhaps some twenty Senators and fifty or sixty Representatives, with seventy to eighty votes in the electoral college, and with them a flood of Spanish-American politics, notoriously the most disorderly, tricky and corrupt politics on the face of the earth. What thinking American who has the future of the Republic at heart will not stand appalled at such a prospect?"

He used similar arguments about the Philippines, inhabited by "a large mass of more or less barbarous Asiatics . . . far less good-natured, tractable and orderly than the negro is." He did not consider himself racist, believing that the tropics, not race, debilitated people. "Show me," argued this northern European, "a single instance of the successful establishment and peaceable maintenance, for a respectable period, of republican institutions, based upon popular self-government, under a tropical sun." Schurz's emphasis on climate helped explain his imperialist views on Canada. It was natural to incorporate the northern and mostly Anglo-Saxon Canadians into the United States, but unnatural to bring in Filipinos or Hawaiians.

Schurz's other arguments against imperialism showed considerable sensitivity toward the native peoples in lands conquered by the United States. He was concerned that undemocratic behavior toward them would end by endangering America's democracy at home, but he was also appalled at the effect on the indigenous peoples themselves. As he wrote Charles Francis Adams, another league member, while the American war against Aguinaldo was going on, "The story of our attempted conquest of the Philippines is a story of deceit, false pretense, brutal treachery to friends, unconstitutional assumption of power, betrayal of the fundamental principles of our democracy, wanton sacrifice of our soldiers for an unjust cause, cruel slaughter of innocent people, and thus of horrible blood guiltiness without parallel in the history of republics." The rhetorical exaggeration of the last phrase underlines the degree to which Schurz believed the Filipino people had been betrayed.

As a former general, senator, and cabinet secretary Schurz had a rich governmental experience on which he did not hesitate to expatiate to the president and his senior advisers. He suggested to McKinley on September 22, 1898, that Cuba and Puerto Rico should be independent and joined with Santo Domingo and Haiti in an Antilles confederation supervised by the United States. When war broke out between Aguinaldo and the American Army in February 1899, he called for immediate Philippine independence under U.S. protection. He recommended the appointment of an American statesman to supervise the functioning of the Philippine government, support it in what it wanted, and protect it from interference by other countries. This was too much for his erstwhile admirer Hay, who became as impatient with Schurz as he had been with Carnegie. Hay described Schurz's program in three points: "1. Surrender to Aguinaldo. 2. Make the other tribes surrender to him. 3. Fight any nation he quarrels with." With all his importuning, Schurz accomplished little more than make himself an object of ridicule at the very level of government he wanted to influence.

Despite his arrogance, pomposity, and ultimate ineffectiveness, Schurz was a major figure, for he expressed better than anyone else the fundamental contradiction between maintaining democracy at home and denying it to colonial peoples. He had lived his beliefs as a freedom fighter in the German revolutions of 1848 and the American Civil War. His physical and moral force, his decades of public service, his rough honesty, and his eloquence and passion in invoking an American heritage to which he had come by choice rather than birth gave him a unique stature in the cause of anti-imperialism.

5.

The intellectual element of the debate between jingoes and goo-goos was strongly affected by the popularity in late-nineteenth-century America of social Darwinism. The doctrine's contention—that some races were better than others and that the fittest would and should survive—gave imperialists inside and outside U.S. universities a formidable debating tool. Brooks Adams, Henry's bellicose younger brother and a philosopher of imperialism, took a social Darwinist line in arguing that "since time began, no race has won for itself supremacy without paying a price in gold or blood to other races as ambitious and almost as powerful as itself." Lodge's talk of "advancement of the race," Mahan's description of "the struggle of life," and Roosevelt's references to the "great masterful races" all showed the debt that imperialism owed to the social Darwinist doctrine.

But the doctrine cut both ways. If "survival of the fittest" could be invoked to justify American expansion overseas, it could also be used in the argument that Americans ought to keep their distance from lesser races. Carnegie, Godkin, and Schurz all cited social Darwinist ideas in opposing the social Darwinist ideas arrayed against them. Schurz, a professed admirer of Herbert Spencer's, wrote: "The prospect of the consequences which follow the admission of the Spanish creoles and the negroes of the West India islands and of the Malays and Tagals of the Philippines to participate in the conduct of our government is so alarming that you instinctively pause before taking the step." David Starr Jordan, the Stanford eugenicist, based his opposition to annexing the Philippines on a horror of the tropics that he shared with Schurz. He called the torrid zone "nature's asylum for degenerates" where civilization suffocated and argued that "if we govern the Philippines, so in their degree must the Philippines govern us." Jordan also opposed war on social Darwinist grounds because it destroyed the flower of the race.

Yale economist William Graham Sumner's embrace of the laissez-faire side of social Darwinism led him to the anti-imperialist camp. He favored the international extension of American commerce but agreed with Schurz that imperial acquisitions were both unnecessary and wrong because imperialists, in the name of civilizing lower races, simply exterminated them. Sumner also abominated war and flatly disagreed with Roosevelt's emphasis on preparedness. "Readiness for war," he warned, "calls for never ending sacrifices" that would "absorb all the resources and activity of the state."

There was more than a little racism among social Darwinist opponents of imperialism, just as there was among its defenders. Most anti-imperialists believed in the superiority of the Anglo-Saxon race, and they feared that imperialism would undermine the institutions and values that were the glory of Anglo-Saxon achievement. Sumner, for example, argued that "the prospect of adding to the present Senate a number of Cuban Senators, either native or carpet-bag, is one whose terrors it is not necessary to unfold." John W. Burgess, Roosevelt's Columbia Law School professor, opposed imperialism for fear that it would bring "mongrel races" to the United States.

Not all anti-imperialist intellectuals were seduced by social Darwinism with its racial overtones. Moorfield Storey—Mugwump, Boston lawyer, political reformer, and president for fifteen years of the Anti-Imperialist League—was one of the few Americans who had praise for Aguinaldo. At home Storey fought for civil rights; he was to become the first president of the National Association for the Advancement of Colored People in 1911. On foreign issues he believed that imperial ventures would be even more dangerous if they succeeded than if they failed. He told a bemused audience at the Naval War College in 1897 that he could imagine "no greater calamity to this country than a successful war, which should lead us to enlarge our boundaries and to assume greater responsibilities." As McKinley was preparing to send his war message to the Congress, Storey described with considerable eloquence the probable consequences of victory: "We would reach out for fresh territory, and to our present difficulties would be added an agitation for the annexation of new regions which, unfit to govern themselves, would govern us. We should be fairly launched upon a policy of military aggression, of territorial expansion, of standing armies and growing navies, which is inconsistent with the continuance of our institutions. God grant that such calamities are not in store for us."

Mahan was given to celebrating Rome's military victories and analyzing the losses of its enemies. Storey also liked to cite Rome, but mainly to remind his listeners of the disaster visited on the empire as a result of its imperial rule. In his keynote speech at the Anti-

Imperialist League's first meeting on June 15, 1898, he warned: "When Rome began her career of conquest, the Roman Republic began to decay. . . . Let us once govern any considerable body of men without their consent, and it is a question of time how soon this republic shares the fate of Rome."

At Harvard, a hotbed of anti-imperial sentiment, the celebrated professor of art history Charles Eliot Norton, another founder of the Anti-Imperialist League, shared Storey's emphasis on lost ideals. The United States, he lamented, "has lost her unique position as a leader in the progress of civilization and has taken up her place simply as one of the grasping and selfish nations of the present day." Norton went so far as to urge his students not to enlist in the American armed forces. But he showed little sympathy for foreigners and favored restrictive ways to keep Irish and Jews from flooding New England.

Probably the most principled of the anti-imperialist intellectuals was Roosevelt's psychology professor at Harvard, William James, who was neither attracted by the doctrine of Anglo-Saxon superiority nor troubled by the adulterating effect of Asians or Hispanics on American traditions and institutions. Rare among jingoes and goo-goos alike, James favored immigration and saw in the discontent of the working class "a most healthy phase of evolution, a little costly, but normal, and sure to do lots of good to all hands in the end." He distrusted democracy for its tendency to breed mediocrity and stifle individual expression, but he held no brief for government by elites. Unlike his expatriate brother, Henry, he was not an Anglophile; he believed in American values and was optimistic about their future.

James's opposition to war and imperialism arose from his low view of human nature. He thought of man as essentially a belligerent savage dressed in the threadbare clothing of civilization. "Man is once for all a fighting animal; centuries of peaceful history could not breed the battle-instinct out of us." The task of civilized people was to contain their warlike drive. James saw his former pupil Roosevelt doing precisely the opposite by inciting war for its own sake: "One foe is as good as another, for aught he tells us." While Roosevelt was in his early months as governor of New York, James wrote that he "is still mentally in the *Sturm und Drang* period of early adolescence, treats human affairs, when he makes speeches about them, from the sole point of view of the organic excitement and difficulty they may bring, gushes over war as the ideal condition of human society, for the manly strenuousness which it involves, and treats peace as a condition of blubberlike and swollen ignobility, fit only for huckstering weaklings, dwelling in gray twilight and heedless of the higher life."

James passionately opposed the American annexation of the Philippines and the war it engendered: "God damn the U.S. for its vile conduct." American intervention, he wrote, would destroy "the one sacred thing in the world, the spontaneous budding of a national life [for Filipinos]. . . . We can destroy their ideals but we can't give them ours." Any thought to the contrary was "snivelling" and "loathsome." In a striking foreshadowing of the debates that later raged over Vietnam, James expressed horror at the spilling of Filipino blood in the name of abstract ideas. His sympathy for the Philippine people, unusual even for anti-imperialists, was matched by his concern for how the war was damaging American values.

6.

Below the academic level, imperialism was debated among men who worked in the world of practical affairs: businessmen, labor leaders, and politicians. Businessmen had been split before the war, but after the victories in the Philippines and Cuba they tended to accept the outcome and see what they could do to profit from it. An exception, like Carnegie, was Edward Atkinson, a Massachusetts insurance executive who had not attended Harvard or any other college and in whose office the Anti-Imperialist League was born. Unlike many league members, he went beyond rhetoric to the distribution of antiwar pamphlets to the American soldiers fighting Aguinaldo, an act that was disavowed by his anti-imperialist friends and nearly got him arrested.

Atkinson's overall approach to imperialism was too impractical to be much help to the movement he had helped start. He devised a scheme for neutralizing the Philippines by turning them into an economic protectorate of the great powers, with the United States as chief protector. This utopian concept assumed the existence of peace and amity among the United States, Germany, Japan, and Great Britain, whereas in fact all of them coveted the islands. He envisaged an informal American empire of trade rather than territory, a concept with which Carnegie, Schurz, and Sumner also flirted. This approach could hardly remain consistent with a true anti-imperialism since it reduced the problem to whether empire was defined as territorial control or economic hegemony, an issue that was to be debated again after World War II, when the United States enjoyed global economic dominance.

If the message from business was confused, the message from labor was clear. Union leaders did not want underpaid Asians or Hispanics usurping American jobs. "If the Philippines are annexed, what is to prevent the Chinese, the Negritos, and the Malays coming to our own country?" asked Samuel Gompers, president of the American Federation of Labor and a founding vice-president of the Anti-Imperialist League. Gompers, an immigrant himself, had conducted Assemblyman Roosevelt through the sweatshops of New York City and had made him a steadfast supporter of better working conditions and political rights for immigrants. But for Gompers rights stopped at the water's edge. He opposed the annexation of Hawaii as leading to the decadence of the United States and the degeneration of its people and to "an inundation of Mongolians to overwhelm the free laborers of our country." Then, as now, the American labor movement believed that its mission was not to generate more immigrants but to protect American workers against foreign competition.

The debate in the U.S. Congress was dominated by the anti-imperialists Thomas B. Reed and George Frisbie Hoar and by the imperialist Albert J. Beveridge. Reed, a Republican congressman from Maine, had won the speakership of the House in 1889 with Lodge's help against McKinley, for whom Reed developed an ill-disguised dislike. Reed was well over six feet tall and close to three hundred pounds in weight, a "gelatinous walrus of a man," according to the Kansas journalist William Allen White. His learning was as massive as his physique. He was famous less for long speeches than for epigrams. He tweaked Roosevelt's pomposity by congratulating him for his "original discovery of the ten commandments." It was Reed who characterized Lodge as "thin soil highly cultivated" and McKinley as "the Emperor of Expediency." He earned a place in the political anthologies by defining a statesman as "a successful politician who is dead."

Reed's opposition to imperialism was based on his fear of its effect at home. Before 1898 "we were at peace within our own borders and with all the world," he lamented. Like Moorfield Storey, he thought an imperial United States would go the way of Rome and other earlier empires into decay. He urged focus on domestic, rather than foreign, opportunities, emphasizing that much of the continental United States lay undeveloped: "Not every opportunity for aggrandizement should be seized. Too much food may mean indigestion." Reed was a fabled parliamentary tactician; during 1898 he had some success in blocking money for new battleships. But he did not prevail for long, and he retired from Congress in 1899.

A more formidable opponent of imperialism was the rotund Senator Hoar of Massachusetts, who boasted an even more distinguished ancestry than Lodge, his Massachusetts colleague and rival; it included a president of Harvard, a signer of the Declaration of Independence, and several fighters in the American Revolution. Hoar combined immense learning (he was president of the American Historical Association) with a vanity that was conspicuous even in the Senate. After a shaky record on imperialism—he had supported the annexation of Hawaii—he became an implacable foe during 1898 and 1899, when he came out for the independence of Cuba, Puerto Rico, and the Philippines and voted against the Treaty of Paris.

His arguments against empire were primarily constitutional. In an impassioned and sophisticated speech on January 9, 1899, opposing the annexation of the Philippines, he asked: "Have we the right, as doubtless we have the physical power, to enter upon the government of ten or twelve million subject people without constitutional restraint?" He found nothing in the Constitution to support "any fancied or real obligation to take care of distant peoples beyond our boundaries." The issue was "whether Congress may conquer and may govern, without their consent and against their will, a foreign nation, a separate, distinct, and numerous people, a territory not hereafter to be populated by Americans [or] to be formed into American states. . . ." Hoar's answer was a resounding no.

Hoar ridiculed the notion, strongly argued by Lodge, that "you cannot take down a national flag where it has once floated in time of war." Such a position would pledge every nation "to the doctrine that wherever it puts its military foot or its naval power with the flag over it, that must be a war to the death and to extermination or the honor of the state is disgraced by the flag of the nation being withdrawn." He conceded only two cases in which conquered territory could be retained: if it was to become a state or if there were clear reasons of national security. The Philippines did not fit either case. In his cause he invoked the Declaration of Independence: "Now, I claim that under the Declaration of Independence you cannot govern a foreign territory, a foreign people, another people than your own; that you cannot subjugate them and govern them against their will, because you think it is for their good, when they do not; because you think you are going to give them the blessings of liberty. You have no right at the cannon's mouth to impose on an unwilling people your Declaration of Independence and your Constitution and your notions of freedom and notions of what is good."

Unlike many anti-imperialists, Hoar kept the interests of the Filipino people in the forefront of his concerns. He dismissed the argument that Americans had governed the Indians, so why not the Filipinos? He contended that "the people of the Philippine Islands are clearly a nation—a people three and one-third times as numerous as our fathers were when they set up this nation." He noted that they had provincial governments with courts and judges. He did not defend the American treatment of the Indians but claimed that the issue was different: "a great many million square miles of forests and a few hundred or thousand men roaming over it [*sic*] without any national life, without the germ of national life, without the capacity for self-government, without self-government, without desiring self-government. . . ." On other occasions Hoar compared Aguinaldo with the Founding Fathers. When the United States went to war with the Filipino leader, Hoar used words like "brutal selfishness," "shame," "perfidy," and "torture."

The primary champion of imperialism in the Senate, the antithesis of his fellow Republican Hoar, was Beveridge of Indiana. Hoar was a Boston Brahmin educated at Harvard; Beveridge was the Hoosier son of an unsuccessful farmer. Hoar was comfortably wealthy; Beveridge exhausted his meager savings to attend De Pauw University. In 1898 Hoar was seventy-two; Beveridge as a newly elected senator was thirty-six. Finley Peter Dunne's fictional pundit, Mr. Dooley, enjoyed the disparity: "At th' age iv eight he was illicted to th' United States Sinit, rayjoocin' [reducing] th' average age iv that body to ninety-three years."

From an early age Beveridge revealed a stellar talent for oratory, a skill that had furthered the careers of such giants as Webster, Lincoln, and Bryan. He could speak for hours, word perfectly and without notes. His oratorical prizes at De Pauw brought him fame throughout Indiana and launched him on a legal career that propelled him to the Senate. He did not take his seat until well after the Treaty of Paris had won Senate approval, but even before the war began, his rhetorical prowess had established him from Chicago to Boston as a tribune of imperialism, inciting war and annexation among enthusiastic audiences.

It was almost a year from Beveridge's election by the Indiana legislature to his swearing in as a U.S. senator. He used the time in an unusual way: He visited the Philippines, China, and Japan. In the Philippines he conferred with the U.S. Army command, which was heavily engaged in the war against Aguinaldo's rebels, and made an extensive investigation of several islands. By his return in September 1899 he possessed more firsthand knowledge of the Philippines than anybody in the Senate. He was summoned to brief President McKinley and Secretary of War Root—he saw the president in three separate sessions—then went to Oyster Bay to fill in Governor Roosevelt. His trip was worthwhile; Roosevelt recommended Beveridge to Lodge, who, after complaining about Beveridge's lack of respect for the Senate's seniority system, placed the freshman on the important new Committee on the Philippines.

The bumptious rookie wasted little time in making his views known. A speech in the Senate on January 9, 1900, outlining an Asia strategy and a proposed course of action in the Philippines made him nationally famous. Newspapers trumpeted it as a classic expression of the philosophy of American imperialism. Indeed, in his characteristic dramatic style, Beveridge argued the case for imperialism even better than Roosevelt, Lodge, or Mahan.

Beveridge set the Philippines directly in his Asia strategy; they were the "base at the door of all the East" on which all lines of navigation converged. As the gateway to the "illimitable" China market they must be "ours forever." The Pacific was "our ocean"; "our natural customer" was China. "Most future wars will be conflicts for commerce. The power that rules the Pacific, therefore, is the power that rules the world. And, with the Philippines, that power is and will forever be the American Republic." Victory in the war between the United States and Aguinaldo's forces would "establish the supremacy of the American republic over the Pacific and throughout the East till the end of time."

Beveridge urged that the war be pressed to total victory. In a revealing historical aside, he contended that the Indian wars would have been shortened—and soldiers, settlers, and Indians alike benefited—"had we made continuous and decisive war." He rejected the charge that the conduct of the American Army in the Philippines was cruel. Drawing, as he constantly did, on his personal experience there, he asserted that the Filipino wounded were "as carefully, tenderly cared for as our own." But "Senators must remember that we are not dealing with Americans or Europeans. We are dealing with Orientals. . . . They mistake kindness for weakness, forbearance for fear."

Beveridge then turned on the anti-imperialists, whom he accused of prolonging the fighting by misleading Aguinaldo about America's purpose. He claimed that the American tradition of free speech was deluding the rebels into thinking that President McKinley was not supported, that they simply had to hold on until the next presidential election. The blood of American dead, he charged, "in sorrow rather than anger," was on the hands of the opponents of the war.

The young senator brushed aside the anti-imperialist argument for Filipino self-government. "They are not capable of self-government. How could they be? They are not of a self-governing race. . . . Self-government is no base and common thing to be bestowed on the mere audacious. . . . Savage blood, Oriental blood, Malay blood, Spanish example—are these the elements of self-government?" Again referring to his firsthand experience ("I have talked with hundreds of these people"), Beveridge concluded that "the great majority simply do not understand any participation in any government whatever." Deprived by race and history of any claim to self-government, the Filipinos were also, in Beveridge's eyes, "children." They needed strong parents in the form of an all-powerful American governor general and a lieutenant governor in each province. The American administrators should be "the highest examples of our civilization." If they were not, however, the alternative was not self-government but continued military rule.

Beveridge also disputed the contention of Hoar and others that the

Declaration of Independence compelled the U.S. government to rule with the consent of the governed. He pointed out that American Indians had not been offered self-government and argued that the Declaration appled only to people capable of self-government. He worried this point at considerable length in his speech because it was essential to his grand global strategy: "The Declaration of Independence does not forbid us to do our part in the regeneration of the world. If it did, the Declaration would be wrong." He also disputed Schurz's assertion that the Philippine climate debilitated the natives and would debilitate American settlers. On the contrary, he exulted, the Philippines had "the best tropical climate in the world," and Americans could certainly live there.

As he drove to his conclusion, Beveridge made a frankly racial appeal: "God has not been preparing the English-speaking and Teutonic peoples for a thousand years for nothing but vain and idle self-contemplation and self-admiration. No! He has made us the master organizers of the world to establish system where chaos reigns." The primary mission was awarded to the United States: "And of all our race He has marked the American people as His chosen nation to finally lead in the regeneration of the world. This is the divine mission of America. . . . We are trustees of the world's progress, guardians of its righteous peace."

Beveridge, who had chosen not to fight in the Spanish-American War, argued that not even the need to sacrifice lives should divert the United States from this divine mission. "As a nation, every historic duty we have done, every achievement we have accomplished has been by the sacrifice of our noblest sons." Using his favorite prop, the American flag, he concluded: "Every holy memory that glorifies the flag is of those heroes who have died that its onward march might not be stayed. It is the nation's dearest lives yielded for the flag that makes it dear to us; it is the nation's most precious blood poured out for it that makes it precious for us."

Here were nearly all the themes of American imperialism at the century's turn in one speech: the assertion that war was inevitable and glorious, the prediction of endless commercial competition, the geopolitical view that the Pacific was the key to ruling the world, the strident militarism, the conviction that Americans were the chosen people for a divine mission, the confidence in American racial superiority, the contention that the United States should rule its colonies forever, the patronizing approach to lesser breeds, the easy rejection of the consent of the governed, the belief in relentless war against native rebellion, the contempt for Americans who disagreed with him, the hyperbolic style pitched to emotions, yet the cool analysis rooted in sophisticated legal theory.

No wonder Roosevelt considered Beveridge a potent weapon in the imperialist battle; he cabled congratulations to him for his January 9 speech from the statehouse in Albany. No wonder too that Senator Hoar recognized a dangerous adversary. Following Beveridge's speech, he rose in the Senate to say: "I heard much calculated to excite the imagination of youth seeking wealth, or the youth charmed by the dream of empire. But the words Right, Duty, Freedom, were absent, my friend must permit me to say, from that eloquent speech."

7.

Contentious debates over imperialism raged on an even broader field of battle, publications directed at large segments of the American people. During the 1880s the evangelical minister Josiah Strong had conditioned a huge Protestant readership to a crude form of social Darwinism and imperialism. Other writers with a mass audience, like Twain and Dunne, set the anti-imperialist case before a different group of readers. In most, but not all, cases, the large-circulation newspapers tended to favor red-blooded solutions to the country's foreign policy challenges. Potentially, all these appeals might have helped determine the country's attitude toward overseas possessions. Actually, however, advocates and opponents of imperialism tended to cancel each other out, and the rantings of the jingo press were in any case directed mainly at readers with little power to affect events.

Mark Twain was arguably the most famous man in the United States around the turn of the nineteenth century. He was certainly its best-known writer. After supporting the American victories of 1898, he turned sharply against imperialism, particularly the annexation of the Philippines and the war against Aguinaldo. When that war had been under way for nearly a year, he gave vent to his democratic and anticlerical convictions, complaining to a friend: "Apparently we are not proposing to set the Filipinos free and give their islands to them;

and apparently we are not proposing to hang the priests and confiscate their property. If these things are so, the war out there has no interest for me."

Later that year he told reporters that the war was "a mess, a quagmire from which each fresh step renders the difficulty of extrication immensely greater." He had once favored putting "a miniature of the American constitution afloat in the Pacific," but now it was clear that "we have gone there to conquer, not to redeem." Acting on his convictions, Twain joined the Anti-Imperialist League and served as a vicepresident from 1901 until his death in 1910. When the league split over Philippine policy, Twain and Schurz stuck with the faction advocating immediate independence.

Twain's hostility to American policy in the war against the Philippine rebels was so great that he abandoned his habitual form of humorous satire and simply lashed out. Believing that Filipinos were capable of self-government, he rejected the view that American democracy should apply only to the continental United States. But he worried about the growth of an American military state and its potential turn toward domestic oppression. Like Hoar, he idealized Aguinaldo, comparing him somewhat incongruously with Joan of Arc, about whom he had recently written a book. Unlike other antiimperialists, he blamed America's errors on the malign influence of Europe, picturing the U.S. Army's iniquities in the Philippines as a replay of British atrocities in the Boer War. For a man of such a subtle mind, Twain's views were Manichaean and simplistic, and that was perhaps why he was unable to express them in his customary satirical style.

His most powerful and influential published article on the Philippines appeared in the *North American Review* in February 1901. "To the Person Sitting in Darkness" was a stinging attack on the war against the Philippine rebels. Twain accused the United States of stringing the Filipinos along until "Manila was ours and we could get along without them. . . . What we wanted, in the interest of Progress and Civilization, was the Archipelago unencumbered by patriots struggling for independence; and War was what we needed. . . . We forced a war, and we have been hunting America's guest and ally through the woods and swamps ever since." At the peak of his passion, he wrote:

. . . we have crushed a deceived and confiding people; we have turned against the weak and the friendless who trusted us; we have stamped out a just and intelligent and well-ordered republic; we have stabbed an ally in the back and slapped the face of a guest; . . . we have robbed a trusting friend of his land and liberty; . . . we have debauched America's honor and blackened her face before the world.

Twain longed to see the United States return to its state of innocence (in his imagination) under George Washington: "We shall let go our obsequious hold on the rear-skirts of the sceptered land-thieves of Europe, and be what we were before, a *real* World Power, and the chiefest of them all, by right of the only clean hands in Christendom, the only hands guiltless of the sordid plunder of any helpless people's stolen liberties, hands recleansed in the patriotism of Washington, and once more fit to touch the hem of the revered Shade's garment and stand in its presence unashamed."

For all his historical romanticism, Twain focused unerringly on the worst feature of American imperialism, the conduct of the war against Philippine citizens. Strangely, much of his writing on this subject was never published, either because he never submitted it or because it was turned down. He suppressed a brilliant satire on "The Battle Hymn of the Republic" that began: "Mine eyes have seen the orgy of the launching of the Sword." He wrote a sardonic "War Prayer" asking for God's help in tearing the Filipino soldiers "to bloody shreds with our shells" and drowning "the thunder of the guns with the shrieks of the wounded." This language may have been too raw to publish anywhere, but Twain's choice of *Harper's Bazaar* was odd; not surprisingly, the piece was rejected as being unsuitable for a women's magazine. It was as if Twain cared so deeply about the Philippines that he turned his pen from a rapier to a hammer but feared to indulge his passions by writing for the public. He thus lost his chance to be the American Zola.

Unlike Twain, Dunne, the creator of the Irish-American pundit Martin Dooley, maintained a consistent and brilliant level of satire in his anti-imperialist writings. Dunne's ridicule of the patriotic jingoism of the Spanish-American War, his exposure of the moral dilemmas inherent in the conquest of the Philippines, and his lampoons of the pretensions of Roosevelt, Beveridge, and others were insufficiently judgmental and too funny to create a coherent opposition to the war. Yet he undercut the jingo philosophy more skillfully than any other American with access to a mass audience. The extended conversations between Mr. Dooley, the wise and witty barkeeper of 9009 Archey Road, Chicago, and Mr. Hennessy, his friend and straight man, left the pretensions of the imperialists in a condition somewhat similar to that of the battleship *Maine*.

Before 1898 Mr. Dooley was familiar only to readers of the Chicago newspaper for which Dunne wrote, but the war against Spain gave the sagacious bartender a nationwide following. Dunne's subtly hilarious account of the Battle of Manila Bay brought him, at the age of thirty-one, national syndication and opened the way to a steady stream of books recapitulating the columns. The first, published in 1899 and containing the Manila Bay essay, was a best-seller for a whole year. In Mr. Dooley's retelling, Manila Bay became a quilting party against an underarmed enemy. Playing on the closeness of the names Dooley and Dewey, he claimed the American commodore as a cousin ("we're th' same breed iv fightin' men") as he chronicled the ease of his victory in Irish dialect:*

> "Cousin George . . . prances up to th' Spanish forts, an' hands thim a few oranges. Tosses thim out like a man throwin' handbills f'r a circus. 'Take that,' he says, 'an' raymimber th' Maine,' he says. An' he goes into th' harbor, where Admiral What-th'-'ell is, an', says he, 'Surrinder,' he says. 'Niver,' says th' Dago. 'Well,' says Cousin George, 'I'll just have to push ye ar-round,' he says. An' he tosses a few slugs at th' Spanyards. Th' Spanish admiral shoots at him with a bow an' arrow, an' goes over and writes a cable. 'This mornin' we was attackted,' he says. 'An,' he says, 'we fought the inimy with great courage,' he says. 'Our vichtry is com-plete,' he says. 'We have lost ivrything we had,' he says. 'Th' treachrous foe,' he says, 'afther destroyin' us, sought refuge behind a mud-scow,' he says; 'but nawthin' daunted us. What boats we cudden't r-run ashore we surrindered,'

---

*The reader is urged not to be intimidated by Dunne's use of the dialect form, which is now discarded. If the words are sounded out phonetically, their meaning will readily become clear. It would be a pity to miss the satire of one of America's greatest comic writers.

he says. 'I cannot write no more,' he says, 'as me coat-tails are afire,' he says; 'an' I am bravely but rapidly leapin' fr'm wan vessel to another, followed be me valiant crew with a fire-engine,' he says. . . . 'Long live Spain, long live mesilf.' "

Not the least delight of that passage was the Spanish admiral Montojo's dispatch claiming victory while describing defeat. Mr. Dooley knew that Montojo was trying to save his skin from a court-martial; in real life, Dewey's intervention helped avert Montojo's judicial punishment before a Spanish military court.

Mr. Dooley had little regard for policy makers. He pictured the members of Mahan's Naval War Board sitting "in a room with a checker-board on th' end iv a flour bar'l," clueless as to the location of the Spanish fleet or, for that matter, their own. Their orders were frenzied, contradictory, and incomprehensible: "R'rush eighty-three millyon throops an' four mules to Tampa, to Mobile, to Chickenmaha [Chickamauga Park, one of the U.S. Army's staging areas in Florida], to Coney Island, to Ireland, to th' divvle, an' r-rush thim back again. Don't r-rush thim."

He enjoyed the foppishness of Roosevelt, whose name he Semiticized: "Teddy Rosenfelt's r-rough r-riders ar-re downstairs, havin' their uniforms pressed. Ordher thim to the goluf links at wanst." Pretentious generals were an easy mark: "Seize Gin'ral Miles' uniform. We must strengthen th' gold resarve." Mr. Dooley's mock tribute to the strategists was eloquent: "Day by day we r-read th' tur-rble story iv our brave sthrateejans sacrificin' their time on th' altar iv their counthry. . . . Little we thought iv th' mothers at home weepin' f'r their brave boys down at Washin'ton hurtin their poor eyes over a checkerboard." The result of all this hard work? "Th' ordhers fr'm Washin'ton," observed Mr. Dooley about the Cuban campaign, "is perfectly comprehinsible to a jackass, but they don't mane annything to a poor, foolish man."

Dunne had a fine time with the self-serving aspects of Roosevelt's account of the Cuban campaign in his 1899 memoir *The Rough Riders*, which Mr. Dooley "reviewed." The sage of Archey Road played with several alternative subtitles for the book—e.g., *Th' Biography iv a Hero be Wan Who Knows* and *The Darin' Exploits iv a Brave Man be an Actual Eye Witness.* The passage "quoting" Roosevelt's account of San Juan Hill made his claims of heroism seem absurd:

> ". . . I sint the ar-rmy home an' attackted San Joon Hill. . . . I climbed that precipitous ascent in th' face iv th' most gallin' fire I iver knew or heerd iv. . . . I dashed madly on cheerin' as I wint. Th' Spanish throops was drawn up in a long line in the formation known among military men as a long line. I fired at th' man nearest to me an' I knew be the expression iv his face that th' trusty bullet wint home. It passed through his frame, he fell, an' wan little home in far-off Catalonia was made happy be th' thought that their riprisintative had been kilt be th' future governor iv New York. The bullet sped on its mad flight an' passed through th' intire line fin'lly imbeddin' itself in th' abdomen iv th' Ar-rch-bishop of Santago eight miles away. This ended th' war."

Roosevelt, not a man to sneer at publicity from any quarter, took the ribbing in good spirit; in fact he invited Dunne repeatedly to stay with him in Oyster Bay and later the White House.

Dunne was as perceptive about policy issues as he was about the military aspects of the Spanish-American War. Mr. Dooley's friend Hennessy, a jingo, said he would "take the whole lot" of the Philippines, even though he admitted not knowing where they were. Mr. Dooley took a more reflective view:

> "Th' war is still goin' on; an' ivry night, whin I'm countin' up the cash, I'm askin' mesilf will I annex Cubia or lave it to the Cubians? Will I take Porther Ricky [Puerto Rico] or put it by? An' what shud I do with the Ph'lippeens? Oh, what shud I do with him? I can't annex thim because I don't know where they ar-re. I can't let go iv them because some wan else'll take thim if I do. They are eight thousan' iv thim islands, with a popylation iv wan hundherd millyon naked savages; an' me bedroom's crowded now with me an' th' bed. How can I take thim in, an' how on earth am I goin' to cover th' nakedness iv thim savages with me wan shoot iv clothes? An' yet 'twud break me heart to think iv givin' people I niver see or heerd tell iv back to other people I don't know. An', if I don't take thim, Schwartzmeister down th' sthreet [a rival publican and symbol of Germany], that has half me thrade already, will grab thim sure."

These verbal meanderings illuminated two of the main postwar issues: the jingo concern that if not annexed, the Philippines would be taken by another power and the goo-goo fear that the United States would be overrun by barbarians.

Mr. Dooley's tongue sharpened when he addressed the Filipinos under American occupation:

> "In ivry city in this unfair land we will erect school-houses an' packin' houses an' houses iv correction; an' we'll larn ye our language, because 'tis aisier to larn ye ours than to larn oursilves yours. An' we'll give ye clothes, if ye pay f'r thim; an', if ye don't, ye can go without. An', whin ye're hungry, ye can go to th' morgue—we mane th' resth'rant—an' ate a good square meal iv ar-rmy beef. . . . We can't give you anny votes, because we haven't more thin enough to go round now; but we'll threat ye th' way a father shud threat his childher if we have to break ivry bone in ye'er bodies. So come to our ar-rms, says we."

Mr. Dooley admitted to not being much of an expansionist. He described America as an "indulgent parent kneelin' on th' stomach iv his adopted child, while a dillygation fr'm Boston bastes him with an umbrella. . . . [T]wud be a disgrace f'r to lave befure we've pounded these frindless an' ongrateful people into insinsibility."

Unlike Twain, Dunne was not a great admirer of the revolutionaries in Cuba or the Philippines, though he clearly believed that the American occupiers were treating them badly. He agreed with Roosevelt's view of the Cuban rebels as lazy and cowardly—an amusing passage described General García's fast-deserting army—but he respected their dignity, as Roosevelt did not. Mr. Dooley depicted García as refusing to carry General Shafter's trunk: "I'm a sojer, . . . not a baggage car." Dunne did not share Twain's veneration for Aguinaldo, but he considered the Filipino leader "a good noisy man" with "a very superyor brand iv home-made liberty," a patriot who had helped the Americans take Manila. Mr. Dooley sympathized with Aguinaldo's refusal to surrender to the U.S. Army: " 'Aggynaldo didn't hear th' whistle blow. He thought th' boom was still on in th' hero business.' "

Dunne's satires on American imperialism must have caused discomfort, but they did not inflame. Assessing his own work more than three decades after the events, Dunne claimed to have been following, rather than shaping, public opinion. "I have always attributed [my popularity] to the possibility that the articles reflected the feeling of the public about this queer war. It was a feeling made up of contempt for the foe with quite a distinct apprehension that perhaps our fighting establishment was as stupid as our politicians and as unprepared for war. It was. But fortunately for us the Spaniards were far stupider and were unprepared too."

He may have been overly modest about his influence, which in fact extended to the White House. From time to time, at the close of President McKinley's cabinet meetings, Lyman J. Gage, the secretary of the treasury and a Chicagoan, read Mr. Dooley's observations aloud for the amusement of the men charged with U.S. strategy on war and annexation. It may not be too much to speculate that these genial satires on militarism, patriotism, and imperialism helped temper the extremes of America's expansionist policies.

Even more broadly, the major influencers of mass opinion were the daily papers, which enjoyed a near monopoly in the pre–radio and television era on how the news was presented and interpreted. The *New York Herald*, which opposed the war, polled 498 newspapers nationwide during the Senate debate on the Treaty of Paris. The percentage of papers favoring the treaty (sixty-one) approximated the two-thirds vote needed and achieved in the Senate. It is not clear whether the editorials were reflecting public opinion or guiding it. Given their information monopoly, they must have had considerable effect.

The newspaper that probably did the most to shape opinion on Cuban issues and the war itself was the *New York Journal*, which Hearst bought in 1895 in a moribund state and turned almost overnight into a high-circulation paper. Hearst decided at the very outset that Spain's mistreatment of Cubans had all the ingredients needed to swell his readership, but as a populist and natural friend of the underdog he also felt genuine sympathy for the Cuban rebels. The *Journal* lobbied vigorously for the United States to go to war with Spain. When it did, Hearst took the credit. HOW DO YOU LIKE THE JOURNAL'S WAR? one of its headlines proclaimed. For Hearst this was not just hype; as he wrote his mother, "I really believe I brought on the war." The boast was only partly true.

The pioneer of mass journalism was not Hearst, but Joseph Pulitzer, an immigrant from Hungary who bought the *New York World* in 1883. Within a year he had tripled the circulation and, by the time Hearst blew in from San Francisco, had the largest readership in the United States. Pulitzer's secret was to pitch his appeal to the burgeoning immigrant populations. He gave them smaller pages (for ease of reading in horsecars and elevated railroad trains), multicolumn headlines, pictures, cartoons, women's features, and a heavy dose of implicit sex and explicit violence. The *World's* politics were Democratic and populist. Cuba made good copy, and the paper sent a correspondent there. But it was not until Hearst arrived that Pulitzer, out of competitive spirit, moved to a strongly jingoist position.

Hearst's *Journal* took its inspiration from Pulitzer's *World*, but it went much farther. When Pulitzer failed to support Bryan in 1896, Hearst displayed his Democratic credentials by backing Bryan and ridiculing McKinley and Hanna in stories and cartoons. The day after the election Hearst got his reward with a record-breaking sale of newspapers. On Cuba, the top foreign story, the *Journal's* reporting was not only imaginative but often imaginary. It published Remington's prurient, but faked, drawing of three young Cuban women being strip-searched by lascivious Spanish policemen.

Hearst's vendetta against Spanish rule made for good copy, but except in one case, there is little evidence that its influence transcended the circulation area of metropolitan New York or San Francisco, the only other city where he was publishing a newspaper. The exception concerned the case of the imprisoned revolutionary beauty Evangelina Cisneros, on whose behalf the *Journal* sent to the queen regent Maria Christina tens of thousands of petitions signed by Americans whom the paper had encouraged to seek Evangelina's release; one of the petitioners was President McKinley's mother. After the queen regent made an unsuccessful appeal to General Weyler, Hearst engineered a jail break through bribery and had the comely Cuban brought to the United States, where he used her to harvest another crop of publicity.

With the *Journal*, the *World*, and several smaller papers urging war with Cuba, nearly 90 percent of New York's newspaper readers were exposed to shrill prowar propaganda. The Republican press, with its much smaller but more elite readership, was more balanced; only the *Times*, one of three papers that McKinley read, strongly favored war. The New York business community reflected this ambivalence. Wall

Street was concerned that war would interrupt recovery from the 1893 panic. While the working-class readers of the *Journal* and the *World* favored a war, the economic interests that wielded real power tended to be undecided or opposed.

The sinking of the *Maine*, followed by Senator Proctor's speech describing Spanish atrocities, brought business leaders around. It was only then that J. P. Morgan, John Jacob Astor, and other New York leaders of corporate America decided that war was inevitable. The loss of 268 American lives in Havana Bay also had a galvanizing effect on the country at large and on local newspapers, which began clamoring for war. Hearst and Pulitzer may have conditioned the American power structure for a turn to war, and they certainly contributed to the enthusiasm with which Americans answered McKinley's call for enlistments. But it took a national disaster that reached every American home, and was easy for Roosevelt and the other war hawks to exploit, to bring the nation and Congress to a pitch of belligerence high enough to erase McKinley's final doubts.

Hearst's huge ego probably did convince him that he had started the war. He was alleged (perhaps apocryphally) to have cabled Havana to his ace artist Remington, who was convinced there would be no war and anxious to return home: "Please remain. You furnish the pictures and I'll furnish the war." But he exaggerated. There had been strong but fruitless pressure in the U.S. press for American war against Spain during the 1868–78 war in Cuba. The difference now was not Hearst but the dramatic loss of American lives in circumstances implying the guilt of the Spanish, who were already diabolized in the press and even in schoolbooks. The "Hearst effect" in 1898 was much like the "CNN effect" during the Bosnian War in 1992–95. In both cases media images raised public awareness of major human rights violations but were insufficient in themselves to provoke intervention.

If Hearst did not start the war, he conducted it in a manner that was unique for any newspaper publisher before or since: He acted like a chief of state. He sent correspondents on clandestine missions—e.g., to free Evangelina Cisneros. He petitioned the Spanish chief of state—and got a response. He offered a reward for information proving how the *Maine* had been sunk. He recruited athletes (including the heavyweight champion James J. Corbett) to fight in Cuba.

He offered McKinley a fully equipped cavalry regiment and gave the U.S. Navy his steam yacht. He tried to blockade the Suez Canal to prevent the passage of Spanish ships. Beating the invasion force to Cuba, he arrived as a war correspondent on a steamer carrying several *Journal* correspondents and two chorus girls. After interviewing American and Cuban generals and covering the Battle of El Caney, he followed up the naval victory at Santiago Bay by personally taking the surrender of twenty-nine Spanish sailors.

In his belligerence and flamboyance, Hearst would have seemed a natural ally for Theodore Roosevelt. In fact the two hated each other. Hearst, four and a half years younger, had followed Roosevelt at Harvard. Like Roosevelt, he made Porcellian but was otherwise known for behavior that would have rankled Roosevelt's prudish sensibilities. He flaunted a mistress, played bizarre practical jokes (like painting his teachers' faces on the business side of chamber pots), and neglected his studies. After giving him several chances, Harvard expelled him for poor grades. Roosevelt's success seemed to arouse his jealousy; he wrote his mother after the war: "I made the mistake of my life in not raising the cowboy regiment I had in mind before Roosevelt raised his."

Unlike Roosevelt, Hearst was a Democrat and a populist, but their political differences do not account for the savagery with which the *Journal* assailed Roosevelt in his campaign for governor in 1898 and again in his vice presidential bid in 1900. Roosevelt replied in kind: As president he dispatched Root to New York in 1904 to blacken Hearst in his run for governor. Root, an inexperienced but effective hatchet man, accused Hearst of corruption, tax evasion, and even the murder of McKinley; the attacks helped ensure Hearst's loss.

The American press was not as rabid about annexing the Philippines as it was about going to war with Cuba, but most newspapers did favor annexation. A July 1898 *Literary Digest* count of editorials in leading Republican dailies showed support for annexation in New York, Philadelphia, Baltimore, Chicago, Milwaukee, Minneapolis, Topeka, St. Louis, Louisville, and San Francisco. By September the *Literary Digest* reported eighty-four papers favoring the annexation of the whole of the Philippines. President McKinley, that voracious consumer of public opinion, cannot have ignored these indicators of national sentiment as he sought divine guidance on what to do with the islands.

8.

The jingoes could count on powerful factors supporting expansion: a growing sense in the country that the United States had earned the right to be a great power; a military strategy, devised primarily by Mahan, that required a large navy and overseas bases; a press that was usually sympathetic to and often fervent about imperialism; a president who was hesitant but malleable; a small group of insiders, led by Roosevelt and Lodge, who were determined on war and annexation; and a Senate that could produce, if only barely, the two-thirds needed for expansionist legislation. But the goo-goos commanded a formidable arsenal as well. It included some of the most respected intellectuals in the United States, a trade union movement spearheaded by Gompers that could weaken the appeals of Hearst and Pulitzer to the working classes, a significant segment of the business community behind Carnegie, the prestige of the popular former president Cleveland, the celebrity pen of Twain and the satire of Dunne, and an eloquent appeal to traditional constitutional values.

The force of anti-imperialism, and its variety, showed that the imperial style was not unanimously acceptable to the American people. The Senate came close to rejecting the Treaty of Paris and, in a vote taken shortly after, failed by only one vote to pass a resolution guaranteeing eventual independence to the Philippines. Some of the dissenters' arguments, especially those contrasting imperial activity with America's core values, were revived during the Vietnam War and are still relevant today. Yet the anti-imperialists failed utterly in all their major objectives. McKinley's reelection in 1900 weakened them mortally, and Roosevelt's election in 1904 destroyed them as a political force.

Why did they fail? In the first place, their base was too narrow. While Schurz, Twain, Carnegie, Dunne, and Gompers exemplified the diversity of the movement, most anti-imperialists were rooted in the northeastern United States, not far from Harvard Yard, and drew their inspiration from the Puritan, abolitionist, and Mugwump traditions of liberal Republicanism. One measure of the weakness of Harvard's influence was the fact that William James taught Roosevelt and Charles Norton taught Hearst, yet neither goo-goo professor had any effect on the jingoism of his former student. Given these limiting factors, the anti-imperialists could hardly afford the internal bickering and lack of clarity that plagued their brief existence as a policy lobby.

In the second place, the anti-imperialists' own values were sometimes inconsistent with the movement's high-minded ideals. Though all of them protested the annexation of the Philippines, many had earlier supported the incorporation of Hawaii and the war against Cuba. Moreover, some goo-goos came to anti-imperialism because of their feeling of superiority to Asians and Hispanics, who, they believed, threatened to disturb the traditional racial structure of the United States, a point of view that matched poorly with their often eloquent defense of the rights of American blacks. The anti-imperialists' fear of foreign contamination, from which only William James seems to have been totally immune, dislodged them from the moral high ground that was so important to their appeal.

Finally, and most important, the anti-imperialists looked and acted out of touch. There were significant age differences between jingoes and goo-goos. In 1898 Schurz was sixty-nine, Hoar was seventy-two, Norton and Atkinson were seventy-one, and Carnegie and Twain were sixty-three. Dunne, at thirty-one, was the only young man in the group. By contrast Mahan was fifty-eight, Lodge forty-eight, Roosevelt forty, and Beveridge thirty-six. Anti-imperialist philosophy was backward-looking: to the ideal America of the Declaration of Independence and the Constitution, to the speeches of Washington and Jefferson, to a country framed by its territorial boundaries, and to the kind of stability that comes from tradition, good breeding, and the primacy of principle over power.

This conservatism made their response to the cataclysmic events of 1898 reactive rather than creative. They saw the dangers, and missed the opportunities, of the new American world. They were on the losing end of historical change. Their links were with a mythic American past. The American people were not too sure they wanted an imperial future, but they did want to go forward, not back. It was Roosevelt and his friends who defined the future with the most clarity and exuberance, who laid claim to its riches, and who set America squarely in the center of it.

10. The White Man's Burdens

1.

Rudyard Kipling knew the United States well. He married an American, Caroline Balestier, a month after the death of her brother Wolcott, a close friend of Kipling's. In 1892 the young couple—Kipling was only twenty-six, but already famous—settled in Brattleboro, Vermont, where off and on they lived for four years. He was not an admirer of the country of his chosen residence. In an earlier visit in 1889 he had disparaged America's aggressive capitalism. Now he found Americans lawless and greedy, eaten by "moral dry rot" and polluted by "barbarism" amid the material wealth of telephones, electric lights, railroads, and "suffrage."

Kipling made his first trip to Washington in 1895. True to form, he lambasted the Cleveland administration as "a colossal agglomeration of reeking bounders." Despite his undisguised hostility, the celebrated author of *Plain Tales from the Hills*, *Barrack-Room Ballads*, and *The Jungle Book* did not escape the admiring attention of the small segment of Washington society that took books seriously. Henry Adams swept him into his salon, where he met Hay and Roosevelt. Perhaps to counter Kipling's pugnacious anti-Americanism, Hay treated him to the standard American opinion of an Englishman: "When a man comes up out of the sea, we say to him: 'See that big bully over there in the East? He's English! Hate him, and you're a good American.'" Roosevelt found Kipling, who was even more precocious than he was, "nervous, voluble, rather underbred" but admitted to his sister Bamie that he was a genius. The night of their first meeting Kipling and Roosevelt had what the latter described as a "rough-and-tumble," with each defending his respective nationalism. Kipling was on his best behavior thereafter, and the two developed considerable respect for each other.

Roosevelt worked to persuade the British writer of the virtues of American expansion. He took Kipling to the Smithsonian to see Indian artifacts and to the National Zoo to watch grizzly bears. The tutorial did not work. As Kipling wrote in his autobiography, "I never got over the wonder of a people who, having extirpated the aboriginals of their continent more completely than any modern race had ever done, honestly believed that they were a godly little New England community, setting examples to brutal mankind. This wonder I used to explain to Theodore Roosevelt, who made the glass cases of Indian relics shake with his rebuttals."

Kipling's American sojourn ended badly, in an argument with his alcoholic and aggressive brother-in-law. The Englishman took the dispute to a Vermont court, where he won his case but at the cost of humiliating publicity, which drove him back to England. There in 1897 he wrote a stanza of verse about British imperialism for Queen Victoria's Diamond Jubilee; it began "Take up the white man's burden." The poetry was stirring but the theme inappropriate: Britain was hardly at the beginning of its imperial career, having taken up the burden long before. Kipling put the verses aside and wrote instead "Recessional," with its magnificent themes of pride and withdrawal:

> *Far-called, our navies melt away;*
> *On dune and headland sinks the fire:*
> *Lo, all our pomp of yesterday*
> *Is one with Nineveh and Tyre!*

After the United States defeated Spain and became embroiled in the debate over whether to annex the Philippines, Kipling was stirred to action. He decided to write for an American audience a poem that would revive the theme of his debates with Roosevelt. Summoning the experience of an old imperial power to the task of instructing a new one, the poem would proclaim the sacred duty of imperialism and alert the Americans to its difficulties, to the dangers, frustrations, ingratitude, thanklessness, and criticism. Kipling took the fragment he had begun in 1897 and expanded it. "The White Man's Burden" appeared in the American magazine *McClure's* in February 1899, just as the Congress was confirming McKinley's decision to turn the Philippines into a colony.

The White Man's Burden

Take up the White Man's burden—
 Send forth the best ye breed—
Go, bind your sons to exile
 To serve your captives' need;
To wait, in heavy harness,
 On fluttered folk and wild—
Your new-caught sullen peoples,
 Half devil and half child.

Take up the White Man's burden—
 In patience to abide,
To veil the threat of terror
 And check the show of pride;
By open speech and simple,
 An hundred times made plain,
To seek another's profit
 And work another's gain.

Take up the White Man's burden—
 The savage wars of peace—
Fill full the mouth of Famine,
 And bid the sickness cease;
And when your goal is nearest
 (The end for others sought)
Watch sloth and heathen folly
 Bring all your hope to nought.

Take up the White Man's burden—
 No iron rule of kings,
But toil of serf and sweeper—
 The tale of common things.
The ports ye shall not enter,
 The roads ye shall not tread,
Go, make them with your living
 And mark them with your dead.

Take up the White Man's burden,
   And reap his old reward—
The blame of those ye better
   The hate of those ye guard—
The cry of hosts ye humour
   (Ah, slowly!) toward the light:—
"Why brought ye us from bondage,
   Our loved Egyptian night?"

Take up the White Man's burden—
   Ye dare not stoop to less—
Nor call too loud on Freedom
   To cloak your weariness.
By all ye will or whisper,
   By all ye leave or do,
The silent sullen peoples
   Shall weigh your God and you.

Take up the White Man's burden!
   Have done with childish days—
The lightly-proffered laurel,
   The easy ungrudged praise:
Comes now, to search your manhood
   Through all the thankless years,
Cold, edged with dear-bought wisdom,
   The judgment of your peers.

Kipling's poem was an instant sensation in a United States enthused with its imperial conquests. But it angered his anti-imperialist friends in Boston, like Charles Eliot Norton, who underrated its cautionary tone. Godkin exploded in all his Irishness: "I think most of the current jingoism on both sides of the water is due to him. He is the poet of the barracks room cads." Kipling's companionable nemesis Roosevelt sent a copy to Lodge with the comment "Rather poor poetry, but good sense from the expansion standpoint." "The White Man's Burden" was much more than a defense of imperialism. It was a challenge to the Americans to treat their new colonies with the same sense of duty, responsibility, and moral high-mindedness that the British, at their best, had shown.

Kipling's own colonial experience had been in India, where he had spent his boyhood. One of the ablest British viceroys of India, Lord George Curzon, took up his position there in the same year that the United States annexed the Philippines. Curzon reflected the standard that Kipling described in the poem. As the viceroy explained to British businessmen in Bengal, "If I thought it were all for nothing, and that you and I . . . were simply writing inscriptions on the sand to be washed out by the next tide, if I felt that we were not working here for the good of India in obedience to a higher law and to a nobler aim, then I would see the link that holds England and India together severed without a sigh. But it is because I believe in the future of this country, and in the capacity of our own race to guide it to goals that it has never hitherto attained, that I keep courage and press forward."

Kipling—and British example—thus set a test for the American imperialists. Nobody surpassed American politicians in their high-flown defense of the superiority of their country's unique values and traditions. Now those values and traditions were to be put to an unprecedented examination. Would the Americans, with their spotty conduct toward the natives of their own continent, treat their new subjects with dignity and respect? Or would they be driven by power and greed and tempted into brutal behavior? Could they live with the fact that they enjoyed the full measure of liberty guaranteed by the U.S. Constitution while their colonial subjects did not? Would they act with the "fine good nature" that John Hay had called for as a sequel to the "splendid little war"? In short, just how would the United States rate as a colonial power?

2.

Nobody was more concerned about these questions than William McKinley. Not only was the president required to protect the new U.S. holdings from outside pressures and internal weaknesses, but he also had to find ways to promote the well-being of multiethnic, mostly non-English-speaking colonial populations far more impoverished than the meanest American state or territory—and, to some degree, hostile. For much of the population of Cuba, Puerto Rico, and the Philippines, one colonial dictatorship had been replaced by another. In Cuba McKinley had to square the Teller Amendment's commit-

ment to independence with the exclusively American military rule
that had been declared. In the Philippines there had been no public
American assurance of independence and therefore no inducement to
Aguinaldo's liberation army to cease its resistance.

McKinley wanted desperately to rule the Caribbean and Pacific islands in the interests of their inhabitants. But how was a benevolent
approach possible if the United States was unwilling to cede complete sovereignty to the local populations? Was empire compatible
with democracy? McKinley, though a lifelong optimist, was not sure
he knew the answers. What he did know was that U.S. colonial rule
had to be carried out, at least initially, through military occupation
and government. That mission naturally belonged in the War, rather
than the State, Department. But the bumbling secretary Alger was
clearly not the man for the job.

After the Spanish-American War the attacks on Alger actually increased. Lodge launched a scathing denunciation of the shortage of
artillery pieces and smokeless (invisible) powder. While the actual
fighting in Cuba, the Philippines, and Puerto Rico had been creditable, the logistical effort to transport the army to Cuba and back to
the mainland after the war had been a scandal. So had the poor quality of food supplied to the troops and the lack of medical resources to
deal with malaria, typhoid, and other sicknesses, which took the lives
of ten times more soldiers than did combat. What was forgotten was
that the secretary of war had succeeded in the largest overseas military transport and supply operation in American history. What was remembered were the flaws, which his pomposity and self-importance
only exaggerated. Too kind to wield a hatchet, the president did not
act on Roosevelt's recommendation for Alger's removal before the
1898 election but let him hang on until July 1899. His successor was
his opposite in every respect, a problem-solving lawyer with outstanding political skills and clean hands, Elihu Root.

Having been surprised by McKinley's insistence that he take over
the government's colonial responsibilities, Root moved reluctantly to
Washington in late July 1899. Neither he nor Clara ever managed to
feel at home there. Clara saw little of her husband, who imported his
workaholic New York ways to a still-southern city where six hours
constituted more than a good day's work. Intelligent and amusing
though they were, the Roots were practically invisible on the Wash-

ington social scene. Hay, Lodge, and Adams liked Root enormously but were rarely able to entice him to dine. Typically he lunched at his desk in his high-ceilinged office in the State, War, and Navy Building on sandwiches, olives, and a bottle of Apollinaris water sent over from the Metropolitan Club a block away. His one indulgence was cigars, which he smoked throughout the day.

Root's assignment was to establish U.S. colonial government on all the islands taken from Spain and to prepare Cuba for independence. Without significant experience in either government or foreign affairs, he took the British Empire as his model and immersed himself in British colonial history. He quickly established a close working relationship with Secretary of State Hay, who had preceded him to Washington by nearly a year and had recommended him to the president for the War Department. Hay, who had no interest in battles for bureaucratic turf, made no effort to challenge Root's sweeping responsibilities in the Caribbean and Pacific or even to dispute McKinley's selection of Root to run the State Department in the summer of 1900, when he was ill.

Root proved an extraordinarily quick study. In his first annual report to Congress at the end of 1899, when he had been in office less than half a year, he set out an approach to colonial policy that combined firm military rule with a generous paternalism. Root asserted that the subject peoples could make no claim to the constitutional rights enjoyed by American citizens or even by the inhabitants of Alaska and Hawaii, other territories not designated for statehood. In his view they had no rights except what the United States gave them. Within this matrix of dictatorship, however, Root emphasized the responsibility of the United States to work on behalf of its colonial subjects. The American people had an "implied contract" with them: ". . . it is our unquestioned duty to make the interests of the people over whom we assert sovereignty the first and controlling consideration in all legislation and administration which concerns them, and to give them, to the greatest possible extent, individual freedom, self-government in accordance with their capacity, just and equal laws, and opportunity for education, for profitable industry, and for development in civilization."

For the neophyte colonial manager, Puerto Rico offered an initial laboratory for the combination of authority and solicitude that Root professed. The island was extremely poor, with a population density seven times Cuba's, the highest illiteracy rate in the Caribbean— more than 80 percent—and no significant resource base. Just two weeks after Root was sworn in, Puerto Rico was devastated by a hurricane that killed over three thousand people and destroyed two-thirds of the coffee crop. It was Root's first challenge, and he met it well, turning the entire U.S. Army on the island into a relief corps. Longer-term reforms followed: a mass vaccination program; a near tripling of the school population; penal and tax reforms; and the successful, though not immediate, achievement of congressional authority for most Puerto Rican products to enter the United States duty-free. In the first decade of the century trade between the island and the mainland was to increase fourfold from a low base.

Root inherited a tense political situation in Puerto Rico. The U.S. military government had dismissed the elected ministry of Luis Muñoz Rivera in 1898 and had clamped down on the press, causing Puerto Ricans to lament their barely tasted autonomy under Spain. Root quickly saw the defects of military rule, but he was not ready to give Puerto Rico the self-determination planned for Cuba. He reported to Congress at the end of 1899 that the people "have not yet been educated in the art of self-government, or any really honest government." In his opinion they were not qualified for what both main local parties sought: independence, autonomy, or statehood.

Wisely, Root did not impose an American system of municipal law on Puerto Ricans, believing, as he said later, that the Spanish legal system "was far better for them than anything we could produce out of our own experience." He decided that a civilian government should replace military rule but insisted that the governor and his cabinet be appointed by the president; he opposed the creation of a legislature. Senator J. B. Foraker of Ohio, an 1898 war hawk who nevertheless opposed excessive American control over the island dependencies, sold Root on a slightly more liberal approach, which took effect on May 1, 1900. The Foraker Act exchanged military for civilian government and provided for a bicameral legislature, one chamber of which was to be elected by Puerto Ricans. But the civilian governor and upper chamber of the legislature were to be appointed by the U.S. president, and the justices of the Puerto Rican Supreme Court by the governor. Foraker and Root treated the island as a colony rather

than a territory, effectively giving Washington a veto on its every political act.

In a 1901 decision designed to determine the status of the new
U.S. territories, the U.S. Supreme Court confirmed Root's hybrid approach to Puerto Rico, ruling that the island belonged to but was not
a part of the United States. Puerto Ricans were not citizens, nor were
they protected by the U.S. Constitution. The ruling relieved Puerto
Ricans of federal taxes, but the unequal status it implied disillusioned
two generations of moderate Puerto Rican politicians. Among these
were Muñoz Rivera and his son Luis Muñoz Marín, who felt compelled to forgo the objectives of independence or statehood and con-
centrate instead on the more modest goals of home rule and
improvement in the standard of living.

The Supreme Court decision meant that Puerto Rico ranked below
the forty-five states of the Union; below the "incorporated territories"
of Oklahoma, Arizona, and New Mexico, destined to become states;
and below the territories of Alaska and Hawaii, which benefited from
the Constitution though they were not on the statehood track. Puerto
Rico was thus relegated to the fourth-class status of "unincorporated
dependency." In the words of Chief Justice Melville W. Fuller, who
dissented from the Court's decision, Puerto Rico was left "like a disembodied shade in an intermediate state of ambiguous existence." A
Puerto Rican politician put it more graphically: "We are Mr. Nobody
from Nowhere."

Cuba was the most predictable of Root's colonial problems since
the Teller Amendment committed the United States to the island's independence once "pacification" was achieved. But Root, on taking office, found no American strategy for Cuba's independence. Nobody
was clear when pacification would come, though during the period of
transition it was assumed that the Cuban rebels would be given no
major role in governing. The freeze-out had begun with General
Shafter's refusal to let rebel forces participate in the surrender of Santiago. This American policy of exclusion had a devastating effect on
soldiers who in some cases had been fighting the Spanish for three
decades and had materially assisted the American victory.

José Martí would not have been surprised at the American
takeover. He saw the United States as compulsively predatory, writing
in 1895 of his duty "to prevent, through the independence of Cuba,

the U.S.A. from spreading over the West Indies and falling with added weight upon other lands of Our America." Martí had lived in the United States for fourteen years and planned the 1895 revolution from his small apartment in New York City. He admired the individualism of Americans but hated their materialism; the last thing he wanted was an American conquest of Cuba. "Once the United States is in Cuba," he wrote, "who will get her out?"

The disenchantment of the rebels was compounded by their debarment from the Paris Peace Conference and their enforced absence from the Havana ceremony transferring the government from Spain to the United States. The American soldiers in the occupying force, many of them southerners, did not get along with the insurrectionary forces, which were mostly black. President McKinley issued a proclamation stating the advisability of keeping on in the civil government officials who had served in the Spanish regime. Given the need to avoid governmental chaos, the decision was understandable, but it made the Cubans wonder why the Americans had come at all. It was particularly insulting when the Americans decided to appoint as civil governor of Santiago Province, where the rebels had been most active, the former mayor of Santiago city.

Fatefully this American tilt toward the Spanish authorities failed to convince one Spanish soldier who turned out to play a role in later history. Ángel Castro, a subaltern in the Spanish Army, had been transferred to military duty from Spain to Cuba following the 1895 revolution. He hated the Americans for preventing his army from defeating the rebels; this hostility burned throughout his long life. No doubt he vented it in front of his son Fidel, born in 1926.

American authority in Cuba was a military dictatorship from the start. The military governor was in charge of both branches of government, military and civil. His authority on the island was supreme; his only superiors were the president and the secretary of war. Before Root joined McKinley's administration, the military governor was General John R. Brooke, a Civil War veteran, who tried to balance the retention of local Spanish law—anathema to Cubans who had fought Spain—with the hiring of Cuban revolutionaries to positions in government.

Brooke's most difficult task was to disband the Cuban revolutionary army, a mission that became more urgent with the outbreak of war in the Philippines the month after he assumed charge. It might have seemed contradictory for the United States to want to demobilize the army of a country to which it had pledged independence, but the pressure from Congress to avoid the risk of wars on two fronts was extreme. The Americans were fortunate in the character of General Máximo Gómez, commander in chief of the Cuban Army and the most revered war hero in Cuba, who agreed to dissolve the army and accept the three million dollars offered by the McKinley administration as demobilization pay for the soldiers, who were in dire need.

Despite the short-lived opposition of the anti-American Cuban Assembly, whose existence ended in April 1899, Gómez's conciliatory views prevailed, the army was disbanded, and the threat of armed rebellion in Cuba passed away. When some of his generals came to Gómez to ask him to negotiate with the United States on behalf of the army, he answered in a voice of disappointed realism: "We must recognize that the only power today in Cuba is the power of those who have intervened, and therefore for the present, thoughts of a Cuban independent government can be no more than a dream."

Brooke's refusal to delegate authority to subordinate officers was not popular among the American generals in charge of the Cuban provinces and was especially hated by Leonard Wood, ex-commander of the Rough Riders, Roosevelt's soldierly model, and now the military governor of Santiago Province. A haughty and confrontational soldier, Wood protested, inter alia, about Brooke's decree that the revenues from the port of Santiago be directed to the Cuban treasury, thus depriving him of funds needed for local public works projects. Such grievances, immemorially an obstacle to good relations between a leader at the center and a subordinate in the field, degenerated in this case into a nasty blood feud. Brooke sent withering orders to Wood: "Your estimate for August is wrong and cannot be allowed"; "The haphazard methods . . . must cease instantly"; "The accounts rendered for the last six months are a disgrace to the army."

In retaliation, Wood used his powerful friends at home against his chief. In the United States Wood was considered a war hero, whereas Brooke, who had never gotten past the training camps of Florida, was a nonentity. Wood had the ear of Roosevelt, Congress, and even his former medical patient the president. He complained to them all. When Root took office, he listened sympathetically to the replay of

Wood's grievances and became convinced that Wood had the dynamism, independent-mindedness, and youth (he was not yet forty, younger than Roosevelt) necessary in a proconsul. Overriding the objections of the army, which opposed Wood as too junior and as a medical rather than line officer, McKinley acted on Root's recommendation and appointed Wood to replace Brooke as military commander of Cuba. Wood took over on December 13, 1899, and from that time served as an energetic executor of Root's policy toward Cuba.

In his first annual report in late 1899 Root confirmed the American pledge, embodied in the Teller Amendment and reaffirmed by the president as a sacred obligation, that Cuba would become independent and that the U.S. occupation was therefore limited in function and temporary:

> The control which we are exercising in trust for the people of Cuba should not be, and of course will not be, continued any longer than is necessary to enable that people to establish a suitable government to which the control shall be transferred, which shall really represent the people of Cuba and be able to maintain order and discharge international obligations. . . . Our present duty is limited to giving every assistance in our power to the establishment of such a government, and to maintaining order and promoting the welfare of the people of Cuba during the period necessarily required for that process.

Even in affirming the Teller Amendment, Root seemed to be sliding away from its categorical determination "to leave the government and control of the island to its people." What did Root mean by a "suitable" government? Suitable to whom? When would it be established? Were the maintenance of order and the discharge of international obligations a condition of its establishment? McKinley, in his own annual message at the end of 1899, compounded the ambiguity. In a passage probably drafted by Root, the president stated that an independent Cuba "must needs be bound to us by ties of singular intimacy and strength. . . . Whether these ties shall be organic or conventional, the destinies of Cuba are in some rightful form and manner irrevocably linked to our own, but how and how far is [*sic*] for the future to determine in the ripeness of events." The reference to "organic" ties provoked a rush of hope among American annexationists. It soon dissipated, but clearly McKinley and Root were beginning to think about how they could balance the commitment to Cuba's independence against a continuation of American influence there.

In accepting a moral obligation toward Cuba, Root encouraged Wood in his efforts to improve the lives of ordinary Cubans. He told Wood: ". . . if we once got into a position where we are retaining our hold on Cuba, to the injury of the Cuban people, doing them an injustice, refusing to properly care for them while we prevent them from caring for themselves, the position will be untenable, and I am not willing to occupy it." Still, Root realized that humanitarian concern was not the only or even the primary American interest in Cuba. "The trouble about Cuba," as he described it with his customary clarity, "is that, although technically a foreign country, practically and morally it occupies an intermediate position, since we have required it to become a part of our political and military system, and to form a part of our lines of exterior defense." Echoing Mahan and his friend Roosevelt, Root saw Cuba as a vital strategic necessity for the United States. But how could its place in "our political and military system" be reconciled with the legislative requirement for its independence? He struggled with that question.

Meanwhile he immersed himself in the details of Cuba's problems, visiting the island three times on inspections, spending hours with Wood in Havana and Washington, and corresponding frequently with the military governor. Under Root's guidance Wood plunged into the task of comprehensive reform. The military governor was a forerunner of several American military commanders in Vietnam, energetic, dedicated, attentive to details, and result-oriented but impatient with the inefficiencies of the local population and myopic about political realities.

Wood was prepared to include in his administration Cubans who had fought against Spain, but he was most comfortable with upper-class Cuban conservatives desirous of a close economic relationship with the United States. He accepted the requirement of the Teller Amendment that Cuba be prepared for independence, but he believed personally that Cuba should be annexed and, listening to the wrong people, thought that most Cubans agreed with him. He assured McKinley in September 1899 that "the people who are talking 'Cuba Libre' and the total withdrawal of the American Army in the daily press represent at most not over five percent of the Cuban people."

Wood's strength lay in his determination and ability to attack the problems of everyday life in Cuba. Enlarging programs started by Brooke, he reformed the penal system, freed prisoners improperly held, sped up judicial procedures, and rid the courts of traditional corrupt practices. He improved sanitation and hygiene in orphanages, reform schools, mental institutions, and other public places. He cleaned up the cities; Roosevelt's sister Corinne, after a midnight inspection of Havana in Wood's company, stated boldly that she would be willing to eat breakfast off the street. The military governor tasked Cuban civil officials with building roads, bridges, and wharves; dredging harbors; and paving streets. He pressed education reform, giving it a heavy American character. A vigorous American educator, recommended by President Eliot of Harvard, arrived with a mandate to build a school in every village. Wood arranged for more than a thousand Cuban teachers to be sent to Harvard to study American education.

His medical training made Wood particularly alert to the dangers of yellow fever, which in the aftermath of the war was sweeping Cuba in epidemic proportions. He launched a campaign to eradicate it, taking inspiration from a Cuban doctor, Carlos Finlay, who had theorized in 1881 that the disease was carried by mosquitoes. Wood encouraged Walter Reed, a major in the Medical Corps, to test Finlay's theory and supported him through a series of unsuccessful experiments. Reed's eventual success led directly to the reduction of yellow fever in Cuba and later worldwide. To the fire of all these reforms Wood was the essential spark; he was a dervish of activity, inspecting, inspiring, and inciting all over the island. In his reforms on behalf of the Cuban people, he earned comparison with his great British contemporaries, Lord Cromer in Egypt and Lord Curzon in India.

Wood tested his success in stabilizing Cuba against economic criteria, whether money could be borrowed at a reasonable rate of interest and whether American capital would be willing to invest there. He was sympathetic to American businessmen seeking franchises and contracts from the War Department. But the Senate had other ideas. Before Wood had been elevated to governor, Senator Foraker, concerned to limit American economic power, had succeeded in winning passage of an amendment to prohibit the U.S. government from granting property franchises or concessions in Cuba during the occupation. Foraker's Amendment, consistent with Teller's Amendment mandating Cuba's independence, was designed to prevent the economic exploitation of Cuba and to shorten the American presence there. Foraker predicted that if the United States established an economic foothold on the island, it would not leave for a century.

Wood advocated repeal of the Foraker Amendment and in the meantime managed to get around it in some areas. Mining claims, for example, were simply considered not to be concessions, and public works projects were ruled to be in the interest of Cuban development. Wood persuaded the president of the Canadian Pacific Railway to undertake a railroad from Havana to Santiago; it was operating in less than three years, cutting the travel time from ten days to one. Also, American sugar interests were able to locate, or in some cases relocate, in Cuba during the occupation. Their control of the market, however, was not overwhelming; in 1905 American-owned mills produced only 21 percent of Cuba's sugar. By contrast, during the occupation nearly half the island's manufacture of cigars and cigarettes was in American hands. In opposition to Republican party policy, Wood urged tariff relief for Cuba in sugar and tobacco. Taken overall, his economic programs favored Cuban development as well as American capitalism. The evidence does not support charges, made at the time and later, that the McKinley administration provided a cover for a massive American economic penetration of Cuba.

3.

On political issues Root and Wood began cautiously. Root authorized municipal elections in Cuba for February 1900, perhaps believing that he could do the right thing at negligible risk since Wood had predicted a victory for pro-American Cubans. As in Puerto Rico, the franchise was limited—in the Cuban case to those who were either literate or owners of valuable property. The American aim was to reduce the vote of the nearly one-third of the Cuban population that was black. Both Root and Wood were seeking to avoid the tumultuous and unstable rule, often by black dictators, that was prevalent in Haiti and Santo Domingo on the island just east of Cuba.

In Cuba, however, stability could be just as threatened by disenfranchising the black population as by empowering it, so Root and Wood conceded the vote to former soldiers in the Cuban Army, most of whom were black. When, against Wood's prediction, the radicals won, both American officials absorbed the rebuff as good sports. They claimed a victory for democracy, and Wood authorized the flying of the Cuban flag from municipal buildings. But the Americans concluded that an independent Cuba could not be trusted to cooperate closely with the United States. Root and Wood now acted to construct a policy that would limit the damage of Cuba's impending independence.

After consulting with Root in Washington, Wood issued instructions in late July 1900 for the election of delegates to a convention that was "to frame and adopt a constitution for the people of Cuba, and as a part thereof, to provide for and agree with the Government of the United States upon the relations to exist between that Government and the Government of Cuba. . . ." This passage, no doubt Root's handiwork, undercut Cuban sovereignty in two important ways. First, there was to be no nationwide popular vote on the constitution. The instructions left not only the drafting but also the adoption of the constitution in the hands of thirty-one delegates rather than the people of Cuba. Moreover, the agreement on bilateral relations desired by the United States would be an integral part of the constitution, not a separate document.

In the face of this blatant American effort to manipulate Cuba's future, only 30 percent of the qualified voters participated in the election of delegates. Moreover, despite Wood's intrusive efforts to encourage Cubans to "send their very best men" to the convention, he admitted that "some of the worst agitators and political rascals" had been elected. The constitutional convention convened on November 5, 1900, the day before McKinley won reelection, in a theater ironically named after José Martí. By then the furor in Cuba had caused Wood to persuade Washington to back off its insistence that the agreement on bilateral relations be part of the constitution. Instead the convention was instructed to consider the bilateral agreement right after adopting the constitution. Thus an attenuated linkage remained, and the founding document of independent Cuba would still be irrevocably connected to the new state's relationship with its northern neighbor.

The convention produced the blueprint for a republican system of government resembling that of the United States: separated powers, with a president, vice president, bicameral legislature, and supreme court; separation of church and state; and universal male suffrage (a far more liberal electoral system than the American occupiers had permitted in the two earlier elections they had supervised). Root gave the new constitution a grudging and provisional seal of approval:

> I do not fully agree with the wisdom of some of the provisions of this constitution, but it provides for a republican form of government; it was adopted after long and patient consideration and discussion; it represented the views of the delegates elected by the people of Cuba; and it contains no features which would justify the assertion that a government organized under it will not be the one to which the United States may properly transfer the obligation for the protection of life and property under international law, assumed in the Treaty of Paris.

The passing grade Root gave the constitution was not enough to allay his concerns. There also had to be a built-in guarantee of American influence. Except where the British, French, and Danes ruled colonial possessions, the Caribbean was a sea of unrest, the worst of it right across the narrow Windward Passage from Cuba. An unstable Cuba would be intolerable for the United States. American economic interests in sugar and tobacco would be threatened. A hostile power like Germany might take advantage of domestic unrest, perhaps even occupy Cuba. The Monroe Doctrine, never enshrined in international law, might come under challenge. America's all-important strategic interest in Cuba as the gateway to the Caribbean and to the planned isthmian canal might be menaced. Any one of these negative factors would be troubling. Taken together, they led Root's coldly logical mind to the conclusion that as the price for independence, the United States had to compel the Cubans to limit their sovereignty.

Root's thinking was set forth clearly in a letter he wrote to Wood on January 9, 1901. The secretary of war urged the military governor to press the convention to outline the relationship it wanted between Cuba and the United States. The Cuban delegates should be disabused of any notion that they would be protected by the United States whatever they did. "If Cuba declines to accord to this government the authority and facilities for her protection, she will have to look out for herself in case of trouble with any other nation." Root then sketched a formula for making protection mandatory: The Cubans should accept a "reservation" to carry the American right to "protect" the island into the period of independence. Root's argument here was highly legalistic, but it formed the base on which rested all the subsequent American actions to curb Cuba's sovereignty:

> Another fact which the Cubans should consider is that in international affairs the existence of a right recognized by international law is of the utmost importance. We now have[,] by virtue of our occupation of Cuba and the terms under which sovereignty was yielded by Spain, a right to protect her which all foreign nations recognize. It is of great importance to Cuba that that right, resting upon the treaty of Paris and derived through that treaty from the sovereignty of Spain, should never be terminated but should be continued by a reservation, with the consent of the Cuban people, at the time when the authority which we now exercise is placed in their hands. If we should simply turn the government over to the Cuban administration, retire from the island, and then turn round to make a treaty with the new government, just as we would make treaties with Venezuela, and Brazil, and England, and France, no foreign State would recognize any longer a right on our part to interfere in any quarrel which she might have with Cuba, unless that interference were based upon an assertion of the Monroe Doctrine. But the Monroe Doctrine is not a part of international law and has never been recognized by European nations.

For Root Cuba was too important and too weak to be dealt with as if it were Venezuela or Brazil. There would be too much risk in treating it as a fully independent country. As he wrote Wood five weeks later, there must be safeguards for the United States: "The preservation of that independence by a country so small as Cuba, so incapable, as she must always be, to contend by force against the great powers of the world, must depend upon her strict performance of international obligations, upon her giving due protection to the lives and property of the citizens of all other countries within her borders, and upon her never contracting any public debt which in the hands of citizens of foreign powers shall constitute an obligation she is unable to meet."

Root was not just a brilliant lawyer but also a skillful politician. Not only had he thought through the legal basis, tenuous as it might be, for the assertion of a special American right in Cuba, but he had also determined the specific and politically feasible steps the United States could take. He described these in a January 11 letter to Secretary of State Hay outlining the provisions that in his view should be incorporated into Cuban law. Independent Cuba was expected to lock in all the decisions of the military occupation, to provide to the United States naval bases on its territory, to give the United States a determining role in the conduct of its foreign relations, and, most important of all, to allow the United States to intervene when the latter decided that stability was threatened. There was some slight precedent for the blockbuster clause on intervention: A decade earlier Secretary of State Blaine had tried to negotiate the right to land U.S. troops in Hawaii but had backed off when King Kalakaua objected. Root's four points, soon to become demands, seriously undercut the independence promised by the Teller Amendment.

The secretary of war had tested the political waters for his extraordinary initiative and was sure of congressional support. Indeed, when Senator Orville Platt of Connecticut, chairman of the Senate Committee on Relations with Cuba, suggested to him a resolution ending the military occupation and prescribing certain conditions on Cuba, Root was ready with his four points, which were incorporated into Platt's legislation with minimal additions. The Platt Amendment, as it is known to history, passed the Senate on February 27, 1901, by a vote of 43–20. Fourteen senators who had supported the Teller Amendment, including Senator Teller himself, voted in favor, thus making a mockery of their principled support for Cuban independence. After passage by the House McKinley signed the bill on March 2. One of the key documents in the entire history of American foreign policy, the amendment was the handiwork of Elihu Root, who devised its key provisions:

> [ART. I.] That the government of Cuba shall never enter into any treaty or other compact with any foreign power or powers which will impair or tend to impair the independence of Cuba, nor in any manner authorize or permit any foreign power or powers to obtain by colonization or for military or naval purposes, or otherwise, lodgment in or control over any portion of said island.

[ART. III.] That the government of Cuba consents that the United States may exercise the right to intervene for the preservation of Cuban independence, the maintenance of a government adequate for the protection of life, property, and individual liberty, and for discharging the obligations with respect to Cuba imposed by the Treaty of Paris on the United States, now to be assumed and undertaken by the government of Cuba.

[ART. IV.] That all Acts of the United States in Cuba during its military occupancy thereof are ratified and validated . . .

[ART. VII.] That . . . the government of Cuba will sell or lease to the United States lands necessary for coaling or naval stations at certain specified points. . . .

Root's defense of the Platt demands, intended for the delegates to the Cuban Constitutional Convention, combined a soft and a hard approach. The soft approach was legalistic, designed to prove that the American claim to the right of intervention under Article III sprang naturally from the original U.S. intervention against Spain and from the terms of the Treaty of Paris. Root argued that Article III was really in the interests of Cuban independence because it turned the Monroe Doctrine from a declaratory to a legal principle, compelling European nations to recognize the American right to intervene in Cuba and thus protecting Cuba from them. In invoking the Monroe Doctrine, Root was giving it an unprecedented scope beyond the rhetorical use made of it by earlier American statesmen. Traditionally it had been designed to keep the Europeans out of the hemisphere; in Root's definition it now gave the United States the right, sanctioned by international law, to intervene. Not even Roosevelt, in a magazine article in 1897 on the doctrine, had claimed this much for it.

Root, Wood, and Platt all professed themselves unable to understand how anyone could read the intervention article in the amendment as undermining Cuba's independence. Platt wrote Root that "the amendment was drafted with a view to avoid any possible claim that its acceptance by the Cuban Constitutional Convention would result in the establishment of a protectorate or suzerainty, or in any way interfere with the independence or sovereignty of Cuba, and speaking for myself, it seems impossible that any such construction can be placed upon that clause." Root expressed the hope to Wood that "you have been able to disabuse the minds of members of the

Convention of the idea that the intervention described in the Platt amendment is synonymous with intermeddling or interference with the affairs of a Cuban Government." But in case Root's tortuous legalisms failed to convince the Cuban delegates, the Americans simultaneously deployed a tougher approach: There would be no Cuban independence unless the Platt Amendment was incorporated in the constitution. Platt warned that if all the articles of the amendment were not accepted, "we shall occupy until they are."

Even before the amendment passed, Wood began a lobbying campaign in Cuba. His characteristically rosy assessments were partially confirmed by the support of the sugar interests and of two of Cuba's grand old revolutionary icons, General Gómez, the rebel military leader, and Tomás Estrada Palma, who had been president of the provisional rebel government in the Ten Years' War and later chief of the Cuban junta in New York during the 1895–98 revolution. But the American view that the amendment reinforced rather than undermined Cuba's independence failed to persuade the elected constitutional convention. The committee of the convention responsible for relations with the United States found some of the Platt points unacceptable "because they impair the independence and sovereignty of Cuba":

> Our duty consists in making Cuba independent of every other nation, the great and noble American nation included, and if we bind ourselves to ask the governments of the U.S. for their consent to our international dealings, if we admit that they shall receive and retain the right to intervene in our country to maintain or precipitate conditions and fulfil duties pertaining solely to Cuban governments and . . . if we grant them the right to acquire and preserve titles to lands for naval stations and maintain these in determined places along our coast, it is clear that we would seem independent of the rest of the world although we were not in reality, but never would be in reference to the U.S.

Juan Gualberto Gómez, a radical black delegate from Santiago and a determined opponent of the Platt Amendment, made a graphic point about Article III: "To reserve to the United States the faculty of deciding for themselves when independence is menaced and when therefore they ought to intervene to preserve it is equivalent to delivering up the key to our house so that they can enter it at all hours when the desire takes them, day or night. . . ." The committee produced counterproposals that failed to meet the American requirements on intervention, debt, and naval stations and that, moreover, were not designed to be included in the Cuban constitution, as the Americans insisted.

A determined American administration and Congress were in no mood to compromise. Even some anti-imperialists accepted Root's argument that Cuba's independence could be enhanced by limiting it. Too late as usual, the Anti-Imperialist League held a mass meeting to denounce the amendment in Faneuil Hall on March 28, nearly four weeks after it had become law. Missing was Massachusetts's venerable anti-imperialist Senator Hoar, who had voted for the amendment. On this issue, as on the Treaty of Paris and on the Philippine war, the anti-imperialists were too weak and too divided to make a difference.

In Cuba the convention voted to refuse incorporation of the Platt Amendment into the new constitution. From Washington Root sent a private note to Wood threatening strong measures if the Cubans finally rejected it: "[T]he Convention . . . will have failed to perform the duty for which it was elected and the duty must be performed by others." Having badly underestimated Cuban opposition to the amendment, Wood now persuaded Root to receive a visit to Washington from a five-member delegation of the convention that, Wood thought, was seeking a cover for capitulation.

The delegation enjoyed high-level treatment: a lunch hosted by Root at the Metropolitan Club with Senator Platt, General Miles, and other key officials and senators; a short meeting with President McKinley, who was friendly but opaque; and several long meetings with Root, who deployed his now-familiar argument that American policy was designed to advance Cuban independence. Hinting at a possible trade-off, the Cubans urged American agreement to a reciprocity treaty that would allow Cuban sugar and other products free access to the U.S. market. Root replied that negotiations on reciprocity would be possible when a representative Cuban government was in place, implying that the Platt Amendment first had to be accepted so that the Cuban constitution could take effect.

The Cubans' visit tipped the convention toward a settlement.

American intransigence had exposed the weakness of the Cuban hand. The alternative to capitulation was continued American occupation, making Cuba a colony rather than a protectorate. A truncated independence, with the vague prospect of a reciprocity treaty to help the Cuban economy, seemed to offer a more honorable future. After unsuccessful efforts to rewrite or interpret some of the provisions, the convention voted sixteen to eleven to accept the amendment, which became an integral part of the Cuban constitution as an appendix. With a military government sitting over them, the Cubans had little choice, but there could have been no doubt on either side that the independence of Cuba was a relative term. In a burst of candor Wood wrote Roosevelt, by then vice president: "There is, of course, little or no independence left Cuba under the Platt Amendment."

Did Root act cynically to produce this result? There is little reason to think so. From the beginning of his tenure he had seen himself as performing "a lawyer's duty upon the call of the greatest of all our clients." That client, the U.S. government, had been ambivalent from the start about Cuban independence. McKinley's war message had contained not a word about it. It was the Senate, via the Teller Amendment, that had injected independence into the picture, and now Teller was happy to circumscribe that independence. Root had every reason to believe that in his hard line, he was negotiating for the State Department, the navy, the Senate, and President McKinley himself.

Moreover, he undoubtedly had faith in what he was doing. Root was a pragmatist. He understood, even if he may have exaggerated, the risks of untrammeled independence for Cuba. His legal arguments were, to say the least, tricky—he could have argued the other side just as effectively—but he was undoubtedly convinced that their objective was worthy. Moreover, on the nuts-and-bolts issues Root made every effort to keep faith with the Cuban people. He gave Wood unstinting support in his health, education, and development efforts. He also threw himself into the bruising debate to win trade reciprocity for Cuba's fragile economy. Thanks largely to his efforts, and Wood's, a reciprocity treaty of benefit to Cuba was signed in December 1902 and took effect three months later.

In the context of the world imperialism of the time, the American decision to give Cuba even partial independence was unusual. Even the most enlightened colonial power, Great Britain, fought a war to deny independence to the Boer republics of South Africa. Curzon, one of the ablest of the British colonial governors, would never have imagined offering imminent, or even eventual, independence to the three hundred million Indians he ruled. As for the Americans, it would have been difficult to deliver fully on the obligation they had assumed in the Teller Amendment. Their strategic requirements, their terror of instability, their fear of foreign encroachment, and their sense of racial superiority made the bestowal of genuine independence too much for them. All these concerns were almost certainly exaggerated, but they were nevertheless taken seriously. Root's policy of partial independence accurately reflected the basic American consensus on Cuba.

Leonard Wood had consistently advocated an alternative to partial independence, annexation. Juan Gualberto Gómez, the Santiago radical, speculated rhetorically that it might be better for Cuba "to be officially and openly administered from Washington" than governed by "discredited Cuban functionaries, pliable instruments of a foreign and irresponsible power." The case for annexation was not absurd. If Cuba had been administered as a U.S. territory with solicitude for its welfare and ample resource allocations, it might have reached the point at which it could choose its future from strength rather than weakness. In this palmiest of scenarios, in time it could have become independent without the residue of anti-Americanism that was to give Fidel Castro a significant measure of his appeal. Or it might eventually have become, like noncontiguous Alaska and even more distant Hawaii, a state in the American Union.

In actuality Cuba became a semi-independent country defined by the reality of American influence and by the shadow of American intervention. The navy constructed a naval base at Guantánamo Bay— an American Gibraltar—on the eastern end of the island, under a lease that contained no termination date. The threat of intervention, as much as the future interventions themselves, assured a heavy American weight on Cuban decisions. Article III of the Platt Amendment distorted the entire bilateral relationship and established a principle for intervention to be invoked in the future in Cuba and in other Latin American countries as well.

In Cuba independence began in controversy. The first political act, the election of a president, produced a charge from the left that Wood had rigged the electoral commission. The favored American candidate, the cooperative Estrada Palma, who had taught school in upstate New York, ran unopposed, the anti-Platt candidate having withdrawn. Estrada Palma thus became the first president of Cuba in a tainted election. On May 20, 1902, Wood transferred to him and to the Cuban Congress "the government and control of the Island" on the condition that they undertake the obligations assumed by the United States in the Treaty of Paris with Spain. After the raising of the Cuban flag, Wood sailed away past the wreck of the *Maine* on the *Brooklyn*, an armored cruiser that had participated in the destruction of Cervera's squadron in Santiago Bay.

4.

The first years of American occupation of the Philippines were marked by full-scale war. As Cabot Lodge commented disingenuously, "The people whom we liberated down there have turned against us." From the outbreak of violence on February 4, 1899, it took the United States more than three years to subdue what was to the Americans an insurrection and to the Filipinos a war for independence. At its height the American troop presence constituted three-quarters of the entire U.S. Army. Casualties on both sides far exceeded the killed and wounded in the three weeks of fighting in Cuba.

The shape of the Philippines, an archipelago of more than seven thousand islands stretching a thousand miles from north to south, complicated the task of the U.S. Army. Also, Aguinaldo's forces at first outnumbered the Americans by about seventy-five thousand to twenty-four thousand. Rapid American buildups reduced the advantage; by 1900 the U.S. Army had seventy thousand troops in the Philippines. The Filipinos were well armed, with Mauser rifles as good as the Americans' Krag-Jorgensens. While the war progressed, the parity in weaponry eroded as an American naval blockade impeded Aguinaldo's efforts to resupply arms to his forces. In the arts of war the Americans were superior in generalship and strategy. Aguinaldo was a political leader with little military expertise of his own. His officers, unskilled in tactics and ineffective in the command of troops, were largely chosen for political rather than military reasons. His army was inexperienced in guerrilla war, where its comparative advantages lay. On the other side, twenty-six of the thirty American generals who served in the Philippines were veterans of the Indian wars and well trained in irregular operations.

Aguinaldo's movement also suffered from inherent weaknesses. Only 30 percent of the Filipino population spoke Tagalog, the language of his ethnic group, which was concentrated on one island (albeit the largest and most populous), Luzon. Moreover, the rebel leader remained bound to his middle-class heritage; his appeal was to Filipinos of privilege. He eschewed the opportunity to proclaim a social revolution that would have attracted the masses to his cause. Yet despite these drawbacks, Aguinaldo was a redoubtable adversary. His soldiers were fighting in their own country against a foreign foe threatening their dreams of liberation. Carl Schurz had put it presciently: "The Filipinos fought against Spain for their freedom and independence, and unless they abandon their recently proclaimed purpose for their freedom and independence, they will fight against us."

In these challenging and unaccustomed conditions, the Americans were nevertheless able to develop a political-military strategy that ultimately won the war without irrevocably alienating the population. It was based on McKinley's strong sense of responsibility toward the Philippine people. Six weeks before the war broke out, in his instruction to the U.S. forces to occupy the entire archipelago, the president had emphasized that "we come, not as invaders or conquerors, but as friends." The instruction concluded: "Finally, it should be the earnest and paramount aim of the military administration to win the confidence, respect, and affection of the inhabitants of the Philippines by assuring them in every possible way that full measure of individual rights and liberties which is the heritage of a free people, and by proving to them that the mission of the United States is one of benevolent assimilation, substituting the mild sway of justice and right for arbitrary rule."

After the fighting began, "benevolent assimilation" came under attack by American opponents of the war, who saw it as a cynical mask for a policy of repression. But the president was serious about it and remained so right up to his death. In January 1899 McKinley seized on a proposal by Admiral Dewey, always more sensitive than his fellow officers to Philippine concerns, and sent to Manila an investigative commission headed by the president of Cornell University, Jacob Gould Schurman. The commission was intended to supplement, rather than replace, U.S. military rule; its mandate was to facilitate "the most humane, pacific and effective extension" of America's authority and to secure "the benefits of a wise and generous protection of life and property to the inhabitants." Its arrival roughly coincided with the outbreak of war in February, giving new urgency to its role of ensuring civilian participation in an increasingly military operation.

Before accepting his mission, Schurman had opposed the U.S. annexation of the Philippines, but his experience there changed his mind. The commission report strongly backed the U.S. military objective: "Only through American occupation . . . is the idea of a free, self-governing and united Philippine commonwealth at all conceivable." Though he did not undermine the army, Schurman did lay the groundwork for a significant effort to make the civilian population more sympathetic to the occupation by proposing to put municipal and provincial governments largely in the hands of local officials.

The military commander, General Elwell S. Otis, recognized and accepted the importance of this endeavor. An arrogant and irascible armchair commander who rarely visited the front, he was not popular among the hard-charging generals under his command. Yet he was a man of parts: a graduate of Harvard Law School, a hero at Gettysburg, and the organizer of the smooth transport of troops to the Philippines. He also presided over significant military successes in the early stages of the war; by the autumn of 1899 he had driven Aguinaldo to abandon conventional warfare and to fall back on guerrilla tactics. Otis was also a military intellectual who believed in McKinley's instruction to make the army the agent of civil reform. Like Wood in Cuba, he plunged his men into civic action programs like food distribution, sewer construction, smallpox vaccination, and legal and educational reforms.

Elihu Root was an ideal secretary of war for a strategy of combining military power with civil pacification. Although (or perhaps because) he was a military neophyte, he made sure the army had all the soldiers it needed. He sent Otis more troops than the commander had requested and initiated, over Otis's objection, a program to train and deploy native soldiers. At the same time Root gave top priority to pacification efforts. He established a policy of bringing civil law to all territory occupied by U.S. troops. Aguinaldo's decision in November 1899 to disband his army and launch a guerrilla war enabled Otis to devote more of his resources to civic action programs. The flagship model of pacification was the island of Negros, where an anti-Aguinaldo population welcomed the American establishment of municipal government, public order, and education and health programs.

McKinley and Root operated in the shadow of the 1900 presidential election. They knew that the anti-imperialists would launch a campaign to defeat the president's bid for a second term, and they feared that Bryan, again the Democratic candidate, would make the Philippines the core issue in the contest. By 1900 the war had become a series of regional conflicts, not particularly threatening to the American forces but not susceptible to quick victories either. Otis's arrogance had annoyed the military establishment and, more seriously, the press; it was time to replace him with a commander who inspired confidence. A civilian leader was needed as well. The Schurman commission finished its work in April 1900; its successor would have to convince the American people of the administration's determination to win the allegiance of the local population. The president and Root thus faced two major personnel decisions. One turned out to be only a partial success; the other was brilliant.

Brigadier General Arthur MacArthur was appointed to succeed Otis as military commander in May 1900. An imperious, self-promoting officer with a striking physical resemblance to Theodore Roosevelt, MacArthur disliked his predecessor's cautious approach to battle. He compared Otis to "a locomotive bottomside up on the track, with its wheels revolving at full speed." MacArthur's locomotive, in contrast, would steam forward on a cleared track, bowling over all Filipinos who resisted. The new leader encouraged regional offensives throughout the archipelago and authorized the ruthless approaches favored by many of his regional commanders. MacArthur's strategy was effective in a military sense; by the time he turned over command to his successor a year later, all but three areas had been brought under control. But the harshness of his methods undercut the pacification policy so important to the president.

McKinley reinforced that policy with the choice of William Howard Taft as president of the Second Philippine Commission. Taft was a big man in every respect, especially physically. A highly respected judge and member of the Ohio political establishment, he had set his sights on an appointment to the Supreme Court. He was not pleased to be asked to go to Manila, having shared with President McKinley his dovish position on the annexation (if a 325-pound man can be compared to a small bird). Taft recalled his conversation with the president:

> "Judge," he said, "I'd like to have you go to the Philippines." I said, "Mr. President, what do you mean by going to the Philippines?" He replied, "We must establish a government there and I would like you to help." "But, Mr. President," I said, "I am sorry we have got the Philippines. I don't want them and I think you ought to have some man who is more in sympathy with the situation." "You don't want them any less than I do," replied the President, "but we have got them and in dealing with them I think I can trust the man who didn't want them better than I can the man who did."

The dispatch of such a formidable figure as Taft symbolized McKinley's determination gradually to establish civilian rule in the Philippines. The first step was to be the shifting in September 1900 of legislative, though not executive, power from the military governor to Taft's commission. The second would be the transfer of every province, once it had been pacified, to civilian rule until the entire Philippines were under Taft's governorship. McKinley was doing in the Philippines, in conditions of open warfare, what he did not do in Cuba, where there was no fighting. In Cuba Wood remained military commander until the handover to a Cuban president in May 1902; in the Philippines MacArthur was to transfer power to Taft almost a year earlier than that. For the Filipinos the contrast with Spanish rule would have been striking since to the end Spain had maintained military governors in all its colonies.

It was Root who wrote the president's instructions to Taft embodying this novel colonial concept. The secretary of war envisioned a "considerable period" before the complete military to civilian transfer could be completed; meanwhile executive powers would continue to be vested in the military commander. But the commission was charged with establishing municipal and provincial governments immediately. The legislative authority scheduled for September 1, 1900, provided for the enactment of laws on taxes, public spending, and the establishment of schools, civil service, and courts. Governmental power was to be decentralized to small units, as far as possible, and Filipinos were to be given preference for offices. Freedoms patterned after those guaranteed in the U.S. Bill of Rights, including due process, protection of private property, speedy and public trials, and freedom of speech and the press, were declared to take precedence over local laws. Primary education would be free and in English.

Root's instruction to Taft's commission attested to the president's concern for the welfare of the Philippine people:

> . . . the commission should bear in mind that the government which they are establishing is designed, not for our satisfaction or for the expression of our theoretical views, but for the happiness, peace, and prosperity of the people of the Philippine Islands, and the measures adopted should be made to conform to their customs, their habits, and even their prejudices, to the fullest extent consistent with the accomplishment of the indispensable requisites of just and effective government.
>
> . . . Upon all officers and employees of the United States, both civil and military, should be impressed a sense of the duty to observe not merely the material but the personal and social rights of the people of the islands, and to treat them with the same courtesy and respect for their personal dignity which the people of the United States are accustomed to require from each other.

Taft reached Manila with the members of his commission on June 3, 1900. One person who was not glad to see them was Arthur MacArthur. The inherent incompatibility between overlapping civilian and military jurisdictions would have been enough to guarantee friction between the commissioner and any general. But MacArthur's vanity, abrasiveness, and contempt for civilian authority, traits he passed on to his son, Douglas, made conflict inevitable. MacArthur tried to humble the commissioners by keeping them waiting all day in the blistering heat, then receiving them like an Asian potentate. He complained to them that their existence was "humiliating" to him. His obstructiveness spurred Taft to inform his excellent connections in Washington, from the president on down, about what was going on.

The dispute between MacArthur and Taft was not just between two strong personalities bent on amassing power. It was also a duel between concepts. Taft believed the Filipinos were inherently sympathetic to the United States, while MacArthur was convinced that Aguinaldo's support spread far beyond Luzon and his Tagalog group. The first analysis argued for pacification; the second for a military solution. The battle was soon joined over whether the Philippines was better run by a military autocracy or a civilian government. Taft was to win it.

In his four years in the Philippines, Taft proved an extraordinary proconsul. Despite his girth, he got around the archipelago and checked the condition of the people for himself. On one occasion, shortly after he had been ill, Root cabled to ask about his health. Taft replied that he felt so well that he had just taken a long horseback trip into the mountains. Root, always fast with a quip, cabled back: "Fine. How's the horse?" Taft's five-man commission was the smallest legislature in the world and one of the busiest, passing 441 measures in its first year. Taft took a hard line on pressing the war to victory and had little respect for the political capacities of Filipinos. The condescension in his reference to them as "little brown brothers" was real (for a man of Taft's bulk, everyone was little), but so was his dream of a civil society for the islands. In his view it could be achieved by enticing native elites to oppose Aguinaldo and bringing them into the colonial government. While the larger units, the provinces, remained under American control, he established governments at the municipal level under elected Filipino leadership.

Under Taft's governorship, half of it in wartime conditions, the literacy rate rose to the highest in Southeast Asia; malaria and cholera were reduced; infrastructure (dams, ports, roads) was improved; and the judicial and tax systems were made more effective. Taft redistributed the lands of the corrupt and unpopular Catholic friars and urged Congress to allow American investors to purchase large tracts of Philippine land. In this he was opposed by a potent coalition of the virtuous (anti-imperialists) and the voracious (beet sugar interests). In the end Senator Hoar achieved legislation to limit the acreage that Americans could buy, as Foraker had done with Cuba. Taft also fought, with some success, to give Philippine sugar, hemp, coconut oil, and tobacco free access to the U.S. market. Taft's qualities of determination, goodwill, and optimism were key to building stable political institutions and to improving living standards. But he was not a man of vision, and he failed to understand the strong desire for independence among many Filipinos. He was content to sacrifice some democracy in order to govern through the conservative elite. He never considered independence an option.

Aguinaldo, on the run and increasingly desperate, put his faith in a Democratic victory in the U.S. elections of 1900. In September he launched attacks designed to disillusion the American electorate with the war. They boomeranged, for the Filipinos' initial successes were followed by crippling U.S. counterattacks. The election was a huge disappointment to the Philippine cause. Bryan made "imperialism" the primary issue of his campaign, berating his opponent for denying the Filipino people their rights, but he failed to shake the popularity of McKinley's foreign and domestic policies. The president swept to reelection by the largest electoral margin since 1872, and Republicans also won majorities in both houses. The victory gave MacArthur the opportunity to toughen his tactics and further weaken Aguinaldo's forces.

Finally, on March 23, 1901, the rebel leader was captured in northern Luzon via a brilliant ruse designed by a flamboyant Kansan, Colonel Frederick Funston. After a harrowing hundred-mile march, Funston, accompanied by an eighty-man detachment of loyal Filipino Macabebe troops, infiltrated Aguinaldo's camp. The Macabebes impersonated rebel soldiers, while Funston and four other Americans masqueraded as their prisoners. Aguinaldo was seized and returned to Manila, where MacArthur, to Taft's horror, treated him like a guest in his palace. The flattery paid off. In a near replica of what he had done with the Spanish in 1897, Aguinaldo issued a proclamation entreating the guerrillas to stop fighting and the Philippine people to recognize American authority. Although the war continued for more than a year, the capture and defection of the Filipino leader had determined its outcome.

Root now moved to bury the independence movement and establish American civilian control over the Philippines. He had prepared his ground carefully. He had disparaged Aguinaldo's claim to authority by unfairly representing him as a military dictator and a "Chinese half-breed" and arguing that he represented only one tribe out of sixty.

Citing Schurman and Taft, he had scoffed at assertions that the Filipinos were ready for self-government. He had quoted back to Schurz the great anti-imperialist's fashionable belief that democracy does not thrive in the tropics. He had developed an elaborate argument, based on Jefferson's congressional authority to govern the Louisiana Territory, to overturn the hallowed principle set forth in the Declaration of Independence that government derives its just powers from the consent of the governed.

Root's policy toward the Philippines, as toward Puerto Rico and Guam, profited from a series of three decisions by the Supreme Court in 1901 that determined the status of the new island possessions. In these Insular Cases, Attorney General John W. Griggs, arguing personally before the Court, successfully established that the Constitution did not automatically apply to the people of an annexed territory or confer on them all the privileges of U.S. citizenship. The Court ruled that only Congress could extend such constitutional provisions. This finding allowed Root to maintain the islands in a colonial status, in contrast with territories in the continental United States. As he said in interpreting the decision, "As near as I can make out the Constitution follows the flag—but doesn't quite catch up with it."

One issue remained to be resolved. The Treaty of Paris stipulated that the "civil rights and political status" of the native inhabitants of the islands taken from Spain "shall be determined by the Congress." Root wanted to transfer that authority to the executive branch. He worked closely with the scholarly Republican senator from Wisconsin John C. Spooner on an amendment that would vest in the president "all military, civil, and judicial powers necessary to govern the Philippine Islands." Although Senate Democrats, plus that protector of senatorial prerogatives Henry Cabot Lodge, were wary about this massive derogation of legislative power, the amendment went through on March 2, 1901.

As it happened, the Spooner Amendment on the Philippines and the Platt Amendment on Cuba both were attached to the same army appropriations bill. In one piece of legislation, Congress had given the president considerable power in Cuba, which was to become nominally independent, and nearly total power in the Philippines, which was to remain a colony. Root was responsible for both accretions of executive authority. Comfortable as he was with power, he was also mindful of the responsibilities that went with it. The last thing he wanted in the Philippines was a continuation of military dictatorship under the likes of MacArthur. Effective July 4, 1901, he appointed Taft civil governor of the Philippines, to exercise all the civil duties previously exercised by the military governor. The military governor was left in control of those areas, now quite few, in which public order had not been restored. Mr. Dooley noted the contradiction between military and civilian rule in quoting his "frind" Taft: "[I]vry wanst in a while whin I think iv it, an illiction is held. Unforchnitly it usually happens that those illicted have not yet surrindhered."

Root understood that in the new conditions it would be impossible for a demoted MacArthur, susceptible to the smallest bruise to his ego, to work with Taft. The general was relieved and replaced by General Adna Chaffee, who had won praise as commander of the American expeditionary force in China during the Boxer Rebellion. Root held Chaffee on a short leash, warning him that his duties would be strictly military. To Taft he wrote that Chaffee "should get the Army out of the business of government and restore it to its proper and natural place as an adjunct of civil government." As head of the army Root might have been expected to expand its powers into the civilian realm. But as an admirer of British colonial policy, which had placed powerful colonial governors in charge of India, Egypt, and South Africa, he was determined to put Filipinos under clear civilian authority with as many of the protections of the American constitutional system as possible. But he remained equally determined not to make them sovereign. He wrote in 1904 that independence would be "the most fatal possible gift to the people of the Philippine Islands."

5.

For the first two years of American colonial rule in Cuba and the Philippines, Theodore Roosevelt was a bystander, though a highly interested one. From the statehouse in Albany and his house in Oyster Bay, he deluged friends in high places with cascades of analysis and advice. He reacted to Aguinaldo's February 1899 insurrection in Manila with a diatribe against his goo-goo bugbears: "[O]ur friends, the peace-at-any-price Senators and publicists have on their shoulders a heavy load of responsibility." He showered Secretary of State

Hay with praise for the passage of the Treaty of Paris following "the most important year this Republic has seen since Lincoln died": "You have indeed led a life eminently worth living, oh writer of books and doer of deeds!" He lectured Lodge unnecessarily that "unyielding resolution" was the key to victory in the Philippines.

Though meddlesome and belligerent, Roosevelt also showed some sensitivity to the political complexities of America's new imperial obligations. In a long letter to Hay in July 1899, he observed that Puerto Ricans seemed to regret the end of Spanish rule; they must therefore be given "the best type of government." He pushed Wood for the top job in Havana because "we need tact and judgment just as much as we need firmness in Cuba now." By contrast, the war in the Philippines awakened his primordial bellicosity. Tact, judgment, and good government gave way to the need to "smash the insurgents in every way until they are literally beaten into peace." He met with the president shortly after his letter to the secretary of state, presumably to press those points.

A few months later, to another correspondent, Roosevelt exhibited his continued fidelity to the martial spirit: "Oversentimentality, oversoftness, in fact, washiness and mushiness are the great dangers of this age and of this people. Unless we keep the barbarian virtues, gaining the civilized ones will be of little avail. . . . A nation that cannot fight is not worth its salt, no matter how cultivated and refined it may be." Along with the "barbarian virtues" went his core belief in the ennobling qualities of conquest, which he hoped would enhance the American character as in his view, they had enhanced the English. "I am an expansionist," he admitted to Finley Peter Dunne, who was certainly not one.

Roosevelt's deep interest in America's new global mission did not divert him from being a reformist governor in his short two-year term in Albany. His greatest obstacle was Tom Platt, ensconced in Washington as a U.S. senator but still the powerful boss of the state Republican machine and a man full of distrust for Roosevelt and his reformist ideas. For both political and personal reasons, Roosevelt had either to co-opt or to neutralize Platt, who, if antagonized, was strong enough to defeat his legislative program and even to destroy his career. The young governor approached the task with Machiavellian subtlety. He wrote Platt adulatory, sometimes even obsequious letters and met him regularly on Saturdays in New York City, neutral ground between Albany and Washington. Avoiding Platt's headquarters at the Fifth Avenue Hotel, Roosevelt used Corinne's or Bamie's apartment. Before his appointment to Washington, Root, with a foot in both camps, often attended; so did Bamie, whose political judgment her brother always esteemed. Roosevelt's careful handling of Platt proved indispensable because he had resolved on a reform program for the state that would be anathema to the conservative boss.

The issue was joined when the governor supported legislation to tax corporations on the public franchises they controlled, a blow at big business and at Platt's machine. Close as he was to Roosevelt, Root, then still a corporation lawyer, opposed the legislation to the point that it caused a temporary rift between the two men. Platt was as livid as his smooth demeanor allowed. He accused Roosevelt of being "a little loose on the relations of capital and labor," as well as "altruistic" and "populist." The boss squirmed and maneuvered, but Roosevelt won. For good measure, he also succeeded in dismissing the machine-backed superintendent of insurance, a corrupt official in the pocket of the large insurance companies. That was enough for Platt, who decided that Roosevelt had to be removed from New York to a position where he could wield no power and do no harm. Platt publicly suggested that Roosevelt should be the Republican candidate for vice president in 1900.

As Platt and Roosevelt both knew, the vice presidency was a political graveyard. In fact, McKinley's first vice president, a New Jersey politician with no prospects named Garret A. Hobart, died in office. No vice president since Thomas Jefferson had directly succeeded a living president. Roosevelt emphatically did not want the job. He considered it a boring figurehead position, "an irksome, wearisome place where I could do nothing," and a financial drain as well. The costly social obligations would overwhelm the modest annual salary of eight thousand dollars. Though he did not talk about it much, Roosevelt wanted to be president in 1904, after McKinley had finished his second term. He attended a Rough Rider reunion in New Mexico in June 1899 and was thrilled by the crowds thronging the stations along the way, "exactly as if I had been a presidential candidate." He disembarked in Kansas for a chat with William Allen White, the newspaper editor, who immediately wrote: "He is more than a presidential possibility in 1904, he is a presidential probability. . . . He is the coming American of the twentieth century."

For Roosevelt 1899 was not too soon to consider possible paths to the Executive Mansion. The vice presidency was for him the least promising of them. He preferred to run for reelection as governor and for a while persuaded himself that he would have Platt's support. But the hardening enmity of Platt's Republican machine and of the large corporations began to erode his belief in the viability of a second term. For this intensely ambitious governor, the other options were not much better. He continued to covet a place in the foreign affairs spotlight and would have liked to run American policy in the Philippines, either as governor general or as secretary of war. Unfortunately the first position would open too late, not until after Aguinaldo's uprising had been quelled. The second would open too soon; by early 1899 Secretary Alger, thanks partly to Roosevelt's sniping, was on the way out, but Roosevelt was inconveniently just beginning his term as governor. When McKinley appointed Root secretary of war in July 1899, Roosevelt was surprised and a bit jealous, but he had already told the president that he himself could not be a candidate for the position. He briefly considered the Senate, not a natural habitat for such an energetic executive, but was blocked here as well since Platt was planning to run again in 1900 and Roosevelt considered the boss unchallengeable.

As usual, the adviser with the steadiest and surest instincts was Roosevelt's old friend Lodge, who argued consistently that the vice presidency was the best alternative: "If I were a candidate for the Presidency I would take the Vice-Presidency in a minute." Roosevelt admitted Lodge's logic (though Edith did not) but continued to resist. As he mulled his other options, his friend took the initiative of securing agreement in principle from a cautious McKinley that Roosevelt would be an acceptable running mate. As a sweetener, Lodge also suggested to Roosevelt that once Aguinaldo's insurrection was overcome, Roosevelt might move from vice president to governor general of the Philippines. Lodge also persuaded Platt, with little difficulty, to say that Roosevelt had "merely to say the word to have the V.P." Roosevelt, though flattered by Lodge's devotion and activity, continued to ignore his advice. As he wrote Bamie, "the dear old goose actually regards me as a presidential possibility of the future, which always makes me thoroughly exasperated. . . ."

Throughout 1899 and early 1900 Roosevelt debated with himself and with his friends. Much as he despised the vice presidency, he never fully wrote it off. Also, much as he proclaimed his desire to run for a second term in New York, he never could dismiss the dangers. He admitted to Bamie that his chances of reelection in New York were no better than even and that even if he won a second term, the Democrats would probably turn the Republicans out in 1902, auguring for him a decline into obscurity. Still, he persevered. "I myself realize all these chances, but am not only willing, but anxious, to take them," he told his sister.

Lodge persisted. Two months before the Republican National Convention, set for June 1900, he put it to Roosevelt squarely: "If you go to that Convention . . . as a delegate, as I see stated in the newspapers, you will be nominated, . . . and if you are nominated in that Convention you will be unable to refuse." Playing on Roosevelt's Republican loyalties, Lodge circled back to the 1884 convention, when he and Roosevelt had resolved to remain true to the party: "The general feeling is that you are the one man for the Vice-Presidency among those who are looking solely for the interests of the party at large." But he warned that if Roosevelt refused the nomination, he would harm his future national prospects.

In May Roosevelt made a reconnaissance trip to Washington to see the president and apparently to explain why he should not be on the ticket. He seems nevertheless to have expected to be talked out of his reluctance and was outraged when McKinley took him at his word. Hay chortled to a mutual friend: "Teddy has been here; have you heard of it? It was more fun than a goat. He came down with a sombre resolution thrown on his strenuous brow to let McKinley and Hanna know once and for all that he would not be Vice President, and found to his stupefaction that nobody in Washington except Platt had ever dreamed of such a thing."

Despite (or perhaps because of) Lodge's prediction, Roosevelt did attend the convention—"I would be looked upon as rather a coward if I didn't go" made himself as conspicuous as possible in a cowboy hat, and was nominated easily. Only Roosevelt's old nemesis Mark

Hanna expressed fury at the party's decision. "Don't any of you realize," he exploded with more foresight than anybody could know, "that there's only one life between this madman and the Presidency?" Lodge, in order to elevate him, and Platt, in order to get rid of him, had colluded to push Roosevelt into high national office. In the end their victim was all too happy to jump into the briar patch. After the convention he wrote Bamie: "The thing could not be helped. There were two entirely different forces at work. The first was the desire to get me out of New York. . . . [The second] was the feeling of the great bulk of the Republicans that I could strengthen the National ticket and they wanted me on it at all hazards. . . . While of course I should have preferred to stay where there was more work, I would be both ungrateful and a fool not to be deeply touched by the way in which I was nominated." To Lodge he wrote: "Well, old man, I am completely reconciled and I believe it all for the best as regards my own personal interests and it is a great load of personal anxiety off me."

Roosevelt waged the most active vice presidential campaign in history, arguing that McKinley's policy of expansion was neither imperialism nor militarism but a vital part of the history of America from the day it became a nation. In citing the movement west, subject of his own four-volume study, and the acquisition of Florida, Alaska, and Hawaii, he contended that 1898 had brought "no new departures." Driving out Spain was actually "anti-imperialistic," and fighting Aguinaldo was in the interests of the majority of Filipinos. Under Aguinaldo they would simply be put at the mercy of a syndicate of "Chinese half-breeds" (the favored Republican term of art for Aguinaldo), under whom "corruption would flourish far more freely than ever it flourished under Tweed." Tempering his belligerence slightly, Roosevelt did add that the Filipinos "must, of course, be governed primarily in the interests of their own citizens. Our first care must be for the people of the islands who have come under our guardianship as a result of the most righteous foreign war that has been waged within the memory of the present generation."

McKinley's landslide victory, to which Roosevelt's popularity and vigorous campaigning undoubtedly contributed, made the forty-two-year-old governor nominally the second man in the United States. To prepare for his onerous duties as vice president, he took himself off to Colorado for five weeks in pursuit of cougars. (He killed twelve.) After the swearing in he exercised his constitutional role of presiding over the Senate for less than one week, whereupon Congress adjourned for eight months. Roosevelt found the vice presidency just as boring as he had feared. Alfred Mahan consoled him as if he were a convalescent: "You are withdrawn perforce, and not by your own volition, for a prolonged rest from the responsibilities and cares of office." Mahan even compared his situation to Saint Paul's four years of "enforced inactivity" in prison.

Except for a week or two in Washington, Roosevelt divided most of his vice presidential term between Oyster Bay and hunting trips in the West. It was clear that McKinley saw him only as a campaign asset, not as an adviser. To friends Roosevelt complained that the president "does not intend that I shall have any influence of any kind, sort or description in the administration from the top to the bottom." His analysis of the problem was accurate: "Neither he nor Hanna (although I really like both) sympathize with my feelings or feel comfortable about me, because they cannot understand what it is that makes me act in certain ways at certain times, and therefore think me indiscreet and overimpulsive." He told Wood that the vice presidency was "an utterly anomalous office" that ought to be abolished. "The man who occupies it may at any moment be everything, but meanwhile he is practically nothing." In general, in his own words, this was a "time of slack water."

It was also a time of long-range political planning. His popularity with the crowds in Illinois, Missouri, and Kansas along his route to Colorado in August had started the political sap rising. When he returned, he sent Lodge, who was traveling in Europe, a detailed analysis of his presidential chances for 1904, based on the support he was shown in the West. "The trip was a revelation to me . . . the men who spoke to me were not nobodies." On the negative side was his belief that his own state of New York would be against him, but he felt confident about New England and parts of the South. A week after his letter to Lodge, he wrote William Allen White that he was working out a presidential strategy.

The irony of this planning was that it was unnecessary. Ten days after Roosevelt's letter to White, on September 6, 1901, President McKinley was shot by a deranged young man at the mammoth Pan-American Exposition in Buffalo. As the assailant was knocked down and beaten and the stricken president helped to a chair, McKinley, courteous to the last, said, "Don't let them hurt him," then implored an aide to take care how he informed the president's wife. McKinley hung on for eight days, during which time there was hope for his recovery. But gangrene set in, and he died on September 14.

McKinley died as he had lived, an enigmatic figure. The most pacific and civil of men, he had nevertheless launched a war that led to the subjugation of Cuba and Puerto Rico and to a three-year conflict in the Philippines. He never could bring himself to be proud of what he had accomplished. The year before his death, as the U.S. Army was locked in the conflict with Aguinaldo's forces, he confided to his former private secretary that "the declaration of war against Spain was an act which has been and will always be the greatest grief of my life." Whether he liked it or not, McKinley's greatest legacy was America's overseas empire. His next greatest was the quality of the men he chose to run it. Henry Adams was right that he was a "magnificent manager of men." Hay for the State Department, Wood for Cuba, Root for the War Department, and Taft for the Philippines: All were McKinley's personal choices, and the last two were unexpected and unorthodox. All four made a genuine effort to carry out McKinley's wish that the United States should govern for the benefit of the native populations. McKinley also selected Roosevelt twice—for assistant secretary of the navy and for vice president—although both times he made the choice with well-founded trepidation.

Roosevelt had sped to Buffalo from an island in Lake Champlain after receiving word of the shooting, then left the president's bedside when he improved. The news of McKinley's death found him in an even more remote place, a mountain in the Adirondacks. Having rushed back to Buffalo, he was sworn in as the twenty-sixth president of the United States in the library of the house in which he had stayed the week before. Root, the senior cabinet official present, presided. In formulaic and reassuring words on taking the oath of office, Roosevelt pledged to continue the policy of President McKinley "for the peace, the prosperity, and the honor of our beloved country." In a mixture of humility and resolve, he wrote Lodge the week after: "It is a dreadful thing to come into the Presidency this way; but it would be a far worse thing to be morbid about it. Here is the task, and I have got to do it to the best of my ability; and that is all there is about it."

Thus Theodore Roosevelt achieved, by tragic accident, the goal on which he had set his heart for most of his adult life. It is perhaps too much to state categorically that he would never have won it without the wisdom and persistence of Henry Cabot Lodge. Roosevelt was after all the most dynamic politician in the United States and one of the youngest. With or without Lodge, his chances for the presidency would have seemed bright. Still, Lodge gave him two things he lacked, self-confidence and an effective political strategy. Except for the governorship of New York, which fell in Roosevelt's lap, Lodge was involved in virtually every career move that made him a phenomenon in American politics: the decision not to quit the party in 1884, the decision to go on the Civil Service Commission, the decision to accept New York City police commissioner, the campaign to become assistant secretary of the navy, the difficult decision to run for vice president. Roosevelt credited Lodge with all his successes. Even before McKinley's death, he wrote his friend: "You are the only man whom, in all my life, I have met who has repeatedly and in every way done for me what I could not do for myself, and what nobody else could do, and done it in a way that merely makes me glad to be under obligation to you."

Young as he was—not yet forty-three, the youngest president in history—Roosevelt was superbly prepared for the office. He was a war hero and a popular writer who had held high political office in city, state, and national government. He was known and respected in all parts of the country. Moreover, having gained an office for which he had not run, he was not saddled with the usual campaign commitments. At the same time, he had inherited McKinley's problems without having had the prior opportunity to deal with them on any level beyond the rhetorical. Not the least of these problems was the war in the Philippines, which was winding down but also growing more brutal and provoking more intense criticism in the United States. It was now Roosevelt's war.

6.

The new president's private views about the Philippines were more thoughtful than the militant themes he had hammered during the 1900 campaign. He was still a militarist, an expansionist, and a worshiper of British imperialism, but part of him doubted the justice and stamina of a colonial vocation for the United States. Two months before McKinley's assassination, for example, he wrote a New York lawyer: "While I have never varied in my feeling that we had to hold the Philippines, I have varied very much in my feelings whether we were to be considered fortunate or unfortunate in having to hold them, and I most earnestly hope that the trend of events will as speedily as may be justify us in leaving them. . . . I am perfectly clear that we do not want to expand over another people capable of self-government unless that people desires to go with us—and not necessarily even then." Even on the Caribbean, he sounded strikingly moderate: "Barring the possible necessity of fortifying the Isthmian canal, or getting a naval station, I hope it will not become our duty to take a foot of soil south of us."

There was, however, no ambivalence in his first public treatment of colonial issues in his first message to Congress in December 1901. He defended the acquisition of Hawaii and the Spanish islands, called for strengthening the Monroe Doctrine against European threats, urged a near doubling of battleship construction, and advocated the building of an isthmian canal as "one of those great works which only a great nation can undertake with prospects of success." He made a bow toward self-government in the Philippines but not at the cost of abandoning them: "To leave the islands at this time would mean that they would fall into a welter of murderous anarchy. Such dereliction of duty on our part would be a crime against humanity."

On the ground, the Philippine war had become dirtier as it fragmented into a series of regional struggles. In a classic, if one-sided, description of the challenge of guerrilla war to an army unaccustomed to it, Root told the Congress after it had ended that U.S. forces were

required to crush out a general system of guerrilla warfare conducted among a people speaking unknown tongues, from whom it was almost impossible to obtain the information necessary for successful pursuit or to guard against surprise and ambush.

The enemies by whom they were surrounded were regardless heedless of all obligations of good faith and of all the limitations which humanity has imposed upon civilized warfare. Bound themselves by the laws of war, our soldiers were called upon to meet every device of unscrupulous treachery and to contemplate without reprisal the infliction of barbarous cruelties upon their comrades and friendly natives. They were instructed, while punishing armed resistance, to conciliate the friendship of the peaceful, yet had to do so with a population among whom it was impossible to distinguish friend from foe, and who in countless instances, used a false appearance of friendship for ambush and assassination.

In support of his assertion that the Filipinos inflicted "barbarous cruelties," Root and other American spokesmen were wont to quote an order allegedly issued during the Battle of Manila by the rebel general Antonio Luna calling for the extermination of non-Filipinos. Whether the order was authentic or not, it was not an adequate description of Filipino behavior during the course of the war. Neither Aguinaldo nor his senior officers pursued a policy of systematic terrorism against Americans. In fact Aguinaldo insisted that American prisoners be treated humanely, and with some notable exceptions, they were. The exceptions were certainly barbaric. Some American prisoners were buried alive with their heads coated with molasses to attract ants; some had their feet cut off or their eyes gouged out; some were simply shot.

The Filipino view of the morality of their guerrilla tactics was colored by the conviction that they were fighting in their own country for their own freedom and that the Americans were invaders sent to crush a native revolution. The guerrillas were systematically savage with Filipinos who opposed them, particularly those who had collaborated with the Americans. Rebel-committed atrocities increased toward the end of the war as the pacification program took hold, the insurgents suffered severe military losses, and the U.S. Army started to execute guerrillas for war crimes.

For its part, the American command adopted, and sought to implement, principles of humane conduct. The strong instructions to the Schurman and Taft commissions to act in the interests of the Philippine people were reinforced by General Otis's April 1899 military directive calling for "kind and considerate treatment" of Philippine citizens. American military occupiers were also restrained by General Orders 100, signed by Abraham Lincoln during the Civil War and enjoining U.S. troops to maintain order, respect private property, and treat the local population justly and humanely. These inhibitions did not apply to continued resistance, however; retaliation against guerrillas was condoned. McKinley, Taft, and Otis believed strongly in the morality of their actions; they believed that the war was by and large clean and that they were altruistically assisting a backward civilization with schools, hospitals, and roads.

That was not, however, the way many officers and men saw the war. The cruder among them dismissed the Filipinos as small, dark, and treacherous barbarians and defined the army's mission as pushing them out of the way. Racial slurs abounded; the rebels were "niggers," "savages," or "goo-goos." (The other "goo-goos," the anti-imperialists at home, were subjected to the same invective by the troops.) The experience of generals and other officers in fighting Indians contributed to the view that the Filipinos should be handled in the same way. One Kansas soldier told a reporter: "The country won't be pacified until the niggers are killed off like the Indians." In fact the triumphal spirit with which American soldiers looked back on the conquest of the West became a corrupting motivation in the war against Filipinos.

Taft's civic program did not go down well with such soldiers, who believed that it weakened their military purpose and dignified a malicious enemy. A jingle made the rounds of the camps satirizing the governor's reference to the Filipinos as "little brown brothers":

> *They say I've got brown brothers here,*
> *But still I draw the line.*
> *He may be a brother of Big Bill Taft,*
> *But he ain't no brother of mine.*

An even coarser marching song castigated the enemy in tones both frustrated and aggressive:

> *Damn, damn, damn the Filipinos!*
> *Cut-throat Khakiac ladrones [thieves]!*
> *Underneath the starry flag*
> *Civilize them with a Krag*
> *And return us to our beloved home.*

The pacification policy favored by Otis and Taft—a "grandmother-ish system," according to one private—was not based on civilizing them "with a Krag." But Otis's successor MacArthur began to down-play pacification in the interest of harsher methods aimed at military successes; he initiated or augmented coercive and brutal measures that stretched the restraints in the general orders. In parts of the country MacArthur adopted a "concentration" policy of herding civilians into "protected zones," outside which the army could treat everyone as an enemy. The similarity with General Weyler's reconcen-tration policy in Cuba was not lost on the anti-imperialists at home, although the American version was less widespread and less costly in human lives.

Outside the "protected zones," the Americans launched a cam-paign of property destruction, mostly by wholesale burnings. General Samuel Young, a cavalry brigade commander who had won Roosevelt's admiration in Cuba, considered "the judicious application of the torch" the most humane way of waging a conflict between races. Un-fortunately, Young's brand of humanity consisted of burning to the ground villages suspected of sympathy to the guerrillas, sometimes with the villagers inside their houses. He also advocated to his superi-ors the summary execution of guerrillas.

Retributive tortures and executions increased. MacArthur ordered that captured guerrillas be denied prisoner of war status. Thus it be-came easier for American soldiers to take revenge for such enemy tac-tics as attacks by guerrillas disguised as civilians, violations of flags of truce, and the torture of U.S. prisoners. Torture became a common American practice during searches for information or weapons. Se-nior officers, if not confronted with evidence of torture, often looked the other way. Some officers were themselves liable to murderous be-havior; the charismatic Funston was one. He bragged in one case of executing twenty-four prisoners in revenge for a fellow officer butchered by rebels; in another he boasted of hanging thirty-five civil-ians suspected of rebel activity. The most notorious interrogation technique was the so-called water cure, in which (as described by an eyewitness) "the victim is laid flat on his back and held down by his tormentors. Then a bamboo tube is thrust into his mouth and some dirty water, the filthier the better, is poured down his unwilling throat." This form of torture, which sometimes proved fatal, was never officially sanctioned but was in common use.

Toward the end of the war, after Roosevelt had become president, atrocities on both sides multiplied. General Chaffee proved to be as tough a commander as his predecessor MacArthur. He authorized General J. Franklin Bell to carry out a murderous sweep of Batangas Province in southwestern Luzon. Acting under orders he had written himself, Bell ordered the execution of prisoners by lot in retaliation for assassinations. He punished priests, local officials, and community leaders for refusing to provide information. He told his men that the innocent must inevitably suffer with the guilty and encouraged young officers to act without restraint or senior review. Taking MacArthur's protected zones approach to its limit, Bell forced villagers into camps, then destroyed what was outside: crops, animals, houses, even human beings. Even after he knew of the deadly results of Bell's zeal, Chaffee endorsed his approach as necessary.

The most baleful encounter of the war occurred on the eastern island of Samar at Balangiga. The American company commander, an idealistic and priggish West Pointer named Thomas W. Connell, had set out to improve the morals of the village and of his own troops. Somehow he managed to antagonize both sides; worse, his intelligence failed to pick up the hundred guerrillas who had infiltrated a native work crew. At reveille on a Sunday morning, the guerrillas threw off their disguises and attacked. Connell, his two fellow officers, and fifty-six American soldiers were killed, some horribly mutilated.

It was the worst massacre of American soldiers since Custer's debacle at Little Bighorn a quarter century before, and it provoked a bloody retaliation. Chaffee gave the Samar command to General Jacob Smith, one of the most primitive of the American officers and a veteran of the U.S. massacre of Sioux Indians at Wounded Knee in 1890. Smith's orders, according to the testimony of a subordinate, were: "I want no prisoners. I wish you to kill and burn, the more you kill and burn the better it will please me. I want all persons killed who are capable of bearing arms in actual hostilities against the United States." Asked the minimum age of a person capable of bearing arms, Smith replied, "Ten years of age." He later allegedly declared that "the interior of Samar must be made a howling wilderness."

Whether Smith actually made the statements attributed to him, he and his subordinates acted as if he had. The Samar campaign was characterized by wholesale destruction of property, execution of prisoners, kidnapping of civilians, and outright murder. When American marines came upon any possessions belonging to a soldier massacred at Balangiga, they killed virtually everyone in the area. The conduct of American forces on Samar under Smith, as well as in Batangas under Bell, departed further from the laws of war than U.S. actions in any other parts of the Philippines. Smith was court-martialed and convicted in May 1902. But after the war Generals Young, Chaffee, and Bell, three of the most ruthless American commanders in the Philippines, were named successively by Roosevelt as army chiefs of staff, an indication of what the president, even on reflection, really thought about the harshness of the U.S. Army's conduct.

Roosevelt was close to General Chaffee; he had fought alongside him in Cuba and had helped persuade McKinley to give him the Philippine command. As president Roosevelt encouraged Chaffee in his tough approach toward the rebels. He did not want to hear bad news about atrocities, and he dismissed the attacks by Twain, Hoar, and the other goo-goos as serving the enemy. It was unfortunate that the only case made from inside the government on behalf of the victims of the army's brutality should have been pursued by General Miles, the army chief of staff and a man universally despised as vain and ambitious by Roosevelt and his cabinet.

Miles made an inspection tour of the Philippines with the president's reluctant acquiescence. He returned with scathing evidence against Bell and others and publicized his findings, enraging a president who had assured his secretary of war that "the warfare in the Philippines has been conducted by our troops with very great leniency." In retaliation Roosevelt prevailed on France to withdraw the award of the Legion of Honor that had been planned for Miles. The chief of staff's efforts did lead to the trial of three more officers, including Major Edwin Glenn, a notorious sadist who admitted to ordering forty-seven prisoners bayoneted and clubbed to death. All three were acquitted on the ground that they were simply following General Chaffee's orders to gain information "no matter what measures have to be adopted."

Roosevelt's natural militancy, plus his desire to end the war, would probably have blinded him to reports of brutality by American forces even if they had not been spread by his domestic enemies. Several months later, in a more reflective mood, he wrote a German friend, the diplomat Hermann Speck von Sternberg, that "there have been some blots on the record." He seemed most disturbed by officers "talking with loose and violent brutality" and singled out General Smith for having spoken about "shooting niggers." But Roosevelt dismissed the water cure as an "old Filipino method of mild torture" in which "nobody was seriously damaged," and his summary arguments to Speck would not have inspired confidence in his humane convictions: "I have taken care that the army should understand that I thoroughly believe in severe measures when necessary, and am not in the least sensitive about killing any number of men if there is adequate reason. But I do not like torture or needless brutality of any kind, and I do not believe in the officers of high rank continually using language which is certain to make the less intelligent or more brutal of their subordinates commit occasional outrages."

The outcry in the American press about atrocities was so strong that the Senate, pushed by Hoar, held hearings beginning in January 1902. Lodge, as head of the Standing Committee on the Philippines, was in the chair. He was not sympathetic to the charges against the army or to investigating them. His own view of the war was narrow: "We make no hypocritical pretense of being interested in the Philippines solely on account of others. While we regard the welfare of these people as a sacred trust, we regard the welfare of the American people first." He ensured that favorable witnesses dominated the hearings and tried to turn them against anti-imperialist critics. Taft, whose testimony took up most of the first month, was honest enough to admit occasional use of the water cure but contended that "there never was a war conducted, whether against inferior races or not, in which there were more compassion and more restraint and more generosity . . . than there have been in the Philippine Islands."

General R. P. Hughes, who had served under all three military commanders, did not help the hard-liners when he defended the U.S. Army's departure from the rules of civilized warfare by arguing that the Filipinos were not civilized. David P. Barrows, who had run the school system in the Philippines, downplayed the water cure as harmless and claimed incredibly that the natives flocked to the camps of their own free will. The three former commanders made ineffective witnesses. Admiral Dewey used the hearings to backtrack on his earlier expressed admiration for Aguinaldo. General Otis maintained that the war had ended when he departed two years before and claimed that Spanish and other European military observers laughed at the Americans "for the humanity we exercised." General MacArthur numbed his audience with an impenetrable bombast that rarely touched on the Philippines. Senator Beveridge removed from the transcript the criticisms of the army by other witnesses before publishing it as a Senate document.

Root believed, as he said in a letter in 1899, that "it is not a function of law to enforce the rules of morality." He had paid no attention to charges of atrocity until the Senate hearings alerted him to this major public relations problem. His first instinct was to defend the army with a show of reasonableness. He rushed into print a white paper purporting to show that brutal conduct by American soldiers was rare and was severely punished. The anti-imperialists had a field day with the document. Moorfield Storey published a long pamphlet claiming that the trials were pro forma and the punishments light and that Root was guilty of suppressing or misstating information. Storey cited one instance in which Root buried a report, filed by a West Pointer serving as governor in a province adjoining Batangas, that charged General Bell with causing one hundred thousand deaths. Storey's verdict was that Root "was silent in the face of certain knowledge and by his silence he made himself responsible for all that was done with his acquiescence."

As there was mounting evidence of atrocities, especially General Smith's rampage in Samar, Root became more attentive to moral principle. He ordered courts-martial for officers accused of using the water cure and also pressed for military trials of mid-level officers involved in other atrocities. He was probably behind Smith's court-martial, which was opposed by Chaffee, the military commander, who may have feared he would be next in the dock. But Root had no answer to the army's judicial leniency; except for Smith, the most infamous, if not the most egregious, example the culprits were getting off lightly. In April 1902 Root issued a tardy but strong instruction to Chaffee—immediately leaked to the press by the administration—on the subject of courts-martial:

you will spare no effort . . . to uncover every such case which may have occurred and bring the offenders to justice.

The President desires to know in the fullest and most circumstantial manner all the facts, nothing being concealed, and no man being for any reason favored or shielded. . . . Great as the provocation has been in dealing with foes who habitually resort to treachery, murder and torture against our men, nothing can justify or will be held to justify, the use of torture or inhuman conduct of any kind on the part of the American Army.

Had instructions of this rigor been issued earlier in the war, many atrocities might have been prevented. Of all people, Root, with his passion for the establishment of civil government in the Philippines, should have seen the damage military brutality did to the aims of pacification. Yet even after the war's end Root remained defensive. Acts of cruel and inhuman treatment, he said in September 1902, "were not justified, and they could not be justified, but spread over years of conflict, over a vast extent of territory, over thousands of engagements and skirmishes and expeditions, in which, first and last, 130,000 of our troops were engaged, they were few and far between—exceptions in a uniform course of self-restraint, humanity and kindness." The laxity of his moral standards could be measured by his praise of the execrable Funston as "gallant and fearless." The defender of Boss Tweed had once again let his lawyerly instincts overcome his moral sense.

Roosevelt, like Root, was embarrassed but not outraged by the atrocities. In May 1902 he told Root to have Taft appoint a commission to report on the conduct of General Chaffee and "whether or not any brutalities or indignities are inflicted by the army upon the natives." The president suggested it be composed of three men, including one Filipino. The commission turned out to be a whitewash operation and seems to have been intended as such. On the basis of its investigations the president reported to the Congress that there had been "individual instances of wrong-doing" accounted for by the climate and native provocations but that the guilty, like General Smith, had been sought out and punished. On the whole, Roosevelt reported, "few indeed have been the instances in which war has been waged by a civilized power against semi-civilized or barbarous forces where there has been so little wrong-doing by the victors as in the Philippine Islands."

On July 4, 1902, the president declared the war officially over, calling it the most glorious war in the nation's history. Pockets of resistance remained in Luzon, Samar, and—most tenaciously—Mindanao, where a Muslim sect (the Moros) harassed the American occupiers for decades. When Wood became military governor of Moro province in 1903, he fought the rebels with such ruthlessness that Mark Twain and other anti-imperialists accused him of massacres. John J. Pershing made his career in fighting the Moros; Roosevelt jumped his promotion to brigadier general after his first campaign against them. But these military side issues apart, America had won the war, though how gloriously is debatable. It had cost the United States some four hundred million dollars, twenty times the price paid to Spain for the Philippines. U.S. killed were 4,234, a creditable casualty rate for a three-year engagement; Shafter had lost 1,000 in Cuba in only three weeks. By U.S. Army estimates Filipino military losses were about 20,000. As in Cuba, there were many civilian deaths from disease—up to 200,000, according to most estimates.

While the U.S. Army was fighting the rebels in the Philippines, the scramble for Africa by the European powers was just ending. How the Americans dealt with Filipinos on their own territory warrants comparison with the European treatment of native Africans on theirs. Unlike the American experience in the Pacific, much of European colonialism in Africa was driven by explorers rather than governments, which were reluctant to assume the costs of exploration. Adventurers like Henry Morton Stanley and Cecil Rhodes operated with a latitude that American military officers did not have; these and other empire builders were prone to promiscuous violence.

The comparison is most apt in African areas where European governments were directly involved. At their worst they far surpassed the Americans in brutality. King Leopold II of Belgium presided over a rapacious system in the Congo designed to extract rubber through the use of forced labor; its effect on the population was genocidal. In Southwest Africa the German military commander issued an "extermination order" against the members of a rebellious tribe. On pain of being shot if found on German territory, men, women, and children were driven into the desert, where more than twenty thousand died.

Even the British, so admired by Roosevelt, Root, and Hay, had their lapses. The famous General Horatio Kitchener commanded British troops in the Boer War, which was fought at the same time as the Philippine war, to put down a rebellion by Dutch inhabitants of southern Africa against British colonial rule. Kitchener set up a system of concentration camps—the euphemism was "camps of refuge"—into which he herded neutral Boer refugees and the families of Boers engaged in fighting the British. Outside the camps he burned the farms of combatants and drove off their horses and cattle. Inside the camps the hygiene was so poor that women and children died in droves of typhoid, dysentery, and measles, a third of the camp population, by one estimate. Far from being punished, Kitchener went on to become a field marshal, an earl, and a cabinet minister. As a result of the war won by his ruthless methods, the British government approved a constitution for a South African union that, to appease the Boers, was blatantly racist against the black population.

Against these European outrages—one of them perpetrated against a "civilized" people—American atrocities appeared less extreme. Nevertheless, they fell far short of the God-driven definition of American ideals that Beveridge and Lodge in the Senate and Roosevelt and Root in the administration persisted in using. If what America stood for in the world was so exceptional, as they asserted, then American standards were loftier than those of cynical Europe. In failing to meet them, the country failed not its European rivals but itself.

The Vietnam War of the 1960s and 1970s was the only other war in U.S. history to rival the Philippine war in provoking widespread condemnation by Americans. In one sense the wars were not really comparable. The Philippine conflict was a classical colonial war, whereas in Vietnam the United States was fighting to reestablish the authority of an internationally recognized local regime. The government of the Republic of Vietnam, through its weakness and corruption, proved as much a liability as an asset to the Americans. The Americans had a huge preponderance in firepower in Vietnam, much greater than in the Philippines, but here too the advantage was at least partly negated by the character of the war.

In virtually all other respects the American effort in the Philippines enjoyed assets that were lacking in the Vietnam counterinsurgency. They explain why the United States won the first war and lost the second. Aguinaldo had no recourse to outside aid, which helped the North Vietnamese forces narrow the military disparity. He did not have officers to compare with those of North Vietnam, who had gained valuable experience in their earlier successful rebellion against France. Nor could his forces use sanctuaries comparable to Laos, Cambodia, and North Vietnam itself. The Filipinos were disunited both ethnically and socially, while the North Vietnamese had on their side a common ethnicity, a strong ideology, and a willingness to sacrifice themselves. As William Bundy, an American official who helped prosecute the Vietnam War, observed, the North Vietnamese were prepared to die more than the Americans were prepared to kill.

Finally, the American pacification effort, which was to fail in Vietnam, proved in the Philippines a key factor in weakening rebel unity and support. Pacification had benefits that lasted beyond the war. The determination of Root and Taft to establish a legal and fair civil society as early as possible, even in wartime conditions, paid dividends. Pacification brought more democracy to Filipinos than other Asian peoples enjoyed; by 1907 the Philippines had the first elected legislature in Asia.

The Philippines had now become a vital possession and a necessity to America's status as a great power. If the United States rejected them, Lodge said on the floor of the Senate, "it would be inevitable that we should sink out from among the great powers of the world." The grand alternative, he proclaimed, was to "follow the laws of our being, the laws in obedience to which we have come to be what we are, and then we shall stretch out into the Pacific; we shall stand in the front rank of the world powers; we shall give to our labor and our industry new and larger and better opportunities . . . ; we shall prosper ourselves; and we shall benefit mankind." He concluded on a messianic note: "I do not believe that this nation was an accident. I do not believe that it is the creation of blind chance. I have faith that it has a great mission in the world—a mission of good, a mission of freedom."

With the end of the wars of 1898–1902, the United States was already, as Lodge said, "in the front rank of the world powers." Moreover, as Kipling predicted, Americans had been through "a savage war of peace" and had won it at some cost to their innocence. They now had colonial possessions in the Philippines and Puerto Rico and a protectorate in Cuba. The first years of their colonial authority exposed characteristically American traits, both admirable and condemnable. A superior attitude toward the natives, sometimes descending into racism, prevailed on all three islands. It came in different varieties, from the soldiers' crude contempt for the "niggers" to the more intellectualized views of the civilian leaders that the local peoples were not ready for self-government. In both Cuba and the Philippines, the United States had behaved with considerable arrogance toward people who sought to map their own future on their own land and had thus managed to alienate an insurgent population that wanted to be on the American side.

At the same time, Americans deeply and generously felt an obligation to improve the condition of their colonial subjects. In the Senate this obligation could deteriorate into the bombast of Beveridge or the intolerance of Lodge. But Congress also tried to protect the Philippines and Cuba from predatory American business interests, liberalized the suffrage in Hawaii, and granted at least partial independence to Cuba. In the executive branch and in the field, reform was pursued with tenacity, setting American colonialism above its European (even its British) counterparts. Root was a colonial strategist of genius, and Wood and Taft were as effective colonial administrators as any in the world. The inspiration for their progressive approach came from William McKinley, who translated his own common decency and generous spirit into a genuine concern for the island peoples. Many of the best elements of American colonialism are traceable to this modest president.

Unfortunately America's leaders betrayed a timidity of approach that deprived them of what might have been admirable foreign policy achievements. American brutality in the Philippines could not be explained away by the exigencies of guerrilla warfare. Root, letting his legal instincts dominate his moral ones, was too cautious to take on the army, even though its chief of staff would have helped him. Roosevelt, in the early months of his presidency, was too obsessed with his vicarious experience with American Indians and the mystique of his Cuban exploits to do anything that smacked of weakness. In writing and action, he had crudely and blindly exalted the splendors of war, and he applied the same spurious euphoria to the grubby war in the Philippines, worrying more about what American commanders said to their troops than about what they were doing to Filipino soldiers and civilians. Roosevelt and Root tolerated the atrocities, finding a scapegoat here and there but essentially explaining away and covering up. It was a black mark on Roosevelt's young presidency.

The Americans were also unwilling to devolve sovereignty on to peoples clearly eager to run their own affairs. Colonial administrators preferred to deal with conservative local oligarchs who often misled them about the strength of anti-American feelings in the population. Naïvely sensing popular support for their rule, they believed they were free to limit self-government. There were no early thoughts of awarding a higher status to Puerto Rico or the Philippines within the United States or of giving them independence, even though a large proportion of Filipinos had fought for their freedom. The Cuban solution was even murkier: independence with so many strings attached that significant elements of sovereignty remained with the United States. It was a poor outcome for Cuba, and not much better for the United States, which now had to influence Cuban affairs by remote control. If Root and his colonial managers had transformed their energy from a commendable paternalism to a greater trust in their colonial subjects, the new empire might have embarked on a course more in keeping with the richer elements of American tradition. As it was, the expansionist tradition overwhelmed the democratic one.

11. The Imperial Presidency

1.

Theodore Roosevelt's presidency, from 1901 to 1909, marked the consolidation of the United States as a world power. Building on the triumphs of 1898, America became the dominant force in the Caribbean and a major presence in Asia. Its navy ranked with the best; Roosevelt sent it around the world in a show of strength that won the respect of some and aroused the consternation of others. It established a "special relationship," which would last out the century, with the foremost naval power, Great Britain. It came to be consulted on the important issues of the day; Roosevelt himself negotiated an end to the Russo-Japanese War. In the words of Alfred Mahan, now a full-time pundit, "Imperialism, the extension of national authority over alien communities, is a dominant note in the world-politics of to-day." With its new empire, small as it was compared with European colonial holdings, the United States had won a place at the table of world powers.

Roosevelt's first term, though truncated by half a year, was a particularly fecund period in the growth of America's status as a great power. Elihu Root, as secretary of war, established mechanisms for government in Cuba, Puerto Rico, and the Philippines. At the State Department John Hay was charged with clearing the diplomatic path toward the construction of an isthmian canal, securing hegemony in the Caribbean and Central America, establishing American credentials in the scramble to open up the enticing market with China, and resolving disputes with the British, including defining the boundary between Canada and Alaska. With hands-on leadership from an activist president, Hay managed all these challenges with conspicuous success.

If Hay had not already been in office when President McKinley was assassinated, he would probably not have been Roosevelt's choice for secretary of state. The new president had promised continuity; keeping Hay and Root in place would fulfill that pledge. But Roosevelt gave an early indication of his opinion of the two men: he cancelled McKinley's plan to move the colonial administration from Root's war department to Hay's state department. The president kept Hay on because he was fond of him and because the secretary was highly regarded in the country. Roosevelt had a long and deep relationship with Hay, his father's friend and benefactor. He liked Hay's company, enjoyed his wit, and admired his modesty. "There was not in his nature the slightest touch of the demagogue," he told Lodge. After church on Sundays the president was given to stopping off at Hay's grand house on Lafayette Park for an hour's chat on his way back to the White House. When Hay gave him a ring containing a lock of Lincoln's hair, he wrote: "I wonder if you have any idea what your strength and wisdom and sympathy, what the guidance you have given me and the mere delight in your companionship, have meant to me."

Yet behind Hay's back and after his death, Roosevelt was not so respectful. He considered Hay weak in conviction, insufficiently committed to a muscular policy of expansion, and so friendly to Britain and hostile to Germany that he could not be trusted to deal with either. He ridiculed Hay's devotion to all things British and took jealous umbrage that the secretary, in congratulating Arthur Balfour's elevation to British prime minister in 1902, had called that position "the most important official post known to modern history." After Hay's death in 1905, Roosevelt, writing to Lodge, pronounced him "not a great Secretary of State. . . . He had a very ease-loving nature and a moral timidity which made him shrink from all that was rough in life, and therefore from practical affairs. He was at his best at a dinner table or in a drawing room, and in neither place have I ever seen anyone's best that was better than his. . . . In public life during the time he was Secretary of State under me he accomplished little. . . . In the Department of State his usefulness to me was almost exclusively the usefulness of a fine figurehead." Roosevelt distrusted Hay's competence: "I had to do all the big things myself, and the other things, I always feared would be badly done." This crabby evaluation was partly true but unfair. It was surely influenced by Roosevelt's resentment that the media-savvy Hay sometimes got more credit than his chief and by the marked difference in their hare vs. tortoise operating styles. In fact Hay's fingerprints were all over most of Roosevelt's first-term foreign policy successes.

Hay considered Roosevelt something of a blowhard and enjoyed lampooning him. For Hay it had been "more fun than a goat" when Roosevelt made a fool of himself in Washington over the vice presidency. Once Roosevelt ascended to the presidency, however, Hay gave him total loyalty, at the expense of his own feeble and declining health. But he chafed at the president's frenetic management style. He recalled wistfully that McKinley had seen him less than once a month; with Roosevelt it was every day. Hay hated the frequent summonses to Oyster Bay and the way he was treated when he got there: "When McKinley sent for me he gave me all his time till we got through; but I always find TR engaged with a dozen other people, and it is an hour's wait and a minute's talk." He recoiled at Roosevelt's impetuosity: "The President is all right, provided you can restrain him for the first fifteen minutes after he has conceived a new idea."

While the secretary was too loyal to disagree with the president, his views tended to be softer than Roosevelt's. He was less than a fervent imperialist. In 1884 he had published an antiannexation poem about Hawaii pleading: "Oh, may we long postpone the evil hour, / When in our zeal for making others free, / We join them with us." More recently he had remarked to Henry Adams that Roosevelt was trying to "steal" Panama. As ambassador in London he had not welcomed the war against Spain and, even after his appointment as secretary of state, had told Andrew Carnegie so. Once in office, however, he had sent tough instructions to the team negotiating the peace treaty.

Hay's early thinking on the Philippines had been marked more by concern for fair treatment of the natives than by strategic objectives. Like Root, he was uncomfortable with Roosevelt's animosity toward big business. He refused to hide his Anglophilia or to cater to the Britain bashing pushed mainly by Irish-Americans. Why, he wondered, should "we . . . be compelled to refuse the assistance of the greatest Power in the world, in carrying out our own policy, because all Irishmen are Democrats and some Germans are fools."

Hay lacked the dynamism and fervor that Roosevelt embodied and increasingly saw in Root. Unlike his chief, Hay was almost entirely without ambition. He had not wanted to be secretary of state when McKinley named him; as Henry Adams wrote, "his obedience to the President's order was the gloomiest acquiescence he had ever smiled." Still less did he want to continue after McKinley was killed. The dead president was the third assassinated leader, after Lincoln and Garfield, to whom Hay had been close. In that same terrible year of 1901, Hay lost his son Del (who fell out of a window at his Yale reunion), his close friend and Five of Hearts member Clarence King, and his lifelong friend and Lincoln coauthor John Nicolay. "I have acquired the funeral habit," he mused. He tried to resign at the beginning of Roosevelt's presidency, citing "my grief for the President mingled and confused with that for my boy." But the new president insisted on his remaining in office.

The State Department that Hay took over was far from the expert-laden, high-tech, rapid-reaction institution of today. It shared with the War and Navy departments the French Second Empire building at Pennsylvania and Seventeenth streets next door to the White House. It was and is a structure that in its flamboyance contrasts with the dour and immobile monstrosities in the style of classical Greece that house much of official Washington. In these ornate premises, with their high ceilings, grand staircases, and omnipresent marble, Hay presided in a large office now used as a conference room.

But his domain was minuscule for a burgeoning country like the United States. The department had a mere eighty-two employees, and even they were not allocated enough space. Abroad America's thirty-five diplomatic missions were staffed by fewer than seventy diplomats—the number had not increased since Hay had begun his diplomatic career three decades before—plus sixteen military attachés. The rank of ambassador had been created only five years before; Hay in London had been one of the first ambassadors. A vast consular corps of more than a thousand people (not all Americans) populated 323 consular posts, many of them targets of political patronage.

The foreign service, according to Andrew Dickson White, the first president of Cornell and a distinguished diplomat, was "not a democratic service resting upon merit, but an aristocratic service resting largely upon wealth." Moreover, there were no professional foreign service officers as such, though some political appointees served long enough to become professionals. Appointees got their posts through the kindness of influential friends, as young Hay himself had done thanks to Secretary of State Seward. In 1895 Cabot Lodge unsuccessfully sponsored a bill to take the consular service out of politics. That same year President Cleveland issued an executive order setting standards, based on testing or experience, for middle-level consular positions. It was not until after Hay's death in 1905 that President Roosevelt, who had professionalized the civil service in the 1880s, established examinations for prospective young diplomats.

Under McKinley and his political mentor Mark Hanna the spoils system was rampant. So Hay had to live with a system that, according to Lodge, put the United States at a disadvantage with every other civilized nation. McKinley, Hay quipped, had already promised all the consulates, but importuning senators would "refuse to believe me disconsulate." Despite his lightheartedness, the pressures of patronage took their toll. "The worst," he wrote Whitelaw Reid, "is the constant solicitations for office . . . the strain of mind and nerves in explaining why things can't be done, and the consciousness that the seekers and their 'influence' think I am lying." Hay discovered that he could not even choose his own clerk "as a friend of the President's from Canton had the place."

Despite the vagaries of the spoils system, Hay got professional assistance from his senior deputies. The first assistant secretary was Francis Loomis, a younger man in his early forties, with experience abroad and a penchant for imperialist activism. John Bassett Moore, the most eminent international lawyer of his time, shuttled from his professorship at Columbia to Washington to provide legal counsel. Moore's agility in giving legal cover to preferred policy options established a principle followed by future legal advisers: not to tell the secretary what he cannot do but rather to find legal support for what he wants to do.

The second assistant secretary, Alvey A. Adee, was even more indispensable to Hay. A fixture at State since the 1870s (he was to serve until 1924), Adee was a walking encyclopedia of diplomatic history, practice, protocol, communication, and style. An indefatigable worker, he participated in debates on every major foreign policy issue and most minor ones. Adee was a unique, even a bizarre character. At just over five feet, he was shorter than Hay himself. A shy bachelor, he had a falsetto voice and a gathering deafness that necessitated ever-enlarging ear trumpets. When he traveled, he always carried three spoons, not trusting alien utensils. His memos, written in red ink on green slips, were classics of brevity and wit. This effete and puckish character maintained a consistent and determined position against imperialism and its excesses, competing for Hay's ear against the more jingoistic Loomis and Moore. Roosevelt did not take Adee seriously, considering him a hopeless fuddy-duddy entombed in the fatuous language of diplomatic delicacy. He may also have resented Adee's skepticism about his imperial ventures.

Hay's routine as secretary would appear leisurely by today's standards. From his house on Lafayette Square it was only a five-minute walk to his office or to the White House, where the cabinet met on Tuesdays. On Thursdays he received the entire diplomatic corps, which could fit into his office. Typical mornings at State were devoted to conferring with Adee or other aides, going over diplomatic dispatches, generating instructions to the field, or dictating to his male secretary. Typewriters were a rarity, and there were only three or four telephones in the entire department. Papers were moved from office to office by messengers who appeared to be walking in their sleep. The telegraph did exist for urgent messages. Hay walked home for lunch, then back to the office for a short afternoon of work, following which he strolled for a hour with Henry Adams; the two then took a cup of tea with Clara Hay. Since Hay reveled in company, his extravagant after-hours social life, where business was also transacted, was more a pleasure than a burden to him.

What was a burden was his relationship with senators. Unlike his colleague Root, who invested infinite charm and patience on influential legislators, Hay could be imperious, dismissive, or patronizing with them. He railed against the Senate's inability to understand the value of compromise in negotiation and its view that, as he put it, "we must get everything and give nothing." His experience with the ratification of the Treaty of Paris, which he thought should have taken one day instead of six weeks, made him regret that the Constitution required a two-thirds vote by the Senate for treaties. He complained to Henry Adams: "The worst of all is the uncertainty about what the Senate may do in any given case. You may work for months over a Treaty, and at last get everything satisfactorily arranged, and send it into the Senate, when it is met by every man who wants to get a political advantage, or to satisfy a personal grudge, everyone who has asked for an office and not got it, everyone, whose wife may think mine has not been attentive enough,—if they can muster one-third of the Senate and one, your Treaty is lost without any reference to its merits."

In his chronic pique with the Senate, Hay ignored the fluctuations in its power since the Civil War. When he took office as secretary, there had not been a strong president since Lincoln; for decades Congress had asserted dominance over the executive branch. This phenomenon received a scholarly analysis in 1879 from a Princeton senior named Woodrow Wilson, whose article, later to inspire his famous book *Congressional Government*, condemned this trend toward legislative control and advocated a strong presidency. Ironically, Henry Cabot Lodge, who had accepted Wilson's article for the *International Review*, came to represent the very symbol of senatorial power that Hay and Wilson resented. Hay understood neither the traditional strength of the Congress nor the fact that by the time of McKinley's presidency the legislature was again growing more malleable to presidential leadership. Roosevelt was to restore much of the president's earlier power. But not all. Lodge administered a lesson on congressional government to Wilson himself when he led the successful assault on the League of Nations treaty in 1919.

2.

Hay's deficiencies with the denizens of Capitol Hill gave him a bad start on the effort to build a canal across the narrow waist of land separating the Atlantic and Pacific oceans. Ever since Balboa discovered the Pacific, romantics had dreamed of linking the two oceans. John Keats, mixing up his conquistadors, wrote of

> . . . *stout Cortez when with eagle eyes*
> *He star'd at the Pacific—and all his men*

> *Look'd at each other with a wild surmise—*
> *Silent, upon a peak in Darien.*

Darién was an old name for Panama, where the isthmus was at its narrowest, only forty-seven miles. A quarter century after Keats's death, this territory became the subject of a historic treaty between the United States and the country that owned it, Colombia, then called New Granada, which had become independent from Spain in 1821. The "wild surmise" of Keats's roving imagination was converted to ink and parchment in 1846, when Colombia, geographically cut off from Panama by dense jungle, ceded to the United States transit rights across the isthmus in return for an American pledge to guarantee its "rights of sovereignty."

Four years after the Bidlack Treaty, named for the American diplomat who had negotiated it, the United States and Great Britain reached an agreement on building a canal. The water route envisaged by the Clayton-Bulwer Treaty of 1850 assumed a new urgency during the next years, after gold had been discovered in California. The increasing number of U.S. settlers bound for the West Coast had difficulty crossing Panama by land. The 1850 treaty stipulated that neither party would maintain exclusive control over a future canal or fortify it; passage would be unrestricted for all countries. These and other clauses made the treaty hugely unpopular in the United States, but it was not until the end of the century that it came under heavy fire.

Mahan, Lodge, and Roosevelt all attacked Clayton-Bulwer as a major obstacle to the construction of a water route across the Isthmus of Panama. Mahan spoke from firsthand experience, having sailed the sea approaches to Panama during the Civil War and having crossed the isthmus by train two decades later. As the three saw it, if the United States took on the risk and expense of building a canal, it should not then have to share control with the British, undertake not to fortify it, and be compelled to let through the ships of other nations—even the warships of an enemy.

The war of 1898 clinched their case. The seizure of the Philippines and the annexation of Hawaii made the United States a Pacific, as well as an Atlantic and a Caribbean, power. The U.S. Navy had to be able to move between the two oceans without taking the long route around Cape Horn at the bottom of South America. The experience of the battleship *Oregon* proved that; it had been compelled to round the Horn to get from Puget Sound to Santiago Bay and almost missed the battle for Cuba. Had there been a canal, its voyage of sixty-seven days might have been cut by two-thirds.

Sensing these new realities, McKinley assigned Hay as secretary of state to clear away the legal and political underbrush so that work could begin on a canal. The first step was to negotiate with the British a canal treaty to replace Clayton-Bulwer. In his usual dyspepsia, Hay was not keen on a canal; he thought transcontinental railroads, in which he was an investor, would provide sufficient linkage between the East and West coasts. Nor did he accept the primacy of the military and strategic factors that energized Mahan, Roosevelt, and Lodge. Thus in his negotiations with the British he aimed too low. He began with a cardinal diplomatic error: He asked the genial and able British ambassador in Washington, Lord Julian Pauncefote, to write the first draft of a revision of Clayton-Bulwer. Working from that draft, which naturally contained all the British desiderata, the two concluded on February 3, 1900, a treaty allowing the United States to build and own a canal. That was an advance, but the draft's retention of the neutrality principle and of the ban on fortification was not.

When the text of the treaty reached the governor's mansion in Albany, Theodore Roosevelt got so angry at Hay's concessions that he issued a statement opposing them. The governor believed that a canal built under Hay-Pauncefote rules would have been counterproductive in the war of 1898, since Spanish warships would have been free to use the canal to get to the Pacific and ravage the American West Coast or the Philippines. The exchange of letters between the two men captured the complexity of their relationship. Hay admonished the governor to mind his own business: "Et Tu? Cannot you leave a few things to the President and the Senate, who are charged with them by the Constitution?" Roosevelt's response was both defiant and obsequious. He reiterated his strong opposition to the treaty but assured Hay that he was "the greatest Secretary of State I have seen in my time."

Even worse for Hay, Cabot Lodge, whose support was critical for Senate approval, declared himself an implacable opponent of the new treaty and led the successful battle to kill it. The two men had a serious falling-out, as Hay accused Lodge of reneging on his promise to support a treaty to succeed Clayton-Bulwer. Henry Adams, ghoulishly relishing the feud between his two friends, wrote: "So [Lodge] has thrown Hay over; declared against his treaty; alienated the Major [McKinley], and destroyed all the credit with the administration which he has labored so hard to create. . . ." Hay, in disgust, agreed with Adams about Lodge: "He would cut my throat or yours for a favorable notice in the newspapers."

But Hay himself was the principal author of his own defeat. He had been insufficiently firm with the British and insufficiently flexible with the Senate. He had disastrously failed to consult Lodge and his colleagues on the Foreign Relations Committee during the negotiations and had withheld all texts from them. After this defeat Hay tried to resign; McKinley would not let him and sent him back to the negotiating table. The British were more than willing to renegotiate, in itself an indication that Hay had not bargained hard enough the first time around. This time Hay brought Lodge in at the outset; the senator worked assiduously on behalf of the new treaty and won public credit for shepherding it through the Senate less than a month after signature. In December 1901 the newly inaugurated President Roosevelt could hail it as his first foreign policy achievement. Hay wrote his wife: "Theodore was very funny about Cabot. He says 'Cabot thinks he made the Treaty.' I said, 'I wanted him to think so.' "

The second Hay-Pauncefote Treaty plugged the main leak of the first by giving the United States by implication the right to fortify a canal. Of note was the cooperative attitude of the British. Embroiled as they were in the Boer War, they were not in a strong position to play tough. But they had also decided that American strength in the Caribbean could serve as a proxy for British interests. That assumption determined their position on the canal, just as it had guided their wartime support for the United States against Spain. A few years after the ratification of the second Hay-Pauncefote Treaty, Britain reduced the military garrisons in its West Indian colonies and its overall naval presence in the Caribbean. It was learning to use American power to its advantage.

With the legal problems finally settled, President Roosevelt moved briskly to the next question of where to build an American canal under U.S. control. Colombia and Nicaragua both were competing for the large boons that construction, revenues, and commerce would bring. Two days after the signing of the Hay-Pauncefote Treaty, a presidential commission recommended Nicaragua as the more "practicable and feasible" route. It was much closer to the United States, posed less complex a construction problem because the canal would be at sea level, and had won favorable evaluations in the engineering reports. Six weeks later the House of Representatives approved Nicaragua by a 308–2 vote.

But Panama had formidable advocates. The prospect of Keats's "realms of gold" brought to Washington a rare assortment of adventurers, promoters, con artists, and shysters. The most important, if not the most respectable, of these soldiers of fortune were an American lawyer, William Nelson Cromwell, founding partner of the New York law firm of Sullivan and Cromwell, and a French engineer named Philippe Bunau-Varilla. Both were associated with Panama's interest against Nicaragua's in winning a canal contract.

Bunau-Varilla, a tiny Frenchman of charm and ingenuity, was a protégé of Ferdinand de Lesseps, the French engineer who had built the Suez Canal and had toiled unsuccessfully to achieve an even larger canal across the Isthmus of Panama. Bunau-Varilla had been chief engineer for de Lesseps's company, which finally went bankrupt, leaving behind huge earthworks and deteriorating machinery. He was a knight-errant whose grail was a canal across Panama. He was also acutely interested in a large share of the profits that would accrue from reviving the canal project. His single-mindedness and brilliance made him one of the most skillful lobbyists ever to hit Washington.

Cromwell, equally diminutive, fastidious in dress, devious, and highly articulate, represented the New Panama Canal Company, the Paris-based successor to the original company; he was also a stockholder and a director. Cromwell's aim was to sell the company—with its property holdings, railroad, and rusting equipment splayed along the canal route—to the U.S. government at a large profit to himself. Like Bunau-Varilla, he was a world-class lobbyist with a keen instinct for using money to buy influence. He even donated sixty thousand dollars to the Republican National Committee to sweeten its views on the Panama option, charging the contribution to his French clients. His greed, unlike Bunau-Varilla's, was unflecked by any particles of altruism.

The Nicaragua option had no champions to compete with these two Lilliputian giants. They lobbied the Washington power structure with single-minded determination, reaching First Assistant Secretary of State Loomis, the State Department lawyer Moore, Secretary Hay himself, and Senators Hanna and Spooner. Cromwell even got access to Roosevelt through Hanna, whom the slick lawyer had sold on the Panama route. The energetic and resourceful Bunau-Varilla persuaded the New Panama Canal Company to cut its price for its Panama properties from $109 million to $40 million, a reduction that made Panama a cheaper bet for the United States than Nicaragua. With the Senate he played on the recent devastation of Martinique by a volcano to stress the risks in Nicaragua, which is also situated in a volcano belt. In making his point, he circulated to each senator a one-centavo Nicaraguan stamp proudly dispaying an active volcano puffing away.

By January 1902 Roosevelt, who was impressed by the pro-Panama arguments of George S. Morison, an engineer and fellow Harvard man, had made up his mind to support the Panama route. Sniffing the political wind, the presidential commission discovered reasons to switch its allegiance to Panama, thus reversing a recommendation of only six weeks earlier. Congress, under intense lobbying, also came around; the Senate vote in favor of Panama on June 19 was 67–6. On June 28 the president signed into law Senator Spooner's bill designating Panama as the site. Now the negotiation with the government of Colombia could begin in earnest.

Washington had been involved in a close relationship with Bogotá ever since the Bidlack Treaty of 1846. Because impenetrable jungle denied Colombia effective control over Panama, a pattern had formed in which Colombia would call on the United States to defend its sovereignty against armed Panamanian bids for independence. According to Roosevelt's probably exaggerated count, there had been an average of one Panamanian uprising a year since Bidlack; the United States had intervened to protect Colombia in thirteen of them and had landed troops seven times, occupying Panama for a total of two hundred days.

Less than three months after the U.S. Congress had selected the Panama route, Panamanian nationalists staged another revolt. Without consulting Colombia, Roosevelt ordered marines landed to protect the railroad across the isthmus between Colón on the Caribbean side and Panama City on the Pacific. Although the United States finally brokered an end to the hostilities—on an American battleship—this unilateral action left a stain of bad blood on the subsequent negotiations. The Americans had acquired the habit of dominance over Colombia, the Colombians a feeling of victimization.

The negotiations in Washington nevertheless began well. Hay opened them in January 1903 with the Colombian chargé d'affaires, Tomás Herrán, a fluent English speaker and a graduate of Georgetown College in Washington, D.C. The secretary of state, aware of his reputation as a weak negotiator, took a firm position, even threatening to revive the Nicaragua option if Herrán did not agree to the American terms. Intimidated, the Colombian diplomat signed prematurely, three days before receiving a cable from Bogotá instructing him to hold off. The treaty, excellent from the U.S. point of view, provided for a canal zone six miles wide to be leased to the United States. The term was for a hundred years, renewable at American option, with a one-time payment of $10 million to the Colombian government plus an annual rent of $250,000. The treaty specifically recognized Colombian sovereignty over Panama but diluted it by authorizing U.S. judicial and police rights within the zone. Cromwell, who had been camping out at the State Department, was present at the signing. In recognition of his effort to achieve the treaty, Hay presented him with the pen he had used. The Senate quickly voted its approval on March 17, 1903.

Then the trouble began. The reaction in Colombia was negative, and, under Cromwell's greedy importuning, Hay inflamed it further. Cromwell feared that Colombia might delay any deal with the United States until the New Panama Canal Company's concession expired in a year's time, then seize the company's property without compensation and sell it to the United States. So he persuaded Hay to guarantee that the huge profits from the sale of the company's holdings on the isthmus would accrue not to Colombia but to the company—and of course to Cromwell as an officer of the company.

Hay had no reason to follow Cromwell's advice on this question. The United States was ready to pay the French company forty million dollars, the largest real estate price ever up to that time. If it had waited for Colombia to possess the property, it might even have gotten it for less. It was the price, not the identity of the seller, that ought to have mattered. But Hay instructed the U.S. minister in Bogotá to inform the Colombian government that the United States would not condone any Colombian effort to deal independently with the New Panama Canal Company. In cutting off this potential path to additional Colombian profits, the United States administered a rebuff to Colombian sovereignty, Colombian interests, and Colombian pride. Prodded by the president, Hay then conveyed a threat to Bogotá: Delay or rejection by Colombia might produce congressional action, "which every friend of Colombia might regret." Several days later a newspaper article planted by Cromwell just after his meeting with the president alleged that the Americans were ready to support a revolution in Panama.

In a mixture of vexation and voracity, the Colombian Senate procrastinated and then voted unanimously against the Hay-Herrán Treaty on August 12. Cromwell had meanwhile been feeding the White House and the State Department scurrilous reports about Colombian politicians. The competent and experienced U.S. minister in Bogotá, Arthur Beaupré, had a much better feel for the country than Cromwell did, but Washington preferred to listen to Cromwell's tendentious distortions. When Roosevelt, thus conditioned, got the news of the vote, he exploded. In invective usually reserved for the likes of Carl Schurz or Henry James, he flailed the Colombians as "blackmailers," "homicidal corruptionists," "cut throats," and—the unkindest cut—"jack rabbits."

The man who had urged the U.S. Senate to reject Hay's first treaty with Pauncefote was now castigating the Colombian Senate for exercising the same prerogative. The president's explosion was partly understandable. Greed was undoubtedly one factor in the Colombians' maneuvering, making their negotiating style tricky and exasperating. As Roosevelt complained, "You could no more make an agreement with the Colombian rulers than you could nail currant jelly to a wall." Hay had an equally striking phrase: "Talking with those fellows down there . . . is like holding a squirrel in your lap and trying to keep up the conversation." Whatever their motives, the Colombians were shortsighted in giving up certain profits for the uncertain prospect of greater ones. Still, it was the right of the Colombian Senate, as it was of the U.S. Senate, to reject a treaty negotiated by its government.

Following the Colombian vote, the key American officials managed to fit into their summer vacation schedules a discussion of next steps. As Roosevelt fulminated from Long Island, Hay in New Hampshire suggested a return to the Nicaragua alternative. Alvey Adee, sweltering in Washington, far from the cooling breezes of Lake Sunapee or Oyster Bay, also pressed the Nicaragua option and warned against American involvement in a revolution in Panama. Three decades of foreign policy experience had convinced this canny veteran that the United States had a moral responsibility not to subvert Colombia's legitimate, if unwelcome, decision. "Our policy before the world should stand, like Mrs. Caesar, without suspicion," he wrote Hay, adding: "We are very sorry, but really we can't help it if Colombia doesn't want the Canal on our terms."

Roosevelt had no intention of impersonating "Mrs. Caesar." Logically, the obvious recourse was to go back to the Nicaragua option. Nicaragua had considerable assets in its proximity, its friendly government, and the fact that no revolution was required to make a canal possible there. Yet Roosevelt never wavered in his determination to build in Panama. He set his staff to devising ways to achieve a route through Panama even in the teeth of Colombia's opposition. John Bassett Moore helpfully decided that Colombia's frequent requests for U.S. intervention in Panama under the Bidlack Treaty made the United States in effect the responsible sovereign on the isthmus and thus free to complete the canal even without Colombia's consent. Moore's opinion transformed a treaty authorizing U.S. intervention on behalf of the interests of Colombia into a treaty authorizing U.S. intervention *against* the interests of Colombia.

Hay, back from vacation, sensitive to the president's wishes, and exposed to the blandishments of the Panama lobby, was wracked with an ambivalence that led him to caution Roosevelt against seizing Panama while noting that a war would be brief, inexpensive, and legally justified. The secretary started telling people that Colombia would not be allowed to stand in the way of a U.S.-built canal. Moreover, he added, in the event of a revolution in Panama the U.S. Navy would prevent the landing of Colombian troops. At the same time, Lodge was urging Roosevelt to proceed with the canal, either invoking the Bidlack Treaty or pointing to the likelihood of Panama's secession. Roosevelt confided in his autobiography that he was determined to seize the isthmus and build the canal whether Panama seceded or not.

Panama's impending loss of a canal as the result of the Colombian decision produced an immediate alliance between Panamanian dissidents and operators like Bunau-Varilla and Cromwell. The Panamanians resolved to launch a revolution against Colombia; the two lobbyists undertook to ensure that it had American support. Under Cromwell's sponsorship, one of the principal conspirators spent two and a half hours with Hay on September 3. On October 10, Bunau-Varilla called on Roosevelt for the first time and emerged with a wink, if not a promise. The Frenchman told Elihu Root afterward that his talk with the president had convinced him that the United States would not let Colombia crush a revolution.

In fact American military activity, the result of careful preparation, was decisive to the outcome. Roosevelt had sent two U.S. Army officers to Panama in secret to evaluate anti-Colombian feeling; they reported to him on October 16 that revolution was certain. After Bunau-Varilla told the State Department that the revolution was scheduled for November 3, the president dispatched ten warships to the scene. One arrived in time to be useful. The USS *Nashville* put in at Colón, on the Carribean side of the isthmus, on November 2; Bunau-Varilla, probably tipped off by American officials, had alerted the insurrectionists to its arrival. Heartened by this show of force, they used persuasive arguments and even more persuasive money to win the defection of the Colombian general in command of the Panama garrison. The *Nashville* prevented Colombian troops from landing, and some fifty marines disembarked to secure the transisthmian railroad against use by the Colombian Army. Thus the U.S. Navy, which had acted as guarantor of Colombia's sovereignty over Panama for half a century, assisted in the destruction of that sovereignty. Independence was accomplished with ridiculous ease; a new government of Panama sought recognition from the United States on November 4 and received it in slightly over an hour.

The light-opera character of the Panama affair reached its final crescendo with the appearance in Washington of Bunau-Varilla in the guise of envoy of the new state of Panama. He claimed to be empowered to conclude a canal agreement with the United States. It was the easiest agreement John Hay ever negotiated, and it was rushed to signature just before the arrival of the genuine representatives of the new government of Panama. They denounced Bunau-Varilla as acting without authority but could do nothing to change the treaty in the face of strong American pressure.

By the Hay–Bunau-Varilla Treaty the width of the canal zone was increased from six miles to ten, and four islands were added to it. Judicial powers, formerly to be shared, were awarded exclusively to the Americans. The United States switched from Colombia to Panama its payment of $10 million plus $250,000 a year in rent. Most important of all, the United States was given rights in the zone as if "it were the sovereign . . . to the entire exclusion of the exercise by the Republic of Panama of any such sovereign rights, power or authority." The United States guaranteed the independence of Panama, a mixed blessing since this could imply the right of intervention in the spirit of the Platt Amendment. The zone was to be held by the United States not for any fixed period but "in perpetuity."

Hay wrote to Senator Spooner: "You and I know too well how many points there are in this treaty to which a Panamanian patriot could object." Not without charges of piracy and dishonor, the Senate on February 23, 1904, approved the treaty by a 66–14 vote. The initial cost to the United States was higher than the price of Louisiana, Alaska, and the Philippines combined: ten million dollars to Panama and forty million to the New Panama Canal Company, with Bunau-Varilla and especially Cromwell reaping significant financial rewards. Construction on the canal began later the same year.

Just after the revolution Roosevelt played coy about the U.S. role, disclaiming prior knowledge of the uprising or support for it. To the Congress he justified his action on universal grounds: It was in "the interests of collective civilization. If ever a Government could be said to have received a mandate from civilization . . . the United States holds that position with regard to the interoceanic canal." As he was preparing to leave office in late 1908, he was ready to take all the credit. He wrote to a London editor: "This I can say absolutely was my own work, and could not have been accomplished save by me or by some man of my temperament." Once out of office, he was even more boastful. To an audience at the University of California at Berkeley, he said: "I am interested in the Panama Canal because I started it. If I had followed traditional, conservative methods I would have submitted a dignified State paper of probably 200 pages to Congress and the debates on it would have been going on yet; but I took the Canal Zone and let Congress debate; and while the debate goes on the Canal does also."

Roosevelt was proud of his canal; in 1906 he made the first trip abroad by a president of the United States to inspect the construction work. But the story of its inception casts little glory on his administration. The arrogant dismissal of the constitutional practices of Colombia, the cynical rewriting of international law to fit U.S. policy, the unacknowledged role of the U.S. Navy, and the punitive treaty imposed on the fledging republic of Panama: None of these actions comported with Roosevelt's pious rationalizations. The Panama affair was also one of the most conspicuous examples of aggressive lobbying in American history. The machinations of Cromwell and Bunau-Varilla were visible at every stage in the process: in the selection of Panama over Nicaragua, in the Panamanian revolution, and in the one-sided treaties with Colombia and Panama. Roosevelt and Hay should never have allowed their government to be so manipulated by unscrupulous men who had a clear financial stake in the outcome.

Yet the president, convinced by the engineers and captivated by the con men, was keen to charge ahead. Hay did nothing to stop him. The secretary's occasional and all-too-temporary second thoughts— for example, his pursuit of the Nicaragua option after Colombia had rejected the treaty—usually came only when he was out of Washington and away from the lobbyists' pressures. They never coalesced into a reasoned effort, which Adee would have enthusiastically supported, to press an alternative strategy on the president. Perhaps Hay was not the man to do it; he was not a confronter, and Roosevelt considered him too soft anyway. After Roosevelt's determined actions had proved successful, Hay was all too happy to bask in the glow of a triumph achieved without the direct use of force. As he wrote to Root, "How on earth a fair-minded man could prefer that the President should have taken possession of the Isthmus with the mailed hand, and built a canal in defiance of the Constitution, the laws, and the treaties, rather than the perfectly regular course which the President did follow, passes my comprehension."

In Cuba and the Philippines the United States had managed to alienate revolutionary groups that had urged American intervention and pleaded common cause with American values. Now, in Panama, Roosevelt's "perfectly regular course" treated in the same cavalier fashion the revolutionaries who had made a canal possible. The new Panamanian government, a liberal one, took office with a grudge against the United States. Like many of its successors, it objected to having become an American protectorate.

Colombia was an even bigger loser. Partly by its own action it had lost ten million dollars plus annual revenues of half a million from the U.S. rent and the payment by the railroad. It had also lost Panama, and in violation of tradition and perhaps even international law, the United States had connived in that loss. Colombia had been insulted and humiliated by its northern neighbor and would not soon forget. Hay considered compensating Colombia, but Bunau-Varilla talked him out of it. Other Latin American countries quickly adjusted to reality and recognized the new Panamanian republic, but even with them Roosevelt's display of force left a residue of suspicion and fear.

In Roosevelt's defense, it must be said, there was a powerful argument for the Panama Canal that did not depend on specious appeals to duty, necessity, or the mandate of civilization. It was Mahan's old strategic conviction that a canal was necessary for the United States to build a great navy and become a great power. When the canal was finally opened under President Wilson, it undoubtedly increased both the perception and the reality of American power vis-à-vis the rest of the world.

But there had been other ways to accomplish this; Mahan himself assumed that a canal across the Nicaragua route would be favored. The way chosen by Roosevelt was described with appropriate cynicism by Root, who had been on a ship en route from Liverpool to New York at the time of the Panamanian revolution but thereafter defended the president's actions. At a cabinet meeting shortly after the Panama affair, Roosevelt launched into a long defense of his position, then turned to Root and asked if he had answered the charges. "You certainly have, Mr. President," Root responded. "You have shown that you were accused of seduction and you have conclusively proved that you were guilty of rape." A more contemporary conclusion was delivered by California senator S. I. Hayakawa during the Senate debate in 1977 over returning the canal to Panama. A professor of linguistics and a man who chose his words carefully, Hayakawa captured Roosevelt's blend of legalistic sanctimony and ruthless action over the canal when he said: "We stole it fair and square."

3.

In his memoirs Theodore Roosevelt wrote that his action over the Panama Canal was the most important foreign policy achievement of his entire presidency. Indeed, while he was in office, the strategic imperative of creating a water passage between the Atlantic and Pacific outweighed all other considerations in his approach to the Caribbean and Central America. The growth of trade with Latin America, the primacy of American investment in the hemisphere, the need for friendly local governments and for dominant U.S. influence over them, the importance of stability, and the endorsement of the Caribbean as an American lake: All these elements of Roosevelt's policy flowed from his determination to guarantee to the U.S. Navy monopolistic control over the isthmian passage. As Elihu Root wrote in 1905, "The inevitable effect of our building the Canal must be to require us to police the surrounding premises. In the nature of things, trade and control, and the obligation to keep order which go with them, must come our way."

Roosevelt set two priorities regarding the Caribbean and Latin America. The first was the traditional Monroe Doctrine consideration that no foreign power must be allowed to establish a foothold. This meant, after Spain's expulsion from the hemisphere, avoiding a vacuum and preventing local governments, whether out of greed or weakness, from attracting the influence of European powers. The second priority was new or, more accurately, was more available to Roosevelt than to his predecessors. This was a license to control local regimes whose activity or fecklessness might affect U.S. interests, and it came to be known as the Roosevelt Corollary. Roosevelt, Hay, and Root exercised caution and subtlety in the development of their Latin American policy, but the net result was to establish a tradition of American hegemony that was to set an example for their successors.

With Great Britain no longer a competitor, the only serious foreign challenge in the Caribbean came from Germany. German pugnacity with Dewey in the Philippines was a fresh memory. Concern that the Germans might buy the Virgin Islands, with their excellent harbor on

St. Thomas, prompted Hay to make a purchase offer to their owner, Denmark. He concluded a treaty in 1902 and actually got it through the Senate (one of his rare victories), but the Danish parliament— under German pressure, some alleged—voted it down. The United States had to wait until World War I to buy the islands.

A sharper confrontation between Roosevelt's America and Kaiser William II's Germany arose in Venezuela. The dictator in Caracas, Cipriano Castro, had run through the national treasury and foreign loans to support a voluptuary's life-style: twenty-three houses, twenty-two mistresses, and a bunch of cronies with fingers as sticky as his. The Germans and the British, whose investments had suffered the most, were eager to intervene to collect their debts. In principle Roosevelt was not opposed. While vice president, he had written Speck von Sternberg, his German diplomatic friend: "If any South American State misbehaves towards any European country, let the European country spank it." Faced with the issue as president, however, he felt constrained to be precise about the conditions under which European spanking would be permitted. In his annual message of December 1901 he called the Monroe Doctrine the "cardinal feature" of U.S. foreign policy and warned non-American powers against "territorial aggrandizement . . . at the expense of any American power on American soil."

In December 1902 Germany and Britain blockaded La Guaira, the port of Caracas, and four other ports and seized several Venezuelan gunboats. Castro gave in, while beseeching American arbitration under the Monroe Doctrine. The Germans contributed to their bad reputation by destroying a Venezuelan village, and the blockade continued until February 1903, long enough to arouse the American public against Germany. Years later, when he was pressing for U.S. entry into the world war against Germany, Roosevelt retrospectively burnished his belligerency in the Venezuelan affair by claiming that he had threatened to send Admiral Dewey, fortuitously stationed in Puerto Rico, to drive the Germans out of Venezuela. The former president seems to have wildly overstated the sharpness of the crisis and of his "threat," though if he had provoked a skirmish with the Germans, he might well have had the country behind him. A journalist in Minnesota, a state with many German immigrants, wrote:

Yankee Dewey's near La Guayra,
Yankee Dewey Dandy,
Maybe just as well to have our
Yankee Dewey handy.

In the end the blockade was lifted without the use of American force. Roosevelt was not eager to take the side of Castro, whom he called a "villainous little monkey." The financial issues were settled by arbitration, with the United States acting as broker between Venezuela and the European powers. This Venezuelan affair showed Roosevelt and Hay in a moderate light. The president clearly did not want to be the savior of last resort in every hemispheric dispute and thus a dupe for hysterical and sybaritic local dictators or for European countries desirous of using American power to advance their own interests. So he sensibly tempered his insistence on recognition of American hegemony. Still, the ultimate German climb-down dispelled any doubt about which power was dominant in the area.

The Venezuela incident spawned an attempt by the foreign minister of Argentina, Luis M. Drago, to win international acceptance for the proposition that European powers could not resort to armed intervention or territorial occupation in order to collect debts. With American support a diluted version of the Drago Doctrine ultimately won international adoption at the Hague Conference of 1907; it banned the use of force except in cases where the debtor state did not cooperate in arbitration.

The U.S. government showed less restraint in the next Caribbean crisis, though Roosevelt moved carefully at the end. The Windward Passage, the most direct approach from the Atlantic to Panama, lies between Cuba and the island of Hispaniola. The Dominican Republic and Haiti, which share Hispaniola, were notorious for corruption and instability; in fact their wretched political condition had been one argument for establishing the Platt Amendment in Cuba. Since Seward's time the U.S. Navy had been interested in the deepwater Samaná Bay in the Dominican Republic. As secretary of state Hay had resisted efforts by the Dominican dictator Ulises Heureaux, a sophisticated version of Venezuela's Castro, to cede the use of Samaná Bay in exchange for making his country an American protectorate. In

1903, four years after Heureaux's assassination, a revolution broke out against the successor government. Panicked at the prospect of violence and instability, the American financial community, which had large investments in the country and to which Hay was close, joined the U.S. Navy in pressing for action to protect the government.

Early in 1904 the navy landed troops, one of whom was killed in the capital, Santo Domingo; the insurgents also fired on a U.S. cruiser. The navy responded by shelling rebel positions and landing marines. No sooner had the shaky government been buttressed than the country went bankrupt, bringing its European creditors, including Germany, to the point of armed intervention. Like the Venezuelan government before, the Dominican government appealed for help to the United States. Hay resisted pressure from his own deputy Loomis, from British, German, and French property owners, and from the Dominican government, to authorize U.S. seizure of the customshouses. Instead he developed an arbitration mechanism that produced in December 1904 a U.S. decision to establish an American collector of customs who would distribute revenues to the Dominican government and to European creditors. Over Loomis's objections, Hay insisted that the agreement guarantee the republic's territorial integrity and disavow annexation. With American naval vessels standing offshore, the arrangement worked to the benefit of everybody: the United States, the Europeans, and the Dominican treasury.

The U.S. government's Dominican fix was a pragmatic response to a particular challenge in a country at that time more important to American interests than Venezuela was. Except for the British, who applauded the American action, the Europeans grumbled but reconciled themselves to getting their money out. The Dominican people gained a few years of respite from the rapacious incompetence of their rulers. Roosevelt never thought of annexation; as he told a friend, "I have about the same desire to annex it as a gorged boa constrictor might have to swallow a porcupine wrong-end-to." Only the U.S. Senate caused difficulties with the customs agreement on constitutional grounds; it took Hay two years to get it through.

In the process Roosevelt devised a policy that was designed to apply not just to the Dominican Republic but to the entire hemisphere. As he described it in his annual message in December 1904, "Chronic wrongdoing, or an impotence which results in a general loosening of the ties of civilized society, may in America [i.e., the American hemisphere], as elsewhere, ultimately require intervention by some civilized nation, and in the western hemisphere the adherence of the United States to the Monroe Doctrine may force the United States, however reluctantly, in flagrant cases of such wrongdoing or impotence, to the exercise of an international police power."

This was the Roosevelt Corollary, which extended the Monroe Doctrine beyond preventing foreign intervention in the hemisphere to privileging American intervention there. It was born of a specific need and hedged with limiting words like "chronic," "ultimately," "flagrant," and "reluctantly." Roosevelt took pains to disclaim aggressive intent: "It cannot be too often and too emphatically asserted that the United States has not the slightest desire for territorial aggrandizement at the expense of any of its southern neighbors, and will not treat the Monroe Doctrine as an excuse for such aggrandizement on its part." Root, who wrote the Platt Amendment, may have had a hand in the Roosevelt Corollary as well; certainly he and the president had discussed the issue. Both of them considered that the corollary limited, as well as expanded, American power. In a speech given several weeks after Roosevelt's, Root described the president's view as "[arrogating] to ourselves, not sovereignty over the American continent, but only the right to protect."

Despite such caveats, Roosevelt had taken a momentous step. He had warned the Europeans that if there were any spanking to be done in the hemisphere, the United States would do it. And he had alerted the "Dagoes" (his favorite derogatory word for Latin American leaders) that incompetence or iniquity could bring American power down on them. The Roosevelt Corollary expanded both the Monroe Doctrine, by authorizing American intervention, and the Platt Amendment, by extending the right of intervention beyond Cuba to the entire hemisphere. It also illustrated the increasing influence of economic interests on U.S. policy in Latin America. American business, which had been ambivalent about getting into war over Cuba, was now behind much of the pressure to enforce stability in the hemisphere.

Not long after, in 1906, Roosevelt took the Platt Amendment off the shelf of principle and put it into practice. Again, he acted with great reluctance. In Cuba, Tomás Estrada Palma, the venerable politician to whom Leonard Wood had turned over power when he sailed

away in May 1902, had gotten into serious difficulties. After a disputed election in 1905, the opposition Liberal party launched a somewhat languid insurrection in the late summer of 1906, which inspired
a classic cable to Washington from the U.S. chargé d'affaires: "Revolution spreading. Everything quiet." Estrada Palma, invoking the Platt
Amendment, appealed to Roosevelt for warships and marines.

American intervention in Cuba was the last thing Roosevelt
wanted, but he would not shrink from it if, as he warned the Cuban
minister in Washington on September 14, "Cuba herself shows that
she has fallen into the insurrectionary habit, that she lacks the self-
restraint necessary to secure peaceful self-government, and that her
contending factions have plunged the country into anarchy." He
ordered naval vessels carrying marines to position themselves off
Havana, but he also sought an urgent diplomatic solution, sending
William H. Taft, by then secretary of war, and Assistant Secretary of
State Robert Bacon (a Harvard boxing friend of Roosevelt's and a partner of J. P. Morgan's) to Havana. They began talks with both sides on
September 19 and worked out a potential compromise by which
Estrada Palma would be a caretaker president until a new temporary
government could be inaugurated. On September 25 Roosevelt implored the Cuban leader through Taft not to resign and cause "the
death of the republic." But Estrada Palma did resign, leaving Cuba
with the prospect of escalating violence and the destruction of foreign
property.

Roosevelt believed that he had no choice but to intervene quickly.
Two thousand marines landed on September 29, six weeks after the
revolt had begun, and quelled the gathering violence. The president
passed over Wood, the obvious choice to govern Cuba, and sent a
civilian judge, Charles Magoon of Minnesota, with full powers to run
the country. Judiciously choosing to fly the Cuban rather than the
American flag, Magoon stayed for two years, backed by six thousand
mostly invisible U.S. troops. The verdict of the British historian Hugh
Thomas, in defending Magoon's poor reputation among Cuban historians, is that he contributed positively to the Cuban electoral system,
to the foundation of the army, to education, and to road building and
that the country he turned back to its people in 1909 was in better
shape than it had been at the end of the Spanish-American War.

The Cuban crisis did not set off appeals for annexation in the

United States, except from Senator Beveridge. Even Beveridge's fellow jingo Cabot Lodge showed a measure of restraint. A week after Estrada Palma's appeal for intervention, Lodge wrote the president from Massachusetts: "Disgust with the Cubans is very general. Nobody wants to annex them, but the general feeling is that they ought to be taken by the neck and shaken until they behave themselves." Roosevelt himself continued to see the American intervention in Cuba as an unwanted duty. In a letter to Taft several weeks after the marines had landed, he wrote:

> There can be no talk of a protectorate by us. Our business is to establish peace and order on a satisfactory basis, start the new government, and then leave the Island; the Cuban government taking the reins into its own hands; tho of course it might be advisable for some little time that some of our troops should stay in the Islands to steady things. I will not even consider the plan of a protectorate, or any plan which would imply our breaking our explicit promise because of which we were able to prevent a war of devastation last fall. The good faith of the United States is a mighty valuable asset and must not be impaired.

Thus did America's strategic interests in the Caribbean, intensified by the need to protect the Panama Canal and its approaches, pull Roosevelt toward a hegemonic position with which even he did not feel entirely comfortable. Venezuela, the Dominican Republic, and Cuba had been of ascending strategic importance, and the degree of American intervention in each ascended correspondingly. In the Roosevelt Corollary the president left his successors a principle of intervention; in his actions he left them a set of precedents. American interests in the Caribbean and Central America did not diminish after Roosevelt, and American interventions increased considerably.

4.

As Mahan had argued long before, a U.S. Navy with a two-ocean capability would need coaling stations, bases, in the Pacific. It had been this strategic consideration that dictated Roosevelt's enthusiasm for acquiring the Philippines and Hawaii. As with most imperial acquisitions, these new possessions expanded appetites and obligations even as they satisfied them. It was now possible to look on the Asian main-land with new eyes. As Mahan wrote in 1901, the canal, Hawaii, and the Philippines "are important as facilitating our access to the seas of China and to the valley of the Yangtse, and as furnishing territorial support to our action there."

As he surveyed the Pacific during his presidency, Roosevelt could take satisfaction in the U.S.-held islands that formed stepping-stones in a generally east-west direction across the vast ocean to the shores of the Asian continent. The easternmost was the Hawaiian archipel-ago, twenty-four hundred miles west of San Francisco. Another thir-teen hundred miles to the west was Midway, American since 1867, when it had become Secretary Seward's only acquisition besides Alaska. Southwest of Midway by just over one thousand miles was Wake Island, seized by the U.S. Navy on its way to the Philippines in 1898 and formally annexed in January 1899. Guam, also captured by the navy en route to the Philippines, lay fifteen hundred miles west of Wake. From Guam to Manila was another fifteen hundred miles. The Philippines themselves were twelve hundred miles from Japan and only half that distance from the Chinese mainland.

In the South Pacific, south of this line of possessions, lay the Samoan islands, which had been the subject of U.S. interest and con-tention with Germany since the Civil War. They were finally divided with Germany in late 1899, with the United States getting the best harbor, at Pago Pago. During the first Cleveland administration State Department veteran Alvey Adee had put the case for acquisition of the Samoan islands (and inferentially for the others as well): ". . . in the hands of a naval Power they threaten our Pacific flank, and indeed they threaten all the Pacific Coast of South America too, and Hawaii besides." For a country with two coasts to protect, the Monroe Doc-trine to uphold, a growing navy to supply, and interests that it had begun to define in global terms, even remote islands had become important.

The heaviest American strategic, political, and economic in-vestments were naturally in Hawaii and the Philippines. During Roosevelt's presidency Hawaii had a small population of 150,000 in-habitants, more than half of whom were aliens, mostly Japanese work-ers in the sugar fields. Political and economic power was still in the

hands of the white oligarchy, which was linked to the islands' missionary past and had been the motive force behind the 1898 annexation.
However, thanks to an act passed by Congress in 1900 against the
wishes of the white supremacists in the Hawaiian government, native
Hawaiians automatically became U.S. citizens (though without the
right to vote for president) and were not subjected to a property qual-
ification, which would have restricted their right to vote. These circumstances made for a kind of stability. Native Hawaiians had some
rights (aliens had none), the white power structure exercised a cen-
tralized but paternalistic rule, and there was no agitation for independence or statehood. The situation was ideal for the army, which
established at Schofield Barracks the largest U.S. Army post, and for
the navy, which made Pearl Harbor home base for its Pacific fleet.

The Philippines, with their insurrectionary past, presented a
greater problem for the Americans. Roosevelt quickly grew apprehensive about the consequences of this colonial acquisition, which he
had done so much to promote. As usual, he saw things in strategic
terms. The Philippines were too far from the United States and too
close to the growing power in Asia, Japan. In fact Manila is as close to
Dublin as it is to San Francisco. The president lamented to Taft in
August 1907 that "in the physical sense I don't see where they are of
any value to us or where they are likely to be of any value." In fact,
"The Philippines form our heel of Achilles. They are all that makes
the present situation with Japan dangerous. . . . Personally I should be
glad to see the islands made independent, with perhaps some kind of
international guarantee for the preservation of order, or with some
warning on our part that if they did not keep order we would have to
interfere again; this among other reasons because I would rather see
this nation fight all her life than to see her give them up to Japan or
any other nation under duress."

The essence of this visionary passage is not that Roosevelt had
been so soon wrong about the Philippines, or that he was honest
enough to admit it, or that he was considering a Platt Amendment for
the country. What stands out is his extraordinary prescience in want-
ing to give the Philippines independence before Japan could attack
the islands. This idea was not a passing fancy; in the 1912 presidential campaign Roosevelt was to come out for Philippine indepen-

dence. He was long dead when Japan captured the Philippines from the United States in 1942, but he had warned of just such a risk thirty-five years before.

The acquisition of Hawaii and the Philippines expanded the American interest in the mainland of Asia, a continent where U.S. involvement had previously been episodic. A special target was China, a weak and sprawling giant whose vast potential market had provoked a competition among the European powers for influence and territory. In his seven years as secretary of state, particularly the three under McKinley, Hay developed the first modern U.S. policy toward China. It was based on America's new pretensions as an Asian power.

Before 1898 the United States had been a bystander rather than a participant in what Hay called "the great game of spoliation" in China. As an advocate of business he focused on America's burgeoning commercial interests in China, though they represented only 2 percent of global foreign trade and only 1 percent of America's foreign trade. He did not want to see the Chinese Empire broken up into pieces that the European powers could swallow. Now that the United States had acquired important holdings in the Pacific, he explored ways that it could inject itself into the "great game." Hay was not a profound strategic thinker, but he showed considerable foresight when he said: "The storm center of the world has shifted . . . to China. Whoever understands that mighty Empire . . . has a key to world politics for the next five centuries."

After China's loss of a war with Japan over Korea in 1895, Great Britain, France, Germany, and Russia had put pressure on the weakened country to cede territory to them. In the next few years all had gained land from China, either by lease or by outright seizure. Britain, whose interest in China was primarily commercial, began to grow concerned at the prospect that China would be partitioned among its rival great powers. Just before the outbreak of the Spanish-American War, the British had sought American cooperation in keeping China open to all foreign commerce. McKinley, preoccupied with the Caribbean, had brushed them off, but in the fall of 1899 Hay returned to the British concept of an Open Door to China, this time as an American initiative. He sent diplomatic notes to Britain, Russia, Germany, France, and Japan, soliciting support, in guarded language, for an agreement by which the parties would respect equal commercial opportunities in China. The replies were positive but conditioned, except for Russia's, which was a polite turndown. Counting on the fact that no government wanted to be seen opposing fair play, Hay asserted in March 1900 that he had "final and definitive" agreement. No country demurred.

Open Doors are for those who are not already inside. Hay was negotiating from weakness since the United States was far behind in the scramble for China. The Open Door notes had no practical effect on the commercial competition in China. "Your open door is already off its hinges," Henry Adams told his friend before the policy was six months old. Hay himself recognized the shaky underpinnings of his approach. He lamented that there was not a single country which the Open Door policy could compel, adding: "The inherent weakness of our position is this: we do not want to rob China ourselves, and our public opinion will not permit us to interfere, with an army, to prevent others from robbing her. Besides, we have no army. The talk of the papers about 'our preeminent moral position giving us the authority to dictate to the world' is mere flap-doodle."

The Open Door was more perception than substance, a policy temporarily and conditionally accepted by the great powers for their own reasons. Yet perceptions often count. Hay's diplomatic legerdemain made him a celebrated figure in the United States and a potential asset to Roosevelt in his 1904 presidential campaign. Americans were pleased that their country was finally welcome at the international high table. They liked Hay's high-sounding opposition to spheres of influence in China, not noticing that the United States had no sphere to renounce. They were also glad that their country was thought of as a power with influence in Asia. The perception of other countries was changing as well. The United States, heretofore a power of the second rank, was now insisting on equal treatment with the traditional great powers and was to continue to insist on such treatment.

As evidence, in the summer of 1900 the United States sent five thousand troops to join an international force to rescue the besieged diplomatic legations in Beijing from the murderous Boxers, members of a secret society dedicated to expelling foreigners from China. The U.S. soldiers came from the Philippines; two years before there would have been no significant American military presence anywhere near China. During the Boxer crisis Hay issued a second set of notes, this time without requesting a response, advocating the territorial integrity of China. Again perception trumped substance, since the disintegration of China continued, and indeed Hay himself contributed to it. Under pressure from the navy, he violated his own precepts by trying unsuccessfully to acquire a naval base in southern China. The Japanese, who had prior rights, quoted his own policy back at him.

With all the mirrors he had skillfully deployed, Hay set the United States on the way to becoming an Asian power. The Open Door policy was one of his two great contributions to American foreign policy. The other was a rapprochement with Great Britain that was to solidify into permanence. The China initiative engaged Hay's mind; his approach toward Britain was an affair of the heart. The close relationship between Washington and London that ensued, and that has lasted ever since Hay's term of office, can easily be taken for granted. But in 1900 Britain was still considered an adversary, as it had been during the American Revolution and in the War of 1812, when the British burned Washington, and during the American Civil War, when they tilted toward the Confederacy.

As recently as 1885, the normally unaggressive President Cleveland had assumed a belligerent stance toward Britain over the Venezuelan boundary. Irish-Americans, a growing factor in American politics, were automatically anti-British, often defining their entire foreign policy in terms of what might injure their erstwhile colonial oppressor. In the 1896 presidential election the Democrats charged that McKinley was pro-British; the Republicans defended their candidate by issuing a pamphlet describing how deeply the president was hated in England. For Root, British imperialism was a paradigm of colonial government; for Mahan, part Irish himself, the British Navy was a model to be emulated. But for both Britain remained a rival.

At loftier intellectual and social levels there was closer understanding. Roosevelt and his friends had grown up with the English classics, and American authors like Hawthorne, Cooper, Twain, Dreiser, and Wharton were popular in England. The bond among living literati was strong. Writers traded domiciles, Kipling to Vermont, Henry James to London. During the run-up to the American war with Spain, Alfred Austin limned the relationship in a verse whose quality provides no clue to how he had bested Swinburne to succeed Tennyson as England's poet laureate:

Yes, this is the Voice on the bluff March gale,
"We severed have been too long:
But now we have done with a worn-out tale,
The tale of an ancient wrong,
And our friendship shall last long as Love doth last,
  and be stronger than Death is strong."

Hay, then ambassador in London, responded to the poem in less fevered tones: "We are bound by a tie which we did not forge and which we cannot break; we are joint ministers of the same sacred mission of liberty and progress. . . ."

The wellborn of both countries mingled freely. Cabot Lodge, who courted Irish-American votes in Massachusetts, saw no contradiction in taking anti-British positions in the Senate and then, during its recesses, sailing off to vacations in England. The two aristocracies, one based on birth, the other on wealth, made some prominent mergers in the late nineteenth century. Joseph Chamberlain, Randolph Churchill, and George Curzon all took American wives. Anthony Trollope ended his Palliser novels with the grand wedding of the future Duke of Omnium, who did not need the money, and the beautiful and wealthy Miss Isabel Boncassen of New York. Economic ties were close. British investment in the United States far outweighed Germany's, and the market in Canada, a British dominion, was lucrative for Americans.

British statesmen meanwhile began to see the merits of a policy that favored the United States, with its growing power, as an effective counterweight to Germany, fast becoming Britain's real adversary. Chamberlain, colonial secretary in a Conservative government, confirmed the change in a speech three weeks after the outbreak of the Spanish-American War. Exceeding his previous assertion that Britain and America were "more closely allied in sentiment and interest than any other nations on the face of the earth," he hinted at an actual alliance between them. Chamberlain's extravagant language represented more than the zeal of a man who had married the daughter of President Cleveland's secretary of war and had succumbed to the inducements of the charming Ambassador Hay. A British strategy shift was under way. It was first visible in Central America, which the British had dominated throughout the century, and the Caribbean, where they now seemed ready to cede domination to America.

Britain's support for the United States in 1898 had to overcome some dynastic and political sympathy for Spain; the Spanish queen regent Maria Christina was a niece of Queen Victoria's. But Maria Christina complained in vain that the British were letting the U.S. Navy use their facilities in the Caribbean. The British Navy also helped Dewey in his Hong Kong preparations for the attack on the Philippines and again in Manila Bay in his confrontation with von Diederichs. The British backdown in Venezuela in 1895, their support for the United States in 1898, and their concessions over the canal in 1901 were not intended as a renunciation of influence but rather, from a geopolitical standpoint, as a means to put American power at the service of British interests. As Kipling described it, "After a nation has pursued certain paths alone in the face of some slight misrepresentations, it is consoling to find another nation (which one can address without a dictionary) preparing to walk along the same lines to, I doubt not, the same ends."

British support was noticed and appreciated by Americans, as Lodge, a recovering Anglophobe, gracefully observed in his history of the Spanish-American War. The United States reciprocated by sympathizing with Britain's fight against the Boer rebellion; even Theodore Roosevelt's Dutch heritage and his exasperation at British treatment of the Boers did not prevent him from favoring a British victory. Mahan's writings took on a markedly pro-British cast when he began to share London's view of the dangers posed by Germany; to count the British fleet as a potential asset was no small thing. Having branded Britain before the war as "undoubtedly the most formidable of our possible enemies," he wrote in 1901 that "the British Empire is in external matters our natural though not our formal ally."

Talk by Roosevelt and others about annexing Canada subsided. The annexation plank that had been inserted in the Republican platform in the 1896 campaign was dropped in 1900. In fact, with America's new power and confidence, Canada, indefensible against an American land attack, came to be seen as a useful hostage to British behavior. Roosevelt, who had many close British friends, wrote to one of them, Arthur Lee, that British support in 1898 "worked a complete revolution in my feelings," that "the English-speaking peoples are now closer together than for a century and a quarter, and that every effort should be made to keep them close together." To his closest British friend, Spring Rice, he wrote: "I am greatly mistaken if we ever slide back into the old condition of bickering and angry distrust."

Hay, the most fervent Anglophile among American leaders, was of course conscious of these trends and worked to translate them into policy. As he was settling in as secretary, he wrote to Henry White, his former deputy in London: "As long as I stay here, no action shall be taken contrary to my conviction that the one indispensable feature of our foreign policy should be a friendly understanding with England." Hay's first try at that understanding was the ill-starred Hay-Pauncefote Treaty. His second try at an isthmian treaty was a success because this time it was the British who compromised.

The British were driven to an even more important concession in a dispute with the United States over Canada's border with the panhandle of Alaska. Gold had been discovered in 1897 in the Canadian Yukon, so the issue was not trivial, since it concerned ownership of harbors and water passages to the goldfields. Before then even the British had assumed the area belonged to the United States; now the Canadians convinced them to reverse themselves. Britain demanded arbitration, a no-lose proposition, since at worst its phony claim would be rejected.

Hay, who cared more for improving the bilateral relationship with Great Britain than for harbors in the frozen north, probed for a modus vivendi. But his suggestions on the modalities of an arbitration tribunal were unacceptable to the Canadians, and a British proposal fell afoul of the Senate, eliciting a new round of complaints from Hay about senatorial fecklessness. In the end Hay managed to stall the Alaska issue until completion of the isthmian negotiations removed a British bargaining chip. By then Roosevelt was president, and his determination to preserve the maritime approaches to Alaska was positively bellicose. He told Hay Canada's claim was "an outrage pure and simple"; to pay the Canadians anything would be "dangerously near blackmail."

Under his new chief Hay faced the challenge of working out a procedure to resolve the dispute that would be acceptable to London yet tough enough to overcome Roosevelt's suspicion that he was soft toward the British. He came up with the idea of compulsory arbitration by "six impartial jurists of repute," three to be chosen by the United States and three by the British government. Even with the assurance that the United States could get no worse than a tie, which would leave it with a preponderant military position in the region, he had difficulty persuading Roosevelt and the Senate. They finally succumbed on the understanding that the three American commissioners would be selected for their steadfast commitment to the U.S. position. Roosevelt thereupon appointed Lodge, who met none of the agreed-on criteria, being neither "impartial" nor a "jurist," and his only "repute" in Britain being ill. The second selection, of Root, was almost as blatant a disregard of the criteria; as Roosevelt's secretary of war, he was under discipline to vote as instructed. The third commissioner was a retired senator from Washington, a state with a clear financial interest in a pro-American outcome. The British members were two Canadians and Lord Alverstone, a jurist of distinction, who was the lord chief justice.

Roosevelt rattled sabers during the six-week deliberations of the commission in September and October 1903, threatening a military occupation of the disputed territory if the decision went the wrong way. Not surprisingly, the Americans and Canadians, both on instruction, voted their national positions; the Americans had been instructed by Roosevelt not to compromise on "the principle involved." Alverstone—because he was intimidated, or because the British government had grown tired of supporting Canada's dubious claim, or because he felt an obligation to do the right thing—voted with the Americans. In a letter to his wife, Hay paid him generous tribute: "I think myself that Lord Alverstone is the hero of the hour. No American statesman would have dared to give a decision on his honor and conscience directly against the claim of his own country."

Resolution of the Alaska dispute was the final settlement of the long border between the United States and the British dominion of Canada. More than that, as Roosevelt wrote Mahan, it "settled the last serious trouble between the British Empire and ourselves." Henry Adams could observe in 1904: "I no longer feel the old acute pleasure in vilifying the British." Mr. Dooley, that quintessential Irishman, also saw the writing on the wall. Following Roosevelt's election in 1904, he observed that "th' king sint f'r Ambassadure Choate, who came as fast as his hands an' knees wud carry him."

Hay's affection for England and his skill as a diplomatist ensured that the opportunity for change was exploited and that the change was not episodic or short-lived. He probably needed the toughening that Roosevelt gave him both on the isthmian issue and on the Alaska boundary, but he in turn moderated Roosevelt's excessive demands and belligerent rhetoric. More than the president, he saw that the overall connection with Britain would transcend ephemeral wins or losses. Above all, Hay was responsible for establishing the civilized and friendly tone of a relationship that, more than a century later, is still seen on both sides of the Atlantic as a family one.

The rigors of Hay's stewardship during an exceptionally important and demanding period of foreign policy took their toll on him. Never robust, he suffered from a variety of physical and mental ailments, including chronic depression. The Senate, and particularly Lodge, wore him down. Since becoming secretary of state, he came to consider this erstwhile friend, with whom he had been exchanging Christmas presents for decades, as obstructive, duplicitous, narrow-minded, and marred by "infirmity of his mind and character." He told Henry Adams that Lodge gave him more trouble than "all the governments of Europe, Asia and the Sulu Islands, and all the Senators from the wild West and the Congressmen from the rebel confederacy." One may wonder if Hay saw his trials with Lodge as unwitting punishment for his once having cuckolded him.

Yet even in his decline Hay's humor remained as sharp as ever. He described to a friend a meeting during the Boxer Rebellion with the Chinese minister Wu Ting-fang, who was not noted for clarity of expression: "Minister Wu came by this morning and stayed for two hours, at the conclusion of which Wu was Hazy and Hay was Woozy." One of Hay's last acts occurred after a Moroccan bandit called Raisuli had kidnapped and held for ransom a presumed American citizen, Ion Perdicaris. Hay sent the Moroccan government an ultimatum that was gleefully read to cheers at the 1904 Republican National Convention: "We want Perdicaris alive or Raisuli dead." When Perdicaris was freed to nationwide acclamation, Hay wrote in his diary: "It is curious how a concise impropriety hits the public."

But Hay's lifelong bouts of depression increased after he lost King, Nicolay, McKinley, and his son Del in 1901, the same year in which he had to juggle the isthmian and Alaskan negotiations. His absences from Washington after 1901 lengthened as he sought the quiet of Lake Sunapee. His friends wondered if he was really sick, while President Roosevelt assumed he was malingering. Early in Roosevelt's second term, on a recuperative trip to Europe with Henry Adams, Hay remarked on shipboard that a dozen treaties were "hung up in the Senate Committee-room like lambs in a butcher's shop." When he returned, he could endure only a week in Washington before fleeing to New Hampshire. He died there on July 1, 1905, at sixty-six. As his biographer Tyler Dennett remarked, "John Hay had to die to prove that he was unwell."

Two weeks before his death Hay dreamed that he had gone to the White House to report to the president, "who turned out to be Mr. Lincoln." Lincoln was sympathetic about his illness and kindly gave him two unimportant letters to answer. The dream left Hay melancholy. A day later he wrote the final entry in his diary: "I say to myself that I should not rebel at the thought of my life ending at this time. I have lived to be old; something I never expected in my youth. I have had many blessings, domestic happiness being the greatest of all. I have lived my life. I have had success beyond all the dreams of my boyhood. My name is printed in the journals of the world without descriptive qualifications, which may, I suppose, be called fame. By mere length of service I shall occupy a modest place in the history of my time."

Roosevelt was right that Hay had not been a great secretary of state. Still, his two great contributions to American foreign policy merit him a place much higher than he would have given himself, in fact not far below his own model, Seward. With his ability, through the Open Door, to convince the American people of their stake in China and the Asian mainland, Hay helped ensure that the acquisition of Hawaii and the Philippines led to an American Asian strategy. The enormous U.S. economic and political interests in Asia today, as well as the commitments reflected in wars fought by American soldiers in Japan, Korea, and Vietnam during the twentieth century, trace some of their origin to his Asian diplomacy.

In addition, Hay's establishment of a special relationship with Great Britain created a catalyst for the growth and conduct of America's responsibilities as a great power in the twentieth century. The Venezuelan crisis of 1895 marked the last time the two countries almost went to war. In the twentieth century the dynamic combination of the two English-speaking peoples helped overcome the threats to peace posed first by Nazi Germany and then by Soviet Russia. Often reluctantly America took on the burdens of global responsibility in the two world wars and at the beginning of the Cold War. Almost certainly it would not have done so without the influence of Great Britain. In every case British diplomacy, persuasion, example, and sometimes weakness weighed heavily in the American decisions to engage. The relationship survived, and even gained from, the power shift from Britain to the United States. As a future British prime minister, Harold Macmillan, told a colleague in 1943, "We . . . are Greeks in the American Empire. You will find the Americans much as the Greeks found the Romans—great big, vulgar, bustling people, more vigorous than we are."

Hay's career in all its variety embodied some of the reasons for America's emergence as a great power. His work with Lincoln during the Civil War contributed to uniting and strengthening the country in the dynamic postwar decades. As a successful businessman he caught the rising tide of America's economic expansion. As a secretary of state who knew both the world and his own country, he presided over a period of expansion with modesty, civility, and a self-deprecating humor that excluded arrogance. As a writer—novelist, poet, historian, and journalist—he immersed himself in the human condition and made himself a man of uncommon humanity. He himself was the best example of the "fine good nature" that he urged on Americans after they had won their "splendid little war."

5.

The years between the Spanish-American War and the end of Theodore Roosevelt's presidency were distinguished by an unprecedented projection of power and influence outward from America's shores. But they were also marked by an extraordinary movement in the opposite direction, a mass migration of people from all over Europe and parts of Asia to the United States. During the first decade of the twentieth century nearly nine million legal immigrants entered the country, more than in any other decade until the 1990s. It was the largest concentrated migration in all human history up to that time. By 1910 more than one in seven Americans was foreign-born, more than twice the proportion of today.

The current of imperial expansion flowing out and the current of immigration flowing in did not always keep to separate channels. Sometimes they intersected, enriching or polluting each other, and when they did so, the element that joined them was race. A nineteenth-century American's views on race influenced his reaction to his country's expansion, to immigration, and to the connection between the two. This linkage was especially important with Theodore Roosevelt and Henry Cabot Lodge, because they were in a position to affect both directions of the two-way traffic: how the United States exported its power abroad and how it treated the millions of foreigners seeking its shores.

America was almost entirely open to newcomers throughout the nineteenth century. Immigration was unregulated at the federal level from the time of the ineffective Alien Acts of 1798, which were directed mainly against radical French and Irish refugees, until the early 1890s. During the century immigrants were enormously important to the growing American economy. When their numbers increased after the Civil War, primarily as the result of the advent of the steamship, they became even more essential for the growth industries of railroads, steel, mining, textiles, meatpacking, and construction. Immigrants were welcomed not only as laborers but also as settlers; midwestern states and land-grant railroads actually advertised for them.

For many Americans, the racial mixture that these new immigrants enhanced was a good thing. Herman Melville exulted: "Our blood is as the flood of the Amazon, made up of a thousand noble currents all pouring into one." The Statue of Liberty was dedicated in New York Harbor in 1886, with Emma Lazarus's words "Give me your tired, your poor, / Your huddled masses yearning to breathe free" engraved on its pedestal. Ralph Waldo Emerson praised the America emerging from the "smelting pot" of Europe. Oliver Wendell Holmes compared Americans with Romans, "the great assimilating people."

At the same time the foreign-born arrivals were often swamped by the waves of anti-immigrant bigotry that swept the United States, especially during periods of economic distress. Immigrants were made to pay for the anti-Catholic, antiradical, and pro–Anglo-Saxon prejudices that typified this American nativism. The decade of the 1890s, which included an economic collapse in 1893, was also a time when more and more immigrants were arriving from southern and eastern European countries. These less educated, often swarthier, and less familiar Italians, Russians, and Habsburg Empire Slavs were distrusted by Americans disposed toward Anglo-Saxon racism. This new immigration did not so much create the nativist offensive as intensify it. In their search for a promised land the immigrants often found themselves in the wrong place at the wrong time.

The xenophobia of the 1890s had two main elements. First was the fear, usually exaggerated, of radicalism. An immigrant anarchist tried unsuccessfully to kill the steel baron Henry Clay Frick in 1891, and President McKinley's assassin had been on the fringes of the anarchist movement. But most immigrants actually tended toward political conservatism. Coming for the most part from European autocracies, they were used to keeping their heads down and to prizing order over social or political instability. In the cities where most of them lived, they fell under the protection of mainly Irish urban political machines and were more inclined to tolerate corrupt paternalism than to flock to join reform movements. They were generally patriotic and loyal to their chosen country. Foreign-born accounted for 20 percent of the Union army in the Civil War, a higher figure than their proportion of the U.S. population.

Fear of immigrant radicalism made capitalists like Carnegie, Frick, and Hay weigh the value of immigrant labor against the supposed dangers of imported disorder. Still, Carnegie came down on the side of continued high immigration. The institutional voice of capitalism, the National Association of Manufacturers, also maintained a consistent proimmigration position. Less affluent Americans—the urban working class, the lower middle class, anti-Catholic Protestants, members of earlier waves of immigration—clung to the proposition that the new immigrants were a threat to their livelihood, their way of life, and even their safety.

These lower-class anti-immigrants had at least experienced in their own lives the actual effect of the huge waves of immigration. Those who constituted the second nativist element had no such excuse since they were among the wealthiest and best-educated men in America. Their hostility to immigration was almost entirely an intellectual construct, acquired not in the sooty mill cities of Pittsburgh, Cleveland, or Fall River but on the leafy campuses of Harvard, MIT,

Yale, Columbia, Johns Hopkins, Cornell, Wisconsin, and Stanford. Theirs was an upper-class nationalism suffused by bizarre theories of race and directed against people presumptuous enough to bring their alleged inferior civilization to America's shores.

Intellectuals who were influenced by social Darwinism and/or Anglo-Saxonism brought a racial emphasis to American imperialism, whether they supported imperial expansion because it was part of the march of civilization against savagery or opposed it because it might bring undesirables to the United States. But they displayed no division in their views on the immigration of non-Anglo-Saxons; to a man they opposed it. Nathaniel Shaler, Roosevelt's professor at Harvard, found "non-Aryan" peoples lacking in the correct "ancestral experience" and impossible to Americanize. John W. Burgess, Roosevelt's law teacher at Columbia, warned of "mongrel races" and the "rabble" immigrating from southern Europe. Francis A. Walker, president of MIT and of the American Economic Association, conducted a study that claimed the declining birth rate of native Americans was due to immigrants, "beaten men from beaten races; representing the worst failures in the struggle for existence."

Eugenics, which became a fad in the United States, inevitably fueled the anti-immigrant fire. The idea of eugenics, an offshoot of Darwinism started by Darwin's cousin Francis Galton, in its crudest application (most of its applications were crude) held that race determined social conditions and that biological deficiencies rather than environmental factors condemned the poor to misery and vice. In a famous American study of a degraded family, *The Jukes* (1877), Richard Dugdale concluded that heredity determined disease, pauperism, and immorality. American eugenicists, who were devoted to selective breeding (as if people were racehorses), managed to persuade the legislatures of twelve states to pass laws favoring sterilization. To the eugenicist mind, immigration was a purely biological issue: Since the degenerate genes of new immigrants could never be improved by the American environment, the best immigrant stock had to be selected at the start and the rest discarded.

Paradoxically, no city in the United States was more affected by anti-immigrant nativism than the town that had stood so firmly against slavery in generations before, Cambridge, Massachusetts.

Considering the intellectual brawn of Harvard and MIT, it would have been possible to stand in Harvard Square and be no more than a few miles from many of the most prominent social Darwinists, Anglo-Saxonists, and eugenicists in the entire United States. In that environment it may not be surprising that the American politician most imbued with this patrician nationalism was Henry Cabot Lodge of Boston, Cambridge, and Nahant. Restriction of immigration was one of the most consistent and important objectives in his long political career.

He was not an ideologue on race. He was a leading spokesman in the Senate for African American rights, and in 1890 he sponsored a Senate bill to expand them. He had adjusted pragmatically to the Irish immigration in the Boston area and was well tuned to the fact that the Irish voted and wielded political power. His efforts were concentrated on keeping southern and eastern Europeans out of the United States. As a student of, and writer about, the Teutonic influence on American civilization Lodge was fascinated by genealogies, especially his own. His pedigree on his father's side was suitably Teutonic, and he managed to upgrade the Cabots of his mother's lineage, who were of Norman descent. In obeisance to his intellectual mentors, he wrote: "Darwin and Galton have lived and written, Mendel [who gave heredity priority over environment] has been discovered and revived, and the modern biologists have supervened, so that a man's origin has become a recognized part of his biographer's task." Applying genealogy to American life, Lodge produced in 1891 a study that, using a biographical encyclopedia, argued that it was the English racial strain that had contributed most to the development of the United States.

Lodge believed that racial characteristics were immutable. "The men of each race," he wrote, "possess an indestructible stock of ideas, traditions, sentiments, modes of thought, an unconscious inheritance from their ancestors, upon which argument has no effect." The races arriving from southern and eastern Europe, he believed, brought with them negative qualities that could not be changed and would be passed on to their descendants. This new immigration was "most alien to the body of the American people" and "a great and perilous change in the very fabric of our race." To combat it, Lodge became the spokesman for the Immigration Restriction League, founded in Boston in 1894 by several young Harvard graduates and a key organization for the next quarter century.

Lodge's greatest effort to stem immigration was through legislation. Early in his political career he adopted an idea that was making the rounds of restrictionist circles, a literacy test as a requirement for immigration. In his version a prospective immigrant had to be able to read forty words in his own or any other language in order to be admitted to the United States. Everybody knew that this would apply mainly to the poorest immigrants from southern and eastern Europe. It was a clever and indirect way to keep them out. Lodge first introduced a bill to make the literacy test law in 1891 and repeatedly thereafter. The wonder was that it kept failing. It was defeated in Congress in 1898, 1902, and 1906; it passed both houses in 1896, 1913, and 1915, but was vetoed successively by Presidents Cleveland, Taft, and Wilson. It finally passed in 1917, over Wilson's veto, during a wartime frenzy of hostility against foreigners. Lodge failed for so long with the literacy test because he had only lukewarm labor support—Samuel Gompers was caught between protecting immigrants and protecting jobs—and because immigrants had begun to constitute a formidable voting bloc increasingly attractive to Republican candidates. In 1924, the year of his death, the legislative efforts of Lodge and his anti-immigration colleagues culminated in the passage of the most restrictive immigration law ever approved by the U.S. Congress.

Theodore Roosevelt was a much more complex figure when it came to race. He was obsessed with the issue, studying and discussing it all his life. But his views were often contradictory. He defended the rights of blacks and extolled the bravery of Indians, but he caricatured both groups and was likely to fasten similar stereotypes onto Filipinos, Cubans, and Latin Americans in general. His scathing description of Cuban soldiers after the American landing in 1898 focused on their ragged appearance and untrustworthy behavior, not on their three-year struggle, which crucially helped the Americans by weakening Spanish rule there. Like American Indians and Aguinaldo's Filipinos, Cubans were for Roosevelt inconvenient occupants of real estate that he would have preferred to find unencumbered by lesser breeds.

With all his prejudices, Roosevelt's innate sense of fairness set him well above Lodge and others of his class on racial issues. He named his beloved Oyster Bay house Sagamore Hill in compliment to the Indians of New York State, for whom the word "Sagamore" means "chieftain." In the glow of hindsight, he recalled in his autobiography that he had promoted Jews and blacks in the New York City police force, had helped create a level playing field in the U.S. civil service, had appointed the first Jewish cabinet member (Oscar Straus, of the New York family of merchants and philanthropists), and had invited Booker T. Washington to dinner at the White House (once). He talked the talk of equal opportunity, telling a Republican audience in 1905: "Our effort must be to secure to each man, whatever his color, equality of opportunity, equality of treatment before the law."

Roosevelt's racial ambivalence carried over to his views on immigration. In *The Winning of the West* he made a point of emphasizing that his backwoods heroes were not recent immigrants but of Scotch-Irish stock, longer in America. He supported Lodge's efforts to curb immigration, though he lacked his friend's zeal on the issue. During the 1890s he favored restricting and regulating immigration "by much more drastic laws than now exist." As president he presided over increases in the head tax for immigrants and the extension of entry restrictions to epileptics, prostitutes, beggars, anarchists, imbeciles, tuberculosis sufferers, and persons who had committed crimes involving moral turpitude. He kept up a running and friendly correspondence with racist intellectuals like Madison Grant, a Yale-educated blue-blooded eugenicist who wrote a virulent book attacking blacks and non-Nordic immigrants. He counted among his good friends racial bigots like the artist Frederic Remington, who once boasted of his desire to massacre "Jews, Injuns, Chinamen, Italians, Huns—the rubbish of the earth," and Owen Wister, who complained that urban civilization was being debased by "encroaching alien vermin."

Still, Roosevelt had a vision of America that depended critically on its immigrants. "Americanization," as he called it, featured the power not of race but of the American environment. His view, influenced by the writings of his friend Frederick Jackson Turner, was that the frontier Americanized people: "A single generation of life upon it has invariably beaten all the frontiersmen of whatever stock into one mould, and this a mould different from any in Europe." In contrast with

Lodge's view of the immutability of race, Roosevelt's consistent belief was that America itself wrought a benevolent transformation on the people who came to it and lived in it, regardless of their ethnic background. He loved the jumble of races and made his Rough Riders a living symbol of it.

The idea of America as a "melting pot" captivated his imagination. Israel Zangwill dedicated his 1908 play of that name to the president, who attended the premiere with Mrs. Zangwill. In *The Melting Pot*, two immigrants from Russia fall in love in America. One is a Jewish boy; the other a Russian girl whose nobleman father was implicated in a pogrom in which the boy's parents died. At the play's end the boy proclaims the victory of the melting pot over ethnic antagonisms: "Celt and Latin, Slav and Teuton, Greek and Syrian—black and yellow . . . how the great Alchemist melts and fuses them with his purging flame!" Four years after the play opened, Roosevelt assured Zangwill of his continued dedication to its theme. He wrote to him that the play "not merely dealt with the 'melting pot,' with the fusing of all foreign nationalities into an American nationality, but it also dealt with the great ideals which it is just as essential for the native born as for the foreign to realize and uphold if the new nationality is to represent a real addition to the sum total of human achievement."

Roosevelt treasured the melting pot not only for its leveling value and its lessons in egalitarian responsibility but also for the evils it warded off. He warned somewhat defensively: "The one absolutely certain way of bringing this nation to ruin, of preventing all possibility of its continuing as a nation at all, would be to permit it to become a tangle of squabbling nationalities." The melting pot was a valuable preventative and thus vital to national security. However, to his mind the pot did not melt all who fell into it equally. Roosevelt was clearly more anxious for the new immigrants to become Americans like him than for the reverse transformation to take place. He did not need melting; they did. This failure to transcend his time and his class prevented him from moving into an intellectual world free of racial bias. Still, his basic goodwill allowed him to distance himself considerably from the world of Darwin, Galton, Lodge, and the racist professors of his youth.

Roosevelt's presidency reflected both sides of his ambivalence on immigration. He signed restrictive, if relatively minor, laws on the subject. He supported the exclusion of Chinese, a subject on which his mentor was Edward Alsworth Ross, a University of Wisconsin sociologist who described immigrants as "hirsute, low-brained, big-faced persons of obviously low mentality." At the same time, drawing on his experience as New York City police commissioner, Roosevelt took reformist actions that improved the lot of immigrants: He attacked corruption in the immigration program by cleansing Ellis Island, the main reception center in New York Harbor, of bribery, shakedowns, and the sale of entry documents, and in 1906 he backed a law to end the practice of naturalizing masses of immigrants on the eve of elections. Since most immigrants voted Democratic, in this latter case Roosevelt was probably influenced by politics, as he often was.

With an eye to the Jewish vote, he responded to the massacre of Jews by Russians in 1903 with diplomatic démarches directed at St. Petersburg. His appointment of Oscar Straus as secretary of commerce and labor was aimed in part at stealing Jewish votes from William Randolph Hearst's bid for the governorship of New York in 1906. Straus's duties included immigration, in which he strongly believed. He talked Roosevelt out of intervening on behalf of the 1906 version of Lodge's ultimately unsuccessful bill to institute the literacy test, despite the president's previously declared support for such legislation.

Roosevelt's earlier experience with the cigar makers kept fresh his concern about the economic exploitation of immigrants. He sought and valued the advice of Frances Kellor, a dynamic social worker and muckraker who went on to transform the living conditions of immigrants in New York State. Roosevelt also presided over, if he did not originate, fairly permissive policies concerning migration from and to America's new overseas territories. Filipinos could come to Hawaii as sugarcane workers, and Puerto Ricans after 1900 had the right of entry to the United States. In addition, large-scale Mexican immigration north of the border began during his presidency. On the other hand, Roosevelt believed that the Anglo-Saxon race was committing "suicide" by allowing itself to be outnumbered by foreigners, a view developed under the influence of Professors Ross and Walker. But his solution, unlike theirs, was not to cut immigration sharply but to encourage old-stock families to have more children.

The close relationship between American expansion outward and immigration inward was full of ambiguities. Some immigrants supported the expansion of the American empire; some opposed it. The working-class immigrants who were the principal readers of Hearst's warmongering newspapers clearly thirsted for a war with Spain, as their purchases of the *New York Journal* in record numbers showed. They thus contributed to heating the war fever to which McKinley responded. On the other hand, prominent immigrant intellectuals like Schurz, Carnegie, and Godkin opposed imperialism and helped lead the political fight against it. So did the American Federation of Labor, which contained many immigrant members.

On the other side of the coin, the jingoes who supported imperial expansion tended to oppose mass immigration, and their denigration of non–Anglo-Saxon cultures augmented existing prejudices against immigrants. As Fritz Stern, one of the foremost historians of modern racism, has written, "the tacit or unquestioned acceptance of imperialism depended on a presumption of racial inequalities." Imperialism is inherently racist. People like Lodge, who wanted to project superior Anglo-Saxon power and values abroad, also wanted to protect their American homeland from the onslaught of inferior cultures. Other Americans took a restrictive view of immigration out of horror that their traditions would be contaminated by foreigners. Gompers forever wavered on this issue, and the Irish-born Godkin supplemented his anti-imperialism with an anti-immigration position just as strong. It was left to a lonely few, led by Senator Hoar, Carnegie, and Schurz, to reject racial arguments and make the parallel cases against imperialism and for immigration.

Legislation shutting down the immigration of non–Anglo-Saxons did not come until 1924, but pressure for such laws was building for decades. The first signal was the Chinese Exclusion Act of 1882. Since 1850 some three hundred thousand Chinese had emigrated to the West Coast to find employment as gold miners, railroad workers, farm laborers, and small businessmen. (Chinese laundries, nonexistent in China, proliferated in the American West.) Their presence provoked a torrent of bigotry led by the Workingmen's party, headed by Denis Kearney, an Irish immigrant. Under popular pressure from California, where Kearney was based, Congress passed an act to suspend Chinese immigration for ten years and deny naturalization to Chinese already in the country. Senator Hoar denounced it as the legalization of racial discrimination, but it was renewed in 1892; in 1902, under Roosevelt, Chinese immigration was suspended indefinitely.

Racial feeling against Chinese was not limited to California; it was shared by American imperialists in general. Mahan, in a letter to the *New York Times* in 1893, wrote that "the vast mass of China—now inert—may yield to one of those impulses which have in past ages buried civilization under a wave of barbaric invasion." Hay's Open Door policy had originated not in respect for China but rather in a desire to prevent the division of its markets by America's European rivals. The door was open to American interests in China but firmly closed to Chinese who wanted to emigrate to the United States.

The racial superiority flaunted by many Americans over Filipinos, Cubans, and Puerto Ricans probably stimulated the efforts made in Congress to close the doors on Chinese and on southern and eastern Europeans. Although Roosevelt, Lodge, Root, Mahan, and Hay all were unfriendly to mass immigration, their views varied in stridency. Hay, for example, regretted what was happening to the Chinese, though he did nothing about it. Two weeks before his death he wrote in his diary that the exclusion of Chinese was "barbarous." Root deplored the "dreadful" treatment of Chinese immigrants in California. When it came to the Japanese, it was Roosevelt and Root who took a moderate position in ensuring that they were not treated as cavalierly as the Chinese had been. Roosevelt's relationship with Japan was in fact a curious amalgam of his views on global strategy and on race.

6.

Roosevelt considered his accomplishments with Japan the major foreign policy achievement of his second term. He was not disposed to believe Asian nations should be admitted into the restricted club of superior Anglo-Saxons, but he made an exception for the Japanese. "The Japs interest me and I like them," he wrote his British friend Spring Rice. To another friend he called the Japanese "a wonderful and civilized people" who were "entitled to stand on an absolute equality with all the other peoples of the civilized world." What impressed him was Japan's energy, technical prowess, culture, industrial achievement, and growing military strength. Japan, like America, was in a heroic phase of political and economic development.

Roosevelt was not just a starry-eyed admirer; he had solid strategic reasons for his pro-Japanese attitude. In Europe he considered Germany a potential enemy and Britain, having conceded the Caribbean to the United States, a budding friend. In Asia he most feared the expansive inclinations of Nicholas II's Russia, against which Japan could be a useful buffer. The Anglo-Japanese alliance of 1902 strengthened ties between two countries friendly to the United States; Roosevelt warmly approved it. He also welcomed Japan's surprise attack on Russia in February 1904, though as the conflict between them wore on, he went beyond being a cheerleader. In fact his analysis of the global geopolitical situation reflected an impressive sophistication.

Now that the United States had made its great imperial thrusts in the Caribbean, the Pacific, and Panama, what Roosevelt cared for most in foreign, as in domestic, affairs was order. He wanted order on America's two long land borders with Canada and Mexico, order in the Caribbean and Central America, and order for the protection of the new Pacific holdings of Hawaii and the distant and vulnerable Philippines. He involved the U.S. government in Venezuela in 1903 and intervened in the Dominican Republic in 1904 and in Cuba in 1906 for the purpose of establishing order. The principle of intervention enshrined in the Roosevelt Corollary was intended to be invoked in disorderly countries, not in stable ones like Argentina or Brazil.

With America's new and significant assets in the Pacific, a similar regime of order was required for Asia. Roosevelt believed this could be achieved through a balance of power between the two major nations, Japan and Russia. The war between them was thus convenient, but only if neither side won convincingly; a "yellow peril" or a "Slav peril" would be equally dangerous. He wanted Japan to succeed but not too overwhelmingly. To ensure such a result, Roosevelt thought it necessary to inject himself into the situation.

Throughout 1904 the president operated with great diplomatic skill on the principal global powers: Germany and France as a means of moderating Russia, Britain as an ally of Japan, and of course Russia and Japan directly. He made use of old and new friends. Spring Rice was in the British Embassy in St. Petersburg, and Speck von Sternberg was the German ambassador in Washington. A Japanese who had gone to Harvard, the influential Baron Kantaro Kaneko, became his back channel to the Japanese government. The president did not trust the Russian ambassador in Washington, so he appointed an able American diplomat, George von Lengerke Meyer, U.S. ambassador to St. Petersburg to give him access to the tsar. He wrote Meyer's detailed instructions himself; Secretary Hay described them admiringly as being so direct as to be indiscreet.

As always when a president pursues personal diplomacy, the professional diplomats were cut out, and though this usually acts to the detriment of good policy, that was not the case this time. The U.S. ambassadors in Berlin and Tokyo were told no more about American negotiations with the Germans and Japanese than successive U.S. ambassadors in Moscow knew about U.S.-Soviet relations during much of the Cold War, when bilateral business was transacted in Washington with an experienced Soviet ambassador. After Roosevelt's victory in the 1904 election, as Hay sickened and died, the president's hands-on involvement became even greater. In Washington he initiated with a special Japanese envoy discussions so secret that even Japan's ally Britain had no inkling of them. But his ingenious diplomacy foundered on Russia's refusal to make peace, even after defeats at Port Arthur and Mukden in northeastern China. The destruction of the Russian fleet in the Tsushima Strait in late May 1905 finally persuaded the tsar of the weakness of his position.

Roosevelt was the choice of both sides to broker a peace. In his memoirs he claimed that this was his own idea; the diplomatic record indicates that the Japanese put him up to it. In any case he was willing, even eager to accept a global mediating assignment larger than any president had undertaken before. The predictable bickering over the venue for the talks drew from Roosevelt a diplomatic patience hitherto unfeatured in his character but left him sputtering privately about Russian treachery and Japanese selfishness. With great reluctance he finally offered the United States as the site in July 1905; the negotiations were held in Portsmouth, New Hampshire, and at Oyster Bay.

The Japanese, preening as victors, stunned the Russians with a set of severe demands (a dry run for the even harsher ones imposed twelve years later by Germany on the new Bolshevik regime). In addition to major territorial changes, Japan insisted on a large monetary indemnity and the cession of Russian-held Sakhalin Island, which the tsar's police had turned into a place of exile for political prisoners.

The Russians, already humiliated militarily, were aggrieved, aggressive, and so opposed to concessions that a renewal of the war was a real possibility. Not even the presence in Portsmouth of a first-rate Russian envoy, Sergei Witte, an important prerevolutionary economic reformer and prime minister, could soften the government's obduracy. Witte towered over his Japanese counterpart by more than a foot—a physical intimidation that symbolized the toughness of the Russian negotiating position. Despite Japan's military advantage, therefore, a solution was by no means inevitable.

Given the keen attention the American press paid to the negotiations and to Roosevelt's involvement, a breakdown of the talks would not have been cost-free for a president just beginning his second term. Roosevelt thought that the Japanese had the better of the argument—they had won after all—so he tried a full diplomatic onslaught on the Russian government, using all the instruments of modern diplomacy except his personal presence, which was not an option since St. Petersburg was weeks away by steamship. He persuaded the Japanese to compromise on the lesser issue, Sakhalin Island, which they agreed to split with Russia. Then, in the improved atmosphere, he sent Ambassador Meyer to Nicholas with a personal letter that emphasized Japan's flexibility and urged similar moderation from Russia. Roosevelt warned the tsar not too gently that if hostilities were renewed, Russia might well lose eastern Siberia. Expanding the points of persuasion, the president got Kaiser William II to exhort his Russian cousin on behalf of compromise and the French to weigh in as well.

Roosevelt's efforts, brilliant as they were, failed. The tsar, in a cable to the president and a two-hour meeting with Meyer, refused to give up either territory or money. As often happens, however, the sobering prospect of diplomatic failure provokes reassessments that begin to change rigid positions. Roosevelt made sure that both sides saw the abyss before them. Finally Witte broke the impasse. He cabled home his belief that Russia's "peace-loving public opinion" (an obvious euphemism in that tsarist police autocracy) would not accept the loss of dignity implied by an indemnity but might accept the partial cession of Sakhalin. He emphasized the dangers if Russia were seen as wrecking the negotiations and the future benefits if Russia won Europe and America to its side. For those reasons, Witte concluded, "we must take Roosevelt's opinion into consideration." He was recognizing, and using as an argument with his monarch, the fact that America's new power had made its voice worth listening to. This time the tsar agreed.

Roosevelt now exploited Russia's concession on Sakhalin to press Japan to drop its demand for indemnity. His arguments, made in a personal message to the emperor, were trenchant. Russia would refuse to pay, so Japan would gain nothing and the war would resume. As he had told the tsar, he now told the emperor that the Japanese could take eastern Siberia, but it would be worthless to them. They would have spent millions of dollars and shed rivers of blood, and worst of all, they would have the whole world against them because nobody would understand their waging war over an issue of money alone. Prudently the president took the precaution of putting his démarche in writing; he suspected that the mikado was usually told what he wanted to hear, not what Roosevelt wanted to tell him.

As the Japanese pondered, Roosevelt blanketed the diplomatic field with further pleas to Japan to give up the indemnity and to Russia to pay it. A week dragged by in extreme tension and with no sign of hope; the Russians even asked for their hotel bill. Roosevelt concentrated on emphasizing to both sides the consequences of failure and decided privately to blame that failure on Russia. At that point the Japanese gave in. Terms were agreed on August 30 on the basis of no indemnity and the division of Sakhalin.

In Japan the peace agreement set off street riots among Japanese angry that it had deprived them of the fruits of their military victory. Russia's obstinacy had indeed achieved more than a defeated country could expect, but the war itself had produced enormous gains for Japan in territory and economic privileges. It had also established Japan as the strongest power in Asia; the Portsmouth Treaty effectively ratified that status. For Roosevelt, it had been a signal victory. The balance of power had been established: Russia had been humbled but not destroyed, and Japan's increase in power had been stopped short of hegemony.

Roosevelt was also able to use the crisis in the Far East to win additional acceptance of America's hold on the Philippines. As a believer in spheres of influence he saw the Yellow Sea as a Japanese sphere, just as he expected the Japanese and others to recognize an American sphere in the Caribbean. But the Philippines, much closer to Japan than to the United States, could not be protected in any American sphere. During the discussions leading to Portsmouth, Roosevelt sent Secretary of War Taft to Tokyo, where he worked out an arrangement to solve this problem. The two sides agreed that the United States, in violation of an 1882 pledge to support Korea's independence, would not interfere with any Japanese claim to Korea. Japan in return would respect U.S. ownership of the Philippines. Taft was accompanied to Japan by Roosevelt's eldest and still-single daughter Alice, a vivacious beauty of twenty. While Alice reaped the publicity, Taft, to protect a vulnerable American acquisition close to the Asian mainland, quietly made the deal to sell out the Koreans.

The Portsmouth negotiation was a masterpiece of classical diplomacy. While he was not present the whole time, Roosevelt set the strategy and did most of the negotiating himself, without a secretary of state, Hay having died six weeks before the first meeting at Portsmouth. As a mediator and negotiator Roosevelt was informed, focused, understanding, sympathetic, firm when he had to be, trustworthy, and decisive. He had learned to speak softly without a big stick. His achievement received due credit throughout the world, including from the two protagonists. "Your personal energetic efforts," cabled Nicholas II, "brought the peace." "Your advice," his Japanese friend Kaneko told him, "was very powerful and convincing, by which the peace of Asia was assured."

These references to peace were strange accolades for a man who had spent most of his life lauding the glories of war. Even stranger was the Nobel Peace Prize he was awarded a year later. Yet he deserved it. He had ended a war that was causing horrific human carnage. He had also taken the United States another rung up the ladder of world power as a successful mediator between the two leading Asian states, as a country that had won recognition of its interests in Asia, and as a growing military giant. Because of Portsmouth, Roosevelt's America now occupied a larger place on the political map of the world.

There was a domestic coda to Roosevelt's foreign policy encounters with Japan. Japanese emigrants to the continental United States and to Hawaii contributed greatly to the American economy. Like the Chinese, however, they were the targets of restrictionists who wanted to exclude them as the Chinese had been excluded since 1882. In California racial feeling welled over in the year after Roosevelt scored his victory at Portsmouth. In October 1906 the San Francisco School Board ordered Asian students into segregated schools; the ruling affected ninety-three Japanese children. Japan erupted into anti-American rioting, and its government protested to Washington. Roosevelt, whose sympathies on this issue lay entirely with the Japanese, acted to head off restrictive federal legislation. He told Congress that the school board's act was a "wicked absurdity" and urged fair treatment for the Japanese.

Once again a mediator, Roosevelt worked out with the San Francisco authorities and the Japanese government a "gentleman's agreement" that dealt with the larger issue involved, Japanese immigration. The Japanese, but not the other Asian, children returned to the public schools, and the Japanese government agreed to restrict immigration by denying passports to Japanese workers heading directly to the United States. Roosevelt also plugged a loophole by prohibiting Japanese in Hawaii from entering the United States. The president had averted a bilateral crisis at the expense of the free immigration of Japanese. The outcome entirely satisfied him, for though he was no fan of mass immigration, he did insist that immigrants, once they had arrived, be treated just like Americans. "We cannot afford to regard any immigrant as a laborer; we must regard him as a citizen," he wrote in 1907.

In addition to his sophisticated approach to Japanese issues, Roosevelt expanded the American presence on the world stage in other ways. Most important, he continued the naval buildup he had advocated since before the Spanish-American War. He never ceased to believe in the vital role of naval power in defining a country's strength and influence. The United States had succeeded abroad, he wrote a congressman in 1904, "because, and only because . . . we possess a navy which makes it evident that we will not tamely submit to injustice or tamely acquiesce in breaking the peace."

In the diplomacy of his second term Roosevelt was greatly assisted by Elihu Root, whom he had named—inevitably—secretary of state as Hay's successor. Root had been back in private law practice for eighteen months but seemed to have had no hesitation about returning to Washington at one-twenty-fifth his law income. He already had considerable diplomatic experience as administrator of America's colonial acquisitions and as acting secretary of state during the Boxer Rebellion when Hay was ill. He brought to the position an enormous capacity for work (not a feature of Hay's tenure), natural diplomatic skill, and fearlessness in exposing brutal realities.

Root had proved himself as a manager in reorganizing the War Department and creating a general staff. Now he presided over a department that, though boasting twice the personnel numbers of 1898, still had fewer than two hundred people. He reformed the patronage-stained consular service by introducing a competitive examination. Unlike Hay, he was an adept with the Senate. He wore down Lodge's fidelity to the Gloucester fishermen to win the help of "the Senior Senator from the fishing grounds" in negotiating an arbitration treaty with Great Britain over fishing rights in Newfoundland. To an unrivaled degree he had the lawyer's skill of understanding an adversary's case as well as he understood his own. Lord Bryce, the British ambassador, described a démarche in Root's office, at which the secretary argued the British case more cogently than the instructions from London that Bryce clutched in his hand. Root then proceeded to demolish the British position. Roosevelt considered Root the greatest statesman of his time. Indeed he might be remembered as a great secretary of state if there had been major crises during his four years in office.

Like Roosevelt, Root took a sympathetic view toward Japanese immigration and helped the president quell the disputes that continued to bubble between California and Japan. He defused the extremism of the California authorities, which was provoking fear of war among the more nervous observers, by initiating secret conferences—the Clam Club, as he called it—between them and the president. On this, as on other subjects, Root showed no fear of his boss. When Roosevelt began to threaten the Californians, Root brought him into line with a tap of his pencil on the mahogany table.

Working with the Japanese ambassador in Washington, Kotaro Takahira, Root in 1908 formalized the agreement Taft had reached three years earlier in Tokyo by which Japan agreed to respect U.S. ownership of the Philippines and Hawaii, in return for American recognition of Japan's hold over Korea. He continued Roosevelt's work in making the United States a global arbiter. In a dispute in 1905 between Germany and France over Morocco, Kaiser William II urged Roosevelt to become involved, and the president reluctantly used his good offices to call a conference at Algeciras in Spain. Roosevelt and Root did not attend in person; the United States was represented by Henry White, who had been Hay's able deputy in the London embassy. The Root-White combination helped produce a facesaving formula for lowering the tension. It was not an important accomplishment and the American part was not decisive. Nevertheless, for the first time the United States helped settle a major regional dispute in which neither its geographical nor its political interests were directly involved. In the second half of the century it was to do this again and again.

Root made his most significant contribution in Latin America. Like Roosevelt, he was reluctant to push for military intervention to restore order in chronically unstable countries; he preferred negotiation. Working with Mexico, he engineered a calming of tensions between Guatemala and Honduras, and later he tried unsuccessfully to mediate a dispute between Nicaragua and Honduras. His approach derived from his moderate view of the Monroe Doctrine, which he did not see as a "warrant for interference" in Latin America. On the other hand, he took it as given that strong powers were bound to exert certain rights over weaker ones. After all, he had forced the Platt Amendment on Cuba, had probably taken a hand in writing the Roosevelt Corollary to the Monroe Doctrine, and had prosecuted the war in the Philippines.

His strongest belief was that because of geography, Latin America was a vital interest for the United States, and it was therefore important to be a "good neighbor," a phrase he coined in 1907. He understood the bruises that America's Cuba and Panama policy had inflicted on Latin American trust in the United States. To heal them as well as to reinforce U.S. interests, he made a three-month trip to Latin America by steamship in 1906, visiting Puerto Rico, Brazil, and Argentina on the eastern side, and then—having passed through the Strait of Magellan—Chile, Peru, Colombia, and Panama in the west. It was the longest visit to Latin America by a secretary of state ever. It revived the hemispheric concentration of James G. Blaine and foreshadowed the Good Neighbor policy of Franklin D. Roosevelt.

Theodore Roosevelt's diplomacy, skillful as it was, had little lasting effect on the course of world history. In Europe the U.S. mediation over Morocco did not curb the growing hostility between Germany and France, which were at war within a decade. In Asia the Russo-Japanese War proved that as he himself admitted, the Open Door closed as soon as a powerful nation showed itself willing to run the risk of war in order to disregard it. His Portsmouth mediation did prevent further military horrors but did not deter Japan's drive toward militarism. But it was the effect of these actions on the American position that counted. Roosevelt wrote in 1910: "We ourselves are becoming, owing to our strength and geographical situation, more and more the balance of power of the whole world." Seven years after that statement, and partly at Roosevelt's urging, the United States was finally to enter the world war to restore the balance between Germany and the Western democracies.

Roosevelt's two terms constituted America's first imperial presidency, in the sense that the country for the first time was administering possessions near and far, had achieved dominant influence over the Caribbean and Central America, had built its navy into the second strongest in the world, and had convinced the world to take its counsel and its policies seriously. When Roosevelt saw off the U.S. battleship fleet for its round-the-world cruise in December 1907, he was sending three messages. To Japan and Europe he was proclaiming that the United States was both a Pacific and an Atlantic power. To the world at large he was broadcasting that America now had global scope and influence. To the American people he was celebrating the fact that their country had finally achieved the status of a great power.

12. America's Century

1.

Events from 1898 through the Roosevelt presidency were the direct result of expansionist policies that began overland during the nineteenth century and reflected an ambition to extend American influence overseas as well. By the last years of the nineteenth century economic and cultural conditions had coalesced in favor of expansion, the weakness of Spain had provided the opportunity, and exceptional men had been there to stiffen a reluctant president. The emergence of the United States as a world power was a culmination, not an aberration.

That emergence was followed not by a retreat to isolation but by an increasingly confident American acceptance of the mantle of a great power. The progress toward global involvement was often hesitant and erratic, and Americans were pulled reluctantly into the two world wars. But as we can see in the hindsight of a century, the direction was steady. The United States did involve itself, late but decisively, in both world conflicts, then led a Western alliance in successfully opposing the challenge from Soviet communism. It was in large part because of America's actions as a great power that the twentieth century was not the "Century of the Third Reich" or the "Century of the Glorious Victory of World Communism."

There was no retreat from the high imperial moment of the Theodore Roosevelt era. During the Taft administration (1909–13) the policy of Dollar Diplomacy, in the spirit of the Platt Amendment, gave the United States increased influence in Central America and the Caribbean. In 1912 Taft sent marines into Cuba to help quell a revolt and into Nicaragua to defeat an uprising against a government that had accepted considerable U.S. control over its finances. Taft's successor Woodrow Wilson (1913–21) proved as imperially inclined as Roosevelt himself. From his base at Princeton, where he was a professor and then president, Wilson had applauded the American attack on Spain, supported the annexation of the Philippines and the war against Aguinaldo's forces, and backed Roosevelt's intervention in Panama.

As president Wilson practiced a classic Rooseveltian diplomacy, seeking to remove threats close to American shores and to protect the sea routes to the Panama Canal, which opened for business in his first term. In 1914 he unsuccessfully sought Senate approval for a U.S. protectorate over Nicaragua that was designed to protect an alternate canal route from foreign incursions. Out of fear that Germany would exploit Haiti's endemic violence in order to gain control of sea access to Panama, Wilson landed troops in 1915, and Haiti became an American protectorate for nineteen years. A year later American marines occupied the Dominican Republic and installed a U.S. dictatorship that lasted for eight years. Wilson also intervened repeatedly in Mexico. In 1916 he turned over to his secretary of state Robert Lansing a draft of a speech he was proposing to give on self-determination; it began: "It shall not lie with the American people to dictate to another people what their government shall be. . . ." Lansing, a finicky stickler for accuracy, wrote on the margin: "Haiti, S. Domingo, Nicaragua, Panama." The draft was rewritten.

When European war broke out in 1914, Wilson saw it initially as a conflict without innocent parties that could end in "peace without victory," and he was cautious about any U.S. involvement. In the view of most Americans, the national interest was not directly involved in this European war. Wilson had to deal with that political fact and resolved to do so through a policy of strict neutrality. Roosevelt, Lodge, and Root, by then a senator from New York, all favored neutrality as well; none of them publicly urged American participation until late in the war. But they considered Germany the clear aggressor and wanted a neutrality combined with "preparedness" (a euphemism for a military buildup) and a tilt toward Britain and its allies.

When the British liner *Lusitania* was sunk in May 1915 by a German submarine with the loss of 128 Americans, the two protest notes Wilson sent to Germany proved too strong for his pacifist secretary of state William Jennings Bryan, who resigned over them. But they were too weak for Roosevelt and company; as Root put it acerbically, they were like shaking your fist at a man and then shaking your finger at him. Lodge opposed as anti-British Wilson's plan to buy German ships that had been trapped in U.S. harbors at the outbreak of the war and helped defeat the proposal in the Senate. But until U.S. interests became unmistakably threatened, neither Wilson nor his Republican tormentors were willing to commit the United States to a European war that was causing unimaginable numbers of casualties.

In early 1917 the Germans made two dangerous and disastrous decisions. They resumed unrestricted submarine warfare against neutral as well as belligerent ships, an act that imperiled American merchant shipping and American lives, and they were caught trying to enlist Mexico in a plan to attack the United States. The British intercepted a telegram sent by German foreign minister Arthur Zimmermann to his minister in Mexico City. It described a desired alliance between Germany and Mexico by which Germany and Japan would support a Mexican attack on the United States aimed at the return to Mexico of Texas, New Mexico, and Arizona. These two German actions plainly threatened important American interests and led to Wilson's declaration of war in April 1917.

All the major factors that brought the United States for the first time into a European war developed from the earlier tradition of American expansion. First, the Republican concern with preparedness was a direct descendant of Roosevelt's, Lodge's, and Mahan's emphasis on militarization in the 1890s, and it finally won a convert in Wilson himself. Second, the response to the German threat to merchant shipping was based on the dictum by Mahan and other naval supremacists that great powers must have powerful navies not subject to intimidation. Third, Germany's attempt to attack the United States from the south violated not only the original Monroe Doctrine but the reasserted policy of the 1898 period that Central America and the Caribbean were vital American interests. Finally, the sympathy toward Great Britain, which overcame the predilections of many Americans of Irish or German background, owed much to John Hay's efforts to promote a special American relationship between the two countries. For the United States, therefore, the Great War was not a diversion from 1898 but an extension of it.

Wilson's losing battle to have America participate in the League of Nations also turned on issues rooted in the Spanish-American War. The president's nemesis in this battle, Henry Cabot Lodge, was never an isolationist but always a consistent advocate of extending American power in the world. Nor was Lodge opposed in principle to a world organization with political and judicial powers. In 1915 he had himself proposed "a union of civilized nations . . . to put a controlling force behind the maintenance of peace and international order." Roosevelt, even earlier, had suggested a similar global body. The heart of the dispute was the League of Nations Covenant, which Wilson insisted be incorporated textually in the Versailles Treaty. Article X of the covenant obligated states to assist a fellow member subjected to external aggression. This was originally a French idea, but Wilson defended it doggedly as part of the negotiated outcome.

Lodge opposed Article X just as strongly, charging that it was wrong to have America's hands tied by an international organization in which it was not a dominant influence. He feared that the League would be condemned to a collective security mission that it could not fulfill and that could only undermine the sovereignty of its members. A firm unilateralist, the Massachusetts senator had fought all his career for a militarily and politically powerful United States. He did not wish to see that power ceded to an organization with amorphous mandates and possibly inimical members. His fight against the League was connected to, and consistent with, the positions he had taken in 1898.

Quantities of ink, paper, and software have been devoted to the question of whether the battle over the League of Nations would have been resolved differently if Wilson had not been in ill health, had not broken with his most sensible adviser, Colonel Edward M. House, and had not been devastated by a stroke in September 1919, just when a final decision was imminent. The stroke nullified the president's formidable powers of persuasion and gave his jealously protective wife effective control over policy. While she dreaded the prospect of a presidential failure, Edith Wilson lacked the constitutional standing, the professional capacity, and the personal inclination to work with the Senate toward passage of a compromise treaty containing reservations. Five years later Lodge argued in his own book on the crisis that the treaty would have passed if Wilson had accepted the reservations Lodge had introduced.

On the other hand, Wilson showed little flexibility—none at all on Article X—and Lodge was equally implacable. The senator had no use for Wilson as a human being. Privately he called the president mean, selfish, unenlightened, self-righteous, stupid, and totally lacking in intellectual integrity. For his part, Wilson callously disdained Lodge's well-known sensitivities toward the Senate's prerogatives, which included the constitutional duty of advice and consent to treaties. Unlike McKinley, Wilson named no senators to his negotiating team, nor did he take any to Paris as observers. He also insulted Lodge personally when on his return to America in February 1919 he traveled to the senator's own city of Boston to make a speech promoting his views, instead of going straight to Washington to report to the Senate.

Lodge's vanity was a factor as well. In 1899, when he led the battle in the Senate for approval of the Treaty of Paris, he was a junior member of the Senate Foreign Relations Committee. Now he was its chairman as well as Senate majority leader. He had told Roosevelt in 1899 that there would never be another battle like the one over ratification of the treaty ending the Spanish-American War. Now there was an even larger fight, and he was in the middle of it. Lodge had thought nothing of savaging treaties submitted by a Republican president, William McKinley, and by his friend poor John Hay. He was certainly not going to balk at attacking a treaty that was splitting the Republican party, that failed in his view to advance U.S. strategic interests, and that had been proposed by an arrogant and sanctimonious Democratic president whose person and principles he despised equally.

The defeat of the League of Nations in the U.S. Senate should not be seen as a step toward isolationism. There were isolationists in the Senate, men who had opposed U.S. entry into the war and were adamantly set against the policy of making the United States a global power. But Lodge and the Republican leadership were not among them. The vote against Wilson's treaty was as much an assertion of the values of 1898 as a vote for the treaty would have been. It proclaimed, among other things, that the United States intended to be a strong nation that would determine its global policies independently. If a historic opportunity for cooperative internationalism was missed, it was not because the United States intended to withdraw behind its continental boundaries. It still had overseas possessions, important economic links to other countries, and a sense of international vocation that the Spanish-American War and its aftermath had helped to shape. Eventual U.S. participation in World War I, by expanding to Europe the orbit of America's global engagements, automatically implied a far broader definition of U.S. interests than William McKinley had ever put forward.

Nevertheless, U.S. nonmembership in the League of Nations lowered the American voice in the world, although three Americans were awarded the Nobel Peace Prize between 1925 and 1931 (after Wilson had already won it in 1919). One casualty of the battle over the League was the internationalist bent of the Republican party. When Roosevelt's death in January 1919 removed the front-runner for the 1920 Republican nomination, the party slipped back into the hands of an old guard, typified by Wilson's successors, Warren G. Harding and Calvin Coolidge, more interested in domestic "normalcy" than in foreign commitments. In a dramatic reversal the Democrats now became the party of internationalism.

Only a generation later the issue of America's participation in a world conflict arose again as a result of Hitler's aggressions. It is unclear whether the United States would have entered World War II if Japan had not attacked it in 1941 and if Hitler, as Japan's ally, had not declared war against it right after Pearl Harbor. But it is likely that America would have at least fought against Germany. Hitler represented a far greater threat to American security than Kaiser William had, as Winston Churchill reminded his future partner Franklin Roosevelt. Moreover, the British factor in shaping American opinion was even more important than in 1914 because by 1940 Britain was fighting for its life alone. British and American planners actually began working out a joint strategy a year before Pearl Harbor. In the Pacific the war imposed on the United States was a direct result of earlier American sanctions aimed at deterring Japan's aggressive bid for the oil and raw materials in the Asian colonies of Britain, France, and the Netherlands. The vulnerability of the U.S. Pacific islands gave Japan the opportunity to strike the American outposts fast and hard. The earliest victims of the Japanese attack were territories that the United States had taken in 1898, Hawaii, Guam, and the Philippines.

The American entry into World War II was critical to the defeat of both Japan and Germany, and continuing U.S. willingness to commit itself to the defense of its friends was the decisive factor during the Cold War against the Soviet Union. After the 1947–49 period, when President Truman convinced the U.S. Congress to support the Truman Doctrine for the defense of Greece and Turkey, the Marshall Plan for the recovery of Europe, and Point Four for the economic development of poorer countries, isolation was no longer even an option. With the birth of NATO and the growth of the American policy of containment, America's commitment to global peace and stability grew even deeper. For more than forty years U.S. troops were stationed in the most forward area of NATO Europe, Berlin, where a Soviet ground attack would have brought the United States into the conflict within the very first minutes. The habitual appointment of an American general as supreme allied commander in Europe provided additional insurance that the United States would defend its allies. Moreover, by the strategic doctrine of nuclear deterrence, the United States, in order to protect Western Europe, undertook to put American cities at risk of destruction by a Soviet nuclear attack.

The Soviet Union collapsed in 1991 primarily because of its own internal contradictions, but NATO's strength and determination over more than four decades had sharpened those contradictions while deterring Moscow's efforts to intimidate Western Europe. When the final crisis came under Mikhail Gorbachev, the steadiness of the Western alliance helped ensure that three of the most extraordinary events of the entire twentieth century—the liberation of Eastern Europe, the reunification of Germany, and the disintegration of the Soviet Empire—all took place without bloodshed.

In retrospect, the twentieth century, for all the brilliance of its intellectual and technological accomplishments, was a time of violence and horror unprecedented in world history. The First World War planted two time bombs that were to explode in 1917 and 1933. First, by weakening Russia, which had finally begun to move toward constitutional reform and economic regeneration, the war helped lead to the most tragic historical accident of the century, the seizure of power by a tiny Bolshevik party lacking significant popular support. Second, the Versailles Treaty, in saddling a defeated Germany with excessive reparation costs, an approach strenuously and shortsightedly advocated by Lodge, helped encourage a vindictive nationalism leading to the Third Reich.

The threat posed by Hitler's Germany became the major international preoccupation from 1933 until the German defeat in 1945. The threat of Stalin's Russia succeeded it as the main concern. Neither challenge could have been dealt with successfully without the full engagement of the United States. The imperial initiation at the end of the nineteenth century had prepared Americans for the great power role that, in the twentieth century, only they could play.

2.

All five founders of American imperialism lived into the twentieth century, but only Root survived beyond its first quarter. Mahan died in December 1914, soon after the outbreak of a global conflict during which the U.S. Navy was to grow more than eightfold in officers and men. But ships were no longer the focus of attention. The war's military leaders were understandably preoccupied with land combat and its murderous consequences. They were also beginning to see the possibilities of the air as a new arena for warfare. In the year of the Spanish-American War, the Wright brothers had been running a bicycle shop in Ohio; their first flight at Kitty Hawk five years later changed military strategy forever. By the end of the First World War the naval aviation force numbered more than two thousand planes. Mahan, the aging naval strategist and historian of sail, was slow to adapt to the military consequences of airplanes, submarines, and amphibious warfare. He grew less relevant even though several of his core precepts—concentration of force, primacy of the offense, and destruction of the enemy's fleet ahead of his bases—survived into the air age. According to one historian, the 1941–45 naval war against Japan was fought on Mahanian principles.

Mahan continued to write furiously and was elected president of the American Historical Association in 1902, but changing times deprived his last years of the acclaim he had enjoyed before 1898. In 1906 the U.S. Navy finally got around to promoting him to rear admiral on the retired list—not because he had won it a global reputation but because he had served in the Civil War. He maintained his quarter century correspondence with Roosevelt but was given no significant post during his friend's presidency. Roosevelt, a keen judge of men, evidently decided that his naval adviser was no longer as useful

as he had been in the 1890s. He ignored Mahan's ill-considered recommendation that the navy avoid building huge battleships of the
type the British had introduced.

Mahan died as he had lived, a fractious combination of sincerity
and insubordination. Looking back over his career, the State Department legal counselor John Bassett Moore credited him with "a peculiar power to grasp principles which others had seen only dimly and to
set them forth with such clearness and force that all could understand them." It was his intellect, not his character, that impressed
people. This fact made him less complete as a person than Roosevelt,
Hay, Root, or Lodge. Mahan, not Root, was the real thinking machine. When the march of events made the machine rusty, he became
a relic.

Theodore Roosevelt, at fifty a young and vigorous former president,
spent the last ten years of his life trying to replay the glories of his
past. After his election victory in 1904 he had injudiciously pledged
not to run for a third term. As the 1908 election approached, he
mightily regretted the pledge. Instead of reneging on it by issuing a
"clarification," as any modern politician might have done ("Changing
circumstances have compelled me to reconsider . . ."), he honored it.
Following his return from a year's safari in Africa, he decided that his
chosen successor, William Howard Taft, was ruining his legacy by being too conservative on domestic issues, too inept in politics, and too
beholden to big business and the party bosses.

After 1910, when the Republicans lost the House for the first time
since 1894, Roosevelt resolved to run for president in 1912. He failed
in his challenge for the Republican nomination against Taft, then
bolted the party to run independently as a Progressive. As expected,
he outpolled Taft in the election, but the split in the Republican
ranks delivered victory to Wilson. The Democrat took less of the popular vote than Roosevelt and Taft combined, but carried forty states to
win by a landslide in electoral votes. Had Roosevelt followed Root
and Lodge's advice and shown more patience, a trait not usually associated with him, he would surely have won the Republican nomination and probably the presidency in 1916. He, not Wilson, would
have been the war president.

U.S. entry into the war on April 6, 1917, provided Roosevelt with
another outlet for his restless energy. Four days later he traveled to

Washington as a supplicant to ask Wilson for permission to raise a division of volunteers to ship out to France before the regulars could be trained. Premier Georges Clemenceau was enthusiastic about this grand gesture of early American support. Wilson was taken by Roosevelt's charm in this only extended meeting between the two men. But he remembered how Roosevelt had won the governorship of New York, and he was not about to award a political rival a platform for some heroic deed. Moreover, the generals dug in against giving a major command to a fifty-eight-year-old politician with limited military experience and a reputation for grandstanding and insubordination. When Wilson turned the proposal down, Roosevelt reacted personally and vindictively. For the rest of the war he volleyed intemperate and abusive public attacks at the president.

In his last decade Roosevelt abandoned much of the balance, restraint, and judgment that had marked his presidency. His rupture with his protégé Taft, his willingness to split his own party, his vainglorious effort to get into the war, his calumnies against ethnic Germans and Irish, whom he considered insufficiently "American," his efforts to curb the civil liberties of domestic opponents of the war, his insistence on unconditional surrender and a punitive peace for Germany, his public disparagement of a U.S. president during wartime— these were actions of a man who seemed to have lost his compass. Roosevelt was like a locomotive whose brakes were failing.

With all his setbacks, the thing that gave him the most pride was the distinguished military service of his sons. He went to great lengths to ensure that all four boys saw combat, including writing a letter to Prime Minister David Lloyd George to get Kermit into the British forces. There was a compulsion here, traceable right back to his own father's failure to serve in the Civil War. Like any father, he feared for his sons' safety, but being the father he was, he saw no alternative. Tragically, the god of war played a cruel and final trick on his faithful acolyte. In mid-July 1918 a reporter turned up at Sagamore Hill to tell Roosevelt that his youngest son, Quentin, a U.S. Army flier, had been shot down behind German lines. Expecting the worst, Roosevelt stoically went through with a political speech at Saratoga. At one point he spoke off the cuff: "The finest, the bravest, the best of our young men have sprung eagerly forward to face death for the sake of a high ideal; and thereby they have brought home to us the great truth that life consists of more than easygoing pleasures, and more than hard, conscienceless, brutal striving after purely material success." Two days later came the news that Quentin had been killed.

Theodore Roosevelt died less than six months later. His health had not been good since a near-death experience on a trip down the Amazon with Kermit in 1913. But there seems little doubt that it was the grief over Quentin's death that really killed him. In turning down the opportunity to run for governor of New York in 1918, he had told Corinne: "I have only one fight left in me, and I think I should reserve my strength in case I am needed in 1920." But a coronary embolism took him at Sagamore Hill on January 6, 1919, at the age of sixty.

Like Roosevelt and Hay, Lodge also lost an adored son. Bay Lodge, a promising young poet, died of a heart attack in 1909. Bay was a throwback to the more aesthetic and tolerant side of his father, the side that Lodge had consciously set aside at twenty-two on the death of his friend Michael Simpson. Nannie Lodge was devastated by the loss of her only son; she died in 1915. But Lodge was not deflected from the single-minded political course he had pursued since the imperial days: domestic conservatism combined with a strong belief that the United States must maintain a place among the great powers.

In 1912 Lodge broke with Roosevelt's Progressivism; popular recall of judges and other forms of direct democracy were too much for him. He did not like Taft and had urged Roosevelt to contest him for the Republican nomination. But after Roosevelt's failure at the Chicago convention, Lodge could not follow his friend into a third party. In 1884 he had rejected the "rope of sand" of an independent party; he did it again in 1912, declaring for Taft and the Republican party. Four years later, in the Senate race of 1916, he defeated John F. Kennedy's grandfather John F. ("Honey Fitz") Fitzgerald. (That loss was avenged in 1952, when Kennedy defeated Lodge's grandson and namesake, Bay's son Henry Cabot Lodge, to win his first Senate seat.)

Lodge's historic battle with Wilson absorbed his penultimate term in the Senate, overshadowing his strong positions on other issues. Nonetheless, he remained a firm protectionist, a defender of civil service reform and a professional foreign service, an advocate of a big navy, and a battler to reduce immigration. The literacy test for prospective immigrants, which he had championed for decades, finally passed over Wilson's veto in 1917. His legislative skills did not dim with age. His management, at the age of sixty-nine, of the Senate's defeat of the League of Nations, however costly to American interests, was a masterpiece of parliamentary leadership, "one of the greatest," said Root, "that I have ever known or known of." Taft, who worked on behalf of the treaty, had a less glowing view. Lodge and Wilson, he remarked, "exalt their personal prestige and the saving of their ugly faces above the welfare of the country and the world."

In his final years Lodge became still more conservative, supporting Warren G. Harding, the candidate of the Republican old guard, in 1920. He showed a flash of moderation as a delegate to the Washington Disarmament Conference of 1921, when he went along with great power naval limitations, then guided the agreement through the Senate. But he remained hostile to unilateral disarmament and intransigent on immigration. A key element in his opposition to the League of Nations was his fear that it would one day challenge America's right to keep immigrants out. He was particularly adamant against the entry of Japanese and was instrumental in ensuring that the draconian National Origins Act of 1924 excluded both Japanese and Chinese. That act, the culmination of Lodge's restrictive efforts, set a ceiling on immigration and based it on racial criteria, assigning quotas to most nationalities according to their percentage of the U.S. population in 1920. As one scholar has written, "After three centuries of free immigration, America all but completely shut her doors on newcomers."

Woodrow Wilson, three years out of office, died on February 3, 1924. Edith Wilson, finally in a position to exact revenge on her husband's tormentor, refused to invite Lodge to the funeral even though he was the Senate majority leader. Lodge himself died nine months later, aged seventy-four. To the end he remained an imperialist and a unilateralist, but also a man who based his activism on a close reading of U.S. interests. In a late speech he said: "There is a wide difference between taking a suitable part and bearing due responsibility in world affairs and plunging the United States into every controversy and conflict on the face of the globe."

After his years as Roosevelt's secretary of state, Elihu Root served as Republican senator from New York during the Taft and early Wilson presidencies. His falling-out with his friend and patron, later repaired, was painful to him. "I care more for one button on Theodore

Roosevelt's waistcoat," he told a friend, "than for Taft's whole body."
Root was not really at home in the Senate, where his colleagues' long-
windedness bored him. There was sadness in his epigram that "Congress is not a mirror of anything because it never reflects." Still, he
worked hard there. He championed the merit system in government
and, deserting his ties with big business, supported a corporation tax
and a constitutional amendment to institute an income tax. He was
instrumental in reclaiming the mud flats along the Potomac, previously used for hospital buildings, cattle depots, and train sheds, and
turning them into a spacious mall to set off the Washington Monument and the planned Lincoln Memorial. But he opposed both the
direct election of senators, which passed in 1913, and Wilson's nomination of the liberal Louis Brandeis to the Supreme Court.

On foreign policy Root preached restraint toward Latin America
and respect for the independence of its countries, elements that were
integral to Franklin Roosevelt's subsequent Good Neighbor policy. He
opposed Wilson's efforts to establish a protectorate over Nicaragua
and to meddle in the unstable situation in Mexico following the revolution of 1910. But he opposed legislation to award independence to
the Philippines. Out of loyalty to John Hay and his treaty with Britain,
he bucked his own party and contested a U.S. exemption from tolls
for American ships passing through the Panama Canal. By 1914 Root
was an advocate of military preparedness and of a neutrality slanting
against Germany. He was not enthusiastic about a League of Nations
but was willing to look for compromises to enable its creation.
Though he did not like Article X, he believed the treaty should be ratified for the sake of cooperation with the European allies and urged
Lodge in vain to give the Democrats "some face-saving modifications." After its defeat, during the presidential campaign of 1920, he
tried, again unsuccessfully, to get Harding to endorse the League.

For this supple conservative there was one principle that guided his
entire international career, the rule of law among states. Root worked
tirelessly to establish the principles of compulsory arbitration, winning the Nobel Peace Prize in 1912 for his efforts. Once out of office,
he helped condition international opinion to the enactment of laws of
war, and his work contributed to the convocation of a World Disarmament Conference in Geneva in 1927. He inspired the creation of a
Central American Court of Justice. He was a leading advocate of the

World Court, defending it in 1935 in his eighty-ninth year, when a proposal to support it lost narrowly in the Senate. The International Court of Justice, finally established with U.S. membership in 1945, redeemed Root's vision.

Though an elitist, Root instinctively understood that foreign policy in a democracy needs a broad public base. He became a pioneer in the establishment of nongovernmental organizations devoted to promoting knowledge of international affairs, helping found and lead the Carnegie Endowment for International Peace and the Council on Foreign Relations. Neither of these institutions has a grassroots character, but both continue to educate businesspeople, lawyers, academics, and other middle-class Americans in their country's international responsibilities. In a seminal article published in the first issue of *Foreign Affairs* in 1921, Root wrote presciently that the days of secret diplomacy were largely over and that the American people would henceforth insist on a place at the policy table. Until his death in 1937, at age ninety-one, Root continued to contribute a fund of sensible policy suggestions that outlived even him.

Root's long, smooth life was uniformly successful and, unlike Hay's, Mahan's, Lodge's, or Roosevelt's, unpunctuated either by career setbacks or by personal tragedies. Yet Root was more human than his aloof and unsentimental demeanor might suggest. Roosevelt's valet, who saw him often, wrote: "Mr. Root is known to the world as a great lawyer and is generally regarded as a man of austere manner and cold, unemotional character. And yet some of us in the White House used to call him 'Cry Baby' . . . because several times we had seen him moved to tears."

Root's passion for international law was motivated by an innate sense of fairness. He believed in helping underdogs—Japanese and Chinese immigrants, Jews in Morocco and Russia, Liberian blacks— but he was opposed to using human rights as a principle of policy. In resisting efforts in the early twentieth century to put pressure on King Leopold for atrocities committed in the Belgian Congo, he wrote: "The very people who are most ardent against entangling alliances insist most fanatically on our doing one hundred things a year on humanitarian grounds, which would lead to immediate war." He added, referring back to 1898: "That attitude practically put us into the war for Cuba."

3.

The territories of America's overseas empire developed differently during the course of the twentieth century. Independent Cuba remained an American obsession, susceptible to U.S. influence and vulnerable to U.S. intervention. Hawaii, counter to the original intention, became a state. The Philippines, following a brutal Japanese occupation during World War II, received their independence in 1946 after nearly a half century of American rule. Puerto Rico continued in its own shadowland, partly American, partly not—still "Mr. Nobody from Nowhere."

American concessions to Puerto Rico tended to come late and often in response to external factors. The island's strategic importance during World War I facilitated the passage of the Jones Act in 1917, which awarded Puerto Ricans U.S. citizenship, gave them an elected legislature, but kept them under governors appointed by the president of the United States and varying in quality from statesmen to hacks. In 1947, following World War II, in which Puerto Ricans fought with distinction in the U.S. Army, they were allowed to elect their own governor. Puerto Rico was accorded its current status as a commonwealth on July 25, 1952, the fifty-fourth anniversary of the U.S. invasion. Puerto Ricans receive federal benefits and do not pay federal taxes, but they cannot vote for the president or Congress unless they live on the mainland.

In recent decades the U.S. government has left it to the Puerto Rican people to choose their status. In a referendum held in 1998 the statehood option won a near majority, with independence and the existing commonwealth status each getting less than 3 percent. More than half of the vote went to "none of the above," a backhanded acceptance of the status quo as a commonwealth but also a signal that Puerto Ricans are not comfortable with their relationship to their former colonial overlord.

The two Asian acquisitions of 1898, the Philippines and Hawaii, developed in opposite directions under the pressures of colonial rule and of World War II. Hawaiians chafed under a political system in which the U.S. president appointed the governor and the U.S. Congress exercised residual control over the elected legislature. In 1940 they voted two to one for statehood. Hawaii represented America's largest military investment in Asia, a condition that brought upon it the full force of Japanese aggression in 1941. Its victimization and its contribution of thirty thousand citizens to the U.S. military effort made the desire for statehood irresistible. Admission to the Union of this ethnically heterogeneous territory came in 1959. It was a fitting historical rebuff to those jingoes and goo-goos who had argued at the end of the nineteenth century that the United States should be protected from "mongrel races."

By contrast, Filipinos, living some four thousand miles west of Hawaii, saw their future in separation from the United States. Aguinaldo's original dream, an independent Philippines based on the American model and organized with American support, remained the objective of most of his countrymen. This consistent desire, combined with the Philippines' distance from the United States, finally persuaded the U.S. government to follow Theodore Roosevelt's advice and divest itself of its "heel of Achilles." American economic nationalists and anti-immigration zealots, arguing respectively that the Philippines were an economic burden and a racial threat, also favored cutting the islands loose.

These strategic, economic, and racist arguments for separation coalesced with the Japanese occupation of the Philippines to make future independence a reality. After the Japanese attack in 1942, President Franklin Roosevelt pledged independence, a promise that his successor, Harry Truman, kept in 1946. But the United States compelled the Philippines, as it had Cuba, to concede several important military bases as a condition. Unlike Cuba, the Manila government was able to repossess those bases at the end of the Cold War, when the Soviet threat disappeared and a friendly and democratic Philippine government energetically urged their return. America's overall record as a colonial power in the Philippines received a compliment from an unlikely source. Ho Chi Minh, the leader of the North Vietnamese resistance against France and later the United States, commented to an American military officer in 1945: "If the Americans had been our masters, they would now be giving us our freedom."

Throughout the century the United States went a long way toward offsetting the hostile commencement of its relationship with the Philippines. Beginning with Taft, the government sent some of its ablest civil servants and soldiers to Manila. Leonard Wood and Henry Stimson, Elihu Root's law partner and protégé, served as colonial governors in the 1920s. General Douglas MacArthur, based in Manila as commander of U.S. forces in the Far East, urged American defense of the islands before the Japanese attack and led the liberation of the country in 1944. Under the temperate guidance of such proconsuls, Philippine governments, though sometimes corrupt and—in the case of Ferdinand Marcos—oppressive, set the standard for democracy in East Asia. Some of the U.S. Foreign Service's ablest diplomats served as ambassadors to the postwar Philippines. The first in this distinguished group, Charles Bohlen, closed a historical chapter in 1960, when he returned to Emilio Aguinaldo, the man whom Elihu Root had dismissed as a "Chinese half-breed" and who was now at ninety-two his country's national hero, the sword that Aguinaldo had been wearing when he was captured by the U.S. Army in 1901.

In independent Cuba the pattern of American intervention set in 1906 continued throughout the century. Cuban presidents for the first thirty years of independence were former officers in the war against the Spanish. In general they saw an interest in ingratiating themselves with the United States, a dynamic that sometimes put the Americans, intentionally or unwittingly, on the side of dictatorship. The United States became effectively the underwriter of the entire Cuban economy. To protect political order and American sugar interests, marines landed in 1912 and again in 1917. American influence also manifested itself in more subtle and sometimes corrupt ways; the American ambassador was traditionally the second most powerful man in the country.

Even after the abrogation in 1934 of the Platt Amendment (except for the retention of the naval base at Guantánamo Bay), America continued to exercise power without responsibility in Cuba. Both major Cuban political figures of the twentieth century, Fulgencio Batista and Fidel Castro, defined themselves in the light of that political reality. Both were children of the Spanish-American War; paradoxically, Batista's father had fought for the revolutionaries against the Spanish while Castro's had fought for the Spanish against the revolutionaries.

Batista dominated Cuban political life for a quarter century, from 1933, when he led an army coup driving the president from office, until 1959, when he was overthrown by Castro. Increasingly dictatorial, Batista decreed the elimination of constitutional government in 1952, an act that opened the way for serious opposition to him from the left. Castro proved the ablest of Batista's foes. A gifted student, debater, and athlete, the twenty-seven-year-old Castro invoked Cuba's violent political tradition in 1953 to attack the Moncada army barracks in Santiago, the city the Americans had taken in 1898. His failure brought him a ridiculously short jail sentence of twenty months, following which he fled to Mexico, where he prepared a more viable revolutionary plan.

In December 1956 Castro landed a small band of guerrillas in eastern Cuba, where they used the nearly impenetrable Sierra Maestra as a safe haven for the launching, by newspaper and radio, of revolutionary appeals. In his two years in the mountains, he won by not losing; Batista's regime undermined its own support by not being able to find and destroy him. Castro also made canny use of the American press. Speaking to a *New York Times* correspondent in conditions of romantic clandestinity, he portrayed himself as a Cuban Robin Hood with many more guerrillas and arms than he actually had.

Castro finally won Cuba with the capture of Santiago on January 1, 1959. In a speech that night he set his achievement in a historical context going back to the revolutions of 1868 and 1895. He reminded the people of Santiago how General Shafter had kept the Cuban general Calixto García from participating in the city's surrender in 1898, and he blamed Americans for depriving Cuba of the fruits of its 1895 revolution. He painted the victory of 1959 as a culmination of what José Martí and his predecessors had begun.

Castro did not require his father's hatred of America or his idol Martí's deep suspicion of the United States to adopt an early anti-American attitude. What he did need, as a leftist leader, was an enemy once Batista had fled Cuba. The American humiliation of the Cuban revolutionaries in 1898, plus the maladroit U.S. bids for hegemony in the years since, made the United States a perfect choice. Conveniently Castro's demonization of the United States absolved him of responsibility for the disastrous effects of his resort to Communist political and economic models. For him the revolution began, rather than ended, with his victory over Batista. With his conquest of Cuba only four weeks old, he was already exhorting the entire nation to become a guerrilla army.

John F. Kennedy's reformist political and economic approach to Latin America began to move the United States away from its exploitative hemispheric record so reviled by Castro. Yet it was Kennedy who secretly launched an invasion of Cuba in 1961 and who threatened war in 1962 over Cuba's clandestine acceptance of Soviet nuclear missiles. Since then the American obsession with Cuba, as strong today as it was in 1898, has prevented a rational U.S. policy toward the island. By its fierce refusal to have anything to do with Castro, the United States has given him far more international stature than he deserves and has deprived itself of the ability to compete directly with his dictatorship for the goodwill of the Cuban people.

4.

A fragile Hispanic commonwealth, an economically weak though independent Asian republic, a far-flung state of the union, and a failed Caribbean protectorate: This might seem a modest bequest by the five men who launched the United States on its imperial course. But the legacies left to twentieth-century America by Roosevelt, Mahan, Lodge, Hay, and Root were broader than may be immediately apparent.

First, they created an authentic American imperialism that was confident in its objectives but modest in its application. As with the earlier conquests across the North American continent, this imperialism had both negative and positive elements. On the negative side the war against Filipinos, the cynicism involved in the annexation of Hawaii, and the compulsion to control Cuba from outside exposed an arrogant aspect to this expansion of American power. So did the overbearing insistence throughout the twentieth century on dominating the internal politics of Latin American countries. On the positive side America's colonialism encouraged political and economic development in the Spanish colonies and began a tradition of helping poor societies everywhere. This enlightened approach matured in Truman's Marshall Plan for Europe and his Point Four program for underdeveloped countries and in Kennedy's Alliance for Progress and Peace Corps. As Theodore Roosevelt put it, "Our chief usefulness to humanity rests on our combining power with high purpose."

Unlike Britain and France, the United States had no professional colonial service and did not develop one. Theodore Roosevelt, Jr., the able governor of Puerto Rico, 1929–31, complained that Americans were incapable of a consistent long-range colonial policy. There was at least one advantage in this deficiency: American imperialists, lacking overseas traditions and institutions, were less likely to treat their subjects as permanent charges. At its best, American imperialism was an inspired amateurism, whose practitioners did not feel comfortable if the Constitution, in Root's figure of speech, lagged too far behind the flag.

Would things have been better for Hawaiians, Cubans, Puerto Ricans, and Filipinos if they had never been under American rule? The answer is certainly no for Hawaiians and probably no for the others. If Cuba, Puerto Rico, and the Philippines had remained under the increasingly feckless rule of Spain, their peoples' lives would surely have been harder than under the Stars and Stripes. Nor would potential alternative colonialists like Germany, Japan, or even Great Britain have seemed more promising. If the Cuban and Philippine revolutions had succeeded even in the absence of American support, as would probably have been the case, two weak independent countries would have emerged as a prey to domestic division and foreign penetration. America's constitutional errors as a colonial power lay less in taking control of the islands than in curtailing the sovereignty of independent Cuba and delaying the independence of the Philippines.

American imperialism began in a progressive atmosphere. Theodore Roosevelt and Woodrow Wilson, the foremost imperialists of modern America, were progressives in their domestic policies. While reasons of state dictated their foreign interventions, they were always conscious of the need to create democratic institutions and project democratic values. Roosevelt even thought it was possible to have an "imperialist democracy," as he told British friends in 1910. But in this he was wrong. As shown by the American experience, imperialism, like slavery, debases rather than enhances democracy. It may well have been the perception of this truth that made Americans so uncomfortable with the colonial status of their territories and so willing to promote them out of it.

The second legacy of the founders of American imperialism was their preparation of the United States to be a great power. Pragmatic as they were, Roosevelt and his friends understood that they were embarked on a grand adventure. The "first great triumph" that Roosevelt foresaw on the troopship to Cuba did indeed become a "world movement." American statesmen then sensed a destiny that was pressing their country toward a glorious future. For McKinley it was the "march of events" that "rules and overrules human action." For Hay it was "the stars in their courses," a "cosmic tendency," and the "spirit of the age" that could not be deflected. Hay could not define America's journey, but he knew the direction: "The United States of today can not go back to what the country was fifty or a hundred years ago. Whether we will or not, whether for better or for worse, we must go forward."

None of these men could foresee the exact course of international affairs during the twentieth century. They would probably have been surprised at the hegemonic position the United States was to win after World War II. They expected their country to become a strong competitor in the world balance of power, not to dominate that balance. Nevertheless, they would not have been astonished at the international burdens that the United States was to assume during the twentieth century. They would have been proud of laying the groundwork for America's global actions. They did not believe in formal alliances, but they did believe in the close relationship with Britain, from which NATO was eventually to grow. They also believed that the United States was destined to be a moral leader in expanding democracy around the globe. Those who survived into the First World War strongly supported the American defense of fellow democracies. Henry Cabot Lodge combined vision with sanctimony when he wrote in 1914: "A world power we had been for many long years, but we had at last become a world power in the finer sense, a power whose active participation and beneficent influence were recognized and desired by other nations in those great questions which concerned the welfare and happiness of all mankind."

The United States entered the world of the great powers through its territorial conquests. But those conquests in themselves did not make the country a great power. America's utility to Britain and France as an ally in the First World War and its indispensability to the Western alliance in the Second World War and the Cold War derived not from American territorial acquisitions but from the new power realities that accompanied them. In the twentieth century, as Mahan

wrote at its outset, imperialism was "the extension of national authority over alien communities." The American "empire" was an empire of
authority, not simply territory.

Third, these five imperialists produced the first comprehensive assertion of U.S. security interests abroad. Those interests were acquired incrementally, sometimes misguidedly, often hypocritically,
and occasionally for the wrong reasons, as in Roosevelt's idiotic assertions that America needed a war. The conviction expressed most
strongly was that America's security depended on effective hegemony
in its own hemisphere. To the north, hegemony over Canada was impossible because of the military strength of Great Britain, Canada's
great power overlord. The critical requirement was therefore to ensure a friendly Canada, which was achieved through pacifying the
three-thousand-mile border by treaty making and by turning Britain
into an ally. These key developments were major achievements of
Theodore Roosevelt and John Hay.

In contrast, Latin America was always in crisis. The interventions
by Roosevelt, Taft, and Wilson in Central America and the Caribbean
were followed by strikingly similar actions by U.S. presidents after
World War II. The protection of America's perceived security from
"Communism"—a specter often as exaggerated as the earlier fears of
Wilhelmine Germany or simply disorder—began with Dwight D.
Eisenhower's ill-advised elimination in 1954 of a leftist Guatemalan
government. American leaders also followed the alternative, softer approaches pioneered by Elihu Root as secretary of state. John F.
Kennedy made a conscious and partially successful effort to promote
democracy and economic development in the hemisphere. Jimmy
Carter's courageous negotiation of a 1977 treaty relinquishing American control of the Panama Canal would have been recognized as
judicious by Root and Hay. Even Roosevelt, rarely bothered by consistency, might have understood it, though the ghost of Henry Cabot
Lodge would surely have fluttered in fierce opposition.

The acquisition of Hawaii and the Philippines had not been dictated by concern about security. Nevertheless, their existence as
American outposts became a key factor in an Asia policy that involved
the United States in three wars during the twentieth century—against
Japan, North Korea, and North Vietnam—and in a commitment to
support Taiwan against potential Chinese aggression. Hawaiian and

Philippine bases provided the forward military deployments for these ambitious objectives. The American defense of South Korea and Taiwan has represented a responsible policy for a global superpower. But the Vietnam debacle was a major error based on the faulty assumption that the North Vietnamese were primarily carrying out expansive designs on behalf of China and the Soviet Union. It is questionable whether any of these U.S. policies could have been pursued with the same intensity had Hawaii and the Philippines not been available to the U.S. armed forces.

It seems paradoxical for the United States to have awarded early independence to Cuba, where its security interests were deeply engaged, yet to have denied it to the Philippines, where they were not. Measures short of annexation—for example, a security guarantee to an independent Philippine government in exchange for basing rights—were available after 1898. We cannot know whether Japan would have gone to war against the United States in 1941 if the Philippines had not been an American bridgehead so close to the Asian mainland. What is indisputable is that by acquiring Hawaii and especially the Philippines in 1898, the United States took on a security commitment in Asia that it found difficult to defend. In the Philippine case the founders of American imperialism may have made a costly mistake.

Latin America and Canada remain to this day the front lines of American security. The men of 1898 established that truism. They also, less wittingly, foreshadowed the expansion of the security perimeter to Europe and Asia. U.S. leadership in World War II and the Cold War was consistent with the view of American interests developed during the time of Theodore Roosevelt. It may even have been a natural consequence of that view, through certainly not an inevitable one.

The fourth legacy of the founders was the creation of two foreign policy priorities, human rights and stability, that have remained in tension with each other ever since. There was more than a little irony in the U.S. government's proclamation of the importance of rights for Cubans less than a decade after it had completed the devastation of a domestic Indian population. Still, human rights was one of the primary reasons why the United States went to war with Spain. Ever since 1898 American statesmen have continued to invoke universal moral values in defense of U.S. actions and interventions overseas. For Woodrow Wilson the war against Germany was a war to end all wars. For Franklin Roosevelt World War II was a war to preserve democracy. Harry Truman, in urging a large appropriation for Greece and Turkey in 1947, told the Congress that "it must be the policy of the United States to support free peoples who are resisting attempted subjugation by armed minorities or by outside pressure." John F. Kennedy's stirring inaugural address pledged the United States to "pay any price" to assure the survival of liberty. Gerald Ford braved protests from the right to sign a document in Helsinki with the Soviet Union and the rest of Europe that established a legitimate international concern over the way governments treat their own citizens. Jimmy Carter elevated human rights to the pinnacle of foreign policy priorities.

Emphasis on human rights was in keeping with the American Revolution and the country's democratic tradition. But U.S. interests as defined in 1898 and during Theodore Roosevelt's presidency also dictated that the government make an effort to preserve domestic stability in areas where American security might be threatened. The natural focus was Latin America, where the United States became the guardian of the status quo. Elihu Root's guidelines—trade, control, order—fitted the second half of the twentieth century as well as the first half.

In the interest of regional order, successive American administrations supported such right-wing dictators as Rafael Trujillo in the Dominican Republic, Anastasio Somoza in Nicaragua, and Fulgencio Batista in Cuba. Some American businesses demonstrated a far greater determination to control local governments than had the vacillating Sugar Trust in Cuba in 1898. The most aggressive of these, the United Fruit Company, reinforced American presidents in their perfervid fear of communism and sparked the U.S. overthrow of Guatemalan president Jacobo Arbenz in 1954. There followed a parade of interventions in Latin America, most of them propelled by fear of Communist-driven instabilities: Kennedy's attack on Cuba in 1961, Johnson's temporary occupation of the Dominican Republic in 1965, the involvement of Nixon's CIA in the ouster of Chilean president Salvador Allende in 1973, Reagan's assault on tiny Grenada in 1983 and his long clandestine struggle against the Sandinista government of Nicaragua (named after the Sandino who had fought U.S. marines in 1928–33), Bush's capture and abduction of the Panamanian dictator Antonio Noriega in 1990, and Clinton's expulsion of the Haitian junta in 1994. All of these actions can be seen as consistent with Theodore Roosevelt's corollary to the Monroe Doctrine.

As U.S. interests broadened globally, the quest for stability was projected worldwide in support of dictators like Ferdinand Marcos in the Philippines, Ngo Dinh Diem in South Vietnam, and Chiang Kai-shek on Taiwan, who were seen as bulwarks against Communism or other forms of left-wing extremism. Despite his preoccupation with human rights, President Carter managed to find words of praise for the autocratic shah of Iran. The folly of this compulsive dependence on the status quo was that in almost every case, it failed to promote stability. Marcos, Diem, Trujillo, Batista, Somoza, and the shah all were deposed, the last three by revolutionaries who based their hostility to the United States on its support of their predecessors. Human rights cannot provide a catchall guide to American policy in the real world, where interests intersect and conflict. But neither Theodore Roosevelt nor his successors managed to understand that regimes not based on popular consent are inherently unstable and that, in fact, stability is usually served best by supporting democratic values and institutions. None of them has dealt successfully with the contradiction inherent in the joint pursuit of democracy, a dynamic concept, and stability, a static one.

The fifth consequence of the work done by the men who launched America as a great power was to strengthen the American presidency. All five were followers of Alexander Hamilton and believers in activist government. Roosevelt was the first strong president since Lincoln, closing a gap of nearly fifty years in which Congress had dominated both domestic and foreign policy. Once America had moved onto the world stage, powerful presidents were the rule rather than the exception. Woodrow Wilson, Franklin Roosevelt, Harry Truman, Lyndon Johnson, Richard Nixon, and Ronald Reagan all were heirs of the first Roosevelt in that sense. They understood that legislatures can never make effective foreign policy; only strong executives can. Professor Woodrow Wilson wrote in 1900: "When foreign affairs play a prominent part in the politics and policy of a nation, its Executive must of necessity be its guide." And President Theodore Roosevelt wrote in

1906: "In any nation which amounts to anything, those in the end must govern who are willing actually to do the work of governing and in so far as the Senate becomes a merely obstructionist body, it will run the risk of seeing its power pass into other hands."

In his book *Diplomacy*, Henry Kissinger draws a sharp distinction between Theodore Roosevelt, the sphere of influence realist, and Wilson, the crusading idealist, and contends Wilson had the more enduring legacy. But surely the contrast is exaggerated, and Roosevelt's effect underrated. Wilson, the man of principle, saw the importance of a sphere of influence when it affected U.S. interests in Latin America, and Roosevelt profoundly believed in the morality of his diplomatic actions, even the most Machiavellian ones. While they did diverge on the uses of American power, they were both pragmatists and visionaries. Their legacy to the twentieth century was a joint one. Roosevelt—for his part in helping create an authentic American imperialism, preparing the United States to be a great power, developing a modern definition of American security interests, generating the tension between human rights and status quo diplomacy, and bequeathing a strong presidency—was as much the father of modern American diplomacy as Wilson.

5.

The imperial America inaugurated in 1898 by Roosevelt, Hay, Mahan, Root, and Lodge lasted almost exactly a century. The United States went from a neophyte imperialist to a mature great power. Though marred by error, arrogance, and even brutality, its international actions during that period were for the most part motivated by a humane and principled sense of the interests of people in general. With exceptions, America acted as an exemplar of democratic values and democratic conduct and led in defeating the antidemocratic challenges from Hitler's Berlin and Stalin's Moscow. But since the end of the Cold War both the power and self-confidence that sustained this century-long international influence have been eroding.

A basic factor contributing to this erosion has been the weakening of the U.S. presidency, the one institution indispensable to the conduct of an energetic and coherent foreign policy. Because of the swelling role of private money in campaigns to elect the president and the Congress, policies that cater to special interests have become the norm rather than the exception. Moreover, the legislative branch has returned to its late-nineteenth-century influence in the management of key foreign policy issues. The president's authority on U.S. policy toward the United Nations, toward the Arab-Israeli conflict, toward trade negotiations, toward bilateral relations with key countries like Cuba and Iran, and toward a host of other issues has been held hostage to the prejudices of Congress and even to the whims of individual members. An influence-ridden, Congress-dominated president will have neither the capacity nor the motivation to provide the leadership that began in the time of Theodore Roosevelt. As with all crises, the disaster of September 11, 2001, strengthened the president's power, but there is little reason to believe in the depth and durability of that change. The political decline of President George W. Bush's own father after the U.S. victory in the Gulf War in 1991 makes this point.

Another weakening factor is the decline of usable American power. By almost all measures of military strength, the United States is unchallenged in the world. But uncertainty has crept in about when and how to use that power. American forces withdrew from Somalia prematurely in 1993 at the first loss of life, and it took three years of a savage war in Bosnia before the United States decided to intervene militarily in 1995. The trend toward military noninvolvement is not inexorable. The Gulf War of 1991 was a textbook example of combining U.S. military power and coalition diplomacy to defeat aggression; the Kosovo campaign in 1999, sloppy as it was, foiled the genocidal plans of a Serbian dictator; and the Afghanistan war of 2001 was the necessary response to a vital threat to American security. But overall there seems less will in both the legislative and executive branches to commit U.S. forces where risk to them is involved and the outcome uncertain. Many in Congress still remain wedded to triumphal rhetoric about the primacy of U.S. power without doing much to make that power relevant or acceptable to others.

Scholars have given considerable recent attention to the fact that America's power extends well beyond the military and political spheres. Joseph S. Nye, Jr., of Harvard has identified the importance of "soft power," by which America exerts a tremendous financial, technological, ideological, and cultural influence upon the rest of the world. Many believe that soft power will enable the United States to retain the kind of global dominance that it had during the Cold War. Similar claims are made with regard to globalization, an abstruse term that implies a growing economic, cultural, and political interdependence among countries and peoples. According to these claims, the United States with its soft power should be best placed to reap the benefits of globalization.

The terrorist attacks on American territory in September 2001 cast serious doubt on these assumptions. Indeed they appear to represent a backlash, not only against American policies but also against the cultural, ideological, and economic principles that guide the United States. They have shown that soft power can be a liability as well as an asset. Terrorism is not new as a weapon directed against the United States. In fact it was a greatly feared phenomenon more than a century ago, when Henry Clay Frick was nearly murdered by an anarchist and William McKinley was assassinated by a man with anarchist connections. But the terrorism conducted by the al Qaeda organization presents more disturbing and potentially longer-term challenges. It is a systematic and well-organized effort to destroy what America stands for. It has used the advances of technology against the most technologically adept country. Moreover, its members have typically never lived under direct American rule, are thus attacking an abstraction rather than a reality, and may be impervious to rational argument or propaganda. It is an ironic compliment to the founders of U.S. imperialism that African Americans, American Indians, Filipinos, or Cubans have never launched a systematic campaign of terrorism against the United States.* Americans are not particularly unpopular among peoples they have ruled.

The elements of power, will, and leadership that had made the United States the dominant country in the century after 1898 were already beginning to decline in the decade after the Cold War. The September 11, 2001, catastrophe has probably hastened the deterioration process. This does not mean that Americans, who are among the most resilient peoples in the world, will not find solutions to the

---

*The attacks against President Truman and the U.S. Congress in 1950 and 1954, respectively, by Puerto Rican nationalists constitute a partial exception. Even so, the attackers represented a tiny minority.

current scourge of terrorism and to the other problems of a young century. It does mean that the solutions will almost certainly be different from those that Theodore Roosevelt and his friends applied.

Arthur O'Shaughnessy, a young Irishman working in the British Museum in the late nineteenth century, displayed a striking insight about the movement of history in his ode to imperialism, quoted at the beginning of Part One of this book. He wrote that "each age is a dream that is dying,/Or one that is coming to birth." We are today at a transition point between two ages, just as O'Shaughnessy was. The age of imperialism that Roosevelt and his friends inspired is dying, perhaps already dead. The content and contours of the age that is coming to birth are still undefined. One can hope nonetheless that statesmen in the new age will remember some of the sobering lessons of the previous period: the iniquity of treating alien peoples as inferior, the folly of exaggerating the value of war, the errors in assuming American omniscience. They would also do well to recall the positive legacies of 1898: the confidence in America's founding principles, the generosity of spirit, the conviction that America is a natural leader in the world, the clear sense of U.S. interests, and, most of all, the understanding that power must be combined with what Theodore Roosevelt called high purpose.

Notes

Theodore Roosevelt is referred to as TR, and the eight-volume collection of his letters edited by Elting E. Morison et al. as *TR Letters*.

INTRODUCTION: RISING EMPIRE

4 *Over a year has passed*: TR, *An Autobiography*, 573–74.
6 *the Pacific was as much our home waters*: Ibid., 563.
6 *new empire* and *rising empire*: Flexner, *George Washington*, 518, and Van Alstyne, *The Rising American Empire*, 1.
6 *However unimportant America may be considered*: Van Alstyne, *The Rising American Empire*, 69.
14 *We gave the fighting instinct*: Beale, *TR and the Rise of America to World Power*, 460.

CHAPTER 1: THE EXPANSIONIST IMPULSE

18 *a rival who*: Ambrose, *Undaunted Courage*, 101.
19 *It is confidently believed*: Haynes, *James K. Polk*, 92.
20 *Our confederacy*: Ambrose, *Undaunted Courage*, 56.
21 *the delegates of Canada*: Thompson and Randall, *Canada and the United States*, 11.
22 *marching*: Ibid., 22.
24 *The existence of an area*: Turner, *The Frontier in American History*, 1.
24 *And now, four centuries*: Ibid., 38.
24 *That these energies*: Ibid., 219.
26 *all American business*: Wall, *Andrew Carnegie*, 192.
26 *The day of combination*: Chernow, *Titan: The Life of John D. Rockefeller, Sr.*, 148.
28 *stare and gawk*: Burns, *The Workshop of Democracy*, 221.
28 *Give me fifty*: Bailey, *A Diplomatic History of the American People*, 392.

29 *the chief theatre of events*: LaFeber, *The New Empire*, 417.

30 *of value enough*: Ibid., 110.

30 *We are not seeking*: Ibid., 106.

31 *America does not go abroad*: McDougall, *Promised Land, Crusader State*, 11.

32 *Hereafter no territory*: LaFeber, *The New Empire*, 28.

32 *the policy of this country*: Bailey, *A Diplomatic History of the American People*, 432.

32 *our rightful and long established claim*: Ibid., 434.

32 *as though the Pacific Ocean*: LaFeber, *The New Empire*, 55.

32 *enters more and more*: LaFeber, *The Cambridge History of American Foreign Relations*, vol. 2, The American Search for Opportunity 1865–1913, 12.

32 *practically sovereign*: Bailey, *A Diplomatic History of the American People*, 482.

33 *The far-reaching*: Stephanson, *Manifest Destiny*, 40.

33 *The work which the English race began*: Brands, *The Reckless Decade*, 288.

34 *It is your duty*: Burns, *The Workshop of Democracy*, 159.

35 Quotes from Josiah Strong: Strong, *Our Country*, 159–80.

35 *stamps the Teutonic*: Hofstadter, *Social Darwinism in American Thought*, 175.

36 *The primacy of the world*: Ibid., 174.

36 *poverty, dirt, and crime*: Ibid., 164.

36 *obediently into the arms*: Ibid., 173.

CHAPTER 2: THE FAVOR OF FORTUNE

40 *The first ancestors I ever heard of*: Hay, *Addresses of John Hay*, 220.

41 *Hay that is green*: Thayer, *The Life and Letters of John Hay*, vol. 1, 35.

41 Excerpts from class poem: Hay, "Erato."

42 *I have wandered*: Thayer, *The Life and Letters of John Hay*, vol. 1, 66.

42 *I am not suited for a reformer*: Ticknor, *A Poet in Exile*, 24.

42 *I never read of a man*: Thayer, *The Life and Letters of John Hay*, vol. 2, 408.

43 *We can't take all Illinois*: Ibid., 87.

44 *At dinner*: Ibid., 139.

44 *The shells*: Ibid., 160.

44 *Nothing new*: Ibid., 145.

45 *Three Indians*: Ibid., 106.

45 *At a dark period*: Hay, *At Lincoln's Side*, xvi.

45 *Today came into the Executive Mansion*: Symington, "A Hayride with Lincoln."

46 *A little after midnight*: Thayer, *The Life and Letters of John Hay*, vol. 1, 198–99.

46 *went with him to the Soldiers' Home*: Ibid., 198.

46 *I consider Lincoln*: Hay letter to Herndon.

47 *Perhaps I may have too little*: Thayer, *The Life and Letters of John Hay*, vol. 1, 216.

47 *One of the most tender*: Hay, *At Lincoln's Side*, 139.

47 *In the morning*: Thayer, *The Life and Letters of John Hay*, vol. 1, 206.

47 *The Tycoon is in fine whack*: Ibid., 196–97.

48 *It is absurd*: Hay letter to Herndon.

48 *No matter how intimate*: Thayer, *The Life and Letters of John Hay*, vol. 1, 330.

48 *He no more resembles*: P. O'Toole, *The Five of Hearts*, 365.

49 *I am thoroughly sick*: Hay *Letters of John Hay*, vol. 1, 253.

49 *placid, philosophic optimist*: Thayer, *The Life and Letters of John Hay*, vol. 1, 255.

49 *Hay is a bright*: Ibid., 222.

50 *a person who having failed*: Bierce, *The Collected Writings of Ambrose Bierce*, 214.

51 *John Hay passed through London*: Henry Adams, *The Education of Henry Adams*, 913.

52 *make their living*: P. O'Toole, *The Five of Hearts*, 41.

52 *Description of Napoleon III's court*: Thayer, *The Life and Letters of John Hay*, vol. 1, 234–36.

53 *I have forgotten*: P. O'Toole, *The Five of Hearts*, 41.

53 *He spoke of the difficult position*: Thayer, *The Life and Letters of John Hay*, vol. 1, 297.

54 *The great calamity*: Ibid., 303–04.

55 *stooping, dirty figures*: Ibid., 293.

55 *In America*: Ibid., 294.

55 *can catch each other's eyes*: Ibid., 312.

56 *Afraid to fight*: Ibid., 229.

56 *If ever, in my green and salad days*: Ibid., 313.

56 *most Americans will agree*: Hay, *Castilian Days*, 400.

56 *I am afraid Cuba is gone*: Thayer, *The Life and Letters of John Hay*, vol. 1, 324.

57 *I am sure that by hanging around*: Dennett, *John Hay: From Poetry to Politics*, 65.

57 *whiteheaded old shyster*: P. O'Toole, *The Five of Hearts*, 41.

57 *No one would have picked*: Henry Adams, *The Education of Henry Adams*, 935.

57 *I am confronted*: P. O'Toole, *The Five of Hearts*, 41.

58 *I have read a million*: Thayer, *The Life and Letters of John Hay*, vol. 1, 331.

58 *For out of that house*: P. O'Toole, *The Five of Hearts*, 44.

59 *Bishop's description of Hay*: Bishop, *Notes and Anecdotes of Many Years*, 45–50.

59 *in substance and perfection of form*: Clymer, *John Hay*, 6.

60 *Pike County Ballads*: Hay, *Pike County Ballads*, 13–24.

61 *I am no poet*: Thayer, *The Life and Letters of John Hay*, vol. 1, 361–62.

61 *I shudder and hide*: Ibid., 374.

62 *You may murder*: Dennett, *John Hay, From Poetry to Politics*, 79.

62 *better than anything*: P. O'Toole, *The Five of Hearts*, 45.

63 *Now the bull is baited*: Hay, *Castilian Days*, 76.

63 *There are those who think*: Ibid., Foreword.

63 *fantastic bigot*: Ibid., 217.

63 *The current cannot be turned*: Ibid., 370.

63 *a picture to look at*: P. O'Toole, *The Five of Hearts*, 56.

64 *Try not to beat back*: Thayer, *The Life and Letters of John Hay*, vol. 1, 382.

64 *a passionate belief*: Turner, *The Frontier in American History*, 358.

64 *John Hay was as strange*: Henry Adams, *The Education of Henry Adams*, 1145–46.

65 *large, handsome, and good*: *Letters of John Hay*, vol. 2, 14.

65 *chats for two*: P. O'Toole, *The Five of Hearts*, 69.

65 King on Clara Hay: Ibid., 92.

65 *had been chatting*: Twain, *Autobiography*, 233–34.

67 *a little like the loyalty*: Henry Adams, *The Education of Henry Adams*, 1014.

67 *the nadir of diplomacy*: Bailey, *A Diplomatic History of the American People*, 426–42.

67 *the nearest approach to a patent of nobility*: Henry Adams, *Democracy*, 29.

67 Captain Brownell, General McCook, Senator Cameron: Hay, "Diary, 1879–1881."

69 George Washington and the dollar: According to James W. Symington, Hay's great-grandson, this story, though not authenticated, is one of the most durable family legends about Hay.

69 *always unselfish*: Henry Adams, *The Education of Henry Adams*, 1063.

69 *a singular facility*: Ibid., 1017.

69 *[He] has always managed to keep*: Samuels, *Henry Adams*, 178.

69 *My beloved Mentor, etc.*: *Letters of John Hay*, vol. 2, 182, 248, 260, 280, 360.

69 *a novel*: Conroy, *Refinements of Love*.

70 *a stable-companion to statesmen*: Thayer, *The Life and Letters of John Hay*, vol. 2, 54.

70 *a bore from Boresville*: Ibid., 111.

70 *not up to it*: Thayer, *The Life and Letters of John Hay*, vol. 1, 456.

70 *With all his gaiety of manner*: Henry Adams, *The Education of Henry Adams*, 1054.

71 *The contact with the greed*: Thayer, *The Life and Letters of John Hay*, vol. 1, 443–44.

72 *The government is utterly helpless*: Ibid., vol. 2, 2–4.

75 *This is a government*: LaFeber, *The New Empire*, 17.

76 *I have given up all hopes*: Thayer, *The Life and Letters of John Hay*, vol. 1, 413.

77 *off her feed*: Samuels, *Henry Adams*, 199.

77 *I can neither talk*: Hay, "Letters of John Hay," vol. 2, 98.

78 *We had the Roosevelts*: Dennett, *John Hay: From Poetry to Politics*, 339.

79 *I feel stricken*: P. O'Toole, *The Five of Hearts*, 228–29.

80 *I have never met a reformer*: Kushner and Sherrill, *John Milton Hay*, 159.

80 *Hay had treated the world*: Henry Adams, *The Education of Henry Adams*, 1063.

81 *He inspired men*: Carnegie, *Autobiography*, 358.

81 *I hate to lose my own friends*: Clymer, *John Hay*, 2.

81 *Cabot [Lodge] and Teddy*: Thayer, *The Life and Letters of John Hay*, vol. 2, 152.

82 *I spent yesterday*: Ibid., 153.

82 *There has been so much talk*: P. O'Toole, *The Five of Hearts*, 288.

83 *sorry and ashamed*: Clymer, *John Hay*, 29.

84 *My early dreams*: Kushner and Sherrill, *John Milton Hay*, 163.

CHAPTER 3: A PEN-AND-INK SAILOR

86 *foot-ball for local politicians*: Mahan, *Letters and Papers*, vol. 1, 440.

86 *scoundrel*: Ibid., 442.

86 *men eminent for nothing creditable*: Ibid., 592.

86 *The air is rife*: Ibid., 573.

87 *The question of landing troops*: Ibid., 573–74.

87 *[W]e have not six ships*: Ibid., 544.

87 *The country cares nothing*: Ibid., 558.

87 *It was a summary of American naval policy*: Mahan, *From Sail to Steam*, 197–98.

88 *I shared the prepossession*: Ibid., 275.

89 *how different things might have been*: Ibid., 277.

89 *My self-assigned task*: Ibid., 283.

89 *Every faculty I possessed*: Ibid., 278.

90 *No less a task is proposed*: Millett and Mazlowski, *For the Common Defense*, 259.

92 *to her knees*: Mahan, *From Sail to Steam*, 269.

93 *in the atmosphere of the single cruiser*: Ibid., 274.

95 *these matters, simply presented*; Mahan, *The Influence of Sea Power upon History*, vi.

95 *the teachings of the past*: Ibid., 9.

95 *applicable to all ages*: Ibid., 22.

96 *great highway*: Ibid., 25.

96 *that thus sail to and fro*: Ibid., 26.

96 *as a nation*: Ibid., 27–28.

96 *geographical position*: Ibid., 28.

96 *the Caribbean will be changed*: Ibid., 33.

97 *enable her fleets*: Ibid., 34.

97 *physical conformation*: Ibid., 35.

97 *almost every one of the original colonies*: Ibid., 39.

97 *Those who follow the limitations*: Ibid.

98 *the United States in her turn*: Ibid., 42.

98 *extent of territory*: Ibid.

98 *national character*: Ibid., 50.

98 *character of the government*: Ibid., 58.

99 *such free governments*: Ibid.

99 *popular governments*: Ibid., 67.

99 *suitable naval stations*: Ibid., 82.

99 *England's naval bases*: Ibid., 83.

99 *attached to the mother-country*: Ibid.

99 *Having therefore no foreign establishments*: Ibid.

100 *a decisive naval superiority*: Ibid., 397.

100 *our coasts were insulted*: Ibid., 137.

100 *During the last two days*: TR Letters, vol. 1, 221.

100 *Captain Mahan has written*: Puleston, *Mahan*, 117.

102 *From my derivation*: Mahan, *From Sail to Steam*, xii.

103 *smartest man in the class*: Mahan, *Letters and Papers*, vol. 1, 55.

103 *the most serious infraction*: Ibid., 71.

104 *It takes at least twenty gentlemen*: Ibid., 41.

104 *[Y]ou can form no idea*: Ibid., 3.

104 *every great man that ever lived*: Ibid., 72.

104 *In a stiff breeze*: Puleston, *Mahan*, 39.

105 *These eternities of the heavens*: Mahan, *From Sail to Steam*, 135.

105 *pervading odor*: Ibid., 147.

105 *delight in a pretty face*: Puleston, *Mahan*, 46.

106 *War, even in its incipiency*: Mahan, *From Sail to Steam*, 158.

106 *one of the prettiest gunboats*: Seager, *Alfred Thayer Mahan*, 36.

106 *desperately tedious work*: Mahan, *From Sail to Steam*, 174.

106 *our men's minds*: Ibid., 177.

108 *more the ideal*: Mahan, *Letters and Papers*, vol. 1, 107.

108 *brutalized by ages*: Mahan, *From Sail to Steam*, 220.

108 *The unmarried girls*: Mahan, *Letters and Papers*, vol. 1, 337.

108 *As for the exposure*: Ibid.

108 *Long as American eyes*: Mahan, *From Sail to Steam*, 227.

109 *The more I reflect on my temper*: Seager, *Alfred Thayer Mahan*, 58.

109 *Elly had a big Mahan*: Puleston, *Mahan*, 65.

109 *Certainly not a great beauty*: Mahan, *Letters and Papers*, vol. 1, 368.

112 *It is not the business*: Mahan, *From Sail to Steam*, 311.

113 *Except Roosevelt*: Mahan, *Letters and Papers*, vol. 2, 122.

113 *England had no army*: Puleston, *Mahan*, 125.

113 *The world has never seen*: Mahan, *The Influence of Sea Power upon the French Revolution and Empire*, vol. 2, 118.

113 *cordial recognition*: Mahan, *The Interest of America in Sea Power, Present and Future*, 27.

114 *unusual eloquence*: Mahan, *From Sail to Steam*, 307.

114 *The besetting anxiety*: Ibid., 288.

114 *invent first*: Mahan, *From Sail to Steam*, 286.

114 *It is better to say*: Mahan, *Letters and Papers*, vol. 1, 575–76.

115 *To retain . . . the undisturbed enjoyment*: Mahan, *The Interest of America in Sea Power, Present and Future*, 9.

115 *Like the Canadian Pacific*: Ibid., 12.

116 *The piercing of the Isthmus*: Ibid., 13.

116 *If my belief*: Mahan, *Letters and Papers*, vol. 2, 28.

117 *all the people of intelligence*: Puleston, *Mahan*, 143.

117 *not reading but devouring it*: Ibid., 160.

117 French, Spanish, English women: Mahan, *Letters and Papers*, vol. 2, 151, 167, 348.

118 *pen-and-ink sailor*: Puleston, *Mahan*, 152.

118 *Captain Mahan always appears*: Mahan, *Letters and Papers*, vol. 2, 211.

120 *As I am responsible for bad results*: Ibid., 323.

120 *has always struck me*: Ibid., 239.

120 *in philosophic spirit*: Puleston, *Mahan*, 129.

120 *I am frankly an imperialist*: Mahan, *From Sail to Steam*, 324.

121 *May God always bless the day*: Mahan, *Letters and Papers*, vol. 2, 286.

122 a *gentleman*: Ibid., 292.

122 *willfully disagreeable*: Ibid., 243.

122 *in the singular beauty*: Mahan, *The Harvest Within*, 106.

122 *However men severally*: Ibid., 180.

CHAPTER 4: A LAWYER'S DUTY

126 *One of his conclusions*: Jessup, *Elihu Root*, vol. 1, 47.

126 *Olympian gods*: Ibid., 47.

126 *very tall; very shy*: Ibid., 56.

127 *a lawyer needs*: Ibid., 57.

127 *position and influence*: Ibid., 58.

127 *It is right that we should be ambitious*: Ibid., 59.

128 *blue . . . I enjoy myself*: Ibid., 64–65.

128 *next below that of patent-medicine mongering*: Burrows and Wallace, *Gotham*, 968.

129 *No matter how vile*: Jessup, *Elihu Root*, vol. 1, 93.

130 *You know, my dear*: Ibid., 83.

130 *You will not let your ambition*: Ibid., 84.

130 *I will not for a moment, believe*: Ibid., 86.

130 *Why do you try to do anything more*: Ibid., 87.

130 *I know how young lawyers*: Ibid., 88.

131 *knock Judge Davis down*: Ibid.

132 *Sir: Your impertinent note*: Ibid., 95.

132 *My dear Sir:—I have received*: Ibid., 103.

132 *I hereby vest that $10*: Ibid.

133 *Nothing in the east*: Ibid., 115.

134 *If I sent you any bill*: Ibid., 112.

134 *The evil which makes all other evils possible*: Ibid., 116.

135 *The governor did not count*: Root, *Addresses on Government and Citizenship*, 202.

136 *a liar and a horse thief*: Jessup, *Elihu Root*, vol. 1, 119.

136 *We are not to be intimidated*: Ibid., 130.

136 *Arthur's period*: Ibid., 128.

136 *I can never forget*: Root, *Addresses on Government and Citizenship*, 203.

139 *The location of their residence*: Jessup, *Elihu Root*, vol. 1, 163.

139 *Great moneyed interests*: Root, *Addresses on Government and Citizenship*, 143.

140 *To be a lawyer*: Jessup, *Elihu Root*, vol. 1, 194.

140 *You will strive*: Root, *Addresses on Government and Citizenship*, 430.

140 *I do not remember*: Ibid., 202–03.

141 *I have had many lawyers*: Jessup, *Elihu Root*, vol. 1, 185.

141 *a lawyer's chief business*: Ibid., 133.

141 *about half the practice*: Ibid.

142 *You have made a good start in life*: Ibid., 191.

142 *frank and murderous smile*: Thayer, *The Life and Letters of John Hay*, vol. 2, 342.

143 *Everybody knows that some rules*: Jessup, *Elihu Root*, vol. 1, 187.

143 *All he wanted*: Ibid., 202.

143 *a conflict of interests*: Ibid., 207.

144 *We can never throw off*: Root, *Miscellaneous Addresses*, 127.

144 *In politics there is struggle*: Jessup, *Elihu Root*, vol. 1, 178.

145 *I am a convinced and uncompromising nationalist*: Root, *Addresses on Government and Citizenship*, 252.

145 *He understood the necessity*: Root, *Men and Policies*, 74–75.

146 *Above all things let us be just*: Root, *Miscellaneous Addresses*, 272.

147 *There is danger of war*: Ibid., 250.

147 *I was called to the telephone*: Jessup, *Elihu Root*, vol. 2, 215.

CHAPTER 5: DAUNTLESS INTOLERANCE

150 *men of American blood*: Lodge, *Speeches and Addresses*, 161.

150 *I do not mean*: Ibid., 167.

150 *I cannot bear to see*: Ibid., 177.

151 *even if they were populated*: Ibid., 182.

151 *The sea power*: Ibid.

151 *has always opposed*: Ibid., 184–85.

151 *the backbone of the modern navy*: Ibid., 187.

151 *commerce follows the flag*: Ibid., 189.

151 *We have spent enough money*: Ibid., 193.

152 *It was the sea power*: Ibid., 185.

152 *grotesque and miserable*: Garraty, *Henry Cabot Lodge*, 151.

152 *The great nations*: Lodge, *The Forum*, 19 (March 1895), 8–17.

152 *We have a record of conquest*: Lodge, *North American Review*, 160 (June 1895), 651–58.

153 *If Great Britain*: Ibid.

153 *an absolute violation*: Lodge, *Speeches and Addresses*, 235.

153 *little better than a British lake*: Ibid., 238.

153 *because it is essential to our safety*: Ibid., 235.

154 *You never saw such desolate*: Lodge, ed., *Selections from the Correspondence of TR and Henry Cabot Lodge*, vol. 1, 187.

155 *The issues of war and peace*: Garraty, *Henry Cabot Lodge*, 182.

155 *There is Cuba*: Lodge, *Speeches and Addresses*, 279–80.

157 *cheap pathos*: Lodge, *Early Memories*, 192–93.

157 *Mr. Adams roused the spirit*: Ibid. 186–87.

157 *To him and to the family*: Ibid., 194.

158 *opened our hearts*: Ibid., 233.

158 *to cherish some vague desires*: Ibid., 234.

158 *drifting vaguely*: Ibid., 236–37.

159 *Keep clear of mere sentiment*: Henry Adams, *Letters of Henry Adams*, vol. 1, 228.

160 *unexpressibly dreary*: Lodge, *Early Memories*, 239.

160 *one of the youngest members*: Ibid., 270.

161 *many of our Boston worthies*: Ibid., 273.

161 *To the modern and recent plutocrat*: Ibid., 209.

161 *their lawlessness, their disregard*: Ibid., 211.

161 a *certain formality of address*: Ibid., 217.

161 *the old and graceful art*: Ibid., 219.

161 *the careful establishment of standards*: Ibid., 224.

162 *work, after all, is the best of friends*: Ibid., 244.

162 *New England has a harsh climate*: Lodge, *Speeches and Addresses*, 4.

162 *The destiny of the republic*: Ibid., 9.

162 *how a part of the world lives*: Lodge, *Early Memories*, 242.

162 *to take money*: Ibid., 212.

163 *crime against humanity*: Ibid., 133.

163 *the story of some Americans*: Lodge and Roosevelt, *Hero Tales from American History*, ix.

163 *The time given to athletic contests*: Lodge, *Speeches and Addresses*, 293.

164 *with both body and brain*: Lodge, *Alexander Hamilton*, 123.

164 *Your danger is a very simple one*: Widenor, *Henry Cabot Lodge and the Search for an American Foreign Policy*, 3–4.

164 *An excellent talker*: Henry Adams, *The Education of Henry Adams*, 1103–04. This long passage has been divided into three paragraphs for ease of reading.

167 *the worst stump speaker*: Garraty, *Henry Cabot Lodge*, 91.

168 *with the tips of their fingers*: Ibid., 78.

168 *It was the bitterest thing*: Ibid., 79.

168 *degenerated sons of Harvard*: Schiftgiesser, *The Gentleman from Massachusetts: Henry Cabot Lodge*, 160.

169 *The more you try to satisfy them*: McCullough, *Mornings on Horseback*, 309.

169 *things political*: Garraty, *Henry Cabot Lodge*, 84.

170 *Only God and his mother*: Ibid., 85.

171 *all our fellow-Republicans*: Lodge, ed., *Selections from the Correspondence of TR and Henry Cabot Lodge*, vol. 1, 13–14.

171 *my evil and unfortunate influence*: Ibid., 11.

172 *I have pretty nearly finished Benton*: Ibid., 41.

172 *among these harum-scarum roughriders*: Ibid., 45.

173 *For the last fortnight*: Robinson, *My Brother TR*, 153–55.

173 *To my friend Theodore Roosevelt*: Lodge, *Speeches and Addresses*, dedication page.

173 *brilliant scholar and statesman*: Robinson, *My Brother TR*, 228.

173 *From [the 1884 Republican convention]*: *TR Letters*, vol. 6, 935.

174 *I can judge of your standing*: Lodge, ed., *Selections from the Correspondence of TR and Henry Cabot Lodge*, vol. 1, 179–80.

175 *one personal favor*: Ibid., 242.

175 *You will be kind enough to remember*: Ibid.

176 *for I don't suppose that between you and me*. Ibid., 243.

176 *a little like bawling*: Ibid., 254.

176 *Sinbad has evidently landed*: Ibid., 266.

176 *highly cultivated but very thin*: Schiftgiesser, *The Gentleman from Massachusetts: Henry Cabot Lodge*, 130.

176 *the fleshpots of Cleveland*: Marian Adams, *The Letters of Mrs. Henry Adams*, 250–51.

176 *a wide stretch of cheap little brick houses*: Twain, *The Gilded Age*, vol. 1, 238.

176 *a long snowy palace*: Ibid., 235.

177 *Beyond the Treasury*: Ibid., 238.

178 *architectural infant asylum*: Green, *Washington: Capital City 1879–1950*, 140.

178 *Such a place for wild flowers*: Henry Adams, *Letters of Henry Adams 1858–1891*, 157.

178 *I know of no other capital*: Ibid., 148.

178 *as wild as a stream*: TR, *An Autobiography*, 46.

178 *a brag shopping place*: Green, *Washington: Capital City 1879–1950*, 11.

178 *Compared with New York or Chicago*: Ibid., 77.

179 *the city of magnificent intentions*: Ibid., 189.

179 *As there are so few cultivated people*: Henry Adams, *Letters of Henry Adams 1858–1891*, 161–62.

179 *One . . . (nicknamed the Antiques)*: Twain, *The Gilded Age*, vol. 2, 9–10.

180 *the great Don*: Marian Adams, *The Letters of Mrs. Henry Adams*, 306.

180 *the water flowed like champagne*: This phrase may have been the creation of William M. Evarts, President Hayes's secretary of state and one of Clover Adams's favorite wits.

180 *gorging on Potomac*: Marian Adams, *The Letters of Mrs. Henry Adams*, 269.

180 *a Voltaire in petticoats*: P. O'Toole, *The Five of Hearts*, 88.

180 *The craving for the meanest kind*: Marian Adams, *The Letters of Mrs. Henry Adams*, 286.

180 *that beast Conkling*: Ibid., 263.

180 *the rat*: Ibid., 337.

180 *vulgar cad*: Ibid., 352, 328.

180 *if nothing happens to it*: Henry Adams, *Letters of Henry Adams 1858–1891*, 302.

180 *the drollest place*: Ibid., 148.

180 *a monkey-show*: Ibid., 311.

180 *prolonged circus*: Marian Adams, *Letters of Mrs. Henry Adams*, 334.

180 *I think the real, live, vulgar*: Ibid., 320.

180 *the big bow-wow style*: Ibid., 306.

180 *A man's house is not his castle*: Ibid., 272.

181 *city of conversation*: Green, *Washington: Capital City 1879–1950*, 190.

181 *No dinner, however superb*: Ibid., 85.

182 *You will one day feel the advantage*: Henry Adams, *Letters of Henry Adams 1858–1891*, 292.

182 *Social influence counts*: Ibid., 318.

182 *I am much touched*: Ibid., 323.

182 *earnest wish*: P. O'Toole, *The Five of Hearts*, 309.

183 *fascination possessed by no other*: Robinson, *My Brother TR*, 250.

183 *She was one of those rare personalities*: Garraty, *Henry Cabot Lodge*, 101.

183 *looked as queens ought to look*: Ibid., 101.

183 *Our little family*: P. O'Toole, *The Five of Hearts*, 213.

184 *the senior senator from the fishing grounds*: Widenor, *Henry Cabot Lodge and the Search for an American Foreign Policy*, 147.

184 *The personal qualities and individual abilities*: Ibid., 13.

184 *We are a great nation*: Ibid., 76.

184 *human environment has altered*: Lodge, *Early Memories*, 200.

185 *these bewildering metamorphoses*: Ibid., 202.

185 *We learned that weak defencelessness*: Garraty, *Henry Cabot Lodge*, 154.

185 *The only peace worth having*: Lodge and Roosevelt, *Hero Tales from American History*, ix.

185 *to meet the encroachments of a foreign power*: Widenor, *Henry Cabot Lodge and the Search for an American Foreign Policy*, 72.

185 *large policy*: See, for example, Lodge, ed., *Selections from the Correspondence of TR and Henry Cabot Lodge*, vol. 2, 300.

185 *the greatest authority*: Widenor, *Henry Cabot Lodge and the Search for an American Foreign Policy*, 88.

186 *He knew that the first rule*: Lodge, *Alexander Hamilton*, 63.

186 *Where there is no moral question*: Lodge, *Speeches and Addresses*, 19–20.

186 *a compromiser on moral questions*: Garraty, *Henry Cabot Lodge*, 28.

186 *formed a museum of wax figures*: Ibid., 128.

186 *a clever man*: P. O'Toole, *The Five of Hearts*, 372.

186 *exceed the endurance of a coral reef*: Henry Adams, *Letters of Henry Adams, 1892–1918*, 318.

186 *the furious kicking of his enemies*: Garraty, *Henry Cabot Lodge*, 129.

186 *a trick, even among his friends*: Ibid., 372.

186 *in discussion he was one of those*: Ibid., 127.

187 *dreary Senatorial drivel*: Henry Adams, *Letters of Henry Adams 1892–1918*, 195.

187 *In the thirteenth century*: Henry Adams, *The Education of Henry Adams*, 1044.

187 *a delightful, big-boyish personage*: Garraty, *Henry Cabot Lodge*, 124.

187 *It is unmitigated Boston*: Widenor, *Henry Cabot Lodge and the Search for an American Foreign Policy*, 3.

CHAPTER 6: SO BRILLIANT AND AGGRESSIVE A MAN

189 *maniacal benevolence*: McCullough, *Mornings on Horseback*, 28.
189 *leonine*: TR, *An Autobiography*, 9.
189 *He was the only man*: Ibid., 8.
190 *One of my memories*: Ibid., 14.
190 *you must* make *your body*: Robinson, *My Brother TR*, 50.
191 *the best man I ever knew*: TR, *An Autobiography*, 7.
191 *with great love and patience*: Ibid., 7.
191 *heart filled with gentleness*: Ibid., 9.
192 *always afterward felt*: McCullough, *Mornings on Horseback*, 57.
194 *From reading of the people I admired*: TR, *An Autobiography*, 29.
194 *they found that I was a foreordained*: Ibid., 30.
195 *a bundle of eccentricities*: Thayer, *TR: An Intimate Biography*, 21.
195 *sharp, ungreased squeak*: Morris, *The Rise of TR*, 64.
196 *I thoroughly enjoyed Harvard*: TR, *An Autobiography*, 24.
196 *purely a science of the laboratory*: Ibid., 26.
196 *had no more desire or ability*: Ibid., 27.
196 *I realize more and more*: Morris, *The Rise of TR*, 96.
196 *How I wish I could ever do something*: Ibid.
197 *We're dining out*: Ibid., 142.
198 *At midday of June 1, 1812*: TR, *The Naval War of 1812*, 102.
199 *gaunt of form*: Ibid., 255.
199 *they would have made a dictionary*: TR, *An Autobiography*, 24.
199 *It is folly for the great English-speaking Republic*: TR, *The Naval War of 1812*, xxiv.
199 *the men in the clubs*: TR, *An Autobiography*, 57.
199 *saloon-keepers*: Ibid.
200 *His hair was parted*: Morris, *The Rise of TR*, 161–62.
200 a swelled head: Thayer, *TR: An Intimate Biography*, 39.
201 *the wealthy criminal class*: Morris, *The Rise of TR*, 193.
202 *Some of them sneered*: McCullough, *Mornings on Horseback*, 254.
202 *a man to be trusted*: TR, *An Autobiography*, 61.
202 *as fearless as he was honest*: Ibid., 67.
202 *I do not think that a man is fit to do good work*: TR, *An Autobiography*, 64.
203 *In the overwhelming majority of cases*: TR, *An Autobiography*, 82.
204 *She was beautiful*: Morris, *The Rise of TR*, 284–85.
205 *not a particle of genius*: Bishop, *Notes and Anecdotes of Many Years*, 116.
205 *I never won anything*: TR, *An Autobiography*, 53.
205 *Young gentlemen*: Morris, *The Rise of TR*, 185–86.
205 *Black care*: Ibid., 273.
206 *I owe more than I can ever express*: TR, *An Autobiography*, 121.
207 *When the days have dwindled*: Morris, *The Rise of TR*, 294.
208 *all teeth and eyes*: Ibid., 329.

208 *meanness, cowardice:* McCullough, *Mornings on Horseback,* 340.

208 *taught him the immense diversity:* Thayer, *TR: An Intimate Biography,* 68.

209 *I told my wife:* McCullough, *Mornings on Horseback,* 348.

209 *You will become President:* Morris, *The Rise of TR,* 337.

209 *In all probability this campaign:* Lodge, ed., *Selections from the Correspondence of TR and Henry Cabot Lodge,* vol. 1, 49.

209 *Am badly defeated:* Ibid., 50.

210 *a roaring good time:* Morris, *The Rise of TR,* 370.

210 *I generally take a moderate walk:* Robinson, *My Brother TR,* 128.

210 *I have very little expectation:* Thayer, *TR: An Intimate Biography,* 44.

210 *I shall probably never be in politics again:* Morris, *The Rise of TR,* 386.

211 *My real trouble in regard to Mr. Roosevelt:* Garraty, *Henry Cabot Lodge,* 104.

212 *I do wish the President:* TR Letters, vol. 1, 175.

212 *applied idealism:* TR, *An Autobiography,* 132–71.

212 *I have been a real force:* TR Letters, vol. 2, 167.

212 *spent and exhausted:* Lodge, ed., *Selections from the Correspondence of TR and Henry Cabot Lodge,* vol. 2, 113.

212 *I do not see any element of permanence:* TR Letters, vol. 2, 334.

212 *My victory here:* Lodge, ed., *Selections from the Correspondence of TR and Henry Cabot Lodge,* vol. 1, 168.

213 *I used to walk by the White House:* Morris, *The Rise of TR,* 423.

213 *I always eat and drink too much:* TR Letters, vol. 1, 428.

213 *pure act:* Henry Adams, *The Education of Henry Adams,* 1101.

213 *make his name well known:* Robinson, *My Brother TR,* 9.

213 *face the rather intimate association:* McCullough, *Mornings on Horseback,* 276.

214 *as Theodore would now:* TR, *Letters from TR to Anna Roosevelt Cowles,* 145.

214 *New York has always had a low political standard:* TR, *Thomas H. Benton,* 73.

215 *glimpse of the real life:* TR, *Letters from TR to Anna Roosevelt Cowles,* 158.

215 *I am more than glad:* Ibid., 169.

215 *not work that can be done on a rose-water basis:* Ibid., 185.215

216 *was fundamentally a struggle:* TR, *The Winning of the West,* vol. 2, 374–75.

216 *represented a people already holding:* Ibid., 376.

217 *emphatically American worthies:* Ibid., 382.

217 *the movement of a whole, free people:* Ibid., 381.

217 *one in speech, thought, and character:* TR, *The Winning of the West,* vol. 1, xv.

217 *Nowhere else on the continent:* Ibid., vol. 3, 207.

218 *We . . . have seized the waste solitudes:* TR, *Thomas H. Benton,* 236.

218 *Unless we were willing that the whole continent:* TR, *The Winning of the West,* vol. 4, 87–88.

218 *of incalculable importance:* TR, *The Winning of the West,* vol. 3, 45–46.

218 *The conquest and settlement by the whites:* Ibid., 174–75.

219 *Whether the whites won the land:* Ibid., 44

219 *filthy, cruel, lecherous:* TR, *The Winning of the West,* vol. 2, 147–48.

219 *but a few degrees less meaningless:* Ibid., vol. 3, 44.

219 *The most ultimately righteous of all wars*: Ibid., 45.

219 *Every such submersion or displacement*: Ibid., 176.

220 *Every good hunting-ground*: TR, *The Winning of the West*, vol. 2, 88.

220 *As for the whites themselves*: Ibid., 91–92.

220 *It was our manifest destiny*: TR, *Thomas H. Benton*, 36.

220 *Any peace which did not surrender*: TR, *The Winning of the West*, vol. 4, 121.

221 *shameful wrong*: TR, *The Winning of the West*, vol. 4, 150, and vol. 1, 331.

221 *great . . . leader*: TR, *Thomas H. Benton*, 186–87.

221 *the most cruel wrongs*: Ibid., 187.

221 *the most formidable savage foes*: TR, *The Winning of the West*, vol. 1, 17.

221 *were the bravest of all the Indian tribes*: TR, *The Winning of the West*, vol. 2, 132.

221 *as wary and able as he was brave*: TR, *The Winning of the West*, vol. 1, 220.

221 *valiant and able warrior*: TR, *The Winning of the West*, vol. 3, 34.

221 *a mighty warrior*: Ibid., 291.

221 *utterly abhorrent*: TR, *The Winning of the West*, vol. 2, 148.

221 *More than a hundred years have passed*: Ibid., 156–57.

222 *on the whole as righteous*: TR, *Thomas H. Benton*, 187.

222 *certain most objectionable details*: Ibid.

222 *We neither wrong them*: TR, *Hunting Trips of a Ranchman and the Wilderness Hunter*, 102.

223 *We of this generation*: TR, *The Winning of the West*, vol. 2, xxxiii.

223 *The whole western movement*: Ibid., xxxiv–xxxv.

223 *At bottom the question of expansion*: Ibid., xxxvi.

223 *During the past three centuries*: Ibid., 1.

223 *a region larger than all Europe*: TR, *The Winning of the West*, vol. 3, 105.

223 *The British fought against the stars*: Ibid., 53.

223 *Her colonial system*: TR, *The Winning of the West*, vol. 4, 267.

224 *The time to have taken the lands*: TR, *Thomas H. Benton*, 235–36.

224 *no State was subject to another*: TR, *The Winning of the West*, vol. 3, 262.

224 *We want no unwilling citizens*: TR, *Thomas H. Benton*, 235.

225 *Much had been accomplished*: TR, *The Winning of the West*, vol. 4, 342–43.

225 *men of the present day*: Ibid., 98.

226 *I am a bit of a believer*: TR Letters, vol. 1, 313.

226 *goes about hissing through his clenched teeth*: Morris, *The Rise of TR*, 444.

226 *I hope there is no truth*: TR Letters, vol. 1, 378.

226 *Great Britain's conduct*: Lodge, ed. *Selections from the Correspondence of TR and Henry Cabot Lodge*, vol. 2, 145.

226 *If there is a muss*: TR, *Letters from TR to Anna Roosevelt Cowles*, 165.

227 *I see that President Eliot*: Lodge, ed., *Selections from the Correspondence of TR and Henry Cabot Lodge*, vol. 1, 218.

227 *the ultimate removal of all European powers*: TR, *Letters from TR to Anna Roosevelt Cowles*, 180.

227 *I am a quietly rampant "Cuba Libre" man*: Ibid., 201.

227 *no preconceived plans*: Lodge, ed., *Selections from the Correspondence of TR and Henry Cabot Lodge*, vol. 1, 241.

228 *I want peace*: Morris, *The Rise of TR*, 555.

228 *McKinley himself is an upright*: TR, *Letters from TR to Anna Roosevelt Cowles*, 182–83.

229 *Roosevelt was a many-sided man*: Memorial Addresses (on TR), Century Association Archives.

CHAPTER 7: ISLAND FORTRESS, CUBAN BLOOD

234 *a certain remorse*: Hay, *Letters of John Hay*, vol. 3, 116.

234 *McKinley has had a terrible stress*: Ibid., 117.

234 *I do not know whether you especially value*: Thayer, *The Life and Letters of John Hay*, vol. 2, 165–66.

234 *You may imagine what it is to me*: Ibid., 166.

235 *from time to time*: Puleston, *Mahan*, 181–82.

235 *No nation, as no man*: Mahan, *The Interest of America in Sea Power, Present and Future*, 239.

235 *receive into its own bosom*: Ibid., 243.

235 *world of civilized Christianity*: Ibid.

235 *In the cluster of island fortresses*: Ibid., 261.

236 *positional value*: Ibid., 292.

236 *could very seriously incommode*: Ibid., 303.

236 *no military rival*: Ibid., 310.

237 *How absurd that the U.S. should be anxious*: Mahan, *Letters and Papers*, vol. 2, 544.

237 *no more backbone*: Morris, *The Rise of TR*, 610.

237 *The year 1898*: Mahan, *Letters and Papers*, vol. 2, 548.

238 *a broken race*: Garraty, *Henry Cabot Lodge*, 160.

238 *just a dear*: Lodge, ed., *Selections from the Correspondence of Theodore Roosevelt and Henry Cabot Lodge*, vol. 2, 279–80.

239 *peace at any price*: TR, *An American Mind*, 175.

239 *All the great masterful races*: Ibid., 174.

239 *education merely serves*: Ibid., 175.

239 *the men who have dared greatly*: Ibid., 174.

239 *No triumph of peace*: Morris, *The Rise of TR*, 569.

240 *I suspect that Roosevelt is right*: Ibid., 572.

240 *at once*: TR Letters, vol. 1, 607–08.

240 *I speak to you with the greatest freedom*: Ibid.

240 *it would be everything for us to take firm action*: Lodge, ed., *Selections from the Correspondence of TR and Henry Cabot Lodge*, vol. 2, 268.

240 *If we don't take Hawaii*: TR Letters, vol. 2, 747.

241 *Now stay there*: Morris, *The Rise of TR*, 581.

241 *entirely independently*: Lodge, ed., *Selections from the Correspondence of TR and Henry Cabot Lodge*, vol. 1, 280.

241 *what I thought ought to be done*: Ibid., 278.

241 *he may have conned Roosevelt*: In his autobiography Roosevelt describes forming his high opinion of Dewey's insistence on preparedness when Dewey, on assignment in South America, risked the censure of his superiors by purchasing coal for a move around Cape Horn that had not yet been ordered. If this incident really happened, neither Dewey in his autobiography nor his biographer, Ronald Spector, mentions it.

242 *I am a bit of a jingo*: TR Letters, vol. 1, 707.

242 *First, the advisability*: Pringle, *TR*, 123.

242 *The blood of the Cubans*: TR Letters, vol. 1, 798.

242 *The Maine was sunk*: Ibid., 774–75.

243 *Do not take any such step*: Musicant, *Empire by Default*, 152.

243 *ORDER THE SQUADRON*: TR Letters, vol. 1, 784.

243 *I find that Roosevelt*: Pringle, *TR*, 124.

244 *ever faithful isle*: Millis, *The Martial Spirit*, 10.

244 *Spaniards sooner than see the island*: Carr, *Spain 1808–1939*, 379.

247 *full powers*: Thomas, *Cuba or the Pursuit of Freedom*, 326–27.

248 *a salutary rigor*: Musicant, *Empire by Default*, 67.

252 *I have been through one war*: Trask, *The War with Spain in 1898*, 58.

252 *the happiest man in the world*: Ibid., 13.

252 *We want no wars of conquest*: May, *Imperial Democracy*, 120.

253 *at all hazards*: Elihu Root, *Miscellaneous Addresses*, 250.

253 *you may be sure there will be no jingo nonsense*: Beisner, *Twelve Against Empire*, 24.

253 *a secretary who knew nothing*: Leech, *In the Days of McKinley*, 152–53.

255 *reasonable chance*: Annals of America, vol. 12, 166.

255 *all Spain has been led to believe*: Trask, *The War with Spain in 1898*, 32.

255 *the Queen will have to choose*: Ibid., 23.

256 *weak . . . a would-be politician*: May, *Imperial Democracy*, 137.

257 *struggling for freedom*: Millis, *The Martial Spirit*, 124.

257 *so powerfully affected the public sentiment*: Linderman, *The Mirror of War*, 38.

257 *Proctor's position might have been expected*: Trask, *The War with Spain in 1898*, 36.

258 *The unanimity with which you are supported*: Linderman, *The Mirror of War*, 34.

258 *I have advised the President*: TR Letters, vol. 2, 804.

258 *The President is resolute*: Ibid., 805.

259 *when it is once certain*: Jessup, *Elihu Root*, vol. 1, 197.

260 *final arbiter*: May, *Imperial Democracy*, 153.

260 *full self-government*: Ibid.

260 *the President's desire is for peace*: Millis, *The Martial Spirit*, 126.

261 *Would the peace you are so confident of*: May, *Imperial Democracy*, 154.

261 *this means peace*: Millis, *The Martial Spirit*, 135.

261 *I hope that nothing will now be done*: Ibid., 137.

261 *the present condition of affairs in Cuba*: Annals of America, vol. 12, 177.

262 *cruel, barbarous, and uncivilized*: Ibid., 54.

262 *dependent people*: Ibid.

262 *people perishing*: Ibid., 174.

262 *It is no answer to say*: Ibid., 177.

262 *To commit this country now*: Ibid., 176.

263 *there is within the island*: Ibid., 176–77.

263 *I should be doubtful about annexing Cuba*: TR Letters, vol. 2, 814.

264 *the people of the island of Cuba*: Lodge, The War with Spain, 238.

264 *the United States hereby disclaims*: Millis, The Martial Spirit, 143.

264 *directed and empowered*: Lodge, The War with Spain, 238.

265 *to move at once to Blockade Cuba*: Musicant, Empire by Default, 188.

265 *a marvelous manager of men*: Henry Adams, The Education of Henry Adams, 1061.

265 *led his country*: May, Imperial Democracy, 159.

266 *if the administration does not turn its face*: Ibid., 152.

267 *My purpose is not to accuse*: G. J. A. O'Toole, The Spanish War, 121.

267 *Do we not owe to our country*: Trask, The War with Spain in 1898, 63–64.

267 *It would be foolish to deny*: G. J. A. O'Toole, The Spanish War, 141.

CHAPTER 8: THE SUPREME TRIUMPHS OF WAR

268 *It was my fortune*: Dewey, Autobiography, v.

268 *War has commenced*: Ibid., 195. The scholarly consensus is that this telegram was drafted by the naval command, but it was delivered to the president by Secretary Long, which raises the possibilitiy that Long's energetic deputy was also involved.

269 *without cohesion or a history*: Musicant, Empire by Default, 213.

270 *Didn't Admiral Dewey do wonderfully well?*: TR Letters, vol. 2, 823.

270 *dash . . . the highest credit*: Mahan, Lessons of the War with Spain, 101.

270 *mingled wisdom and daring*: Dewey, Autobiography, 229.

271 *individual responsibility*: Mahan, Letters and Papers, vol. 2, 552.

272 *Remember . . . how limited my power is*: TR Letters, vol. 2, 804.

272 *One of the commonest taunts*: Ibid., 803.

272 *I had always felt*: TR, An Autobiography, 222.

272 *he ought to be willing*: Ibid.

273 *My Assistant Secretary, Roosevelt*: G. J. A. O'Toole, The Spanish War, 195.

273 *almost the only member of the Administration*: TR, An Autobiography, 223.

274 *You would be amused*: TR Letters, vol. 2, 831.

274 *as typical an American regiment*: Ibid., 832–33.

274 *frightful mismanagement*: Ibid., 840.

275 *men should be appointed as Generals*: Ibid., 842.

275 *Hard it is to realize*: Hagedorn, Leonard Wood, 160.

275 *It is a great historical expedition*: Ibid., 843.

276 *If only the Army*: TR Letters, vol. 2, 818.

276 *radically vicious*: Musicant, *Empire by Default*, 355.

278 *singing through the trees*: TR, *The Rough Riders*, 89.

278 *Indian and cow-boy*: Ibid., 109.

280 *On the day of the big fight*: TR Letters, vol. 2, 852.

281 *We are within measurable distance*: Ibid., 846.

281 *too unwieldy*: Ibid.

281 *Not since the campaign of Crassus*: Ibid., 849.

281 *darkest day of the war*: Alger, *The Spanish-American War*, 172.

282 *The sound of my bugles*: Musicant, *Empire by Default*, 442.

282 *judgment, energy, and watchfulness*: Mahan, *Lessons of the War with Spain*, 182.

282 *Don't cheer, boys*: Musicant, *Empire by Default*, 459.

283 *The fleet under my command*: Ibid., 466.

287 *The Hawaiian pear*: Bailey, *A Diplomatic History of the American People*, 470.

289 *superior force of the United States*: Daws, *Shoal of Time*, 276.

290 *beheaded*: Kuykendall, *The Hawaiian Kingdom*, vol. 3, 642.

291 *We need Hawaii*: Trask, *The War with Spain in 1898*, 389.

291 *The issue in Hawaii*: Musicant, *Empire by Default*, 657.

291 *a duty that has its origin*: Millis, *The Martial Spirit*, 123.

292 *How can we endure our shame*: Daws, *Shoal of Time*, 290.

292 *Hurrah for Hawaii!*: TR Letters, vol. 2, 851.

292 *Did I tell you that I killed a Spaniard*: Ibid., 853.

292 *to walk out unmolested*: Ibid., 850.

292 *stupidity and inefficiency*: Ibid., 862.

294 *a treacherous, lying*: Trask, *The War with Spain in 1898*, 210.

294 *as fine a type of the American fighting soldier*: TR, *The Rough Riders*, 73.

294 *a lot of degenerates*: Millis, *The Martial Spirit*, 362.

294 *no more fit for self-government*: Trask, *The War with Spain in 1898*, 210.

294 *We are not savages*: Ibid., 322–23.

295 *Porto Rico is not forgotten*: Lodge, ed., *Selections from the Correspondence of TR and Henry Cabot Lodge*, vol. 1, 299–300.

296 *bombarded with cigars and bananas*: Carr, *Puerto Rico*, 28.

296 *We are Spaniards*: Musicant, *Empire by Default*, 521.

296 *Having soundly thrashed*: Hagedorn, *Leonard Wood*, 180.

296 *In my opinion there is but one course to take*: Musicant, *Empire by Default*, 513.

296 *like rotten sheep*: Trask, *The War with Spain in 1898*, 330.

298 *as good as any regulars*: TR Letters, vol. 2, 859.

298 *I suggest that*: Ibid., 860.

298 *We weren't out more than a dozen strokes*: Morris, *The Rise of TR*, 658.

299 *I am feeling disgracefully well!*: Ibid., 664.

299 *Oh, but we have had a bully fight!*: Ibid., 664.

299 *He simply can't do better*: Ibid., 872.

299 *this peculiarly American regiment*: Ibid., 673.

300 *completing the reduction of Spanish power*: Linn, *The Philippine War 1899–1902*, 5.

300 *that if Dewey had just sailed away*: Brands, *The Reckless Decade*, 329.

301 *a period of anxiety*: Dewey, *Autobiography*, 252.

302 *by order of the Kaiser*: Ibid., 257.

303 *as soon as possible*: Trask, *The War with Spain in 1898*, 400.

304 *these little men*: Ibid., 400, 402.

305 *Obviously, as our purpose was to weaken the Spaniards*: Dewey, *Autobiography*, 246.

305 *it is desirable*: Ibid., 311.

306 *any conferences, relations*: Ibid.

306 *kept me advised of his progress*: Ibid., 312.

306 *In my opinion, these people are far superior*: Ibid.

306 *within easy striking distance*: Ibid., 269.

306 *They are not ignorant, savage tribes*: Miller, *"Benevolent Assimilation,"* 40.

308 *niggers*: Musicant, *Empire by Default*, 569.

309 *a large and gradually increasing*: Ibid., 584–85.

309 *We don't want a war*: Ibid., 585.

309 *now . . . we must establish our authority by force*: Dewey, *Autobiography*, 285.

309 *no serious statesman can accept a favor*: Henry Adams, *The Education of Henry Adams*, 1053.

310 *permanent amity*: Trask, *The War with Spain in 1898*, 424.

310 *You and I had better have no opinion*: Dennett, *John Hay: From Poetry to Politics*, 189–90.

310 *It has been a splendid little war*: Thayer, *The Life and Letters of John Hay*, vol. 2, 337.

311 *You have written your name*: Ibid.

311 *Ordinary rules do not apply to you*: Lodge, ed., *Selections from the Correspondence of TR and Henry Cabot Lodge*, vol. 1, 324.

311 *the good people in New York*: TR Letters, vol. 2, 863.

312 *One of the most important is the friendly relations*: Nevins, *Henry White*, 137.

312 *"We're a gr-reat people"*: Dunne, *Mr. Dooley in Peace and War*, 9.

312 *What a wonderful war it has been*: Garraty, *Henry Cabot Lodge*, 195.

312 *We have never in all our history*: Trask, *The War with Spain in 1898*, 427.

CHAPTER 9: JINGOES AND GOO-GOOS

316 *Do not forget we are poor*: Trask, *The War with Spain in 1898*, 443.

316 *dropped into our laps*: Musicant, *Empire by Default*, 591.

316 *hitching post*: Ibid., 590.

316 *a little timid*: Lodge, ed., *Selections from the Correspondence of TR and Henry Cabot Lodge*, vol. 1, 323.

316 *in full right and sovereignty*: Trask, *The War with Spain in 1898*, 441.

316 *It is my earnest wish*: Annals of America, vol. 12, 232–33.

317 . . . *without any original thought*: Ibid.

319 Tamar, Iowa: May, *Imperial Democracy*, 258–59; Musicant, *Empire by Default*, 614–15.

320 *I walked the floor of the White House*: May, *Imperial Democracy*, 252–53.

321 *I consider . . . that the intention of the Americans*: Trask, *The War with Spain in 1898*, 457.

321 *all claim of sovereignty*: Lodge, *The War with Spain*, 268.

321 *civil rights and political status*: Ibid., 273.

322 *cowardly and dishonorable*: Musicant, *Empire by Default*, 591.

323 *a mess of Asian pottage*: Paterson, *American Imperialism and Anti-Imperialism*, 114.

323 *Are we to have a Mongolian state*: Tompkins, *Anti-Imperialism in the United States*, 108.

323 *crazy: [H]e thinks Germany*: Leech, *In the Days of McKinley*, 354.

323 *We were down in the engine room*: Ibid., 392.

324 *It was the closest, hardest fight*: Lodge, ed., *Selections from the Correspondence of TR and Henry Cabot Lodge*, vol. 1, 391.

324 *One word from Mr. Bryan*: Millis, *The Martial Spirit*, 401.

325 *With the signature of the treaty*: Ibid., 396.

325 *the confidence, respect, and affection*: Ibid.

325 *we come, not as invaders*: Ibid.

325 *My government is ready to open hostilities*: Brands, *Bound to Empire*, 49.

325 *It is always the unexpected*: Trask, *The War with Spain in 1898*, 470.

326 *their welfare is our welfare*: Leech, *In the Days of McKinley*, 362.

327 *for the liberator to submit*: Ibid., 362.

327 *I cannot bound my vision*: Ibid.

327 *No imperial designs*: Trask, *The War with Spain in 1898*, 472.

328 *a dangerous and ominous jingo*: Morris, *The Rise of TR*, 468.

328 *jingo*: Bartlett, *Familiar Quotations*, 598.

328 *unhung traitors*: Beisner, *Twelve Against Empire*, 237.

328 *I do not favor a policy of acquisition*: McDougall, *Promised Land, Crusader State*, 101.

328 *Hawaiian monstrosity*: Nevins, *Grover Cleveland*, 743.

328 *the mission of our nation*: Ibid., 745.

328 *the greatest expansionist in our history*: Lodge, *Speeches and Addresses*, 330.

328 *merely the last and final step*: Lodge, *The War with Spain*, 4.

329 *What the nation has gained*: Mahan, *Retrospect and Prospect*, 17.

331 *I was opposed*: TR Letters, vol. 2, 889.

332 *put all good eggs*: Carnegie, *Autobiography*, 176.

333 *America is going to control anything*: Wall, *Andrew Carnegie*, 675.

333 *Are we to exchange Triumphant Democracy*: Ibid., 694.

333 *Andrew Carnegie really seems to be off his head*: Thayer, *The Life and Letters of John Hay*, vol. 2, 199.

333 *It is a matter of congratulation*: Millis, *The Martial Spirit*, 406.

333 *a dangerous man*: Wall, *Andrew Carnegie*, 709.

334 *restore our Republic*: Ibid., 695.

334 *As long as we remain free*: Ibid., 694.

334 *foreign races*: Ibid.

334 *a disgusting country*: Beisner, *Twelve Against Empire*, 71.

334 *un-American*: Ibid., 76.

334 *alien, inferior, and mongrel races*: Ibid.

335 *social and political problems*: Tompkins, *Anti-Imperialism in the United States*, 46.

335 *malignant and dishonest liar*: Beisner, *Twelve Against Empire*, 56.

335 *Schurz is a wonderful man*: Thayer, *The Life and Letters of John Hay*, vol. 1, 103.

335 *He will make a wonderful land pirate*: Ibid., 103.

336 *prattling foreigner*: TR Letters, vol. 2, 1086.

336 *a champion of dishonor*: Ibid., 928.

336 *My country, right or wrong*: Trefousse, *Carl Schurz*, 180.

336 *yield to the allurements*: Tompkins, *Anti-Imperialism in the United States*, 53.

336 *a barbarous notion*: Ibid., 212.

337 *Our real compensation*: Millis, *The Martial Spirit*, 160–61.

337 *If we turn this war*: Tompkins, *Anti-Imperialism in the United States*, 122.

337 *That would bring us another lot*: Schurz, *The Reminiscences of Carl Schurz*, vol. 3, 440

337 *a large mass*: Beisner, *Twelve Against Empire*, 26.

337 *Show me*: Root, *The Military and Colonial Policy of the United States*, 43.

338 *The story of our attempted conquest*: Schurz, *The Reminiscences of Carl Schurz*, 446–47.

338 *1. Surrender to Aguinaldo*: Beisner, *Twelve Against Empire*, 31–32.

339 *since time began*: Annals of America, vol. 12, 427.

339 *The prospect of the consequences*: Paterson, *American Imperialism and Anti-Imperialism*, 115.

339 *nature's asylum for degenerates*: Ibid.

339 *if we govern the Philippines*: Ibid.

340 *Readiness for war*: Annals of America, vol. 12, 506.

340 *the prospect of adding to the present Senate*: Millis, *The Martial Spirit*, 77.

340 *mongrel races*: Gossett, *Race: The History of an Idea in America*, 114.

340 *no greater calamity*: Tompkins, *Anti-Imperialism in the United States*, 83.

340 *We would reach out for fresh territory*: Trask, *The War with Spain in 1898*, 53–54.

341 *When Rome began her career*: Tompkins, *Anti-Imperialism in the United States*, 124–25.

341 *has lost her unique position*: Tuchman, *The Proud Tower*, 161.

341 *a most healthy phase of evolution*: Beisner, *Twelve Against Empire*, 37.

341 *Man is once for all*: Ibid., 42.

341 *One foe is as good as another*: Hofstadter, *Social Darwinism in American Thought*, 195.

341 *is still mentally in the Sturm und Drang period*: Beisner, *Twelve Against Empire*, 43.

342 *God damn the U.S.*: Ibid., 44.

342 *the one sacred thing*: Ibid.

342 *snivelling, loathsome*: Ibid.

343 *If the Philippines are annexed*: Paterson, *American Imperialism and Anti-Imperialism*, 115.

343 *an inundation of Mongolians*: Tompkins, *Anti-Imperialism in the United States*, 109.

343 *gelatinous walrus of a man*: Beisner, *Twelve Against Empire*, 204.

343 *original discovery of the ten commandments*: Ibid.

343 *thin soil highly cultivated*: Ibid., 205.

343 *the Emperor of Expediency*: Ibid.

343 *a successful politician*: Ibid.

344 *we were at peace within our own borders*: Ibid., 208.

344 *Not every opportunity*: *Annals of America*, vol. 12, 161.

344 *Have we the right*: Ibid., 248.

344 *any fancied or real obligation*: Ibid., 249.

344 *whether Congress may conquer*: Ibid.

344 *you cannot take down a national flag*: Ibid., 250.

344 *to the doctrine*: Ibid.

345 *Now, I claim that under the Declaration*: Ibid., 252.

345 *the people of the Philippine Islands*: Ibid.

345 *a great many million square miles*: Ibid.

345 *brutal selfishness*: Beisner, *Twelve Against Empire*, 162.

345 *At th' age iv eight*: Dunne, *Mr. Dooley's Philosophy*, 129.

346 *base at the door of all the East*: *Annals of America*, vol. 12, 337.

346 *illimitable* China market: Ibid., 336.

346 *ours forever*: Ibid.

346 *our ocean*: Ibid.

346 *our natural customer*: Ibid., 337.

346 *Most future wars*: Ibid.

347 *establish the supremacy*: Ibid., 338.

347 *had we made continuous and decisive war*: Ibid., 337–38.

347 *as carefully, tenderly cared for as our own*: Ibid., 338.

347 *Senators must remember*: Ibid.

347 *in sorrow rather than anger*: Ibid., 339.

347 *They are not capable*: Ibid.

347 *I have talked with hundreds*: Ibid.

347 *the great majority*: Ibid.

347 *children*: Ibid., 340

347 *the highest examples of our civilization*: Ibid.

348 *The Declaration of Independence*: Ibid., 341.

348 *the best tropical climate*: Bowers, *Beveridge and the Progressive Era*, 120.

348 *God has not been preparing*: *Annals of America*, vol. 12, 343.

348 *And of all our race*: Ibid.

348 *As a nation*: Ibid., 344.

348 *Every holy memory*: Ibid.

349 *I heard much calculated to excite*: Bowers, *Beveridge and the Progressive Era*, 122.

349 *Apparently we are not proposing*: Zwick, *Mark Twain's Weapons of Satire*, xx.

350 *a mess, a quagmire*: Ibid., xx.

350 *a miniature of the American constitution*: Ibid.

350 *Manila was ours*: Ibid., 35–36.

351 *. . . we have crushed a deceived and confiding people*: Ibid., 37.

351 *We shall let go our obsequious hold*: Ibid., 122–24.

351 *Mine eyes have seen the orgy*: Ibid., 40.

351 *War Prayer*: Ibid., 159.

352 *we're th' same breed*: Dunne, *Mr. Dooley in Peace and War*, 20.

352 *Cousin George*: Ibid., 21–22.

353 *in a room with a checker-board*: Ibid., 30.

353 *R'rush eighty-three millyon throops*: Ibid., 31.

353 *Teddy Rosenfelt's r-rough r-riders*: Ibid., 32.

353 *Seize Gin'ral Miles' uniform*: Ibid.

353 *Day by day*: Ibid., 32–33.

353 *Th' ordhers fr'm Washin'ton*: Ibid., 17.

354 *. . . I sint the ar-rmy home*: Dunne, *Mr. Dooley at His Best*, 101–02.

354 *take the whole lot*: Dunne, *Mr. Dooley in Peace and War*, 43.

354 *Th' war is still goin' on*: Ibid., 44–45.

354 *In ivry city*: Dunne, *Mr. Dooley in the Hearts of His Countrymen*, 4.

354 *indulgent parent*: Ibid., 6.

355 *I'm a sojer*: Dunne, *Mr. Dooley in Peace and War*, 64–65.

355 *a good noisy man*: Dunne, *Mr. Dooley in the Hearts of His Countrymen*, 10.

355 *a very superyor brand*: Ibid., 5.

355 *Aggynaldo didn't hear th' whistle blow*: Ibid., 12.

356 *I have always attributed*: Dunne, *Mr. Dooley at His Best*, xxv–vi.

356 *I really believe I brought on the war*: Nasaw, *The Chief: The Life of William Randolph Hearst*, 145.

358 *Please remain*: Ibid., 127.

359 *I made the mistake of my life*: Ibid., 145.

CHAPTER 10: THE WHITE MAN'S BURDENS

362 *moral dry rot*: Ricketts, *The Unforgiving Minute: A Life of Rudyard Kipling*, 197.

362 *a colossal agglomeration*: Ibid., 212.

362 *When a man comes up out of the sea*: Ibid.

362 *nervous, voluble, rather underbred*: TR Letters, vol. 1, 433.

362 *rough-and-tumble*: TR, *Letters from TR to Anna Roosevelt Cowles*, 150.

362 *I never got over the wonder*: Ricketts, *The Unforgiving Minute: A Life of Mark Twain*, 213.

364 *Take up the white man's burden*: Ibid., 232–33.

365　*I think most of the current jingoism*: Perkins, *The Great Rapprochement*, 76.

365　*Rather poor poetry*: Lodge, ed., *Selections from the Correspondence of TR and Henry Cabot Lodge*, vol. 1, 384.

366　*If I thought that it were all for nothing*: Gilmour, *Curzon*, 166.

368　*it is our unquestioned duty*: Root, *The Military and Colonial Policy of the United States*, 162.

369　*have not yet been educated*: Ibid., 163.

370　*like a disembodied shade*: Morales Carrión, *Puerto Rico: A Political and Cultural History*, 157.

370　*We are Mr. Nobody*: Carr, *Puerto Rico: A Colonial Experiment*, 33.

370　*to prevent, through the independence of Cuba*: Thomas, *Cuba or the Pursuit of Freedom*, 310.

371　*Once the United States is in Cuba*: Jacobsen, *Barbarian Virtues*, 43.

372　*We must recognize*: Foner, *The Spanish-Cuban-American War and the Birth of American Imperialism 1895–1902*, vol. 2, 445.

372　*Your estimate for August*: Hagedorn, *Leonard Wood*, vol. 1, 247–48.

373　*The control which we are exercising*: Root, *The Military and Colonial Policy of the United States*, 171.

373　*must needs be bound to us*: Foner, *The Spanish-Cuban-American War and the Birth of American Imperialism 1895–1902*, vol. 2, 525.

374　*if we once got into a position*: Hagedorn, *Leonard Wood*, vol. 1, 343.

374　*The trouble about Cuba*: Jessup, *Elihu Root*, vol. 1, 327.

374　*the people who are talking "Cuba Libre"*: Foner, *The Spanish-Cuban-American War and the Birth of American Imperialism 1895–1902*, vol. 2, 456.

377　*to frame and adopt a constitution*: Ibid., 541.

377　*send their very best men*: Hagedorn, *Leonard Wood*, vol. 1, 322.

377　*some of the worst agitators*: Ibid.

378　*I do not fully agree*: Root, *The Military and Colonial Policy of the United States*, 215.

378　*If Cuba declines*: Jessup, *Elihu Root*, vol. 1, 309.

379　*Another fact which the Cubans should consider*: Ibid.

379　*The preservation of that independence*: Ibid., 313.

380　*[ART. I]: That the government of Cuba*: Root, *The Military and Colonial Policy of the United States*, 213–14.

381　*the amendment was drafted*: Jessup, *Elihu Root*, vol. 1, 320.

381　*you have been able to disabuse*: Ibid., 316.

382　*we shall occupy*: Foner, *The Spanish-Cuban-American War and the Birth of American Imperialism 1895–1902*, vol. 2, 619.

382　*because they impair the independence*: Thomas, *Cuba or the Pursuit of Freedom*, 454.

382　*Our duty consists*: Ibid.

382　*To reserve to the United States*: Ibid.

383　*[T]he Convention. . . . will have failed*: Foner, *The Spanish-Cuban-American War and the Birth of American Imperialism 1895–1902*, vol. 2, 601.

384 *There is, of course, little or no independence*: Ibid., 632.

385 *to be officially and openly administered*: Ibid., 605.

386 *the government and control of the Island*: Hagedorn, *Leonard Wood*, vol. 1, 390.

386 *The people whom we liberated*: Seager, *Alfred Thayer Mahan*, 419.

387 *The Filipinos fought against Spain*: Brands, *Bound to Empire*, 41.

387 *we come, not as invaders*: Millis, *The Martial Spirit*, 396.

387 *Finally, it should be the earnest and paramount aim*: Miller, "Benevolent Assimilation," title page.

388 *the most humane*: Karnow, *In Our Image: America's Empire in the Philippines*, 151.

388 *Only through American occupation*: Root, *The Military and Colonial Policy of the United States*, 44.

389 *a locomotive bottomside up*: Karnow, *In Our Image: America's Empire in the Philippines*, 132.

390 *"Judge," he said*: Leech, *In the Days of McKinley*, 484.

391 *. . . the commission should bear in mind*: Root, *The Military and Colonial Policy of the United States*, 291, 294.

391 *humiliating*: Linn, *The Philippine War 1899–1902*, 216.

392 *Fine. How's the horse?*: Jessup, *Elihu Root*, vol. 1, 363.

393 *Chinese half-breed*: Root, *The Military and Colonial Policies of the United States*, 36.

394 *As near as I can make out*: Jessup, *Elihu Root*, vol. 1, 348.

394 *all military, civil, and judicial powers*: Root, *The Military and Colonial Policy of the United States*, 255.

395 *[I]vry wanst in a while*: Dunne, *Mr. Dooley, Now and Forever*, 188.

395 *should get the Army out of the business*: Jessup, *Elihu Root*, vol. 1, 360.

395 *the most fatal possible gift*: Ibid., 370.

395 *[O]ur friends, the peace-at-any-price Senators*: TR Letters, vol. 2, 933.

396 *the most important year*: Ibid., 934.

396 *unyielding resolution*: Ibid., 998.

396 *the best type of government*: Ibid., 1024.

396 *we need tact and judgment*: Ibid., 1025.

396 *smash the insurgents*: Ibid.

396 *Oversentimentality, over-softness*: Ibid., 1100.

396 *I am an expansionist*: Ibid., 1134.

397 *a little loose*: Morris, *The Rise of TR*, 700–01.

397 *an irksome, wearisome place*: TR, *Letters from TR to Anna Roosevelt Cowles*, 233.

397 *exactly as if I had been a presidential candidate*: Morris, *The Rise of TR*, 704.

397 *He is more than a presidential possibility*: Ibid.

398 *If I were a candidate for the Presidency*: Lodge, ed., *Selections from the Correspondence of TR and Henry Cabot Lodge*, vol. 1, 424.

398 *merely to say the word*: Ibid., 431.

398 *the dear old goose*: TR, *Letters from TR to Anna Roosevelt Cowles*, 241.

399 *I myself realize all these chances*: Ibid., 244.

399 *If you go to that Convention*: Lodge, ed., *Selections from the Correspondence of TR and Henry Cabot Lodge*, vol. 1, 459.

399 *The general feeling*: Ibid.

399 *Teddy has been here*: Morris, *The Rise of TR*, 721.

399 *I would be looked upon as rather a coward*: Lodge, ed., *Selections from the Correspondence of TR and Henry Cabot Lodge*, vol. 1, 460.

400 *Don't any of you realize*: Morris, *The Rise of TR*, 724.

400 *The thing could not be helped*: TR, *Letters from TR to Anna Roosevelt Cowles*, 245.

400 *Well, old man*: Lodge, ed., *Selections from the Correspondence of TR and Henry Cabot Lodge*, vol. 1, 465.

400 *no new departures*: TR Letters, vol. 2, 1402–03.

400 *anti-imperialistic*: Ibid., 1403.

400 *Chinese half-breeds*: Ibid., 1405.

400 *corruption would flourish*: Ibid.

400 *must, of course, be governed*: Ibid., 1404.

401 *You are withdrawn perforce*: Mahan, *Letters and Papers*, vol. 2, 706–07.

401 *does not intend that I shall have any influence*: TR Letters, vol. 3, 60.

401 *Neither he nor Hanna*: Ibid.

401 *an utterly anomalous office*: Ibid.

401 *time of slack water*: TR Letters, vol. 3, 120.

401 *The trip was a revelation*: Lodge, ed., *Selections from the Correspondence of TR and Henry Cabot Lodge*, vol. 1, 498.

402 *Don't let them hurt him*: Leech, *In the Days of McKinley*, 595.

402 *the declaration of war against Spain*: Linderman, *The Mirror of War*, 35.

402 *for the peace, the prosperity*: Harbaugh, *Power and Responsibility: The Life and Times of TR*, 146.

402 *It is a dreadful thing*: Lodge, ed., *Selections from the Correspondence of TR and Henry Cabot Lodge*, vol. 1, 506.

403 *You are the only man*: Ibid., 443.

404 *While I have never varied*: TR Letters, vol. 3, 105.

404 *Barring the possible necessity*: Ibid.

404 *one of those great works*: Brands, *TR: The Last Romantic*, 429.

404 *To leave the islands at this time*: Ibid.

404 *[U.S. forces were] required to crush*: Root, *The Military and Colonial Policy of the United States*, 330.

405 *kind and considerate treatment*: Linn, *The Philippine War 1899–1902*, 220.

406 *The country won't be pacified*: Miller, "Benevolent Assimilation," 179.

406 *They say I've got brown brothers here*: Karnow, *In Our Image: America's Empire in the Philippines*, 174.

406 *Damn, damn, damn the Filipinos!*: Ibid., 155.

407 *grandmotherish system*: Miller, "Benevolent Assimilation," 179.

407 *the judicious application of the torch*: Ibid., 220.

407 *the victim is laid flat on his back*: Ibid., 223.

408 *I want no prisoners*: Miller, *"Benevolent Assimilation,"* 220.

408 *Ten years of age*: Ibid.

408 *the interior of Samar*: Ibid.

409 *the warfare in the Philippines*: TR Letters, vol. 3, 245.

409 *no matter what measures have to be adopted*: Miller, *"Benevolent Assimilation,"* 258.

410 *there have been some blots*: TR Letters, vol. 3, 297–98.

410 *We make no hypocritical pretense*: Miller, *"Benevolent Assimilation,"* 147.

410 *there never was a war conducted*: Jessup, *Elihu Root*, vol. 1, 340.

411 *for the humanity we exercised*: Miller, *"Benevolent Assimilation,"* 216.

411 *it is not a function of law*: Maguire, *Law and War: An American Story*, 52.

411 *was silent in the face of certain knowledge*: Jessup, *Elihu Root*, vol. 1, 339.

412 *you will spare no effort*: Ibid., 342–43.

412 *were not justified*: Root, *The Military and Colonial Policy of the United States*, 92.

412 *gallant and fearless*: Ibid., 93.

412 *whether or not any brutalities*: TR, *Letters*, vol. 3, 260.

412 *individual instances of wrong-doing*: Ibid.

412 *few indeed have been the instances*: Ibid.

414 *camps of refuge*: Pakenham, *The Scramble for Africa 1876–1912*, 577.

415 *it would be inevitable that we should sink*: Lodge, *Speeches and Addresses*, 369–70.

415 *follow the laws of our being*: Ibid., 372–73.

CHAPTER 11: THE IMPERIAL PRESIDENCY

418 *Imperialism, the extension of national authority*: Mahan, *Retrospect and Prospect*, 111.

419 *There was not in his nature*: TR Letters, vol. 4, 1271.

419 *I wonder if you have any idea*: Ibid., 1131.

419 *the most important official post*: Dennett, *John Hay: From Poetry to Politics*, 223.

419 *not a great Secretary of State*: TR Letters, vol. 4, 1490.

420 *I had to do all the big things*: Ibid., 1271.

420 *When McKinley sent for me*: Dennett, *John Hay: From Poetry to Politics*, 347.

420 *The President is all right*: Clymer, *John Hay: The Gentleman as Diplomat*, 198.

420 *Oh, may we long postpone the evil hour*: Ibid., 101.

420 *steal Panama*: Ibid., 204.

420 *we . . . be compelled*: Dennett, *John Hay: From Poetry to Politics*, 334.

421 *his obedience to the President's order*: Henry Adams, *The Education of Henry Adams*, 1054.

421 *I have acquired the funeral habit*: Thayer, *The Life and Letters of John Hay*, vol. 2, 268.

421 *my grief for the President*: Ibid., 344.

422 *not a democratic service*: White, *The Autobiography of Andrew Dickson White*, 358.

422 *refuse to believe me disconsulate*: Henry Adams, *The Education of Henry Adams*, 1080.

422 *The worst is the constant solicitations*: Thayer, *The Life and Letters of John Hay*, vol. 2, 191–92.

422 *as a friend of the President's*: Ibid., 192.

423 *we must get everything*: Hay, "Letters," vol. 3, 185.

424 *The worst of all is the uncertainty*: Ibid., 160–61.

426 *Et Tu?*: P. O'Toole, *The Five of Hearts*, 314.

426 *the greatest Secretary of State*: TR Letters, vol. 2, 1192.

427 *So [Lodge] has thrown Hay over*: Clymer, *John Hay: The Gentleman as Diplomat*, 178.

427 *He would cut my throat*: Ibid., 182.

427 *Theodore was very funny about Cabot*: Ibid., 188.

428 *practicable and feasible*: Morris, *Theodore Rex*, 67.

431 *which every friend of Colombia*: McCullough, *The Path Between the Seas*, 334.

431 *You could no more make an agreement*: Thayer, *The Life and Letters of John Hay*, vol. 2, 327–28.

432 *Our policy before the world*: McCullough, *The Path Between the Seas*, 340.

434 *as if it were the sovereign*: Ibid., 393.

434 *in perpetuity*: Ibid.

434 *You and I know too well*: Ibid., 392.

434 *the interests of collective civilization*: Bailey, *A Diplomatic History of the American People*, 544.

434 *This I can say absolutely was my own work*: TR Letters, vol. 6, 1444.

434 *I am interested in the Panama Canal*: Bailey, *A Diplomatic History of the American People*, 545.

435 *How on earth a fair-minded man*: Thayer, *The Life and Letters of John Hay*, vol. 2, 324.

436 *You certainly have, Mr. President*: Brands, TR: *The Last Romantic*, 488.

437 *We stole it fair and square*: joelmartin.com

437 *The inevitable effect of our building the Canal*: Jessup, *Elihu Root*, vol. 1, 471.

438 *If any South American State misbehaves*: TR Letters, vol. 3, 115.

438 *territorial aggrandizement*: TR, Annual Message, December 3, 1901, www.theodore-roosevelt.com, Almanac of TR, 17.

439 *Yankee Dewey's near La Guayra*: Bailey, *A Diplomatic History of the American People*, 552.

439 *villainous little monkey*: TR Letters, vol. 4, 1156.

440 *I have about the same desire to annex it*: Ibid., 734.

440 *Chronic wrongdoing*: Brands, TR: *The Last Romantic*, 527.

441 *It cannot be too often and too emphatically asserted*: Divine, *American Foreign Policy: A Documentary History*, 161.

441 *[arrogating] to ourselves, not sovereignty*: Jessup, *Elihu Root*, vol. 1, 470.

442 *Revolution spreading. Everything quiet*: Thomas, *Cuba or the Pursuit of Freedom*, 475.

442 *Cuba herself shows:* TR Letters, vol. 5, 412.

442 *the death of the Republic:* Ibid., 422.

442 *Hugh Thomas:* Thomas, *Cuba or the Pursuit of Freedom,* 481–93.

443 *Disgust with the Cubans:* Lodge, ed., *Selections from the Correspondence of TR and Henry Cabot Lodge,* vol. 2, 233.

443 *There can be no talk of a protectorate:* TR Letters, vol. 5, 560.

444 *are important as facilitating our access:* Mahan, *Retrospect and Prospect,* 34.

444 *. . . in the hands of a naval Power:* LaFeber, *The Cambridge History of American Foreign Relations,* vol. 2, 90.

445 *in the physical sense:* TR Letters, vol. 5, 761.

445 *The Philippines form our heel of Achilles:* Ibid., 762.

446 *the great game of spoliation:* Thayer, *The Life and Letters of John Hay,* vol. 2, 241.

446 *The storm center of the world:* Moon, *Imperialism and World Politics,* 321.

447 *Your open door is already off its hinges:* Samuels, *Henry Adams,* 338.

447 *The inherent weakness of our position:* LaFeber, *The Cambridge History of American Foreign Relations,* vol. 2, 175.

449 *We are bound by a tie:* Perkins, *The Great Rapprochement,* 87.

450 *After a nation has pursued certain paths:* Ibid., 51.

450 *undoubtedly the most formidable:* Mahan, *The Interest of America in Sea Power, Present and Future,* 27.

450 *the British Empire is in external matters:* Mahan, *Retrospect and Prospect,* 34.

450 *worked a complete revolution:* TR Letters, vol. 2, 890.

451 *I am greatly mistaken:* Ibid., 1050–54.

451 *As long as I stay here:* Perkins, *The Great Rapprochement,* 57–58.

451 *an outrage pure and simple:* TR Letters, vol. 3, 287–88.

451 *six impartial jurists of repute:* Bailey, *A Diplomatic History of the American People,* 556.

452 *the principle involved:* Tilchin, *TR and the British Empire,* 41.

452 *I think myself that Lord Alverstone:* Dennett, *John Hay: From Poetry to Politics,* 360.

452 *settled the last serious trouble:* Tilchin, *TR and the British Empire,* 48.

452 *I no longer feel the old acute pleasure:* Perkins, *The Great Rapprochement,* 154.

452 *th' king sint f'r Ambassadure Choate:* Dunne, *Dissertations by Mr. Dooley,* 213–14.

453 *infirmity of his mind and character:* Dennett, *John Hay: From Poetry to Politics,* 358.

453 *all the governments of Europe:* Henry Adams, *Letters of Henry Adams, 1892–1918,* 196.

453 *Minister Wu came by this morning:* I am indebted for this story to James W. Symington, John Hay's great-grandson.

453 *We want Perdicaris alive:* Thayer, *The Life and Letters of John Hay,* vol. 2, 383.

453 *It is curious how a concise impropriety:* Ibid., 383.

454 *hung up in the Senate Committee-room:* Henry Adams, *The Education of Henry Adams,* 1180.

454 *John Hay had to die*: Dennett, *John Hay: From Poetry to Politics*, 439.

454 *who turned out to be Mr. Lincoln*: Thayer, *The Life and Letters of John Hay*, vol. 2, 405.

454 *I say to myself that I should not rebel*: Hay, *Letters of John Hay*, vol. 3, 350.

455 *We . . . are Greeks*: Renwick, *Fighting with Allies*, vii.

456 *Our blood is as the flood*: Strout, *The American Image of the Old World*, 135.

456 *smelting pot*: Jones, *American Immigration*, 137–38.

456 *the great assimilating people*: Higham, *Strangers in the Land*, 21.

458 *non-Aryan*: Ibid., 141; Jones, *American Immigration*, 221.

458 *mongrel races*: Gossett, *Race: The History of an Idea*, 114.

458 *beaten men from beaten races*: Higham, *Strangers in the Land*, 143.

459 *Darwin and Galton have lived*: Gossett, *Race: The History of an Idea*, 159.

459 *The men of each race*: Widenor, *Henry Cabot Lodge and the Search for an American Foreign Policy*, 60.

459 *most alien to the body*: Jacobsen, *Barbarian Virtues*, 196.

461 *Our effort must be to secure to each man*: TR, *An American Mind: Selected Writings*, 332

461 *by much more drastic laws*: TR, *American Ideals*, 29.

461 *Jews, Injuns, Chinamen*: Slotkin, *Gunfighter Nation*, 97.

461 *encroaching alien vermin*: Townsend, *Manhood at Harvard*, 268.

461 *A single generation of life*: TR Letters, vol. 1, 787.

462 *Celt and Latin*: Jacobsen, *Barbarian Virtues*, 204.

462 *not merely dealt with the "melting pot"*: Dyer, *TR and the Idea of Race*, 131.

462 *The one absolutely certain way*: Schlesinger, *The Disuniting of America*, 118.

463 *hirsute, low-brained*: Kraut, *The Huddled Masses: The Immigrant in American Society 1880–1921*, 153.

464 *the tacit or unquestioned acceptance*: Stern, *Einstein's German World*, 234.

465 *the vast mass of China*: Mahan, *Letters and Papers*, vol. 1, 92–93.

465 *barbarous*: Thayer, *The Life and Letters of John Hay*, vol. 2, 406–07.

465 *dreadful treatment*: Jessup, *Elihu Root*, vol. 2, 44.

465 *The Japs interest me*: Brands, *TR: The Last Romantic*, 531.

465 *a wonderful and civilized people*: Beale, *TR and the Rise of America to World Power*, 268–69.

466 *yellow peril*: Ibid., 271.

468 *peace-loving public opinion*: Ibid., 299.

468 *we must take Roosevelt's opinion*: Ibid.

470 *Your personal energetic efforts*: Ibid., 306.

470 *Your advice was very powerful*: Ibid., 307.

471 *wicked absurdity*: Harbaugh, *Power and Responsibility: The Life and Times of TR*, 299.

471 *We cannot afford to regard any immigrant*: Brands, *TR: The Last Romantic*, 581.

471 *because, and only because . . . we possess a navy*: TR Letters, vol. 4, 737.

472 *the Senior Senator from the fishing grounds*: Jessup, *Elihu Root*, vol. 2, 85.

473 *warrant for interference*: Jessup, *Elihu Root*, vol. 1, 561.

473 *good neighbor*: Ibid., 563.
474 *We ourselves are becoming*: Beale, *TR and the Rise of America to World Power*, 447.

CHAPTER 12: AMERICA'S CENTURY

476 *It shall not lie with the American people*: LaFeber, *Inevitable Revolutions: The United States in Central America*, 55.
478 *a union of civilized nations*: Garraty, *Henry Cabot Lodge*, 344.
482 *the 1941–45 naval war against Japan*: Weigley, *The American Way of War*, 311.
483 *a peculiar power to grasp principles*: Puleston, *Mahan*, 199.
484 *The finest, the bravest*: Brands, *TR: The Last Romantic*, 800.
485 *I have only one fight left in me*: Ibid., 810.
486 *one of the greatest*: Garraty, *Henry Cabot Lodge*, 379.
486 *exalt their personal prestige*: Ibid.
486 *After three centuries*: Jones, *American Immigration*, 238.
486 *There is a wide difference between taking a suitable part*: Widenor, *Henry Cabot Lodge and the Search for an American Foreign Policy*, 326.
486 *I care more for one button*: Jessup, *Elihu Root*, vol. 2, 202.
487 *Congress is not a mirror*: Ibid., 205.
487 *some face-saving modifications*: Garraty, *Henry Cabot Lodge*, 383.
488 *Mr. Root is known to the world*: Jessup, *Elihu Root*, vol. 2, 137–38.
488 *The very people who are most ardent*: Ibid., 61–62.
493 *Our chief usefulness to humanity*: McDougall, *Promised Land, Crusader State*, 120.
494 *imperialist democracy*: Cooper, *The Warrior and the Priest: Woodrow Wilson and TR*, 144.
495 *march of events*: *Annals of America*, vol. 12, 232.
495 *cosmic tendency*: Hay, *Addresses*, 250.
495 *A world power we had been for many long years*: Widenor, *Henry Cabot Lodge and the Search for an American Foreign Policy*, 134.
498 *it must be the policy of the United States*: McCormick, *America's Half-Century*, 75.
499 *When foreign affairs play a prominent part*: Heckscher, *Woodrow Wilson*, 130.
500 *In any nation which amounts to anything*: Collin, *Theodore Roosevelt's Caribbean*, 445.
501 *soft power*: Joseph S. Nye, Jr., "Redefining the National Interest," *Foreign Affairs* (July–August 1996), 22–36.

Bibliography

Aaron, Daniel, ed. *America in Crisis.* New York: Alfred A. Knopf, 1952.

Abbot, Willis John. *Blue Jackets of '98: A History of the Spanish-American War.* New York: Dodd, Mead, 1899.

Adams, Brooks. *The Law of Civilization and Decay: An Essay on History.* New York: Macmillan, 1896.

Adams, Henry. *The Degeneration of the Democratic Dogma.* New York: Peter Smith, 1949.

———. *Democracy. An American Novel.* New York: Airmont, 1968.

———. *The Education of Henry Adams.* New York: Library of America, 1983.

———. *Letters of Henry Adams 1858–1918,* ed. Worthington Chauncey Ford. Boston: Houghton Mifflin, 1930 and 1938. 2 vols.

———. *Letters of John Hay,* ed. Henry Adams. Washington: 1908.

———. *Selected Letters,* ed. Ernest Samuels. Cambridge: Belknap Press of Harvard University Press, 1992.

Adams, Marian. *The Letters of Mrs. Henry Adams 1865–1883,* ed. Ward Thoron. Boston: Little, Brown, 1936.

Alger, Russell A. *The Spanish-American War.* Freeport, N.Y.: Books for Libraries Press, 1971.

Ambrose, Stephen E. *Undaunted Courage: Meriwether Lewis, Thomas Jefferson, and the Opening of the American West.* New York: Simon & Schuster, 1996.

Andriote, John-Manuel. *The Metropolitan Club of the City of Washington,* Washington, D.C.: The Club, 1997.

Annals of America, vol. 12, *1895–1904: Populism, Imperialism, and Reform.* Chicago: Encyclopaedia Britannica, 1976.

Bailey, Thomas A. *A Diplomatic History of the American People.* New York: F. S. Crofts, 1947.

Barnes, William, and John Heath Morgan. *The Foreign Service of the United States: Origins, Development, and Functions.* Washington, D.C.: Department of State, 1961.

Bartlett, John. *Familiar Quotations.* Boston: Little, Brown, 1980.

Beale, Howard K. *Theodore Roosevelt and the Rise of America to World Power.* Baltimore: Johns Hopkins University Press, 1956.

Bederman, Gail. *Manliness and Civilization: A Cultural History of Gender and Race in the United States 1880–1917.* Chicago: University of Chicago, 1995.

Beisner, Robert L. *Twelve Against Empire: The Anti-Imperialists 1898–1900.* New York: McGraw-Hill, 1968.

Bemis, Samuel Flagg. *A Diplomatic History of the United States.* New York: Henry Holt, 1942.

Benjamin, Jules R. *The United States and Cuba, Hegemony and Dependent Development 1880–1934.* Pittsburgh: University of Pittsburgh Press, 1974.

———. *The United States and the Origins of the Cuban Revolution.* Princeton: Princeton University Press, 1990.

Bierce, Ambrose. *The Collected Writings of Ambrose Bierce.* New York: Citadel Press, 1974.

Bishop, Joseph Bucklin. *Notes and Anecdotes of Many Years.* New York: Charles Scribner's Sons, 1925.

Blum, John Morton. *The Republican Roosevelt.* Cambridge: Harvard University Press, 1993.

Boorstein, Daniel. *The Americans: The Democratic Experience.* New York: Random House, 1973.

Bowers, Claude G. *Beveridge and the Progressive Era.* Cambridge: Houghton Mifflin, 1932.

Brands, H. W. *Bound to Empire: The United States and the Philippines.* New York: Oxford University Press, 1992.

———. *The Reckless Decade: America in the 1890's.* New York: St. Martin's, 1995.

———. *TR: The Last Romantic.* New York: Basic Books, 1997.

Burns, James MacGregor. *The Workshop of Democracy.* New York: Alfred A. Knopf, 1985.

Burrows, Edwin G., and Mike Wallace. *Gotham: A History of New York City to 1898.* New York: Oxford University Press, 1999.

Burton, Theodore E. *John Sherman.* Boston: Houghton Mifflin, 1906.

Carnegie, Andrew. *Autobiography of Andrew Carnegie.* Boston: Houghton Mifflin, 1920.

Carr, Raymond. *Modern Spain 1875–1980.* Oxford: Oxford University Press, 1980.

———. *Puerto Rico: A Colonial Experiment.* New York: New York University Press, 1984.

———. *Spain, 1808–1939.* London: Oxford University Press, 1966.

Chanler, Mrs. Winthrop. *Autumn in the Valley.* Boston: Little, Brown,1936.

Chernow, Ron. *The House of Morgan: An American Banking Dynasty and the Rise of Modern Finance.* New York: Atlantic Monthly Press, 1990.

———. *Titan: The Life of John D. Rockefeller, Sr.* New York: Random House, 1998.

Clymer, Kenton J. *John Hay: The Gentleman as Diplomat.* Ann Arbor: University of Michigan Press, 1975.

Coletta, Paolo E., ed. *Threshold to American Internationalism: Essays on the Foreign Policy of William McKinley.* New York: Exposition Press, 1970.

Collin, Richard H. *Theodore Roosevelt's Caribbean: The Panama Canal, the Monroe Doctrine, and the Latin American Context.* Baton Rouge: Louisiana State University Press, 1990.

Conroy, Sarah Booth. *Refinements of Love.* New York: Pantheon, 1993.

Cooper, John Milton, Jr. *The Warrior and the Priest: Woodrow Wilson and Theodore Roosevelt.* Cambridge: Harvard University Press, 1983.

Corry, John A. *1898: Prelude to a Century.* New York: Fordham University Press, 1998.

Cowles, Anna Roosevelt. *Letters of Theodore Roosevelt to Anna Roosevelt Cowles, 1870–1918.* New York: Charles Scribner's Sons, 1924.

Crane, Katharine. *Mr. Carr of State: Forty-Seven Years in the Department of State.* New York: St. Martin's, 1960.

Daniels, Roger. *Coming to America, A History of Immigration and Ethnicity in American Life.* New York: HarperCollins, 1990.

Daws, Gavan. *Shoal of Time: A History of the Hawaiian Islands.* Honolulu: University of Hawaii Press, 1974.

Dennett, Tyler. *John Hay: From Poetry to Politics.* Port Washington, N.Y.: Kennikat Press, 1963.

Dewey, George. *Autobiography of George Dewey, Admiral of the Navy.* New York: Charles Scribner's Sons, 1913.

Divine, Robert A., ed. *American Foreign Policy: A Documentary History.* New York: Meridian, 1960.

Dunne, Finley Peter. *Dissertations by Mr. Dooley.* New York: Harpers, 1906.

———. *Mr. Dooley at His Best.* New York: Charles Scribner's Sons, 1949.

———. *Mr. Dooley in Peace and War.* Boston: Small, Maynard, and Co., 1905.

———. *Mr. Dooley in the Hearts of His Countrymen.* Boston: Small, Maynard, and Co., 1899.

———. *Mr. Dooley: Now and Forever,* ed. Louis Filler. Palo Alto, Calif: Stanford University, 1954.

———. *Mr. Dooley's Philosophy.* New York: R. H. Russell, 1900.

Dyer, Thomas G. *Theodore Roosevelt and the Idea of Race.* Baton Rouge: Louisiana State University Press, 1980.

Flexner, James Thomas. *George Washington: Anguish and Farewell 1793–1799.* Boston: Little, Brown, 1969.

Foner, Philip S. *The Spanish-Cuban-American War and the Birth of American Imperialism 1895–1902,* vol. 2, 1898–1902. New York: Monthly Review Press, 1972.

Freidel, Frank. *The Splendid Little War.* Boston: Little, Brown, 1958.

Furnas, J. C. *The Americans: A Social History of the United States 1587–1914.* New York: G. P. Putnam's Sons, 1969.

Garraty, John A. *Henry Cabot Lodge: A Biography.* New York: Alfred A. Knopf, 1953.

Gilmour, David. *Curzon.* London: John Murray, 1994.

Gossett, Thomas F. *Race: The History of an Idea in America*. Dallas: Southern Methodist University Press, 1963.

Green, Constance McLaughlin. *Washington: Capital City 1879–1950*. Princeton: Princeton University Press, 1962.

Hagedorn, Hermann. *Leonard Wood: A Biography*. New York: Harper, 1931. 2 vols.

Halevy, Elie. *Imperialism and the Rise of Labour* (vol. 5 of *A History of the English People in the Nineteenth Century*). London: Ernest Benn, 1929.

Handlin, Oscar. *The Uprooted*. Boston: Little, Brown, 1979.

Hansen, Marcus Lee. *The Immigrant in American History*. Cambridge: Harvard University Press, 1948.

Harbaugh, William Henry. *Power and Responsibility: The Life and Times of Theodore Roosevelt*. New York: Farrar, Straus and Cudahy, 1961.

Hay, John (and John G. Nicolay). *Abraham Lincoln: A History*. New York: Century Co., 1886.

——. *Addresses of John Hay*. New York: Century Co., 1906.

——. *At Lincoln's Side: John Hay's Civil War Correspondence and Selected Writing*, ed. Michael Burlingame. Carbondale: Southern Illinois University Press, 2000.

——. *The Breadwinners*. New Haven: Yale College and University Press, 1973.

——. *Castilian Days*. Boston: James R. Osgood and Co., 1871.

——. "Diary 1879–1881," private collection of James W. Symington.

——. "Erato: A Poem by John M. Hay of Warsaw, Illinois: The Class Poem delivered in the Chapel of Brown University Class Day June 10, 1858." Providence: Knowles, Anthony, and Co., 1858. Library of Congress.

——. Letter on Lincoln to William Herndon from Paris, September 5, 1866. Library of Congress.

——. "Letters of John Hay and Extracts from His Diary," ed. Henry Adams, 1908. 3 vols. Unpublished. Library of Congress.

——. "Memorial Address on the Life and Character of William McKinley," delivered before the two houses of Congress, February 27, 1902. Library of Congress.

——, and Elihu Root. "A Party Fit to Govern." Privately printed. Library of Congress.

——. *Pike County Ballads and Other Pieces*. Boston: Houghton Mifflin, 1886.

——. "The Pioneers of Ohio: An Address Before the Pioneers' Association of the Western Reserve at Burgess' Grove, Cuyahoga County, Ohio, August 27, 1879." Cleveland: Leader Publishing Co., 1879.

——. *A Poet in Exile: Early Letters of John Hay*, ed. Caroline Ticknor. Boston: Houghton Mifflin, 1910.

Hayes, Carlton J. H. *A Generation of Materialism 1871–1900*. New York: Harper and Brothers, 1941.

Haynes, Sam W. *James K. Polk and the Expansionist Impulse*. New York: Longman, 1997.

Healy, David F. *Drive to Hegemony: The United States in the Caribbean, 1898–1907*. Madison: University of Wisconsin Press, 1988.

————. *U.S. Expansionism: The Imperialist Urge in the 1890's.* Madison: University of Wisconsin Press, 1970.

————. *The United States in Cuba, 1898–1902.* Madison: University of Wisconsin Press, 1963.

Heckscher, August. *Woodrow Wilson: A Biography.* New York: Charles Scribner's Sons, 1991.

Heilbroner, Robert, and Aaron Singer. *The Economic Transformation of America, 1600 to the Present.* Fort Worth: Harcourt Brace, 1999.

Herring, Hubert. *A History of Latin America from the Beginnings to the Present.* New York: Alfred A. Knopf, 1961.

Higham, John. *Strangers in the Land: Patterns of American Nativism 1860–1925.* New Brunswick, N.J.: Rutgers University Press, 1994.

Hitchens, Christopher. *Blood, Class, and Nostalgia: Anglo-American Ironies.* London: Chatto and Windus, 1990.

Hobsbawm, Eric. *The Age of Empire 1875–1914.* New York: Pantheon, 1987.

Hobson, J. A. *Imperialism: A Study.* London: George Allen and Unwin, 1938.

Hofstadter, Richard. *The Age of Reform.* New York: Vintage, 1960.

————. *The American Political Tradition and the Men Who Made It.* New York: Vintage, 1989.

————. "Manifest Destiny and the Philippines." In Daniel Aaron, ed., *America in Crisis: Fourteen Crucial Episodes in American History.* New York: Alfred A. Knopf, 1952.

————. *The Paranoid Style in American Politics and Other Essays.* Chicago: University of Chicago, 1965.

————. *Social Darwinism in American Thought.* Boston: Beacon Press, 1992.

Hogan, J. Michael. *The Panama Canal in American Politics.* Carbondale: Southern Illinois University Press, 1986.

Hoge, James F., Jr., and Fareed Zakaria. *The American Encounter: The United States and the Making of the Modern World: Essays from 75 Years of Foreign Affairs.* New York: Basic Books, 1997.

Holbrook, Stewart H. *The Age of the Moguls.* Garden City, N.Y.: Doubleday, 1954.

Homans, Abigail Adams. *Education by Uncles.* Boston: Houghton Mifflin, 1966.

Howells, William Dean. *The Rise of Silas Lapham.* Oxford: Oxford University Press, 1998.

Hunt, Michael H. *Ideology and U.S. Foreign Policy.* New Haven: Yale University Press, 1987.

Isaacson, Walter, and Evan Thomas. *The Wise Men: Six Friends and the World They Made.* New York: Simon & Schuster, 1986.

Jacobson, Matthew Frye. *Barbarian Virtues: The United States Encounters Foreign Peoples at Home and Abroad, 1876–1917.* New York: Hill and Wang, 2000.

Jeffers, H. Paul. *Colonel Roosevelt: Theodore Roosevelt Goes to War, 1897–1898.* New York: John Wiley and Sons, 1996.

Jessup, Philip C. *Elihu Root.* New York: Dodd, Mead, 1938. 2 vols.

Jones, Maldwyn Allen. *American Immigration.* Chicago: University of Chicago Press, 1992.

Kaplan, Amy, and Donald E. Pease. eds. *Cultures of United States Imperialism.* Durham, N.C.: Duke University Press, 1993.

Karnow, Stanley. *In Our Image: America's Empire in the Philippines.* New York: Random House, 1989.

Kennan, George F. *American Diplomacy 1900–1950.* Chicago: University of Chicago Press, 1951.

Kennedy, Charles Stuart. *The American Consul: A History of the United States Consular Service 1776–1914.* New York: Greenwood Press, 1990.

Kennedy, Paul. *The Rise and Fall of the Great Powers: Economic Change and Military Conflict from 1500 to 2000.* New York: Random House, 1987.

Kissinger, Henry. *Diplomacy.* New York: Simon & Schuster, 1994.

Kraut, Alan M. *The Huddled Masses: The Immigrant in American Society 1880–1921.* Arlington Heights, Ill.: Harlan Davidson, Inc., 1982.

Kushner, Howard I., and Anne Hummel Sherrill. *John Milton Hay: The Union of Poetry and Politics.* New York: Twayne Publishers, 1977.

Kuykendall, Ralph S. *The Hawaiian Kingdom 1874–1893,* Vol. 3, *The Kalakaua Dynasty.* Honolulu: University of Hawaii Press, 1967.

LaFeber, Walter. *The Cambridge History of American Foreign Relations,* vol. 2, *The American Search for Opportunity, 1865–1913.* Cambridge: Cambridge University Press, 1993.

———. *Inevitable Revolutions: The United States in Central America.* New York: W. W. Norton, 1993.

———. *The New Empire: An Interpretation of American Expansion 1860–1898.* Ithaca, N.Y.: Cornell University Press, 1993.

Latourette, Kenneth Scott. *A Short History of the Far East.* New York: Macmillan, 1947.

Leech, Margaret. *In the Days of McKinley.* New York: Harper and Brothers, 1959.

Leopold, Richard W. *Elihu Root and the Conservative Tradition.* Boston: Little, Brown, 1954.

Linderman, Gerald F. *The Mirror of War: American Society and the Spanish-American War.* Ann Arbor: University of Michigan Press, 1974.

Linn, Brian McAllister. *The Philippine War 1899–1902.* Lawrence: University Press of Kansas, 2000.

Lodge, Henry Cabot. *Alexander Hamilton.* Boston: Houghton Mifflin, 1898.

———. *Early Memories.* New York: Charles Scribner's Sons, 1913.

———. *George Washington.* Boston: Houghton Mifflin, 1898.

———, and Theodore Roosevelt. *Hero Tales from American History.* New York: Century Co., 1895.

———, ed., *Selections from the Correspondence of Theodore Roosevelt and Henry Cabot Lodge, 1884–1918.* New York: Charles Scribner's Sons, 1925. 2 vols.

———. *Six Popular Tales.* Boston: George A. Smith and Co., 1879.

———. *Speeches and Addresses, 1884–1909.* Boston: Houghton Mifflin, 1909.

———. *The War with Spain.* New York: Harper and Brothers, 1899.

Maguire, Peter. *Law and War: An American Story.* New York: Columbia University Press, 2000.

Mahan, Alfred Thayer. *From Sail to Steam: Recollections of Naval Life*. New York: Harper and Brothers, 1907.

———. *The Harvest Within: Thoughts on the Life of the Christian*. Boston: Little, Brown, 1909.

———. *The Influence of Sea Power upon History 1660–1783*. New York: Dover, 1987.

———. *The Influence of Sea Power upon the French Revolution and Empire 1793–1812*. Boston: Little, Brown, 1894. 2 vols.

———. *The Interest of America in International Conditions*. Boston: Little, Brown, 1910.

———. *The Interest of America in Sea Power, Present and Future*. Boston: Little, Brown, 1897.

———. *Lessons of the War with Spain and Other Articles*. Boston: Little, Brown, 1899.

———. *Letters and Papers of Alfred Thayer Mahan*, ed. Robert Seager II and Doris D. Maguire. Annapolis: Naval Institute Press, 1975. 3 vols.

———. *Retrospect and Prospect: Studies in International Relations, Naval and Political*. Boston: Little, Brown, 1902.

Marryat, Captain Frederick. *Mr. Midshipman Easy*. Ithaca, N.Y.: McBooks Press, 1998.

Mattox, Henry F. *The Twilight of Amateur Diplomacy: The American Foreign Service and Its Senior Officers in the 1890's*. Kent, Ohio: Kent State University Press, 1989.

May, Ernest R. *Imperial Democracy: The Emergence of America as a Great Power*. Chicago: Imprint Publications, 1991.

May, Glenn Anthony. *A Past Recovered*. Quezon City, Philippines: New Day Publishers, 1987.

McCormick, Thomas J. *America's Half-Century: United States Foreign Policy in the Cold War and After*. Baltimore: Johns Hopkins University Press, 1995.

McCullough, David G. *Mornings on Horseback*. New York: Simon & Schuster, 1981.

———. *The Path Between the Seas: The Creation of the Panama Canal 1870–1914*. New York: Simon & Schuster, 1977.

McDougall, Walter A. *Promised Land, Crusader State: The American Encounter with the World Since 1776*. Boston: Houghton Mifflin, 1997.

McNaught, Kenneth. *The Penguin History of Canada*. London: Penguin Books, 1988.

Memorial Addresses (on Theodore Roosevelt) delivered before the Century Association, February 9, 1919. New York: 1919.

Merk, Frederick. *History of the Westward Movement*. New York: Alfred A. Knopf, 1978.

———. *Manifest Destiny and Mission in American History*. Cambridge: Harvard University Press, 1995.

Miller, Stuart Creighton. *"Benevolent Assimilation": The American Conquest of the Philippines, 1899–1903*. New Haven: Yale University Press, 1982.

Millett, Allan R., and Peter Maslowski. *For the Common Defense: A Military History of the United States of America*. New York: Free Press, 1984.

Millis, Walter. *The Martial Spirit: A Study of Our War with Spain.* Boston: Houghton Mifflin, 1931.

Moon, Parker Thomas. *Imperialism and World Politics.* New York: Macmillan, 1926.

Morales Carrión, Arturo. *Puerto Rico: A Political and Cultural History.* New York: W. W. Norton, 1983.

Morison, Samuel Eliot. *The Oxford History of the American People.* New York: Oxford University Press, 1965.

Morris, Edmund. *The Rise of Theodore Roosevelt.* New York: Coward, McCann, and Geoghegan, 1979.

———. *Theodore Rex.* New York: Random House, 2001.

Morris, Sylvia Jukes. *Edith Kermit Roosevelt: Portrait of a First Lady.* New York: Coward, McCann, and Geoghegan, 1980.

Musicant, Ivan. *Empire by Default: The Spanish-American War and the Dawn of the American Century.* New York: Henry Holt, 1998.

Nagel, Paul C. *John Quincy Adams: A Public Life, A Private Life.* New York: Alfred A. Knopf, 1998.

Nasaw, David. *The Chief: The Life of William Randolph Hearst.* Boston: Houghton Mifflin, 2000.

Nevins, Allan. *Grover Cleveland: A Study in Courage.* New York: Dodd, Mead, 1932.

———. *Henry White: Thirty Years of American Diplomacy.* New York: Harper and Brothers, 1930.

Osgood, Robert Endicott. *Ideals and Self-Interest in America's Foreign Relations: The Great Transformation of the Twentieth Century.* Chicago: University of Chicago Press, 1964.

O'Toole, G. J. A. *The Spanish War: An American Epic 1898.* New York: W. W. Norton, 1984.

O'Toole, Patricia. *The Five of Hearts: An Intimate Portrait of Henry Adams and His Friends 1880–1918.* New York: Clarkson Potter, 1990.

Pakenham, Thomas. *The Scramble for Africa 1876–1912.* New York: Random House, 1991.

Paret, Peter, ed. *Makers of Modern Strategy: From Machiavelli to the Nuclear Age.* Princeton: Princeton University Press, 1986.

Paterson, Thomas G., ed. *American Imperialism and Anti-Imperialism.* New York: Thomas Y. Crowell, 1973.

Penczer, Peter R. *Washington, D.C., Past and Present.* Arlington, Va.: Oneonta Press, 1998.

Perez, Louis A., Jr. *The War of 1898: The United States and Cuba in History and Historiography.* Chapel Hill: University of North Carolina Press, 1998.

Perkins, Bradford. *The Great Rapprochement: England and the United States, 1865–1914.* New York: Atheneum, 1968.

Pratt, Julius W. *Expansionists of 1898: The Acquisition of Hawaii and the Spanish Islands.* Baltimore: Johns Hopkins University Press, 1936.

Pringle, Henry F. *The Life and Times of William Howard Taft.* New York: Farrar and Rinehart, 1939. 2 vols.

———. *Theodore Roosevelt: A Biography.* San Diego: Harcourt Brace, 1956.

Puleston, Captain W. D., USN. *Mahan: The Life and Work of Captain Alfred Thayer Mahan, USN.* London: Jonathan Cape, 1939.

Rafael, Vicente L. *White Love and Other Events in Filipino History.* Durham, N.C.: Duke University Press, 2000.

Reckner, James R. *Teddy Roosevelt's Great White Fleet.* Annapolis: Naval Institute Press, 1988.

Renwick, Sir Robin. *Fighting with Allies: America and Britain in Peace and at War.* New York: Times Books, 1996.

Ricketts, Harry. *The Unforgiving Minute: A Life of Rudyard Kipling.* London: Chatto and Windus, 1899.

Robinson, Corinne Roosevelt. *My Brother Theodore Roosevelt.* New York: Charles Scribner's Sons, 1923.

Roosevelt, Theodore. *American Ideals and Other Essays Social and Political.* New York: G. P. Putnam's Sons, 1897.

———. *An American Mind, Selected Writings,* ed. Mario R. DiNunzio. New York: Penguin Books, 1994.

———. *An Autobiography.* New York: Da Capo Press, 1985.

———. *Fear God and Take Your Own Part.* New York: George H. Doran, 1916.

———. *Gouverneur Morris.* Boston: Houghton Mifflin, 1898.

———. *Hunting Trips of a Ranchman and The Wilderness Hunter.* New York: Modern Library, 1996.

———. *The Letters of Theodore Roosevelt,* ed. Elting E. Morison et al. Cambridge: Harvard University Press, 1951–54. 8 vols.

———. *Letters from Theodore Roosevelt to Anna Roosevelt Cowles 1870–1918.* New York: Charles Scribner's Sons, 1924.

———. *The Naval War of 1812.* New York: Modern Library, 1999.

———. *Ranch Life and the Hunting Trail.* New York: Gramercy Books, 1995.

———. *The Rough Riders.* New York: Da Capo Press, 1990.

———. *Selections from the Correspondence of Theodore Roosevelt and Henry Cabot Lodge 1884–1918,* ed. Henry Cabot Lodge. New York: Charles Scribner's Sons, 1925. 2 vols.

———. *The Strenuous Life: Essays and Addresses.* New York: Century Co., 1901.

———. *Thomas H. Benton.* Boston: Houghton Mifflin, 1899.

———. *The Winning of the West.* New York: G. P. Putnam's Sons, 1889. 4 vols.

Root, Elihu. *Addresses on Government and Citizenship,* ed. Robert Bacon and James Brown Scott. Freeport, N.Y.: Books for Libraries Press, 1969.

———. *Addresses on International Subjects,* ed. Robert Bacon and James Brown Scott. Cambridge: Harvard University Press, 1916.

———. *Men and Policies: Addresses by Elihu Root,* ed. Robert Bacon and James Brown Scott. Cambridge: Harvard University Press, 1925.

———. *The Military and Colonial Policy of the United States: Addresses and Reports,* ed. Robert Bacon and James Brown Scott. Cambridge: Harvard University Press, 1916.

————. Miscellaneous Addresses, ed. Robert Bacon and James Brown Scott. Cambridge: Harvard University Press, 1917.

————. "A Requisite for the Success of Popular Diplomacy," *Foreign Affairs* (September 1922). In Hoge and Zakaria, *The American Encounter.*

Russ, William Adam, Jr. *The Hawaiian Republic (1894–1898) and Its Struggle to Win Annexation.* Selinsgrove, Pa.: Susquehanna University Press, 1961.

Samuels, Ernest. *Henry Adams.* Cambridge: Harvard University Press, 1989.

Schiftgiesser, Karl. *The Gentleman from Massachusetts: Henry Cabot Lodge.* Boston: Little, Brown, 1944.

Schlesinger, Arthur M., Jr. *The Disuniting of America: Reflections on a Multicultural Society.* New York: W. W. Norton, 1992.

Schurz, Carl. *The Reminiscences of Carl Schurz.* New York: McClure Co., 1907.

Seager, Robert, II. *Alfred Thayer Mahan: The Man and His Letters.* Annapolis: Naval Institute Press, 1977.

Sears, Lorenzo. *John Hay: Author and Statesman.* New York: Dodd, Mead, 1914.

Slotkin, Richard. *Gunfighter Nation: The Myth of the Frontier in Twentieth-Century America.* Norman: University of Oklahoma Press, 1998.

Spector, Ronald. *Admiral of the New Empire: The Life and Career of George Dewey.* Baton Rouge: Louisiana State University Press,1974.

Spence, Jonathan D. *The Search for Modern China.* New York: W. W. Norton, 1990.

Stanwood, Edward. *James Gillespie Blaine.* Boston: Houghton Mifflin, 1905.

Stephanson, Anders. *Manifest Destiny: American Expansion and the Empire of Right.* New York: Hill and Wang, 1995.

Stern, Fritz. *Einstein's German World.* Princeton: Princeton University Press, 1999.

Stewart, J. I. M. *Rudyard Kipling.* New York: Dodd, Mead, 1966.

Strong, Josiah. *Our Country.* New York: Baker and Taylor Co., 1885.

Strouse, Jean. *Morgan: American Financier.* New York: Random House, 1999.

Strout, Cushing. *The American Image of the Old World.* New York: Harper and Row, 1963.

Sullivan, Mark. *Our Times: The United States 1900–1925*, vol. 1, *The Turn of the Century.* New York: Charles Scribner's Sons, 1927.

Sumida, Jon Tetsuro. *Inventing Grand Strategy and Teaching Command: The Classic Works of Alfred Thayer Mahan Reconsidered.* Washington, D.C.: Woodrow Wilson Center Press, 1997.

Swanberg, W. A. *Citizens Hearst: A Biography of William Randolph Hearst.* New York: Bantam Books, 1963.

Symington, James W. "A Hayride with Lincoln," address to the John Hay National Wildlife Refuge, Lake Sunapee, N.H., October 3, 1998, private collection of James W. Symington.

Syrett, Harold C., ed. *American Historical Documents.* New York: Barnes and Noble, 1960.

Takaki, Ronald. *Strangers from a Different Shore: A History of Asian Americans.* New York: Penguin Books, 1989.

Taylor, Charles. *The Life of Admiral Mahan: Naval Philosopher.* London: John Murray, 1920.

Thayer, William Roscoe. *The Life and Letters of John Hay.* Boston: Houghton Mifflin, 1929.

———. *Theodore Roosevelt: An Intimate Biography.* Boston: Houghton Mifflin, 1919.

Thomas, Hugh. *Cuba or the Pursuit of Freedom.* New York: Da Capo Press, 1998.

———. "Remember the Maine," *New York Review of Books,* April 23, 1998.

Thompson, John Herd, and Stephen J. Randall. *Canada and the United States: Ambivalent Allies.* Athens: University of Georgia Press, 1997.

Tilchin, William N. *Theodore Roosevelt and the British Empire: A Study in Presidential Statecraft.* New York: St. Martin's, 1997.

Tompkins, E. Berkeley. *Anti-Imperialism in the United States: The Great Debate 1890–1920.* Philadelphia: University of Pennsylvania Press, 1970.

Townsend, Kim. *Manhood at Harvard: William James and Others.* Cambridge: Harvard University Press, 1996.

Trask, David F. *The War with Spain in 1898.* Lincoln: University of Nebraska Press, 1996.

Traxel, David. *1898: The Birth of the American Century.* New York: Alfred A. Knopf, 1998.

Trefousse, Hans L. *Carl Schurz, a Biography.* Knoxville: University of Tennessee Press, 1982.

Trend, J. B. *The Civilization of Spain.* London: Oxford University Press, 1960.

Trías Monge, José. *Puerto Rico: The Trials of the Oldest Colony in the World.* New Haven: Yale University Press, 1997.

Tuchman, Barbara W. *The Proud Tower: A Portrait of the World Before the War 1890–1914.* New York: Macmillan, 1966.

Turk, Richard W. *The Ambiguous Relationship: Theodore Roosevelt and Alfred Thayer Mahan.* New York: Greenwood Press, 1987.

Turner, Frederick Jackson. *The Frontier in American History.* Tucson: University of Arizona Press, 1997.

Twain, Mark. *Mark Twain's Autobiography,* with an introduction by Albert Bigelow Paine. New York: Harper, 1924. 2 vols.

———. *The Gilded Age.* New York: Harper and Brothers, 1915.

Van Alstyne, R. W. *The Rising American Empire.* New York: Oxford University Press, 1960.

Vidal, Gore. *Empire.* New York: Random House, 1987.

Vilar, Pierre. *Spain: A Brief History.* Oxford: Pergamon, 1977.

Wagenheim, Olga Jiménez de. *Puerto Rico: An Interpretive History from Pre-Colombian Times to 1900.* Princeton: Marcus Wiener, 1998.

Walker, Dale L. *The Boys of '98: Theodore Roosevelt and the Rough Riders.* New York: Tom Doherty Associates, 1998.

Wall, Joseph Frazier. *Andrew Carnegie.* Pittsburgh: University of Pittsburgh Press, 1970.

Weigley, Russell F. *The American Way of War: A History of United States Military Strategy and Policy.* Bloomington: Indiana University Press, 1977.

Weston, Rubin Francis. *Racism in U.S. Imperialism: The Influence of Racial Assumptions on American Foreign Policy, 1893–1946.* Columbia, S.C.: University of South Carolina Press, 1972.

White, Andrew Dickson. *The Autobiography of Andrew Dickson White.* New York: Century Co., 1905.

Widenor, William C. *Henry Cabot Lodge and the Search for an American Foreign Policy.* Berkeley: University of California Press, 1980.

Williams, William Appleman. *The Tragedy of American Diplomacy.* New York: Dell, 1972.

Wilson, Woodrow. *Congressional Government: A Study in American Politics.* Gloucester, Mass.: Peter Smith, 1973.

Wolman, Paul. *Most Favored Nation: The Republican Revisionists and U.S. Tariff Policy, 1897–1912.* Chapel Hill: University of North Carolina Press, 1992.

Zakaria, Fareed. *From Wealth and Power: The Unusual Origins of America's World Role.* Princeton: Princeton University Press, 1998.

Zwick, Jim, ed. *Mark Twain's Weapons of Satire: Anti-Imperialist Writings on the Philippine-American War.* Syracuse: Syracuse University Press, 1992.

Acknowledgments

Why would a career diplomat be moved to write a book about America's imperial past? The answer is that, having been a U.S. foreign service officer through much of the Cold War, when the United States was the world's dominant power, I have always been fascinated by the questions of when and how we achieved that status. My assignments in Russia and the Balkans also persuaded me of the importance of individuals in influencing major historical transitions. These concerns led me inexorably back to the period of the Spanish-American War when, it seemed to me, the United States emerged for the first time as a world power and when a few key Americans had a critical role in that dramatic transformation.

Fortunately, the period around the turn of the twentieth century is rich with excellent historical writing. Among the books that contributed to my understanding and enthusiasm, Margaret Leech's classic *In the Days of McKinley* was the first. Also important as I sought to define my approach were two brilliant biographies of the young Theodore Roosevelt: Edmund Morris's *The Rise of Theodore Roosevelt* and David McCullough's *Mornings on Horseback*, both of them contributions to literature as well as history. By my side during the whole project was Thomas A. Bailey's *A Diplomatic History of the American People*, surely one of the sprightliest textbooks ever written. Patricia O'Toole's elegantly written social history *The Five of Hearts* gave the period immediacy and vivacity. Walter Isaacson and Evan Thomas's first-rate study *The Wise Men*, a biography of six creators of U.S. Cold War strategy, convinced me that group biography can sometimes be the best means for describing the essentials of a historical period.

I am grateful to the people who helped me get started. The late Don Cook, a master journalist of the entire Cold War period and author of several fine popular histories, gave me the confidence to take on a large subject. Ronald Steel and Michael Beschloss encouraged me to undertake the project and helped me define its parameters. The book began as an essay for the Literary Society of Washington, D.C. Wilton Dillon, a fellow member, put me in touch with *The Wilson Quarterly*, which turned the essay into an article which in turn became the basis for a book proposal. Jay Tolson, then managing editor of the *Quarterly*, helped me enormously at this early stage.

Dolores Martin introduced me to the Hispanic Division of the Library of Congress, where the director, Georgette Dorn, and her staff kept me generously supplied with research materials over four years; Tracy North in particular was remarkable in her resourcefulness and speed in finding books and documents. The Prints and Photographs Division of the Library of Congress was accommodating and efficient. Robert Lewis, the librarian at the Metropolitan Club, cheerfully made available the club's fine collection of works by and about its five distinguished members. Dr. Russell Flinchum, archivist at the Century Association, dug into the association's files for useful information. Robert Moskin shared with me his extensive research on the U.S. Foreign Service. Many museum professionals went out of their way to chase down pictures: Carrie Foley at the Massachusetts Historical Society, Randy W. Hackenburg at the U.S. Army Military History Institute, John Pemberton at The Mariner's Museum, Dawn Stitzell at the U.S. Naval Institute, Walter Dailey at the Theodore Roosevelt Collection of Harvard University, and Yvette Stickell at the National Portrait Gallery of the Smithsonian Institution.

I owe a large debt to Stanley Karnow, author of a prizewinning book on the Philippines, who encouraged me from the start, lent me part of his library, and helped me with the entire text. I am also grateful to Professor David P. Calleo of the Johns Hopkins School of Advanced International Studies; Henry S. F. Cooper, former secretary of the Century Association; and Dr. Nicholas X. Rizopoulos, director of the Foreign Policy Roundtable at the Carnegie Council on Ethics and International Affairs, for giving me the opportunity to try out my ideas before an audience. Dr. Rizopoulos also made extremely useful suggestions for the final chapter. Stephen Rosenfeld helped me considerably with the sections on Puerto Rico. Alfred Friendly reviewed the manuscript thoroughly and suggested dozens of valuable improvements. Jenonne Walker and Helmut Sonnenfeldt contributed helpful insights based on their experience with foreign policy and strategic issues. Anders Stephanson, my colleague at Columbia University and author of an important study of the intellectual background of imperialism, also read the whole manuscript; his thoughtful comments were all the more valuable for having come from a political orientation different from mine. Gail Ross, my agent, contributed much-needed expertise about the publishing business.

James W. Symington, like his great-grandfather John Hay a gifted conversationalist and storyteller, encouraged me in many ways and offered stories, documents, and pictures. John B. Root searched out and supplied an original picture of his grandmother. Others who provided information, advice, technical help, or overall encouragement are Jodie T. Allen, Albert J. Beveridge III, Sally Boasberg, Professor Ronald T. Curran, Professor Carol Feldman, Dr. Sedi Flugelman, Professor Robert L. Gale, Jane Hughes, C. P. Hyland, Ambassador Peter Jay, Ulrike Klopfer, Ambassador Paul Leifer, Gordana Logar, Andrew Loomis, Joanne Myers, Peter Rosenblatt, Dr. Joel H. Rosenthal, Ambassador Javier Ruperez, Helena Santina, Professor Fritz Stern, Jennifer Stuart, Bardyl Tirana, Professor Douglas Wilson, Tim Zimmermann, and Professor Aristide R. Zolberg.

Every writer should be fortunate enough to have Elisabeth Sifton as an editor. Somehow she managed to will herself into the world of my subjects so that her changes reflected and enlivened the historical context. Try as I might, I could rarely if ever improve on her recommendations. She has been exactly the experienced, thoughtful, critical, and encouraging editor that I needed. Elisabeth's assistant, Danny Mulligan, kept on top of the growing administrative needs toward the end of the project.

My family has been a huge support. My son, Tim, engaged in his own book, made time to help me through the byways of the Internet. My daughters, Quinny and Lily, were always ready to offer up a grandchild or two for diversion. My wife, Teeny, though a great-granddaughter of Theodore Roosevelt's sister Corinne, announced that she would never have read this kind of book if it hadn't been written by me. Nevertheless she applied her considerable editorial talent to the entire manuscript, mainly in the interest of depriving me of my favorite clichés. Equally important, she provided and protected the best working environment that anyone who writes at home could ever want. Thanks to her, the entire five-year project was, day by day, an unalloyed pleasure rather than a burden.

Index